Less managing. More teaching. Greater learning.

Q: INSTRUCTORS...

Would you like your **students** to show up for class more **prepared**? *(Let's face it, class is much more fun if everyone is engaged and prepared...)*

Want ready-made application-level **interactive assignments**, student progress reporting, and auto-assignment grading? *(Less time grading means more time teaching...)*

Want an **instant view of student or class performance** relative to learning objectives? *(No more wondering if students understand...)*

Need to **collect data and generate reports** required for administration or accreditation? *(Say goodbye to manually tracking student learning outcomes...)*

Want to **record and post your lectures** for students to view online?

A: With **McGraw-Hill's Connect™ Management,**

INSTRUCTORS GET:

- Interactive Applications – **book-specific interactive assignments** that require students to APPLY concepts and tools of strategic analysis.

- Simple **assignment management**, allowing you to spend more time teaching.

- **Auto-graded** assignments, quizzes, and tests.

- **Detailed Visual Reporting** where student and section results can be viewed and analyzed.

- Sophisticated **online testing** capability.

- A **filtering and reporting** function that allows you to easily assign and report on materials that are correlated to accreditation standards, learning outcomes, and Bloom's taxonomy.

- An easy-to-use **lecture capture** tool.

Q: STUDENTS...

Want to get more **value** from your textbook purchase?

Think learning strategic management should be a bit more **interesting**?

Check out the STUDENT RESOURCES section under the *Connect*™ Library tab.

Here you'll find a wealth of resources designed to help you achieve your goals in the course. You'll find things like **quizzes**, **PowerPoints, and Case Grid** to help you study. Every student has different needs, so explore the STUDENT RESOURCES to find the materials best suited to you.

Q: INSTRUCTORS...

McGraw-Hill Higher Education and Blackboard have teamed up. What does this mean **for you**?

- **Your life, simplified.** Now you and your students can access McGraw-Hill's Connect™ and Create™ right from within your Blackboard course—all with one single sign-on.

- **Deep integration of content and tools.** Whether you're choosing a book for your course or building Connect™ assignments, all the tools you need are right where you want them—inside of Blackboard.

- **Seamless Gradebooks.** Multiple gradebooks? No thanks! When a student completes an integrated Connect™ assignment, the grade for that assignment automatically (and instantly) feeds your Blackboard grade center.

- **A solution for everyone.** Whether your institution is already using Blackboard or you just want to try Blackboard on your own, we have a solution for you. Be sure to ask your local McGraw-Hill representative for details.

The **Best** of **Both Worlds**

www.domorenow.com

Strategic
Management

creating competitive advantages

sixth edition

Gregory G. Dess
University of Texas at Dallas

G. T. Lumpkin
Syracuse University

Alan B. Eisner
Pace University

Gerry McNamara
Michigan State University

Strategic Management

creating competitive advantages

sixth edition

McGraw-Hill Irwin

The McGraw·Hill Companies

McGraw-Hill
Irwin

STRATEGIC MANAGEMENT: CREATING COMPETITIVE ADVANTAGES
Published by McGraw-Hill/Irwin, a business unit of The McGraw-Hill Companies, Inc., 1221 Avenue of the Americas, New York, NY, 10020. Copyright © 2012, 2010, 2008, 2007, 2006, 2004 by The McGraw-Hill Companies, Inc. All rights reserved. Printed in the United States of America. No part of this publication may be reproduced or distributed in any form or by any means, or stored in a database or retrieval system, without the prior written consent of The McGraw-Hill Companies, Inc., including, but not limited to, in any network or other electronic storage or transmission, or broadcast for distance learning.

Some ancillaries, including electronic and print components, may not be available to customers outside the United States.

This book is printed on acid-free paper.

1 2 3 4 5 6 7 8 9 0 DOW/DOW 1 0 9 8 7 6 5 4 3 2 1

ISBN 978-0-07-743956-9
MHID 0-07-743956-2

Vice president and editor-in-chief: *Brent Gordon*
Editorial director: *Paul Ducham*
Executive editor: *Michael Ablassmeir*
Executive director of development: *Ann Torbert*
Development editor II: *Laura Griffin*
Editorial coordinator: *Andrea Heirendt*
Vice president and director of marketing: *Robin J. Zwettler*
Marketing director: *Amee Mosley*
Executive marketing manager: *Anke Braun Weekes*
Marketing specialist: *Elizabeth Steiner*
Vice president of editing, design, and production: *Sesha Bolisetty*
Lead project manager: *Harvey Yep*
Buyer II: *Debra R. Sylvester*
Interior designer: *Pam Verros*
Senior photo research coordinator: *Jeremy Cheshareck*
Lead media project manager: *Kerry Bowler*
Cover/interior design: *Pam Verros*
Cover image: © *Getty Images*
Typeface: *10/12 Times Roman*
Compositor: *Laserwords Private Limited*
Printer: *R. R. Donnelley*

Library of Congress Cataloging-in-Publication Data

Strategic management : creating competitive advantages / Gregory G. Dess ... [et al.]. — 6th ed.
   p. cm.
   Includes index.
   ISBN-13: 978-0-07-743956-9 (alk. paper)
   ISBN-10: 0-07-743956-2 (alk. paper)
   1. Strategic planning. I. Dess, Gregory G.
HD30.28.D4743 2012
658.4'012—dc23

2011027545

www.mhhe.com

Dedication

To my family, Margie and Taylor;
my parents, Bill and Mary Dess;
and Glenn F. Kirk
–Greg

To my lovely wife, Vicki,
and my students and colleagues
–Tom

To my family, Helaine, Rachel, and Jacob
–Alan

To my wonderful wife, Gaelen;
my children, Megan and AJ;
and my parents, Gene and Jane
–Gerry

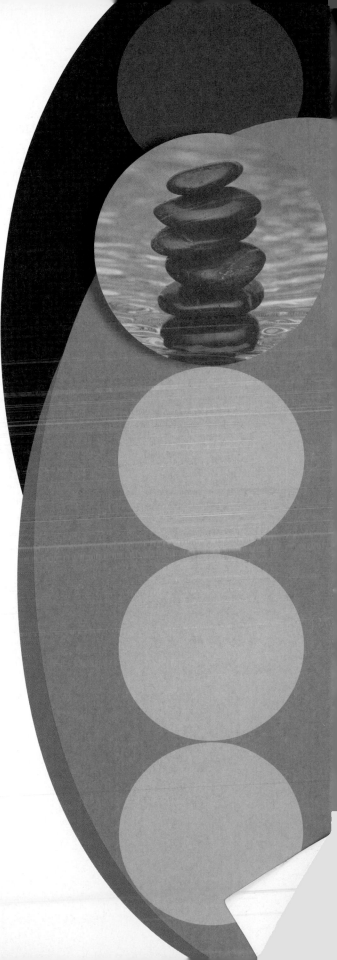

About the Authors

Gregory G. Dess is the Andrew R. Cecil Endowed Chair in Management at the University of Texas at Dallas. His primary research interests are in strategic management, organization–environment relationships, and knowledge management. He has published numerous articles on these subjects in both academic and practitioner-oriented journals. He also serves on the editorial boards of a wide range of practitioner-oriented and academic journals. In August 2000, he was inducted into the *Academy of Management Journal*'s Hall of Fame as one of its charter members. Professor Dess has conducted executive programs in the United States, Europe, Africa, Hong Kong, and Australia. During 1994 he was a Fulbright Scholar in Oporto, Portugal. In 2009, he received an honorary doctorate from the University of Bern (Switzerland). He received his PhD in Business Administration from the University of Washington (Seattle) and a BIE degree from Georgia Tech.

G. T. (Tom) Lumpkin is the Chris J. Witting Chair and Professor of Entrepreneurship at Syracuse University in New York. Prior to joining the faculty at Syracuse, Tom was the Kent Hance Regents Endowed Chair and Professor of Entrepreneurship at Texas Tech University. His research interests include entrepreneurial orientation, opportunity recognition, strategy-making processes, social entrepreneurship, and innovative forms of organizing work. He has published numerous research articles in journals such as *Strategic Management Journal, Academy of Management Journal, Academy of Management Review, Journal of Business Venturing,* and *Entrepreneurship: Theory and Practice.* He is a member of the editorial review boards of *Strategic Entrepreneurship Journal, Entrepreneurship Theory & Practice,* and the *Journal of Business Venturing.* He received his PhD in management from the University of Texas at Arlington and MBA from the University of Southern California.

Alan B. Eisner is Professor of Management and Department Chair, Management and Management Science Department, at the Lubin School of Business, Pace University. He received his PhD in management from the Stern School of Business, New York University. His primary research interests are in strategic management, technology management, organizational learning, and managerial decision making. He has published research articles and cases in journals such as *Advances in Strategic Management, International Journal of Electronic Commerce, International Journal of Technology Management, American Business Review, Journal of Behavioral and Applied Management,* and *Journal of the International Academy for Case Studies.* He is the former Associate Editor of the Case Association's peer reviewed journal, *The CASE Journal.*

Gerry McNamara is a Professor of Management at Michigan State University. He received his PhD from the Carlson School of Management at the University of Minnesota. His research focuses on strategic decision making, organizational risk taking, and mergers and acquisitions. His research has been published in numerous journals, including the *Academy of Management Journal, Strategic Management Journal, Organization Science, Organizational Behavior and Human Decision Processes, Journal of Management,* and *Journal of International Business Studies.* His research on mergers and acquisitions has been abstracted in the *New York Times, Bloomberg Businessweek, The Economist,* and *Financial Week.* He is currently an Associate Editor for the *Academy of Management Journal*

Preface

Welcome to the Sixth Edition of *Strategic Management: Creating Competitive Advantages* We're very pleased with the positive market response to our previous editions. We are always striving to improve our work, and we appreciate the extensive and constructive feedback that many strategy professionals have graciously given us. We have worked hard to incorporate many of their ideas into the Sixth Edition—as we have in previous editions as well. We acknowledge these many contributions later in the Preface.

As you noticed on the cover, we have added Gerry McNamara of Michigan State University as a coauthor. We are very excited to welcome him—he has certainly added a lot of value to our collective work. Gerry has an outstanding record as a strategy scholar—and his writing style is consistent with that of the other authors on the book. As we worked on the Sixth Edition, it was great to have, in the vernacular, "fresh blood" to provide new perspectives. Gerry certainly did not let us down!

We'd like to revisit a fundamental question: Why did we write the book in the first place? All of us would agree that there have always been some solid strategy textbooks on the market. However, we felt that there was a strong need for a book that students and faculty would think satisfied the three *R*'s that we always kept in mind while we worked: relevant, rigorous, and readable. That is, our tagline (paraphrasing the well-known Secret deodorant commercial) is: "Strong enough for the professor; made for the student." We are quite pleased that we have received such feedback over the years from faculty who have used our book. Perhaps Professor Stephen Vitucci (Tarleton State University) said it best:

> I want it to be rigorous but something that they can read and understand. The Dess, Lumpkin, and Eisner text I am currently using is exactly what I like and, more importantly, what my students need and like.

We were also recently contacted by Liz Welch and Sabina Nawaz, former General Manager and Senior Director, respectively, at Microsoft. They are now external consultants who conduct course offerings for Microsoft, several divisions of ITT, and other well-known firms. The author team was very gratified by their strong support of our text, which we feel verifies the "external validity" and practical relevance of our work:

> As organizational and leadership development consultants, we are always looking for great tools, case studies, and examples to better deliver core strategy concepts to our clients. Not only does DLE's *Strategic Management* provide us with that, it is almost a "one-stop shop" in this regard. The book has a comprehensive conceptual model with timely, relevant, and well-researched examples and cases. We have found it to be of conceptual as well as practical use and highly recommend it to consultants and leaders alike.

We were quite pleased with such praise. But to continue to earn it, we strive to use an engaging writing style that minimizes unnecessary jargon and covers all of the traditional bases. We also integrate some central themes throughout the book—such as globalization, technology, ethics, environmental sustainability, and entrepreneurship—that are vital in understanding strategic management in today's global economy. We draw on short examples from business practice to bring concepts to life by providing 103 Strategy Spotlights (more detailed examples in sidebars).

Unlike other strategy texts, we provide three separate chapters that address timely topics about which business students should have a solid understanding. These are the role of intellectual assets in value creation (Chapter 4), entrepreneurial strategy and competitive dynamics (Chapter 8), and fostering entrepreneurship in established organizations (Chapter 12). We also provide an excellent set of cases to help students analyze, integrate, and apply strategic management concepts.

In developing *Strategic Management: Creating Competitive Advantage,* we certainly didn't forget the instructors. As we all know, you have a most challenging (but rewarding) job. We did our best to help you. We provide a variety of supplementary materials that should help you in class preparation and delivery. For example, our chapter notes do not simply summarize the material in the text. Rather (and consistent with the concept of strategy!), we ask ourselves: "How can we add value?" Thus, for each chapter, we provide numerous questions to pose to help guide class discussion, at least 12 boxed examples to supplement chapter material, and three detailed "teaching tips" to further engage students. Also, the author team completed the chapter notes—along with the entire test bank—ourselves. That is, unlike many of our rivals, we didn't simply farm the work out to others. Instead, we felt that such efforts help to enhance quality and consistency—as well as demonstrate our personal commitment to provide a top-quality total package to strategy instructors.

Let's now address some of the key substantive changes in the Sixth Edition. Then we will cover some of the major features that we have had in previous editions.

What's New? Highlights of the Sixth Edition

We worked hard to add new material to the chapters that reflects both the feedback that we have received from reviewers as well as the challenges and opportunities that face today's managers. This involved an extensive amount of time carefully reviewing a wide variety of books, academic and practitioner journals, and the business press.

We also endeavored to avoid "chapter creep." That is, when we added new material, we deleted others (which included culling out redundant examples). We certainly benefited from the work of Rae Pinkham, a professional editor. She diligently pored over the chapter material and helped tighten our writing. The overall result was that we were able to update our material, add new material, as well as keep the chapters about the same length. We certainly appreciate her excellent contribution!

Here are some major changes in the Sixth Edition:

- **All of the 12 opening "Learning from Mistakes" vignettes that lead off each chapter are totally new.** Unique to this text, they are all examples of what can go wrong, and they serve as an excellent vehicle for clarifying and reinforcing strategy concepts. After all, what can be learned if one simply admires perfection!
- **Well over half of our "Strategy Spotlights" (sidebar examples) are brand new, and many others have been thoroughly updated.** We have a total of 103 Spotlights—by far the most sidebar examples in the strategy market. We are still able to conserve space because we focus on bringing the most important strategy concepts to life in a concise and highly readable manner. We work hard to eliminate unnecessary detail that detracts from the main point we are trying to make.
- **We have added 4 exhibits to the text and have carefully revised many other exhibits.** This, along with the four-color pictures in each chapter, aids learning and improves visual appeal. To further enhance readability, we focus on writing short paragraphs and provide many indented examples throughout the book.

- **We have increased the number of "Strategy Spotlights" that focus on three issues that are critical in today's leading-edge organizations—ethics, environmental sustainability, and crowdsourcing.** We have included an icon to identify each of these topics, We have 10 "Spotlights" on ethics that include such issues as the role of nongovernmental organizations (NGOs) as an important stakeholder group (Chapter 1) and how some power companies engaged in "greenwashing"—making unsubstantiated claims about how environmental friendly their products or services really are (Chapter 11)! We include 10 "Spotlights" on environmental sustainability, such as Timberland's detoxification initiative as a means to create an efficient supply chain (Chapter 3) and why Shell's innovative gasoline product worked in Thailand—but failed miserably in Holland (Chapter 7). Finally, we have 8 "Spotlights" on crowdsourcing. These include topics such as how Goldcorp used crowdsourcing to strike gold (literally!) (Chapter 1) and how IBM's "Innovation Jam" helped it create new products and services (Chapter 12).

Key content changes for the chapters include:

- **Chapter 1 introduces the concept of "shared value," which was coined by Michael Porter and Mark Kramer in a 2011 *Harvard Business Review* article.** Shared value involves practices that enhance the competitiveness of a company while simultaneously advancing the economic and social conditions in which it operates. Such an approach goes beyond narrowly focusing on shareholder returns—it enhances the satisfaction of multiple shareholders.
- **Chapter 3 addresses a novel perspective—"The Prosumer"—that has important implications for today's organizations.** Here, the customer becomes engaged in the actual production process. Not only can this generate greater customer satisfaction, but also it has the potential to result in significant cost savings and generate innovative ideas for the firm.
- **Chapter 4 provides insights on how firms can successfully achieve integration when they engage in collaborative efforts.** We address four barriers (e.g., people aren't willing to provide help, people are unable to work with people they don't know well) that need to be overcome before effective collaboration can be achieved. Such barriers must be identified, and we discuss how managers can devise appropriate ways to overcome them.
- **Chapter 5 now includes a detailed discussion on the sustainability of competitive advantage that integrates key strategy concepts that are addressed in the first four chapters of the text.** We include the concepts of stakeholder analysis, industry five-forces analysis, the resource-base view of the firm, and social capital (both within and outside the firm's boundaries). We address how such strategic management concepts provide us with a means to address whether or not the strategy of a firm (Atlas Door) is sustainable over time.
- **Chapter 7 discusses "reverse innovation" a trend whereby many developing countries are becoming hotbeds for innovation.** Also referred to as "frugal innovation," such initiatives serve to expand potential markets in both developing and mature economies.
- **Chapter 9 addresses one of the most controversial topics in corporate governance—duality. That is, should a firm's Chief Executive Officer also serve as Chairman of the Board?** We address "pro" and "con" positions and explain why there is a trend toward less duality in large corporations as well as what the implications are for other governance mechanisms, such as the appointing of a lead director.

- **Chapter 11 introduces a rather new idea—the ambicultural leader.** Here, leaders can benefit by drawing on the best of different philosophies and business practices while avoiding the negatives of each. To illustrate, we provide the example of combining both Chinese and Western philosophies and practices.
- **Chapter 12 explains the idea of an "Innovator's D.N.A" and its importance in enhancing a firm's capacity for innovation and creativity.** We address the five key traits (e.g., questioning, observing, experimenting) and provide examples of how well-known entrepreneurs applied them to launch extremely successful enterprises.
- **Chapter 13 updates our Appendix: Sources of Company and Industry Information.** Here, we are most indebted to Ruthie Brock and Carol Byrne. These library professionals at the University of Texas at Arlington have graciously provided us with comprehensive and updated information that is organized in a range of issues. These include competitive intelligence, annual report collections, company rankings, business websites, and strategic and competitive analysis. Such information is invaluable in analyzing companies and industries.

WHAT REMAINS THE SAME: KEY FEATURES OF EARLIER EDITIONS

Let's now briefly address some of the exciting features that remain from the earlier editions.

- **Traditional organizing framework with three other chapters on timely topics.** Crisply written chapters cover all of the strategy bases and address contemporary topics. First, the chapters are divided logically into the traditional sequence: strategy analysis, strategy formulation, and strategy implementation. Second, we include three chapters on such timely topics as intellectual capital/knowledge management, entrepreneurial strategy and competitive dynamics, and fostering corporate entrepreneurship and new ventures.
- **"Learning from Mistakes" chapter-opening cases.** To enhance student interest, we begin each chapter with a case that depicts an organization that has suffered a dramatic performance drop, or outright failure, by failing to adhere to sound strategic management concepts and principles. We believe that this feature serves to underpin the value of the concepts in the course and that it is a preferred teaching approach to merely providing examples of outstanding companies that always seem to get it right! After all, isn't it better (and more challenging) to diagnose problems than admire perfection? As Dartmouth's Sydney Finkelstein, author of *Why Smart Executives Fail,* notes: "We live in a world where success is revered, and failure is quickly pushed to the side. However, some of the greatest opportunities to learn—both for individuals and organizations—come from studying what goes wrong."* We'll see how, for example, Nokia, the Finnish phone manufacturer, saw its reputation as the industry's most powerful brand eroded when it failed to meet customers' needs in the emerging smartphone revolution. Clearly, its focus on mobile phones for voice communication was its most disastrous call in the past 10 years. We will also explore why AOL's $850 million acquisition of Bebo, a social networking firm, failed. AOL,

*Personal communication, June 20, 2005.

a provider of Internet service, unloaded it two years later for only $10 million. Not a good return on their investment, to say the least! And we discuss why Carrefour, Europe's largest retailer, failed in both Thailand and Malaysia. Its key rival, Tesco, not only was much savvier in figuring out customer needs in these markets but also picked strong local partners.

- **Consistent chapter format and features to reinforce learning.** We have included several features in each chapter to add value and create an enhanced learning experience. First, each chapter begins with an overview and a set of bullets pointing to key learning objectives. Second, as previously noted, the opening case describes a situation in which a company's performance eroded because of a lack of proper application of strategy concepts. Third, at the end of each chapter there are four different types of questions/exercises that should help students assess their understanding and application of material:

  1. Summary review questions.
  2. Experiential exercises.
  3. Application questions and exercises.
  4. Ethics questions

Given the emergence of the Internet and e-commerce, each chapter contains at least one exercise that involves the use of the Internet.

- **"Reflecting on Career Implications" for each chapter.** This feature—at the end of each chapter—will help instructors drive home the immediate relevance/value of strategy concepts. It focuses on how an understanding of key concepts helps business students early in their careers.
- **Key Terms.** Approximately a dozen key terms for each chapter are identified in the margins of the pages. This addition was made in response to reviewer feedback and improves students' understanding of core strategy concepts.
- **Clear articulation and illustration of key concepts.** Key strategy concepts are introduced in a clear and concise manner and are followed by timely and interesting examples from business practice. Such concepts include value-chain analysis, the resource-based view of the firm, Porter's five-forces model, competitive advantage, boundaryless organizational designs, digital strategies, corporate governance, ethics, and entrepreneurship.
- **Extensive use of sidebars.** We include 103 sidebars (or about eight per chapter) called "Strategy Spotlights." The Strategy Spotlights not only illustrate key points but also increase the readability and excitement of new strategy concepts.
- **Integrative themes.** The text provides a solid grounding in ethics, globalization, environmental substainability and technology. These topics are central themes throughout the book and form the basis for many of the Strategy Spotlights.
- **Implications of concepts for small businesses.** Many of the key concepts are applied to start-up firms and smaller businesses, which is particularly important since many students have professional plans to work in such firms.
- **Not just a textbook but an entire package.** *Strategic Management* features the best chapter teaching notes available today. Rather than merely summarizing the key points in each chapter, we focus on value-added material to enhance the teaching (and learning) experience. Each chapter includes dozens of questions to spur discussion, teaching tips, in-class group exercises, and about a dozen detailed examples from business practice to provide further illustrations of key concepts.

Student Support Materials

Online Learning Center (OLC)

The following resources are available to students via the publisher's OLC at www.mhhe .com/dess6e:

- Chapter quizzes students can take to gauge their understanding of material covered in each chapter.
- A selection of PowerPoint slides for each chapter.
- Links to strategy simulations the Business Strategy Game & GLO-BUS. Both provide a powerful and constructive way of connecting students to the subject matter of the course with a competition among classmates on campus and around the world.

Instructor Support Materials

Instructor's Manual (IM)

Prepared by the textbook authors, the accompanying IM contains summary/objectives, lecture/discussion outlines, discussion questions, extra examples not included in the text, teaching tips, reflecting on career implications, experiential exercises, and more.

Test Bank

Prepared by the authors, the test bank contains more than 1,000 true/false, multiple-choice, and essay questions. It has now been tagged with learning objectives as well as Bloom's Taxonomy and AACSB criteria.

- **Assurance of Learning Ready.** Assurance of Learning is an important element of many accreditation standards. Dess 6e is designed specifically to support your Assurance of Learning initiatives. Each chapter in the book begins with a list of numbered learning objectives that appear throughout the chapter, as well as in the end-of-chapter questions and exercises. Every test bank question is also linked to one of these objectives, in addition to level of difficulty, topic area, Bloom's Taxonomy level, and AACSB skill area. *EZ Test,* McGraw-Hill's easy-to-use test bank software, can search the test bank by these and other categories, providing an engine for targeted Assurance of Learning analysis and assessment.
- **AACSB Statement.** The McGraw-Hill Companies is a proud corporate member of AACSB International. Understanding the importance and value of AACSB accreditation, Dess 6e has sought to recognize the curricula guidelines detailed in the AACSB standards for business accreditation by connecting selected questions in Dess 6e and the test bank to the general knowledge and skill guidelines found in the AACSB standards. The statements contained in Dess 6e are provided only as a guide for the users of this text. The AACSB leaves content coverage and assessment within the purview of individual schools, the mission of the school, and the faculty. While Dess 6e and the teaching package make no claim of any specific AACSB qualification or evaluation, we have labeled selected questions within Dess 6e according to the six general knowledge and skills areas.
- **Computerized Test Bank Online.** A comprehensive bank of test questions is provided within a computerized test bank powered by McGraw-Hill's flexible electronic testing program, *EZ Test Online* (www.eztestonline.com). *EZ Test Online* allows you to create paper and online tests or quizzes in this easy-to-use program!

Imagine being able to create and access your test or quiz anywhere, at any time without installing the testing software. Now, with *EZ Test Online,* instructors can select questions from multiple McGraw-Hill test banks or author their own, and then either print the test for paper distribution or give it online.

- **Test Creation.**
  - Author/edit questions online using the 14 different question type templates.
  - Create printed tests or deliver online to get instant scoring and feedback.
  - Create questions pools to offer multiple versions online – great for practice.
  - Export your tests for use in *WebCT, Blackboard, PageOut,* and Apple's *iQuiz.*
  - Compatible with *EZ Test Desktop* tests you've already created.
  - Sharing tests with colleagues, adjuncts, TAs is easy.
- **Online Test Management.**
  - Set availability dates and time limits for your quiz or test.
  - Control how your test will be presented.
  - Assign points by question or question type with drop-down menu.
  - Provide immediate feedback to students or delay until all finish the test.
  - Create practice tests online to enable student mastery.
  - Your roster can be uploaded to enable student self-registration.
- **Online Scoring and Reporting.**
  - Automated scoring for most of *EZ Test*'s numerous question types.
  - Allows manual scoring for essay and other open response questions.
  - Manual rescoring and feedback is also available.
  - *EZ Test*'s grade book is designed to easily export to your grade book.
  - View basic statistical reports.
- **Support and Help.**
  - User's guide and built-in page-specific help.
  - Flash tutorials for getting started on the support site.
  - Support website: *www.mhhe.com/eztest*
  - Product specialist available at 1-800-331-5094.
  - Online Training: *http://auth.mhhe.com/mpss/workshops/.*

PowerPoint Presentation

Prepared by Brad Cox of Midlands Tech, it consists of more than 400 slides incorporating an outline for the chapters tied to learning objectives. Also included are multiple-choice questions that can be used as Classroom Performance System (CPS) questions as well as additional examples outside of the text to promote class discussion.

Instructor's Resource CD-ROM

All instructor supplements are available in this one-stop multimedia resource, which includes the Instructor's Manual, Test Bank, and PowerPoint Presentations.

McGraw-Hill Connect™ Management

Less Managing. More Teaching. Greater Learning. McGraw-Hill *Connect Management* is an online assignment and assessment solution that connects students with the tools and resources they'll need to achieve success.

- **McGraw-Hill *Connect Management* Features.** *Connect Management* offers a number of powerful tools and features to make managing assignments easier, so faculty can spend more time teaching. With *Connect Management,* students can engage with their coursework anytime and anywhere, making the learning process more accessible and efficient. *Connect Management* offers you the features described below.

  - There are chapter quizzes for the 12 chapters, consisting of 15–25 multiple-choice questions, testing students' overall comprehension of concepts presented in the chapter.
  - There are 2 specially crafted interactives for each of the 12 chapters that drill students in the use and application of the concepts and tools of strategic analysis.
  - The majority of the *Connect* exercises are automatically graded, thereby simplifying the task of evaluating each class member's performance and monitoring the learning outcomes.

- **Student Progress Tracking.** *Connect Management* keeps instructors informed about how each student, section, and class is performing, allowing for more productive use of lecture and office hours. The progress-tracking function enables you to

  - View scored work immediately and track individual or group performance with assignment and grade reports.
  - Access an instant view of student or class performance relative to learning objectives.
  - Collect data and generate reports required by many accreditation organizations, such as AACSB.

- **Smart Grading.** When it comes to studying, time is precious. *Connect Management* helps students learn more efficiently by providing feedback and practice material when they need it, where they need it. When it comes to teaching, your time also is precious. The grading function enables you to

  - Have assignments scored automatically, giving students immediate feedback on their work and side-by-side comparisons with correct answers.
  - Access and review each response, manually change grades, or leave comments for students to review.
  - Reinforce classroom concepts with practice tests and instant quizzes.

- **Simple Assignment Management.** With *Connect Management,* creating assignments is easier than ever, so you can spend more time teaching and less time managing. The assignment management function enables you to

  - Create and deliver assignments easily with selectable test bank items.
  - Streamline lesson planning, student progress reporting, and assignment grading to make classroom management more efficient than ever.
  - Go paperless with online submission and grading of student assignments.

- **Instructor Library.** The *Connect Management* Instructor Library is your repository for additional resources to improve student engagement in and out of class. You can select and use any asset that enhances your lecture. The *Connect Management* Instructor Library includes

  - Instructor Manual
  - PowerPoint® files
  - Test Bank

Online Learning Center (OLC)

The instructor section of *www.mhhe.com/dess6e* also includes the Instructor's Manual, PowerPoint Presentations, as well as additional resources.

The Business Strategy Game and GLO-BUS Online Simulations

Both allow teams of students to manage companies in a head-to-head contest for global market leadership. These simulations give students the immediate opportunity to experiment with various strategy options and to gain proficiency in applying the concepts and tools they have been reading about in the chapters. To find out more or to register, please visit *www.mmhe.com/thompsonsims*.

Additional Resources

Create

Craft your teaching resources to match the way you teach! With McGraw-Hill *Create*, *www.mcgrawhill-create.com* you can easily rearrange chapters, combine material from other content sources, and quickly upload content you have written, like your course syllabus or teaching notes. Find the content you need in *Create* by searching through thousands of leading McGraw-Hill textbooks. Arrange your book to fit your teaching style. *Create* even allows you to personalize your book's appearance by selecting the cover and adding your name, school, and course information. Order a *Create* book and you'll receive a complimentary print review copy in 3–5 business days or a complimentary electronic review copy (eComp) via e-mail in about one hour. Go to *www.mcgrawhillcreate.com* today and register. Experience how McGraw-Hill *Create* empowers you to teach *your* students *your* way.

e-book Options

e-books are an innovative way for students to save money and to "go-green", McGraw-Hill's e-books are typically 40% of bookstore price. Students have the choice between an online and a downloadable CourseSmart e-book.

Through *CourseSmart*, students have the flexibility to access an exact replica of their textbook from any computer that has internet service without plug-ins or special software via the version, or create a library of books on their harddrive via the downloadable version. Access to the CourseSmart e-books is 1 year.

Features: *CourseSmart* e-books allow students to highlight, take notes, organize notes, and share the notes with other *CourseSmart* users. Students can also search terms across all e-books in their purchased *CourseSmart* library. *CourseSmart* e-books can be printed (5 pages at a time).

More info and purchase: Please visit *www.coursesmart.com* for more information and to purchase access to our e-books. *CourseSmart* allows students to try 1 chapter of the e-book, free of charge, before purchase.

McGraw-Hill Higher Education and Blackboard

McGraw-Hill Higher Education and Blackboard have teamed up. What does this mean for you?

1. **Your life, simplified.** Now you and your students can access McGraw-Hill's *Connect*™ and *Create*™ right from within your Blackboard course—all with one single sign-on. Say goodbye to the days of logging in to multiple applications.

2. **Deep integration of content and tools.** Not only do you get single sign-on with *Connect* and *Create,* you also get deep integration of McGraw-Hill content and content engines right in Blackboard. Whether you're choosing a book for your course or building Connect assignments, all the tools you need are right where you want them—inside of Blackboard.

3. **Seamless gradebooks.** Are you tired of keeping multiple gradebooks and manually synchronizing grades into Blackboard? We thought so. When a student completes an integrated Connect assignment, the grade for that assignment automatically (and instantly) feeds your Blackboard grade center.

4. **A solution for everyone.** Whether your institution is already using Blackboard or you just want to try Blackboard on your own, we have a solution for you. McGraw-Hill and Blackboard can now offer you easy access to industry-leading technology and content, whether your campus hosts it or we do. Be sure to ask your local McGraw-Hill representative for details.

The **Best** of **Both Worlds**

McGraw-Hill Customer Care Contact Information

At McGraw-Hill, we understand that getting the most from new technology can be challenging. That's why our services don't stop after you purchase our products. You can e-mail our product specialists 24 hours a day to get product training online. Or you can search our knowledge bank of Frequently Asked Questions on our support website, For customer support, call 800-331-5094, e-mail *hmsupport@mcgraw-hill.com*, or visit *www.mhhe.com/support*. One of our technical support analysts will be able to assist you in a timely fashion.

Acknowledgments

Strategic Management represents far more than just the joint efforts of the four co-authors. Rather, it is the product of the collaborative input of many people. Some of these individuals are academic colleagues, others are the outstanding team of professionals at

McGraw-Hill/Irwin, and still others are those who are closest to us—our families. It is time to express our sincere gratitude.

First, we'd like to acknowledge the dedicated instructors who have graciously provided their insights since the inception of the text. Their input has been very helpful in both pointing out errors in the manuscript and suggesting areas that needed further development as additional topics. We sincerely believe that the incorporation of their ideas has been critical to improving the final product. These professionals and their affiliations are:

The Reviewer Hall of Fame

Moses Acquaah, *University of North Carolina–Greensboro*

Todd Alessandri, *Northeastern University*

Larry Alexander, *Virginia Polytechnic Institute*

Brent B. Allred, *College of William & Mary*

Allen C. Amason, *University of Georgia*

Kathy Anders, *Arizona State University*

Peter H. Antoniou, *California State University, San Marcos*

Dave Arnott, *Dallas Baptist University*

Marne L. Arthaud-Day, *Kansas State University*

Jay Azriel, *York University of Pennsylvania*

Jeffrey J. Bailey, *University of Idaho*

Dennis R. Balch, *University of North Alabama*

Bruce Barringer, *University of Central Florida*

Barbara R. Bartkus, *Old Dominion University*

Barry Bayon, *Bryant University*

Brent D. Beal, *Louisiana State University*

Joyce Beggs, *University of North Carolina–Charlotte*

Michael Behnam, *Suffolk University*

Kristen Bell DeTienne, *Brigham Young University*

Eldon Bernstein, *Lynn University*

Daniela Blettner, *Tilburg University*

Dusty Bodie, *Boise State University*

William Bogner, *Georgia State University*

Jon Bryan, *Bridgewater State College*

Charles M. Byles, *Virginia Commonwealth University*

Mikelle A. Calhoun, *Valparaiso University*

Thomas J. Callahan, *University of Michigan, Dearborn*

Samuel D. Cappel, *Southeastern Louisiana State University*

Gary Carini, *Baylor University*

Shawn M. Carraher, *Texas A&M University, Commerce*

Tim Carroll, *University of South Carolina*

Don Caruth, *Amberton University*

Maureen Casile, *Bowling Green State University*

Gary J. Castrogiovanni, *Florida Atlantic University*

Radha Chaganti, *Rider University*

Erick PC Chang, *Arkansas State University*

Theresa Cho, *Rutgers University*

Bruce Clemens, *Western New England College*

Betty S. Coffey, *Appalachian State University*

Wade Coggins, *Webster University, Fort Smith Metro Campus*

Susan Cohen, *University of Pittsburgh*

George S. Cole, *Shippensburg University*

Joseph Coombs, *Texas A & M University*

Christine Cope Pence, *University of California, Riverside*

James J. Cordeiro, *SUNY Brockport*

Jeffrey Covin, *Indiana University*

Keith Credo, *Auburn University*

Deepak Datta, *University of Texas at Arlington*

James Davis, *University of Notre Dame*

David Dawley, *West Virginia University*

Helen Deresky, *State University of New York, Plattsburgh*

Rocki-Lee DeWitt, *University of Vermont*

Jay Dial, *Ohio State University*

Michael E. Dobbs, *Arkansas State University*

Jonathan Doh, *Villanova University*

Tom Douglas, *Clemson University*

Jon Down, *Oregon State University*

Alan E. Ellstrand, *University of Arkansas*

Dean S. Elmuti, *Eastern Illinois University*

Clare Engle, *Concordia University*

Tracy Ethridge, *Tri-County Technical College*

William A. Evans, *Troy State University, Dothan*

Frances H. Fabian, *University of Memphis*

Angelo Fanelli, *Warrington College of Business*

Michael Fathi, *Georgia Southwestern University*

Carolyn J. Fausnaugh, *Florida Institute of Technology*

Tamela D. Ferguson, *University of Louisiana at Lafayette*

David Flanagan, *Western Michigan University*

Dave Foster, *Montana State University*

Isaac Fox, *University of Minnesota*

Deborah Francis, *Brevard College*

Steven A. Frankforter, *Winthrop University*

Vance Fried, *Oklahoma State University*

Naomi A. Gardberg, *CNNY Baruch College*

Mehmet Erdem Genc, *Baruch College, CUNY*

J. Michael Geringer, *California Polytechnic State University*

Diana L. Gilbertson, *California State University, Fresno*

Matt Gilley, *St. Mary's University*

Debbie Gilliard, *Metropolitan State College–Denver*

Yezdi H. Godiwalla, *University of Wisconsin–Whitewater*

Sanjay Goel, *University of Minnesota, Duluth*

Sandy Gough, *Boise State University*

Allen Harmon, *University of Minnesota, Duluth*

Niran Harrison, *University of Oregon*

Paula Harveston, *Berry College*

Ahmad Hassan, *Morehead State University*

Donald Hatfield, *Virginia Polytechnic Institute*

Kim Hester, *Arkansas State University*

John Hironaka, *California State University, Sacramento*

Alan Hoffman, *Bentley College*

Gordon Holbein, *University of Kentucky*

Stephen V. Horner, *Arkansas State University*

Jill Hough, *University of Tulsa*

John Humphreys, *Eastern New Mexico University*

James G. Ibe, *Morris College*

Jay J. Janney, *University of Dayton*

Lawrence Jauch, *University of Louisiana–Monroe*

Dana M. Johnson, *Michigan Technical University*

Homer Johnson, *Loyola University, Chicago*

James Katzenstein, *California State University, Dominguez Hills*

Joseph Kavanaugh, *Sam Houston State University*

Franz Kellermanns, *University of Tennessee*

Craig Kelley, *California State University, Sacramento*

Donna Kelley, *Babson College*

Dave Ketchen, *Auburn University*

John A. Kilpatrick, *Idaho State University*

Helaine J. Korn, *Baruch College, CUNY*

Stan Kowalczyk, *San Francisco State University*

Daniel Kraska, *North Central State College*

Donald E. Kreps, *Kutztown University*

Jim Kroeger, *Cleveland State University*

Subdoh P. Kulkarni, *Howard University*

Ron Lambert, *Faulkner University*

Theresa Lant, *New York University*

Ted Legatski, *Texas Christian University*

David J. Lemak, *Washington State University Tri-Cities*

Cynthia Lengnick-Hall, *University of Texas at San Antonio*

Donald L. Lester, *Arkansas State University*

Wanda Lester, *North Carolina A&T State University*

Benyamin Lichtenstein, *University of Massachusetts at Boston*

Jun Lin, *SUNY at New Paltz*

Zhiang (John) Lin, *University of Texas at Dallas*

Dan Lockhart, *University of Kentucky*

John Logan, *University of South Carolina*

Kevin Lowe, *University of North Carolina, Greensboro*

Doug Lyon, *Fort Lewis College*

Hao Ma, *Bryant College*

Rickey Madden, *Ph.D., Presbyterian College*

James Maddox, *Friends University*

Ravi Madhavan, *University of Pittsburgh*

Paul Mallette, *Colorado State University*

Santo D. Marabella, *Moravian College*

Catherine Maritan, *Syracuse University*

Daniel Marrone, *Farmingdale State College, SUNY*

Sarah Marsh, *Northern Illinois University*

John R. Massaua, *University of Southern Maine*

Larry McDaniel, *Alabama A&M University*

Abagail McWilliams, *University of Illinois, Chicago*

John E. Merchant, *California State University, Sacramento*

John M. Mezias, *University of Miami*

Michael Michalisin, *Southern Illinois University at Carbondale*

Doug Moesel, *University of Missouri Columbia*

Fatma Mohamed, *Morehead State University*

Mike Montalbano, *Bentley University*

Debra Moody, *University of North Carolina, Charlotte*

Gregory A. Moore, *Middle Tennessee State University*

James R. Morgan, *Dominican University and UC Berkeley Extension*

Sara A. Morris, *Old Dominion University*

Carolyn Mu, *Baylor University*

Stephen Mueller, *Northern Kentucky University*

John Mullane, *Middle Tennessee State University*

Gerry Nkombo Muuka, *Murray State University*

Chandran Mylvaganam, *Northwood University*

Anil Nair, *Old Dominion University*

V.K. Narayanan, *Drexel University*

Maria L. Nathan, *Lynchburg College*

Louise Nemanich, *Arizona State University*

Charles Newman, *University of Maryland, University College*

Stephanie Newport, *Austin Peay State University*

Bill Norton, *University of Louisville*

Yusuf A. Nur, *SUNY Brockport*

Jeffrey R. Nystrom, *University of Colorado*

d.t. ogilvie, *Rutgers University*

William Ross O'Brien, *Dallas Baptist University*

Floyd Ormsbee, *Clarkson University*

Karen L. Page, *University of Wyoming*

Jacquelyn W. Palmer, *University of Cincinnati*

Julie Palmer, *University of Missouri, Columbia*

Daewoo Park, *Xavier University*

Gerald Parker, *Saint Louis University*

Ralph Parrish, *University of Central Oklahoma*

Douglas K. Peterson, *Indiana State University*

Edward Petkus, *Mary Baldwin College*

Michael C. Pickett, *National University*

Peter Ping Li, *California State University, Stanislaus*

Michael W. Pitts, *Virginia Commonwealth University*

Laura Poppo, *Virginia Tech*

Steve Porth, *Saint Joseph's University*

Jodi A. Potter, *Robert Morris University*

Scott A. Quatro, *Grand Canyon University*

Nandini Rajagopalan, *University of Southern California*

Annette L. Ranft, *Florida State University*

Abdul Rasheed, *University of Texas at Arlington*

Devaki Rau, *Northern Illinois University*

George Redmond, *Franklin University*

Kira Reed, *Syracuse University*

Clint Relyea, *Arkansas State University*

Barbara Ribbens, *Western Illinois University*

Maurice Rice, *University of Washington*

Violina P. Rindova, *University of Maryland, College Park*

Ron Rivas, *Canisius College*

David Robinson, *Indiana State University–Terre Haute*

Kenneth Robinson, *Kennesaw State University*

Simon Rodan, *San Jose State University*

Patrick R. Rogers, *North Carolina A&T State University*

John K. Ross III, *Texas State University, San Marcos*

Robert Rottman, *Kentucky State University*

Matthew R. Rutherford, *Gonzaga University*

Carol M. Sanchez, *Grand Valley State University*

William W. Sannwald, *San Diego State University*

Yolanda Sarason, *Colorado State University*

Marguerite Schneider, *New Jersey Institute of Technology*

Roger R. Schnorbus, *University of Richmond*

Terry Sebora, *University of Nebraska–Lincoln*

John Seeger, *Bentley College*

Jamal Shamsie, *Michigan State University*

Mark Shanley, *University of Illinois at Chicago*

Lois Shelton, *California State University, Northridge*

Herbert Sherman, *Long Island University*

Weilei Shi, *Baruch College–CUNY*

Chris Shook, *Auburn University*

Jeremy Short, *Texas Tech University*

Mark Simon, *Oakland University, Michigan*

Rob Singh, *Morgan State University*

Bruce Skaggs, *University of Kentucky*

Wayne Smeltz, *Rider University*

Anne Smith, *University of Tennessee*

Andrew Spicer, *University of South Carolina*

James D. Spina, *University of Maryland*

John Stanbury, *George Mason University & Inter-University Institute of Macau, SAR China*

Timothy Stearns, *California State University, Fresno*

Elton Stephen, *Austin State University*

Alice Stewart, *Ohio State University*

Ram Subramanian, *Grand Valley State University*

Roy Suddaby, *University of Iowa*

Michael Sullivan, *UC Berkeley Extension*

Marta Szabo White, *Georgia State University*

Justin Tan, *York University, Canada*

Qingju Tao, *Lehigh University*

Linda Teagarden, *Virginia Tech*

Bing-Sheng Teng, *George Washington University*

Alan Theriault, *University of California–Riverside*

Tracy Thompson, *University of Washington, Tacoma*

Karen Torres, *Angelo State University*

Robert Trumble, *Virginia Commonwealth University*

K.J. Tullis, *University of Central Oklahoma*

Craig A. Turner, *Ph.D., East Tennessee State University*

Beverly Tyler, *North Carolina State University*

Rajaram Veliyath, *Kennesaw State University*

S. Stephen Vitucci, *Tarleton State University–Central Texas*

Jay A. Vora, *St. Cloud State University*

Jorge Walter, *Portland State University*

Bruce Walters, *Louisiana Tech University*

Edward Ward, *St. Cloud State University*

N. Wasilewski, *Pepperdine University*

Andrew Watson, *Northeastern University*

Larry Watts, *Stephen F. Austin University*

Paula S. Weber, *St. Cloud State University*

Kenneth E. A. Wendeln, *Indiana University*

Robert R. Wharton, *Western Kentucky University*

Laura Whitcomb, *California State University–Los Angeles*

Scott Williams, *Wright State University*

Diana Wong, *Bowling Green State University*

Beth Woodard, *Belmont University*

John E. Wroblewski, *State University of New York–Fredonia*

Anne York, *University of Nebraska, Omaha*

Michael Zhang, *Sacred Heart University*

Monica Zimmerman, *Temple University*

Second, the authors would like to thank several faculty colleagues who were particularly helpful in the review, critique, and development of the book and supplementary materials. Greg's colleagues at the University of Texas at Dallas also have been helpful and supportive. These individuals include Mike Peng, Joe Picken, Kumar Nair, John Lin, Roberto Ragozzino, Seung-Hyun Lee, Tev Dalgic, and Jane Salk. His administrative assistant, Mary Vice, has been extremely helpful. Two doctoral students, Brian Pinkham and Ciprian Stan, have provided many useful inputs and ideas, along with a research associate, Yolanda Tsang. He also appreciates the support of his dean and associate dean, Hasan Pirkul and Varghese Jacob, respectively. Tom would like to thank Gerry Hills, Abagail McWilliams, Rod Shrader, Mike Miller, James Gillespie, Ron Mitchell, Kim Boal, Keith Brigham, Jeremy Short, Tyge Payne, Bill Wan, Andy Yu, Abby Wang, Johan Wiklund, Mike Haynie, Alex McKelvie, Cathy Maritan, Ravi Dharwadkar, and Pam Brandes. Special thanks also to Jeff Stambaugh for his vital contribution to new materials prepared for the sixth Edition. Tom also extends a special thanks to Benyamin Lichtenstein for his support and encouragement. Both Greg and Tom wish to thank a special colleague, Abdul Rasheed at the University of Texas at Arlington, who certainly has been a valued source of friendship and ideas for us for many years. He provided many valuable contributions to the sixth Edition. Alan thanks his colleagues at Pace University and the Case Association for their support in developing these fine case selections. Special thanks go to Jamal Shamsie at Michigan State University for his support in developing the case selections for this edition. He is also very grateful to Panline Assenza at Berkeley College for her superb work as case teaching notes and powerpoints editor. And we appreciate Doug Sanford, at University of Towson for his expertise with one of our new pedagogical features—the key terms in each chapter. Gerry thanks all of his colleagues at Michigan State University for their help and support over the years. He also thanks his co-authors, including Phil Bromiley, Paul Vaaler, Cindy Devers, Federico Aime, Mike Mannor, John Haleblian, Kalin Kolev, Seungho Choi, Don Conlon, Bob Wiseman, Rebecca Luce, Kathie Sutcliffe, Jody Tompson, David Deephouse, Bernadine Dykes, Mathias Arrfelt, Mason Carpenter, Rob Davison, and Dustin Sleesman, for their role in helping him grow as a scholar.

Third, we would like to thank the team at McGraw-Hill/Irwin for their outstanding support throughout the process. This begins with John Biernat, formerly Publisher, who signed us to our original contract. John was always available to provide support and valued input during the entire process. In editorial, Paul Ducham, editorial director, executive editor Mike Ablassmeir, development editor Laura Griffin, and editorial coordinator Andrea Heirendt, kept things on track, responded quickly to our never-ending needs and requests, and offered insights and encouragement. Once the manuscript was completed and revised, lead project manager Harvey Yep expertly guided us through the production process. Rachel Townsend, media project manager, did an outstanding job in helping us with the digital materials. Jeremy Cheshareck, senior photo research coordinator, and freelance designer Pam Verros provided excellent design, photo, and art work. We also appreciate executive marketing manager Anke Weekes and marketing specialist Liz Steiner for their energetic, competent, and thorough marketing efforts. Last, but certainly not least, we thank MHI's 70 plus outstanding book reps—who serve on the "front lines." Clearly, they deserve a lot of credit for our success.

Finally, we would like to thank our families. For Greg this includes his parents, William and Mary Dess, who have always been there for him. His wife, Margie, and daughter, Taylor, have been a constant source of love and companionship. Greg would also like to recognize Glenn F. Kirk. He was one of Greg's first managers in industry (Western Electric Company), and he certainly led by example. Glenn was also very patient (and forgiving) with Greg's limited engineering and "collaboration" skills(!). Tom thanks his wife Vicki for her constant love and companionship. Tom also thanks Lee Hetherington and Thelma Lumpkin for their inspiration, as well as his mom Katy, and his sister Kitty, for a lifetime of support. Alan thanks his family—his wife Helaine and his children Rachel and Jacob—for their love and support. He also thanks his parents, Gail Eisner and the late Marvin Eisner, for their support and encouragement. Gerry thanks his wife, Gaelen, for her love, support, and friendship and his children, Megan and AJ, for their love and the joy they bring to his life. He also thanks his parents, Gene and Jane, for their encouragement and support in all phases of his life. Finally, he thanks Phil Bromiley, his academic mentor, for helping him grow as a scholar.

guided tour

Learning Objectives

Learning Objectives numbered LO4.1, LO4.2, LO4.3, etc. with corresponding icons in the margins to indicate where learning objectives are covered in the text.

Learning from Mistakes

Learning from Mistakes are examples of where things went wrong. Failures are not only interesting but also sometimes easier to learn from. And students realize strategy is not just about "right or wrong" answers, but requires critical thinking.

Learning from Mistakes

Toyota Motor Company had developed an industry-leading strategy that focused on value innovation and cost reduction.[1] For many years it was a solid strategy for both the company and its customers. Over the years, Toyota built a reputation for engineering excellence and cost cutting. Its engineers collaborated with suppliers to extract cost-savings without compromising quality. Yet, by the middle of the last decade, Toyota's virtue had become a vice and eventually led to recalled vehicles, lawsuits, and a damaged reputation. What went wrong?

Toyota's problems stemmed from an overwhelming desire to cut costs. This, in turn, led to a product that did not meet the same high quality that its customers had come to expect. When a North American parts supplier interested in working with the automaker did a teardown of a 2007 Camry, its engineers were surprised by how much the traditional Toyota craftsmanship had been watered down by years of nips and tucks. One example of this came to light in 2006, when a redesigned Camry revealed an embarrassing flaw in its headliner (the lining that covers the inside of the roof). Under pressure to cut costs, a Toyota affiliate chose a carbon fiber material that had not yet been approved by Toyota engineers. Unfortunately, the new carbon fiber material required so much heat to mold during production that it would catch fire. Thus, as many as 30 percent of the parts were scrapped—compared to a normal scrap rate for headliners of about 5 percent.

6.6 strategy spotlight

Crowdsourcing: How a Strategic Alliance Will Benefit Both Parties

MRM Worldwide, a New York-based advertising firm, has entered into a strategic alliance with Aniboom, a "virtual" animation company. The alliance is designed to bring MRM's clients quicker and more cost-efficient animation services

in the future as clients seek more efficient ways of doing business.

MRM's plans are to have animators compete for work: "MRMs clients can launch a content creation competition in the Aniboom community for advertising solutions and have the community at large or a panel of judges select the top finalists and ultimate winner of the assign-

Sources: Van Hoven, M. 2009. Strategic Alliances: MRM and Aniboom Team Up, Crowdsource. www.mediabistro.com. August 31. np; and McClellan, S. 2009. MRM, Aniboom Team Up. www.adweek.com. August 31. np.

crowdsourcing

Strategy Spotlight

These boxes weave themes of ethics, globalization, and technology into every chapter of the text, providing students with a thorough grounding necessary for understanding strategic management. Select boxes incorporating crowdsourcing, environmental sustainability, and ethical themes include the following icons:

8.2 strategy spotlight

Entrepreneurial Vision to Revitalize Detroit

Detroit is the poorest major city in America. With an unemployment rate of 26 percent and a declining population, it

that is surrounded by the Great Lakes and having served as a member of the Detroit Water and Sewerage Board of Commissioners, Oliver appreciated the value of water as a critical resource needed for economic development. Fresh water is a commodity increasingly demanded around the

Although these businesses span a wide range of industries, they demonstrate that entrepreneurial vision often arises out an individual's experiences and can encompass both a business idea as well as a vehicle with which to improve conditions in a larger community.

Sources: Suhail, F. 2010. Alternative Energy: Creating Non-exportable Jobs. Forbes.com. June 30. np; Easton, N. 2010. If You Can Remake Yourself Here. Fortune. November 1: 59–63; Gray, S. 2010. When Entrepreneurs Need Nerves of Steel. Fortune. October 18: 63–66; Saulny, S. 2010. Detroit Entrepreneurs Opt to Look Up. The New York Times, January 10: A18; Anonymous. 2010. Champions of the New Economy. eBusiness. Mar/June np; Whitford, D. 2010. Can Farming Save Detroit? Fortune. January 10: 78–84.

crowdsourcing   **environmental sustainability**   **ethics**

Key Terms

Key Terms defined in the margins have been added to improve students' understanding of core strategy concepts.

human capital the individual capabilities, knowledge, skills, and experience of a company's employees and managers.

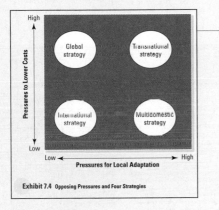

Exhibit 7.4 Opposing Pressures and Four Strategies

Exhibits

Both new and improved exhibits in every chapter provide visual presentations of the most complex concepts covered to support student comprehension.

Reflecting on Career Implications

This new section before the summary of every chapter consists of examples on how understanding of key concepts helps business students early in their careers.

Reflecting on Career Implications . . .

- *Creating the Environmentally Aware Organization:* In your career, what are some ways in which you can engage in scanning, monitoring, and intelligence gathering for future job opportunities? Consider, for example, subscribing to your field's professional publications and becoming actively involved in relevant professional organizations.
- *SWOT Analysis:* From a career standpoint, periodically evaluate your strengths and weaknesses as well as potential opportunities and threats to your career. In addition, strive to seek input from trusted peers and superiors.
- *General Environment:* Carefully evaluate the elements of the general environment facing your firm. Identify factors (e.g., rapid technological change) that can provide promising career opportunities as well as possibilities for you to add value for your organization. In doing this, don't focus solely on "internal factors" of your organization.
- *Five-Forces Analysis:* Consider the five forces affecting the industry within which your organization competes. If the "forces" are unfavorable, the long-term profit potential of the industry may be unattractive. And, there will likely be fewer resources available and—all other things being equal—fewer career opportunities.

support materials

Online Learning Center (OLC)

The website *www.mhhe.com/dess6e* follows the text chapter-by-chapter. OLC content is ancillary and supplementary germane to the textbook. As students read the book, they can go online to take self-grading quizzes, review material, or work through interactive exercises. It includes chapter quizzes, student PowerPoint slides, and links to strategy simulations The *Business Strategy Game* and GLO-BUS.

The instructor section also includes the Instructor's Manual, PowerPoint Presentations, Test Bank as well as all student resources.

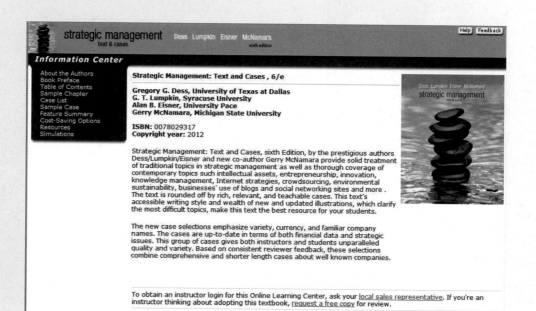

Brief Contents

Contents

part 2 Strategic Formulation

Chapter 5

Business-Level Strategy: Creating and Sustaining Competitive Advantages. 160

Chapter 6

Corporate-Level Strategy: Creating Value through Diversification 200

part 3 Strategic
Implementation

Chapter 9
Strategic Control and Corporate
Governance 316

Chapter 10
Creating Effective Organizational
Designs 354

part 4 Case Analysis

Strategic Management

creating competitive advantages

sixth edition

The Strategic Management Process

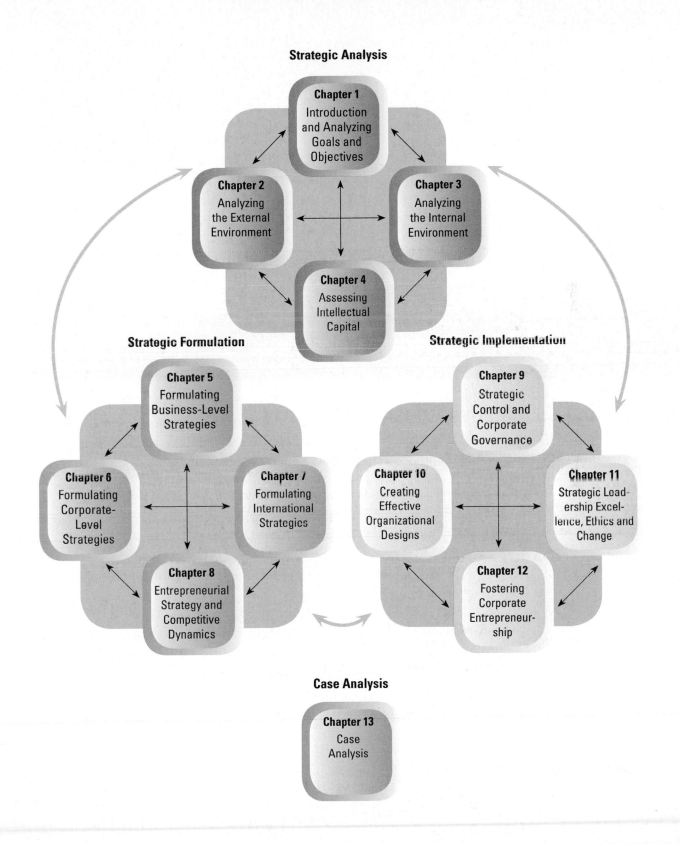

Strategic Analysis

Chapter 1
Introduction and Analyzing Goals and Objectives

Chapter 2
Analyzing the External Environment

Chapter 3
Analyzing the Internal Environment

Chapter 4
Assessing Intellectual Capital

Strategic Formulation

Chapter 5
Formulating Business-Level Strategies

Chapter 6
Formulating Corporate-Level Strategies

Chapter 7
Formulating International Strategies

Chapter 8
Entrepreneurial Strategy and Competitive Dynamics

Strategic Implementation

Chapter 9
Strategic Control and Corporate Governance

Chapter 10
Creating Effective Organizational Designs

Chapter 11
Strategic Leadership Excellence, Ethics and Change

Chapter 12
Fostering Corporate Entrepreneurship

Case Analysis

Chapter 13
Case Analysis

Strategic Management:

Creating Competitive Advantages

After reading this chapter, you should have a good understanding of:

LO1.1 The definition of strategic management and its four key attributes.

LO1.2 The strategic management process and its three interrelated and principal activities.

LO1.3 The vital role of corporate governance and stakeholder management as well as how "symbiosis" can be achieved among an organization's stakeholders.

LO1.4 The importance of social responsibility, including environmental sustainability, and how it can enhance a corporation's innovation strategy.

LO1.5 The need for greater empowerment throughout the organization.

LO1.6 How an awareness of a hierarchy of strategic goals can help an organization achieve coherence in its strategic direction.

LEARNING OBJECTIVES

We define strategic management as *consisting of the analyses, decisions, and actions an organization undertakes in order to create and sustain competitive advantages.* At the heart of strategic management is the question: How and why do some firms outperform others? Thus, the challenge to managers is to decide on strategies that provide advantages that can be sustained over time. There are four key attributes of strategic management. It is directed at overall organizational goals, includes multiple stakeholders, incorporates short-term as well as long-term perspectives, and recognizes trade-offs between effectiveness and efficiency. We discuss the above definition and the four key attributes in the first section.

The second section addresses the strategic management process. The three major processes are strategy analysis, strategy formulation, and strategy implementation. These three components parallel the analyses, decisions, and actions in the above definition. We discuss how each of the 12 chapters addresses these three processes and provide examples from each chapter.

The third section discusses two important and interrelated concepts: corporate governance and stakeholder management. Corporate governance addresses the issue of who "governs" the corporation and determines its direction. It consists of three primary participants: stockholders (owners), management (led by the chief executive officer), and the board of directors (elected to monitor management). Stakeholder management recognizes that the interests of various stakeholders, such as owners, customers, and employees, can often conflict and create challenging decision-making dilemmas for managers. However, we discuss how some firms have been able to achieve "symbiosis" among stakeholders wherein their interests are considered interdependent and can be achieved simultaneously. We also discuss the important role of social responsibility and explain the concept of "shared value." Further, we emphasize the need for corporations to incorporate environmental sustainability in their strategic actions.

The fourth section addresses factors in the business environment that have increased the level of unpredictable change for today's leaders. Such factors have also created the need for a greater strategic management perspective and reinforced the role of empowerment throughout the organization.

The final section focuses on the need for organizations to ensure consistency in their vision, mission, and strategic objectives which, collectively, form a hierarchy of goals. While visions may lack specificity, they must evoke powerful and compelling mental images. Strategic objectives are much more specific and are essential for driving toward overall goals.

Learning from Mistakes

What makes the study of strategic management so interesting? For one, struggling firms can become stars, while high flyers can become earthbound very rapidly. As colorfully noted by Arthur Martinez, Sears' former chairman: "Today's peacock is tomorrow's feather duster." Consider, for example, the change in membership on the prestigious *Fortune 500* list of the largest U.S. firms:[1]

- Of the 500 companies that appeared on the first list in 1955, only 62, ranked by revenue, have appeared on the list every year since.
- Some of the most powerful companies on today's list—businesses like Intel, Apple, and Google—grew from nothing to great on the strength of new technologies, bumping venerable old companies off the list.
- Nearly 2,000 companies have appeared on the list since its inception, and most are long gone from it. Just making the list guarantees nothing about your ability to endure.
- In 2009 and 2010, admittedly more volatile years than most, 71 companies—including Bear Stearns, Circuit City, Merrill Lynch, and Tribune—dropped off the 500.

Let's take a look at another fallen star, Nokia, the Finnish phone manufacturer. Nokia captured the emerging market for mobile phones and built the industry's most powerful brand in the 1990s.[2] Its handsets virtually defined the industry from the time it launched the first GSM phone in 1992. Then from 1996 to 2001, its revenues increased almost fivefold, and in 1998 it was the world's largest mobile manufacturer. In 2005 it sold its billionth handset, an 1100 model, to a customer in Nigeria. Unfortunately, Nokia's market dominance was short-lived. What happened?

While Nokia focused on emerging markets, it took its eye off the ball in developed economies, where the smartphone revolution was on its way. Nokia's focus on mobile phones for voice communication turned out to be their most disastrous call in the past 10 years. In addition to voice communications, customers also demanded interactive applications, Web browsing, and global positioning systems—as provided by Apple's iPhone and RIM's BlackBerry. As noted in *The Economist:* "Apple's iPhone and Google's Android range compete on 'cool.' BlackBerry is synonymous with business. But what does Nokia stand for?"

Nokia's inability to meet customer needs in both established and emerging markets resulted in a significant drop in its market share. It dropped from almost 51 percent in the fourth quarter of 2007 to less than 41 percent in the fourth quarter of 2008.

Since Apple introduced its first iPhone on January 9, 2007, Nokia's stock dropped 45 percent over the next three years—wiping out about $77 billion in the firm's market capitalization. Over the same period, Apple's shares soared 234 percent! Further, the 2010 global brands ranking by Millward Brown Optimor, placed Nokia in 43rd place, i.e., 30 places down compared to its position in 2009. Its profit margins had also been shrinking, along with its market share and the average price of its phones. Finally, at its peak, Nokia accounted for 4 percent of Finland's gross national product—by 2009, that share was down to only 1.6 percent, according to Helsinki-based economic research institute, ETLA.

Nokia also suffered from its location. Building a mobile telephone giant in Finland was a great achievement. However, Nokia wasn't surrounded by Internet companies or consumer electronics manufacturers. It wasn't exposed to a culture of innovation which would have forced it to question its assumptions and business decisions. Maybe in short, Nokia needed to be where the action was, that is, in the middle of the computer industry as well as the film, music, and Internet businesses. As suggested by *Bloomberg BusinessWeek:*

> Nokia should have relocated to California a decade ago. It would have caused an outcry in Finland, and probably Brussels as well. And it would have been worth it. Nokia needed to pitch itself into the cauldron of technological change. Maybe that way it could have held onto its brand leadership, rather than surrender it to a computer manufacturer that looked dead on its feet a decade ago.

The cruel truth—for all its residual market share—is that Nokia misread the way the mobile phone industry was merging with the computer industry and social networking. And now, maybe it's too late to turn that around.

Today's leaders, such as those at Nokia, face a large number of complex challenges in the global marketplace. In considering how much credit (or blame) they deserve, two perspectives of leadership come immediately to mind: the "romantic" and "external control" perspectives.[3] First, let's look at the **romantic view of leadership.** Here, the implicit assumption is that the leader is the key force in determining an organization's success—or lack thereof.[4] This view dominates the popular press in business magazines such as *Fortune, BusinessWeek,* and *Forbes,* wherein the CEO is either lauded for his or her firm's success or chided for the organization's demise.[5] Consider, for example, the credit that has been bestowed on leaders such as Jack Welch, Andrew Grove, and Herb Kelleher for the tremendous accomplishments of their firms, General Electric, Intel, and Southwest Airlines, respectively.

romantic view of leadership
situations in which the leader is the key force determining the organization's success—or lack thereof.

Similarly, Apple's success in the last decade has been attributed almost entirely to Steve Jobs, its CEO.[6] Apple's string of hit products such as iMac computers, iPods, and iPhones are testament to his genius for developing innovative, user-friendly, and aesthetically pleasing products. In addition to being a perfectionist in product design, Jobs also is a master showman with a cult following. On January 14, 2009, he announced that he was taking a medical leave through June. Perhaps not surprisingly, Apple's stock immediately dropped 10 percent. And, almost exactly two years later, on January 17, 2011, Jobs announced that he was taking another medical leave. The immediate reaction: Apple's shares went down 6 percent the following week—this reflects a drop of around $20 billion in the firm's market value.[7]

Finally, consider how George Buckley reinvigorated 3M's focus on innovation. 3M, with $23 billion in 2010 revenues, produces an astonishing 55,000 different products. Its goal has always been to generate 30 percent of its sales from products introduced in the past five years. However, when the board asked Buckley in 2005 to assume the CEO position, this benchmark had dropped to only 21 percent. Strategy Spotlight 1.1 describes Buckley's strong initiatives to accelerate 3M's rate of innovation.

● The BP oil spill in April 2010, severely affected many industries along the Gulf Coast.

How CEO George Buckley Turned Around 3M

Why is innovation important to 3M? As their older products become outmoded or become commodities, they must be replaced. According to Larry Wendling, head of 3M's corporate research, "Our business model is literally new-product innovation." However, when James McNerney left the company to become Boeing's CEO, the percentage had slid to 21 percent. And, what's worse, much of the new product revenue came from a single category: optical films.

The board went outside the firm for its new CEO and appointed George Buckley, who had previously served as CEO of Brunswick, an Illinois company known for bowling gear and boats. What is perhaps most important to know about Buckley, however, is that he has a Ph.D. in electrical engineering and is a scientist at heart, with several patents to his name. He states: "This is to me an engineer's and scientist's Toys'R'Us," and "There is no company like it in America. There is no company like it in the world."

When Buckley took over 3M, he quickly set some clear business goals for the company. He wanted his managers to protect and strengthen 3M's core businesses, which included abrasives, optical film, and industrial tapes. He also wanted 3M to develop lower-cost products to compete in emerging markets, as well as for the firm to play a key role in future growth markets such as renewable energy, water infrastructure, and mobile digital media.

Perhaps most important, Buckley has been an outspoken champion for 3M's labs. In 2009, despite the deep recession, he kept R&D spending at more than $1 billion and asserted that "even in the worst economic times in memory, we released over 1,000 new products." He also removed the stringent focus on efficiency, particularly in basic research. This had a huge psychic payoff for staff at the science-centric company. Ram Charan, a world-famous consultant who advises the firm claims "George has accelerated the innovation machine by devoting his personal time, his energy, his focus, to empowering the researchers, opening up their minds and urging them to restore the luster of 3M." Buckley's results are impressive: The percentage of 3M's revenue from products introduced in the past five years is back to 30 percent and is expected to reach the mid-30s by 2012.

In closing, Marc Gunther, a contributing editor at *Fortune* magazine, provides some interesting personal insights: "Buckley is a charming and, above all, enthusiastic guy . . . who, in his spare time, likes taking apart and putting together old motorcycles or restoring Victorian furniture . . . While he surely needs traditional management skills to oversee a global company of 75,000 people, my sense is that his scientific curiosity about how the world works and boyish delight in how things get invented make him a perfect fit for 3M."

Sources: Gunther, M. 2010. 3M's innovation revival. *Fortune.* September 27: 73–76; Hindo, B. 2007. 3M chief plants a money tree. *www.businessweek.com.* June 11: np; and, Gunther, M. Why 3M is unique. *theenergycollective.com.* December 10: np.

On the other hand, when things don't go well, much of the failure of an organization can also, rightfully, be attributed to the leader.[8] Nokia's leadership failed to see the changes taking place in the mobile phone industry. In contrast, Apple fully capitalized on the emerging trend toward sophisticated smartphones.

The contrasting fortunes of Hewlett-Packard under two different CEOs also demonstrate the influence leadership has on firm performance.[9] When Carly Fiorina was fired as CEO of the firm, HP enjoyed an immediate increase in its stock price of 7 percent—hardly a strong endorsement of her leadership! Her successor, Mark Hurd, led the firm to five years of outstanding financial results. Interestingly, when he abruptly resigned on August 6, 2010, the firm's stock dropped 12 percent almost instantly! (To provide some perspective, this represents a decrease in HP's market value of about $12 billion.)

However, this reflects only part of the picture. Consider another perspective called the **external control view of leadership.** Here, rather than making the implicit assumption that the leader is the most important factor in determining organizational outcomes, the focus is on external factors that may positively (or negatively) affect a firm's success. We don't have to look far to support this perspective. Developments in the general environment,

external control view of leadership situations in which external forces—where the leader has limited influence—determine the organization's success.

such as economic downturns, governmental legislation, or an outbreak of major internal conflict or war, can greatly restrict the choices that are available to a firm's executives. In addition, major unanticipated developments can often have very negative consequences for businesses regardless of how well formulated their strategies are.

Let's look at a few recent examples:[10]

- Hurricane Katrina in 2007 had a disastrous effect on businesses located along the Gulf Coast.
- The financial meltdown of 2008 and the resultant deep recession during the following two years forced once proud corporations like General Motors and Citigroup to ask for government bailouts. Others, such as Merrill Lynch and Washington Mutual, had to be acquired by other firms.
- In the aftermath of BP's disastrous oil well explosion on April 20, 2010, the fishing and tourism industries in the region suffered significant downturns. BP itself was forced to pay a $20 billion fine to the U.S. government.
- In April 2010, a volcanic eruption in Iceland disrupted air traffic all over Europe for well over a week. It is estimated that major airlines lost approximately $1.7 billion.
- On March 11, 2011, a 9.0 earthquake and tsunami devastated Japan and resulted in the loss of more than 20,000 lives. During the next two trading days, the country's stock exchange (Nikkei) suffered its biggest loss in 40 years. The disaster hit nearly every industry hard—especially energy companies. For example, Tokyo Electric Power Co., which operates a nuclear power plant that was severly damaged, fell 24.7 percent, and Toshiba Corp., a maker of nuclear power plants, slid 19.5 percent. Firms as diverse as Toyota, Honda, and Sony were forced to halt production because extensive damage to roads and distribution systems made it nearly impossible to move products.

Before moving on, it is important to point out that successful executives are often able to navigate around the difficult circumstances that they face. At times it can be refreshing to see the optimistic position they take when they encounter seemingly insurmountable odds. Of course, that's not to say that one should be naïve or Pollyannaish. Consider, for example, how one CEO is handling trying times:[11]

Name a general economic woe, and the chances are that Charles Needham is dealing with it.

- Market turmoil has knocked 80 percent off the shares of South Africa's Metorex, the mining company that he heads.
- The plunge in global commodities is slamming prices for the copper, cobalt, and other minerals Metorex unearths across Africa. The credit crisis makes it harder to raise money.
- And fighting has again broken out in the Democratic Republic of Congo, where Metorex has a mine and several projects in development.

Such problems might send many executives to the window ledge. Yet Needham appears unruffled as he sits down at a conference table in the company's modest offices in a Johannesburg suburb. The combat in northeast Congo, he notes, is far from Metorex's mine. Commodity prices are still high, in historical terms. And Needham is confident he can raise enough capital, drawing on relationships with South African banks. "These are the kinds of things you deal with, doing business in Africa," he says.

What Is Strategic Management?

Given the many challenges and opportunities in the global marketplace, today's managers must do more than set long-term strategies and hope for the best.[12] They must go beyond what some have called "incremental management," whereby they view their job as making

strategic management the analyses, decisions, and actions an organization undertakes in order to create and sustain competitive advantages.

a series of small, minor changes to improve the efficiency of their firm's operations.[13] That is fine if your firm is competing in a very stable, simple, and unchanging industry. But there aren't many of those left. The pace of change is accelerating, and the pressure on managers to make both major and minor changes in a firm's strategic direction is increasing.

Rather than seeing their role as merely custodians of the status quo, today's leaders must be proactive, anticipate change, and continually refine and, when necessary, make dramatic changes to their strategies. The strategic management of the organization must become both a process and a way of thinking throughout the organization.

Defining Strategic Management

>LO1.1

The definition of strategic management and its four key attributes.

Strategic management consists of the analyses, decisions, and actions an organization undertakes in order to create and sustain competitive advantages. This definition captures two main elements that go to the heart of the field of strategic management.

First, the strategic management of an organization entails three ongoing processes: *analyses, decisions,* and *actions.* Strategic management is concerned with the *analysis* of strategic goals (vision, mission, and strategic objectives) along with the analysis of the internal and external environment of the organization. Next, leaders must make strategic decisions. These *decisions,* broadly speaking, address two basic questions: What industries should we compete in? How should we compete in those industries? These questions also often involve an organization's domestic and international operations. And last are the *actions* that must be taken. Decisions are of little use, of course, unless they are acted on. Firms must take the necessary actions to implement their **strategies.** This requires leaders to allocate the necessary resources and to design the organization to bring the intended strategies to reality.

strategy The ideas, decisions, and actions that enable a firm to succeed.

Second, the essence of strategic management is the study of why some firms outperform others.[14] Thus, managers need to determine how a firm is to compete so that it can obtain advantages that are sustainable over a lengthy period of time. That means focusing on two fundamental questions:

competitive advantage A firm's resources and capabilities that enable it to overcome the competitive forces in its industry(ies).

- *How should we compete in order to create **competitive advantages** in the marketplace?* Managers need to determine if the firm should position itself as the low-cost producer or develop products and services that are unique and will enable the firm to charge premium prices. Or should they do some combination of both?
- *How can we create competitive advantages in the marketplace that are unique, valuable, and difficult for rivals to copy or substitute?* That is, managers need to make such advantages sustainable, instead of temporary.

Rivals almost always copy ideas that work. In the 1980s, American Airlines tried to establish a competitive advantage by introducing the frequent flyer program. Within weeks, all the airlines did the same thing. Overnight, frequent flyer programs became a necessary tool for competitive parity instead of a competitive advantage. The challenge, therefore, is to create competitive advantages that are sustainable.

operational effectiveness performing similar activities better than rivals.

Sustainable competitive advantage cannot be achieved through operational effectiveness alone.[15] The popular management innovations of the last two decades—total quality, just-in-time, benchmarking, business process reengineering, outsourcing—are all about operational effectiveness. **Operational effectiveness** means performing similar activities better than rivals. Each of these is important, but none lead to sustainable competitive advantage because everyone is doing them. Strategy is all about being different. Sustainable competitive advantage is possible only by performing different activities from rivals or performing similar activities in different ways. Companies such as Walmart, Southwest Airlines, and IKEA have developed unique, internally consistent, and difficult-to-imitate activity systems that have provided them with sustained competitive advantages. A company with a good strategy must make clear choices about what it wants to accomplish. Trying to do everything that your rivals do eventually leads to mutually destructive price competition, not long-term advantage.

The Four Key Attributes of Strategic Management

Before discussing the strategic management process, let's briefly talk about four attributes of strategic management.[16] It should become clear how this course differs from other courses that you have had in functional areas, such as accounting, marketing, operations, and finance. Exhibit 1.1 provides a definition and the four attributes of strategic management.

First, strategic management is *directed toward overall organizational goals and objectives.* That is, effort must be directed at what is best for the total organization, not just a single functional area. Some authors have referred to this perspective as "organizational versus individual rationality."[17] That is, what might look "rational" or ideal for one functional area, such as operations, may not be in the best interest of the overall firm. For example, operations may decide to schedule long production runs of similar products to lower unit costs. However, the standardized output may be counter to what the marketing department needs to appeal to a demanding target market. Similarly, research and development may "overengineer" the product to develop a far superior offering, but the design may make the product so expensive that market demand is minimal. Therefore, in this course you will look at cases and strategic issues from the perspective of the organization rather than that of the functional area(s) in which you have the strongest background.

Second, strategic management *includes multiple stakeholders in decision making.*[18] **Stakeholders** are those individuals, groups, and organizations who have a "stake" in the success of the organization, including owners (shareholders in a publicly held corporation), employees, customers, suppliers, the community at large, and so on. (We'll discuss this in more detail later in this chapter.) Managers will not be successful if they focus on a single stakeholder. For example, if the overwhelming emphasis is on generating profits for the owners, employees may become alienated, customer service may suffer, and the suppliers may resent demands for pricing concessions. However, many organizations can satisfy multiple stakeholder needs simultaneously. For example, financial performance may increase because employees who are satisfied with their jobs work harder to enhance customer satisfaction—leading to higher profits.

Third, strategic management *requires incorporating both short-term and long-term perspectives.*[19] Peter Senge, a leading strategic management author, has referred to this need as a "creative tension."[20] That is, managers must maintain both a vision for the future of the organization as well as a focus on its present operating needs. However, financial

stakeholders
individuals, groups, and organizations who have a stake in the success of the organization, including owners (shareholders in a publicly held corporation), employees, customers, suppliers, and the community at large.

Definition: Strategic management consists of the analyses, decisions, and actions an organization undertakes in order to create and sustain competitive advantages.

Key Attributes of Strategic Management

- Directs the organization toward overall goals and objectives.
- Includes multiple stakeholders in decision making.
- Needs to incorporate short-term and long-term perspectives.
- Recognizes trade-offs between efficiency and effectiveness.

Exhibit 1.1
Strategic Management Concepts

markets can exert significant pressures on executives to meet short-term performance targets. Studies have shown that corporate leaders often take a short-term approach to the detriment of creating long-term shareholder value. Consider the following:

> According to recent studies, only 59 percent of financial executives say they would pursue a positive net present value project if it meant missing the quarter's consensus earnings per-share estimate. Worse, 78 percent say they would sacrifice value—often a great deal of value—to smooth earnings. Similarly, managers are more likely to cut R&D to reverse an earning slide if a significant amount of the company's equity is owned by institutions with high portfolio turnover. Many companies have the same philosophy about long-term investments such as infrastructure and employee training.[21]

Fourth, strategic management *involves the recognition of trade-offs between effectiveness and efficiency.* Some authors have referred to this as the difference between "doing the right thing" **(effectiveness)** and "doing things right" **(efficiency).**[22] While managers must allocate and use resources wisely, they must still direct their efforts toward the attainment of overall organizational objectives. Managers who only focus on meeting short-term budgets and targets may fail to attain the broader goals. Consider the following amusing story told by Norman Augustine, former CEO of defense giant Martin Marietta (now Lockheed Martin):

> I am reminded of an article I once read in a British newspaper which described a problem with the local bus service between the towns of Bagnall and Greenfields. It seemed that, to the great annoyance of customers, drivers had been passing long queues of would-be passengers with a smile and a wave of the hand. This practice was, however, clarified by a bus company official who explained, "It is impossible for the drivers to keep their timetables if they must stop for passengers."[23]

Clearly, the drivers who were trying to stay on schedule had ignored the overall mission. As Augustine noted, "Impeccable logic but something seems to be missing!"

Successful managers must make many trade-offs. It is central to the practice of strategic management. At times, managers must focus on the short term and efficiency; at other times the emphasis is on the long term and expanding a firm's product-market scope in order to anticipate opportunities in the competitive environment. For example, consider Kevin Sharer's perspective. He is CEO of Amgen, the giant $15 billion biotechnology firm:

> A CEO must always be switching between what I call different altitudes—tasks of different levels of abstraction and specificity. At the highest altitude you're asking the big questions: What are the company's mission and strategy? Do people understand and believe in these aims? Are decisions consistent with them? At the lowest altitude, you're looking at on-the-ground operations: Did we make that sale? What was the yield on that last lot in the factory? How many days of inventory do we have for a particular drug? And then there's everything in between: How many chemists do we need to hire this quarter? What should we pay for a small biotech company that has a promising new drug? Is our production capacity adequate to roll out a product in a new market?[24]

Some authors have developed the concept of **"ambidexterity"** which refers to a manager's challenge to both align resources to take advantage of existing product markets as well as proactively explore new opportunities.[25] Strategy Spotlight 1.2 discusses ambidextrous behaviors that are required for success in today's challenging marketplace.

The Strategic Management Process

We've identified three ongoing processes—analyses, decisions, and actions—that are central to strategic management. In practice, these three processes—often referred to as strategy analysis, strategy formulation, and strategy implementation—are highly interdependent and do not take place one after the other in a sequential fashion in most companies.

effectiveness tailoring actions to the needs of an organization rather than wasting effort, or "doing the right thing."

efficiency performing actions at a low cost relative to a benchmark, or "doing things right."

ambidexterity the challenge managers face of both aligning resources to take advantage of existing product markets as well as proactively exploring new opportunities.

strategic management process strategy analysis, strategy formulation, and strategy implementation

>LO1.2
The strategic management process and its three interrelated and principal activities.

Ambidextrous Behaviors: Combining Alignment and Adaptability

A recent study involving 41 business units in 10 multinational companies identified four ambidextrous behaviors in individuals. Such behaviors are the essence of ambidexterity, and they illustrate how a dual capacity for alignment and adaptability can be woven into the fabric of an organization at the individual level.

They take time and are alert to opportunities beyond the confines of their own jobs. A large computer company's sales manager became aware of a need for a new software module that nobody currently offered. Instead of selling the customer something else, he worked up a business case for the new module. With management's approval, he began working full time on its development.

They are cooperative and seek out opportunities to combine their efforts with others. A marketing manager for Italy was responsible for supporting a newly acquired subsidiary. When frustrated about the limited amount of contact she had with her peers in other countries, she began discussions with them. This led to the creation of a European marketing forum which meets quarterly to discuss issues, share best practices, and collaborate on marketing plans.

They are brokers, always looking to build internal networks. When visiting the head office in St. Louis, a Canadian plant manager heard about plans for a $10 million investment for a new tape manufacturing plant. After inquiring further about the plans and returning to

Canada, he contacted a regional manager in Manitoba, who he knew was looking for ways to build his business. With some generous support from the Manitoba government, the regional manager bid for, and ultimately won, the $10 million investment.

They are multitaskers who are comfortable wearing more than one hat. Although an operations manager for a major coffee and tea distributor was charged with running his plant as efficiently as possible, he took it upon himself to identify value-added services for his clients. By developing a dual role, he was able to manage operations and develop a promising electronic module that automatically reported impending problems inside a coffee vending machine. With corporate funding, he found a subcontractor to develop the software, and he then piloted the module in his own operations. It was so successful that it was eventually adopted by operations managers in several other countries.

A recent *Harvard Business Review* article provides some useful insights on how one can become a more ambidextrous leader. Consider the following questions:

- **Do you meet your numbers?**
- **Do you help others?**
- **What do you do for your peers?** Are you just their in-house competitor?
- **When you manage up, do you bring problems—or problems with possible solutions?**
- **Are you transparent?** Managers who get a reputation for spinning events gradually lose the trust of peers and superiors.
- **Are you developing a group of senior-managers who know you and are willing to back your original ideas with resources?**

Source: Birkinshaw, J. & Gibson, C. 2004. Building ambidexterity into an organization. *MIT Sloan Management Review*, 45(4): 47–55; and, Bower, J. L. 2007. Solve the succession crisis by growing inside-out leaders. *Harvard Business Review*, 85(11): 90–99.

Intended versus Realized Strategies

Henry Mintzberg, a management scholar at McGill University, argues that viewing the strategic management process as one in which analysis is followed by optimal decisions and their subsequent meticulous implementation neither describes the strategic management process accurately nor prescribes ideal practice.[26] He sees the business environment as far from predictable, thus limiting our ability for analysis. Further, decisions are seldom based on optimal rationality alone, given the political processes that occur in all organizations.[27]

Taking into consideration the limitations discussed above, Mintzberg proposed an alternative model. As depicted in Exhibit 1.2, decisions following from analysis, in this model, constitute the ***intended* strategy** of the firm. For a variety of reasons, the intended strategy rarely survives in its original form. Unforeseen environmental developments,

intended strategy
strategy in which organizational decisions are determined only by analysis.

Exhibit 1.2   Realized Strategy and Intended Strategy: Usually Not the Same

Source: From Mintzberg, H. & Waters, J. A., "Of Strategies: Deliberate and Emergent," *Strategic Management Journal,* Vol. 6, 1985, pp. 257–272. Copyright © John Wiley & Sons Limited. Reproduced with permission.

unanticipated resource constraints, or changes in managerial preferences may result in at least some parts of the intended strategy remaining *unrealized.* On the other hand, good managers will want to take advantage of a new opportunity presented by the environment, even if it was not part of the original set of intentions. For example, consider the wind energy industry.

> In October 2008, the United States Congress extended a key wind tax credit and many states have mandates requiring utilities to tap renewable energy. Such legislation, combined with falling clean energy costs and wildly cyclical prices for coal, oil, and gas, has created a surge in demand for companies such as GE Wind Energy, which makes large turbines and fan blades. Not surprisingly, such businesses have increased hiring and research and development, as well as profit and revenue forecasts.[28]

Thus, the final **realized strategy** of any firm is a combination of deliberate and emergent strategies.

Next, we will address each of the three key strategic management processes: strategy analysis, strategy formulation, and strategy implementation and provide a brief overview of the chapters.

Exhibit 1.3 depicts the strategic management process and indicates how it ties into the chapters in the book. Consistent with our discussion above, we use two-way arrows to convey the interactive nature of the processes.

Strategy Analysis

Strategy analysis may be looked upon as the starting point of the strategic management process. It consists of the "advance work" that must be done in order to effectively formulate and implement strategies. Many strategies fail because managers may want to formulate and implement strategies without a careful analysis of the overarching goals of the organization and without a thorough analysis of its external and internal environment.

Analyzing Organizational Goals and Objectives (Chapter 1)   A firm's vision, mission, and strategic objectives form a hierarchy of goals that range from broad statements of intent and bases for competitive advantage to specific, measurable strategic objectives.

Analyzing the External Environment of the Firm (Chapter 2)   Managers must monitor and scan the environment as well as analyze competitors. Two frameworks of the external environment are provided: (1) the general environment consists of several elements, such as demographic, technological, and economic segments, and (2) the industry environment consists of competitors and other organizations that may threaten the success of a firm's products and services.

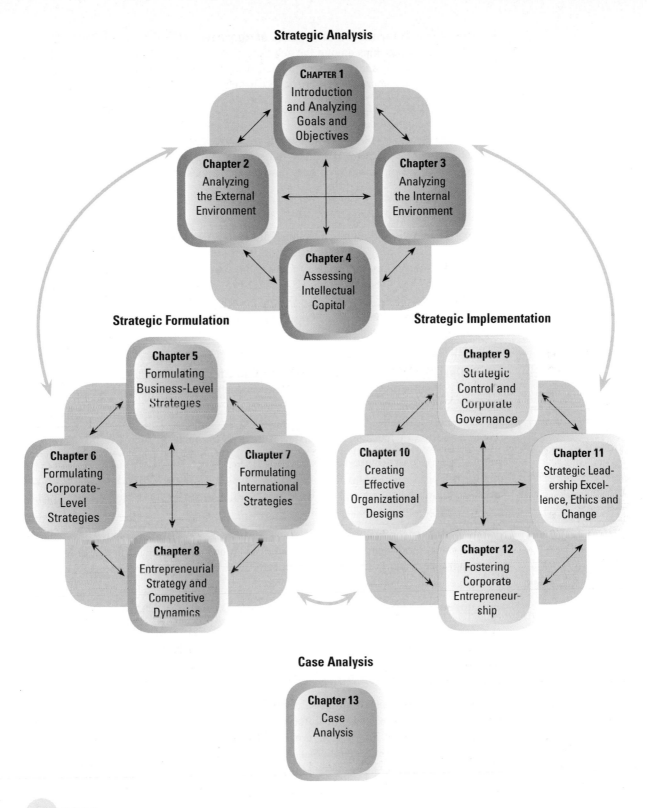

Strategic Analysis

CHAPTER 1
Introduction and Analyzing Goals and Objectives

Chapter 2
Analyzing the External Environment

Chapter 3
Analyzing the Internal Environment

Chapter 4
Assessing Intellectual Capital

Strategic Formulation

Chapter 5
Formulating Business-Level Strategies

Chapter 6
Formulating Corporate-Level Strategies

Chapter 7
Formulating International Strategies

Chapter 8
Entrepreneurial Strategy and Competitive Dynamics

Strategic Implementation

Chapter 9
Strategic Control and Corporate Governance

Chapter 10
Creating Effective Organizational Designs

Chapter 11
Strategic Leadership Excellence, Ethics and Change

Chapter 12
Fostering Corporate Entrepreneurship

Case Analysis

Chapter 13
Case Analysis

Exhibit 1.3 **The Strategic Management Process**

Assessing the Internal Environment of the Firm (Chapter 3) Analyzing the strengths and relationships among the activities that constitute a firm's value chain (e.g., operations, marketing and sales, and human resource management) can be a means of uncovering potential sources of competitive advantage for the firm.[29]

Assessing a Firm's Intellectual Assets (Chapter 4) The knowledge worker and a firm's other intellectual assets (e.g., patents, trademarks) are becoming increasingly important as the drivers of competitive advantages and wealth creation. We also assess how well the organization creates networks and relationships as well as how technology can enhance collaboration among employees and provide a means of accumulating and storing knowledge.[30]

Strategy Formulation

A firm's strategy formulation is developed at several levels. First, business-level strategy addresses the issue of how to compete in a given business to attain competitive advantage. Second, corporate-level strategy focuses on two issues: (a) what businesses to compete in and (b) how businesses can be managed to achieve synergy; that is, they create more value by working together than if they operate as stand-alone businesses. Third, a firm must determine the best method to develop international strategies as it ventures beyond its national boundaries. Fourth, managers must formulate effective entrepreneurial initiatives.

Formulating Business-Level Strategy (Chapter 5) The question of how firms compete and outperform their rivals and how they achieve and sustain competitive advantages goes to the heart of strategic management. Successful firms strive to develop bases for competitive advantage, which can be achieved through cost leadership and/or differentiation as well as by focusing on a narrow or industrywide market segment.[31]

Formulating Corporate-Level Strategy (Chapter 6) Corporate-level strategy addresses a firm's portfolio (or group) of businesses. It asks (1) What business (or businesses) should we compete in? and (2) How can we manage this portfolio of businesses to create synergies among the businesses?

Formulating International Strategy (Chapter 7) When firms enter foreign markets, they face both opportunities and pitfalls.[32] Managers must decide not only on the most appropriate entry strategy but also how they will go about attaining competitive advantages in international markets.[33]

Entrepreneurial Strategy and Competitive Dynamics (Chapter 8) Entrepreneurial activity aimed at new value creation is a major engine for economic growth. For entrepreneurial initiatives to succeed viable opportunities must be recognized and effective strategies must be formulated.

Strategy Implementation

Clearly, sound strategies are of no value if they are not properly implemented.[34] Strategy implementation involves ensuring proper strategic controls and organizational designs, which includes establishing effective means to coordinate and integrate activities within the firm as well as with its suppliers, customers, and alliance partners.[35] Leadership plays a central role, including ensuring that the organization is committed to excellence and ethical behavior. It also promotes learning and continuous improvement and acts entrepreneurially in creating and taking advantage of new opportunities.

Strategic Control and Corporate Governance (Chapter 9) Firms must exercise two types of strategic control. First, informational control requires that organizations continually monitor and scan the environment and respond to threats and opportunities.

---

strategy formulation decisions made by firms regarding investments, commitments, and other aspects of operations that create and sustain competitive advantage.

strategy implementation actions made by firms that carry out the formulated strategy, including strategic controls, organizational design, and leadership.

Second, behavioral control involves the proper balance of rewards and incentives as well as cultures and boundaries (or constraints). Further, successful firms (those that are incorporated) practice effective corporate governance.

Creating Effective Organizational Designs (Chapter 10) To succeed, firms must have organizational structures and designs that are consistent with their strategy. And, in today's rapidly changing competitive environments, firms must ensure that their organizational boundaries—those internal to the firm and external—are more flexible and permeable.[36] Often, organizations develop strategic alliances to capitalize on the capabilities of other organizations.

Creating a Learning Organization and an Ethical Organization (Chapter 11)
Effective leaders set a direction, design the organization, and develop an organization that is committed to excellence and ethical behavior. In addition, given rapid and unpredictable change, leaders must create a "learning organization" to ensure that the entire organization can benefit from individual and collective talents.

Fostering Corporate Entrepreneurship (Chapter 12) With rapid and unpredictable change in the global marketplace, firms must continually improve and grow as well as find new ways to renew their organizations. Corporate entrepreneurship and innovation provide firms with new opportunities, and strategies should be formulated that enhance a firm's innovative capacity.

Chapter 13, "Analyzing Strategic Management Cases," provides guidelines and suggestions on how to evaluate cases in this course. Thus, the concepts and techniques discussed in these 12 chapters can be applied to real-world organizations.

Let's now address two concepts—corporate governance and stakeholder management—that are critical to the strategic management process.

The Role of Corporate Governance and Stakeholder Management

>LO1.3
The vital role of corporate governance and stakeholder management as well as how "symbiosis" can be achieved among an organization's stakeholders.

Most business enterprises that employ more than a few dozen people are organized as corporations. As you recall from your finance classes, the overall purpose of a corporation is to maximize the long-term return to the owners (shareholders). Thus, we may ask: Who is really responsible for fulfilling this purpose? Robert Monks and Neil Minow provide a useful definition of **corporate governance** as "the relationship among various participants in determining the direction and performance of corporations. The primary participants are (1) the shareholders, (2) the management (led by the chief executive officer), and (3) the board of directors."[37] This relationship is illustrated in Exhibit 1.4.

The board of directors (BOD) are the elected representatives of the shareholders charged with ensuring that the interests and motives of management are aligned with those of the owners (i.e., shareholders). In many cases, the BOD is diligent in fulfilling its purpose. For example, Intel Corporation, the giant $43 billion maker of microprocessor chips, is widely recognized as an excellent example of sound governance practices. Its BOD follows guidelines to ensure that its members are independent (i.e., not members of the executive management team and do not have close personal ties to top executives) so that they can provide proper oversight, it has explicit guidelines on the selection of director candidates (to avoid "cronyism"), and it provides detailed procedures for formal evaluations of directors and the firm's top officers.[38] Such guidelines serve to ensure that management is acting in the best interests of shareholders.[39]

Recently, there has been much criticism as well as cynicism by both citizens and the business press about the poor job that management and the BODs of large corporations are doing. We only have to look at the scandals at firms such as Arthur Andersen, WorldCom,

corporate governance the relationship among various participants in determining the direction and performance of corporations. The primary participants are (1) the shareholders, (2) the management (led by the chief executive officer), and (3) the board of directors.

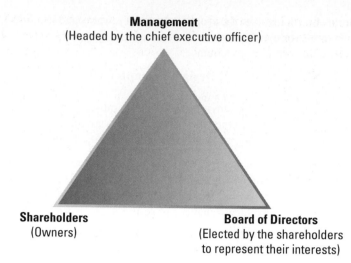

Management
(Headed by the chief executive officer)

Shareholders
(Owners)

Board of Directors
(Elected by the shareholders
to represent their interests)

Exhibit 1.4 **The Key Elements of Corporate Governance**

Enron, Tyco, and ImClone Systems.[40] Such malfeasance has led to an erosion of the public's trust in the governance of corporations. For example, a recent Gallup poll found that 90 percent of Americans felt that people leading corporations could not be trusted to look after the interests of their employees, and only 18 percent thought that corporations looked after their shareholders. Forty-three percent, in fact, believed that senior executives were in it only for themselves. In Britain, that figure, according to another poll, was an astonishing 95 percent.[41] Perhaps worst of all, in another study, 60 percent of directors (the very people who decide how much executives should earn) felt that executives were "dramatically overpaid"![42]

It is now clear that much of the bonus pay awarded to executives on Wall Street in the past few years was richly undeserved.[43] In the three years that led up to the recent collapse of seven big financial institutions, the chief executives of those firms collected a total of $80 million in performance bonuses and raked in $210 million in severance pay and earnings from stock sales. Let's take a closer look at a few of these payouts (the amounts below represent bonus pay, severance, and gains from stock sales from 2005 to late 2008):

- Richard Fuld, Lehman Brothers ($172 million)
- Kerry Killinger, Washington Mutual ($37 million)
- Martin Sullivan, American International Group ($36 million)
- Michael Perry, Indymac, Federal Bank ($20 million)
- Kenneth Thompson, Wachovia Corporation ($14 million)

Clearly, there is a strong need for improved corporate governance, and we will address this topic in Chapter 9.[44] We focus on three important mechanisms to ensure effective corporate governance: an effective and engaged board of directors, shareholder activism, and proper managerial rewards and incentives.[45] In addition to these internal controls, a key role is played by various external control mechanisms.[46] These include the auditors, banks, analysts, an active financial press, and the threat of hostile takeovers.

Alternative Perspectives of Stakeholder Management

stakeholder management a firm's strategy for recognizing and responding to the interests of all its salient stakeholders.

Generating long-term returns for the shareholders is the primary goal of a publicly held corporation.[47] As noted by former Chrysler vice chairman Robert Lutz, "We are here to serve the shareholder and create shareholder value. I insist that the only person who owns the company is the person who paid good money for it."[48]

Despite the primacy of generating shareholder value, managers who focus solely on the interests of the owners of the business will often make poor decisions that lead to negative, unanticipated outcomes.[49] For example, decisions such as mass layoffs to increase profits, ignoring issues related to conservation of the natural environment to save money, and exerting excessive pressure on suppliers to lower prices can certainly harm the firm in the long run. Such actions would likely lead to negative outcomes such as alienated employees, increased governmental oversight and fines, and disloyal suppliers.

Clearly, in addition to *shareholders,* there are other *stakeholders* (e.g. suppliers, customers) who must be explicitly taken into account in the strategic management process.[50] A stakeholder can be defined as an individual or group, inside or outside the company, that has a stake in and can influence an organization's performance. Each stakeholder group makes various claims on the company.[51] Exhibit 1.5 provides a list of major stakeholder groups and the nature of their claims on the company.

Zero Sum or Symbiosis?   There are two opposing ways of looking at the role of stakeholder management in the strategic management process.[52] The first one can be termed "zero sum." In this view, the role of management is to look upon the various stakeholders as competing for the organization's resources. In essence, the gain of one individual or group is the loss of another individual or group. For example, employees want higher wages (which drive down profits), suppliers want higher prices for their inputs and slower, more flexible delivery times (which drive up costs), customers want fast deliveries and higher quality (which drive up costs), the community at large wants charitable contributions (which take money from company goals), and so on. This zero-sum thinking is rooted, in part, in the traditional conflict between workers and management, leading to the formation of unions and sometimes ending in adversarial union–management negotiations and long, bitter strikes.

Consider, for example, the many stakeholder challenges facing Walmart, the world's largest retailer.

Walmart strives to ramp up growth while many stakeholders are watching nervously: employees and trade unions; shareholders, investors, and creditors; suppliers and joint venture partners; the governments of the U.S. and other nations where the retailer operates; and customers. In addition many non-governmental organizations (NGOs), particularly in countries where the retailer buys its products, are closely monitoring Walmart. Walmart's stakeholders have different interests, and not all of them share the firm's goals. Each group has the ability, in various degrees, to influence the firm's choices and results. Clearly, this wasn't the case when Sam Walton built his first store in Rogers, Arkansas, in 1962![53]

Exhibit 1.5
An Organization's Key Stakeholders and the Nature of Their Claims

Stakeholder Group	Nature of Claim
Stockholders	Dividends, capital appreciation
Employees	Wages, benefits, safe working environment, job security
Suppliers	Payment on time, assurance of continued relationship
Creditors	Payment of interest, repayment of principal
Customers	Value, warranties
Government	Taxes, compliance with regulations
Communities	Good citizenship behavior such as charities, employment, not polluting the environment

There will always be conflicting demands on organizations. However, organizations can achieve mutual benefit through stakeholder symbiosis, which recognizes that stakeholders are dependent upon each other for their success and well-being.[54] Consider Procter & Gamble's "laundry detergent compaction," a technique for compressing even more cleaning power into ever smaller concentrations.

In the early 2000s, P&G perfected a technique that could compact two or three times as much cleaning powder into a liquid concentration. This remarkable breakthrough has led to a change not only in consumer shopping habits, but also a revolution in industry supply-chain economics. Let's look at how several key stakeholders are affected along the supply chain:[55]

> *Consumers* love concentrated liquids because they are easier to carry, pour, and store. *Retailers,* meanwhile, prefer them because they take up less floor and shelf space, which leads to higher sales-per-square-foot—a big deal for Walmart, Target, and other big retailers. *Shipping and wholesalers,* meanwhile, prefer reduced-sized products because smaller bottles translate into reduced fuel consumption and improved warehouse space utilization. And, finally, *environmentalists* favor such products because they use less packaging and produce less waste than conventional products.

Strategy Spotlight 1.3 discusses the role of NGOs and their potential influence on companies' operations. While some organizations have been confronted for their controversial impact on the environment, others have made environmental concerns part of their business strategies and have been praised by watchdog groups for being proactive.

Crowdsourcing: Stakeholders Can Fulfill Multiple Roles Thus far, we have implicitly assumed that stakeholders' roles are fixed. That is, a stakeholder is . . . pick one: a customer, supplier, employee, competitor, and so fourth. However, in practice, that is certainly not the case. Consider Shaw Industries, a vertically integrated carpet producer (which we discuss in Chapter 6). It acquired Amoco's polypropylene fiber manufacturing facilities, which provide carpet fibers for both internal use and sale to other manufacturers. Thus, some of Shaw's competitors are also its customers. Similarly, a retailer may share space on tractor trailers that it uses to ship products to its stores. This helps to decrease everyone's logistics costs—hence rivals become customers (or collaborators). And rivals can become key allies (within the boundaries of the same firm) when a firm acquires competitors to consolidate an industry—as has been the case in a myriad of industries such as finance, defense, and funeral homes.

To show how stakeholder roles are becoming more fluid, we'd like to introduce a concept that will be a theme through the text: **crowdsourcing.**[56] When and where did the term originate? In January 2006, open sourcing was, for most businesspeople, little more than an online curiosity. At that time, Jeff Howe of *Wired* magazine started to write an article about the phenomenon. However, he soon discovered a far more important story to be told: Large—as well as small—companies in a wide variety of industries had begun farming out serious tasks to individuals and groups on the Internet. Together with his editor, Mark Robinson, they coined a new term to describe the phenomenon. In June 2006, the article appeared in which *crowdsourcing* was defined as the tapping of the "latent talent of the (online) crowd." It has become the term of choice for a process that is infiltrating many aspects of business life.

Clearly, *crowdsourcing* has claimed some well-known successes, particularly on the product development front: Consider:

- The Linux operating system, created as an open-source alternative to Windows and UNIX, can be downloaded free and altered to suit any user's needs. And, with all the firepower brought to bear by the online open-source community, bugs in the system get fixed in a matter of hours.

crowdsourcing
practice wherein the Internet is used to tap a broad range of individuals and groups to generate ideas and solve problems.

NGOs: A Key Stakeholder Group

Although the number of NGOs worldwide is hard to determine, according to a recent study there are at least 40,000 multinational NGOs. In addition, there are also hundreds of thousands based in individual countries. The focus of most of these is, at least partially, on the welfare of the environment.

What are NGOs? NGOs describe a wide array of groups and organizations—from activist groups "reclaiming the streets" to development organizations delivering aid and providing essential public services. Other NGOs are research-driven policy organizations, looking to engage with decision makers. Still others see themselves as watchdogs, casting a critical eye over current events.

The largest NGOs are multinational operations with enormous reach and influence. They include well-established organizations such as Greenpeace, Sierra Club, World Wildlife Fund, Nature Conservancy, Environmental Defense, Natural Resources Defense Council, Conservation International, Friends of the Earth, and National Wildlife Federation. Many of these established groups have been around for more than 30 years and can still have a major public influence. In fact, according to a recent study that polled opinion leaders, 55 percent trust NGOs, versus only 6 percent that trust businesses.

Some of these organizations are confrontational, taking a range of actions to reach their goals, from making waves in courts (the National Resources Defense Council), to boarding oil rigs (Greenpeace), to illegal activities, exemplified by arsonists' actions in the Colorado mountain resort of Vail. It is impossible for firms to predict all potential actions, especially irrational ones. However, they can reduce the odds of being attacked. In contrast to Vail, other ski resorts, such as Aspen, have confronted environmental issues and made them a central focus of their business strategies. For example, Aspen ski company decided to rely solely on wind power to power all of its operations. As a result, the company was rated as the number one ski resort in the West in addressing environmental issues by respected watchdog groups. Vail, on the other hand, is still trying to catch up.

As another example of a firm's environmentally sensitive behavior, Nike recently announced that it would not source any leather from the Amazon until deforestation for cattle expansion is halted. Their announcement, coupled with a similar one by Timberland, followed the release of a Greenpeace report entitled "Slaughtering the Amazon." It documented a three-year investigation that tracked beef, leather, and other cattle products from ranches involved in deforestation at the heart of the Amazon rainforest.

Sources: Esty, D. C. & Winston, A. S. 2009. *Green to Gold*. Hoboken, NJ: Wiley: 69–70; Anonymous. 2009. Timberland Steps It Up a Notch, Commit to Amazon Protections. *www.greenpeace.org*. July 29: np; and, Anonymous. undated. The Rise and Role of NGOs in Sustainable Development. *www.iisd.org*. np.

ethics

- One of Amazon's smartest moves was to invite their customers to write online reviews. The customers are neither paid nor controlled by the company, but the content that they create adds enormous value to other customers and, therefore, to Amazon.
- Roughly five million users per month swear by Wikipedia, the free online encyclopedia created and updated by Internet volunteers to the tune of roughly two million articles and counting.

Throughout the book, we will introduce examples of *crowdsourcing* to show its relevance to key strategy concepts. For example, in Chapter 3, we describe how RYZ, a tiny high-end sneaker company, relies on its customers to both design and market its products. Chapter 5 discusses Netflix, which recently awarded a $1 million prize to a group of programming experts who built a system that was 10 percent better than Cinematch—its in-house system to personalize movie recommendations. And, in Chapter 6, we discuss how a strategic alliance helped two firms more effectively cultivate and create animation content using the internet.

How Goldcorp Used Crowdsourcing to Strike Gold!

A little over a decade ago, Toronto-based gold mining company Goldcorp was in big trouble. Besieged by strikes, lingering debts, and an exceedingly high cost of production, the firm had terminated mining operations. Conditions in the marketplace were quite poor and the gold market was contracting. Most analysts assumed that the company's 50-year-old mine in Red Lake, Ontario, was nearly dead. Without solid evidence of substantial new gold deposits, Goldcorp was likely to fold.

Clearly, CEO Robert McEwen needed a miracle. He was frustrated with his in-house geologists' reliability in estimating the value and location of gold on his property. He did something that was unprecedented in the industry: He published his geological data on the Web for all to see and he challenged the world to do the prospecting. The "Goldcorp Challenge" posted a total of $575,000 in prize money to be awarded to the participants who submitted the best methods and estimates.

His reasoning: If he could attract the attention of world-class talent to the problem of finding more gold in Red Lake, just as Linux managed to attract world-class programmers to the cause of better software, he could tap into thousands of minds that he wouldn't otherwise

have access to. He could also speed up exploration and improve his odds of discovery.

Although his geologists were appalled at the idea of exposing their super-secret data to the world, the response was immediate. More than 1,400 scientists, engineers, and geologists from 50 countries downloaded the company's data and started their viral exploration. Says McEwen: "We had math, advanced physics, intelligent systems, computer graphics, and organic solutions to inorganic problems. There were capabilities I had never seen before in the industry. When I saw the computer graphics, I almost fell out of my chair."

The panel of five judges was astonished by the creativity of the submissions. The top winner, which won $105,000, was a collaboration by two groups in Australia: Fractal Graphics, of West Perth, and Taylor Wall & Associates, in Queensland, which together had developed a powerful 3-D graphical depiction of the mine. One of the team members humorously stated: "I've never been to a mine. I'd never even been to Canada." Overall, the contestants identified 110 targets on the Red Lake property, more than 80 percent of which yielded substantial quantities of gold. In fact, since the challenge was initiated, an astounding 8 million ounces of gold have been found—worth well over $3 billion (given gold's fluctuating market value). Not a bad return on a half million dollar investment.

As of early 2011, Goldcorp had annual revenues of $3 billion and a market value of $33 billion! Not bad for a once failing firm . . .

Sources: de Castella, T. 2010. Should We Trust the Wisdom of Crowds? *news.bbc.co.uk.* July 5: np; Libert, B. & Spector, J. 2008. *We Are Smarter Than Me.* Philadelphia, PA: Wharton School Publishing; Tapscott, D. & Williams, A. D. 2007. Innovation in the Age of Mass Collaboration. *www.businessweek.com.* February 1: np; and, Tischler, L. 2002. He Struck Gold on the Net (Really). *fastcompany.com.* May 2: np.

crowdsourcing

Strategy Spotlight 1.4 describes how Goldcorp, a Toronto-based mining company, crowdsourced the expertise required to identify the best location to mine gold on the firm's property. Goldcorp invited geologists around the world to compete for $575,000 in prize money for analyzing its geological data. It was a remarkable success!

Social Responsibility and Environmental Sustainability: Moving beyond the Immediate Stakeholders

Organizations cannot ignore the interests and demands of stakeholders such as citizens and society in general that are beyond its immediate constituencies—customers, owners, suppliers, and employees. The realization that firms have multiple stakeholders and that evaluating their performance must go beyond analyzing their financial results has led to a new way of thinking about businesses and their relationship to society. We address this important issue in the following three sections.

First, *social responsibility* recognizes that businesses must respond to society's expectations regarding their obligations to society. Second, an emerging perspective, *shared value,* views social responsibility not just as an added cost to businesses. Instead, it views businesses as creators of value that they then share with society in a mutually beneficial relationship. Finally, we discuss the *triple bottom line approach* to evaluating a firm's performance. This perspective takes into account financial, social, and environmental performance.

Social Responsibility is the expectation that businesses or individuals will strive to improve the overall welfare of society.[57] From the perspective of a business, this means that managers must take active steps to make society better by virtue of the business being in existence.[58] Similar to norms and values, actions that constitute socially responsible behavior tend to change over time. In the 1970s affirmative action was a high priority and during the 1990s and up to the present time, the public has been concerned about environmental quality. Many firms have responded to this by engaging in recycling and reducing waste. And in the wake of terrorist attacks on New York City and the Pentagon, as well as the continuing threat from terrorists worldwide, a new kind of priority has arisen: the need to be vigilant concerning public safety.

social responsibility
the expectation that businesses or individuals will strive to improve the overall welfare of society.

Today, demands for greater corporate responsibility have accelerated.[59] These include corporate critics, social investors, activists, and, increasingly, customers who claim to assess corporate responsibility when making purchasing decisions. Such demands go well beyond product and service quality.[60] They include a focus on issues such as labor standards, environmental sustainability, financial and accounting reporting, procurement, and environmental practices.[61] At times, a firm's reputation can be tarnished by exceedingly poor judgment on the part of one of its managers. For example, BP CEO Tony Hayward's decision to withhold information from the public about the magnitude of the oil spill in the Gulf of Mexico further damaged the firm's reputation.

>LO1.4
The importance of social responsibility, including environmental sustainability, and how it can enhance a corporation's innovation strategy.

A key stakeholder group that appears to be particularly susceptible to corporate social responsibility (CSR) initiatives is customers.[62] Surveys indicate a strong positive relationship between CSR behaviors and consumers' reactions to a firm's products and services.[63] For example:

- Corporate Citizenship's poll conducted by Cone Communications found that "84 percent of Americans say they would be likely to switch brands to one associated with a good cause, if price and quality are similar."[64]
- Hill & Knowlton/Harris's Interactive poll reveals that "79 percent of Americans take corporate citizenship into account when deciding whether to buy a particular company's product and 37 percent consider corporate citizenship an important factor when making purchasing decisions."[65]

Such findings are consistent with a large body of research that confirms the positive influence of CSR on consumers' company evaluations and product purchase intentions across a broad range of product categories.

The Concept of "Shared Value" Capitalism is typically viewed as an unparalleled vehicle for meeting human needs, improving efficiency, creating jobs, and building wealth.[66] However, a narrow conceptualization of capitalism has prevented business from harnessing its full potential to meet society's broader challenges. The opportunities have always been there but have been overlooked. It is increasingly acknowledged that businesses acting as businesses, not as charitable donors, are the most powerful force for addressing the pressing issues that we face. This new conception of capitalism redefines the purpose of the corporation as creating shared value, not just profit per se. This will drive the next wave of innovation and productivity growth in the global economy.

Shared value can be defined as policies and operating practices that enhance the competitiveness of a company while simultaneously advancing the economic and social conditions in which it operates. Shared value creation focuses on identifying and expanding the connections between societal and economic progress.[67]

Shared value is not about personal values. Nor is it about "sharing" the value created by firms—a redistribution approach. Instead, it is about expanding the total pool of economic and social value. A good example of this difference is the fair trade movement:

> Fair trade aims to increase the proportion of revenue that goes to poor farmers by paying them higher prices for the same crops. Though this may be a noble sentiment, fair trade is mostly about redistribution rather than expanding the overall amount of value created.

> A shared value perspective, however, focuses on improving growing techniques and strengthening the local cluster of supporting suppliers and other institutions in order to increase farmers' efficiency, yields, product quality, and sustainability. This leads to a bigger pie of revenue and profits that benefits both farmers and the companies that buy from them. Early studies of cocoa farmers in the Ivory Coast, for example, suggest that while fair trade can increase farmers' incomes by 10 to 20 percent, shared value investments can raise their incomes by more than 300 percent! Initial investment and time may be required to implement new procurement practices and develop the cluster. However, the return will be greater economic value and broader strategic benefits for all participants.

A firm's value chain inevitably affects—and is affected by—numerous societal issues. Opportunities to create shared value arise because societal problems can create economic costs in the firm's value chain. Such external factors inflict internal costs to the firm, even in the absence of regulation or resource taxes. For example, excess product packaging and greenhouse gases are not just costly to the environment but also costly to businesses.

The shared value perspective acknowledges that the congruence between societal progress and value chain productivity is far greater than traditionally believed. The synergy increases when firms consider societal issues from a shared value perspective and invent new ways of operating to address them. So far, however, relatively few firms have reaped the full productivity benefits.

Let's look at what a few companies are doing to reap "win-win" benefits by addressing societal challenges and, in so doing, enjoying higher productivity and profitability:

- Hindustan Unilever is creating a new direct-to-home distribution system. It is operated by underprivileged female entrepreneurs in Indian villages of fewer than 2,000 people. The firm provides microcredit and training and has more than 45,000 entrepreneurs covering about 100,000 villages across 15 Indian states. Project Shakti, the name of the distribution system, provides benefits to communities not only by giving women skills that often double their household income but also by reducing the spread of communicable diseases through increased access to hygiene products. Thus, the unique ability of business to market to hard-to-reach consumers can benefit society by getting life-altering products into the hands of people that need them. Project Shakti now accounts for 5 percent of Unilever's total revenues in India. It has also extended the company's reach into rural areas and built its brand in media-dark regions, creating major economic value for the company.
- Leading companies have learned that because of lost workdays and diminished employee productivity, poor health costs them far more than health benefits do. For example, Johnson & Johnson has helped employees stop smoking (a two-thirds reduction in the past 15 years) and has implemented many other new wellness programs. Such initiatives have saved the company $250 million on health care costs, a return of $2.71 for every dollar spent on wellness from 2002 to 2008. Further, Johnson & Johnson has benefited from a more present and productive workforce.

- Olam International, a leading cashew producer, traditionally shipped its nuts from Africa to Asia for processing. By opening local processing plants and training workers in Tanzania, Mozambique, Nigeria, and the Ivory Coast, Olam cut its processing and shipping costs by as much as 25 percent and greatly reduced carbon emissions! Further, Olam built preferred relationships with local farmers. It has provided direct employment to 17,000 people—95 percent of whom are women—and indirect employment to an equal number of people, in rural areas where jobs otherwise were not available.

The Triple Bottom Line: Incorporating Financial as Well as Environmental and Social Costs   Many companies are now measuring what has been called a **"triple bottom line."** This involves assessing financial, social, and environmental performance. Shell, NEC, Procter & Gamble, and others have recognized that failing to account for the environmental and social costs of doing business poses risks to the company and its community.[68]

triple bottom line assessment of a firm's financial, social, and environmental performance.

The environmental revolution has been almost four decades in the making.[69] In the 1960s and 1970s, companies were in a state of denial regarding their firms' impact on the natural environment. However, a series of visible ecological problems created a groundswell for strict governmental regulation. In the U.S., Lake Erie was "dead," and in Japan, people died of mercury poisoning. Clearly, the effects of global warming are being felt throughout the world. Some other examples include the following:

- Ice roads are melting, so Canadian diamond miners must airlift equipment at great cost instead of trucking it in.
- More severe storms and rising seas mean oil companies must build stronger rigs, and cities must build higher seawalls.
- The loss of permafrost and protective sea ice may force villages like Alaska's Shismaref to relocate.
- Yukon River salmon and fisheries are threatened by a surge of parasites associated with a jump in water temperature.
- Later winters have let beetles spread in British Columbia, killing 22 million acres of pine forests, an area the size of Maine.
- In Mali, Africa, crops are threatened. The rainy season is now too short for rice, and the dry season is too hot for potatoes.[70]

● Windpower is a more sustainable, environmentally friendly option than nuclear power plants or coal- or oil-fired power plants.

Stuart Hart, writing in the *Harvard Business Review,* addresses the magnitude of problems and challenges associated with the natural environment:

> The challenge is to develop a *sustainable global economy:* an economy that the planet is capable of supporting indefinitely. Although we may be approaching ecological recovery in the developed world, the planet as a whole remains on an unsustainable course. Increasingly, the scourges of the late twentieth century—depleted farmland, fisheries, and forests; choking urban pollution; poverty; infectious disease; and migration—are spilling over geopolitical borders. The simple fact is this: in meeting our needs, we are destroying the ability of future generations to meet theirs . . . corporations are the only organizations with the resources, the technology, the global reach, and, ultimately, the motivation to achieve sustainability.[71]

Environmental sustainability is now a value embraced by the most competitive and successful multinational companies.[72] The McKinsey Corporation's survey of more than 400 senior executives of companies around the world found that 92 percent agreed with former Sony President Akio Morita's contention that the environmental challenge will be one of the central issues in the 21st century.[73] Virtually all executives acknowledged their firm's responsibility to control pollution, and 83 percent agreed that corporations have an environmental responsibility for their products even after they are sold.

For many successful firms, environmental values are now becoming a central part of their cultures and management processes.[74] And, as noted earlier, environmental impacts are being audited and accounted for as the "third bottom line." According to one 2004 corporate report, "If we aren't good corporate citizens as reflected in a Triple Bottom Line that takes into account social and environmental responsibilities along with financial ones—eventually our stock price, our profits, and our entire business could suffer."[75] Also, a CEO survey on sustainability by Accenture debunks the notion that sustainability and profitability are mutually exclusive corporate goals. The study found that sustainability is being increasingly recognized as a source of cost efficiencies and revenue growth. In fact, 80 percent of the more than 760 CEOs surveyed indicated that the recent deep recession has only served to heighten the importance of sustainability for their businesses.[76]

Let's take a look at how Dell is making money and helping their customers at the end of their product's technology life cycle:[77]

> Since computers generally have a rather short life cycle, companies are faced with real challenges over environmental and data liabilities when they need to dispose of obsolete equipment. Dell's Asset Recovery System helps customers deal with both the software and environmental cleanup they need.

> For about $25 for a piece of equipment, Dell comes to your office and takes your computer away. They first perform a "destructive data overwrite" to eliminate all digital information on the computer, and then they dismantle the machine. Dell refurbishes and reuses some of the parts, and recycles the plastic. In the end, only 1 percent of the old computer's volume goes to a landfill.

> This environmentally sustainable service enhances customer relationships and helps to drive sales. Dell discovered that the take-back role comes, conveniently, when Dell is delivering the next generation of equipment. Dell's executives would be happy if this service was just breaking even—but they are turning a profit on it. As noted by Daniel Esty and Andrew Winston in their book *Green to Gold,* "They seem a bit sheepish about doing so. We see no need to apologize."

Clearly, there are many other examples of how firms have profited by investing in socially responsible behavior, including those activities that enhance environmental sustainability. However, how do such "socially responsible" companies fare in terms of shareholder returns compared to benchmarks such as the Standard & Poor's 500 index? Strategy Spotlight 1.5 focuses on this issue.

>LO1.5
The need for greater empowerment throughout the organization.

The Strategic Management Perspective: An Imperative throughout the Organization

Strategic management requires managers to take an integrative view of the organization and assess how all of the functional areas and activities fit together to help an organization achieve its goals and objectives. This cannot be accomplished if only the top managers in the organization take an integrative, strategic perspective of issues facing the firm and everyone else "fends for themselves" in their independent, isolated functional areas. Instead, people throughout the organization must strive toward overall goals.

Socially Responsible Investing (SRI): Can You Do Well by Doing Good?

SRI is a broad-based approach to investing that now encompasses an estimated $3.07 trillion out of $25.2 trillion in the U.S. investment marketplace today. SRI recognizes that corporate responsibility and societal concerns are valid parts of investment decisions. With SRI, investors have the opportunity to put their money to work to build a more sustainable world while earning competitive returns both today and over time.

And, as the saying goes, nice guys don't have to finish last. The ING SRI, which tracks the stocks of 50 companies, enjoyed a 47.4 percent return in 2009. That easily beat the 26.5 percent gain of the Standard & Poor's 500-stock index. And a review of the 145 socially responsible equity mutual and exchange-traded funds tracked by Morningstar shows that 65 percent of them outperformed the S&P 500 last year.

Many socially responsible investing funds shun alcohol, tobacco, gambling, and defense companies—while embracing tech. Thus, they clearly benefitted from the 2009 returns of popular holdings, including Cisco (+46.9%), Microsoft (+60.5%), Google (+101.5%), and Intel (+43.9%). Over the recent 10-year period, Parnassus Equity Income and New Alternatives gained nearly 7 percent a year, on average, versus a 9 percent cumulative loss for the S&P 500 over the same period.

Another indication of the competitive performance of SRI funds is the performance of SRI indices over the long term. The longest running SRI index, the FTSE KLD 400, was started in 1990. Since that time, it has continued to perform competitively. It returned an average of 9.51 percent a year from inception through December 31, 2009, compared to 8.66 percent for the S&P 500 over the same period.

Sources: Kaahwarski, T. 2010. It Pays to Be Good. *Bloomberg BusinessWeek.* February 1 & 8. 69; Anonymous. undated. Performance and Socially Responsible Investments. *www.socialinvest.org.* np; Anonymous. Socially Responsible Investing Facts. *www.socialinvest.* np.

ethics

The need for such a perspective is accelerating in today's increasingly complex, interconnected, ever-changing, global economy. As noted by Peter Senge of MIT, the days when Henry Ford, Alfred Sloan, and Tom Watson (top executives at Ford, General Motors, and IBM, respectively) "learned for the organization are gone." He goes on to say:

> In an increasingly dynamic, interdependent, and unpredictable world, it is simply no longer possible for anyone to "figure it all out at the top." The old model, "the top thinks and the local acts," must now give way to integrating thinking and acting at all levels. While the challenge is great, so is the potential payoff. "The person who figures out how to harness the collective genius of the people in his or her organization," according to former Citibank CEO Walter Wriston, "is going to blow the competition away."[78]

To develop and mobilize people and other assets, leaders are needed throughout the organization.[79] No longer can organizations be effective if the top "does the thinking" and the rest of the organization "does the work." Everyone must be involved in the strategic management process. There is a critical need for three types of leaders:

- *Local line leaders* who have significant profit-and-loss responsibility.
- *Executive leaders* who champion and guide ideas, create a learning infrastructure, and establish a domain for taking action.
- *Internal networkers* who, although they have little positional power and formal authority, generate their power through the conviction and clarity of their ideas.[80]

Sally Helgesen, author of *The Web of Inclusion: A New Architecture for Building Great Organizations,* also expressed the need for leaders throughout the organization. She asserted that many organizations "fall prey to the heroes-and-drones syndrome, exalting the value of those in powerful positions while implicitly demeaning the contributions of those who fail to achieve top rank."[81] Culture and processes in which leaders emerge at all levels, both up and down as well as across the organization, typify today's high-performing firms.[82]

Top-level executives are key in setting the tone for the empowerment of employees. Consider Richard Branson, founder of the Virgin Group, whose core businesses include retail operations, hotels, communications, and an airline. He is well known for creating a culture and an informal structure where anybody in the organization can be involved in generating and acting upon new business ideas. In an interview, he stated,

> [S]peed is something that we are better at than most companies. We don't have formal board meetings, committees, etc. If someone has an idea, they can pick up the phone and talk to me. I can vote "done, let's do it." Or, better still, they can just go ahead and do it. They know that they are not going to get a mouthful from me if they make a mistake. Rules and regulations are not our forte. Analyzing things to death is not our kind of thing. We very rarely sit back and analyze what we do.[83]

To inculcate a strategic management perspective throughout the organization, managers must often make a major effort to effect transformational change. This involves extensive communication, incentives, training, and development. For example, under the direction of Nancy Snyder, a corporate vice president, Whirlpool, the world's largest producer of household appliances, brought about a significant shift in the firm's reputation as an innovator.[84] This five-year initiative included both financial investments in capital spending as well as a series of changes in management processes, including training innovation mentors, making innovation a significant portion of leadership development programs, enrolling all salaried employees in online courses in business innovation, and providing employees with an innovation portal that allows them access to multiple innovation tools and data.

We'd like to close with our favorite example of how inexperience can be a virtue. It further reinforces the benefits of having broad involvement throughout the organization in the strategic management process (see Strategy Spotlight 1.6).

hierarchy of goals
organizational goals ranging from, at the top, those that are less specific yet able to evoke powerful and compelling mental images, to, at the bottom, those that are more specific and measurable.

>LO1.6
How an awareness of a hierarchy of strategic goals can help an organization achieve coherence in its strategic direction.

Ensuring Coherence in Strategic Direction

Employees and managers throughout the organization must strive toward common goals and objectives.[85] By specifying desired results, it becomes much easier to move forward. Otherwise, when no one knows what the firm is striving to accomplish, they have no idea of what to work toward.

Organizations express priorities best through stated goals and objectives that form a **hierarchy of goals,** which includes its vision, mission, and strategic objectives.[86] What visions may lack in specificity, they make up for in their ability to evoke powerful and compelling mental images. On the other hand, strategic objectives tend to be more specific and provide a more direct means of determining if the organization is moving toward broader, overall goals.[87] Visions, as one would expect, also have longer time horizons than either mission statements or strategic objectives. Exhibit 1.6 depicts the hierarchy of goals and its relationship to two attributes: general versus specific and time horizon.

Organizational Vision

vision
organizational goal(s) that evoke(s) powerful and compelling mental images.

A **vision** is a goal that is "massively inspiring, overarching, and long term."[88] It represents a destination that is driven by and evokes passion. A vision may or may not succeed; it depends on whether everything else happens according to a firm's strategy. As Mark Hurd, Hewlett-Packard's CEO, humorously pointed out, "Without execution, vision is just another word for hallucination."[89]

Strategy and the Value of Inexperience

Peter Gruber, chairman of Mandalay Entertainment, explained how his firm benefited from the creative insights of an inexperienced intern.

Sometimes life is all about solving problems. In the movie business, at least, there seems to be one around every corner. One of the most effective lessons I've learned about tackling problems is to start by asking not "How to?" but rather "What if?" I learned that lesson from a young woman who was interning on a film I was producing. She actually saved the movie from being shelved by the studio.

The movie, *Gorillas in the Mist*, had turned into a logistical nightmare. We wanted to film at an altitude of 11,000 feet, in the middle of the jungle, in Rwanda—then on the verge of a revolution—and to use more than 200 animals. Warner Brothers, the studio financing the movie, worried that we would exceed our budget. But our biggest problem was that the screenplay required the gorillas to do what we wrote—in other words, to "act." If they couldn't or wouldn't, we'd have to fall back on a formula that the studio had seen fail before: using dwarfs in gorilla suits on a soundstage.

We called an emergency meeting to solve these problems. In the middle of it, a young intern asked, "What if you let the gorillas write the story?" Everyone laughed and wondered what she was doing in the meeting with experienced filmmakers. Hours later, someone casually asked her what she had meant. She said, "What if you sent a really good cinematographer into the jungle with a ton of film to shoot the gorillas. Then you could write a story around what the gorillas did on film." It was a brilliant idea. And we did exactly what she suggested: We sent Alan Root, an Academy Award–nominated cinematographer, into the jungle for three weeks. He came back with phenomenal footage that practically wrote the story for us. We shot the film for $20 million—half of the original budget!

This woman's inexperience enabled her to see opportunities where we saw only boundaries. This experience taught me three things. First, ask high-quality questions, like "What if?" Second, find people who add new perspectives and create new conversations. As experienced filmmakers, we believed that our way was the only way—and that the intern lacked the experience to have an opinion. Third, pay attention to those with new voices. If you want unlimited options for solving a problem, engage the what if before you lock onto the how to. You'll be surprised by what you discover.

Source: Gruber, P. 1998. My greatest lesson. *Fast Company* 15: 88, 90.

Leaders must develop and implement a vision. In a survey of executives from 20 different countries, respondents were asked what they believed were a leader's key traits.[90] Ninety-eight percent responded that "a strong sense of vision" was the most important. Similarly, when asked about the critical knowledge skills, the leaders cited "strategy formulation to achieve a vision" as the most important skill. In other words, managers need

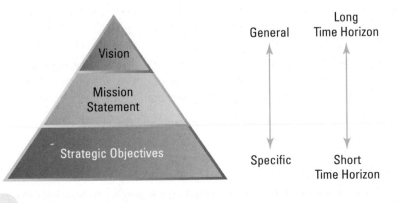

Exhibit 1.6 A Hierarchy of Goals

to have not only a vision but also a plan to implement it. Regretfully, 90 percent reported a lack of confidence in their own skills and ability to conceive a vision. For example, T. J. Rogers, CEO of Cypress Semiconductor, an electronic chipmaker that faced some difficulties in 1992, lamented that his own shortsightedness caused the danger, "I did not have the 50,000-foot view, and got caught."[91]

One of the most famous examples of a vision is Disneyland's: "To be the happiest place on earth." Other examples are:

- "Restoring patients to full life." (Medtronic)
- "We want to satisfy all of our customers' financial needs and help them succeed financially." (Wells Fargo)
- "Our vision is to be the world's best quick service restaurant." (McDonald's)
- "To organize the world's information and make it universally accessible and useful." (Google)

Although such visions cannot be accurately measured by a specific indicator of how well they are being achieved, they do provide a fundamental statement of an organization's values, aspirations, and goals. Such visions go well beyond narrow financial objectives, of course, and strive to capture both the minds and hearts of employees.

The vision statement may also contain a slogan, diagram, or picture—whatever grabs attention.[92] The aim is to capture the essence of the more formal parts of the vision in a few words that are easily remembered, yet that evoke the spirit of the entire vision statement. In its 20-year battle with Xerox, Canon's slogan, or battle cry, was "Beat Xerox." Motorola's slogan is "Total Customer Satisfaction." Outboard Marine Corporation's slogan is "To Take the World Boating."

Clearly, vision statements are not a cure-all. Sometimes they backfire and erode a company's credibility. Visions fail for many reasons, including the following:[93]

The Walk Doesn't Match the Talk   An idealistic vision can arouse employee enthusiasm. However, that same enthusiasm can be quickly dashed if employees find that senior management's behavior is not consistent with the vision. Often, vision is a sloganeering campaign of new buzzwords and empty platitudes like "devotion to the customer," "teamwork," or "total quality" that aren't consistently backed by management's action.

Irrelevance   Visions created in a vacuum—unrelated to environmental threats or opportunities or an organization's resources and capabilities—often ignore the needs of those who are expected to buy into them. Employees reject visions that are not anchored in reality.

Not the Holy Grail   Managers often search continually for the one elusive solution that will solve their firm's problems—that is, the next "holy grail" of management. They may have tried other management fads only to find that they fell short of their expectations. However, they remain convinced that one exists. A vision simply cannot be viewed as a magic cure for an organization's illness.

Too Much Focus Leads to Missed Opportunities   The downside of too much focus is that in directing people and resources toward a grandiose vision, losses can be devastating. Consider, Samsung's ambitious venture into automobile manufacturing:

> In 1992, Kun-Hee Lee, chairman of South Korea's Samsung Group, created a bold strategy to become one of the 10 largest car makers by 2010. Seduced by the clarity of the vision, Samsung bypassed staged entry through a joint venture or initial supply contract. Instead, Samsung borrowed heavily to build a state-of-the-art research and design facility and erect a greenfield factory, complete with cutting-edge robotics. Samsung Auto suffered operating losses and crushing interest charges from the beginning. And within a few years the business was divested for a fraction of the initial investment.[94]

An Ideal Future Irreconciled with the Present   Although visions are not designed to mirror reality, they must be anchored somehow in it. People have difficulty identifying with a vision that paints a rosy picture of the future but does not account for the often hostile environment in which the firm competes or that ignores some of the firm's weaknesses.

Mission Statements

A company's **mission statement** differs from its vision in that it encompasses both the purpose of the company as well as the basis of competition and competitive advantage.

Exhibit 1.7 contains the vision statement and mission statement of WellPoint Health Network, a giant $63 billion managed health care organization. Note that while the vision statement is broad based, the mission statement is more specific and focused on the means by which the firm will compete.

Effective mission statements incorporate the concept of stakeholder management, suggesting that organizations must respond to multiple constituencies. Customers, employees, suppliers, and owners are the primary stakeholders, but others may also play an important role. Mission statements also have the greatest impact when they reflect an organization's enduring, overarching strategic priorities and competitive positioning. Mission statements also can vary in length and specificity. The two mission statements below illustrate these issues.

> **mission statement**
> a set of organizational goals that include both the purpose of the organization, its scope of operations, and the basis of its competitive advantage.

- To produce superior financial returns for our shareholders as we serve our customers with the highest quality transportation, logistics, and e-commerce. (Federal Express)
- To be the very best in the business. Our game plan is status go . . . we are constantly looking ahead, building on our strengths, and reaching for new goals. In our quest of these goals, we look at the three stars of the Brinker logo and are reminded of the basic values that are the strength of this company . . . People, Quality and Profitability. Everything we do at Brinker must support these core values. We also look at the eight golden flames depicted in our logo, and are reminded of the fire that ignites our mission and makes up the heart and soul of this incredible company. These flames are: Customers, Food, Team, Concepts, Culture, Partners, Community, and Shareholders. As keeper of these flames, we will continue to build on our strengths and work together to be the best in the business. (Brinker International, whose restaurant chains include Chili's and On the Border)[95]

Few mission statements identify profit or any other financial indicator as the sole purpose of the firm. Indeed, many do not even mention profit or shareholder return.[96]

Exhibit 1.7
Comparing WellPoint Health Network's Vision and Mission

Vision
WellPoint *will redefine our industry:* Through a new generation of consumer-friendly products that put individuals back in control of their future.

Mission
The WellPoint companies provide health *security* by offering a *choice* of quality branded health and related financial services *designed* to meet the *changing* expectations of individuals, families, and their sponsors throughout a *lifelong* relationship.

Source: WellPoint Health Network company records.

Employees of organizations or departments are usually the mission's most important audience. For them, the mission should help to build a common understanding of purpose and commitment to nurture.

A good mission statement, by addressing each principal theme, must communicate why an organization is special and different. Two studies that linked corporate values and mission statements with financial performance found that the most successful firms mentioned values other than profits. The less successful firms focused almost entirely on profitability.[97] In essence, profit is the metaphorical equivalent of oxygen, food, and water that the body requires. They are not the point of life, but without them, there is no life.

Vision statements tend to be quite enduring and seldom change. However, a firm's mission can and should change when competitive conditions dramatically change or the firm is faced with new threats or opportunities.

The transformation of the James Irvine Foundation is described in Strategy Spotlight 1.7. It changed from a philanthropic foundation with the broad mission of "promoting the welfare of the people of California" to a narrow mission that focuses on the education of youths ages 14 to 24.

strategic objectives
A set of organizational goals that are used to operationalize the mission statement and that are specific and cover a well-defined time frame.

Strategic Objectives

Strategic objectives are used to operationalize the mission statement.[98] That is, they help to provide guidance on how the organization can fulfill or move toward the "higher goals" in the goal hierarchy—the mission and vision. Thus, they are more specific and cover a more well-defined time frame. Setting objectives demands a yardstick to measure the fulfillment of the objectives.[99]

Exhibit 1.8 lists several firms' strategic objectives—both financial and nonfinancial. While most of them are directed toward generating greater profits and returns for the owners of the business, others are directed at customers or society at large.

Exhibit 1.8
Strategic Objectives

Strategic Objectives (Financial)

- Increase sales growth 6 percent to 8 percent and accelerate core net earnings growth from 13 percent to 15 percent per share in each of the next 5 years. (Procter & Gamble)

- Generate Internet-related revenue of $1.5 billion. (AutoNation)

- Increase the contribution of Banking Group earnings from investments, brokerage, and insurance from 16 percent to 25 percent. (Wells Fargo)

- Cut corporate overhead costs by $30 million per year. (Fortune Brands)

Strategic Objectives (Nonfinancial)

- We want a majority of our customers, when surveyed, to say they consider Wells Fargo the best financial institution in the community. (Wells Fargo)

- We want to operate 6,000 stores by 2010—up from 3,000 in the year 2000. (Walgreen's)

- We want to be the top-ranked supplier to our customers. (PPG)

- Reduce greenhouse gases by 10 percent (from a 1990 base) by 2010. (BP Amoco)

Sources: Company documents and annual reports.

How the James Irvine Foundation Redefined Its Mission

Several years ago the James Irvine Foundation, with a $1.5 billion endowment, undertook its first comprehensive strategic planning effort in more than a decade. Its leaders continued to embrace the broad mission that had been set by real estate magnate James Irvine in 1937: to promote the welfare of the people of California.

Over time, however, this inspirational statement had led to a sprawling portfolio of grants, and the foundation's leaders had come to recognize that it was far too open-ended to be useful in making program and funding decisions. To decide where the foundation could have the most lasting impact, they commissioned research on a broad range of issues facing Californians, including education, health, and the environment. Through its research, the foundation found that changing demographics, technology, and audience expectations would influence dramatically how art museums, symphony orchestras, and theaters would run their establishments.

Source: Ditkoff, S. W., & Colby, S. J. 2009. Galvanizing Philanthropy. *Harvard Business Review.* 87(11): 109; Anonymous. undated. A Conversation with John Jenks, Irvine's Chief Investment Officer. *www.irvine.org.* np; and, Emerling, S. 2009. James Irvine Foundation Rewards the Innovators. *www.articles.latimes .com,* June 17: np.

The senior team was soon flooded in data. Some findings leaped out—the significant challenges facing California's youth, for one. But given the magnitude of the state's needs, the team quickly realized that numbers alone could justify a large variety of funding decisions. So it honed in on three critical organizational values: addressing the root causes rather than crises; enabling Californians to help themselves; and working on problems that might attract like-minded partners or funders. Guided by both values and data, the team redefined its mission and selected youths ages 14 to 24 as the primary beneficiaries of its funding, and education as the primary lever for change. Saying yes to those criteria meant exiting other investments in, for example, civic culture and sustainable communities. It was a difficult choice.

The Irvine Foundation had to make some hard decisions: What, for instance, should it do about its long-standing commitment to the arts? The arts did not emerge from the data as a critical challenge, but decades of investment there had given Irvine unique assets in the form of reputation and relationships. Furthermore, its exit would have a disproportionately harsh impact on the field. So the foundation's leaders continued arts funding, albeit at a much lower level.

For objectives to be meaningful, they need to satisfy several criteria. They must be:

- *Measurable.* There must be at least one indicator (or yardstick) that measures progress against fulfilling the objective.
- *Specific.* This provides a clear message as to what needs to be accomplished.
- *Appropriate.* It must be consistent with the organization's vision and mission.
- *Realistic.* It must be an achievable target given the organization's capabilities and opportunities in the environment. In essence, it must be challenging but doable.
- *Timely.* There must be a time frame for achieving the objective. As the economist John Maynard Keynes once said, "In the long run, we are all dead!"

When objectives satisfy the above criteria, there are many benefits. First, they help to channel all employees' efforts toward common goals. This helps the organization concentrate and conserve valuable resources and work collectively in a timely manner.

Second, challenging objectives can help to motivate and inspire employees to higher levels of commitment and effort. Much research has supported the notion that people work harder when they are striving toward specific goals instead of being asked simply to "do their best."

Third, as we noted earlier in the chapter, there is always the potential for different parts of an organization to pursue their own goals rather than overall company goals. Although well intentioned, these may work at cross-purposes to the organization as a whole. Meaningful objectives thus help to resolve conflicts when they arise.

Finally, proper objectives provide a yardstick for rewards and incentives. They will ensure a greater sense of equity or fairness when rewards are allocated.

In summary, an organization must take care to ensure consistency throughout in how it implements strategic objectives. Consider how Textron, an $11 billion conglomerate, ensures that its corporate goals are effectively implemented:

> At Textron, each business unit identifies "improvement priorities" that it must act upon to realize the performance outlined in the firm's overall strategic plan. Each improvement priority is translated into action items with clearly defined accountabilities, timetables, and key performance indicators (KPIs) that enable executives to tell how a unit is delivering on a priority. Improvement priorities and action items cascade to every level at the firm—from the management committee (consisting of Textron's top five executives) down to the lowest levels in each of the company's 10 business units. Says Lewis Campbell, Textron's CEO, "Everyone needs to know: 'If I have only one hour to work, here's what I'm going to focus on.' Our goal deployment process makes each individual's accountabilities and priorities clear."[100]

As indicated in this example, organizations have lower-level objectives that are more specific than strategic objectives. These are often referred to as short-term objectives—essential components of a firm's "action plan" that are critical in implementing the firm's chosen strategy. We discuss these issues in detail in Chapter 9.

Reflecting on Career Implications . . .

- *Attributes of Strategic Management:* How do your activities and actions contribute to the goals of your organization? Observe the decisions you make on the job. What are the short-term and long-term implications of your decisions and actions? Have you recently made a decision that might yield short-term profits but might negatively impact the long-term goals of the organization (e.g., cutting maintenance expenses to meet a quarterly profit target)?
- *Intended versus Emergent Strategies:* Don't be too inflexible in your career strategies; strive to take advantage of new opportunities as they arise. Many promising career opportunities may "emerge" that were not part of your intended career strategy or your specific job assignment. Take initiative by pursuing opportunities to get additional training (e.g., learn a software or a statistical package), volunteering for a short-term overseas assignment, etc.
- *Ambidexterity:* Avoid defining your role in the organization too narrowly; look for opportunities to leverage your talents and your organization's resources to create value for your organization. This often involves collaborating with people in other departments or with your organization's customers and suppliers.
- *Strategic Coherence:* Focus your efforts on the "big picture" in your organization. In doing this, you should always strive to assure that your efforts are directed toward your organization's vision, mission, and strategic objectives.

Summary

We began this introductory chapter by defining strategic management and articulating some of its key attributes. Strategic management is defined as "consisting of the analyses, decisions, and actions an organization undertakes to create and sustain competitive advantages." The issue of how and why some firms outperform others in the marketplace is central to the study of strategic management. Strategic management has four key attributes: It is directed at overall organizational goals, includes multiple stakeholders, incorporates both short-term and long-term perspectives, and incorporates trade-offs between efficiency and effectiveness.

The second section discussed the strategic management process. Here, we paralleled the above definition of strategic management and focused on three core activities in the strategic management process—strategy analysis, strategy formulation, and strategy implementation. We noted how each of these activities is highly interrelated to and interdependent on the others. We also discussed how each of the 12 chapters in this text fits into the three core activities.

Next, we introduced two important concepts corporate governance and stakeholder management which must be taken into account throughout the strategic management process. Governance mechanisms can be broadly divided into two groups: internal and external. Internal governance mechanisms include shareholders (owners), management (led by the chief executive officer), and the board of directors. External control is exercised by auditors, banks, analysts, and an active business press as well as the threat of takeovers. We identified five key stakeholders in all organizations: owners, customers, suppliers, employees, and society at large. Successful firms go beyond an overriding focus on satisfying solely the interests of owners. Rather, they recognize the inherent conflicts that arise among the demands of the various stakeholders as well as the need to endeavor to attain "symbiosis"—that is, interdependence and mutual benefit—among the various stakeholder groups. The emerging practice of crowdsourcing, wherein the Internet is used to generate ideas and solve problems, is leading to an evolution in stakeholder roles. Managers must also recognize the need to act in a socially responsible manner which, if done effectively, can enhance a firm's innovativeness. The "shared value" approach represents an innovative perspective on creating value for the firm and society at the same time. The managers also should recognize and incorporate issues related to environmental sustainability in their strategic actions.

In the fourth section, we discussed factors that have accelerated the rate of unpredictable change that managers face today. Such factors, and the combination of them, have increased the need for managers and employees throughout the organization to have a strategic management perspective and to become more empowered.

The final section addressed the need for consistency among a firm's vision, mission, and strategic objectives. Collectively, they form an organization's hierarchy of goals. Visions should evoke powerful and compelling mental images. However, they are not very specific. Strategic objectives, on the other hand, are much more specific and are vital to ensuring that the organization is striving toward fulfilling its vision and mission.

Summary Review Questions

1. How is "strategic management" defined in the text, and what are its four key attributes?

2. Briefly discuss the three key activities in the strategic management process. Why is it important for managers to recognize the interdependent nature of these activities?

3. Explain the concept of "stakeholder management." Why shouldn't managers be solely interested in stockholder management, that is, maximizing the returns for owners of the firm—its shareholders?

4. What is "corporate governance"? What are its three key elements and how can it be improved?

5. How can "symbiosis" (interdependence, mutual benefit) be achieved among a firm's stakeholders?

6. Why do firms need to have a greater strategic management perspective and empowerment in the strategic management process throughout the organization?

7. What is meant by a "hierarchy of goals"? What are the main components of it, and why must consistency be achieved among them?

Key Terms

romantic view of
  leadership, 05
external control view of
  leadership, 06
strategic management, 08
strategy, 08
competitive advantage, 08
operational
  effectiveness, 08
stakeholders, 09

effectiveness, 10
efficiency, 10
ambidexterity, 10
strategic management
  process, 10
intended strategy, 11
realized strategy, 12
strategy analysis, 12
strategy
  formulation, 14

Experiential Exercise

Using the Internet or library sources, select four organizations—two in the private sector and two in the public sector. Find their mission statements. Complete the following exhibit by identifying the stakeholders that are mentioned. Evaluate the differences between firms in the private sector and those in the public sector.

Name			
Mission Statement			
Stakeholders (✓ = mentioned)			
1. Customers			
2. Suppliers			
3. Managers/employees			
4. Community-at-large			
5. Owners			
6. Others?			
7. Others?			

Application Questions & Exercises

1. Go to the Internet and look up one of these company sites: *www.walmart.com*, *www.ge.com*, or *www.fordmotor.com*. What are some of the key events that would represent the "romantic" perspective of leadership? What are some of the key events that depict the "external control" perspective of leadership?

2. Select a company that competes in an industry in which you are interested. What are some of the recent demands that stakeholders have placed on this company? Can you find examples of how the company is trying to develop "symbiosis" (interdependence and mutual benefit) among its stakeholders? (Use the Internet and library resources.)

3. Provide examples of companies that are actively trying to increase the amount of empowerment in the strategic management process throughout the organization. Do these companies seem to be having positive outcomes? Why? Why not?

4. Look up the vision statements and/or mission statements for a few companies. Do you feel that they are constructive and useful as a means of motivating employees and providing a strong strategic direction? Why? Why not? (*Note:* Annual reports, along with the Internet, may be good sources of information.)

Ethics Questions

1. A company focuses solely on short-term profits to provide the greatest return to the owners of the business (i.e., the shareholders in a publicly held firm). What ethical issues could this raise?

2. A firm has spent some time—with input from managers at all levels—in developing a vision statement and a mission statement. Over time, however, the behavior of some executives is contrary to these statements. Could this raise some ethical issues?

References

1. Gunther, M. 2010. Fallen angels. *Fortune,* November 1: 75–78.

2. Sidhu, I. 2010. *Doing both.* East Saddle River, NJ & London: FT Press; ben-Aaron, D. 2010. After Nokia, can angry birds propel Finland? *Bloomberg BusinessWeek.* December 6–December 12: 48–50; ben-Aaron, D. 2010. Nokia board faces call for change on $77 billion lost value. *http://www.bloomberg.com/news.* July 15: np; Anonymous. 2010. The curse of the alien boss. *The Economist.* August 7: 65; and, Lynn, M. 2010. The fallen king of Finland. *Bloomberg BusinessWeek.* September 26: 6–7. We thank Pratik Kapadia for his valued contribution.

3. For a discussion of the "romantic" versus "external control" perspective, refer to Meindl, J. R. 1987. The romance of leadership and the evaluation of organizational performance. *Academy of Management Journal* 30: 92–109; and Pfeffer, J. & Salancik, G. R. 1978. *The external control of organizations: A resource dependence perspective.* New York: Harper & Row.

4. A recent perspective on the "romantic view" of leadership is provided by Mintzberg, H. 2004. Leadership and management development: An afterword. *Academy of Management Executive,* 18(3): 140–142.

5. For a discussion of the best and worst managers for 2008, read: Anonymous. 2009. The best managers. *BusinessWeek,* January 19: 40–41; and, The worst managers. On page 42 in the same issue.

6. Burrows, P. 2009. Apple without its core*? BusinessWeek.* January 26/February 2: 31.

7. For an insightful discussion of Steve Jobs's impact on Apple, read: Satariano, A. 2011. The essence of Apple. *Bloomberg BusinessWeek.* January 24–January 30: 6–8.

8. For a study on the effects of CEOs on firm performance, refer to: Kor, Y. Y. & Misangyi, V. F. 2008. *Strategic Management Journal,* 29(11):1357–1368.

9. Charan, R. & Colvin, G. 2010. Directors: A harsh new reality. *money.cnn.com.* October 6: np.

10. Dobson, C. 2010. Global airlines lost $1.7 billion due to Iceland ash cloud. *www.theepochtimes.com.* May 23: np, and Pylas, P. 2011. Nikkei slides 11 percent on radiation fears. *www.finance.yahoo.com.* March 14: np.

11. Ewing, J. 2008. South Africa emerges from the shadows. *BusinessWeek.* December 15: 52–56.

12. For an interesting perspective on the need for strategists to maintain a global mind-set, refer to Begley, T. M. & Boyd, D. P. 2003. The need for a global mind-set. *MIT Sloan Management Review* 44(2): 25–32.

13. Porter, M. E. 1996. What is strategy? *Harvard Business Review* 74(6): 61–78.

14. See, for example, Barney, J. B. & Arikan, A. M. 2001. The resource-based view: Origins and implications. In Hitt, M. A., Freeman, R. E., & Harrison, J. S. (Eds.), *Handbook of strategic management:* 124–189. Malden, MA: Blackwell.

15. Porter, M. E. 1996. What is strategy? *Harvard Business Review,* 74(6): 61–78; and Hammonds, K. H. 2001. Michael Porter's big ideas. *Fast Company,* March: 55–56.

16. This section draws upon Dess, G. G. & Miller, A. 1993. *Strategic management.* New York: McGraw-Hill.

17. See, for example, Hrebiniak, L. G. & Joyce, W. F. 1986. The strategic importance of managing myopia. *Sloan Management Review,* 28(1): 5–14.

18. For an insightful discussion on how to manage diverse stakeholder groups, refer to Rondinelli, D. A. & London, T. 2003. How corporations and environmental groups cooperate: Assessing cross-sector alliances and collaborations. *Academy of Management Executive,* 17(1): 61–76.

19. Some dangers of a short-term perspective are addressed in: Van Buren, M. E. & Safferstone, T. 2009. The quick wins paradox. *Harvard Business Review,* 67(1): 54–61.

20. Senge, P. 1996. Leading learning organizations: The bold, the powerful, and the invisible. In Hesselbein, F., Goldsmith, M., & Beckhard, R. (Eds.), *The leader of the future:* 41–58. San Francisco: Jossey-Bass.

21. Samuelson, J. 2006. A critical mass for the long term. *Harvard Business Review,* 84(2): 62, 64; and, Anonymous. 2007. Power play. *The Economist,* January 20: 10–12.

22. Loeb, M. 1994. Where leaders come from. *Fortune,* September 19: 241 (quoting Warren Bennis).

23. Address by Norman R. Augustine at the Crummer Business School, Rollins College, Winter Park, FL, October 20, 1989.

24. Hemp, P. 2004. An Interview with CEO Kevin Sharer. *Harvard Business Review,* 82(7/8): 66–74.

25. New perspectives on "management models" are addressed in: Birkinshaw, J. & Goddard, J. 2009. What is your management model? *MIT Sloan Management Review,* 50(2): 81–90.

26. Mintzberg, H. 1985. Of strategies: Deliberate and emergent. *Strategic Management Journal,* 6: 257–272.

27. Some interesting insights on decision-making processes are found in: Nutt, P. C. 2008. Investigating the success of decision making processes. *Journal of Management Studies,* 45(2): 425–455.

28. Aston, A. 2009. How to bet on cleantech. *BusinessWeek,* January 5: 70–71.

29. A study investigating the sustainability of competitive advantage is: Newbert, S. L. 2008. Value, rareness, competitive advantages, and performance: A conceptual-level empirical investigation of the resource-based view of the firm. *Strategic Management Journal,* 29(7): 745–768.

30. Good insights on mentoring are addressed in: DeLong, T. J., Gabarro, J. J., & Lees, R. J. 2008. Why mentoring matters in a hypercompetitive world. *Harvard Business Review,* 66(1): 115–121.

31. A unique perspective on differentiation strategies is: Austin, R. D. 2008. High margins and the quest for aesthetic coherence. *Harvard Business Review,* 86(1): 18–19.

32. Some insights on partnering in the global area are discussed in: MacCormack, A. & Forbath, T. 2008. *Harvard Business Review,* 66(1): 24, 26.

33. For insights on how firms can be successful in entering new markets in emerging economies, refer to: Eyring, M. J., Johnson, M. W. & Nair, H. 2011. New business models in emerging markets. *Harvard Business Review,* 89(1/2): 88–95.

34. An interesting discussion of the challenges of strategy implementation is: Neilson, G. L., Martin, K. L., & Powers, E. 2008. The secrets of strategy execution. *Harvard Business Review,* 86(6): 61–70.

35. Interesting perspectives on strategy execution involving the link between strategy and operations are addressed in: Kaplan, R. S. & Norton, D. P. 2008. Mastering the management system. *Harvard Business Review,* 66(1): 62–77.

36. An innovative perspective on organizational design is found in: Garvin, D. A. & Levesque, L. C. 2008. The multiunit enterprise. *Harvard Business Review,* 86(6): 106–117.

37. Monks, R. & Minow, N. 2001. *Corporate governance* (2nd ed.). Malden, MA: Blackwell.

38. Intel Corp. 2007. *Intel corporation board of directors guidelines on significant corporate governance issues.* www.intel.com

39. Jones, T. J., Felps, W., & Bigley, G. A. 2007. Ethical theory and stakeholder-related decisions: The role of stakeholder culture. *Academy of Management Review,* 32(1): 137–155.

40. For example, see The best (& worst) managers of the year, 2003. *BusinessWeek,* January 13: 58–92; and Lavelle, M. 2003. Rogues of the year. *Time,* January 6: 33–45.

41. Handy, C. 2002. What's a business for? *Harvard Business Review,* 80(12): 49–55.

42. Anonymous, 2007. In the money. *Economist,* January 20: 3–6.

43. Hessel, E. & Woolley, S. 2008. Your money or your life. *Forbes,* October 27: 52.

44. Some interesting insights on the role of activist investors can be found in: Greenwood, R. & Schol, M. 2008. When (not) to listen to activist investors. *Harvard Business Review,* 66(1): 23–24.

45. For an interesting perspective on the changing role of boards of directors, refer to Lawler, E. & Finegold, D. 2005. Rethinking governance. *MIT Sloan Management Review,* 46(2): 67–70.

46. Benz, M. & Frey, B. S. 2007. Corporate governance: What can we learn from public governance? *Academy of Management Review,* 32(1): 92–104.

47. The salience of shareholder value is addressed in: Carrott, G. T. & Jackson, S. E. 2009. Shareholder value must top the CEO's agenda. *Harvard Business Review,* 67(1): 22–24.

48. Stakeholder symbiosis. 1998. *Fortune,* March 30: S2.

49. An excellent review of stakeholder management theory can be found in: Laplume, A. O., Sonpar, K., & Litz, R. A. 2008. Stakeholder theory: Reviewing a theory that moves us. *Journal of Management,* 34(6): 1152–1189.

50. For a definitive, recent discussion of the stakeholder concept, refer to Freeman, R. E. & McVae, J. 2001. A stakeholder approach to strategic management. In Hitt, M. A., Freeman, R. E., & Harrison, J. S. (Eds.). *Handbook of strategic management:* 189–207. Malden, MA: Blackwell.

51. Harrison, J. S., Bosse, D. A. & Phillips, R. A. 2010. Managing for stakeholders, stakeholder utility functions, and competitive advantage. *Strategic Management Journal,* 31(1): 58–74.

52. For an insightful discussion on the role of business in society, refer to Handy, op. cit.

53. Camillus, J. 2008. Strategy as a wicked problem. *Harvard Business Review,* 86(5): 100–101.

54. Stakeholder symbiosis. op. cit., p. S3.

55. Sidhu, I. 2010. *Doing both.* FT Press: Upper Saddle River, NJ: 7–8.

56. Our discussion of crowdsourcing draws on the first two books that have addressed this concept: Libert, B. & Spector, J. 2008. *We are smarter than me.* Philadelphia: Wharton Publishing; and, Howe, J. 2008. *Crowdsourcing.* New York: Crown Business. Eric von Hippel has addressed similar ideas in his earlier book (2005. *Democratizing innovation.* Cambridge, MA: MIT Press).

57. Thomas, J. G. 2000. Macroenvironmetal forces. In Helms, M. M. (Ed.), *Encyclopedia of management.* (4th ed.): 516–520. Farmington Hills, MI: Gale Group.

58. For a strong advocacy position on the need for corporate values and social responsibility, read Hollender, J. 2004. What matters most: Corporate values and social responsibility. *California Management Review,* 46(4): 111–119.

59. Waddock, S. & Bodwell, C. 2004. Managing responsibility: What can be learned from the quality movement. *California Management Review,* 47(1): 25–37.

60. For a discussion of the role of alliances and collaboration on corporate social responsibility initiatives, refer to Pearce, J. A. II. & Doh, J. P. 2005. The high impact of collaborative social initiatives. *MIT Sloan Management Review,* 46(3): 30–40.

61. Insights on ethical behavior and performance are addressed in: Trudel, R. & Cotte, J. 2009. *MIT Sloan Management Review,* 50(2): 61–68.

62. Bhattacharya, C. B. & Sen, S. 2004, Doing better at doing good: When, why, and how consumers respond to corporate social initiatives. *California Management Review,* 47(1): 9–24.

63. For some findings on the relationship between corporate social responsibility and firm performance, see: Margolis, J. D. & Elfenbein, H. A. 2008. *Harvard Business Review,* 86(1): 19–20.

64. Cone Corporate Citizenship Study, 2002, www.coneinc.com.

65. Refer to www.bsr.org.

66. This section draws on: Porter, M. E. & Kramer, M. R. 2011. Creating shared value. *Harvard Business Review,* 89 (1/2): 62–77.

67. A similar concept is conscious capitalism. Refer, for example, to: Sheth, J. N. 2007. *Firms of endearment: How world-class companies profit from passion and purpose.* Philadelphia, PA: Wharton Publishing.

68. An insightful discussion of the risks and opportunities associated with global warming, refer to: Lash, J. & Wellington, F. 2007. Competitive advantage on a warming planet. *Harvard Business Review,* 85(3): 94–102.

69. This section draws on Hart, S. L. 1997. Beyond greening: Strategies for a sustainable world. *Harvard Business Review,* 75(1): 66–76, and Berry, M. A. & Rondinelli, D. A. 1998. Proactive corporate environmental management: A new industrial revolution. *Academy of Management Executive,* 12(2): 38–50.

70. Carey, J. 2006. Business on a warmer planet. *BusinessWeek,* July 17: 26–29.

71. Hart, op. cit., p. 67.

72. For a creative perspective on environmental sustainability and competitive advantage as well as ethical implications, read Ehrenfeld, J. R. 2005. The roots of sustainability. *MIT Sloan Management Review,* 46(2): 23–25.

73. McKinsey & Company. 1991. *The corporate response to the environmental challenge.* Summary Report, Amsterdam: McKinsey & Company.

74. Delmas, M. A. & Montes-Sancho, M. J. 2010. Voluntary agreements to improve environmental quality: Symbolic and substantive cooperation. *Strategic Management Journal,* 31(6): 575–601.

75. Vogel, D. J. 2005. Is there a market for virtue? The business case for corporate social responsibility. *California Management Review,* 47(4): 19–36.

76. Walsh, D. T. 2010. Harness the profit motive to deliver environmental sustainability. *www.huffingtonpost.com.* November 5: np.

77. Esty, D. C. & Winston, A. S. 2009. *Green to gold.* Hoboken, NJ: Wiley: 124–125.

78. Senge, P. M. 1990. The leader's new work: Building learning organizations. *Sloan Management Review,* 32(1): 7–23.

79. For an interesting perspective on the role of middle managers in the strategic management process, refer to Huy, Q. H. 2001. In praise of middle managers. *Harvard Business Review,* 79(8): 72–81.

80. Senge, 1996, op. cit., pp. 41–58.

81. Helgesen, S. 1996. Leading from the grass roots. In Hesselbein, F., Goldsmith, M., & Beckhard, R. (Eds.), *The leader of the future:* 19–24. San Francisco: Jossey-Bass.

82. Wetlaufer, S. 1999. Organizing for empowerment: An interview with AES's Roger Sant and Dennis Blake. *Harvard Business Review,* 77(1): 110–126.

83. Kets de Vries, M. F. R. 1998. Charisma in action: The transformational abilities of Virgin's Richard Branson and ABB's Percy Barnevik. *Organizational Dynamics,* 26(3): 7–21.

84. Hamel, G. 2006. The why, what, and how of management innovation. *Harvard Business Review,* 84(2): 72–84.

85. An interesting discussion on how to translate top management's goals into concrete actions is found in: Bungay, S. 2011. How to make the most of your company's strategy. *Harvard Business Review,* 89(1/2): 132–40.

86. An insightful discussion about the role of vision, mission, and strategic objectives can be found in: Collis, D. J. & Rukstad, M. G. 2008. Can you say what your strategy is? *Harvard Business Review,* 66(4): 82–90.

87. Our discussion draws on a variety of sources. These include Lipton, M. 1996. Demystifying the development of an organizational vision. *Sloan Management Review,* 37(4): 83–92; Bart, C. K. 2000. Lasting inspiration. *CA Magazine,* May: 49–50; and Quigley, J. V. 1994. Vision: How leaders develop it, share it, and sustain it. *Business Horizons,* September–October: 37–40.

88. Lipton, op. cit.

89. Hardy, Q. 2007. The uncarly. *Forbes,* March 12: 82–90.

90. Some interesting perspective on gender differences in organizational vision are discussed in: Ibarra, H. & Obodaru, O. 2009. Women and the vision thing. *Harvard Business Review,* 67(1): 62–70.

91. Quigley, op. cit.

92. Ibid.

93. Lipton, op. cit. Additional pitfalls are addressed in this article.

94. Sull, D. N. 2005. Strategy as active waiting. *Harvard Business Review,* 83(9): 120–130.

95. Company records.

96. Lipton, op. cit.

97. Sexton, D. A. & Van Aukun, P. M. 1985. A longitudinal study of small business strategic planning. *Journal of Small Business Management,* January: 8–15, cited in Lipton, op. cit.

98. For an insightful perspective on the use of strategic objectives, refer to Chatterjee, S. 2005. Core objectives: Clarity in designing strategy. *California Management Review,* 47(2): 33–49.

99. Ibid.

100. Mankins, M. M. & Steele, R. 2005. Turning great strategy into great performance. *Harvard Business Review,* 83(5): 66–73.

chapter TWO

Analyzing the External Environment of the Firm

Creating Competitive Advantages

After reading this chapter, you should have a good understanding of:

LO2.1 The importance of developing forecasts of the business environment.

LO2.2 Why environmental scanning, environmental monitoring, and collecting competitive intelligence are critical inputs to forecasting.

LO2.3 Why scenario planning is a useful technique for firms competing in industries characterized by unpredictability and change.

LO2.4 The impact of the general environment on a firm's strategies and performance.

LO2.5 How forces in the competitive environment can affect profitability, and how a firm can improve its competitive position by increasing its power vis-à-vis these forces.

LO2.6 How the Internet and digitally based capabilities are affecting the five competitive forces and industry profitability.

LO2.7 The concept of strategic groups and their strategy and performance implications.

LEARNING OBJECTIVES

Strategies are not and should not be developed in a vacuum. They must be responsive to the external business environment. Otherwise, your firm could become, in effect, the most efficient producer of buggy whips, leisure suits, or typewriters. To avoid such strategic mistakes, firms must become knowledgeable about the business environment. One tool for analyzing trends is forecasting. In the development of forecasts, environmental scanning and environmental monitoring are important in detecting key trends and events. Managers also must aggressively collect and disseminate competitor intelligence. The information gleaned from these three activities is invaluable in developing forecasts and scenarios to minimize present and future threats as well as to exploit opportunities. We address these issues in the first part of this chapter. We also introduce a basic tool of strategy analysis—the concept of SWOT analysis (strengths, weaknesses, opportunities, and threats).

In the second part of the chapter, we present two frameworks for analyzing the external environment—the general environment and the competitive environment. The general environment consists of six segments—demographic, sociocultural, political/legal, technological, economic, and global. Trends and events in these segments can have a dramatic impact on your firm.

The competitive environment is closer to home. It consists of five industry-related factors that can dramatically affect the average level of industry profitability. An awareness of these factors is critical in making decisions such as which industries to enter and how to improve your firm's current position within an industry. This is helpful in neutralizing competitive threats and increasing power over customers and suppliers. We also address how industry and competitive practices are being affected by the capabilities provided by Internet technologies. In the final part of this section, we place firms within an industry into strategic groups based on similarities in resources and strategies. As we will see, the concept of strategic groups has important implications for the intensity of rivalry and how the effects of a given environmental trend or event differ across groups.

Learning from Mistakes

The emerging middle-class market in China has grown rapidly, and its appetite for consumerism and savings has skyrocketed.[1] Currently the upper tier of China's wealthiest account for 25 percent of Chinese household savings and will continue to control the bulk of the nation's accumulated wealth—60 percent by 2025. Their importance to banks and other financial-services firms will therefore increase. As the first foreign bank—and now the largest foreign financial institution in Hong Kong—Citibank Hong Kong was counting on over 100 years of successful, award-winning business strategies to help it grow along with China's economy and its increasing consumer financial needs. But it suffered from a misstep . . .

> The company expected favorable results after launching a 15 percent customer discount program in partnership with a restaurant chain. However, Citibank found itself in the hot seat, or bowl for that matter, with many environmentally conscious customers. In a matter of days, social media campaigns had sprung up condemning the promotion. Citibank Hong Kong quickly removed the promotion after being inundated with emails and calls to action. So how did this shining example of a foreign company tarnish its reputation abroad?

> Well . . . the cultural delicacy item that Citibank Hong Kong promoted (with partner Maxim's Chinese Cuisine outlets) was shark fin soup, a soup that is increasingly known for contributing to an estimated 90–100 million shark deaths per year due to definning. The prized fins are collected from live sharks by removing them and then throwing the sharks back in the ocean to die. The company tried to promote a rare, high-status item (US$150/bowl), but ignored the growing sensitivity the market had toward shark fin soup. Citibank Hong Kong lost sight of its environmentally informed market and paid the price when this issue was widely publicized.

Successful managers must recognize opportunities and threats in their firm's external environment. They must be aware of what's going on outside their company. If they focus exclusively on the efficiency of internal operations, the firm may degenerate into the world's most efficient producer of buggy whips, typewriters, or carbon paper. But if they miscalculate the market, opportunities will be lost—hardly an enviable position for their firm. As we saw from the Citibank Hong Kong example, misreading the market can lead to negative consequences—and even adversely affect a firm's reputation.

• Citibank Hong Kong paid a stiff price for promoting shark fin soup for a sales promotion in China.

In *Competing for the Future*, Gary Hamel and C. K. Prahalad suggest that "every manager carries around in his or her head a set of biases, assumptions, and presuppositions about the structure of the relevant 'industry,' about how one makes money in the industry, about who the competition is and isn't, about who the customers are and aren't, and so on."[2] Environmental analysis requires you to continually question such assumptions. Peter Drucker labeled these interrelated sets of assumptions the "theory of the business."[3] The sudden reversal in Nokia's fortunes (chapter 1) clearly illustrates that if a company does not keep pace with changes in the external environment, it becomes difficult to sustain competitive advantages and deliver strong financial results.

A firm's strategy may be good at one point in time, but it may go astray when management's frame of reference gets out of touch with the realities of the actual business situation. This results when management's assumptions, premises, or beliefs are incorrect or when internal inconsistencies among them render the overall "theory of the business" invalid. As Warren Buffett, investor extraordinaire, colorfully notes, "Beware of past performance 'proofs.' If history books were the key to riches, the Forbes 400 would consist of librarians."

In the business world, many once successful firms have fallen. Consider the high-tech company Novell, which went head-to-head with Microsoft. Novell bought market-share loser WordPerfect to compete with Microsoft Word. The result? A $1.3 billion loss when Novell sold WordPerfect to Corel. And today we may wonder who will be the next Blockbuster, Circuit City, or *Encyclopaedia Britannica*.

Creating the Environmentally Aware Organization

So how do managers become environmentally aware?[4] We will now address three important processes—scanning, monitoring, and gathering competitive intelligence—used to develop forecasts.[5] Exhibit 2.1 illustrates relationships among these important activities. We also discuss the importance of scenario planning in anticipating major future changes in the external environment and the role of SWOT analysis.[6]

>LO2.1
The importance of developing forecasts of the business environment.

The Role of Scanning, Monitoring, Competitive Intelligence, and Forecasting

Environmental Scanning **Environmental scanning** involves surveillance of a firm's external environment to predict environmental changes and detect changes already under way.[7,8] This alerts the organization to critical trends and events before changes develop a discernible pattern and before competitors recognize them.[9] Otherwise, the firm may be forced into a reactive mode.[10]

Experts agree that spotting key trends requires a combination of knowing your business and your customer as well as keeping an eye on what's happening around you.[11] Such a big-picture/small-picture view enables you to better identify the emerging trends that will affect your business. We suggest a few tips in Exhibit 2.2.

Leading firms in an industry can also be a key indicator of emerging trends.[11] For example, with its wide range of household goods, Procter & Gamble is a barometer for consumer spending. Any sign that it can sell more of its premium products without cutting prices sharply indicates that shoppers may finally be becoming less price-sensitive with

>LO2.2
Why environmental scanning, environmental monitoring, and collecting competitive intelligence are critical inputs to forecasting.

environmental scanning surveillance of a firm's external environment to predict environmental changes and detect changes already under way.

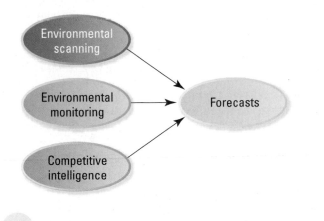

Exhibit 2.1 **Inputs to Forecasting**

- **Listen.** Ask your customers questions about your products and services. Ask what they are looking for next. Find out what media they're watching and what they think of current events.

- **Pay attention.** Read trade publications related to your industry to identify key issues. Watch industries that are always on the cutting edge, such as technology, music, and fashion, in order to discover emerging trends that may affect your business.

- **Follow trends online.** Trend-hunting websites such as trendhunter.com and jwtintelligence.com offer up the trends du jour. Add them to your regular Web-surfing itinerary.

- **Go old school.** Ask your customers what they think. Organize online or in-person focus groups to find out what people are thinking. You can also launch social media groups or chat rooms to gather feedback from your audience.

Source: Moran, G. 2008. Be Your Own Trendspotter. *Entrepreneur,* December: 17.

everyday purchases. In particular, investors will examine the performance of beauty products like Olay moisturizers and CoverGirl cosmetics for evidence that spending on small, discretionary pick-me-ups is improving.

Strategy Spotlight 2.1 addresses how Zara, a Spanish fashion retailer, keeps abreast of trends and promising opportunities.

environmental monitoring a firm's analysis of the external environment that tracks the evolution of environmental trends, sequences of events, or streams of activities.

Environmental Monitoring Environmental monitoring tracks the evolution of environmental trends, sequences of events, or streams of activities. They may be trends that the firm came across by accident or ones that were brought to its attention from outside the organization.[12] Monitoring enables firms to evaluate how dramatically environmental trends are changing the competitive landscape.

One of the authors of this text has conducted on-site interviews with executives from several industries to identify indicators that firms monitor as inputs to their strategy process. Examples of such indicators included:

- *A Motel 6 executive.* The number of rooms in the budget segment of the industry in the United States and the difference between the average daily room rate and the consumer price index (CPI).
- *A Pier 1 Imports executive.* Net disposable income (NDI), consumer confidence index, and housing starts.
- *A Johnson & Johnson medical products executive.* Percentage of gross domestic product (GDP) spent on health care, number of active hospital beds, and the size and power of purchasing agents (indicates the concentration of buyers).

Such indices are critical for managers in determining a firm's strategic direction and resource allocation.

competitive intelligence a firm's activities of collecting and interpreting data on competitors, defining and understanding the industry, and identifying competitors' strengths and weaknesses.

Competitive Intelligence Competitive intelligence (CI) helps firms define and understand their industry and identify rivals' strengths and weaknesses.[13] This includes the intelligence gathering associated with collecting data on competitors and interpreting such data. Done properly, competitive intelligence helps a company avoid surprises by anticipating competitors' moves and decreasing response time.[14]

Examples of competitive analysis are evident in daily newspapers and periodicals such as *The Wall Street Journal, BusinessWeek,* and *Fortune.* For example, banks continually track home loan, auto loan, and certificate of deposit (CD) interest rates charged by rivals. Major airlines change hundreds of fares daily in response to competitors' tactics.

How Zara, a Spanish Retailer, Spots Opportunities

After massive investments in sophisticated IT systems, many companies continue to miss market shifts that their rivals exploit. With IT investments, however, it's not how much you spend but how you spend it. To continually identify gaps in the market, firms need real-time data and the ability to share it widely throughout the organization. Those hard data must be supplemented with direct observations from the field.

Consider Spanish retailer, Zara, whose success is often attributed to its flexible supply chain. Equally impressive is Zara's ability to spot changing preferences among its fickle customers—despite spending only one-quarter of the industry average on IT. Zara's designers, marketing managers, and buyers work side by side in the company's sprawling headquarters. The open office plan fosters frequent discussions and promotes the sharing of real-time data as well as field observations and anecdotes. By colocating employees from different functions, Zara allows them to break out of their silos and develop a holistic feel for the market, see how their work fits, and sense new opportunities as they arise.

Source: Sull, D. 2010. Are You Ready to Rebound? *Harvard Business Review.* 88(3): 72; D'Aveni, R. A. 2010. *Beating the Commodity Trap.* Boston: Harvard Business Press; and, Caesar, J. 2010. Zara Launches Online Retail Store. *www.bbc.co.uk.* September 2: np.

For instance, in the summer of 2007, Zara launched a line of slim-fit clothes, including pencil skirts and tapered jeans, in response to catwalk trends and what celebrities were wearing. Marketing executives projected that the new items would fly off the racks, but the daily statistics revealed that the items were not selling. So Zara marketing managers immediately went into the field to see firsthand what was happening. They talked to managers, employees, and customers and quickly realized that women loved how the clothes looked but struggled to squeeze into their usual size in the dressing room. Zara responded by recalling the items and relabeling them one size smaller. The company then watched sales boom as customers happily fit into their usual size. The shared, real-time data supplemented with firsthand observation helped employees respond quickly and tip the balance from failure to success.

Zara has experienced tremendous growth and increasing market power. By 2007, it was the biggest fashion company in Europe, outpacing H&M as queen of cheap chic. It is committed to international expansion. In 2008, Korea, Ukraine, Montenegro, Egypt, and Honduras were conquered, and, in 2009, Zara announced a joint venture with India's Tata Group to open stores in India.

Finally, in September 2010, Zara launched its first online retail stores in France, Spain, Italy, Portugal, and the United Kingdom. Since Zara is "liked" by more than 4.5 million people who have signed up as fans on Facebook, the key to its success will now be to convert those fans to customers.

Car manufacturers are keenly aware of announced cuts or increases in rivals' production volume, sales, and sales incentives (e.g., rebates and low interest rates on financing). This information is used in their marketing, pricing, and production strategies.

The Internet has dramatically accelerated the speed at which firms can find competitive intelligence. Leonard Fuld, founder of the Cambridge, Massachusetts, training and consulting firm Fuld & Co., specializes in competitive intelligence.[15] His firm often profiles top company and business group managers and considers these issues: What is their background? What is their style? Are they marketers? Are they cost cutters? Fuld has found that the more articles he collects and the more biographies he downloads, the better he can develop profiles.

One of Fuld & Co.'s clients asked it to determine the size, strength, and technical capabilities of a privately-held company. Initially, it was difficult to get detailed information. Then one analyst used Deja News (*www.dejanews.com*), now part of Google, to tap into some online discussion groups. The analyst's research determined that the company had posted 14 job openings on one Usenet group. That posting was a road map to the competitor's development strategy.

At times, a firm's aggressive efforts to gather competitive intelligence may lead to unethical or illegal behaviors.[16] Strategy Spotlight 2.2 provides an example of a company, United Technologies, that has set clear guidelines to help prevent unethical behavior.

Ethical Guidelines on Competitive Intelligence: United Technologies

United Technologies (UT) is a $53 billion global conglomerate composed of world-leading businesses with rich histories of technological pioneering, such as Otis Elevator, Carrier Air Conditioning, and Sikorsky (helicopters). It was founded in 1853 and has an impressive history of technological accomplishments. UT built the first working helicopter, developed the first commercially available hydrogen cells, and designed complete life support systems for space shuttles. UT believes strongly in a robust code of ethics. In the last decade, they have clearly articulated their principles governing business conduct. These include an antitrust guide, an ethics guide when contracting with the U.S. government and foreign governments, a policy on accepting gifts from suppliers, and guidelines for proper usage of e-mail. One such document is the Code of Ethics Guide on Competitive Intelligence. This encourages managers and workers to ask themselves these five questions whenever they have ethical concerns.

1. Have I done anything that coerced somebody to share this information? Have I, for example, threatened a supplier by indicating that future business opportunities will be influenced by the receipt of information with respect to a competitor?

2. Am I in a place where I should not be? If, for example, I am a field representative with privileges to move around in a customer's facility, have I gone outside the areas permitted? Have I misled anybody in order to gain access?

3. Is the contemplated technique for gathering information evasive, such as sifting through trash or setting up an electronic "snooping" device directed at a competitor's facility from across the street?

4. Have I misled somebody in a way that the person believed sharing information with me was required or would be protected by a confidentiality agreement? Have I, for example, called and misrepresented myself as a government official who was seeking some information for some official purpose?

5. Have I done something to evade or circumvent a system intended to secure or protect information?

ethics

Sources: Nelson, B. 2003. The thinker. *Forbes,* March 3: 62–64; and The Fuld war room—Survival kit 010. Code of ethics (printed 2/26/01); and *www.yahoo.com.*

A word of caution: Executives must be careful to avoid spending so much time and effort tracking the actions of traditional competitors that they ignore new competitors. Further, broad environmental changes and events may have a dramatic impact on a firm's viability. Peter Drucker, considered the father of modern management, wrote:

> Increasingly, a winning strategy will require information about events and conditions outside the institution: noncustomers, technologies other than those currently used by the company and its present competitors, markets not currently served, and so on.[17]

Consider the fall of the once-mighty *Encyclopaedia Britannica.*[18] Its demise was not caused by a traditional competitor in the encyclopedia industry. It was caused by new technology. CD-ROMs came out of nowhere and devastated the printed encyclopedia industry. Why? A full set of the *Encyclopaedia Britannica* sells for about $2,000, but an encyclopedia on CD-ROM, such as Microsoft *Encarta,* sells for about $50. To make matters worse, many people receive *Encarta* free with their personal computers.

environmental forecasting the development of plausible projections about the direction, scope, speed, and intensity of environmental change.

Environmental Forecasting Environmental scanning, monitoring, and competitive intelligence are important inputs for analyzing the external environment. **Environmental forecasting** involves the development of plausible projections about the direction, scope, speed, and intensity of environmental change.[19] Its purpose is to predict change.[20] It asks:

How long will it take a new technology to reach the marketplace? Will the present social concern about an issue result in new legislation? Are current lifestyle trends likely to continue?

Some forecasting issues are much more specific to a particular firm and the industry in which it competes. Consider how important it is for Motel 6 to predict future indicators, such as the number of rooms, in the budget segment of the industry. If its predictions are low, it will build too many units, creating a surplus of room capacity that would drive down room rates.

A danger of forecasting is that managers may view uncertainty as black and white and ignore important gray areas.[21] The problem is that underestimating uncertainty can lead to strategies that neither defend against threats nor take advantage of opportunities.

In 1977 one of the colossal underestimations in business history occurred when Kenneth H. Olsen, president of Digital Equipment Corp., announced, "There is no reason for individuals to have a computer in their home." The explosion in the personal computer market was not easy to detect in 1977, but it was clearly within the range of possibilities at the time. And, historically, there have been underestimates of the growth potential of new telecommunication services. The electric telegraph was derided by Ralph Waldo Emerson, and the telephone had its skeptics. More recently, an "infamous" McKinsey study in the early 1980s predicted fewer than 1 million cellular users in the United States by 2000. Actually, there were nearly 100 million.[22]

Obviously, poor predictions never go out of vogue. Consider some of the "gems" associated with the global financial crisis that began in 2008.[23]

- "Freddie Mac and Fannie Mae are fundamentally sound. . . . I think they are in good shape going forward."—Barney Frank (D-Mass.), House Financial Services Committee Chairman, July 14, 2008. (*Two months later, the government forced the mortgage giants into conservatorships.*)
- "Existing home sales to trend up in 2008"—Headline of a National Association of Realtors press release, December 9, 2007. (*On December 23, 2007, the group said November sales were down 11 percent from a year earlier in the worst housing slump since the Great Depression.*)
- "I think you'll see $150 a barrel [of oil] by the end of the year."—T. Boone Pickens, June 20, 2008. (*Oil was then around $135 a barrel. By late December it was around $40.*)
- "I expect there will be some failures. . . . I don't anticipate any serious problems of that sort among the large internationally active banks."—Ben Bernanke, Federal Reserve Chairman, February 28, 2008. (*In September, Washington Mutual became the largest financial institution in U.S. history to fail. Citigroup needed an even bigger rescue in November.*)
- "In today's regulatory environment, it's virtually impossible to violate rules."—Bernard Madoff, money manager, October 20, 2007. (*On December 11, 2008, Madoff was arrested for allegedly running a Ponzi scheme that may have lost investors $50 billion. He was sentenced to 150 years in prison on July 29, 2009.*)

Scenario Analysis is a more in-depth approach to forecasting. It draws on a range of disciplines and interests, among them economics, psychology, sociology, and demographics. It usually begins with a discussion of participants' thoughts on ways in which societal trends, economics, politics, and technology may affect an issue.[24] For example, consider Lego. The popular Danish toy manufacturer has a strong position in the construction toys market. But what would happen if this broadly defined market should change dramatically? After all, Lego is competing not only with producers of similar

> **>LO2.3**
> Why scenario planning is a useful technique for firms competing in industries characterized by unpredictability and change.

scenario analysis an in-depth approach to environmental forecasting that involves experts' detailed assessments of societal trends, economics, politics, technology, or other dimensions of the external environment.

Scenario Planning at PPG

PPG Industries, the Pittsburgh-based manufacturer of paints, coatings, optical products, specialty materials, chemicals, glass, and fiber glass, has paid dividends every year since 1899 and has maintained or increased dividends every year since 1972. With sales over $13 billion and operations in more than 60 countries, PPG is truly a global player. Although considered a very successful company, PPG has had its share of strategic errors. Realizing that business was slowing down in its core businesses, PPG acquired medical electronics businesses from Honeywell and Litton Industries in 1986 and from Allegheny International in 1987. However, these efforts at diversification proved to be failures, as the firm's competence in low-cost, standardized production in stable, mature industries was of little help in the highly volatile biomedical industry, where customization was vital. Seven years later, PPG exited the medical electronics business by selling off these units. To profit from the construction boom in China, PPG entered the Chinese market with a focus on glass. After years of losses, the company realized that it would have to focus on coatings.

These costly failures led PPG to a new emphasis on strategic planning. One of the key tools they use today is scenario planning. They have developed four alternative futures based on differing assumptions about two key variables: the cost of energy (because their manufacturing operations are energy intensive) and the extent of opportunity for growth in emerging markets. In the most favorable scenario, cost of energy will stay moderate and stable and opportunities for growth and differentiation will be fast and strong. In this scenario, they determined that their success will depend on having the resources to pursue new opportunities. On the other hand, in the worst case scenario, cost of energy will be high and opportunities for growth will be weak and slow. This scenario would call for a complete change in strategic direction. Between these two extremes lies the possibility of two mixed scenarios. First, opportunity for growth in emerging markets may be high, but cost of energy may be high and volatile. In this scenario, the company's success will depend on coming up with more efficient processes. Finally, cost of energy may remain moderate and stable, but opportunities for growth in emerging markets may remain weak and slow. In this situation, the most viable strategy may be one of capturing market share with new products.

Developing strategies based on possible future scenarios seems to be paying off for PPG Industries. The company currently boasts a return on equity of 19.1 percent and its stock has had a total return of over 43 percent over the most recent 52-week period.

Source: Camillus, J. C. 2008. Strategy as a Wicked Problem. *Harvard Business Review*, 86 (5): 98–106; *www.ppg.com.*; and *www.finance.yahoo.com.*

products but also on a much broader canvas for a share of children's playtime. In this market, Lego has a host of competitors, many of them computer based; still others have not yet been invented. Lego may end up with an increasing share of a narrow, shrinking market (much like IBM in the declining days of the mainframe computer). To avoid such a fate, managers must consider a wider context than their narrow, traditional markets, by laying down guidelines for at least 10 years in the future to anticipate rapid change. Strategy Spotlight 2.3 provides an example of scenario planning at PPG Industries.

SWOT Analysis

To understand the business environment of a particular firm, you need to analyze both the general environment and the firm's industry and competitive environment. Generally, firms compete with other firms in the same industry. An industry is composed of a set of firms that produce similar products or services, sell to similar customers, and use similar methods of production. Gathering industry information and understanding competitive dynamics among the different companies in your industry is key to successful strategic management.

One of the most basic techniques for analyzing firm and industry conditions is **SWOT analysis.** SWOT stands for strengths, weaknesses, opportunities, and threats. It provides "raw material"—a basic listing of conditions both inside and surrounding your company.

The Strengths and Weaknesses refer to the internal conditions of the firm—where your firm excels (strengths) and where it may be lacking relative to competitors (weaknesses). Opportunities and Threats are environmental conditions external to the firm. These could be factors either in the general or competitive environment. In the general environment, one might experience developments that are beneficial for most companies such as improving economic conditions, that lower borrowing costs or trends that benefit some companies and harm others. An example is the heightened concern with fitness, which is a threat to some companies (e.g., tobacco) and an opportunity to others (e.g., health clubs). Opportunities and threats are also present in the competitive environment among firms competing for the same customers.

The general idea of SWOT analysis is that a firm's strategy must:

- build on its strengths,
- remedy the weaknesses or work around them,
- take advantage of the opportunities presented by the environment, and,
- protect the firm from the threats.

Despite its apparent simplicity, the SWOT approach has been very popular. First, it forces managers to consider both internal and external factors simultaneously. Second, its emphasis on identifying opportunities and threats makes firms act proactively rather than reactively. Third, it raises awareness about the role of strategy in creating a match between the environmental conditions and the firm's internal strengths and weaknesses. Finally, its conceptual simplicity is achieved without sacrificing analytical rigor. (We will also address some of the limitations of SWOT analysis in Chapter 3.)

The General Environment

The **general environment** is composed of factors that can have dramatic effects on firm strategy.[25] Typically, a firm has little ability to predict trends and events in the general environment and even less ability to control them. When listening to CNBC, for example, you can hear many experts espouse different perspectives on what action the Federal Reserve Board may take on short-term interest rates—an action that can have huge effects on the valuation of entire economic sectors. Also, it's difficult to predict future political events such as the ongoing Middle East peace negotiations and tensions on the Korean peninsula. Dramatic innovations in information technology (e.g., the Internet) have helped keep inflation in check by lowering the cost of doing business in the United States at the beginning of the 21st century.[26]

We divide the general environment into six segments: demographic, sociocultural, political/legal, technological, economic, and global. Exhibit 2.3 provides examples of key trends and events in each of the six segments of the general environment.

The Demographic Segment

Demographics are the most easily understood and quantifiable elements of the general environment. They are at the root of many changes in society. Demographics include elements such as the aging population,[27] rising or declining affluence, changes in ethnic composition, geographic distribution of the population, and disparities in income level.[28]

The impact of a demographic trend, like all segments of the general environment, varies across industries. Rising levels of affluence in many developed countries bode well

SWOT analysis a framework for analyzing a company's internal and external environment and that stands for strengths, weaknesses, opportunities, and threats.

general environment factors external to an industry, and usually beyond a firm's control, that affect a firm's strategy.

>LO2.4
The impact of the general environment on a firm's strategies and performance.

demographic segment of the general environment genetic and observable characteristics of a population, including the levels and growth of age, density, sex, race, ethnicity, education, geographic region, and income.

Exhibit 2.3
General Environment: Key
Trends and Events

Demographic

- Aging population
- Rising affluence
- Changes in ethnic composition
- Geographic distribution of population
- Greater disparities in income levels

Sociocultural

- More women in the workforce
- Increase in temporary workers
- Greater concern for fitness
- Greater concern for environment
- Postponement of family formation

Political/Legal

- Tort reform
- Americans with Disabilities Act (ADA) of 1990
- Repeal of Glass-Steagall Act in 1999 (banks may now offer brokerage services)
- Deregulation of utility and other industries
- Increases in federally mandated minimum wages
- Taxation at local, state, federal levels
- Legislation on corporate governance reforms in bookkeeping, stock options, etc. (Sarbanes-Oxley Act of 2002)

Technological

- Genetic engineering
- Emergence of Internet technology
- Computer-aided design/computer-aided manufacturing systems (CAD/CAM)
- Research in synthetic and exotic materials
- Pollution/global warming
- Miniaturization of computing technologies
- Wireless communications
- Nanotechnology

Economic

- Interest rates
- Unemployment rates
- Consumer Price Index
- Trends in GDP
- Changes in stock market valuations

Global

- Increasing global trade
- Currency exchange rates
- Emergence of the Indian and Chinese economies
- Trade agreements among regional blocs (e.g., NAFTA, EU, ASEAN)
- Creation of WTO (leading to decreasing tariffs/free trade in services)
- Increased risks associated with terrorism

China's Growing Middle Class Helps Cargo Carriers Rebound from the Recession

Increasingly, wealthy Chinese consumers eat more imported fresh fish, lobster, and cheese and wear imported fashions. One implication: They are helping global air cargo revenue rebound from the decline in 2009, the worst year in five decades.

China, with its soaring demand for luxury goods and perishable foods from overseas will lead an 18.5 percent recovery in air shipments in 2010, according to the International Air Transport Association. "China has attracted more investment and luxury brands, as purchasing power has gotten much stronger," said Kelvin Lau, an equity analyst at Daiwa Institute of Research in Hong Kong. For example, Cathay Pacific, the biggest carrier in Hong Kong,

is flying 100 tons of lobster and 150 tons of grouper to China and Hong Kong every month from Australia and Indonesia. It also increased shipments of sashimi-grade fish to the country from Tokyo by 60 percent in the first four months of 2010.

The size of China's middle class could rise to 46 percent of all households by 2020, from 32 percent in 2010, claims the research firm Euromonitor International. The firm defines middle-class households as those with annual disposable incomes equivalent to $5,000 to $15,000.

United Parcel Service, the world's largest package-delivery firm, has added two cargo planes in Hong Kong and one in Shanghai in 2010. FedEx, the world's largest air cargo carrier, is planning to buy more air freighters for its longest routes to Asia.

Shanghai International Port, China's largest port group, had a throughput of 428 million tons in 2010—up from 365 tons the previous year. And Global Logistic Properties Ltd., a logistics company whose customers include Walmart China and FedEx, expects cargo demand through the Beijing airport to increase by 15 percent a year from 2010 to 2015.

Source: Leung, W. & Ling, C. S. 2010. Chinese Consumers' Appetites Fatten Air Shippers. *International Herald Tribune.* July 30: 15; Wong, F. & Lian, R. 2011. Shanghai International Port Posts 44 Percent Jump in 2010 Net. *www.reuters.com.* January 11: np; and, Park, K. 2011. Global Logistic to Expand in Smaller China Cities to Tap on Rental Growth. *www.bloomberg.com.* January 4: np.

for brokerage services as well as for upscale pets and supplies. However, this trend may adversely affect fast-food restaurants because people can afford to dine at higher-priced restaurants. Fast-food restaurants depend on minimum-wage employees to operate efficiently, but the competition for labor intensifies as more attractive employment opportunities become prevalent, thus threatening the employment base for restaurants. Let's look at the details of one of these trends.

The aging population in the United States and other developed countries has important implications. The U.S. Bureau of Statistics states that only 18 percent of American workers were 55 and older in 2008.[29] However, by 2012 that figure will increase to 24 percent, or about one in four, of all U.S. workers. At the same time, the United States is expected to experience a significant drop in younger workers aged 25 to 44 from 68 percent to 64 percent by 2018, making it increasingly important for employers to recruit and retain older workers.

Strategy Spotlight 2.4 discusses how the increasing appetite for high-end consumer goods by China's growing middle class has boosted the revenues for air cargo carriers. This comes at a time when many western economies are still reeling from a recession.

The Sociocultural Segment

Sociocultural forces influence the values, beliefs, and lifestyles of a society. Examples include a higher percentage of women in the workforce, dual-income families, increases in the number of temporary workers, greater concern for healthy diets and physical fitness, greater interest in the environment, and postponement of having children. Such forces enhance sales of products and services in many industries but depress sales in others. The increased number

sociocultural segment of the general environment the values, beliefs, and lifestyles of a society.

of women in the workforce has increased the need for business clothing merchandise but decreased the demand for baking product staples (since people would have less time to cook from scratch). This health and fitness trend has helped industries that manufacture exercise equipment and healthful foods but harmed industries that produce unhealthful foods.

Increased educational attainment by women in the workplace has led to more women in upper management positions.[30] Given such educational attainment, it is hardly surprising that companies owned by women have been one of the driving forces of the U.S. economy; these companies (now more than 9 million in number) account for 40 percent of all U.S. businesses and have generated more than $3.6 trillion in annual revenue. In addition, women have a tremendous impact on consumer spending decisions. Not surprisingly, many companies have focused their advertising and promotion efforts on female consumers. Consider, for example, Lowe's efforts to attract female shoppers:

> Lowe's has found that women prefer to do larger home-improvement projects with a man—be it a boyfriend, husband, or neighbor. As a result, in addition to its "recipe card classes" (that explain various projects that take only one weekend), Lowe's offers co-ed store clinics for projects like sink installation. "Women like to feel they're given the same attention as a male customer," states Lowe's spokesperson Julie Valeant-Yenichek, who points out that most seminar attendees, whether male or female, are inexperienced.[31]

Home Depot recently spent millions of dollars to add softer lighting and brighter signs in 300 stores. Why? It is an effort to match rival Lowe's appeal to women.

The Political/Legal Segment

political/legal segment of the general environment how a society creates and exercises power, including rules, laws, and taxation policies.

Political processes and legislation influence environmental regulations with which industries must comply.[32,33] Some important elements of the political/legal arena include tort reform, the Americans with Disabilities Act (ADA) of 1990, the repeal of the Glass-Steagall Act in 1999 (banks may now offer brokerage services), deregulation of utilities and other industries, and increases in the federally mandated minimum wage.[34]

Government legislation can also have a significant impact on the governance of corporations. The U.S. Congress passed the Sarbanes-Oxley Act in 2002, which greatly increases the accountability of auditors, executives, and corporate lawyers. This act responded to the widespread perception that existing governance mechanisms failed to protect the interests of shareholders, employees, and creditors. Clearly, Sarbanes-Oxley has also created a tremendous demand for professional accounting services.

Legislation can also affect firms in the high-tech sector of the economy by expanding the number of temporary visas available for highly skilled foreign professionals.[35] For example, a bill passed by the U.S. Congress in October 2000 allowed 195,000 H-1B visas for each of the following three years—up from a cap of 115,000. However, beginning in 2006 and continuing through 2010, the annual cap on H-1B visas has shrunk to only 65,000—with an additional 20,000 visas available for foreigners with a Master's or higher degree from a U.S. institution. Many of the visas are for professionals from India with computer and software expertise. As one would expect, this is a political "hot potato" for industry executives as well as U.S. labor and workers' right groups. The key arguments against increases in H-1B visas are that H-1B workers drive down wages and take jobs from Americans.

Strategy Spotlight 2.5 discusses one of the proactive steps that Microsoft has taken to address this issue.

The Technological Segment

technological segment of the general environment innovation and state of knowledge in industrial arts, engineering, applied sciences, and pure science; and their interaction with society.

Developments in technology lead to new products and services and improve how they are produced and delivered to the end user.[36] Innovations can create entirely new industries and alter the boundaries of existing industries.[37] Technological developments and trends include genetic engineering, Internet technology, computer-aided design/computer-aided

How Microsoft "Gets Around" H-1B Visa Restrictions

In March 2008, Microsoft Chairman Bill Gates took one of his company's most problematic issues to the U.S. Senate. During his testimony, he criticized U.S. immigration policy that limits the H-1B visas issued to skilled workers from foreign countries—workers that Microsoft would urgently like to hire. Gates told the lawmakers: "It makes no sense to tell well-trained, highly skilled individuals—many of whom are educated at top universities—that the U.S. does not welcome or value them" and that the U.S. "will find it far more difficult to maintain its competitive edge over the next 50 years if it excludes those who are able and willing to help us compete." Gates also claimed that Microsoft hires four Americans in supporting roles for every high-skilled H-1B visa holder it hires. (This claim was also made in a June 2010 editorial in *Fortune* magazine.) Despite his efforts, the senators ignored his pleas and the visa policy went unchanged.

What to do? Six months later, Microsoft opened an office in Richmond, British Columbia, a suburb of Vancouver. Here, it hopes to place hundreds of workers unable to obtain U.S. visas. Placing workers in the same time zone will help them to collaborate—given that the facility is located just 130 miles north of Microsoft's Redmond, Washington, campus. And it is just a 2½ hour drive on Interstate 5 if one needs face time. It certainly doesn't hurt that Canada does not place limits on visas for skilled workers. An unusually pointed press release by Microsoft stated: "The Vancouver area is a global gateway with a diverse population, is close to Microsoft's offices in Redmond, and allows the company to recruit and retain highly skilled people affected by immigration issues in the U.S."

Sources: Elliott, M. 2010. Opinion. *Fortune.* June 14: 56; MacDonald, I. 2008. Finesse the visa crisis with a worker-mobility plan. *Harvard Business Review,* 86(11): 28–29; Greene, J. 2008. Case study: Microsoft's Canadian solution. *BusinessWeek,* January 28: 51; MacDonald, I. 2008. Tech firms get creative in employing foreigners. *Dallas Morning News,* November 16: 5D; and, Anonymous. 2007. Microsoft to open Canada center in response to U.S. immigration. *www.workpermit.com,* July 10: np.

manufacturing (CAD/CAM), research in artificial and exotic materials, and, on the downside, pollution and global warming.[38] Petroleum and primary metals industries spend significantly to reduce their pollution. Engineering and consulting firms that work with polluting industries derive financial benefits from solving such problems.

Nanotechnology is becoming a very promising area of research with many potentially useful applications.[39] Nanotechnology takes place at industry's tiniest stage: one billionth of a meter. Remarkably, this is the size of 10 hydrogen atoms in a row. Matter at such a tiny scale behaves very differently. Familiar materials—from gold to carbon soot—display startling and useful new properties. Some transmit light or electricity. Others become harder than diamonds or turn into potent chemical catalysts. What's more, researchers have found that a tiny dose of nanoparticles can transform the chemistry and nature of far bigger things.

However, transforming the power of new technologies to commercially viable products can be difficult.[40] For example, the East Japan Railway Company tried to capture tiny amounts of energy from the footsteps of the thousands of commuters who passed through their gates. Unfortunately, they found out that all the energy generated in a day at the station was miniscule: enough to light a 100-watt bulb for a few minutes!

The Economic Segment

The economy affects all industries, from suppliers of raw materials to manufacturers of finished goods and services, as well as all organizations in the service, wholesale, retail, government, and nonprofit sectors.[41] Key economic indicators include interest rates, unemployment rates, the Consumer Price Index, the gross domestic product, and net disposable income.[42] Interest-rate increases have a negative impact on the residential home construction industry but a negligible (or neutral) effect on industries that produce consumer necessities such as prescription drugs or common grocery items.

> **economic segment of the general environment** characteristics of the economy, including national income and monetary conditions.

Other economic indicators are associated with equity markets. Perhaps the most watched is the Dow Jones Industrial Average (DJIA), which is composed of 30 large industrial firms. When stock market indexes increase, consumers' discretionary income rises and there is often an increased demand for luxury items such as jewelry and automobiles. But when stock valuations decrease, demand for these items shrinks. For example, Exhibit 2.4 shows that the sales of value-priced liquor, wine, and beer actually went up, while sales of higher priced alcoholic beverages did not fare so well during the recent recession.

The Global Segment

global segment of the general environment influences from foreign countries, including foreign market opportunities, foreign-based competition, and expanded capital markets.

More firms are expanding their operations and market reach beyond the borders of their "home" country. Globalization provides both opportunities to access larger potential markets and a broad base of production factors such as raw materials, labor, skilled managers, and technical professionals. However, such endeavors also carry many political, social, and economic risks.[43]

Examples of key elements include currency exchange rates, increasing global trade, the economic emergence of China, trade agreements among regional blocs (e.g., North American Free Trade Agreement, European Union), and the General Agreement on Tariffs and Trade (GATT) (lowering of tariffs).[44] Increases in trade across national boundaries also provide benefits to air cargo and shipping industries but have a minimal impact on service industries such as bookkeeping and routine medical services. The emergence of China as an economic power has benefited many industries, such as construction, soft drinks, and computers. However, it has had a negative impact on the defense industry in the United States as diplomatic relations between the two nations improve.

A key factor in the global economy is the rapid rise of the middle class in emerging countries. By 2015, for the first time, the number of consumers in Asia's middle class will equal those in Europe and North America combined. An important implication of this trend is the dramatic change in hiring practices of U.S. multinationals. In 2010, for example, American companies have created 1.4 million jobs overseas—but only 1 million in the United States.[45]

Also, consider the cost of terrorism. A recent survey indicates that for S&P 500 firms, the threat has caused direct and indirect costs of $107 billion a year. This figure includes extra spending (on insurance and redundant capacity, for instance) as well as lost revenues (from fearful consumers' decreased activity).[46]

Relationships among Elements of the General Environment

In our discussion of the general environment, we see many relationships among the various elements.[47] For example, a demographic trend in the United States, the aging of the population, has important implications for the economic segment (in terms of tax policies to

Exhibit 2.4
Alcoholic Beverage Sales during the Recession: Low End versus Premium Products

Percentage changes in dollar sales compared to a year earlier (52 weeks ended March 6, 2010)		
Spirits	Increase in value-priced liquors	+1.4%
	Top-shelf spirits	Flat
Wine	Growth of $9–$12 bottles of table wine	+6%
	Decline of $20 bottles of table wine	−1.6%
Beer	Growth of cheapest beer segment	+7.3%
	Decline in sales of imported beers	−3.8%

Source: Kalwarski, T. 2010. No Recession Hangover for the Booze Business. *Bloomberg Businessweek*, April, 19: 17.

provide benefits to increasing numbers of older citizens). Another example is the emergence of information technology as a means to increase the rate of productivity gains in the United States and other developed countries. Such use of IT results in lower inflation (an important element of the economic segment) and helps offset costs associated with higher labor rates.

The effects of a trend or event in the general environment vary across industries. Governmental legislation (political/legal) to permit the importation of prescription drugs from foreign countries is a very positive development for drugstores but a very negative event for U.S. drug manufacturers. Exhibit 2.5 provides other examples of how the impact of trends or events in the general environment can vary across industries.

Exhibit 2.5 The Impact of General Environmental Trends on Various Industries

Segment/Trends and Events	Industry	Positive	Neutral	Negative
Demographic				
Aging population	Health care	✓		
	Baby products			✓
Rising affluence	Brokerage services	✓		
	Fast foods			✓
	Upscale pets and supplies	✓		
Sociocultural				
More women in the workforce	Clothing	✓		
	Baking products (staples)			✓
Greater concern for health and fitness	Home exercise equipment	✓		
	Meat products			✓
Political/legal				
Tort reform	Legal services			✓
	Auto manufacturing	✓		
Americans with Disabilities Act (ADA)	Retail			✓
	Manufacturers of elevators, escalators, and ramps	✓		
Technological				
Genetic engineering	Pharmaceutical	✓		
	Publishing		✓	
Pollution/global warming	Engineering services	✓		
	Petroleum			✓
Economic				
Interest rate increases	Residential construction			✓
	Most common grocery products		✓	
Global				
Increasing global trade	Shipping	✓		
	Personal service		✓	
Emergence of China as an economic power	Soft drinks	✓		
	Defense			✓

strategy spotlight

2.6

The Internet and Digital Technologies: Affecting Many Environmental Segments

The Internet has dramatically changed the way business is conducted in every corner of the globe. According to digital economy visionary Don Tapscott:

> The Net is much more than just another technology development; the Net represents something qualitatively new—an unprecedented, powerful, universal communications medium. Far surpassing radio and television, this medium is digital, infinitely richer, and interactive. . . . Mobile computing devices, broadband access, wireless networks, and computing power embedded in everything from refrigerators to automobiles are converging into a global network that will enable people to use the Net just about anywhere and anytime.

The Internet provides a platform or staging area for the application of numerous technologies, rapid advances in knowledge, and unprecedented levels of global communication and commerce. Even technologies that don't require the Internet to function, such as wireless phones and GPS, rely on the Internet for data transfer and communications.

Sources: Anonymous. 2005. SMBs believe in the Web. *eMarketer.com*, *www.emarketer.com*, May 16. Downes, L. & Mui, C. 1998. *Unleashing the killer app.* Boston: Harvard Business School Press. Green, H. 2003. Wi-Fi means business. *BusinessWeek*, April 28: 86–92; McGann, R. 2005. Broadband: High speed, high spend. *ClickZ Network*, *www.clickz.com*, January 24; Tapscott, D. 2001. Rethinking strategy in a Networked World. *Strategy and Business*, Third Quarter: 34–41; and, Yang, C. 2003. Beyond wi-fi: A new wireless age. *BusinessWeek*, December 15: 84–88.

Growth in Internet usage has surged in recent years both among individual users as well as businesses. Exhibit 2.6 illustrates (2000–2010) worldwide growth trends in Internet use. Business use of the Internet has become nearly ubiquitous throughout the economy. Major corporations all have a Web presence, and many companies use the Internet to interact with key stakeholders. For example, some companies have direct links with suppliers through online procurement systems that automatically reorder inventories and supplies. Companies such as Cisco Systems even interact with their own employees using the Internet to update employment records, such as health care information and benefits.

Small and medium-sized enterprises (SMEs) are also relying on the Internet more than ever. A recent study found that 87 percent of SMEs are receiving monthly revenue from their Web site, and 42 percent derive more than a quarter of their monthly revenue from their Internet presence. According to Joel Kocher, CEO of Interland, "We are getting to the point in most small-business categories where it will soon be safe to say that if you're not online, you're not really serious about being in business."

Despite these advances, the Internet and digital technologies still face numerous challenges. For example, international standards for digital and wireless communications are still in flux. As a result, cell phones and other devices that work in the United States are often useless in many parts of Europe and Asia. And, unlike analog systems, electronic bits of data that are zooming through space can be more easily lost, stolen, or manipulated. However, even with these problems, Internet and digital technologies will continue to be a growing global phenomenon. As Andy Grove, former chairman of Intel, stated, "The world now runs on Internet time."

Geographic Regions	Internet Users, 2000 (1000s)	Internet Users, 2010 (1000s)	Population Penetration	Usage Growth, 2000–2010
Africa	4,514	110,932	10.9%	2,357%
Asia	114,304	825,094	21.5%	622%
Europe	105,096	475,069	58.4%	352%
Middle East	3,285	63,241	29.8%	1,825%
North America	108,097	266,225	77.4%	146%
Latin America/Caribbean	18,069	204,690	34.5%	1,033%
Oceania/Australia	7,620	21,264	61.3%	179%
World Total	360,985	1,966,515	28.7%	445%

Source: *www.internetworldstats.com*

Exhibit 2.6   **Growth in Internet Activity**

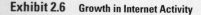

Before moving on, let's consider the Internet. The Internet has been a leading and highly visible component of a broader technological phenomenon—the emergence of digital technology. These technologies are altering the way business is conducted and having an impact on nearly every business domain. Strategy Spotlight 2.6 addresses the impact of the Internet and digital technologies on the business environment.

The Competitive Environment

>LO2.5
How forces in the competitive environment can affect profitability, and how a firm can improve its competitive position by increasing its power vis-à-vis these forces.

Managers must consider the competitive environment (also sometimes referred to as the task or industry environment). The nature of competition in an industry, as well as the profitability of a firm, is often more directly influenced by developments in the competitive environment.

The **competitive environment** consists of many factors that are particularly relevant to a firm's strategy. These include competitors (existing or potential), customers, and suppliers. Potential competitors may include a supplier considering forward integration, such as an automobile manufacturer acquiring a rental car company, or a firm in an entirely new industry introducing a similar product that uses a more efficient technology.

Next, we will discuss key concepts and analytical techniques that managers should use to assess their competitive environments. First, we examine Michael Porter's five-forces model that illustrates how these forces can be used to explain an industry's profitability.[48] Second, we discuss how the five forces are being affected by the capabilities provided by Internet technologies. Third, we address some of the limitations, or "caveats," that managers should be familiar with when conducting industry analysis. Finally, we address the concept of strategic groups, because even within an industry it is often useful to group firms on the basis of similarities of their strategies. As we will see, competition tends to be more intense among firms *within* a strategic group than between strategic groups.

industry
a group of firms that produce similar goods or services.

competitive environment
factors that pertain to an industry and affect a firm's strategies.

Porter's Five-Forces Model of Industry Competition

The "five-forces" model developed by Michael E. Porter has been the most commonly used analytical tool for examining the competitive environment. It describes the competitive environment in terms of five basic competitive forces.[49]

1. The threat of new entrants.
2. The bargaining power of buyers.
3. The bargaining power of suppliers.
4. The threat of substitute products and services.
5. The intensity of rivalry among competitors in an industry.

Each of these forces affects a firm's ability to compete in a given market. Together, they determine the profit potential for a particular industry. The model is shown in Exhibit 2.7. A manager should be familiar with the five-forces model for several reasons. It helps you decide whether your firm should remain in or exit an industry. It provides the rationale for increasing or decreasing resource commitments. The model helps you assess how to improve your firm's competitive position with regard to each of the five forces.[50] For example, you can use insights provided by the five-forces model to create higher entry barriers that discourage new rivals from competing with you.[51] Or you may develop strong relationships with your distribution channels. You may decide to find suppliers who satisfy the price/performance criteria needed to make your product or service a top performer.

Porter's five-forces model of industry competition
a tool for examining the industry-level competitive environment, especially the ability of firms in that industry to set prices and minimize costs.

The Threat of New Entrants The threat of new entrants refers to the possibility that the profits of established firms in the industry may be eroded by new competitors.[52] The extent of the threat depends on existing barriers to entry and the combined reactions from existing competitors.[53] If entry barriers are high and/or the newcomer can

threat of new entrants the possibility that the profits of established firms in the industry may be eroded by new competitors.

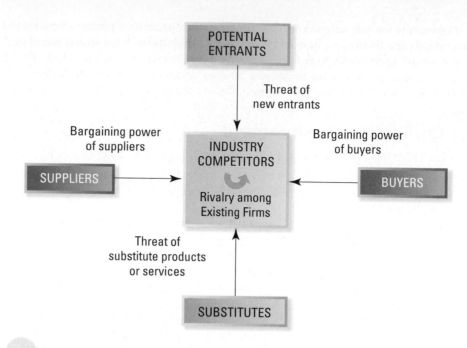

Exhibit 2.7 **Porter's Five-Forces Model of Industry Competition**

Source: Adapted and reprinted with permission of The Free Press, a division of Simon & Schuster Adult Publishing Group, from *Competitive Strategy: Techniques for Analyzing Industries and Competitors* by Michael E. Porter. Copyright © 1980, 1998 by The Free Press. All rights reserved.

anticipate a sharp retaliation from established competitors, the threat of entry is low. These circumstances discourage new competitors. There are six major sources of entry barriers.

economies of scale decreases in cost per unit as absolute output per period increases.

Economies of Scale Economies of scale refers to spreading the costs of production over the number of units produced. The cost of a product per unit declines as the absolute volume per period increases. This deters entry by forcing the entrant to come in at a large scale and risk strong reaction from existing firms or come in at a small scale and accept a cost disadvantage. Both are undesirable options.

Product Differentiation When existing competitors have strong brand identification and customer loyalty, differentiation creates a barrier to entry by forcing entrants to spend heavily to overcome existing customer loyalties.

product differentiation the degree that a product has strong brand loyalty or customer loyalty.

Capital Requirements The need to invest large financial resources to compete creates a barrier to entry, especially if the capital is required for risky or unrecoverable up-front advertising or research and development (R&D).

Switching Costs A barrier to entry is created by the existence of one-time costs that the buyer faces when switching from one supplier's product or service to another.

switching cost one-time costs that a buyer/supplier faces when switching from one supplier/ buyer to another.

Access to Distribution Channels The new entrant's need to secure distribution for its product can create a barrier to entry.

Cost Disadvantages Independent of Scale Some existing competitors may have advantages that are independent of size or economies of scale. These derive from:

- Proprietary products
- Favorable access to raw materials
- Government subsidies
- Favorable government policies

In an environment where few, if any, of these entry barriers are present, the threat of new entry is high. For example, if a new firm can launch its business with a low capital investment and operate efficiently despite its small scale of operation, it is likely to be a threat. One company that failed because of low entry barriers in an industry is ProCD.[54] You probably never heard of this company. It didn't last very long. ProCD provides an example of a firm that failed because it entered an industry with very low entry barriers.

The story begins in 1986 when Nynex (a former Baby Bell company) issued the first electronic phone book, a compact disk containing all listings for the New York City area. It charged $10,000 per copy and sold the CDs to the FBI, IRS, and other large commercial and government organizations. James Bryant, the Nynex executive in charge of the project, smelled a fantastic business opportunity. He quit Nynex and set up his own firm, ProCD, with the ambitious goal of producing an electronic directory covering the entire United States.

The telephone companies, fearing an attack on their highly profitable Yellow Pages business, refused to license digital copies of their listings. Bryant was not deterred. He hired Chinese workers at $3.50 a day to type every listing from every U.S. telephone book into a database. The result contained more than 70 million phone numbers and was used to create a master disk that enabled ProCD to make hundreds of thousands of copies. Each CD sold for hundreds of dollars and cost less than a dollar each to produce.

It was a profitable business indeed! However, success was fleeting. Competitors such as Digital Directory Assistance and American Business Information quickly launched competing products with the same information. Since customers couldn't tell one product from the next, the players were forced to compete on price alone. Prices for the CD soon plummeted to a few dollars each. A high-priced, high-margin product just months earlier, the CD phone book became little more than a cheap commodity.

The Bargaining Power of Buyers   Buyers threaten an industry by forcing down prices, bargaining for higher quality or more services, and playing competitors against each other. These actions erode industry profitability.[55] The power of each large buyer group depends on attributes of the market situation and the importance of purchases from that group compared with the industry's overall business. A buyer group is powerful when:

bargaining power of buyers the threat that buyers may force down prices, bargain for higher quality or more services, and play competitors against each other.

- *It is concentrated or purchases large volumes relative to seller sales.* If a large percentage of a supplier's sales are purchased by a single buyer, the importance of the buyer's business to the supplier increases. Large-volume buyers also are powerful in industries with high fixed costs (e.g., steel manufacturing).
- *The products it purchases from the industry are standard or undifferentiated.* Confident they can always find alternative suppliers, buyers play one company against the other, as in commodity grain products.
- *The buyer faces few switching costs.* Switching costs lock the buyer to particular sellers. Conversely, the buyer's power is enhanced if the seller faces high switching costs.
- *It earns low profits.* Low profits create incentives to lower purchasing costs. On the other hand, highly profitable buyers are generally less price sensitive.
- *The buyers pose a credible threat of backward integration.* If buyers are either partially integrated or pose a credible threat of backward integration, they are typically able to secure bargaining concessions.
- *The industry's product is unimportant to the quality of the buyer's products or services.* When the quality of the buyer's products is not affected by the industry's product, the buyer is more price sensitive.

At times, a firm or set of firms in an industry may increase its buyer power by using the services of a third party. FreeMarkets Online is one such third party.[56] Pittsburgh-based FreeMarkets has developed software enabling large industrial buyers to organize online auctions for qualified suppliers of semistandard parts such as fabricated components,

Tuition Increases: Sometimes Students Have Low Bargaining Power

Students at the University of California at Berkeley got hit with a 32 percent tuition fee increase in 2010. They protested by taking over a classroom building. As noted by *Forbes* writer Asher Hawkins: "It was a futile effort. Students who are already embarked on a four-year program are something of a captive audience, and California's state coffers are empty."

After the increase, the tuition and fees for in-state undergraduate students will come to about $10,000 for the academic year. (This represents a compound annual increase of nearly 10 percent over the past decade.) Although this may still seem like a reasonable price for a high-quality education, there could be more price increases ahead.

At some state schools, the risk of sharp tuition increases is quite high. *Forbes* conducted a study that analyzed university financial data, state budgets, and tuition levels to come up with a "danger list." These are state schools that are most likely to raise tuition or cut the quality of the educational experience over the next four-year period. It should be something for students to consider when deciding where to go for undergraduate school.

Five of the 10 schools on the high-risk short list were part of the University of California system. A big contributing factor is the state's enormous budget deficit. And since Berkeley and UCLA have 10 to 12 applicants for every available spot, they are easy targets for legislators looking for ways to balance the budget. A spokesman for the UC system, Peter King, agrees: "The factors employed by *Forbes* to generate this ranking list capture well the perfect storm that has enveloped the University of California system."

On January 8, 2011, California Governor Jerry Brown proposed cutting a combined $1 billion from the University of California and California State systems, which had a combined $5.6 billion general fund budget in 2010. Mark Yudof, president of the UC system stated, "The collective tuition payments made by UC students for the first time in history would exceed what the state contributes to the system's general fund."

Sources: Staley, O. 2011. California universities feel the squeeze. *Bloomberg Businessweek.* January 24–January 30: 29–30; Hawkins, A. 2010. Tuition risk. *Forbes.* May 10: 36; and, Woo, S. 2011. California governor unveils spending plan. *www.wsj.com.* January 11: np.

packaging materials, metal stampings, and services. By aggregating buyers, FreeMarkets increases the buyers' bargaining power. The results are impressive. In its first 48 auctions, most participating companies saved over 15 percent; some saved as much as 50 percent.

Although a firm may be tempted to take advantage of its suppliers because of high buyer power, it must be aware of the potential long-term backlash from such actions. A recent example (Strategy Spotlight 2.7) is the growing resentment that students have toward state universities in California because of steep increases in tuition. Unfortunately, students are essentially a captive market and have relatively little bargaining power.

bargaining power of suppliers the threat that suppliers may raise prices or reduce the quality of purchased goods and services.

The Bargaining Power of Suppliers   Suppliers can exert bargaining power by threatening to raise prices or reduce the quality of purchased goods and services. Powerful suppliers can squeeze the profitability of firms so far that they can't recover the costs of raw material inputs.[57] The factors that make suppliers powerful tend to mirror those that make buyers powerful. A supplier group will be powerful when:

- *The supplier group is dominated by a few companies and is more concentrated (few firms dominate the industry) than the industry it sells to.* Suppliers selling to fragmented industries influence prices, quality, and terms.
- *The supplier group is not obliged to contend with substitute products for sale to the industry.* The power of even large, powerful suppliers can be checked if they compete with substitutes.
- *The industry is not an important customer of the supplier group.* When suppliers sell to several industries and a particular industry does not represent a significant fraction of its sales, suppliers are more prone to exert power.

- *The supplier's product is an important input to the buyer's business.* When such inputs are important to the success of the buyer's manufacturing process or product quality, the bargaining power of suppliers is high.
- *The supplier group's products are differentiated or it has built up switching costs for the buyer.* Differentiation or switching costs facing the buyers cut off their options to play one supplier against another.
- *The supplier group poses a credible threat of forward integration.* This provides a check against the industry's ability to improve the terms by which it purchases.

The Threat of Substitute Products and Services All firms within an industry compete with industries producing substitute products and services.[58] Substitutes limit the potential returns of an industry by placing a ceiling on the prices that firms in that industry can profitably charge. The more attractive the price/performance ratio of substitute products, the tighter the lid on an industry's profits.

Identifying substitute products involves searching for other products or services that can perform the same function as the industry's offerings. This may lead a manager into businesses seemingly far removed from the industry. For example, the airline industry might not consider video cameras much of a threat. But as digital technology has improved and wireless and other forms of telecommunication have become more efficient, teleconferencing has become a viable substitute for business travel. That is, the rate of improvement in the price–performance relationship of the substitute product (or service) is high.

Teleconferencing can save both time and money, as IBM found out with its "Manager Jam" idea.[59] With 319,000 employees scattered around six continents, it is one of the world's largest businesses (including 32,000 managers) and can be a pretty confusing place. The shift to an increasingly mobile workplace means many managers supervise employees they rarely see face-to-face. To enhance coordination, Samuel Palmisano, IBM's new CEO, launched one of his first big initiatives: a two-year program exploring the role of the manager in the 21st century. "Manager Jam," as the project was nicknamed, was a 48-hour real-time Web event in which managers from 50 different countries swapped ideas and strategies for dealing with problems shared by all of them, regardless of geography. Some 8,100 managers logged on to the company's intranet to participate in the discussion forums.

Renewable energy resources are also a promising substitute product and are rapidly becoming more economically competitive with fossil fuels. Strategy Spotlight 2.8 addresses this critical issue.

The Intensity of Rivalry among Competitors in an Industry Firms use tactics like price competition, advertising battles, product introductions, and increased customer service or warranties. Rivalry occurs when competitors sense the pressure or act on an opportunity to improve their position.[60]

Some forms of competition, such as price competition, are typically highly destabilizing and are likely to erode the average level of profitability in an industry.[61] Rivals easily match price cuts, an action that lowers profits for all firms. On the other hand, advertising battles expand overall demand or enhance the level of product differentiation for the benefit of all firms in the industry. Rivalry, of course, differs across industries. In some instances it is characterized as warlike, bitter, or cutthroat, whereas in other industries it is referred to as polite and gentlemanly. Intense rivalry is the result of several interacting factors, including the following:

- *Numerous or equally balanced competitors.* When there are many firms in an industry, the likelihood of mavericks is great. Some firms believe they can make moves without being noticed. Even when there are relatively few firms, and they are nearly equal in size and resources, instability results from fighting among companies having the resources for sustained and vigorous retaliation.

threat of substitute products and services the threat of limiting the potential returns of an industry by placing a ceiling on the prices that firms in that industry can profitably charge without losing too many customers to substitute products.

substitute products and services products and services outside the industry that serve the same customer needs as the industry's products and services.

intensity of rivalry among competitors in an industry the threat that customers will switch their business to competitors within the industry.

The Growing Viability of Renewable Resources as Substitutes for Fossil Fuels

Renewable resources currently provide just over 6 percent of total U.S. energy. However, that figure could increase rapidly in the years ahead, according to a joint report issued in September 2006 by the Worldwatch Institute and the Center for Progress, entitled "American Energy: The Renewable Path to Energy Security."

The report indicates that many of the new technologies that harness renewables are, or soon will be, economically competitive with fossil fuels. Dynamic growth rates are driving down costs and spurring rapid advances in technologies. And, since 2000, global wind energy generation has more than tripled, solar cell production has risen six-fold, production of fuel ethanol from crops has more than doubled, and biodiesel production has expanded nearly four-fold. Annual global investment in "new" renewable energy has risen almost six-fold since 1995, with cumulative investment over the period nearly $180 billion.

A November 2006 study by the RAND Corporation is consistent with the aforementioned report. It asserts that the economy of the United States would likely benefit, rather than be slowed, if the nation attained the goal of supplying 25 percent of its energy needs from renewable sources by 2025. Such developments would also reduce U.S. dependence on oil, which would mean a substantial start on capping greenhouse gas emissions, which most scientists link to global warming.

Deep Patel, founder of Los Angeles–based online clean-energy technologies retailer *GoGreenSolar.com*, provides some practical insights:

- *Clean energy is regional:* Think solar in sunny climates like California, geothermal in Nevada, and wind in blustery states such as Oklahoma.

- *Big corporations tend to hire established, renewable energy companies.* "But no one's paying as much attention to smaller businesses and homeowners that want to go solar. For entrepreneurs, that represents the biggest untapped market."

- Consumers need help *"taking a staged approach to going solar."* At GoGreenSolar, a "Plug N Play Solar Power Kit" starts consumers off with two solar panels that they can add to later. Patel's prediction: more such modular solutions will become available.

Sources: Anonymous. 2008. Clean Energy. *Entrepreneur,* December: 59; Clayton, M. 2006. Greener, cleaner . . . and competitive. *www.csmonitor.com.* December 4; and, Anonymous. 2006. Renewables becoming cost-competitive with fossil fuels in the U.S. *www.worldwatch.org.* September 18.

environmental sustainability

- ***Slow industry growth.*** Slow industry growth turns competition into a fight for market share, since firms seek to expand their sales.
- ***High fixed or storage costs.*** High fixed costs create strong pressures for all firms to increase capacity. Excess capacity often leads to escalating price cutting.
- ***Lack of differentiation or switching costs.*** Where the product or service is perceived as a commodity or near commodity, the buyer's choice is typically based on price and service, resulting in pressures for intense price and service competition. Lack of switching costs, described earlier, has the same effect.
- ***Capacity augmented in large increments.*** Where economies of scale require that capacity must be added in large increments, capacity additions can be very disruptive to the industry supply/demand balance.
- ***High exit barriers.*** Exit barriers are economic, strategic, and emotional factors that keep firms competing even though they may be earning low or negative returns on their investments. Some exit barriers are specialized assets, fixed costs of exit, strategic interrelationships (e.g., relationships between the business units and others within a company in terms of image, marketing, shared facilities, and so on), emotional barriers, and government and social pressures (e.g., governmental discouragement of exit out of concern for job loss).

Rivalry between firms is often based solely on price, but it can involve other factors. Take Pfizer's market position in the impotence treatment market. Pfizer was the first pharmaceutical firm to develop Viagra, a highly successful drug that treats impotence.

In several countries, the United Kingdom among them, Pfizer faced a lawsuit by Eli Lilly & Co. and Icos Corp. challenging its patent protection. These two pharmaceutical firms recently entered into a joint venture to market Cialis, a drug to compete with Viagra. The U.K. courts agreed and lifted the patent.

This opened the door for Eli Lilly and Icos to proceed with challenging Pfizer's market position. Because Cialis has fewer side effects than Viagra, the drug has the potential to rapidly decrease Pfizer's market share in the United Kingdom if physicians switch prescriptions from Viagra to Cialis. If future patent challenges are successful, Pfizer may see its sales of Viagra erode rapidly.[62] But Pfizer is hardly standing still. It recently doubled its advertising expenditures on Viagra.

Exhibit 2.8 summarizes our discussion of industry five-forces analysis. It points out how various factors such as economies of scale and capital requirements affect each "force."

How the Internet and Digital Technologies Are Affecting the Five Competitive Forces

The Internet and other digital technologies are having a significant impact on nearly every industry. These technologies have fundamentally changed the ways businesses interact with each other and with consumers. In most cases, these changes have affected industry forces in ways that have created many new strategic challenges. In this section, we will evaluate Michael Porter's five-forces model in terms of the actual use of the Internet and the new technological capabilities that it makes possible.

The Threat of New Entrants In most industries, the threat of new entrants has increased because digital and Internet-based technologies lower barriers to entry. For example, businesses that reach customers primarily through the Internet may enjoy savings on other traditional expenses such as office rent, sales-force salaries, printing, and postage. This may encourage more entrants who, because of the lower start-up expenses, see an opportunity to capture market share by offering a product or performing a service more efficiently than existing competitors. Thus, a new cyber entrant can use the savings provided by the Internet to charge lower prices and compete on price despite the incumbent's scale advantages.

Alternatively, because digital technologies often make it possible for young firms to provide services that are equivalent or superior to an incumbent, a new entrant may be able to serve a market more effectively, with more personalized services and greater attention to product details. A new firm may be able to build a reputation in its niche and charge premium prices. By so doing, it can capture part of an incumbent's business and erode profitability. Consider Voice Over Internet Protocol (VOIP), a fast growing alternative to traditional phone service, which is expected to reach 25 million U.S. households by 2012.[63] Savings of 20 to 30 percent are common for VOIP consumers. This is driving prices down and lowering telecom industry profits. More importantly it threatens the value of the phone line infrastructure that the major carriers have invested in so heavily.

Another potential benefit of Web-based business is access to distribution channels. Manufacturers or distributors that can reach potential outlets for their products more efficiently by means of the Internet may enter markets that were previously closed to them. Access is not guaranteed, however, because strong barriers to entry exist in certain industries.[64]

The Bargaining Power of Buyers The Internet and wireless technologies may increase buyer power by providing consumers with more information to make buying decisions and by lowering switching costs. But these technologies may also suppress the power

Internet a global network of linked computers that use a common transmission format, exchange information and store data.

>LO2.6
How the Internet and digitally based capabilities are affecting the five competitive forces and industry profitability.

Threat of New Entrants Is High When:	High	Low
Economies of scale are		X
Product differentiation is		X
Capital requirements are		X
Switching costs are		X
Incumbent's control of distribution channels is		X
Incumbent's proprietary knowledge is		X
Incumbent's access to raw materials is		X
Incumbent's access to government subsidies is		X

Power of Buyers Is High When:	High	Low
Concentration of buyers relative to suppliers is	X	
Switching costs are		X
Product differentiation of suppliers is		X
Threat of backward integration by buyers is	X	
Extent of buyer's profits is		X
Importance of the supplier's input to quality of buyer's final product is		X

Power of Suppliers Is High When:	High	Low
Concentration relative to buyer industry is	X	
Availability of substitute products is		X
Importance of customer to the supplier is		X
Differentiation of the supplier's products and services is	X	
Switching costs of the buyer are	X	
Threat of forward integration by the supplier is	X	

Threat of Substitute Products Is High When:	High	Low
The differentiation of the substitute product is	X	
Rate of improvement in price–performance relationship of substitute product is	X	

Intensity of Competitive Rivalry Is High When:	High	Low
Number of competitors is	X	
Industry growth rate is		X
Fixed costs are	X	
Storage costs are	X	
Product differentiation is		X
Switching costs are		X
Exit barriers are	X	
Strategic stakes are	X	

Exhibit 2.8 **Competitive Analysis Checklist**

of traditional buyer channels that have concentrated buying power in the hands of a few, giving buyers new ways to access sellers. To sort out these differences, let's first distinguish between two types of buyers: end users and buyer channel intermediaries.

End users are the final customers in a distribution channel. Internet sales activity that is labeled "B2C"—that is, business-to-consumer—is concerned with end users. The Internet is likely to increase the power of these buyers for several reasons. First, the Internet provides large amounts of consumer information. This gives end users the information they need to shop for quality merchandise and bargain for price concessions. The automobile industry provides an excellent example. For a small fee, agencies such as Consumers Union (publishers of *Consumer Reports*) will provide customers with detailed information about actual automobile manufacturer costs.[65] This information, available online, can be used to bid down dealers' profits. Second, an end user's switching costs are also potentially much lower because of the Internet. Switching may involve only a few clicks of the mouse to find and view a competing product or service online.

In contrast, the bargaining power of distribution channel buyers may decrease because of the Internet. *Buyer channel intermediaries* are the wholesalers, distributors, and retailers who serve as intermediaries between manufacturers and end users. In some industries, they are dominated by powerful players that control who gains access to the latest goods or the best merchandise. The Internet and wireless communications, however, make it much easier and less expensive for businesses to reach customers directly. Thus, the Internet may increase the power of incumbent firms relative to that of traditional buyer channels. Strategy Spotlight 2.9 illustrates some of the changes brought on by the Internet that have affected the industry's two types of buyers.

The Bargaining Power of Suppliers Use of the Internet and digital technologies to speed up and streamline the process of acquiring supplies is already benefiting many sectors of the economy. But the net effect of the Internet on supplier power will depend on the nature of competition in a given industry. As with buyer power, the extent to which the Internet is a benefit or a detriment also hinges on the supplier's position along the supply chain.

The role of suppliers involves providing products or services to other businesses. The term "B2B"—that is, business-to-business—often refers to businesses that supply or sell to other businesses. The effect of the Internet on the bargaining power of suppliers is a double-edged sword. On the one hand, suppliers may find it difficult to hold onto customers because buyers can do comparative shopping and price negotiations so much faster on the Internet. This is especially damaging to supply-chain intermediaries, such as product distributors, who cannot stop suppliers from directly accessing other potential business customers. In addition, the Internet inhibits the ability of suppliers to offer highly differentiated products or unique services. Most procurement technologies can be imitated by competing suppliers, and the technologies that make it possible to design and customize new products rapidly are being used by all competitors.

On the other hand, several factors may also contribute to stronger supplier power. First, the growth of new Web-based business may create more downstream outlets for suppliers to sell to. Second, suppliers may be able to create Web-based purchasing arrangements that make purchasing easier and discourage their customers from switching. Online procurement systems directly link suppliers and customers, reducing transaction costs and paperwork.[66] Third, the use of proprietary software that links buyers to a supplier's website may create a rapid, low-cost ordering capability that discourages the buyer from seeking other sources of supply. *Amazon.com*, for example, created and patented One-Click purchasing technology that speeds up the ordering process for customers who enroll in the service.[67]

Finally, suppliers will have greater power to the extent that they can reach end users directly without intermediaries. Previously, suppliers often had to work through intermediaries who brought their products or services to market for a fee. But a process known as

Buyer Power in the Book Industry: The Role of the Internet

The $25 billion book publishing industry illustrates some of the changes brought on by the Internet that have affected buying power among two types of buyers—end users and buyer channel intermediaries. Prior to the Internet, book publishers worked primarily through large distributors. These intermediaries such as Tennessee-based Ingram, one of the largest and most powerful distributors, exercised strong control over the movement of books from publishers to bookstores. This power was especially strong relative to small, independent publishers who often found it difficult to get their books into bookstores and in front of potential customers.

Sources: Healy, M. 2009. Book Industry Trends 2009 shows publishers' net revenues rose 1.0 percent in 2007 to reach $40.3 billion. *www.bisg.org.* May 29: np; Books "most popular online buy." 2008. *newsvote.bbc.co.uk.* January 29: np. Hoynes, M. 2002. Is it the same for book sales? *BookWeb.org, www.bookweb.org,* March 20; *www.parapublishing.com;* Teague, D. 2005. U.S. book production reaches new high of 195,000 titles in 2004; Fiction soars.*Bowker.com, www.bowker.com,* May 24; and Teicher, C. M. 2007. March of the small presses. *Publishers Weekly, www.publishersweekly.com,* March 26; and The Nielsen Company, 2010. Global trends in online: A Nielsen global consumer report.

The Internet has significantly changed these relationships. Publishers can now negotiate distribution agreements directly with online retailers such as Amazon and Books-A-Million. Such online bookstores now account for about $4 billion in annual sales. And small publishers can use the Internet to sell directly to end users and publicize new titles, without depending on buyer channel intermediaries to handle their books. By using the Internet to appeal to niche markets, 63,000 small publishers with revenues of less than $50 million each generated $14.2 billion in sales in 2005—over half of the industry's total sales.

Future trends for the industry do not look favorable. The Book Industry Study Group (BISG) released figures in May 2009 which estimated that publishers' revenues in 2008 reached $40.3 billion, up 1 percent from 2007's total. BISG expects revenues to increase to $43.5 billion by the end of 2012. There is also good news for online book sellers: According to results from a 2010 worldwide survey by Nielsen Online, 44 percent of users had bought books online—up from 34 percent just three years earlier.

disintermediation is removing the organizations or business process layers responsible for intermediary steps in the value chain of many industries.[68] Just as the Internet is eliminating some business functions, it is creating an opening for new functions. These new activities are entering the value chain by a process known as *reintermediation*—the introduction of new types of intermediaries. Many of these new functions are affecting traditional supply chains. For example, delivery services are enjoying a boom because of the Internet. Many more consumers are choosing to have products delivered to their door rather than going out to pick them up.

The Threat of Substitutes   Along with traditional marketplaces, the Internet has created a new marketplace and a new channel. In general, therefore, the threat of substitutes is heightened because the Internet introduces new ways to accomplish the same tasks.

Consumers will generally choose to use a product or service until a substitute that meets the same need becomes available at a lower cost. The economies created by Internet technologies have led to the development of numerous substitutes for traditional ways of doing business. For example, a company called Conferenza is offering an alternative way to participate in conferences for people who don't want to spend the time and money to attend. Conferenza's website provides summaries of many conference events, quality ratings using an "event intelligence" score, and schedules of upcoming events.[69]

Another example of substitution is in the realm of electronic storage. With expanded desktop computing, the need to store information electronically has increased dramatically. Until recently, the trend has been to create increasingly larger desktop storage capabilities and techniques for compressing information that create storage efficiencies. But a viable substitute has recently emerged: storing information digitally on the Internet. Companies such as My Docs Online Inc. are providing Web-based storage that firms can access simply by leasing space online. Since these storage places are virtual, they can be accessed anywhere the Web can be accessed. Travelers can access important documents and files without transporting them physically from place to place. Cyberstorage is not free, but it is cheaper and more convenient than purchasing and carrying disk storage.[70]

The Intensity of Competitive Rivalry   Because the Internet creates more tools and means for competing, rivalry among competitors is likely to be more intense. Only those competitors that can use digital technologies and the Web to give themselves a distinct image, create unique product offerings, or provide "faster, smarter, cheaper" services are likely to capture greater profitability with the new technology. Such gains are hard to sustain, however, because in most cases the new technology can be imitated quickly. Thus, the Internet tends to increase rivalry by making it difficult for firms to differentiate themselves and by shifting customer attention to issues of price.

Rivalry is more intense when switching costs are low and product or service differentiation is minimized. Because the Internet makes it possible to shop around, it has "commoditized" products that might previously have been regarded as rare or unique. Since the Internet reduces the importance of location, products that previously had to be sought out in geographically distant outlets are now readily available online. This makes competitors in cyberspace seem more equally balanced, thus intensifying rivalry.

The problem is made worse for marketers by the presence of shopping robots ("bots") and infomediaries that search the Web for the best possible prices. Consumer websites like mySimon and PriceSCAN seek out all the Web locations that sell similar products and provide price comparisons.[71] Obviously, this focuses the consumer exclusively on price. Some shopping infomediaries, such as BizRate and CNET, not only search for the lowest prices on many different products but also rank the customer service quality of different sites that sell similarly priced items.[72] Such infomediary services are good for consumers because they give them the chance to compare services as well as price. For businesses, however, they increase rivalry by consolidating the marketing message that consumers use to make a purchase decision into a few key pieces of information over which the selling company has little control.

Exhibit 2.9 summarizes many of the ways the Internet is affecting industry structure. These influences will also change how companies develop and deploy strategies to generate above-average profits and sustainable competitive advantage.

Using Industry Analysis: A Few Caveats

For industry analysis to be valuable, a company must collect and evaluate a wide variety of information. As the trend toward globalization accelerates, information on foreign markets as well as on a wider variety of competitors, suppliers, customers, substitutes, and potential new entrants becomes more critical. Industry analysis helps a firm not only to evaluate the profit potential of an industry but also consider various ways to strengthen its position vis-à-vis the five forces. However, we'd like to address a few caveats.

First, *managers must not always avoid low profit industries (or low profit segments in profitable industries).*[73] Such industries can still yield high returns for some players who pursue sound strategies. As examples, consider Paychex, a payroll-processing company, and WellPoint Health Network, a huge health care insurer:[74]

> Paychex, with $2 billion in revenues, became successful by serving small businesses. Existing firms had ignored them because they assumed that such businesses could not afford the service. When Paychex's founder, Tom Golisano, failed to convince his bosses at Electronic Accounting Systems that they were missing a great opportunity, he launched the firm. It now serves nearly 600,000 clients in the United States and Germany. Paychex's after-tax-return on sales is a stunning 24 percent.

Exhibit 2.9 How the Internet and Digital Technologies Influence Industry

	Benefits to Industry (+)	Disadvantages to Industry (−)
Threat of New Entrants		• Lower barriers to entry increase number of new entrants. • Many Internet-based capabilities can be easily imitated.
Bargaining Power of Buyers	• Reduces the power of buyer intermediaries in many distribution channels.	• Switching costs decrease. • Information availability online empowers end users.
Bargaining Power of Suppliers	• Online procurement methods can increase bargaining power over suppliers.	• The Internet gives suppliers access to more customers and makes it easier to reach end users. • Online procurement practices deter competition and reduce differentiating features.
Threat of Substitutes	• Internet-based increases in overall efficiency can expand industry sales.	• Internet-based capabilities create more opportunities for substitution.
Intensity of Rivalry		• Since location is less important, the number of competitors increases. • Differences among competitors are harder to perceive online. • Rivalry tends to focus on price and differentiating features are minimized.

Sources: Bodily, S. & Venkataraman, S. 2004. Not walls, windows: Capturing value in the digital age. *Journal of Business Strategy*, 25(3): 15–25; Lumpkin, G. T., Droege, S. B., & Dess, G. G. 2002. E-commerce strategies: Achieving sustainable competitive advantage and avoiding pitfalls. *Organizational Dynamics*, 30 (Spring): 1–17.

In 1986, WellPoint Health Network (when it was known as Blue Cross of California) suffered a loss of $160 million. That year, Leonard Schaeffer became CEO and challenged the conventional wisdom that individuals and small firms were money losers. (This was certainly "heresy" at the time—the firm was losing $5 million a year insuring 65,000 individuals!) However, by the early 1990s, the health insurer was leading the industry in profitability. The firm has continued to grow and outperform its rivals even during economic downturns. By 2010, its revenues and profits were $65 billion and $4.8 billion, respectively—each figure representing an *annual* increase of over 18 percent for the most recent four-year period.

zero-sum game a situation in which multiple players interact, and winners win only by taking from other players.

Second, five-forces analysis implicitly *assumes a zero-sum game, determining how a firm can enhance its position relative to the forces.* Yet such an approach can often be short-sighted; that is, it can overlook the many potential benefits of developing constructive win–win relationships with suppliers and customers. Establishing long-term mutually beneficial relationships with suppliers improves a firm's ability to implement just-in-time (JIT) inventory systems, which let it manage inventories better and respond quickly to market demands. A recent study found that if a company exploits its powerful position against a supplier, that action may come back to haunt the company.[75] Consider, for example, General Motors' heavy-handed dealings with its suppliers:[76]

> GM has a reputation for particularly aggressive tactics. Although it is striving to crack down on the most egregious of these, it continues to rank dead last in the annual supplier satisfaction survey. "It's a brutal process," says David E. Cole, who is head of the Center for Automotive Research in Ann Arbor. "There are bodies lying by the side of the road."
>
> Suppliers point to one particularly nasty tactic: shopping their technology out the back door to see if rivals can make it cheaper. In one case, a GM purchasing manager showed a supplier's new brake design to Delphi Corporation. He was fired. However, in a recent survey, parts executives said they tend to bring hot new technology to other carmakers first. This is yet another reason GM finds it hard to compete in an intensely competitive industry.

Third, the five-forces analysis also has been criticized for *being essentially a static analysis*. External forces as well as strategies of individual firms are continually changing the structure of all industries. The search for a dynamic theory of strategy has led to greater use of game theory in industrial organization economics research and strategy research.

Based on game-theoretic considerations, Brandenburger and Nalebuff recently introduced the concept of the value net,[77] which in many ways is an extension of the five-forces analysis. It is illustrated in Exhibit 2.10. The value net represents all the players in the game and analyzes how their interactions affect a firm's ability to generate and appropriate value. The vertical dimension of the net includes suppliers and customers. The firm has direct transactions with them. On the horizontal dimension are substitutes and complements, players with whom a firm interacts but may not necessarily transact. The concept of complementors is perhaps the single most important contribution of value net analysis and is explained in more detail below.

Complements typically are products or services that have a potential impact on the value of a firm's own products or services. Those who produce complements are usually referred to as complementors.[78] Powerful hardware is of no value to a user unless there is software that runs on it. Similarly, new and better software is possible only if the hardware on which it can be run is available. This is equally true in the video game industry, where the sales of game

complements
products or services that have an impact on the value of a firm's products or services.

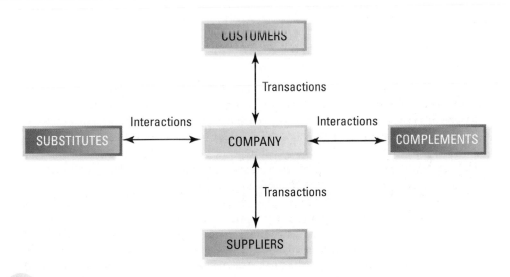

Exhibit 2.10   The Value Net

consoles and video games complement each other. Nintendo's success in the early 1990s was a result of their ability to manage their relationship with their complementors. They built a security chip into the hardware and then licensed the right to develop games to outside firms. These firms paid a royalty to Nintendo for each copy of the game sold. The royalty revenue enabled Nintendo to sell game consoles at close to their cost, thereby increasing their market share, which, in turn, caused more games to be sold and more royalties to be generated.[79]

Despite efforts to create win–win scenarios, conflict among complementors is inevitable.[80] After all, it is naive to expect that even the closest of partners will do you the favor of abandoning their own interests. And even the most successful partnerships are seldom trouble free. Power is a factor that comes into play as we see in Strategy Spotlight 2.10 with the example of Apple's iPod—an enormously successful product.

We would like to close this section with some recent insights from Michael Porter, the originator of the five-forces analysis.[81] He addresses two critical issues in conducting a good industry analysis, which will yield an improved understanding of the root causes of profitability: (1) choosing the appropriate time frame and (2) a rigorous quantification of the five forces.

- *Good industry analysis looks rigorously at the structural underpinnings of profitability. A first step is to understand the time horizon.* One of the essential tasks in industry analysis is to distinguish short-term fluctuations from structural changes. A good guideline for the appropriate time horizon is the full business cycle for the particular industry. For most industries, a three- to five-year horizon is appropriate. However, for some industries with long lead times, such as mining, the appropriate horizon may be a decade or more. It is average profitability over this period, not profitability in any particular year, which should be the focus of analysis.

- *The point of industry analysis is not to declare the industry attractive or unattractive but to understand the underpinnings of competition and the root causes of profitability.* As much as possible, analysts should look at industry structure quantitatively, rather than be satisfied with lists of qualitative factors. Many elements of five forces can be quantified: the percentage of the buyer's total cost accounted for by the industry's product (to understand buyer price sensitivity); the percentage of industry sales required to fill a plant or operate a logistical network to efficient scale (to help assess barriers to entry); and the buyer's switching cost (determining the inducement an entrant or rival must offer customers).

Strategic Groups within Industries

strategic groups
clusters of firms that share similar strategies.

In an industry analysis, two assumptions are unassailable: (1) No two firms are totally different, and (2) no two firms are exactly the same. The issue becomes one of identifying groups of firms that are more similar to each other than firms that are not, otherwise known as **strategic groups.**[82] This is important because rivalry tends to be greater among firms that are alike. Strategic groups are clusters of firms that share similar strategies. After all, is Kmart more concerned about Nordstrom or Walmart? Is Mercedes more concerned about Hyundai or BMW? The answers are straightforward.[83]

These examples are not meant to trivialize the strategic groups concept.[84] Classifying an industry into strategic groups involves judgment. If it is useful as an analytical tool, we must exercise caution in deciding what dimensions to use to map these firms. Dimensions include breadth of product and geographic scope, price/quality, degree of vertical integration, type of distribution (e.g., dealers, mass merchandisers, private label), and so on. Dimensions should also be selected to reflect the variety of strategic combinations in an industry. For example, if all firms in an industry have roughly the same level of product differentiation (or R&D intensity), this would not be a good dimension to select.

What value is the strategic groups concept as an analytical tool? *First, strategic groupings help a firm identify barriers to mobility that protect a group from attacks by other*

>LO2.7
The concept of strategic groups and their strategy and performance implications.

Apple's iPod: Relationships with Its Complementors

In 2002, Steve Jobs began his campaign to cajole the major music companies into selling tracks to iPod users through the iTunes Music Store, an online retail site. Most industry executives, after being burned by illegal file-sharing services like Napster and Kazaa, just wanted digital music to disappear. However, Jobs's passionate vision persuaded them to climb on board. He promised to reduce the risks that they faced by offering safeguards against piracy, as well as a hip product (iPod and iPad Touch) that would drive sales.

However, Apple had a much stronger bargaining position when its contracts with the music companies came up for renewal in April 2005. By then, iTunes had captured 80 percent of the market for legal downloads. The music companies, which were receiving between 60 and 70 cents per download, wanted more. Their reasoning: If the iTunes Music Store would only charge $1.50 or $2.00 per track, they could double or triple their revenues and profits. Since Jobs knew that he could sell more iPods if the music was cheap, he was determined to keep the price of a download at 99 cents and to maintain Apple's

margins. Given iTunes' dominant position, the music companies had little choice but to relent.

Apple's foray into music has been tremendously successful. Between 2006 and 2009, iPod sales increased from $7.7 billion to $9.4 billion—a 22 percent increase. And, other music related products and services soared from $4 billion to $5 billion over the same period. Despite tough competition, Apple still dominates the music player business.

● The iPod is largely responsible for Apple's recent stellar financial performance.

Source: Hesseldahl, A. 2008. Now that we all have iPods. *BusinessWeek*, December 15: 36; Apple Computer Inc. 10-K, 2010; and, Yoffie, D. B. & Kwak, M. 2006. With friends like these: The art of managing complementors. *Harvard Business Review*, 84(9): 88–98.

groups.[85] Mobility barriers are factors that deter the movement of firms from one strategic position to another. For example, in the chainsaw industry, the major barriers protecting the high-quality/dealer-oriented group are technology, brand image, and an established network of servicing dealers.

The second value of strategic grouping is that it *helps a firm identify groups whose competitive position may be marginal or tenuous.* We may anticipate that these competitors may exit the industry or try to move into another group. In recent years in the retail department store industry, firms such as JCPenney and Sears have experienced extremely difficult times because they were stuck in the middle, neither an aggressive discount player like Walmart nor a prestigious upscale player like Neiman Marcus.

Third, strategic groupings *help chart the future directions of firms' strategies.* Arrows emanating from each strategic group can represent the direction in which the group (or a firm within the group) seems to be moving. If all strategic groups are moving in a similar direction, this could indicate a high degree of future volatility and intensity of competition. In the automobile industry, for example, the competition in the minivan and sport utility segments has intensified in recent years as many firms have entered those product segments.

Fourth, strategic groups are *helpful in thinking through the implications of each industry trend for the strategic group as a whole.* Is the trend decreasing the viability of a group? If so, in what direction should the strategic group move? Is the trend increasing or decreasing entry barriers? Will the trend decrease the ability of one group to separate itself from other groups? Such analysis can help in making predictions about industry evolution. A sharp increase in interest rates, for example, tends to have less impact on providers of higher-priced goods (e.g., Porsches) than on providers of lower-priced goods (e.g., Chevrolet Cobalt) whose customer base is much more price sensitive.

Exhibit 2.11 provides a strategic grouping of the worldwide automobile industry.[86] The firms in each group are representative; not all firms are included in the mapping. We have identified four strategic groups. In the top left-hand corner are high-end luxury automakers who focus on a very narrow product market. Most of the cars produced by the members of this group cost well over $100,000. Some cost many times that amount. The 2010 45B Ferrari Italia starts at $225,000, and the 2010 Lamborghini Gallardo will set you back about $221,000 (in case you were wondering how to spend your employment signing bonus). Players in this market have a very exclusive clientele and face little rivalry from other strategic groups. At the other extreme, in the lower left-hand corner is a strategic group that has low-price/quality attributes and targets a narrow market. These players, Hyundai and Kia, limit competition from other strategic groups by pricing their products very low. The third group (near the middle) consists of firms high in product pricing/quality and average in their product-line breadth. The final group (at the far right) consists of firms with a broad range of products and multiple price points. These firms have entries that compete at both the lower end of the market (e.g., the Ford Focus) and the higher end (e.g., Chevrolet Corvette).

The auto market has been very dynamic and competition has intensified in recent years.[87] Many firms in different strategic groups compete in the same product markets, such as minivans and sport utility vehicles. In the late 1990s Mercedes entered the fray with its M series, and Porsche has a recent entry as well with its Cayenne, a 2004 model.

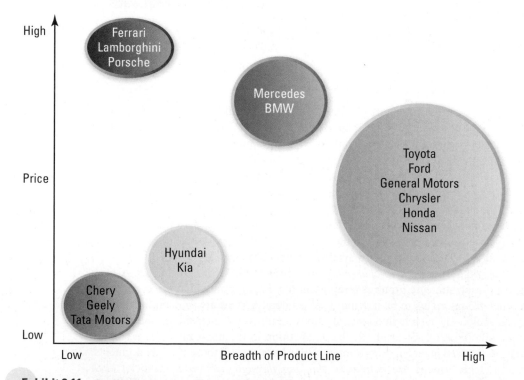

Exhibit 2.11   **The World Automobile Industry: Strategic Groups**

Note: Members of each strategic group are not inclusive, only illustrative.

Some players are also going more upscale with their product offerings. Recently, Hyundai introduced its Genesis, starting at $33,000. This brings Hyundai into direct competition with entries from other strategic groups such as Toyota's Camry and Honda's Accord. Hyundai is offering an extensive warranty (10 years, 100,000 miles) in an effort to offset customer perceptions of their lower quality. To further intensify competition, some key automakers are providing offerings in lower-priced segments. BMW, with their 1-series, is a well-known example. Such cars, priced in the low $30,000s, compete more directly with products from broad-line manufacturers like Ford, General Motors, and Toyota.

Such models are competing in an industry that has experienced relatively flat unit sales in the first half of the last decade. However, in recent years things have turned increasingly sour. U.S. automobile sales dropped from 13.2 million units in 2008 to only 10.4 million units in 2009 (the fewest units since 1982) and 11.3 million units in 2010. This compares to an average of 16.4 million units between 2000 and 2007. And J. D. Power predicts sales of only 13.2 million units for 2011, as the economy emerges from the recession.[88] One can certainly expect incentive-laden offerings to appear on dealer lots for some time to come.

Our discussion would not be complete, of course, without paying some attention to recent entries in the automobile industry that will likely lead to the formation of a new strategic group—placed at the bottom left corner of the grid in Exhibit 2.11. Three firms—China's Zhejiang Geely Holding Company, China's Chery Automobile Company, and India's Tata Motors—have introduced models that bring new meaning to the term "subcompact."[89] Let's take a look at these econoboxes.

Chery's QQ model sells for between $4,000 and $7,000 in the Chinese market and sports horsepower in the range of 51 to 74. Geely's best-selling four-door sedan, the Free Cruiser, retails from $6,300 and $6,900. The firm is planning to go more upscale with the Geely KingKong ($7,500–$10,000), a four-door 1.5- to 1.8-liter sedan, and the Vision ($9,700–$15,300), a 1.8-liter four-door sedan. But, for price-points, India's Tata Motors has everyone beat. In January 2008, it unveiled the Nano with an astonishing retail price of only $2,500. It is a four-door, five-seat hatchback that gets 54 miles per gallon. But before you order one—keep in mind that it only comes with a 30 horsepower engine.

Reflecting on Career Implications . . .

- *Creating the Environmentally Aware Organization:* In your career, what are some ways in which you can engage in scanning, monitoring, and intelligence gathering for future job opportunities? Consider, for example, subscribing to your field's professional publications and becoming actively involved in relevant professional organizations.
- *SWOT Analysis:* From a career standpoint, periodically evaluate your strengths and weaknesses as well as potential opportunities and threats to your career. In addition, strive to seek input from trusted peers and superiors.
- *General Environment:* Carefully evaluate the elements of the general environment facing your firm. Identify factors (e.g., rapid technological change) that can provide promising career opportunities as well as possibilities for you to add value for your organization. In doing this, don't focus solely on "internal factors" of your organization.
- *Five-Forces Analysis:* Consider the five forces affecting the industry within which your organization competes. If the "forces" are unfavorable, the long-term profit potential of the industry may be unattractive. And, there will likely be fewer resources available and—all other things being equal—fewer career opportunities.

Summary

Managers must analyze the external environment to minimize or eliminate threats and exploit opportunities. This involves a continuous process of environmental scanning and monitoring as well as obtaining competitive intelligence on present and potential rivals. These activities provide valuable inputs for developing forecasts. In addition, many firms use scenario planning to anticipate and respond to volatile and disruptive environmental changes.

We identified two types of environments: the general environment and the competitive environment. The six segments of the general environment are demographic, sociocultural, political/legal, technological, economic, and global. Trends and events occurring in these segments, such as the aging of the population, higher percentages of women in the workplace, governmental legislation, and increasing (or decreasing) interest rates, can have a dramatic effect on a firm. A given trend or event may have a positive impact on some industries and a negative, neutral, or no impact at all on others.

The competitive environment consists of industry-related factors and has a more direct impact than the general environment. Porter's five-forces model of industry analysis includes the threat of new entrants, buyer power, supplier power, threat of substitutes, and rivalry among competitors. The intensity of these factors determines, in large part, the average expected level of profitability in an industry. A sound awareness of such factors, both individually and in combination, is beneficial not only for deciding what industries to enter but also for assessing how a firm can improve its competitive position. We discuss how many of the changes brought about by the digital economy can be understood in the context of five-forces analysis. The limitations of five-forces analysis include its static nature and its inability to acknowledge the role of complementors. Although we addressed the general environment and competitive environment in separate sections, they are quite interdependent. A given environmental trend or event, such as changes in the ethnic composition of a population or a technological innovation, typically has a much greater impact on some industries than on others.

The concept of strategic groups is also important to the external environment of a firm. No two organizations are completely different nor are they exactly the same. The question is how to group firms in an industry on the basis of similarities in their resources and strategies. The strategic groups concept is valuable for determining mobility barriers across groups, identifying groups with marginal competitive positions, charting the future directions of firm strategies, and assessing the implications of industry trends for the strategic group as a whole.

Summary Review Questions

1. Why must managers be aware of a firm's external environment?
2. What is gathering and analyzing competitive intelligence and why is it important for firms to engage in it?
3. Discuss and describe the six elements of the external environment.
4. Select one of these elements and describe some changes relating to it in an industry that interests you.
5. Describe how the five forces can be used to determine the average expected profitability in an industry.
6. What are some of the limitations (or caveats) in using five-forces analysis?
7. Explain how the general environment and industry environment are highly related. How can such interrelationships affect the profitability of a firm or industry?
8. Explain the concept of strategic groups. What are the performance implications?

Key Terms

environmental
  scanning, 41
environmental
  monitoring, 42
competitive
  intelligence, 42
environmental
  forecasting, 44
scenario analysis, 45
SWOT analysis, 47
general environment, 47
demographic segment
  of the general
  environment, 47
sociocultural segment
  of the general
  environment, 49
political/legal segment
  of the general
  environment, 50
technological segment of
  the general
  environment, 50

economic segment
  of the general
  environment, 51
global segment
  of the general
  environment, 52
industry, 55
competitive
  environment, 55
Porter's five-forces
  model of industry
  competition, 55
threat of new
  entrants, 55
economies of
  scale, 56
product
  differentiation, 56
switching cost, 56
bargaining power of
  buyers, 57
bargaining power of
  suppliers, 58

Experiential Exercise

Select one of the following industries: personal computers, airlines, or automobiles. For this industry, evaluate the strength of each of Porter's five forces as well as complementors.

Industry Force	High? Medium? Low?	Why?
1. Threat of new entrants		
2. Power of buyers		
3. Power of suppliers		
4. Power of substitutes		
5. Rivalry among competitors		
6. Complementors		

Application Questions & Exercises

1. Imagine yourself as the CEO of a large firm in an industry in which you are interested. Please (1) identify major trends in the general environment, (2) analyze their impact on the firm, and (3) identify major sources of information to monitor these trends. (Use Internet and library resources.)

2. Analyze movements across the strategic groups in the U.S. retail industry. How do these movements within this industry change the nature of competition?

3. What are the major trends in the general environment that have impacted the U.S. pharmaceutical industry?

4. Go to the Internet and look up *www.kroger.com*. What are some of the five forces driving industry competition that are affecting the profitability of this firm?

Ethics Questions

1. What are some of the legal and ethical issues involved in collecting competitor intelligence in the following situations?

   a. Hotel A sends an employee posing as a potential client to Hotel B to find out who Hotel B's major corporate customers are.

   b. A firm hires an MBA student to collect information directly from a competitor while claiming the information is for a course project.

   c. A firm advertises a nonexistent position and interviews a rival's employees with the intention of obtaining competitor information.

2. What are some of the ethical implications that arise when a firm tries to exploit its power over a supplier?

References

1. Heimbuch, J. 2010. Hooray! Hawaii outlaws shark fin soup. *www.treehugger.com*, October 27: np.; Anonymous. 2006. The value of China's emerging middle class. *www.mkq preview.com*. June: np; and, Wassener, B. 2010. A shark fin promotion backfires. *www.green.blogs.nytimes.com*. July 22: np; and, *www.citigroup.com*. We thank Kimberly Kentfield for her valued contributions.

2. Hamel, G. & Prahalad, C. K. 1994. *Competing for the future.* Boston: Harvard Business School Press.

3. Drucker, P. F. 1994. Theory of the business. *Harvard Business Review,* 72: 95–104.

4. For an insightful discussion on managers' assessment of the external environment, refer to Sutcliffe, K. M. & Weber, K. 2003. The high cost of accurate knowledge. *Harvard Business Review,* 81(5): 74–86.

5. For insights on recognizing and acting on environmental opportunities, refer to: Alvarez, S. A. & Barney, J. B. 2008. Opportunities, organizations, and entrepreneurship: Theory and debate. *Strategic Entrepreneurship Journal,* 2(3): entire issue.

6. Charitou, C. D. & Markides, C. C. 2003. Responses to disruptive strategic innovation. *MIT Sloan Management Review,* 44(2): 55–64.

7. Our discussion of scanning, monitoring, competitive intelligence, and forecasting concepts draws on several sources. These include Fahey, L. & Narayanan, V. K. 1983. *Macroenvironmental analysis for strategic management.* St. Paul, MN: West; Lorange, P., Scott, F. S., & Ghoshal,

S. 1986. *Strategic control.* St. Paul, MN: West; Ansoff, H. I. 1984. *Implementing strategic management.* Englewood Cliffs, NJ: Prentice Hall; and Schreyogg, G. & Stienmann, H. 1987. Strategic control: A new perspective. *Academy of Management Review,* 12: 91–103.

8. An insightful discussion on how leaders can develop "peripheral vision" in environmental scanning is found in: Day, G. S. & Schoemaker, P. J. H. 2008. Are you a "vigilant leader"? *MIT Sloan Management Review,* 49 (3): 43–51.

9. Elenkov, D. S. 1997. Strategic uncertainty and environmental scanning: The case for institutional influences on scanning behavior. *Strategic Management Journal,* 18: 287–302.

10. For an interesting perspective on environmental scanning in emerging economies see May, R. C., Stewart, W. H., & Sweo, R. 2000. Environmental scanning behavior in a transitional economy: Evidence from Russia. *Academy of Management Journal,* 43(3): 403–27.

11. Bryon, E. 2010. For insight into P&G, check Olay numbers. *Wall Street Journal.* October 27: C1.

12. Tang, J. 2010. How entrepreneurs discover opportunities in China: An institutional view. *Asia Pacific Journal of Management.* 27(3): 461–480.

13. Walters, B. A. & Priem, R. L. 1999. Business strategy and CEO intelligence acquisition. *Competitive Intelligence Review,* 10(2): 15–22.

14. Prior, V. 1999. The language of competitive intelligence, Part 4. *Competitive Intelligence Review,* 10(1): 84–87.

15. Zahra, S. A. & Charples, S. S. 1993. Blind spots in competitive analysis. *Academy of Management Executive* 7(2): 7–27.

16. Wolfenson, J. 1999. The world in 1999: A battle for corporate honesty. *The Economist* 38: 13–30.

17. Drucker, P. F. 1997. The future that has already happened. *Harvard Business Review,* 75(6): 22.

18. Evans, P. B. & Wurster, T. S. 1997. Strategy and the new economics of information. *Harvard Business Review,* 75(5): 71–82.

19. Fahey & Narayanan, op. cit., p. 41.

20. Insights on how to improve predictions can be found in: Cross, R., Thomas, R. J., & Light, D. A. 2009. The prediction lover's handbook. *MIT Sloan Management Review,* 50 (2): 32–34.

21. Courtney, H., Kirkland, J., & Viguerie, P. 1997. Strategy under uncertainty. *Harvard Business Review,* 75(6): 66–79.

22. Odlyzko, A. 2003. False hopes. *Red Herring,* March: 31.

23. Coy, P. 2009. Worst predictions about 2008. *BusinessWeek,* January 12: 15–16.

24. For an interesting perspective on how Accenture practices and has developed its approach to scenario planning, refer to Ferguson, G., Mathur, S., & Shah, B. 2005. Evolving from information to insight. *MIT Sloan Management Review,* 46(2): 51–58.

25. Dean, T. J., Brown, R. L., & Bamford, C. E. 1998. Differences in large and small firm responses to environmental context: Strategic implications from a comparative analysis of business formations. *Strategic Management Journal,* 19: 709–728.

26. Some insights on management during economic downturns are in: Colvin, G. 2009. How to manage your business in a recession. *Fortune,* January 19: 88–93.

27. Colvin, G. 1997. How to beat the boomer rush. *Fortune,* August 18: 59–63.

28. Porter, M. E. 2010. Discovering—and lowering—the real costs of health care. *Harvard Business Review,* 89 (1/2): 49–50.

29. U.S. Bureau of Labor Statistics. 2009. *Occupational handbook, 2010–2011 edition.* December 19. *www.bls.gov/oco/oco203.htm.*

30. Challenger, J. 2000. Women's corporate rise has reduced relocations. *Lexington* (KY) *Herald-Leader,* October 29: D1.

31. Tsao, A. 2005. Retooling home improvement, *Businesssweek.com,* February, 14; and, Grow, B. 2004.

Who wears the wallet in the family? *BusinessWeek,* August 16:10.

32. Watkins, M. D. 2003. Government games. *MIT Sloan Management Review* 44(2): 91–95.

33. A discussion of the political issues surrounding caloric content on meals is in: Orey, M. 2008. A food fight over calorie counts. *BusinessWeek,* February 11: 36.

34. For a discussion of the linkage between copyright law and innovation, read: Guterman, J. 2009. Does copyright law hinder innovation? *MIT Sloan Management Review,* 50(2): 14–15.

35. Davies, A. 2000. The welcome mat is out for nerds. *BusinessWeek,* May 21: 17; Broache, A. 2007. Annual H-1B visa cap met—already. *news.cnet.com,* April 3: np; and, Anonymous. Undated. Cap count for H-1B and H-2B workers for fiscal year 2009. *www.uscis.gov:* np.

36. Hout, T. M., Ghemawat, P. 2010. China vs. the world: Whose technology is it? *Harvard Business Review,* 88(12): 94–103.

37. Anonymous. Business ready for Internet revolution. 1999. *Financial Times,* May 21: 17.

38. A discussion of an alternate energy—marine energy—is the topic of: Boyle, M. 2008. Scottish power. *Fortune.* March 17: 28.

39. Baker, S. & Aston, A. 2005. The business of nanotech. *BusinessWeek,* February 14: 64–71.

40. Morse, G. 2009. The power of unwitting workers. *Harvard Business Review,* 87(10): 26.

41. For an insightful discussion of the causes of the global financial crisis, read: Johnson, S. 2009. The global financial crisis—What really precipitated it? *MIT Sloan Management Review.* 50(2): 16–18.

42. Tyson, L. D. 2011. A better stimulus for the U.S. economy. *Harvard Business Review,* 89(1/2): 53.

43. A interesting and balanced discussion on the merits of multinationals to the U.S. economy is found in: Mandel, M. 2008. Multinationals: Are they good for America? *BusinessWeek,* March 10: 41–64.

44. Insights on risk perception across countries are addressed in: Purda, L. D. 2008. Risk perception and the financial system. *Journal of International Business Studies,* 39(7): 1178–1196.

45. Gogoi, P. 2010. Many U.S. companies are hiring . . . overseas. *www.msn.com.* December 28: np.

46. Byrnes, N. 2006. The high cost of fear. *BusinessWeek,* November 6: 16.

47. Goll, I. & Rasheed, M. A. 1997. Rational decision-making and firm performance: The moderating role of environment. *Strategic Management Journal,* 18: 583–591.

48. This discussion draws heavily on Porter, M. E. 1980. *Competitive strategy:* Chapter 1. New York: Free Press.

49. Ibid.

50. Rivalry in the airline industry is discussed in: Foust, D. 2009. Which airlines will disappear in 2009? *BusinessWeek,* January 19: 46–47.

51. Fryer, B. 2001. Leading through rough times: An interview with Novell's Eric Schmidt. *Harvard Business Review,* 78(5): 117–123.

52. For a discussion on the importance of barriers to entry within industries, read Greenwald, B. & Kahn, J. 2005. *Competition demystified: A radically simplified approach to business strategy.* East Rutherford, NJ: Portfolio.

53. A discussion of how the medical industry has erected entry barriers that have resulted in lawsuits is found in: Whelan, D. 2008. Bad medicine. *BusinessWeek,* March 10: 86–98.

54. The ProCD example draws heavily upon Shapiro, C. & Varian, H. R. 2000. Versioning: The smart way to sell information. *Harvard Business Review,* 78(1): 106–114.

55. Wise, R. & Baumgarter, P. 1999. Go downstream: The new profit imperative in manufacturing. *Harvard Business Review,* 77(5): 133–141.

56. Salman, W. A. 2000. The new economy is stronger than you think. *Harvard Business Review,* 77(6): 99–106.

57. Mudambi, R. & Helper, S. 1998. The "close but adversarial" model of supplier relations in the U.S. auto industry. *Strategic Management Journal,* 19: 775–792.

58. Trends in the solar industry are discussed in: Carey, J. 2009. Solar: The sun will come out tomorrow. *BusinessWeek,* January 12: 51.

59. Tischler, L. 2002. IBM: Manager jam. *Fast Company,* October: 48.

60. An interesting analysis of self-regulation in an industry (chemical) is in: Barnett, M. L. & King, A. A. 2008. Good fences make good neighbors: A longitudinal analysis of an industry self-regulatory institution. *Academy of Management Journal,* 51(6): 1053–1078.

61. For an interesting perspective on the intensity of competition in the supermarket industry, refer to Anonymous. 2005. Warfare in the aisles. *The Economist,* April 2: 6–8.

62. Marcial, G. 2000. Giving Viagra a run for its money. *BusinessWeek,* October 23: 173.

63. McGann, R. 2005. VOIP poised to take flight? *ClickZ.com,* February 23, *www.clickz.com.*

64. For an interesting perspective on changing features of firm boundaries, refer to Afuah, A. 2003. Redefining firm boundaries in the face of Internet: Are firms really shrinking? *Academy of Management Review,* 28(1): 34–53.

65. *www.consumerreports.org.*

66. Time to rebuild. 2001. *Economist,* May 19: 55–56.

67. *www.amazon.com.*

68. For more on the role of the Internet as an electronic intermediary, refer to Carr, N. G. 2000. Hypermediation: Commerce as clickstream. *Harvard Business Review,* 78(1): 46–48.

69. Olofson, C. 2001. The next best thing to being there. *Fast Company,* April: 175; and *www.conferenza.com.*

70. Lelii, S. R. 2001. Free online storage a thing of the past ? *eWEEK,* April 22.

71. *www.mysimon.com;* and *www.pricescan.com.*

72. *www.cnet.com;* and *www.bizrate.com.*

73. For insights into strategies in a low-profit industry, refer to: Hopkins, M. S. 2008. The management lessons of a beleaguered industry. *MIT Sloan Management Review,* 50(1): 25–31.

74. Foust, D. 2007. The best performers. *BusinessWeek,* March 26: 58–95; Rosenblum, D., Tomlinson, D., & Scott, L. 2003. Bottom-feeding for blockbuster businesses. *Harvard Business Review,* 81(3): 52–59; Paychex 2006 Annual Report; and, WellPoint Health Network 2005 Annual Report.

75. Kumar, N. 1996. The power of trust in manufacturer-retailer relationship. *Harvard Business Review,* 74(6): 92–110.

76. Welch, D. 2006. Renault-Nissan: Say hello to Bo. *BusinessWeek,* July 31: 56–57.

77. Brandenburger, A. & Nalebuff, B. J. 1995. The right game: Use game theory to shape strategy. *Harvard Business Review,* 73(4): 57–71.

78. For a scholarly discussion of complementary assets and their relationship to competitive advantage, refer to Stieglitz, N. & Heine, K. 2007. Innovations and the role of complementarities in a strategic theory of the firm *Strategic Management Journal,* 28(1): 1–15.

79. A useful framework for the analysis of industry evolution has been proposed by Professor Anita McGahan of Boston University. Her analysis is based on the identification of the core activities and the core assets of an industry and the threats they face. She suggests that an industry may follow one of four possible evolutionary trajectories—radical change, creative change, intermediating change, or progressive change—based on these two types of threats of obsolescence. Refer to: McGahan, A. M. 2004. How industries change. *Harvard Business Review,* 82(10): 87–94.

80. Yoffie, D. B. & Kwak, M. 2006. With friends like these: The art of managing complementors. *Harvard Business Review,* 84(9): 88–98.

81. Porter, M. I. 2008. The five competitive forces that shape strategy. *Harvard Business Review,* 86(1): 79–93.

82. Peteraf, M. & Shanley, M. 1997. Getting to know you: A theory of strategic group identity. *Strategic Management Journal,* 18 (Special Issue): 165–186.

83. An interesting scholarly perspective on strategic groups may be found in

Dranove, D., Perteraf, M., & Shanley, M. 1998. Do strategic groups exist? An economic framework for analysis. *Strategic Management Journal,* 19(11): 1029–1044.

84. For an empirical study on strategic groups and predictors of performance, refer to Short, J. C., Ketchen, D. J., Jr., Palmer, T. B., & Hult, T. M. 2007. Firm, strategic group, and industry influences on performance. *Strategic Management Journal,* 28(2): 147–167.

85. This section draws on several sources, including Kerwin, K. R. & Haughton,

K. 1997. Can Detroit make cars that baby boomers like? *BusinessWeek,* December 1: 134–148; and Taylor, A., III. 1994. The new golden age of autos. *Fortune,* April 4: 50–66.

86. Csere, C. 2001. Supercar supermarket. *Car and Driver,* January: 118–127.

87. For a discussion of the extent of overcapacity in the worldwide automobile industry, read: Roberts, D., Matlack, C., Busyh, J., & Rowley, I. 2009. A hundred factories too many. *BusinessWeek,* January 19: 42–43.

88. Naughton, K. 2010. HIS auto trims 2010 U.S. vehicle sales forecast to

11.3 million units. *www.bloomberg.com/news.* September 27: np; and, Woodall, B. 2011. J. D. Power lowers U.S. auto sales forecast. *www.reuters.com.* August 10: np.

89. This discussion draws on: Wojdyla, B. 2008. The $2500 Tata Nano, unveiled in India. *jalopnik.com,* January 10: np; Roberts, D. 2008. China's Geely has global auto ambitions. *businessweek.com,* July 27: np; and, Fairclough, G. 2007. In China, Chery automobile drives an industry shift. *The Wall Street Journal,* December 4: A1, A17.

chapter THREE

Assessing the Internal Environment of the Firm

After reading this chapter, you should have a good understanding of:

LO3.1 The benefits and limitations of SWOT analysis in conducting an internal analysis of the firm.

LO3.2 The primary and support activities of a firm's value chain.

LO3.3 How value-chain analysis can help managers create value by investigating relationships among activities within the firm and between the firm and its customers and suppliers.

LO3.4 The resource-based view of the firm and the different types of tangible and intangible resources, as well as organizational capabilities.

LO3.5 The four criteria that a firm's resources must possess to maintain a sustainable advantage and how value created can be appropriated by employees and managers.

LO3.6 The usefulness of financial ratio analysis, its inherent limitations, and how to make meaningful comparisons of performance across firms.

LO3.7 The value of the "balanced scorecard" in recognizing how the interests of a variety of stakeholders can be interrelated.

LO3.8 How firms are using Internet technologies to add value and achieve unique advantages. (Appendix)

LEARNING OBJECTIVES

Two firms compete in the same industry and both have many strengths in a variety of functional areas: marketing, operations, logistics, and so on. However, one of these firms outperforms the other by a wide margin over a long period of time. How can this be so? This chapter endeavors to answer that question.

We begin with two sections that include frameworks for gaining key insights into a firm's internal environment: value-chain analysis and the resource-based view of the firm. In value-chain analysis, we divide a firm's activities into a series of value-creating steps. We then explore how individual activities within the firm add value, and also how *interrelationships* among activities within the firm, and between the firm and its suppliers and customers, create value.

In the resource-based view of the firm, we analyze the firm as a collection of tangible and intangible resources as well as organizational capabilities. Advantages that tend to be sustainable over time typically arise from creating *bundles* of resources and capabilities that satisfy four criteria: they are valuable, rare, difficult to imitate, and difficult to substitute. Not all of the value created by a firm will necessarily be kept (or appropriated) by the owners. We discuss the four key factors that determine how profits will be distributed between owners as well as employees and managers.

In the closing sections, we discuss how to evaluate a firm's performance and make comparisons across firms. We emphasize both the inclusion of financial resources and the interests of multiple stakeholders. Central to our discussion is the concept of the balanced scorecard, which recognizes that the interests of different stakeholders can be interrelated. We also consider how a firm's performance evolves over time and how it compares with industry norms and key competitors.

In an appendix to this chapter, we explore how Internet-based businesses and incumbent firms are using digital technologies to add value. We consider four activities—search, evaluation, problem solving, and transaction—as well as three types of content—customer feedback, expertise, and entertainment programming. Such technology-enhanced capabilities are providing new means with which firms can achieve competitive advantages.●

Learning from Mistakes

Toyota Motor Company had developed an industry-leading strategy that focused on value innovation and cost reduction.[1] For many years it was a solid strategy for both the company and its customers. Over the years, Toyota built a reputation for engineering excellence and cost cutting. Its engineers collaborated with suppliers to extract cost-savings without compromising quality. Yet, by the middle of the last decade, Toyota's virtue had become a vice and eventually led to recalled vehicles, lawsuits, and a damaged reputation. What went wrong?

Toyota's problems stemmed from an overwhelming desire to cut costs. This, in turn, led to a product that did not meet the same high quality that its customers had come to expect. When a North American parts supplier interested in working with the automaker did a teardown of a 2007 Camry, its engineers were surprised by how much the traditional Toyota craftsmanship had been watered down by years of nips and tucks. One example of this came to light in 2006, when a redesigned Camry revealed an embarrassing flaw in its headliner (the lining that covers the inside of the roof). Under pressure to cut costs, a Toyota affiliate chose a carbon fiber material that had not yet been approved by Toyota engineers. Unfortunately, the new carbon fiber material required so much heat to mold during production that it would catch fire. Thus, as many as 30 percent of the parts were scrapped—compared to a normal scrap rate for headliners of about 5 percent.

The worst of Toyota's problems came in early 2010 when the company recalled around 3.8 million vehicles. The problem with these vehicles occurred when customers complained that their car would suddenly accelerate to speeds of over 100 mph without warning. This recall included America's most popular passenger vehicle, the Camry, and the best-selling gas-electric hybrid, the Prius. Recalls came after the National Highway Traffic Safety Administration received reports of 102 incidents in which the accelerator became stuck. However, safety analysts estimated that there were approximately 2,000 cases in which owners of Toyota vehicles, including Camry, Prius, and Lexus, experienced "runaway cars."

A well-publicized incident that further tarnished Toyota's reputation was the tragic death of the Saylor family. On August 28, 2009, Mark Saylor died alongside his wife Cleofe, and their daughter Mahala, 13, and Mrs. Saylor's brother, Chris Lastrella when the Lexus they had rented accelerated out of control on a highway in San Diego. In the emergency call, Mr. Lastrella was heard saying: "We're in a Lexus . . . and we're going north on 125 and our accelerator is stuck . . . there's no brakes . . . we're approaching the intersection . . . Hold on . . . hold on and pray . . . pray."

Clearly, Toyota got carried away chasing high-speed growth, market share, and productivity gains year in and year out. This focus slowly dulled the commitment to quality embedded in Toyota's corporate culture. In February 2010, Kiichiro Toyoda, the grandson of the company's founder, told a congressional committee: "I fear the pace at which we have grown may have been too quick . . . Priorities became confused, and we were not able to stop, think and make improvements as much as we were able to do before."

Toyota aggressively tried to cut costs at a rate their product could not keep up with. By ignoring key aspects of the value chain, such as operations and R&D, quality was sacrificed within Toyota. This led to products that were faulty as well as a recall that has cost them billions of dollars in repairs and lost revenue—plus a damaged reputation.

In this chapter we will place heavy emphasis on the value-chain concept. That is, we focus on the key value-creating activities (e.g., operations, marketing and sales, and procurement) that a firm must effectively manage and integrate in order to attain competitive advantages in the marketplace. However, firms must not only pay close attention to their own value-creating activities but must also maintain close and effective relationships with key organizations outside the firm boundaries such as suppliers, customers, and alliance partners. Clearly, Toyota's overemphasis on cost cutting—both within the firm and with their suppliers—eroded the quality of their cars as well as their reputation with customers.

Before moving to value-chain analysis, let's briefly revisit the benefits and limitations of SWOT analysis. As discussed in Chapter 2, a SWOT analysis consists of a careful listing of a firm's strengths, weaknesses, opportunities, and threats. While we believe SWOT analysis is very helpful as a starting point, it should not form the primary basis for evaluating a firm's internal strengths and weaknesses or the opportunities and threats in the environment. Strategy Spotlight 3.1 elaborates on the limitations of the traditional SWOT approach.

We will now turn to value-chain analysis. As you will see, it provides greater insights into analyzing a firm's competitive position than SWOT analysis does by itself.

>LO3.1
The benefits and limitations of SWOT analysis in conducting an internal analysis of the firm.

Value-Chain Analysis

Value-chain analysis views the organization as a sequential process of value-creating activities. The approach is useful for understanding the building blocks of competitive advantage and was described in Michael Porter's seminal book *Competitive Advantage*.[2] Value is the amount that buyers are willing to pay for what a firm provides them and is measured by total revenue, a reflection of the price a firm's product commands and the quantity it can sell. A firm is profitable when the value it receives exceeds the total costs involved in creating its product or service. Creating value for buyers that exceeds the costs of production (i.e., margin) is a key concept used in analyzing a firm's competitive position.

Porter described two different categories of activities. First, five **primary activities**—inbound logistics, operations, outbound logistics, marketing and sales, and service—contribute to the physical creation of the product or service, its sale and transfer to the buyer, and its service after the sale. Second, **support activities**—procurement, technology development, human resource management, and general administration—either add value by themselves or add value through important relationships with both primary activities and other support activities. Exhibit 3.1 illustrates Porter's value chain.

value-chain analysis a strategic analysis of an organization that uses value-creating activities.

primary activities sequential activities of the value chain that refer to the physical creation of the product or service, its sale and transfer to the buyer, and its service after sale, including inbound logistics, operations, outbound logistics, marketing and sales, and service.

support activities activities of the value chain that either add value by themselves or add value through important relationships with both primary activities and other support activities; including procurement, technology development, human resource management, and general administration.

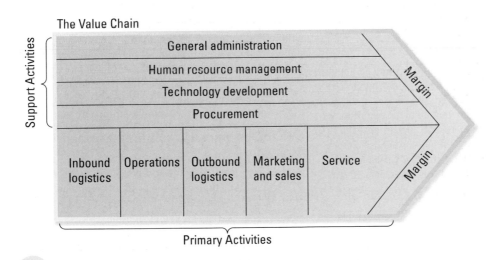

Exhibit 3.1 The Value Chain: Primary and Support Activities

Source: Reprinted with the permission of Free Press, a division of Simon & Schuster Inc., from *Competitive Advantage: Creating and Sustaining Superior Performance* by Michael E. Porter. Copyright © 1985, 1998 The Free Press. All rights reserved.

The Limitations of SWOT Analysis

SWOT analysis is a tried-and-true tool of strategic analysis. SWOT (strengths, weaknesses, opportunities, threats) analysis is used regularly in business to initially evaluate the opportunities and threats in the business environment as well as the strengths and weaknesses of a firm's internal environment. Top managers rely on SWOT to stimulate self-reflection and group discussions about how to improve their firm and position it for success.

But SWOT has its limitations. It is just a starting point for discussion. By listing the firm's attributes, managers have the raw material needed to perform more in-depth strategic analysis. However, SWOT cannot show them how to achieve a competitive advantage. They must not make SWOT analysis an end in itself, temporarily raising awareness about important issues but failing to lead to the kind of action steps necessary to enact strategic change.

Consider the ProCD example from Chapter 2, page 57. A brief SWOT analysis might include the following:

Strengths	Opportunities
First-mover advantage	Demand for electronic phone books
Low labor cost	Sudden growth in use of digital technology

Weaknesses	Threats
Inexperienced new company	Easily duplicated product
No proprietary information	Market power of incumbent firms

The combination of low production costs and an early-mover advantage in an environment where demand for CD-based phone books was growing rapidly seems to indicate that ProCD founder James Bryant had a golden opportunity. But the SWOT analysis did not reveal how to turn those strengths into a competitive advantage, nor did it highlight how rapidly the environment would change, allowing imitators to come into the market and erode his first-mover advantage. Let's look at some of the limitations of SWOT analysis.

Strengths May Not Lead to an Advantage

A firm's strengths and capabilities, no matter how unique or impressive, may not enable it to achieve a competitive advantage in the marketplace. It is akin to recruiting a concert pianist to join a gang of thugs—even though such

Sources: Shapiro, C. & Varian, H. R. 2000. Versioning: The Smart Way to Sell Information. *Harvard Business Review,* 78(1): 99–106; and Picken, J. C. & Dess, G. G. 1997. *Mission Critical.* Burr Ridge, IL: Irwin Professional Publishing.

an ability is rare and valuable, it hardly helps the organization attain its goals and objectives! Similarly, the skills of a highly creative product designer would offer little competitive advantage to a firm that produces low-cost commodity products. Indeed, the additional expense of hiring such an individual could erode the firm's cost advantages. If a firm builds its strategy on a capability that cannot, by itself, create or sustain competitive advantage, it is essentially a wasted use of resources. ProCD had several key strengths, but it did not translate them into lasting advantages in the marketplace.

SWOT's Focus on the External Environment Is Too Narrow

Strategists who rely on traditional definitions of their industry and competitive environment often focus their sights too narrowly on current customers, technologies, and competitors. Hence they fail to notice important changes on the periphery of their environment that may trigger the need to redefine industry boundaries and identify a whole new set of competitive relationships. Reconsider the example from Chapter 2 of *Encyclopaedia Britannica,* whose competitive position was severely eroded by a "nontraditional" competitor—CD-based encyclopedias (e.g., Microsoft *Encarta*) that could be used on home computers.

SWOT Gives a One-Shot View of a Moving Target

A key weakness of SWOT is that it is primarily a static assessment. It focuses too much of a firm's attention on one moment in time. Essentially, this is like studying a single frame of a motion picture. You may be able to identify the principal actors and learn something about the setting, but it doesn't tell you much about the plot. Competition among organizations is played out over time. As circumstances, capabilities, and strategies change, static analysis techniques do not reveal the dynamics of the competitive environment. Clearly, ProCD was unaware that its competitiveness was being eroded so quickly.

SWOT Overemphasizes a Single Dimension of Strategy

Sometimes firms become preoccupied with a single strength or a key feature of the product or service they are offering and ignore other factors needed for competitive success. For example, Toyota, the giant automaker, paid a heavy price for its excessive emphasis on cost control. The resulting problems with quality and the negative publicity led to severe financial losses and an erosion of its reputation in many markets.

SWOT analysis has much to offer, but only as a starting point. By itself, it rarely helps a firm develop competitive advantages that it can sustain over time.

To get the most out of value-chain analysis, view the concept in its broadest context, without regard to the boundaries of your own organization. That is, place your organization within a more encompassing value chain that includes your firm's suppliers, customers, and alliance partners. Thus, in addition to thoroughly understanding how value is created within the organization, be aware of how value is created for other organizations in the overall supply chain or distribution channel.[3]

>LO3.2
The primary and support activities of a firm's value chain.

Next, we'll describe and provide examples of each of the primary and support activities. Then, we'll provide examples of how companies add value by means of relationships among activities within the organization as well as activities outside the organization, such as those activities associated with customers and suppliers.[4]

Primary Activities

Five generic categories of primary activities are involved in competing in any industry, as shown in Exhibit 3.2. Each category is divisible into a number of distinct activities that depend on the particular industry and the firm's strategy.[5]

Inbound Logistics Inbound logistics is primarily associated with receiving, storing, and distributing inputs to the product. It includes material handling, warehousing, inventory control, vehicle scheduling, and returns to suppliers.

inbound logistics receiving, storing, and distributing inputs of a product.

Just-in-time (JIT) inventory systems, for example, were designed to achieve efficient inbound logistics. In essence, Toyota epitomizes JIT inventory systems, in which parts deliveries arrive at the assembly plants only hours before they are needed. JIT systems will play a vital role in fulfilling Toyota's commitment to fill a buyer's new car order in just five days.[6] This standard is in sharp contrast to most competitors that require approximately 30 days' notice to build vehicles. Toyota's standard is three times faster than even Honda Motors, considered to be the industry's most efficient in order follow-through. The five

Exhibit 3.2
The Value Chain: Some Factors to Consider in Assessing a Firm's Primary Activities

Inbound Logistics

- Location of distribution facilities to minimize shipping times.
- Warehouse layout and designs to increase efficiency of operations for incoming materials.

Operations

- Efficient plant operations to minimize costs.
- Efficient plant layout and workflow design.
- Incorporation of appropriate process technology.

Outbound Logistics

- Effective shipping processes to provide quick delivery and minimize damages.
- Shipping of goods in large lot sizes to minimize transportation costs.

Marketing and Sales

- Innovative approaches to promotion and advertising.
- Proper identification of customer segments and needs.

Service

- Quick response to customer needs and emergencies.
- Quality of service personnel and ongoing training.

Source: Adapted from Porter, M.E. 1985. *Competitive Advantage: Creating and Sustaining Superior Performance.* New York: Free Press.

days represent the time from the company's receipt of an order to the time the car leaves the assembly plant. Actual delivery may take longer, depending on where a customer lives. How can Toyota achieve such fast turnaround?

- Its 360 key suppliers are now linked to the company by way of computer on a virtual assembly line.
- Suppliers load parts onto trucks in the order in which they will be installed.
- Parts are stacked on trucks in the same place each time to help workers unload them quickly.
- Deliveries are required to meet a rigid schedule with as many as 12 trucks a day and no more than four hours between trucks.

operations all activities associated with transforming inputs into the final product form.

Operations   Operations include all activities associated with transforming inputs into the final product form, such as machining, packaging, assembly, testing, printing, and facility operations.

Creating environmentally friendly manufacturing is one way to use operations to achieve competitive advantage. Shaw Industries (now part of Berkshire Hathaway), a world-class competitor in the floor-covering industry, is well known for its concern for the environment.[7] It has been successful in reducing the expenses associated with the disposal of dangerous chemicals and other waste products from its manufacturing operations. Its environmental endeavors have multiple payoffs. Shaw has received many awards for its recycling efforts—awards that enhance its reputation.

outbound logistics collecting, storing, and distributing the product or service to buyers.

Outbound Logistics   Outbound logistics is associated with collecting, storing, and distributing the product or service to buyers. These activities include finished goods, warehousing, material handling, delivery vehicle operation, order processing, and scheduling.

● Despite superb logistics and excellent manufacturing operations, Dell's competitive position in personal computers—including desktops and laptops—has eroded in recent years.

Campbell Soup uses an electronic network to facilitate its continuous-replenishment program with its most progressive retailers.[8] Each morning, retailers electronically inform Campbell of their product needs and of the level of inventories in their distribution centers. Campbell uses that information to forecast future demand and to determine which products require replenishment (based on the inventory limits previously established with each retailer). Trucks leave Campbell's shipping plant that afternoon and arrive at the retailers' distribution centers the same day. The program cuts the inventories of participating retailers from about a four- to a two-weeks' supply. Campbell Soup achieved this improvement because it slashed delivery time and because it knows the inventories of key retailers and can deploy supplies when they are most needed.

The Campbell Soup example also illustrates the win–win benefits of exemplary value-chain activities. Both the supplier (Campbell) and its buyers (retailers) come out ahead. Since the retailer makes more money on Campbell products delivered through continuous replenishment, it has an incentive to carry a broader line and give the company greater shelf space. After Campbell introduced the program, sales of its products grew twice as fast through participating retailers as through all other retailers. Not surprisingly, supermarket chains love such programs.

3.2 | strategy spotlight

Security Risks in Mexico Have Led to Higher Shipping Costs

A report in January 2009 by the U.S. Joint Forces Command caught some by surprise with its warning about Mexico's political instability. It stated: "In terms of worst-case scenarios for the Joint Force and indeed the world, two large and important states bear consideration for a rapid and sudden collapse: Pakistan and Mexico." While the report stated that a collapse in Mexico was considered less likely, it went on to say, "The government, its politicians and judicial infrastructure are all under sustained assault and pressure by criminal gangs and drug cartels. How that internal conflict turns out over the next several years will have a major impact on the stability of the Mexican state."

A December 17, 2010, *Wall Street Journal* article also claimed that fights between drug cartels claimed more than 31,000 lives over the most recent four-year period—including 11,000 lives in 2010. Further, crimes such as robbery, extortion, and kidnapping increased. For some companies—especially those that don't yet have operations in Mexico—the violence has become daunting.

Not surprisingly, such instability has implications for quality of life and economic development—as well as the cost of doing business. Let's take a look at how logistics costs are affected.

Ryder Systems, for example, doesn't take any chances when it comes to securing its shipping operations in Mexico. It uses GPS to track every one of its trucks moving manufactured goods in Mexico to the border. Private security agents escort every container before it heads to Texas or elsewhere. It handles about 3,000 border crossings weekly. And if a load arrives late, alarms are raised and the dogs do their inspections—not once, but three times.

Faced with the threat of smuggling attempts by criminal organizations in Mexico, foreign companies are simply forced to do more and spend more. In the process, they are charging consumers more to shore up security in a country where killings, extortions, and kidnappings have become part of daily life. While it is difficult to define the full scope of the problem, those who provide risk analysis can offer some insights.

The share of corporate operating costs dedicated to security has risen by roughly a third in the past two years, according to Julio Millan, a Mexico City–based business consultant. He estimates that security spending in 2010 accounted for 3 percent of corporate operating costs in the northern part of the country, versus only 2 percent in 2009. "That's a huge jump," claims Millan. "The public is paying the cost of security through the price of products."

Sources: Casey, N., & Hagerty, J. R. 2010. Companies Shun Violent Mexico. *www.wsj.com*. December 17: np; Anonymous. 2009. Just How Risky Has Mexico Become as a Sourcing Location? *www.scdigest.com*. February 9: np; and Villagran, L. 2010. Companies Grapple with Mexico Security Risks. *Dallas Morning News*. August 20: 1D, 3D.

Many U.S. companies with manufacturing plants in Mexico took advantage of low labor costs. However, they have experienced a sharp increase in their shipping costs. This is because they have been forced to spend more on security as a result of increasing drug-related violence (see Strategy Spotlight 3.2).

Marketing and Sales These activities are associated with purchases of products and services by end users and the inducements used to get them to make purchases.[9] They include advertising, promotion, sales force, quoting, channel selection, channel relations, and pricing.[10,11]

It is not always enough to have a great product.[12] The key is to convince your channel partners that it is in their best interests not only to carry your product but also to market it in a way that is consistent with your strategy.[13] Consider Monsanto's efforts at educating distributors to improve the value proposition of its line of Saflex® windows.[14] The products had a superior attribute: The window design permitted laminators to form an exceptional type of glass by sandwiching a plastic sheet interlayer between two pieces of glass. This product is not only stronger and offers better ultraviolet protection than regular glass, but also when cracked, it adheres to the plastic sheet—an excellent safety feature for both cars and homes.

marketing and sales activities associated with purchases of products and services by end users and the inducements used to get them to make purchases.

Despite these benefits, Monsanto had a hard time convincing laminators and window manufacturers to carry these products. According to Melissa Toledo, brand manager at Monsanto, "Saflex was priced at a 30 percent premium above traditional glass, and the various stages in the value chain (distributors and retailers) didn't think there would be a demand for such an expensive glass product." What did Monsanto do? It reintroduced Saflex as KeepSafe® and worked to coordinate the product's value propositions. By analyzing the experiences of all of the players in the supply chain, it was able to create marketing programs that helped each build a business aimed at selling its products. Said Toledo, "We want to know how they go about selling those types of products, what challenges they face, and what they think they need to sell our products. This helps us a lot when we try to provide them with these needs."[15]

At times, a firm's marketing initiatives may become overly aggressive and lead to actions that are both unethical and illegal.[16] For example:

- **Burdines.** This department store chain is under investigation for allegedly adding club memberships to its customers' credit cards without prior approval.
- **Fleet Mortgage.** This company has been accused of adding insurance fees for dental coverage and home insurance to its customers' mortgage loans without the customers' knowledge.
- **HCI Direct.** Eleven states have accused this direct-mail firm with charging for panty hose samples that customers did not order.
- **Juno Online Services.** The Federal Trade Commission brought charges against this Internet service provider for failing to provide customers with a telephone number to cancel service.

Strategy Spotlight. 3.3 discusses RYZ, a company which has almost no marketing costs. Why? It relies exclusively on social media such as Myspace and Facebook to create demand for its products.

service actions associated with providing service to enhance or maintain the value of the product.

Service   This primary activity includes all actions associated with providing service to enhance or maintain the value of the product, such as installation, repair, training, parts supply, and product adjustment.

Let's see how two retailers are providing exemplary customer service. At Sephora.com, a customer service representative taking a phone call from a repeat customer has instant access to what shade of lipstick she likes best. This will help the rep cross-sell by suggesting a matching shade of lip gloss. CEO Jim Wiggett expects such personalization to build loyalty and boost sales per customer. Nordstrom, the Seattle-based department store chain, goes even a step further. It offers a cyber-assist: A service rep can take control of a customer's Web browser and literally lead her to just the silk scarf that she is looking for. CEO Dan Nordstrom believes that such a capability will close enough additional purchases to pay for the $1 million investment in software.

Support Activities

Support activities in the value chain can be divided into four generic categories, as shown in Exhibit 3.3. Each category of the support activity is divisible into a number of distinct value activities that are specific to a particular industry. For example, technology development's discrete activities may include component design, feature design, field testing, process engineering, and technology selection. Similarly, procurement may include activities such as qualifying new suppliers, purchasing different groups of inputs, and monitoring supplier performance.

procurement the function of purchasing inputs used in the firm's value chain, including raw materials, supplies, and other consumable items as well as assets such as machinery, laboratory equipment, office equipment, and buildings.

Procurement   Procurement refers to the function of purchasing inputs used in the firm's value chain, not to the purchased inputs themselves.[17] Purchased inputs include raw materials, supplies, and other consumable items as well as assets such as machinery, laboratory equipment, office equipment, and buildings.[18,19]

strategy spotlight

Crowdsourcing: RYZ's Potential Customers Become Its Marketing and Design Staff

What happens when a company lets consumers design and vote on their own products? Quite often, the firm's overhead goes down and profits go up. This business model is an example of using crowdsourcing as a means of community-based design.

One of these companies is RYZ, founded in 2008, with over $1 million in revenues. It doesn't need a large marketing or design staff. Rather, it relies on potential customers for that. Would-be designers use a template from the company's website to create a pair of high-rise sneakers. The designs are posted online, and viewers vote on which ones they like. Winning designs are produced, and designers get $1,000 plus 1 percent of royalties for their efforts.

Sources: Brillen, P. 2010. The Youdesign Movement. *www.nyt.com*, February 25: np; Kaufman, W. 2009. Crowdsourcing Turns Business on Its Head. *www.npr.org*. August 20: np; and *RYZwear.com*.

RYZ runs a weekly contest to cherry pick the best submitted sneaker design, which is then manufactured in a limited edition and sold for $54.99 to $99. And encouraging winners to promote their work makes sense: After all, you are more likely to try to make your design a success when you've invested time and effort. As an additional inducement, the winners get their picture on the company's website—along with a statement touting their work.

Not surprisingly, marketing costs are virtually nil, and relying on customers for design and market research enables the firm to move much more quickly, claims Rob Langstaff, the firm's founder and CEO. Previously head of Adidas North America, he says that it would take about 12 months and a substantial investment to get a design to market in the traditional, large shoe companies. In contrast, he asserts that RYZ can go from design to final product in only about six weeks.

crowdsourcing

Exhibit 3.3   The Value Chain: Some Factors to Consider in Assessing a Firm's Support Activities

General Administration

- Effective planning systems to attain overall goals and objectives.
- Excellent relationships with diverse stakeholder groups.
- Effective information technology to integrate value-creating activities.

Human Resource Management

- Effective recruiting, development, and retention mechanisms for employees.
- Quality relations with trade unions.
- Reward and incentive programs to motivate all employees.

Technology Development

- Effective R&D activities for process and product initiatives.
- Positive collaborative relationships between R&D and other departments.
- Excellent professional qualifications of personnel.

Procurement

- Procurement of raw material inputs to optimize quality and speed and to minimize the associated costs.
- Development of collaborative win-win relationships with suppliers.
- Analysis and selection of alternative sources of inputs to minimize dependence on one supplier.

Source: Adapted from Porter, M.E. 1985. *Competitive Advantage: Creating and Sustaining Superior Performance.* New York: Free Press.

Microsoft has improved its procurement process (and the quality of its suppliers) by providing formal reviews of its suppliers. One of Microsoft's divisions has extended the review process used for employees to its outside suppliers.[20] The employee services group, which is responsible for everything from travel to 401(k) programs to the on-site library, outsources more than 60 percent of the services it provides. Unfortunately, the employee services group was not providing them with enough feedback. This was feedback that the suppliers wanted to get and that Microsoft wanted to give.

The evaluation system that Microsoft developed helped clarify its expectations to suppliers. An executive noted: "We had one supplier—this was before the new system—that would have scored a 1.2 out of 5. After we started giving this feedback, and the supplier understood our expectations, its performance improved dramatically. Within six months, it scored a 4. If you'd asked me before we began the feedback system, I would have said that was impossible."

Technology Development   Every value activity embodies technology.[21] The array of technologies employed in most firms is very broad, ranging from technologies used to prepare documents and transport goods to those embodied in processes and equipment or the product itself.[22] Technology development related to the product and its features supports the entire value chain, while other technology development is associated with particular primary or support activities.

The Allied Signal and Honeywell merger brought together roughly 13,000 scientists and an $870 million R&D budget that should lead to some innovative products and services in two major areas: performance materials and control systems. Some of the possible innovations include:

- *Performance materials.* The development of uniquely shaped fibers with very high absorption capability. When employed in the company's Fram oil filters, they capture 50 percent more particles than ordinary filters. This means that cars can travel further with fewer oil changes.
- *Control systems.* Working with six leading oil companies, Honeywell developed software using "self-learning" algorithms that predict when something might go wrong in an oil refinery before it actually does. Examples include a faulty gas valve or hazardous spillage.[23]

Human Resource Management   Human resource management consists of activities involved in the recruiting, hiring, training, development, and compensation of all types of personnel.[24] It supports both individual primary and support activities (e.g., hiring of engineers and scientists) and the entire value chain (e.g., negotiations with labor unions).[25]

Like all great service companies, JetBlue Airways Corporation is obsessed with hiring superior employees.[26] But they found it difficult to attract college graduates to commit to careers as flight attendants. JetBlue developed a highly innovative recruitment program for flight attendants—a one-year contract that gives them a chance to travel, meet lots of people, and then decide what else they might like to do. They also introduced the idea of training a friend and employee together so that they could share a job. With such employee-friendly initiatives, JetBlue has been very successful in attracting talent.

Jeffrey Immelt, GE's chairman, addresses the importance of effective human resource management:[27]

Human resources has to be more than a department. GE recognized early on—50 or 60 years ago—that in a multibusiness company, the common denominators are people and culture. From an employee's first day at GE, she discovers that she's in the people-development business as much as anything else. You'll find that most good companies have the same basic HR processes that we have, but they're discrete. HR at GE is not an agenda item; it is the agenda.

3.4

Removing Individual Metrics in Performance Evaluations

ITT China President William Taylor wanted to know why employee turnover was so high in the Shanghai sales office. The local manager knew the answer: If the sales manager gave workers an average "3" on the 1-5 performance scale, they'd stop talking to him and, in some cases, quit shortly thereafter. The manager lamented: "They're losing face in the organization. It would be great if we could do something about the scores."

Comments like that popped up around the world. For example, in southern Europe, the focus on individual performance didn't sit well with the region's more "collective

ethos," claims James Duncan, director of ITT's talent development. And in Scandinavia, where there's more of "a sense of equality between bosses and workers," says Duncan, some workers asked, "What gives you the right to rate me a 3?" That led ITT to make the radical decision to ditch performance ratings altogether.

Most employees, who still require a detailed evaluation, cheered the changes. In one of the ITT plants in Shenyang, China, the new system has helped to cut the plant's attrition rate in half. The change isn't as popular in the U.S., where some metrics-loving engineers in the defense business remain attached to the old rankings. Still, most people have come around. Says Duncan, "It's not just Asia and Europe." No matter what culture you are from, everyone "likes the fact that they're treated like an adult in this discussion."

Source: McGregor, J. 2008. Case study: To Adapt, ITT Lets Go of Unpopular Ratings. *BusinessWeek*, January 28: 46.

Strategy Spotlight 3.4 discusses a rather unique approach to individual performance evaluations: eliminate the metrics!

General Administration   General administration consists of a number of activities, including general management, planning, finance, accounting, legal and government affairs, quality management, and information systems. Administration (unlike the other support activities) typically supports the entire value chain and not individual activities.[28]

Although general administration is sometimes viewed only as overhead, it can be a powerful source of competitive advantage. In a telephone operating company, for example, negotiating and maintaining ongoing relations with regulatory bodies can be among the most important activities for competitive advantage. Also, in some industries top management plays a vital role in dealing with important buyers.[29]

The strong and effective leadership of top executives can also make a significant contribution to an organization's success. As we discussed in Chapter 1, chief executive officers (CEOs) such as Herb Kelleher, Andrew Grove, and Jack Welch have been credited with playing critical roles in the success of Southwest Airlines, Intel, and General Electric.

Information systems can also play a key role in increasing operating efficiencies and enhancing a firm's performance.[30] Consider Walgreen Co.'s introduction of Intercom Plus, a computer-based prescription management system. Linked by computer to both doctors' offices and third-party payment plans, the system automates telephone refills, store-to-store prescription transfers, and drug reordering. It also provides information on drug interactions and, coupled with revised workflows, frees up pharmacists from administrative tasks to devote more time to patient counseling.[31]

Interrelationships among Value-Chain Activities within and across Organizations

We have defined each of the value-chain activities separately for clarity of presentation. Managers must not ignore, however, the importance of relationships among value-chain

> **>LO3.3**
> How value-chain analysis can help managers create value by investigating relationships among activities within the firm and between the firm and its customers and suppliers.

> **general administration**
> general management, planning, finance, accounting, legal and government affairs, quality management, and information systems; activities that support the entire value chain and not individual activities.

activities.[32] There are two levels: (1) **interrelationships** among activities within the firm and (2) relationships among activities within the firm and with other stakeholders (e.g., customers and suppliers) that are part of the firm's expanded value chain.[33]

With regard to the first level, consider AT&T's innovative Resource Link program. Here, employees who have reached their plateau may apply for temporary positions in other parts of the organization. Clearly, this program has the potential to benefit all activities within the firm's value chain because it creates opportunities for top employees to lend their expertise to all of the organization's value-creating activities.

With regard to the second level, Campbell Soup's use of electronic networks enabled it to improve the efficiency of outbound logistics.[34] However, it also helped Campbell manage the ordering of raw materials more effectively, improve its production scheduling, and help its customers better manage their inbound logistics operations.

Strategy Spotlight 3.5 discusses an innovative initiative by Timberland, a leading shoe manufacturer, to eliminate toxic adhesives from its shoes. This effort has the potential for long-term cost savings for their suppliers as well as increased market share for their product line.

The "Prosumer" Concept: Integrating Customers into the Value Chain

When addressing the value-chain concept, it is important to focus on the interrelationship between the organization and its most important stakeholder—its customers.[35] A key to success for some leading-edge firms is to team up with their customers to satisfy their particular need(s). As stated in a recent IBM Global CEO Study:

> In the future, we will be talking more and more about the "prosumer"—a customer/producer who is even more extensively integrated into the value chain. As a consequence, production processes will be customized more precisely and individually.[36]

Including customers in the actual production process can create greater satisfaction among them. It also has the potential to result in significant cost savings and to generate innovative ideas for the firm, which can be transferred to the customer in terms of lower prices and higher quality products and services.

In terms of how a firm views its customers, the move to create the prosumer stands in rather stark contrast to the conventional marketing approach in which the customer merely consumes the products produced by the company. Another area where this approach differs from conventional thinking concerns the notion of tying the customer into the company through, for example, loyalty programs and individualized relationship marketing.

How Procter & Gamble Embraced the Prosumer Concept In the early 2000s P&G's people were not clearly oriented toward any common purpose. The corporate mission "To meaningfully improve the everyday lives of the customers" had not been explicitly or inspirationally rolled out to the employees. To more clearly focus everyone's efforts, P&G expanded the mission to include the idea that "the consumer is the boss." This philosophy became one in which people who buy and use P&G products are valued not just for their money but also as *a rich source of information and direction.* "The consumer is the boss" became far more than a slogan in P&G. It became a clear, simple, and inclusive cultural priority for both employees and the external stakeholders such as suppliers.

The P&G efforts in the fragrance areas are one example. P&G transformed this small underperforming business area into a global leader and the world's largest fine fragrance company. They accomplished this by clearly and precisely defining the target consumer for each fragrance brand and by identifying subgroups of consumers for some brands. P&G still kept the partnerships with established fashion houses such as Dolce & Gabbana, Gucci, and Lacoste. However, the main point was to make the consumer the boss, focusing on innovations that were meaningful to consumers, including, for instance, fresh new

strategy spotlight

Timberland's Detoxification Initiative

Making shoes is a surprisingly toxic business. Both the materials and the adhesives that connect them are made of chemicals that are known dangers to the cardiac, respiratory, and nervous systems. One pair of running shoes will hardly harm you. However, workers in the industry face real risks.

Timberland, the second largest company in the outdoor industry, with $1.3 billion in revenues, realized that it needed to rethink the industry's traditional reliance on toxic chemicals. It became the first footwear company to test new water-based adhesives on nonathletic shoes. (Nike and others had already taken the initiatives in the "white shoe," or athletic, part of the industry.) Making such a change required the firm to work closely with Asian suppliers. According to Timberland's website, the company released its long-term strategy in 2008, which included its goal to create products at lower cost and with less harm to the environment. The strategy included eliminating polyvinylchloride (PVC) from its product line and increasing the use of water-based adhesives in its footwear in order to reduce the use of solvents.

Common sense would suggest that Timberland's detoxification efforts would be very costly for its suppliers. And during the test phase it was quite expensive. The new adhesives cost more because economies of scale hadn't yet been achieved. However, over time, Timberland fully expects the process to be at least cost neutral for its business and a money maker for the full value chain.

Sources: Esty, D. C. & Winston, A. S. *Green to Gold*. Hoboken, NJ: Wiley, p: 112–113; *www.community.timberland.com*; and *finance.yahoo.com*.

Why? Water-based adhesives eliminate almost entirely the supplier's expense for handling hazardous materials, including waste disposal, insurance, and training. Manufacturing expenses had already declined during the testing phase, because water-based adhesives go on with one coat instead of two, and the application equipment requires less cleaning. Thus, suppliers can run

● Timberland is well known for their environmental sustainability initiatives.

longer without interruption. The change also improves worker safety as well as reduces both labor costs and time.

Sounds good. But will Timberland be able to capture these supplier savings down the road? Probably not, but over time this strategy should help the firm win market share and drive revenues.

 environmental sustainability

scents, distinctive packaging, and proactive marketing. In addition, P&G streamlined the supply chain to reduce complexity and lower its cost structure.

"The consumer is the boss" idea goes even further. It also means that P&G tries to build social connections through digital media and other forms of interactions (thus incorporating the crowdsourcing concept that we introduced in Chapter 1). Baby diapers are one example. P&G used to use handmade diapers for its product tests. Today, however, this product is shown digitally and created in alternatives in an on-screen virtual world. Changes can be made immediately as new ideas emerge, and it can be redesigned on screen. Thus, P&G is creating a social system with the consumers (and potential consumers) that enable the firm to co-design and co-engineer new innovations with buyers. At P&G the philosophy of "the consumer is the boss" set a new standard.

Applying the Value Chain to Service Organizations

The concepts of inbound logistics, operations, and outbound logistics suggest managing the raw materials that might be manufactured into finished products and delivered to customers. However, these three steps do not apply only to manufacturing. They correspond to any transformation process in which inputs are converted through a work process into outputs that add value. For example, accounting is a sort of transformation process that converts daily records of individual transactions into monthly financial reports. In this example, the transaction records are the inputs, accounting is the operation that adds value, and financial statements are the outputs.

What are the "operations," or transformation processes, of service organizations? At times, the difference between manufacturing and service is in providing a customized solution rather than mass production as is common in manufacturing. For example, a travel agent adds value by creating an itinerary that includes transportation, accommodations, and activities that are customized to your budget and travel dates. A law firm renders services that are specific to a client's needs and circumstances. In both cases, the work process (operation) involves the application of specialized knowledge based on the specifics of a situation (inputs) and the outcome that the client desires (outputs).

The application of the value chain to service organizations suggests that the value-adding process may be configured differently depending on the type of business a firm is engaged in. As the preceding discussion on support activities suggests, activities such as procurement and legal services are critical for adding value. Indeed, the activities that may only provide support to one company may be critical to the primary value-adding activity of another firm.

Exhibit 3.4 provides two models of how the value chain might look in service industries. In the retail industry, there are no manufacturing operations. A firm, such as Best Buy, adds value by developing expertise in the procurement of finished goods and by displaying them in their stores in a way that enhances sales. Thus, the value chain makes procurement activities (i.e., partnering with vendors and purchasing goods) a primary rather than a support activity. Operations refer to the task of operating Best Buy's stores.

Exhibit 3.4 Some Examples of Value Chains in Service Industries

For an engineering services firm, research and development provides inputs, the transformation process is the engineering itself, and innovative designs and practical solutions are the outputs. Arthur D. Little, for example, is a large consulting firm with offices in 20 countries. In its technology and innovation management practice, A. D. Little strives to make the best use of the science, technology and knowledge resources available to create value for a wide range of industries and client sectors. This involves activities associated with research and development, engineering, and creating solutions as well as downstream activities such as marketing, sales, and service. How the primary and support activities of a given firm are configured and deployed will often depend on industry conditions and whether the company is service and/or manufacturing oriented.

Resource-Based View of the Firm

The **resource-based view (RBV) of the firm** combines two perspectives: (1) the internal analysis of phenomena within a company and (2) an external analysis of the industry and its competitive environment.[37] It goes beyond the traditional SWOT (strengths, weaknesses, opportunities, threats) analysis by integrating internal and external perspectives. The ability of a firm's resources to confer competitive advantage(s) cannot be determined without taking into consideration the broader competitive context. A firm's resources must be evaluated in terms of how valuable, rare, and hard they are for competitors to duplicate. Otherwise, the firm attains only competitive parity.

As noted earlier (in Strategy Spotlight 3.1), a firm's strengths and capabilities—no matter how unique or impressive—do not necessarily lead to competitive advantages in the marketplace. The criteria for whether advantages are created and whether or not they can be sustained over time will be addressed later in this section. Thus, the RBV is a very useful framework for gaining insights as to why some competitors are more profitable than others. As we will see later in the book, the RBV is also helpful in developing strategies for individual businesses and diversified firms by revealing how core competencies embedded in a firm can help it exploit new product and market opportunities.

In the two sections that follow, we will discuss the three key types of resources that firms possess (summarized in Exhibit 3.5): tangible resources, intangible resources, and organizational capabilities. Then we will address the conditions under which such assets and capabilities can enable a firm to attain a sustainable competitive advantage.[38]

It is important to note that resources by themselves typically do not yield a competitive advantage. Even if a basketball team recruited an all-star center, there would be little chance of victory if the other members of the team were continually outplayed by their opponents or if the coach's attitude was so negative that everyone, including the center, became unwilling to put forth their best efforts.

In a business context, a firm's excellent value-creating activities (e.g., logistics) would not be a source of competitive advantage if those activities were not integrated with other important value-creating activities such as marketing and sales. Thus, a central theme of the resource-based view of the firm is that competitive advantages are created (and sustained) through the bundling of several resources in unique combinations.[39]

Types of Firm Resources

Firm resources are all assets, capabilities, organizational processes, information, knowledge, and so forth, controlled by a firm that enable it to develop and implement value-creating strategies.

Tangible Resources These are assets that are relatively easy to identify. They include the physical and financial assets that an organization uses to create value for its

---

resource-based view of the firm perspective that firms' competitive advantages are due to their endowment of strategic resources that are valuable, rare, costly to imitate, and costly to substitute.

>LO3.4
The resource-based view of the firm and the different types of tangible and intangible resources, as well as organizational capabilities.

tangible resources organizational assets that are relatively easy to identify, including physical assets, financial resources, organizational resources, and technological resources.

Tangible Resources

Financial	• Firm's cash account and cash equivalents.
	• Firm's capacity to raise equity.
	• Firm's borrowing capacity.
Physical	• Modern plant and facilities.
	• Favorable manufacturing locations.
	• State-of-the-art machinery and equipment.
Technological	• Trade secrets.
	• Innovative production processes.
	• Patents, copyrights, trademarks.
Organizational	• Effective strategic planning processes.
	• Excellent evaluation and control systems.

Intangible Resources

Human	• Experience and capabilities of employees.
	• Trust.
	• Managerial skills.
	• Firm-specific practices and procedures.
Innovation and creativity	• Technical and scientific skills.
	• Innovation capacities.
Reputation	• Brand name.
	• Reputation with customers for quality and reliability.
	• Reputation with suppliers for fairness, non–zero-sum relationships.

Organizational Capabilities

- Firm competencies or skills the firm employs to transfer inputs to outputs.
- Capacity to combine tangible and intangible resources, using organizational processes to attain desired end.

  EXAMPLES:
  - Outstanding customer service.
  - Excellent product development capabilities.
  - Innovativeness of products and services.
  - Ability to hire, motivate, and retain human capital.

Source: Adapted from Barney, J. B. 1991. Firm Resources and Sustained Competitive Advantage. *Journal of Management:* 17: 101; Grant, R. M. 1991. *Contemporary Strategy Analysis:* 100–102. Cambridge England: Blackwell Business and Hitt, M. A., Ireland, R. D., & Hoskisson, R. E. 2001. *Strategic Management: Competitiveness and Globalization* (4th ed.). Cincinnati: South-Western College Publishing.

customers. Among them are financial resources (e.g., a firm's cash, accounts receivables, and its ability to borrow funds); physical resources (e.g., the company's plant, equipment, and machinery as well as its proximity to customers and suppliers); organizational resources (e.g., the company's strategic planning process and its employee development, evaluation, and reward systems); and technological resources (e.g., trade secrets, patents, and copyrights).

Many firms are finding that high-tech, computerized training has dual benefits: It develops more effective employees and reduces costs at the same time. Employees at FedEx take computer-based job competency tests every 6 to 12 months.[40] The 90-minute computer-based tests identify areas of individual weakness and provide input to a computer database of employee skills—information the firm uses in promotion decisions.

Intangible Resources   Much more difficult for competitors (and, for that matter, a firm's own managers) to account for or imitate are **intangible resources**, which are typically embedded in unique routines and practices that have evolved and accumulated over time. These include human resources (e.g., experience and capability of employees, trust, effectiveness of work teams, managerial skills), innovation resources (e.g., technical and scientific expertise, ideas), and reputation resources (e.g., brand name, reputation with suppliers for fairness and with customers for reliability and product quality).[41] A firm's culture may also be a resource that provides competitive advantage.[42]

For example, you might not think that motorcycles, clothes, toys, and restaurants have much in common. Yet Harley-Davidson has entered all of these product and service markets by capitalizing on its strong brand image—a valuable intangible resource.[43] It has used that image to sell accessories, clothing, and toys, and it has licensed the Harley-Davidson Café in New York City to provide further exposure for its brand name and products.

Strategy Spotlight 3.6 discusses how various social networking sites have the potential to play havoc with a firm's reputation.

Organizational Capabilities   **Organizational capabilities** are not specific tangible or intangible assets, but rather the competencies or skills that a firm employs to transform inputs into outputs.[44] In short, they refer to an organization's capacity to deploy tangible and intangible resources over time and generally in combination, and to leverage those capabilities to bring about a desired end.[45] Examples of organizational capabilities are outstanding customer service, excellent product development capabilities, superb innovation processes, and flexibility in manufacturing processes.[46]

In the case of Apple, the majority of components used in their products can be characterized as proven technology, such as touch screen and MP3 player functionality.[47] However, Apple combines and packages these in new and innovative ways while also seeking to integrate the value chain. This is the case with iTunes, for example, where suppliers of downloadable music are a vital component of the success Apple has enjoyed with their iPod series of MP3 players. Thus, Apple draws on proven technologies and their ability to offer innovative combinations of these.

Firm Resources and Sustainable Competitive Advantages

As we have mentioned, resources alone are not a basis for competitive advantages, nor are advantages sustainable over time.[48] In some cases, a resource or capability helps a firm to increase its revenues or to lower costs but the firm derives only a temporary advantage because competitors quickly imitate or substitute for it.[49] Many e-commerce businesses in the early 2000s saw their profits seriously eroded because new (or existing) competitors easily duplicated their business model. For example, Priceline.com, expanded its offerings from enabling customers to place bids online for airline tickets to a wide variety of other products. However, it was easy for competitors (e.g., a consortium of major airlines) to duplicate Priceline's products and services. Ultimately, its market capitalization had plummeted roughly 98 percent from its all-time high.

For a resource to provide a firm with the potential for a sustainable competitive advantage, it must have four attributes.[50] First, the resource must be valuable in the sense that it exploits opportunities and/or neutralizes threats in the firm's environment. Second, it must be rare among the firm's current and potential competitors. Third, the resource must be difficult for competitors to imitate. Fourth, the resource must have no strategically equivalent

intangible resources organizational assets that are difficult to identify and account for and are typically embedded in unique routines and practices, including human resources, innovation resources, and reputation resources.

organizational capabilities the competencies and skills that a firm employs to transform inputs into outputs.

strategic resources (also firm resources or organizational resources) firms' capabilities that are valuable, rare, costly to imitate, and costly to substitute.

>LO3.5
The four criteria that a firm's resources must possess to maintain a sustainable advantage and how value created can be appropriated by employees and managers.

Blogs, Social Networking Sites, and Corporate Reputations: A Lethal Combination?

Customers are now connecting with and drawing power from one another. The mechanism: online social technologies such as blogs, social networking sites like MySpace, user-generated content sites like YouTube, and countless communities across the web. They are defining their own perspective on companies and brands—a perspective that is often at odds with the image a company wants to project. This groundswell of people using technologies to get the things they need from one another, rather than from the companies, has tilted the balance of power from company to customer.

Let's look at an example: Brian Finkelstein, a law student, had trouble with the cable modem in his home. A Comcast Cable repairman arrived to fix the problem. However, when the technician had to call the home office for a key piece of information, he was put on hold for so long that he fell asleep on Finkelstein's couch. Outraged, Finkelstein made a video of the sleeping technician and posted it on YouTube. The clip became a hit—with more than a million viewings. And, to this day, it continues to undermine Comcast's efforts to improve its reputation for customer service.

Source: Bernoff, J. & Li, C. 2008. Harnessing the Power of the Oh-So-Social Web. *MIT Sloan Management Review*, 49(3): 36–42; and, Stelter, B. 2008. Griping Online? Comcast Hears and Talks Back. nytimes.com, July 25: np.

But Comcast is working hard to improve its reputation. It has a lot of work to do—after all, the company was ranked at the bottom of a recent American Customer Satisfaction Index, which tracks consumer opinions of more than 200 companies. And hundreds of customers have filed grievances on a site called comcastmustdie.com.

One of Comcast's initiatives to try to turn things around is headed by Frank Eliason, its digital care manager. He uses readily available online tools to monitor public comments on blogs, message boards, and social networks for any mention of Comcast. When Eliason sees a complaint, he contacts the source and tries to defuse the problem. "When you're having a two-way conversation, you really get to clear the air," says Eliason.

Comcast says the online outreach is part of a larger effort to revamp its customer service. In just five months, Eliason, whose job redefines customer service, has reached out to well over 1,000 customers online.

Comcast is not the only company trying to reach out to customers online. Using the social messaging service Twitter, Southwest Airlines answers customer questions about ticket prices and flight delays, Whole Foods Market posts details about discounts, and the chief executive of the online shoe store Zappos shares details of his life with 7,200 "followers." Many other companies also monitor online discussion groups. But given its track record, Comcast felt they needed to take the extra step: contacting customers who are discussing the company online.

substitutes. These criteria are summarized in Exhibit 3.6. We will now discuss each of these criteria. Then, we will examine how Dell's competitive advantage, which seemed secure as late as 2006, has eroded.

Is the Resource Valuable? Organizational resources can be a source of competitive advantage only when they are valuable. Resources are valuable when they enable a firm to formulate and implement strategies that improve its efficiency or effectiveness. The SWOT framework suggests that firms improve their performance only when they exploit opportunities or neutralize (or minimize) threats.

The fact that firm attributes must be valuable in order to be considered resources (as well as potential sources of competitive advantage) reveals an important complementary relationship among environmental models (e.g., SWOT and five-forces analyses) and the resource-based model. Environmental models isolate those firm attributes that exploit opportunities and/or neutralize threats. Thus, they specify what firm attributes may be considered as resources. The resource-based model then suggests what additional characteristics these resources must possess if they are to develop a sustained competitive advantage.

Is the resource or capability . . .	Implications
Valuable?	• Neutralize threats and exploit opportunities
Rare?	• Not many firms possess
Difficult to imitate?	• Physically unique
	• Path dependency (how accumulated over time)
	• Causal ambiguity (difficult to disentangle what it is or how it could be re-created)
	• Social complexity (trust, interpersonal relationships, culture, reputation)
Difficult to substitute?	• No equivalent strategic resources or capabilities

Is the Resource Rare? If competitors or potential competitors also possess the same valuable resource, it is not a source of a competitive advantage because all of these firms have the capability to exploit that resource in the same way. Common strategies based on such a resource would give no one firm an advantage. For a resource to provide competitive advantages, it must be uncommon, that is, rare relative to other competitors.

This argument can apply to bundles of valuable firm resources that are used to formulate and develop strategies. Some strategies require a mix of multiple types of resources—tangible assets, intangible assets, and organizational capabilities. If a particular bundle of firm resources is not rare, then relatively large numbers of firms will be able to conceive of and implement the strategies in question. Thus, such strategies will not be a source of competitive advantage, even if the resource in question is valuable.

Can the Resource Be Imitated Easily? Inimitability (difficulty in imitating) is a key to value creation because it constrains competition.[51] If a resource is inimitable, then any profits generated are more likely to be sustainable.[52] Having a resource that competitors can easily copy generates only temporary value.[53] This has important implications. Since managers often fail to apply this test, they tend to base long-term strategies on resources that are imitable. IBP (Iowa Beef Processors) became the first meatpacking company in the United States to modernize by building a set of assets (automated plants located in cattle producing states) and capabilities (low-cost "disassembly" of carcasses) that earned returns on assets of 1.3 percent in the 1970s. By the late 1980s, however, ConAgra and Cargill had imitated these resources, and IBP's profitability fell by nearly 70 percent, to 0.4 percent.

Monster.com entered the executive recruiting market by providing, in essence, a substitute for traditional bricks-and-mortar headhunting firms. Although Monster.com's resources are rare and valuable, they are subject to imitation by new rivals—other dot-com firms. Why? There are very low entry barriers for firms wanting to try their hand at recruitment. For example, many job search dot-coms have emerged in recent years, including jobsearch.com, headhunter.com, nationjob.com, and hotjobs.com. In all, there are more than 40,000 online job boards available to job seekers. It would be most difficult for a firm to attain a sustainable advantage in this industry.

Clearly, an advantage based on inimitability won't last forever. Competitors will eventually discover a way to copy most valuable resources. However, managers can forestall them and sustain profits for a while by developing strategies around resources that have at least one of the following four characteristics.[54]

Physical Uniqueness The first source of inimitability is physical uniqueness, which by definition is inherently difficult to copy. A beautiful resort location, mineral rights, or Pfizer's pharmaceutical patents simply cannot be imitated. Many managers believe that several of their resources may fall into this category, but on close inspection, few do.

path dependency
a characteristic of resources that is developed and/or accumulated through a unique series of events.

Path Dependency A greater number of resources cannot be imitated because of what economists refer to as **path dependency.** This simply means that resources are unique and therefore scarce because of all that has happened along the path followed in their development and/or accumulation. Competitors cannot go out and buy these resources quickly and easily; they must be built up over time in ways that are difficult to accelerate.

The Gerber Products Co. brand name for baby food is an example of a resource that is potentially inimitable. Re-creating Gerber's brand loyalty would be a time-consuming process that competitors could not expedite, even with expensive marketing campaigns. Similarly, the loyalty and trust that Southwest Airlines employees feel toward their firm and its cofounder, Herb Kelleher, are resources that have been built up over a long period of time. Also, a crash R&D program generally cannot replicate a successful technology when research findings cumulate. Clearly, these path-dependent conditions build protection for the original resource. The benefits from experience and learning through trial and error cannot be duplicated overnight.

causal ambiguity
a characteristic of a firm's resources that is costly to imitate because a competitor cannot determine what the resource is and/or how it can be re-created.

Causal Ambiguity The third source of inimitability is termed **causal ambiguity**. This means that would-be competitors may be thwarted because it is impossible to disentangle the causes (or possible explanations) of either what the valuable resource is or how it can be re-created. What is the root of 3M's innovation process? You can study it and draw up a list of possible factors. But it is a complex, unfolding (or folding) process that is hard to understand and would be hard to imitate.

Often, causally ambiguous resources are organizational capabilities, involving a complex web of social interactions that may even depend on particular individuals. When Continental and United tried to mimic the successful low-cost strategy of Southwest Airlines, the planes, routes, and fast gate turnarounds were not the most difficult aspects for them to copy. Those were all rather easy to observe and, at least in principle, easy to duplicate. However, they could not replicate Southwest's culture of fun, family, frugality, and focus since no one can clearly specify exactly what that culture is or how it came to be.

Strategy Spotlight 3.7 describes Amazon's continued success as the world's largest online marketplace. Competitors recently tried to imitate Amazon's free shipping strategy, but with limited success. The reason is that Amazon has developed an array of interrelated elements of strategy which their rivals find too difficult to imitate.

social complexity
a characteristic of a firm's resources that is costly to imitate because the social engineering required is beyond the capability of competitors, including interpersonal relations among managers, organizational culture, and reputation with suppliers and customers.

Social Complexity A firm's resources may be imperfectly inimitable because they reflect a high level of **social complexity**. Such phenomena are typically beyond the ability of firms to systematically manage or influence. When competitive advantages are based on social complexity, it is difficult for other firms to imitate them.

A wide variety of firm resources may be considered socially complex. Examples include interpersonal relations among the managers in a firm, its culture, and its reputation with its suppliers and customers. In many of these cases, it is easy to specify how these socially complex resources add value to a firm. Hence, there is little or no causal ambiguity surrounding the link between them and competitive advantage. But an understanding that certain firm attributes, such as quality relations among managers, can improve a firm's efficiency does not necessarily lead to systematic efforts to imitate them. Such social engineering efforts are beyond the capabilities of most firms.

Although complex physical technology is not included in this category of sources of imperfect inimitability, the exploitation of physical technology in a firm typically involves the use of socially complex resources. That is, several firms may possess the same physical technology, but only one of them may have the social relations, culture, group norms, and so on to fully exploit the technology in implementing its strategies. If such complex social resources are not subject to imitation (and assuming they are valuable and rare and no substitutes exist), this firm may obtain a sustained competitive advantage from exploiting its physical technology more effectively than other firms.

Amazon Prime: Very Difficult for Rivals to Copy

Amazon Prime is a free shipping service which guarantees delivery of products within two days for an annual fee of $79. According to *Bloomberg Businessweek,* it may be the most ingenious and effective customer loyalty program in all of e-commerce, if not retail in general. It converts casual shoppers, who gorge on the gratification of having purchases reliably appear two days after they order, into Amazon addicts. Analysts describe Prime as one of the main factors driving Amazon's stock price—up nearly 300 percent from 2008 to 2010. Also, it is one of the main reasons why Amazon's sales grew 30 percent during the recession while other retailers suffered.

Analysts estimate that Amazon Prime has more than 4 million members in the United States, a small slice of Amazon's 121 million active buyers worldwide. However, analysts claim that Prime members increase their purchases on the site by about 150 percent after they join and may be responsible for as much as 20 percent of Amazon's overall sales in the United States. Such shoppers are considered the "whales" of the $140 billion U.S. e-commerce market, one of the fastest growing parts of U.S. retail. And, according to Hudson Square Research, Amazon, with a hefty 8 percent of the U.S. e-commerce market, is the single biggest online retailer in the United States.

Source: Stone, B. 2010. What's in the box? Instant gratification. *Bloomberg Businessweek.* November 29–December 5: 39–40; Klein, E. 2010. The genius of Amazon Prime. *www.voices.washingtonpost.com.* November 29: np; and Fowler, G. A. 2010. Retailers team up against Amazon. *www.wsj.com.* October 6: np.

Prime was introduced in 2004. It was the result of a years-long search for the right loyalty program. An Amazon software engineer named Charlie Ward first suggested the idea of a free shipping service via a suggestion box feature on Amazon's internal website. Bing Gordon, an Amazon board member and venture capitalist, came up with the "Prime" name. Other executives, including Chief Executive Jeffrey Bezos, devised the two-day shipping offer—which exploited Amazon's ability to accelerate the handling of individual items in its distribution centers.

Amazon Prime has proven to be extremely hard for rivals to copy. Why? It enables Amazon to exploit its wide selection, low prices, network of third-party merchants, and finely tuned distribution system. All that while also keying off that faintly irrational human need to maximize the benefits of a club that you have already paid to join.

Now, several years after the program's creation, rivals—both online and off—have realized the increasing threat posed by Prime and are rushing to try to respond. For example, in October 2010, a consortium of more than 20 retailers, including Barnes & Noble, Sports Authority, and Toys 'R' Us, banded together to offer their own copycat $79, two-day shipping program, ShopRunner, which applies to products across their websites. However, as noted by Fiona Dias, the executive who administers the program, "As Amazon added more merchandising categories to Prime, retailers started feeling the pain. They have finally come to understand that Amazon is an existential threat and that Prime is the fuel of the engine.

Strategy Spotlight 3.8 describes how a Chinese beverage firm captured a significant market share in rural China by establishing close relationships with its distributors.

Are Substitutes Readily Available?   The fourth requirement for a firm resource to be a source of sustainable competitive advantage is that there must be no strategically equivalent valuable resources that are themselves not rare or inimitable. Two valuable firm resources (or two bundles of resources) are strategically equivalent when each one can be exploited separately to implement the same strategies.

Substitutability may take at least two forms. First, though it may be impossible for a firm to imitate exactly another firm's resource, it may be able to substitute a similar resource that enables it to develop and implement the same strategy. Clearly, a firm seeking to imitate another firm's high-quality top management team would be unable to copy the team exactly. However, it might be able to develop its own unique management team. Though these two teams would have different ages, functional backgrounds, experience, and so on, they could be strategically equivalent and thus substitutes for one another.

strategy spotlight

How a Chinese Beverage Company Succeeded by Creating Close Partnerships with Its Distributors

In 1998, when Hangzhou Wahaha Co. Ltd (Wahaha), the largest Chinese beverage producer, decided to take on Coca-Cola and PepsiCo, they began their attack in the rural areas of China. Why? They believed that they possessed a competitive advantage over the international giants because of the partnerships that they had built with the distributors across the more remote locations in China. ("Wa ha ha," which sounds like a child laughing, comes from a children's folk song.)

Four years prior to the launch of the "Wahaha Future Cola," the firm developed a policy for how to tie in "channel members" over the long term as a response to the increasing problem of accounts receivable and bad debt. This policy provided incentives for the channel members to pay an annual deposit in advance to cover any potential future bad debt and to operate according to Wahaha's payment policy.

Sounds OK, but what did the distributors get in return? They received an interest rate from Wahaha that was superior to the bank rate. In addition, further discounts were offered for early payment, and annual bonuses were

Source: Anonymous. 2010. Wahaha . . . China's leading beverage producer. *www.chinabevnews.com.* April 11: np; Andersen, M. M., Froholdt, M. & Poulfelt, F. 2010. *Return on Strategy.* New York: Routledge; and Miller, P. M. 2004. The Chinese beverage company's expansion is no laughing matter. *www.chinabuisnessreview.* September–October: np.

awarded to distributors that met the criterion for prompt payment.

Wahaha implemented this model over a two-year period. It effectively struck financial partnerships with existing distributors that led to higher commitment from distributors. This creative strategy became instrumental to Wahaha's success and their ability to deliver products to the rural areas of China. Here, logistics often create unique challenges.

Wahaha's distribution network now consists of about 4,000 first-tier domestic wholesalers and a large number of second- and third-tier wholesalers and outlets to ensure that Wahaha's products reach millions of retailers nationwide within one week of leaving the factory—no small feat with China's vast rural areas and provinces as far out as Xinjiang and Tibet. As CEO Zong Qinghou colorfully points out: "Our rapid and sound network serves as human blood vessels which circulate the bloodstream to every part of the body once the products are ready."

In contrast, domestic and multinational companies established their own distribution networks—not partnerships with local distributors as Wahaha had done. Not surprisingly, Wahaha has managed to capture impressive market share increases in markets traditionally dominated by Coca-Cola and PepsiCo. And its financial results have been stunning. From 2003 to 2009, its revenues have increased from $1.24 billion to $5.2 billion, and its profits have increased from $165 million to $1.5 billion. These figures represent annual compound rate increases of 27 and 45 percent, respectively!

Second, very different firm resources can become strategic substitutes. For example, Internet booksellers such as Amazon.com compete as substitutes for bricks-and-mortar booksellers such as B. Dalton. The result is that resources such as premier retail locations become less valuable. In a similar vein, several pharmaceutical firms have seen the value of patent protection erode in the face of new drugs that are based on different production processes and act in different ways, but can be used in similar treatment regimes. The coming years will likely see even more radical change in the pharmaceutical industry as the substitution of genetic therapies eliminates certain uses of chemotherapy.[55]

To recap this section, recall that resources and capabilities must be rare and valuable as well as difficult to imitate or substitute in order for a firm to attain competitive advantages that are sustainable over time.[56] Exhibit 3.7 illustrates the relationship among the four criteria of sustainability and shows the competitive implications.

In firms represented by the first row of Exhibit 3.7, managers are in a difficult situation. When their resources and capabilities do not meet any of the four criteria, it would be difficult to develop any type of competitive advantage, in the short or long term. The

100 Part 1:: Strategic Analysis

Is a resource or capability ...				
Valuable?	Rare?	Difficult to Imitate?	Without Substitutes?	Implications for Competitiveness?
No	No	No	No	Competitive disadvantage
Yes	No	No	No	Competitive parity
Yes	Yes	No	No	Temporary competitive advantage
Yes	Yes	Yes	Yes	Sustainable competitive advantage

Source: Adapted from Barney, J. B. 1991. Firm Resources and Sustained Competitive Advantage. *Journal of Management*, 17: 99–120.

resources and capabilities they possess enable the firm neither to exploit environmental opportunities nor neutralize environmental threats. In the second and third rows, firms have resources and capabilities that are valuable as well as rare, respectively. However, in both cases the resources and capabilities are not difficult for competitors to imitate or substitute. Here, the firms could attain some level of competitive parity. They could perform on par with equally endowed rivals or attain a temporary competitive advantage. But their advantages would be easy for competitors to match. It is only in the fourth row, where all four criteria are satisfied, that competitive advantages can be sustained over time. Next, let's look at Dell and see how its competitive advantage, which seemed to be sustainable for a rather long period of time, has eroded.

Dell's Eroding (Sustainable?) Competitive Advantage   In 1984, Michael Dell started Dell Inc. in a University of Texas dorm room with an investment of $1,000.[57] By 2006, Dell had attained annual revenues of $56 billion and a net income of $3.6 billion—making Michael Dell one of the richest people in the world. Dell achieved this meteoric growth by differentiating itself through the direct sales approach that it pioneered. Its user-configurable products met the diverse needs of its corporate and institutional customer base. Exhibit 3.8 summarizes how Dell achieved its remarkable success by integrating its tangible resources, intangible resources, and organizational capabilities.

Dell continued to maintain this competitive advantage by strengthening its value-chain activities and interrelationships that are critical to satisfying the largest market opportunities. It achieved this by (1) implementing e-commerce direct sales and support processes that accounted for the sophisticated buying habits of the largest markets and (2) matching its inventory management to its extensive supplier network. Dell also sustained these advantages by investing in intangible resources, such as proprietary assembly methods and packaging configurations, that helped to protect against the threat of imitation.

Dell recognized that the PC is a complex product with components sourced from several different technologies and manufacturers. Thus, in working backward from the customer's purchasing habits, Dell saw that the company could build valuable solutions by organizing its resources and capabilities around build-to-specification tastes, making both the sales and integration processes flexible, and passing on overhead expenses to its suppliers. Even as the PC industry became further commoditized, Dell was one of the few competitors that was able to retain solid margins. It accomplished this by adapting its manufacturing and assembly capabilities to match the PC market's trend toward user compatibility.

For many years, it looked as if Dell's competitive advantage over its rivals would be sustainable for a very long period of time. However, by early 2007, Dell began falling

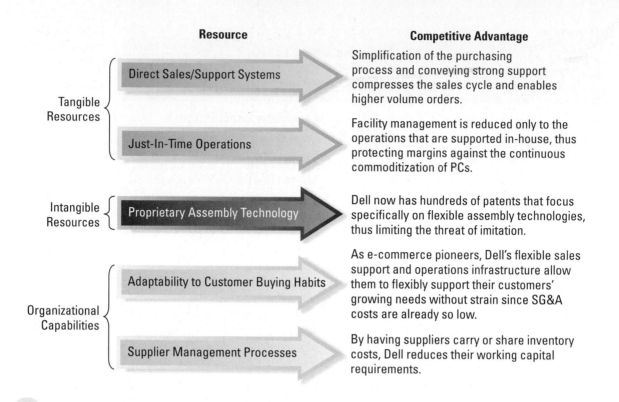

Resource		Competitive Advantage
Tangible Resources	Direct Sales/Support Systems	Simplification of the purchasing process and conveying strong support compresses the sales cycle and enables higher volume orders.
	Just-In-Time Operations	Facility management is reduced only to the operations that are supported in-house, thus protecting margins against the continuous commoditization of PCs.
Intangible Resources	Proprietary Assembly Technology	Dell now has hundreds of patents that focus specifically on flexible assembly technologies, thus limiting the threat of imitation.
Organizational Capabilities	Adaptability to Customer Buying Habits	As e-commerce pioneers, Dell's flexible sales support and operations infrastructure allow them to flexibly support their customers' growing needs without strain since SG&A costs are already so low.
	Supplier Management Processes	By having suppliers carry or share inventory costs, Dell reduces their working capital requirements.

Exhibit 3.8 Dell's Tangible Resources, Intangible Resources, and Organizational Capabilities

behind its rivals in market share. This led to a significant decline in its stock price—followed by a complete shake-up of the top management team. But what led to Dell's competitive decline in the first place?[58]

- Dell had become so focused on cost that it failed to pay attention to the design of the brand. Customers increasingly began to see the product as a commodity.
- Much of the growth in the PC industry today is in laptops. Customers demand a sleeker, better-designed machine instead of just the cheapest laptop. Also, they often want to see the laptop before they buy it.
- When Dell outsourced its customer service function to foreign locations, it led to a decline in customer support. This eroded Dell's brand value.
- Dell's efforts to replicate its made-to-order, no middleman strategy to other products such as printers and storage devices proved to be a failure. This is because customers saw little need for customization of these products.
- Rivals such as HP have been improving their product design and reducing their costs.[59] Thus, they now have cost parity with Dell, while enjoying a better brand image and the support of an extensive dealer network.

Not surprisingly, Dell's performance has suffered. Between 2006 and 2010, its revenues and net income have slumped from $56 billion to $53 billion and $3.6 billion and $1.4 billion, respectively. Inder Sidhu, the author of *Doing Both* (2010), provides a succinct summary of the central lesson in the Dell story:[60]

> Dell illustrates what can happen when a company emphasizes optimization to the exclusion of reinvention. Dell's obsession with operational excellence prevented it from delivering innovations that the market wanted, costing it a great deal of goodwill and prestige. When *Fortune* announced its annual list of "Most Admired Companies" in 2009, Dell, the leader from just four years prior, wasn't even mentioned in the top 50.

The Generation and Distribution of a Firm's Profits: Extending the Resource-Based View of the Firm

The resource-based view of the firm has been useful in determining when firms will create competitive advantages and enjoy high levels of profitability. However, it has not been developed to address how a firm's profits (often referred to as "rents" by economists) will be distributed to a firm's management and employees or other stakeholders such as customers, suppliers, or governments.[61] This becomes an important issue because firms may be successful in creating competitive advantages that can be sustainable for a period of time. However, much of the profits can be retained (or "appropriated") by its employees and managers or other stakeholders instead of flowing to the owners of the firm (i.e., the stockholders).*

Consider Viewpoint DataLabs International, a Salt Lake City–based company that makes sophisticated three-dimensional models and textures for film production houses, video games, and car manufacturers. This example will help to show how employees are often able to obtain (or "appropriate") a high proportion of a firm's profits:

> Walter Noot, head of production, was having trouble keeping his highly skilled Generation X employees happy with their compensation. Each time one of them was lured away for more money, everyone would want a raise. "We were having to give out raises every six months—30 to 40 percent—then six months later they'd expect the same. It was a big struggle to keep people happy."[62]

At Viewpoint DataLabs, much of the profits are being generated by the highly skilled professionals working together. They are able to exercise their power by successfully demanding more financial compensation. In part, management has responded favorably because they are united in their demands, and their work involves a certain amount of social complexity and causal ambiguity—given the complex, coordinated efforts that their work entails.

Four factors help explain the extent to which employees and managers will be able to obtain a proportionately high level of the profits that they generate:[63]

- **Employee Bargaining Power.** If employees are vital to forming a firm's unique capability, they will earn disproportionately high wages. For example, marketing professionals may have access to valuable information that helps them to understand the intricacies of customer demands and expectations, or engineers may understand unique technical aspects of the products or services. Additionally, in some industries such as consulting, advertising, and tax preparation, clients tend to be very loyal to individual professionals employed by the firm, instead of to the firm itself. This enables them to "take the clients with them" if they leave. This enhances their bargaining power.

- **Employee Replacement Cost.** If employees' skills are idiosyncratic and rare (a source of resource-based advantages), they should have high bargaining power based on the high cost required by the firm to replace them. For example, Raymond Ozzie, the software designer who was critical in the development of Lotus Notes, was able to dictate the terms under which IBM acquired Lotus.

- **Employee Exit Costs.** This factor may tend to reduce an employee's bargaining power. An individual may face high personal costs when leaving the organization. Thus, that individual's threat of leaving may not be credible. In addition, an employee's expertise may be firm-specific and of limited value to other firms. Causal ambiguity may make it difficult for the employee to explain his or her specific contribution to a given project. Thus, a rival firm might be less likely to pay a high wage premium since it would be unsure of the employee's unique contribution.

---

* Economists define rents as profits (or prices) in excess of what is required to provide a normal return.

- *Manager Bargaining Power.* Managers' power is based on how well they create resource-based advantages. They are generally charged with creating value through the process of organizing, coordinating, and leveraging employees as well as other forms of capital such as plant, equipment, and financial capital (addressed further in Chapter 4). Such activities provide managers with sources of information that may not be readily available to others. Thus, although managers may not know as much about the specific nature of customers and technologies, they are in a position to have a more thorough, integrated understanding of the total operation.

Chapter 9 addresses the conditions under which top-level managers (such as CEOs) of large corporations have been, at times, able to obtain levels of total compensation that would appear to be significantly disproportionate to their contributions to wealth generation as well as to top executives in peer organizations. Here, corporate governance becomes a critical control mechanism. For example, William Esrey and Ronald T. LeMay (the former two top executives at Sprint Corporation) earned more than $130 million in stock options because of "cozy" relationships with members of their board of directors, who tended to approve with little debate huge compensation packages.[64]

Such diversion of profits from the owners of the business to top management is far less likely when the board members are truly independent outsiders (i.e., they do not have close ties to management). In general, given the external market for top talent, the level of compensation that executives receive is based on factors similar to the ones just discussed that determine the level of their bargaining power.[65]

In addition to employees and managers, other stakeholder groups can also appropriate a portion of the rents generated by a firm. If, for example, a critical input is controlled by a monopoly supplier or if a single buyer accounts for most of a firm's sales, their bargaining power can greatly erode the potential profits of a firm. Similarly, excessive taxation by governments can also reduce what is available to a firm's stockholders.

Evaluating Firm Performance: Two Approaches

This section addresses two approaches to use when evaluating a firm's performance. The first is financial ratio analysis, which, generally speaking, identifies how a firm is performing according to its balance sheet, income statement, and market valuation. As we will discuss, when performing a financial ratio analysis, you must take into account the firm's performance from a historical perspective (not just at one point in time) as well as how it compares with both industry norms and key competitors.[66]

The second perspective takes a broader stakeholder view. Firms must satisfy a broad range of stakeholders, including employees, customers, and owners, to ensure their long-term viability. Central to our discussion will be a well-known approach—the balanced scorecard—that has been popularized by Robert Kaplan and David Norton.[67]

financial ratio analysis a technique for measuring the performance of a firm according to its balance sheet, income statement, and market valuation.

Financial Ratio Analysis

The beginning point in analyzing the financial position of a firm is to compute and analyze five different types of financial ratios:

- Short-term solvency or liquidity
- Long-term solvency measures
- Asset management (or turnover)
- Profitability
- Market value

Exhibit 3.9 summarizes each of these five ratios.

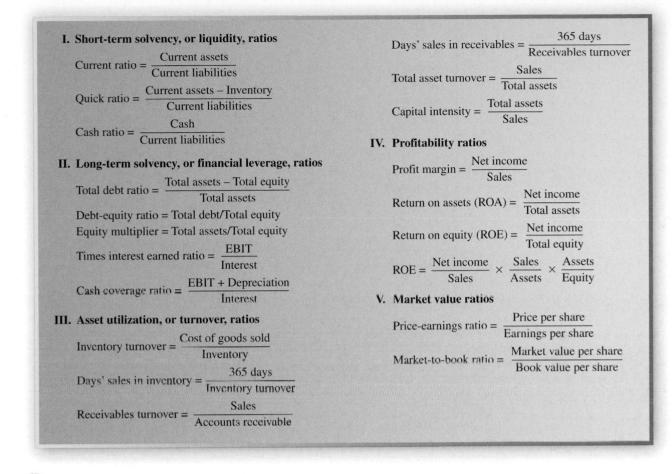

I. Short-term solvency, or liquidity, ratios

$$\text{Current ratio} = \frac{\text{Current assets}}{\text{Current liabilities}}$$

$$\text{Quick ratio} = \frac{\text{Current assets} - \text{Inventory}}{\text{Current liabilities}}$$

$$\text{Cash ratio} = \frac{\text{Cash}}{\text{Current liabilities}}$$

II. Long-term solvency, or financial leverage, ratios

$$\text{Total debt ratio} = \frac{\text{Total assets} - \text{Total equity}}{\text{Total assets}}$$

$$\text{Debt-equity ratio} = \text{Total debt/Total equity}$$

$$\text{Equity multiplier} = \text{Total assets/Total equity}$$

$$\text{Times interest earned ratio} = \frac{\text{EBIT}}{\text{Interest}}$$

$$\text{Cash coverage ratio} = \frac{\text{EBIT} + \text{Depreciation}}{\text{Interest}}$$

III. Asset utilization, or turnover, ratios

$$\text{Inventory turnover} = \frac{\text{Cost of goods sold}}{\text{Inventory}}$$

$$\text{Days' sales in inventory} = \frac{365 \text{ days}}{\text{Inventory turnover}}$$

$$\text{Receivables turnover} = \frac{\text{Sales}}{\text{Accounts receivable}}$$

$$\text{Days' sales in receivables} = \frac{365 \text{ days}}{\text{Receivables turnover}}$$

$$\text{Total asset turnover} = \frac{\text{Sales}}{\text{Total assets}}$$

$$\text{Capital intensity} = \frac{\text{Total assets}}{\text{Sales}}$$

IV. Profitability ratios

$$\text{Profit margin} = \frac{\text{Net income}}{\text{Sales}}$$

$$\text{Return on assets (ROA)} = \frac{\text{Net income}}{\text{Total assets}}$$

$$\text{Return on equity (ROE)} = \frac{\text{Net income}}{\text{Total equity}}$$

$$\text{ROE} = \frac{\text{Net income}}{\text{Sales}} \times \frac{\text{Sales}}{\text{Assets}} \times \frac{\text{Assets}}{\text{Equity}}$$

V. Market value ratios

$$\text{Price-earnings ratio} = \frac{\text{Price per share}}{\text{Earnings per share}}$$

$$\text{Market-to-book ratio} = \frac{\text{Market value per share}}{\text{Book value per share}}$$

Exhibit 3.9 A Summary of Five Types of Financial Ratios

Appendix 1 to Chapter 13 (the Case Analysis chapter) provides detailed definitions for and discussions of each of these types of ratios as well as examples of how each is calculated. Refer to pages 491 to 500.

A meaningful ratio analysis must go beyond the calculation and interpretation of financial ratios.[68] It must include how ratios change over time as well as how they are interrelated. For example, a firm that takes on too much long-term debt to finance operations will see an immediate impact on its indicators of long term financial leverage. The additional debt will negatively affect the firm's short-term liquidity ratio (i.e., current and quick ratios) since the firm must pay interest and principal on the additional debt each year until it is retired. Additionally, the interest expenses deducted from revenues reduce the firm's profitability.

A firm's financial position should not be analyzed in isolation. Important reference points are needed. We will address some issues that must be taken into account to make financial analysis more meaningful: historical comparisons, comparisons with industry norms, and comparisons with key competitors.

Historical Comparisons When you evaluate a firm's financial performance, it is very useful to compare its financial position over time. This provides a means of evaluating trends. For example, Apple Inc. reported revenues of $65 billion and net income of $14 billion in 2010. Virtually all firms would be very happy with such financial success. These

>LO3.6

The usefulness of financial ratio analysis, its inherent limitations, and how to make meaningful comparisons of performance across firms.

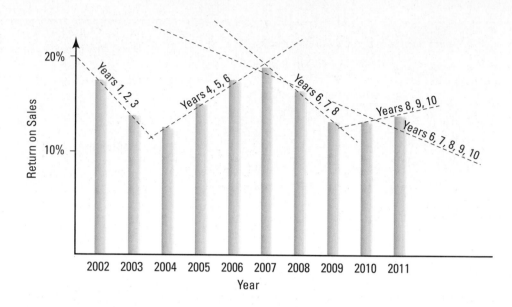

figures represent a stunning annual growth in revenue and net income of 100 percent and 190 percent, respectively, for the 2008 to 2010 time period. Had Apple's revenues and net income in 2010 been $40 billion and $6 billion, respectively, it would still be a very large and highly profitable enterprise. However, such performance would have significantly damaged Apple's market valuation and reputation as well as the careers of many of its executives.

Exhibit 3.10 illustrates a 10-year period of return on sales (ROS) for a hypothetical company. As indicated by the dotted trend lines, the rate of growth (or decline) differs substantially over time periods.

Comparison with Industry Norms When you are evaluating a firm's financial performance, remember also to compare it with industry norms. A firm's current ratio or profitability may appear impressive at first glance. However, it may pale when compared with industry standards or norms.

Comparing your firm with all other firms in your industry assesses relative performance. Banks often use such comparisons when evaluating a firm's creditworthiness. Exhibit 3.11 includes a variety of financial ratios for three industries: semiconductors, grocery stores, and skilled-nursing facilities. Why is there such variation among the financial ratios for these three industries? There are several reasons. With regard to the collection period, grocery stores operate mostly on a cash basis, hence a very short collection period. Semiconductor manufacturers sell their output to other manufacturers (e.g., computer makers) on terms such as 2/15 net 45, which means they give a 2 percent discount on bills paid within 15 days and start charging interest after 45 days. Skilled-nursing facilities also have a longer collection period than grocery stores because they typically rely on payments from insurance companies.

The industry norms for return on sales also highlight differences among these industries. Grocers, with very slim margins, have a lower return on sales than either skilled-nursing facilities or semiconductor manufacturers. But how might we explain the differences between skilled-nursing facilities and semiconductor manufacturers? Health care facilities, in general, are limited in their pricing structures by Medicare/Medicaid regulations and by insurance reimbursement limits, but semiconductor producers have pricing structures determined by the market. If their products have superior performance, semiconductor manufacturers can charge premium prices.

Exhibit 3.11
How Financial Ratios
Differ across Industries

Financial Ratio	Semiconductors	Grocery Stores	Skilled-Nursing Facilities
Quick ratio (times)	1.9	0.6	1.2
Current ratio (times)	3.9	1.9	1.6
Total liabilities to net worth (%)	30.2	71.4	156.9
Collection period (days)	49.0	2.6	30.3
Assets to sales (%)	147.3	19.5	113.9
Return on sales (%)	24	1.1	2.4

Source: Dun & Bradstreet. *Industry Norms and Key Business Ratios, 2007–2008.* One Year Edition, SIC #3600–3699 (Semiconductors); SIC #5400–5499 (Grocery Stores); SIC #8000–8099 (Skilled-Nursing Facilities). New York: Dun & Bradstreet Credit Services.

Comparison with Key Competitors   Recall from Chapter 2 that firms with similar strategies are members of a strategic group in an industry. Furthermore, competition is more intense among competitors within groups than across groups. Thus, you can gain valuable insights into a firm's financial and competitive position if you make comparisons between a firm and its most direct rivals. Consider a firm trying to diversify into the highly profitable pharmaceutical industry. Even if it was willing to invest several hundred million dollars, it would be virtually impossible to compete effectively against industry giants such as Pfizer and Merck. These two firms have 2010 revenues of $68 billion and $46 billion, respectively, and R&D budgets of $9 billion and $11 billion, respectively.[69]

Integrating Financial Analysis and Stakeholder Perspectives: The Balanced Scorecard

It is useful to see how a firm is performing over time in terms of several ratios. However, such traditional approaches to performance assessments can be a double-edged sword.[70] Many important transactions that managers make—investments in research and development, employee training and development, and, advertising and promotion of key brands—may greatly expand a firm's market potential and create significant long-term shareholder value. But such critical investments are not reflected positively in short-term financial reports. Financial reports typically measure expenses, not the value created. Thus, managers may be penalized for spending money in the short term to improve their firm's long-term competitive viability!

Now consider the other side of the coin. A manager may destroy the firm's future value by dissatisfying customers, depleting the firm's stock of good products coming out of R&D, or damaging the morale of valued employees. Such budget cuts, however, may lead to very good short-term financials. The manager may look good in the short run and even receive credit for improving the firm's performance. In essence, such a manager has mastered "denominator management," whereby decreasing investments makes the return on investment (ROI) ratio larger, even though the actual return remains constant or shrinks.

The Balanced Scorecard: Description and Benefits   To provide a meaningful integration of the many issues that come into evaluating a firm's performance, Kaplan and Norton developed a **"balanced scorecard."**[71] This provides top managers with a fast but comprehensive view of the business. In a nutshell, it includes financial measures that reflect the results of actions already taken, but it complements these indicators with measures of customer satisfaction, internal processes, and the organization's innovation and improvement activities—operational measures that drive future financial performance.

>LO3.7
The value of the "balanced scorecard" in recognizing how the interests of a variety of stakeholders can be interrelated.

balanced scorecard
a method of evaluating a firm's performance using performance measures from the customers', internal, innovation and learning, and financial perspectives.

Exhibit 3.12
The Balanced
Scorecard's Four
Perspectives

- How do customers see us? (customer perspective)
- What must we excel at? (internal business perspective)
- Can we continue to improve and create value? (innovation and learning perspective)
- How do we look to shareholders? (financial perspective)

customer perspective measures of firm performance that indicate how well firms are satisfying customers' expectations.

internal business perspective measures of firm performance that indicate how well firms' internal processes, decisions and actions are contributing to customer satisfaction.

innovation and learning perspective measures of firm performance that indicate how well firms are changing their product and service offerings to adapt to changes in the internal and external environments.

financial perspective measures of firms' financial performance that indicate how well strategy, implementation and execution are contributing bottom-line improvement.

The balanced scorecard enables managers to consider their business from four key perspectives: customer, internal, innovation and learning, and financial. These are briefly described in Exhibit 3.12.

Customer Perspective Clearly, how a company is performing from its customers' perspective is a top priority for management. The balanced scorecard requires that managers translate their general mission statements on customer service into specific measures that reflect the factors that really matter to customers. For the balanced scorecard to work, managers must articulate goals for four key categories of customer concerns: time, quality, performance and service, and cost. For example, lead time may be measured as the time from the company's receipt of an order to the time it actually delivers the product or service to the customer.

Internal Business Perspective Customer-based measures are important. However, they must be translated into indicators of what the firm must do internally to meet customers' expectations. Excellent customer performance results from processes, decisions, and actions that occur throughout organizations in a coordinated fashion, and managers must focus on those critical internal operations that enable them to satisfy customer needs. The internal measures should reflect business processes that have the greatest impact on customer satisfaction. These include factors that affect cycle time, quality, employee skills, and productivity. Firms also must identify and measure the key resources and capabilities they need for continued success.

Innovation and Learning Perspective Given the rapid rate of markets, technologies, and global competition, the criteria for success are constantly changing. To survive and prosper, managers must make frequent changes to existing products and services as well as introduce entirely new products with expanded capabilities. A firm's ability to improve, innovate, and learn is tied directly to its value. Simply put, only by developing new products and services, creating greater value for customers, and increasing operating efficiencies can a company penetrate new markets, increase revenues and margins, and enhance shareholder value. A firm's ability to do well from an innovation and learning perspective is more dependent on its intangible than tangible assets. Three categories of intangible assets are critically important: human capital (skills, talent, and knowledge), information capital (information systems, networks), and organization capital (culture, leadership).

Financial Perspective Measures of financial performance indicate whether the company's strategy, implementation, and execution are indeed contributing to bottom-line improvement. Typical financial goals include profitability, growth, and shareholder value. Periodic financial statements remind managers that improved quality, response time, productivity, and innovative products benefit the firm only when they result in improved sales, increased market share, reduced operating expenses, or higher asset turnover.[72]

Consider how Sears, the huge retailer, found a strong causal relationship between employee attitudes, customer attitudes, and financial outcomes.[73] Through an ongoing study, Sears developed (and continues to refine) what it calls its total performance indicators, or

TPI—a set of indicators for assessing their performance with customers, employees, and investors. Sears's quantitative model has shown that a 5.0 percent improvement in employee attitudes leads to a 1.3 percent improvement in customer satisfaction, which in turn drives a 0.5 percent improvement in revenue. Thus, if a single store improved its employee attitude by 5.0 percent, Sears could predict with confidence that if the revenue growth in the district as a whole were 5.0 percent, the revenue growth in this particular store would be 5.5 percent. Interestingly, Sears's managers consider such numbers as rigorous as any others that they work with every year. The company's accounting firm audits management as closely as it audits the financial statements.

A key implication is that managers do not need to look at their job as balancing stakeholder demands. They must avoid the following mind-set: "How many units in employee satisfaction do I have to give up to get some additional units of customer satisfaction or profits?" Instead, the balanced scorecard provides a win–win approach—increasing satisfaction among a wide variety of organizational stakeholders, including employees (at all levels), customers, and stockholders.

Limitations and Potential Downsides of the Balanced Scorecard   There is general agreement that there is nothing inherently wrong with the concept of the balanced scorecard.[74] The key limitation is that some executives may view it as a "quick fix" that can be easily installed. However, implementing a balanced metrics system is an evolutionary process. It is not a one-time task that can be quickly checked off as "completed." If managers do not recognize this from the beginning and fail to commit to it long term, the organization will be disappointed. Poor execution becomes the cause of such performance outcomes. And organizational scorecards must be aligned with individuals' scorecards to turn the balanced scorecards into a powerful tool for sustained performance.[*]

In a recent study of 50 Canadian medium-size and large organizations, the number of users expressing skepticism about scorecard performance was much greater than the number claiming positive results. However, the overwhelming perspective was that balanced scorecards can be worthwhile in clarifying an organization's strategy, and if this can be accomplished, better results will follow. A few companies stated categorically that scorecards have improved their firm's financial results. For example, one respondent claimed that "We did not meet our financial goals previously, but since implementing our balanced scorecard, we have now met our goals three years running."

On the other hand, a greater number of respondents agreed with the statement "Balanced scorecards don't really work." Some representative comments included: "It became just a number-crunching exercise by accountants after the first year," "It is just the latest management fad and is already dropping lower on management's list of priorities as all fads eventually do," and "If scorecards are supposed to be a measurement tool, why is it so hard to measure their results?" There is much work to do before scorecards can become a viable framework to measure sustained strategic performance.

Problems often occur in the balanced scorecard implementation efforts when there is an insufficient commitment to learning and the inclusion of employees' personal ambitions. Without a set of rules for employees that address continuous process improvement and the personal improvement of individual employees, there will be limited employee buy-in and insufficient cultural change. Thus, many improvements may be temporary and superficial. Often, scorecards that failed to attain alignment and improvements dissipated

---

[*] Building on the concepts that are the foundation of the balanced scorecard approach, Kaplan and Norton have recently developed a useful tool called the strategy map. Strategy maps show the cause and effect links by which specific improvements in different areas lead to a desired outcome. Strategy maps also help employees see how their jobs are related to the overall objectives of the organization. They also help us understand how an organization can convert its assets—both tangible and intangible—into tangible outcomes. Refer to Kaplan, R. S. & Norton, D. P. 2000. Having Trouble with Your Strategy? Then Map It. *Harvard Business Review,* 78(10): 167–176.

Exhibit 3.13
Potential Limitations of
the Balanced Scorecard

Most agree that the balanced scorecard concept is a useful and an appropriate management tool. However, there are many design and implementation issues that may short circuit its value, including the following:

- **Lack of a Clear Strategy.** A scorecard can be developed without the aid of a strategy. However, it then becomes a key performance indicator or stakeholder system, lacking in many of the attributes offered from a true balanced scorecard.

- **Limited or Ineffective Executive Sponsorship.** Although training and education are important, without tenacious leadership and support of a scorecard project, the effort is most likely doomed.

- **Too Much Emphasis on Financial Measures Rather than Nonfinancial Measures.** This leads to measures that do not connect to the drivers of the business and are not relevant to performance improvement.

- **Poor Data on Actual Performance.** This can negate most of the effort invested in defining performance measures because a company can't monitor actual changes in results from changes in behavior.

- **Inappropriate Links of Scorecard Measures to Compensation.** Although this can focus managerial and employee attention, exercising it too soon can produce many unintended side effects such as dysfunctional decision making by managers looking to cash in.

- **Inconsistent or Inappropriate Terminology.** Everyone must speak the same language if measurement is to be used to guide change within an organization. Translating strategy into measures becomes even more difficult if everyone cannot agree on (or understand) the same language and terminology.

Sources: Angel, R. & Rampersad, H. 2005. Do Scorecards Add Up? *Camagazine.com.* May: np; and Niven, P. 2002. *Balanced Scorecard Step by Step: Maximizing Performance and Maintaining Results.* New York: John Wiley & Sons.

very quickly. And, in many cases, management's efforts to improve performance were seen as divisive and were viewed by employees as aimed at benefiting senior management compensation. This fostered a "what's in it for me?" attitude. Exhibit 3.13 summarizes some of the potential downsides of the balanced scorecard.

Reflecting on Career Implications . . .

- *The Value Chain:* Carefully analyze where you can add value in your firm's value chain. How might your firm's support activities (e.g., information technology, human resource practices) help you accomplish your assigned tasks more effectively?
- *The Value Chain:* Consider important relationships among activities both within your firm as well as between your firm and its suppliers, customers, and alliance partners.
- *Resource-Based View of the Firm:* Are your skills and talents rare, valuable, difficult to imitate, and have few substitutes? If so, you are in a better position to add value for your firm—and earn rewards and incentives. How can your skills and talents be enhanced to help satisfy these criteria to a greater extent? More training? Change positions within the firm? Consider career options at other organizations?
- *Balanced Scorecard:* In your decision making, strive to "balance" the four perspectives: customer, internal business, innovation and learning, and financial. Do not focus too much on short-term profits. Do your personal career goals provide opportunities to develop your skills in all four directions?

Summary

In the traditional approaches to assessing a firm's internal environment, the primary goal of managers would be to determine their firm's relative strengths and weaknesses. Such is the role of SWOT analysis, wherein managers analyze their firm's strengths and weaknesses as well as the opportunities and threats in the external environment. In this chapter, we discussed why this may be a good starting point but hardly the best approach to take in performing a sound analysis. There are many limitations to SWOT analysis, including its static perspective, its potential to overemphasize a single dimension of a firm's strategy, and the likelihood that a firm's strengths do not necessarily help the firm create value or competitive advantages.

We identified two frameworks that serve to complement SWOT analysis in assessing a firm's internal environment: value-chain analysis and the resource-based view of the firm. In conducting a value-chain analysis, first divide the firm into a series of value-creating activities. These include primary activities such as inbound logistics, operations, and service as well as support activities such as procurement and human resources management. Then analyze how each activity adds value as well as how *interrelationships* among value activities in the firm and among the firm and its customers and suppliers add value. Thus, instead of merely determining a firm's strengths and weaknesses per se, you analyze them in the overall context of the firm and its relationships with customers and suppliers—the value system.

The resource-based view of the firm considers the firm as a bundle of resources: tangible resources, intangible resources, and organizational capabilities. Competitive advantages that are sustainable over time generally arise from the creation of bundles of resources and capabilities. For advantages to be sustainable, four criteria must be satisfied: value, rarity, difficulty in imitation, and difficulty in substitution. Such an evaluation requires a sound knowledge of the competitive context in which the firm exists. The owners of a business may not capture all of the value created by the firm. The appropriation of value created by a firm between the owners and employees is determined by four factors: employee bargaining power, replacement cost, employee exit costs, and manager bargaining power.

An internal analysis of the firm would not be complete unless you evaluate its performance and make the appropriate comparisons. Determining a firm's performance requires an analysis of its financial situation as well as a review of how well it is satisfying a broad range of stakeholders, including customers, employees, and stockholders. We discussed the concept of the balanced scorecard, in which four perspectives must be addressed: customer, internal business, innovation and learning, and financial. Central to this concept is the idea that the interests of various stakeholders can be interrelated. We provide examples of how indicators of employee satisfaction lead to higher levels of customer satisfaction, which in turn lead to higher levels of financial performance. Thus, improving a firm's performance does not need to involve making trade-offs among different stakeholders. Assessing the firm's performance is also more useful if it is evaluated in terms of how it changes over time, compares with industry norms, and compares with key competitors.

In the Appendix to Chapter 3, we discuss how Internet and digital technologies have created new opportunities for firms to add value. Four value-adding activities that have been enhanced by Internet capabilities are search, evaluation, problem solving, and transaction. These four activities are supported by three different types of content that Internet businesses often use—customer feedback, expertise, and entertainment programming. Seven business models have been identified that are proving successful for use by Internet firms. These include commission, advertising, markup, production, referral, subscription, and fee-for-service–based models. Firms also are finding that combinations of these business models can contribute to greater success.

Summary Review Questions

1. SWOT analysis is a technique to analyze the internal and external environment of a firm. What are its advantages and disadvantages?
2. Briefly describe the primary and support activities in a firm's value chain.
3. How can managers create value by establishing important relationships among the value-chain activities both within their firm and between the firm and its customers and suppliers?
4. Briefly explain the four criteria for sustainability of competitive advantages.
5. Under what conditions are employees and managers able to appropriate some of the value created by their firm?
6. What are the advantages and disadvantages of conducting a financial ratio analysis of a firm?
7. Summarize the concept of the balanced scorecard. What are its main advantages?

Key Terms

value-chain analysis, 81
primary activities, 81
support activities, 81
inbound logistics, 83
operations, 84
outbound logistics, 84
marketing and sales, 85
service, 86
procurement, 86
technology
  development, 88
human resource
  management, 88
general
  administration, 89
interrelationships, 90
resource-based view of the
  firm, 93

tangible resources, 93
intangible resources, 95
organizational
  capabilities, 95
strategic resources
  (also firm resources
  or organizational
  resources), 95
path dependency, 98
causal ambiguity, 98
social complexity, 98
financial ratio
  analysis, 104
balanced scorecard, 107
customer
  perspective, 108
internal perspective, 108
innovation and learning

perspective, 108
financial
  perspective, 108
search activities, 117
evaluation activities, 117

problem-solving
  activities, 117
transaction
  activities, 118
business model, 119

Experiential Exercise

Dell Computer is a leading firm in the personal computer industry, with annual revenues of $53 billion during its 2010 fiscal year. Dell had created a very strong competitive position via its "direct model," whereby it manufactures its personal computers to detailed customer specifications. However, its advantage has been eroded recently by strong rivals such as HP.

Below we address several questions that focus on Dell's value-chain activities and interrelationships among them as well as whether they are able to attain sustainable competitive advantage(s). (We discuss Dell in this chapter on pages 101–102.)

1. Where in Dell's value chain are they creating value for their customer?

Value-Chain Activity	Yes/No	How Does Dell Create Value for the Customer?
Primary:		
Inbound logistics		
Operations		
Outbound logistics		
Marketing and sales		
Service		
Support:		
Procurement		
Technology development		
Human resource management		
General administration		

2. What are the important relationships among Dell's value-chain activities? What are the important interdependencies? For each activity, identify the relationships and interdependencies.

	Inbound logistics	Operations	Outbound logistics	Marketing and sales	Service	Procurement	Technology development	Human resource management	General administration
Inbound logistics									
Operations									
Outbound logistics									
Marketing and sales									
Service									
Procurement									
Technology development									
Human resource management									
General administration									

3. What resources, activities, and relationships enable Dell to achieve a sustainable competitive advantage?

Resource/Activity	Is It Valuable?	Is It Rare?	Are There Few Substitutes?	Is It Difficult to Make?
Inbound logistics				
Operations				
Outbound logistics				
Marketing and sales				
Service				
Procurement				
Technology development				
Human resource management				
General administration				

Application Questions & Exercises

1. Using published reports, select two CEOs who have recently made public statements regarding a major change in their firm's strategy. Discuss how the successful implementation of such strategies requires changes in the firm's primary and support activities.

2. Select a firm that competes in an industry in which you are interested. Drawing upon published financial reports, complete a financial ratio analysis. Based on changes over time and a comparison with industry norms, evaluate the firm's strengths and weaknesses in terms of its financial position.

3. How might exemplary human resource practices enhance and strengthen a firm's value-chain activities?

4. Using the Internet, look up your university or college. What are some of its key value-creating activities that provide competitive advantages? Why?

Ethics Questions

1. What are some of the ethical issues that arise when a firm becomes overly zealous in advertising its products?

2. What are some of the ethical issues that may arise from a firm's procurement activities? Are you aware of any of these issues from your personal experience or businesses you are familiar with?

References

1. Anonymous. 2010. 'There's no brakes . . . hold on and pray': Last words of man before he and his family died in Toyota Lexus crash. *www.dailymail.co.uk*. February 3: np. Ohnsman, A. 2010. The Humbling of Toyota. *BusinessWeek,* March 22: 32–36; Anonymous. 2009. Toyota recalls 3.8 million vehicles, *www.msnbc.com*. September 29: np; Ross, B. 2009. Owners of Toyota cars in rebellion over series of accidents caused by sudden acceleration, Part one. *www.abcnews.go.com*. November 3: np; and, Ohnsman, A. 2009. Toyota recall crisis said to lie in cost cuts, growth ambitions, *www.bloomberg.com*. February 26: np. We thank Jason Hirsch for his valued contributions.

2. Our discussion of the value chain will draw on Porter, M. E. 1985. *Competitive advantage:* chap. 2. New York: Free Press.

3. Dyer, J. H. 1996. Specialized supplier networks as a source of competitive advantage: Evidence from the auto industry. *Strategic Management Journal,* 17: 271–291.

4. For an insightful perspective on value-chain analysis, refer to Stabell, C. B. & Fjeldstad, O. D. 1998. Configuring value for competitive advantage: On chains, shops, and networks. *Strategic Management Journal,* 19: 413–437. The authors develop concepts of value chains, value shops, and value networks to extend the value-creation logic across a broad range of industries. Their work builds on the seminal contributions of Porter, 1985, op. cit., and others who have addressed how firms create value through key interrelationships among value-creating activities.

5. Ibid.

6. Maynard, M. 1999. Toyota promises custom order in 5 days. *USA Today,* August 6: B1.

7. Shaw Industries. 1999. Annual report: 14–15.

8. Fisher, M. L. 1997. What is the right supply chain for your product? *Harvard Business Review,* 75(2): 105–116.

9. Jackson. M. 2001. Bringing a dying brand back to life. *Harvard Business Review,* 79(5): 53–61.

10. Anderson, J. C. & Nmarus, J. A. 2003. Selectively pursuing more of your customer's business. *MIT Sloan Management Review,* 44(3): 42–50.

11. Insights on advertising are addressed in: Rayport, J. F. 2008. Where is advertising? Into 'stitials. *Harvard Business Review,* 66(5): 18–20.

12. An insightful discussion of the role of identity marketing—that is, the myriad labels that people use to express who they are—in successful marketing activities is found in Reed, A., II & Bolton, L. E. 2005. The complexity of identity. *MIT Sloan Management Review,* 46(3): 18–22.

13. Insights on the usefulness of off-line ads are the focus of: Abraham, M. 2008. The off-line impact of online ads. *Harvard Business Review,* 66(4): 28.

14. Berggren, E. & Nacher, T. 2000. Why good ideas go bust. *Management Review,* February: 32–36.

15. For an insightful perspective on creating effective brand portfolios, refer to Hill, S., Ettenson, R., & Tyson, D. 2005. Achieving the ideal brand portfolio. *MIT Sloan Management Review,* 46(2): 85–90.

16. Haddad, C. & Grow, B. 2001. Wait a second—I didn't order that! *BusinessWeek,* July 16: 45.

17. For a scholarly discussion on the procurement of technology components, read Hoetker, G. 2005. How much you know versus how well I know you: Selecting a supplier for a technically innovative component. *Strategic Management Journal,* 26(1): 75–96.

18. For a discussion on criteria to use when screening suppliers for back-office functions, read Feeny, D., Lacity, M., & Willcocks, L. P. 2005. Taking the measure of outsourcing providers. *MIT Sloan Management Review,* 46(3): 41–48.

19. For a study investigating sourcing practices, refer to: Safizadeh, M. H., Field, J. M., & Ritzman, L. P. 2008. Sourcing practices and boundaries of the firm in the financial services industry. *Strategic Management Journal,* 29(1): 79–92.

20. Imperato, G. 1998. How to give good feedback. *Fast Company,* September: 144–156.

21. Bensaou, B. M. & Earl, M. 1998. The right mindset for managing information technology. *Harvard Business Review,* 96(5): 118–128.

22. A discussion of R&D in the pharmaceutical industry is in: Garnier, J-P. 2008. Rebuilding the R&D engine in big pharma. *Harvard Business Review,* 66(5): 68–76.

23. Donlon, J. P. 2000. Bonsignore's bid for the big time. *Chief Executive,* March: 28–37.

24. Ulrich, D. 1998. A new mandate for human resources. *Harvard Business Review,* 96(1): 124–134.

25. A study of human resource management in China is: Li, J., Lam, K., Sun, J. J. M., & Liu, S. X. Y. 2008. Strategic resource management, institutionalization, and employment modes: An empirical study in China. *Strategic Management Journal,* 29(3): 337–342.

26. Wood, J. 2003. Sharing jobs and working from home: The new face of the airline industry. AviationCareer.net, February 21.

27. Green, S., Hasan, F., Immelt, J. Marks, M., & Meiland, D. 2003. In search of global leaders. *Harvard Business Review,* 81(8): 38–45.

28. For insights on the role of information systems integration in fostering innovation refer to: Cash, J. I. Jr., Earl, M. J., & Morison, R. 2008. Teaming up to crack innovation and enterprise integration. *Harvard Business Review,* 66(11): 90–100.

29. For a cautionary note on the use of IT, refer to McAfee, A. 2003. When too much IT knowledge is a dangerous thing. *MIT Sloan Management Review,* 44(2): 83–90.

30. Walgreen Co. 1996. *Information technology and Walgreens: Opportunities for employment,* January; and Dess, G. G. & Picken, J. C. 1997. *Beyond productivity.* New York: AMACOM.

31. The important role in IT for a Japanese bank is addressed in: Upton, D. M. & Staats, B. R. 2008. Radically simple IT. *Harvard Business Review,* 66(3): 118–124.

32. For an interesting perspective on some of the potential downsides of close customer and supplier relationships, refer to Anderson, E. & Jap, S. D. 2005. The dark side of close relationships. *MIT Sloan Management Review,* 46(3): 75–82.

33. Day, G. S. 2003. Creating a superior customer-relating capability. *MIT Sloan Management Review,* 44(3): 77–82.

34. To gain insights on the role of electronic technologies in enhancing a firm's connections to outside suppliers and customers, refer to Lawrence, T. B., Morse, E. A., & Fowler, S. W. 2005. Managing your portfolio of connections. *MIT Sloan Management Review,* 46(2): 59–66.

35. This section draws on Andersen, M. M., Froholdt, M. & Poulfelt, F. 2010. *Return on strategy.* New York: Routledge: 96–100.

36. Quote from Hartmut Jenner, CEO, Alfred Karcher GmbH, IBM Global CEO Study, P. 27.

37. Collis, D. J. & Montgomery, C. A. 1995. Competing on resources: Strategy in the 1990's. *Harvard Business Review,* 73(4): 119–128; and Barney, J. 1991. Firm resources and sustained competitive advantage. *Journal of Management,* 17(1): 99–120.

38. For recent critiques of the resource-based view of the firm, refer to: Sirmon, D. G., Hitt, M. A., & Ireland, R. D. 2007. Managing firm resources in dynamic environments to create value: Looking inside the black box. *Academy of Management Review,* 32(1): 273–292; and Newbert, S. L. Empirical research on the resource-based view of the firm: An assessment and suggestions for future research. *Strategic Management Journal,* 28(2): 121–146.

39. For insights into research findings on the linkage between resources and performance, refer to: Crook, T. R., Ketchen, D. J., Jr., Combs, J. G., & Todd, S. Y. 2008. Strategic resources and performance: A meta-analysis. *Strategic Management Journal,* 29(11): 1141–1154.

40. Henkoff, R. 1993. Companies that train the best. *Fortune,* March 22: 83; and Dess & Picken, *Beyond productivity,* p. 98.

41. Gaines-Ross, L. 2010. Reputation warfare. *Harvard Business Review,* 88(12): 70–76.

42. Barney, J. B. 1986. Types of competition and the theory of strategy: Towards an integrative framework. *Academy of Management Review,* 11(4): 791–800.

43. Harley-Davidson. 1993. Annual report.

44. For a rigorous, academic treatment of the origin of capabilities, refer to Ethiraj, S. K., Kale, P., Krishnan, M. S., & Singh, J. V. 2005. Where do capabilities come from and how do they matter? A study of the software services industry. *Strategic Management Journal,* 26(1): 25–46.

45. For an academic discussion on methods associated with organizational capabilities, refer to Dutta, S., Narasimhan, O., & Rajiv, S. 2005. Conceptualizing and measuring capabilities: Methodology and empirical application. *Strategic Management Journal,* 26(3): 277–286.

46. Lorenzoni, G. & Lipparini, A. 1999. The leveraging of interfirm relationships as a distinctive organizational capability: A longitudinal study. *Strategic Management Journal,* 20: 317–338.

47. Andersen, M. M. op. cit. 209.

48. A study investigating the sustainability of competitive advantage is: Newbert, S. L. 2008. Value, rareness, competitive advantages, and performance: A conceptual-level empirical investigation of the resource-based view of the firm. *Strategic Management Journal,* 29(7): 745–768.

49. Arikan, A. M. & McGahan, A. M. 2010. The development of capabilities in new firms. *Strategic Management Journal,* 31(1): 1–18.

50. Barney, J. 1991. Firm resources and sustained competitive advantage. *Journal of Management,* 17(1): 99–120.

51. Barney, 1986, op. cit. Our discussion of inimitability and substitution draws upon this source.

52. A study that investigates the performance implications of imitation is: Ethiraj, S. K. & Zhu, D. H. 2008. Performance effects of imitative

entry. *Strategic Management Journal,* 29(8): 797–818.

53. Sirmon, D. G., Hitt, M. A., Arregale, J.-L. & Campbell, J. T. 2010. The dynamic interplay of capability strengths and weaknesses: Investigating the bases of temporary competitive advantage. *Strategic Management Journal,* 31(13): 1386–1409.

54. Deephouse, D. L. 1999. To be different, or to be the same? It's a question (and theory) of strategic balance. *Strategic Management Journal,* 20: 147–166.

55. Yeoh, P. L. & Roth, K. 1999. An empirical analysis of sustained advantage in the U.S. pharmaceutical industry: Impact of firm resources and capabilities. *Strategic Management Journal,* 20: 637–653.

56. Robins, J. A. & Wiersema, M. F. 2000. Strategies for unstructured competitive environments: Using scarce resources to create new markets. In Bresser, R. F., et al., (Eds.), *Winning strategies in a deconstructing world:* 201–220. New York: John Wiley.

57. For an insightful case on how Dell was able to build its seemingly sustainable competitive advantage in the marketplace, refer to "Matching Dell" by Jan W. Rivkin and Michael E. Porter, Harvard Business School Case 9-799-158 (June 6, 1999).

58. Byrnes, N. & Burrows, P. 2007. Where Dell went wrong. *BusinessWeek,* February 18: 62–63; and Smith, A. D. 2007. Dell's moves create buzz. *Dallas Morning News.* February 21: D1.

59. For an insightful perspective on how HP has increased its market share and profitability in the personal computer market, refer to: Edwards, C. 2008. How HP got the wow! back. *BusinessWeek,* December 22: 60–61. HP surpassed Dell in fall 2006 to become the world's largest PC manufacturer, and it increased its market share from 14.5 percent to 18.8 percent between June 2005 and September 2008.

60. Sidhu, I. op. cit., 61.

61. Amit, R. & Schoemaker, J. H. 1993. Strategic assets and organizational rent. *Strategic Management Journal,* 14(1): 33–46; Collis, D. J. & Montgomery, C. A. 1995. Competing on resources: Strategy in the 1990's. *Harvard Business Review,* 73(4): 118–128; Coff, R. W. 1999. When competitive advantage doesn't lead to performance: The resource-based view and stakeholder bargaining power. *Organization Science,* 10(2): 119–133; and Blyler, M. & Coff, R. W. 2003. Dynamic capabilities, social capital, and rent appropriation: Ties that split pies. *Strategic Management Journal,* 24: 677–686.

62. Munk, N. 1998. The new organization man. *Fortune,* March 16: 62–74.

63. Coff, op. cit.

64. Lavelle, L. 2003. Sprint's board needs a good sweeping, too. *BusinessWeek,* February 24: 40; Anonymous. 2003. Another nail in the coffin. *The Economist,* February 15: 69–70; and Byrnes, N., Dwyer, P., & McNamee, M. 2003. Hacking away at tax shelters, *BusinessWeek,* February 24: 41.

65. We have focused our discussion on how internal stakeholders (e.g., employees, managers, and top executives) may appropriate a firm's profits (or rents).

For an interesting discussion of how a firm's innovations may be appropriated by external stakeholders (e.g., customers, suppliers) as well as competitors, refer to Grant, R. M. 2002. *Contemporary strategy analysis* (4th ed.): 335–340. Malden, MA: Blackwell.

66. Luehrman, T. A. 1997. What's it worth? A general manager's guide to valuation. *Harvard Business Review,* 45(3): 132–142.

67. See, for example, Kaplan, R. S. & Norton, D. P. 1992. The balanced scorecard: Measures that drive performance. *Harvard Business Review,* 69(1): 71–79.

68. Hitt, M. A., Ireland, R. D., & Stadter, G. 1982. Functional importance of company performance: Moderating effects of grand strategy and industry type. *Strategic Management Journal,* 3: 315–330.

69. *finance.yahoo.com.*

70. Kaplan & Norton, op. cit.

71. Ibid.

72. For a discussion of the relative value of growth versus increasing margins, read Mass, N. J. 2005. The relative value of growth. *Harvard Business Review,* 83(4): 102–112.

73. Rucci, A. J., Kirn, S. P., & Quinn, R. T. 1998. The employee-customer-profit chain at Sears. *Harvard Business Review,* 76(1): 82–97.

74. Our discussion draws upon: Angel, R. & Rampersad, H. 2005. Do scorecards add up? *camagazine.com.* May: np.; and Niven, P. 2002. *Balanced scorecard step by step: Maximizing performance and maintaining results.* New York: John Wiley & Sons.

APPENDIX TO CHAPTER 3

How the Internet and Digital Technologies Add Value

>LO3.8

How firms are using Internet technologies to add value and achieve unique advantages. (Appendix)

The Internet has changed the way business is conducted. By providing new ways to interact with customers and using digital technologies to streamline operations, the Internet is helping companies create new value propositions. Let's take a look at several ways these changes have added new value. Exhibit 3A.1 illustrates four related activities that are being revolutionized by the Internet—search, evaluation, problem solving, and transactions.[1]

[1] The ideas in this section draw on several sources, including Zeng, M. & Reinartz, W. 2003. Beyond Online Search: The Road to Profitability. *California Management Review,* Winter: 107–130; and Stabell, C. B. & Fjeldstad, O. D. 1998. Configuring Value for Competitive Advantage: On Chains, Shops, and Networks. *Strategic Management Journal,* 19: 413–437.

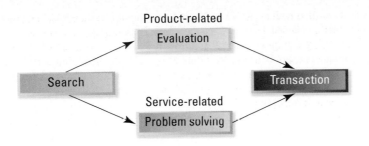

Exhibit 3A.1 Internet Activities that Add Value

Sources: Adapted from Zeng, M., & Reinartz, W. 2003. Beyond online search: The road to profitability. *California Management Review.* Winter: 107–130; and Stabell, C. B., & Fjeldstad, O. D. 1998. Configuring value for competitive advantage: On chains, shops, and networks. *Strategic Management Journal,* 19: 413–437.

Search Activities

Search refers to the process of gathering information and identifying purchase options. The Internet has enhanced both the speed of information gathering and the breadth of information that can be accessed. This enhanced search capability is one of the key reasons the Internet has lowered switching costs—by decreasing the cost of search. These efficiency gains have greatly benefited buyers. Suppliers also have benefited. Small suppliers that had difficulty getting noticed can be found more easily, and large suppliers can publish thousands of pages of information for a fraction of the cost that hard-copy catalogs once required. Additionally, online search engines such as Google, Yahoo and Bing have accelerated the search process to incredible speeds.

Evaluation Activities

Evaluation refers to the process of considering alternatives and comparing the costs and benefits of various options. Online services that facilitate comparative shopping, provide product reviews, and catalog customer evaluations of performance have made the Internet a valuable resource.[2] For example, BizRate.com offers extensive product ratings that can help evaluate products. Sites such as CNET that provide comparative pricing have helped lower prices even for quality products that have traditionally maintained premium prices. Opinion-based sites such as ePinions.com and PlanetFeedback.com provide reports of consumer experiences with various vendors.

Many Internet businesses, according to digital business experts Ming Zeng and Werner Reinartz, could improve their performance by making a stronger effort to help buyers evaluate purchases.[3] Even so, only certain types of products can be evaluated online. Products such as CDs that appeal primarily to the sense of sound sell well on the Internet. But products that appeal to multiple senses are harder to evaluate online. This explains why products such as furniture and fashion have never been strong online sellers. It's one thing to look at a leather sofa, but to be able to sit on it, touch, and smell the leather online are impossible.

Problem-Solving Activities

Problem solving refers to the process of identifying problems or needs and generating ideas and action plans to address those needs. Whereas evaluation is primarily product-related, problem solving is typically used in the context of services. Customers usually have unique problems that are handled one at a time. For example, online travel services such as Travelocity help customers select from many options to form a unique travel package. Furthermore, problem solving often involves providing answers immediately (compared to the creation of a new product). Firms in industries such as medicine, law, and engineering are using the Internet and digital technologies to deliver many new solutions.

search activities a way that digital technologies and the Internet have added value to firms' operations by enhancing the gathering of information and identifying purchase options.

evaluation activities a way that digital technologies and the Internet have added value to firms' operations by facilitating the comparison of the costs and benefits of various options.

problem-solving activities a way that digital technologies and the Internet have added value to firms' operations by identifying problems or needs and generating ideas and action plans to address those needs.

[2] For an interesting discussion of how successful Internet-based companies are using evaluation to add value see Weiss, L. M., Capozzi, M. M., & Prusak, L. 2004. Learning from the Internet Giants. *Sloan Management Review,* 45(4): 79–84.

[3] Zeng & Reinartz, op.cit.

Many products involve both a service and a product component; therefore, both problem solving and evaluation may be needed. Dell Computer's website is an example of a site that has combined the benefits of both. By creating a website that allows for customization of individual computers, they address the unique concerns of customers "one computer at a time." But the site also features a strong evaluative component because it allows users to compare the costs and features of various options. Shoppers can even compare their customized selection to refurbished Dell computers that are available at a substantially lower cost.

Transaction Activities

Transaction refers to the process of completing the sale, including negotiating and agreeing contractually, making payments, and taking delivery. Numerous types of Internet-enabled activities have contributed to lowering this aspect of overall transaction costs. Auctions of various sorts, from raw materials used in manufacturing to collectibles sold on eBay, facilitate the process of arriving at mutually agreed-on prices. Services such as PayPal provide a third-party intermediary that facilitates transactions between parties who never have (and probably never will) meet. Amazon.com's One-Click technology allows for very rapid purchases, and Amazon's overall superiority in managing order fulfillment has made its transactions process rapid and reliable. Amazon's success today can be attributed to a large extent to its having sold this transaction capability to other companies such as Target, Toys "R" Us and even Borders (another bookseller!).[4]

Other Sources of Competitive Advantage

There are other factors that can be important sources of competitive advantage. One of the most important of these is content. The Internet makes it possible to capture vast amounts of content at a very low cost. Three types of content can improve the value proposition of a website—customer feedback, expertise, and entertainment programming.

- *Customer Feedback.* Buyers often trust what other buyers say more than a company's promises. One type of content that can enhance a website is customer testimonials. Remember the leather sofa online? The testimonials of other buyers can build confidence and add to the chances that the purchaser will buy online sight unseen. This is one way that content can be a source of competitive advantage. Being able to interact with like-minded customers by reading their experiences or hearing how they have responded to a new product offering builds a sense of belonging that is otherwise hard to create.
- *Expertise.* The Internet has emerged as a tremendously important learning tool. Fifty-one percent of users compare the Internet to a library.[5] The prime reason many users go to the Web is to gain expertise. Websites that provide new knowledge or unbiased information are highly valuable. Additionally the problem-solving function often involves educating consumers regarding options and implications of various choices. For example, LendingTree.com, the online loan company, provides a help center that includes extensive information and resources about obtaining loans, maintaining good credit, and so forth. Further, the expertise function is not limited to consumer sites. In the case of B2B businesses, websites that facilitate sharing expert knowledge help build a sense of community in industry or professional groups.
- *Entertainment Programming.* The Internet is being used by more and more people as an entertainment medium. With technologies such as streaming media, which allows the Internet to send televisionlike images and sound, computers can provide everything from breaking news to video games to online movies. A study by the Pew Internet and American Life Project indicates that among people using high-speed broadband service, TV viewing is down and online activity has increased. One reason is that the technology is interactive, which means that viewers don't just passively watch, but they use the Web to create art or play online games. Businesses have noticed this trend, of course, and are creating Web content that is not just informative but entertaining.

These three types of content—customer feedback, expertise, and entertainment programming—are potential sources of competitive advantage. That is, they create advantages by making the value creation process even stronger. Or, if they are handled poorly, they diminish performance.

transaction activities a way that digital technologies and the Internet have added value to firms' operations by completing sales efficiently, including negotiating and agreeing contractually, making payments, and taking delivery.

[4] Bayers, C. 2002. The Last Laugh. *Business 2.0,* September: 86–93.
[5] Greenspan, R. 2003. Internet Not for Everyone. *CyberAtlas,* April 16, *www.cyberatlas.com.*

Business Models

business model a method and a set of assumptions that explain how a business creates value and earns profits in a competitive environment.

The Internet provides a unique platform or staging area for business activity, which has become, in some ways, like a new marketplace. How do firms conduct business in this new arena? One way of addressing this question is by describing various Internet business models. A business model is a method and a set of assumptions that explain how a business creates value and earns profits in a competitive environment. Some of these models are quite simple and traditional even when applied in an Internet context. Others have features that are unique to the digitally networked, online environment. In this section, we discuss seven Internet business models that account for the vast majority of business conducted online.[6]

- **Commission-Based Models** are used by businesses that provide services for a fee. The business is usually a third-party intermediary, and the commission charged is often based on the size of the transaction. The most common type is a brokerage service, such as a stockbroker (e.g., Schwab.com), real estate broker (e.g., Remax.com), or transaction broker (e.g., PayPal.com). This category also includes auction companies such as eBay. In exchange for putting buyers and sellers together, eBay earns a commission.

- **Advertising-Based Models** are used by companies that provide content and/or services to visitors and sell advertising to businesses that want to reach those visitors. It is similar to the broadcast television model, in which viewers watch shows produced with advertising dollars. A key difference is that online visitors can interact with both the ads and the content. Large portals such as Yahoo.com are in this category as well as specialty portals such as iNest.com, which provides services for buyers of newly constructed homes. Epinions.com, a recommender system, is just one example of the many types of content that are often available.

- **Markup-Based Models** are used by businesses that add value in marketing and sales (rather than production) by acquiring products, marking up the price, and reselling them at a profit. Also known as the merchant model, it applies to both wholesalers and retailers. Amazon.com is the best-known example in this category. It also includes bricks-and-mortar companies such as Walmart, which has a very successful online operation, and vendors whose products are purely digital such as Fonts.com, which sells downloadable fonts and photographs.

- **Production-Based Models** are used by companies that add value in the production process by converting raw materials into value-added products. Thus, it is also referred to as the manufacturing model. The Internet adds value to this model in two key ways. First, it lowers marketing costs by enabling direct contact with end users. Second, such direct contact facilitates customization and problem solving. Dell's online ordering system is supported by a state-of-the-art customized manufacturing process. Travelocity uses its rich database of travel options and customer profiles to identify, produce, and deliver unique solutions.

- **Referral-Based Models** are used by firms that steer customers to another company for a fee. One type is the affiliate model, in which a vendor pays an affiliate a fee each time a visitor clicks through the affiliate's website and makes a purchase from the vendor. Many name-brand companies use affiliate programs. For example, WeddingChannel.com, which provides a bridal registry where wedding guests can buy gifts from companies such as Tiffany's, Macy's, or Crate & Barrel, receives a fee each time a sale is made through its website. Another referral-based example is Yesmail.com, which generates leads using e-mail marketing.

- **Subscription-Based Models** are used by businesses that charge a flat fee for providing either a service or proprietary content. Internet service providers are one example of this model. Companies such as America Online and Earthlink supply Internet connections for fees that are charged whether buyers use the service or not. Subscription-based models are also used by content creators such as the *Economist* or the *New York Times*. Although these recognizable brands often provide free content, only a small portion is available free. The *Economist,* for example, advertises that 70 percent of its content is available only to subscribers.

- **Fee-for-Service–Based Models** are used by companies that provide ongoing services similar to a utility company. Unlike the commission-based model, the fee-for-service model involves a pay-as-you-go system. That is, activities are metered and companies pay only for the amount of service used. Application service providers fall in this category. For example, eProject.com

---

[6] Afuah, A. & Tucci, C.L. 2003. *Internet Business Models and Strategies* (2nd ed). New York: McGraw-Hill; and, Timmers, P. 1999. *Electronic Commerce.* New York: Wiley.

provides virtual work space where people in different physical locations can collaborate online. Users essentially rent Internet space, and a host of tools that make it easy to interact, for a fee based on their usage.

Exhibit 3A.2 summarizes the key feature of each Internet business model, suggests what role content may play in the model, and addresses how the four value-adding activities—search, evaluation, problem solving, and transaction—can be sources of competitive advantage.

Exhibit 3A.2
Internet Business Models

Type	Features and Content	Sources of Competitive Advantage
Commission-Based	Charges commissions for brokerage or intermediary services. Adds value by providing expertise and/or access to a wide network of alternatives.	Search Evaluation Problem solving Transaction
Advertising-Based	Web content paid for by advertisers. Adds value by providing free or low-cost content—including customer feedback, expertise, and entertainment programming—to audiences that range from very broad (general content) to highly targeted (specialized content).	Search Evaluation
Markup-Based	Resells marked-up merchandise. Adds value through selection, through distribution efficiencies, and by leveraging brand image and reputation. May use entertainment programming to enhance sales.	Search Transaction
Production-Based	Sells manufactured goods and custom services. Adds value by increasing production efficiencies, capturing customer preferences, and improving customer service.	Search Problem solving
Referral-Based	Charges fees for referring customers. Adds value by enhancing a company's product or service offering, tracking referrals electronically, and generating demographic data. Expertise and customer feedback often included with referral information.	Search Problem solving Transaction
Subscription-Based	Charges fees for unlimited use of service or content. Adds value by leveraging strong brand name, providing high-quality information to specialized markets, or providing access to essential services. May consist entirely of entertainment programming.	Evaluation Problem solving
Fee-for-Service–Based	Charges fees for metered services. Adds value by providing service efficiencies, expertise, and practical outsourcing solutions.	Problem solving Transaction

Sources: Afuah, A. & Tucci, C. L. 2003. *Internet Business Models and Strategies* (2nd ed). New York: McGraw-Hill; Rappa, M. 2005. *Business Models on the Web,* digitalenterprise.org/models/models.html; and Timmers, P. 1999. *Electronic Commerce.* New York: Wiley.

chapter FOUR

Recognizing a Firm's Intellectual Assets:

Moving beyond a Firm's Tangible Resources

After reading this chapter, you should have a good understanding of:

LO4.1 Why the management of knowledge professionals and knowledge itself are so critical in today's organizations.

LO4.2 The importance of recognizing the interdependence of attracting, developing, and retaining human capital.

LO4.3 The key role of social capital in leveraging human capital within and across the firm.

LO4.4 The importance of social networks in knowledge management and in promoting career success.

LO4.5 The vital role of technology in leveraging knowledge and human capital.

LO4.6 Why "electronic" or "virtual" teams are critical in combining and leveraging knowledge in organizations and how they can be made more effective.

LO4.7 The challenge of protecting intellectual property and the importance of a firm's dynamic capabilities.

LEARNING OBJECTIVES

One of the most important trends that managers must consider is the significance of the knowledge worker in today's economy. Managers must both recognize the importance of top talent and provide mechanisms to leverage human capital to innovate and, in the end, develop products and services that create value.

The first section addresses the increasing role of knowledge as the primary means of wealth generation in today's economy. A company's value is not derived solely from its physical assets, such as plant, equipment, and machinery. Rather, it is based on knowledge, know-how, and intellectual assets—all embedded in people.

The second section discusses the key resource itself, human capital, which is the foundation of intellectual capital. We explore ways in which the organization can attract, develop, and retain top talent—three important, interdependent activities. With regard to attracting human capital, we address issues such as "hiring for attitude, training for skill." One of the issues regarding developing human capital is encouraging widespread involvement throughout the organization. Our discussion on retaining human capital addresses issues such as the importance of having employees identify with an organization's mission and values. We also address the value of a diverse workforce.

The attraction, development, and retention of human capital are necessary but not sufficient conditions for organizational success. In the third section we address social capital—networks of relationships among a firm's members. This is especially important where collaboration and sharing information are critical. We address why social capital can be particularly important in attracting human capital and making teams effective. We also address the vital role of social networks—both in improving knowledge management and in promoting career success.

The fourth section addresses the role of technology in leveraging human capital. Examples range from e-mail and the use of networks to facilitate collaboration among individuals to more complex forms of technologies, such as sophisticated knowledge management systems. We discuss how electronic teams can be effectively managed. We also address how technology can help to retain knowledge.

The last section discusses the differences between protection of physical property and intellectual property. We suggest that the development of dynamic capabilities may be one of the best ways that a firm can protect its intellectual property.

Learning from Mistakes

Hitachi Ltd., a Japanese multinational corporation, is the world's third largest tech firm.[1] Its first president, Namihei Odaira, believed that "inventions are an engineer's lifeblood," and, not surprisingly, he focused on the company's inventions from the very beginning. He demanded that his tech people apply their engineering skills toward generating inventions and patents. This, he felt, could be the key to value creation and competitive advantage. Sounds good . . . but what problems arose?

In 1970 alone, Hitachi filed 20,000 patent applications. Unfortunately, the emphasis was on the sheer number rather than the quality of each patent. At that time, the company earned a mere $5 million in licensing income but paid out $95 million in licensing fees.

In 1979, Hitachi faced major patent litigation. Westinghouse charged Hitachi, a Hitachi-GE joint venture, and a few other companies with patent infringement and petitioned the U.S. International Trade Commission to block the import of circuit breakers from Japan. By then, Hitachi already had several dozen U.S. patents for electrical power transmission equipment. However, it found that they were all patents for features distinctive to Hitachi products and were not the type that other companies could use. Thus, there were no grounds for countersuing Westinghouse for patent infringement.

Hitachi's second big patent problem occurred in 1986. Texas Instruments sued a total of nine Japanese and Korean semiconductor manufacturers in the U.S. International Trade Commission and Texas courts, arguing that its licensing fee was too low and that it could not renew Hitachi's contract at the terms proposed. It demanded to set the licensing fee for DRAM manufacturing technology at 10 percent of sales.

These were bitter lessons for Hitachi. It initiated four campaigns to double its number of "strategic patents" in 1981, 1985, 1990, and 1995, respectively. The goal was to focus their resources on patents that would create the most value for the firm as well as to gain global patent coverage for the company's world-class products and technologies.

Patents can be very valuable. However, a company must effectively use them to create value. Hitachi realized that there was no point in obtaining a mountain of patents if they were not going to help the company compete in the competitive marketplace.

Managers are always looking for stellar professionals who can take their organizations to the next level. However, attracting talent is a necessary but *not* sufficient condition for success. In today's knowledge economy, it does not matter how big your stock of resources is—whether it be top talent, physical resources, or financial capital. Rather, the question becomes: How good is the organization at attracting top talent and leveraging that talent to produce a stream of products and services valued by the marketplace?

We also address issues associated with intellectual property (IP) and its potential to create value for the firm. The Hitachi example shows how heavy investment in IP alone is insufficient for value creation in the competitive marketplace.

>LO4.1
Why the management of knowledge professionals and knowledge itself are so critical in today's organizations.

The Central Role of Knowledge in Today's Economy

Central to our discussion is an enormous change that has accelerated over the past few decades and its implications for the strategic management of organizations.[2] For most of the 20th century, managers focused on tangible resources such as land, equipment, and money as well as intangibles such as brands, image, and customer loyalty. Efforts were directed more toward the efficient allocation of labor and capital—the two traditional factors of production.

How times have changed. Today, more than 50 percent of the gross domestic product (GDP) in developed economies is knowledge-based; it is based on intellectual assets and intangible people skills.[3] In the U.S., intellectual and information processes create most of the value for firms in large service industries (e.g., software, medical care, communications, and education), which make up 77 percent of the U.S. GDP. In the manufacturing sector, intellectual activities like R&D, process design, product design, logistics, marketing, and technological innovation produce the preponderance of value added.[4] To drive home the point, Gary Hamel and the late C. K. Prahalad, two leading writers in strategic management state:

> The machine age was a physical world. It consisted of things. Companies made and distributed things (physical products). Management allocated things (capital budgets); management invested in things (plant and equipment).
>
> In the machine age, people were ancillary, and things were central. In the information age, things are ancillary, knowledge is central. A company's value derives not from things, but from knowledge, know-how, intellectual assets, competencies—all embedded in people.[5]

In the **knowledge economy,** wealth is increasingly created by effective management of knowledge workers instead of by the efficient control of physical and financial assets. The growing importance of knowledge, coupled with the move by labor markets to reward knowledge work, tells us that investing in a company is, in essence, buying a set of talents, capabilities, skills, and ideas—intellectual capital—not physical and financial resources.[6]

Let's provide a few examples. People don't buy Microsoft's stock because of its software factories; it doesn't own any. Rather, the value of Microsoft is bid up because it sets standards for personal-computing software, exploits the value of its name, and forges alliances with other companies. Similarly, Merck didn't become the "Most Admired" company, for seven consecutive years in *Fortune*'s annual survey, because it can manufacture pills, but because its scientists can discover medicines. P. Roy Vagelos, who was CEO of Merck, the $44 billion pharmaceutical giant, during its long run atop the "Most Admired" survey, said, "A low-value product can be made by anyone anywhere. When you have knowledge no one else has access to—that's dynamite. We guard our research even more carefully than our financial assets."[7]

To apply some numbers to our arguments, let's ask, What's a company worth?[8] Start with the "big three" financial statements: income statement, balance sheet, and statement of cash flow. If these statements tell a story that investors find useful, then a company's market value* should roughly (but not precisely, because the market looks forward and the books look backward) be the same as the value that accountants ascribe to it—the book value of the firm. However, this is not the case. A study compared the market value with the book value of 3,500 U.S. companies over a period of two decades. In 1978 the two were similar: Book value was 95 percent of market value. However, market values and book values have diverged significantly. Within 20 years, the S&P industrials were—on average—trading at 2.2 times book value.[9] Robert A. Howell, an expert on the changing role of finance and accounting, muses that "The big three financial statements . . . are about as useful as an 80-year-old Los Angeles road map."

The gap between a firm's market value and book value is far greater for knowledge-intensive corporations than for firms with strategies based primarily on tangible assets.[10] Exhibit 4.1 shows the ratio of market-to-book value for some well-known companies. In

knowledge economy an economy where wealth is created through the effective management of knowledge workers instead of by the efficient control of physical and financial assets.

---

* The market value of a firm is equal to the value of a share of its common stock times the number of shares outstanding. The book value of a firm is primarily a measure of the value of its tangible assets. It can be calculated by the formula: total assets − total liabilities.

intellectual capital the difference between the market value of the firm and the book value of the firm, including assets such as reputation, employee loyalty and commitment, customer relationships, company values, brand names, and the experience and skills of employees.

human capital the individual capabilities, knowledge, skills, and experience of a company's employees and managers.

social capital the network of friendships and working relationships between talented people both inside and outside the organization.

firms where knowledge and the management of knowledge workers are relatively important contributors to developing products and services—and physical resources are less critical—the ratio of market-to-book value tends to be much higher.

As shown in Exhibit 4.1, firms such as Apple, Google, Microsoft, and Oracle have very high market value to book value ratios because of their high investment in knowledge resources and technological expertise. In contrast, firms in more traditional industry sectors such as International Paper, Nucor, and Southwest Airlines have relatively low market to book ratios. This reflects their greater investments in physical resources and lower investment in knowledge resources. A firm like Intel has a market to book value ratio that falls between the above two groups of firms. This is because their high level of investment in knowledge resources is matched by a correspondingly huge investment in plant and equipment. For example, in 2007, Intel invested $3 billion to build a fabrication facility in Chandler, Arizona.[11]

Many writers have defined **intellectual capital** as the difference between a firm's market value and book value—that is, a measure of the value of a firm's intangible assets.[12] This broad definition includes assets such as reputation, employee loyalty and commitment, customer relationships, company values, brand names, and the experience and skills of employees.[13] Thus, simplifying, we have:

Intellectual capital = Market value of firm − Book value of the firm

How do companies create value in the knowledge-intensive economy? The general answer is to attract and leverage human capital effectively through mechanisms that create products and services of value over time.

First, **human capital** is the "*individual* capabilities, knowledge, skills, and experience of the company's employees and managers."[14] This knowledge is relevant to the task at hand, as well as the capacity to add to this reservoir of knowledge, skills, and experience through learning.[15]

Second, **social capital** is "the network of relationships that individuals have throughout the organization." Relationships are critical in sharing and leveraging knowledge and in acquiring resources.[16] Social capital can extend beyond the organizational boundaries to include relationships between the firm and its suppliers, customers, and alliance partners.[17]

Exhibit 4.1 Ratio of Market Value to Book Value for Selected Companies

Company	Annual Sales ($ billions)	Market Value ($ billions)	Book Value ($ billions)	Ratio of Market to Book Value
Apple	65.2	314.6	47.8	6.6
Google	20.9	196.4	36.0	5.4
Microsoft	65.8	241.3	46.2	5.2
Oracle	32.0	157.0	30.8	5.1
Intel	42.7	116.1	41.7	2.8
International Paper	24.6	12.3	6.0	2.1
Nucor	14.9	13.8	7.4	1.9
Southwest Airlines	11.7	9.9	5.5	1.8

Note: The data on market valuations are as of January 11, 2011. All other financial data are based on the most recently available balance sheets and income statements.

Source: *www.finance.yahoo.com.*

126 Part 1:: Strategic Analysis

Third is the concept of "knowledge," which comes in two different forms. First, there is **explicit knowledge** that is codified, documented, easily reproduced, and widely distributed, such as engineering drawings, software code, and patents.[18] The other type of knowledge is **tacit knowledge.** That is in the minds of employees and is based on their experiences and backgrounds.[19] Tacit knowledge is shared only with the consent and participation of the indivivdual.

New knowledge is constantly created through the continual interaction of explicit and tacit knowledge. Consider, two software engineers working together on a computer code. The computer code is the explicit knowledge. By sharing ideas based on each individual's experience—that is, their tacit knowledge—they create new knowledge when they modify the code. Another important issue is the role of "socially complex processes," which include leadership, culture, and trust.[20] These processes play a central role in the creation of knowledge.[21] They represent the "glue" that holds the organization together and helps to create a working environment where individuals are more willing to share their ideas, work in teams, and, in the end, create products and services of value.[22]

Numerous books have been written on the subject of knowledge management and the central role that it has played in creating wealth in organizations and countries throughout the developed world.[23] Here, we focus on some of the key issues that organizations must address to compete through knowledge.

We will now turn our discussion to the central resource itself—human capital—and some guidelines on how it can be attracted/selected, developed, and retained.[24] Tom Stewart, editor of the *Harvard Business Review,* noted that organizations must also undergo significant efforts to protect their human capital. A firm may "diversify the ownership of vital knowledge by emphasizing teamwork, guard against obsolescence by developing learning programs, and shackle key people with golden handcuffs."[25] In addition, people are less likely to leave an organization if there are effective structures to promote teamwork and information sharing, strong leadership that encourages innovation, and cultures that demand excellence and ethical behavior. Such issues are central to this chapter. Although we touch on these issues throughout this chapter, we provide more detail in later chapters. We discuss organizational controls (culture, rewards, and boundaries) in Chapter 9, organization structure and design in Chapter 10, and a variety of leadership and entrepreneurship topics in Chapters 11 and 12.

> **explicit knowledge**
> knowledge that is codified, documented, easily reproduced, and widely distributed.

> **tacit knowledge**
> knowledge that is in the minds of employees and is based on their experiences and backgrounds.

Human Capital: The Foundation of Intellectual Capital

Organizations must recruit talented people—employees at all levels with the proper sets of skills and capabilities coupled with the right values and attitudes. Such skills and attitudes must be continually developed, strengthened, and reinforced, and each employee must be motivated and her efforts focused on the organization's goals and objectives.[26]

The rise to prominence of knowledge workers as a vital source of competitive advantage is changing the balance of power in today's organization.[27] Knowledge workers place professional development and personal enrichment (financial and otherwise) above company loyalty. Attracting, recruiting, and hiring the "best and the brightest," is a critical first step in the process of building intellectual capital. At a symposium for CEOs, Bill Gates said, "The thing that is holding Microsoft back . . . is simply how [hard] we find it to go out and recruit the kind of people we want to grow our research team."[28]

Hiring is only the first of three processes in which all successful organizations must engage to build and leverage their human capital. Firms must also *develop* employees to fulfill their full potential to maximize their joint contributions.[29] Finally, the first two processes are for naught if firms can't provide the working environment and intrinsic and extrinsic rewards to *retain* their best and brightest.[30]

> **>LO4.2**
> The importance of recognizing the interdependence of attracting, developing, and retaining human capital.

These activities are highly interrelated. We would like to suggest the imagery of a three-legged stool (see Exhibit 4.2).[31] If one leg is weak or broken, the stool collapses.

To illustrate such interdependence, poor hiring impedes the effectiveness of development and retention processes. In a similar vein, ineffective retention efforts place additional burdens on hiring and development. Consider the following anecdote, provided by Jeffrey Pfeffer of the Stanford University Business School:

> Not long ago, I went to a large, fancy San Francisco law firm—where they treat their associates like dog doo and where the turnover is very high. I asked the managing partner about the turnover rate. He said, "A few years ago, it was 25 percent, and now we're up to 30 percent." I asked him how the firm had responded to that trend. He said, "We increased our recruiting." So I asked him, "What kind of doctor would you be if your patient was bleeding faster and faster, and your only response was to increase the speed of the transfusion?"[32]

Clearly, stepped-up recruiting is a poor substitute for weak retention.[33] Although there are no simple, easy-to-apply answers, we can learn from what leading-edge firms are doing to attract, develop, and retain human capital in today's highly competitive marketplace.[34] Before moving on, Strategy Spotlight 4.1 addresses the importance of a firm's "green" or environmental sustainability strategy in attracting young talent.

Attracting Human Capital

> All we can do is bet on the people we pick. So my whole job is picking the right people.
>
> **Jack Welch,** former chairman, General Electric Company[35]

The first step in the process of building superior human capital is input control: attracting and selecting the right person.[36] Human resource professionals often approach employee selection from a "lock and key" mentality—that is, fit a key (a job candidate) into a lock (the job). Such an approach involves a thorough analysis of the person and the job. Only then can the right decision be made as to how well the two will fit together. How can you fail, the theory goes, if you get a precise match of knowledge, ability, and skill profiles? Frequently, however, the precise matching approach places its emphasis on task-specific skills (e.g., motor skills, specific information processing capabilities, and communication skills) and puts less emphasis on the broad general knowledge and experience, social skills, values, beliefs, and attitudes of employees.[37]

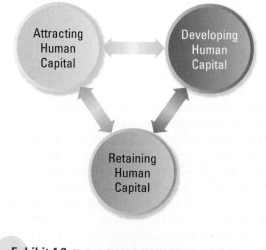

Exhibit 4.2 Human Capital: Three Interdependent Activities

Going "Green" Helps Attract Talent

When companies go "green," they often find that the benefits extend beyond the environment. Eco-friendly strategies can also help attract young talent and reduce costs. According to Lindsey Pollack, author of *Getting from College to Career:*

> Students are looking to work for companies that care about the environment. They are almost expecting greenness like they expect work-life balance, ethnic diversity, and globalization.

A recent poll on green employment by MonsterTRAK.com, a job website geared toward students and entry-level hires, found that 80 percent of young professionals are interested in securing a job that has a positive impact on the environment, and 92 percent would be more inclined to work for a company that is environmentally friendly. And, in another survey, 68 percent of Millennials said they would refuse to work for an employer that is not socially responsible.

In response, paper maker NewPage Corp. distributes a brochure that highlights the firm's commitment to environmental responsibility when it recruits on campuses. It showcases the company's new corporate headquarters, in Miamisburg, Ohio, that uses 28 percent to 39 percent less energy than a standard office building and is furnished with environmentally friendly materials. Says NewPage CEO Mark Sunwyn, "At the end of the day, we are competing with everyone else for the best talent, and this is a generation that is very concerned with the environment."

To meet the growing demand for students interested in working for green companies, MonsterTRAK, a unit of the giant employment firm Monster.com, launched GreenCareers. It was the first online recruitment service that focuses on green employment. EcoAmerica and the Environmental Defense Fund, two environmental nonprofits, are adding their expertise in partnership with MonsterTRAK. "EcoAmerica approached MonsterTRAK to create GreenCareers because there is an urgent need to reach and educate environmentally 'agnostic' audiences, in this case college students, about the ways they can address climate change and other serious environmental problems," claims Mark Charnock, vice president and general manager at MonsterTRAK.

Sources: Luhby, T. 2008. How to Lure Gen Y Workers? *CNNMoney.com*, August 17: np; Mattioli. 2007. How Going Green Draws Talent, Cut Costs. *Wall Street Journal*, November 13: B10; and, Odell, A. M. 2007. Working for the Earth: Green Companies and Green Jobs Attract Employees. *www.socialfunds.com*, October 9: np.

environmental sustainability

Many have questioned the precise matching approach. They argue that firms can identify top performers by focusing on key employee mind-sets, attitudes, social skills, and general orientations. If they get these elements right, the task-specific skills can be learned quickly. (This does not imply, however, that task-specific skills are unimportant; rather, it suggests that the requisite skill sets must be viewed as a necessary but not sufficient condition.) This leads us to a popular phrase today that serves as the title of the next section.

"Hire for Attitude, Train for Skill" Organizations are increasingly emphasizing general knowledge and experience, social skills, values, beliefs, and attitudes of employees.[38] Consider Southwest Airlines' hiring practices, which focus on employee values and attitudes. Given its strong team orientation, Southwest uses an "indirect" approach. For example, the interviewing team asks a group of employees to prepare a five-minute presentation about themselves. During the presentations, interviewers observe which candidates enthusiastically support their peers and which candidates focus on polishing their own presentations while the others are presenting.[39] The former are, of course, favored.

Alan Cooper, president of Cooper Software, Inc., in Palo Alto, California, goes further. He cleverly *uses technology* to hone in on the problem-solving ability of his applicants and their attitudes before an interview even takes place. He has devised a "Bozo

Filter," an online test that can be applied to any industry. Before you spend time on whether job candidates will work out satisfactorily, find out how their minds work. Cooper advised, "Hiring was a black hole. I don't talk to bozos anymore, because 90 percent of them turn away when they see our test. It's a self-administering bozo filter."[40] How does it work?

> The online test asks questions designed to see how prospective employees approach problem-solving tasks. For example, one key question asks software engineer applicants to design a table-creation software program for Microsoft Word. Candidates provide pencil sketches and a description of the new user interface. Another question used for design communicators asks them to develop a marketing strategy for a new touch-tone phone—directed at consumers in the year 1850. Candidates e-mail their answers back to the company, and the answers are circulated around the firm to solicit feedback. Only candidates with the highest marks get interviews.

Sound Recruiting Approaches and Networking   Companies that take hiring seriously must also take recruiting seriously. The number of jobs that successful knowledge-intensive companies must fill is astonishing. Ironically, many companies still have no shortage of applicants. For example, Google, ranked fourth on *Fortune*'s 2011 "100 Best Companies to Work For," is planning to hire thousands of employees—even though its hiring rate has slowed.[41] The challenge becomes having the right job candidates, not the greatest number of them.

GE Medical Systems, which builds CT scanners and magnetic resonance imaging (MRI) systems, relies extensively on networking. They have found that current employees are the best source for new ones. Recently, Steven Patscot, head of staffing and leadership development, made a few simple changes to double the number of referrals. First, he simplified the process—no complex forms, no bureaucracy, and so on. Second, he increased incentives. Everyone referring a qualified candidate received a gift certificate from Sears. For referrals who were hired, the "bounty" increases to $2,000. Although this may sound like a lot of money, it is "peanuts" compared to the $15,000 to $20,000 fees that GE typically pays to headhunters for each person hired.[42] Also, when someone refers a former colleague or friend for a job, his or her credibility is on the line. Thus, employees will be careful in recommending people for employment unless they are reasonably confident that these people are good candidates. This provides a good "screen" for the firm in deciding whom to hire. Hiring the right people makes things a lot easier: fewer rules and regulations, less need for monitoring and hierarchy, and greater internalization of organizational norms and objectives.

Consider some of the approaches that companies are currently using to recruit and retain young talent. As baby boomers retire, people in this demographic group are becoming more and more important in today's workforce. We also provide some "tips" on how to get hired. We address these issues in Exhibit 4.3.

Developing Human Capital

It is not enough to hire top-level talent and expect that the skills and capabilities of those employees remain current throughout the duration of their employment. Rather, training and development must take place at all levels of the organization.[43] For example, Solectron assembles printed circuit boards and other components for its Silicon Valley clients.[44] Its employees receive an average of 95 hours of company-provided training each year. Chairman Winston Chen observed, "Technology changes so fast that we estimate 20 percent of an engineer's knowledge becomes obsolete each year. Training is an obligation we owe to our employees. If you want high growth and high quality, then training is a big part of the equation." Although the financial returns on training may be hard to calculate, most experts believe it is essential. One company that has calculated the benefit from training is Motorola. Every dollar spent on training returns $30 in productivity gains over the following three years.

Exhibit 4.3
**What Companies Are
Doing to Attract and
Retain Young Talent . . .
and What You Should Do
to Get Hired**

Here are some "best practices" that companies are using to help recruit and retain today's high-maintenance Millennials. This generation has also been termed "Generation Y" or "Echo Boom" and includes people born after 1982:

- *Don't fudge the sales pitch.* High-tech presentations and one-on-one attention may be attractive to undergrads, but the pitch had better match the experience. Today's ultraconnected students can get the lowdown on a company by spending five minutes on a social networking site.

- *Let them have a life.* Wary of their parents' 80-hour workweeks, Millennials strive for more balance, so liberal vacations are a must. They also want assurances they'll be able to use it. At KPMG, 80 percent of employees used 40 hours of paid time off in the six months through May 2006.

- *No time clocks, please.* Recent grads don't mind long hours if they can work them on their own time. Lockheed Martin allows employees to work nine-hour days and take every other Friday off.

- *Give them responsibility.* A chance to work on fulfilling projects and develop ones of their own is important to Millennials. Google urges entry-level employees to spend 20 percent of their time developing new ideas. PepsiCo allows promising young employees to manage small teams in six months.

- *Feedback and more feedback.* Career planning advice and frequent performance appraisals are keys to holding on to young hires. Lehman Brothers provides new hires with two mentors—a slightly older peer to help them get settled and a senior employee to give long-term guidance.

- *Giving back matters.* Today's altruistic young graduates expect to have opportunities for community service. Wells Fargo encourages its employees to teach financial literacy classes in the community. Accenture and Bain allow employees to consult for nonprofits.

Some advice on how to get hired (based on Fortune's "100 Best Companies to Work For"):

- **It helps to know someone.** Almost all of the "Best Companies" rely extensively on employee referrals. Principal Financial Group and many others get about 40 percent of new hires this way.

- **Do creative research.** Know more about the place and the industry than your rivals. A Google search is not viewed as a form of "creative research." Says Jay Jones, a recruiting manager for Alcon Laboratories: "Detailed research, including talking to customers, is so rare it will almost guarantee you get hired."

- **Unleash your inner storyteller.** By far the most popular interview style is what's known as behavioral, meaning that you will be asked to describe troublesome situations in past jobs and tell exactly how you handled them.

- **No lone rangers need apply.** By and large, team players are wanted. "I actually count the number of times a candidates says 'I' in an interview," says Adobe's recruiting director, Jeff Vijungco. "We'd rather hear 'we.'"

- **Be open to learning new things.** Showing passion is a must, and most of the "100 Best" pride themselves on creating "learning environments." Thus, talk about the skills you'd like to acquire or polish. Declaring that you're already the best at what you do is a turnoff.

Source: Fisher, A. 2008. How to Get Hired by a "Best" Company. *Fortune*, February 4: 96; and Gerdes, L. 2006. The Top 50 Employers for New College Grads. *BusinessWeek*, September 18: 64–81.

In addition to training and developing human capital, firms must encourage widespread involvement, monitor and track employee development, and evaluate human capital.[45]

Encouraging Widespread Involvement   Developing human capital requires the active involvement of leaders at all levels. It won't be successful if it is viewed only as the responsibility of the human resources department. Each year at General Electric, 200 facilitators, 30 officers, 30 human resource executives, and many young managers actively participate in GE's orientation program at Crotonville, its training center outside New York City. Topics include global competition, winning on the global playing field, and personal examination of the new employee's core values vis-à-vis GE's values. As a senior manager once commented, "There is nothing like teaching Sunday school to force you to confront your own values."

Similarly, A. G. Lafley, Procter & Gamble's former CEO, claimed that he spent 40 percent of his time on personnel.[46] Andy Grove, who was previously Intel's CEO, required all senior people, including himself, to spend at least a week a year teaching high flyers. And Nitin Paranjpe, CEO of Hindustan Unilever, recruits people from campuses and regularly visits high-potential employees in their offices.

Transferring Knowledge   Often in our lives, we need to either transfer our knowledge to someone else (a child, a junior colleague, a peer) or access accumulated bits of wisdom— someone else's tacit knowledge.[47] This is a vital aspect of developing human capital.[48] However, before we can even begin to plan such a transfer, we need to understand how our brains process incoming information. According to Dorothy A. Leonard of Harvard University:

> Our existing tacit knowledge determines how we assimilate new experiences. Without receptors—hooks on which to hang new information—we may not be able to perceive and process the information. It is like being sent boxes of documents but having no idea how they could or should be organized.

This cognitive limitation also applies to the organizational level. When GE Healthcare sets up or transfers operations, it appoints an experienced manager as the "pitcher" and a team in the receiving plant as the "catcher." These two teams work together, often over a period of years—first at the pitcher's location and then at the catcher's. To ensure a smooth transition, the pitching team needs to be sensitive to the catching team's level of experience and familiarity with GE Healthcare procedures.

Strategy Spotlight 4.2 discusses an emerging trend in organizations—reverse mentoring. Here, Internet savvy new hires mentor seasoned executives.

Monitoring Progress and Tracking Development   Whether a firm uses on-site formal training, off-site training (e.g., universities), or on-the-job training, tracking individual progress—and sharing this knowledge with both the employee and key managers— becomes essential. Like many leading-edge firms, GlaxoSmithKline (GSK) places strong emphasis on broader experiences over longer time periods. Dan Phelan, senior vice president and director of human resources, explained, "We ideally follow a two-plus-two-plus-two formula in developing people for top management positions." This reflects the belief that GSK's best people should gain experience in two business units, two functional units (such as finance and marketing), and in two countries.

Evaluating Human Capital   In today's competitive environment, collaboration and interdependence are vital to organizational success. Individuals must share their knowledge and work constructively to achieve collective, not just individual, goals. However, traditional systems evaluate performance from a single perspective (i.e., "top down") and generally don't address the "softer" dimensions of communications and social skills, values, beliefs, and attitudes.[49]

Time Warner's Reverse Mentoring Program

Time Warner recently developed a mentoring program that engages people on both ends of their careers. In this case, some of the company's senior executives were challenged to stay at the forefront of a rapidly evolving new-media landscape. To raise awareness of digital media, Time Warner launched Digital Reverse Mentoring—a program in which tech-savvy college students mentor senior executives on emerging digital trends and technologies such as Facebook, Twitter, and other Web 2.0 applications. Gen Y mentors meet with senior executives for

Source: Hewlett, S. A., Sherbin, L. & Sumberg, K. 2009. How Gen Y & Boomers will reshape your agenda. *Harvard Business Review*, 87(7/8): 76.

one-on-one meetings about writing blogs, posting videos on YouTube, and making imaginative use of new media. The program helps them not only to better understand how new technologies are affecting Time Warner but also to obtain fresh ideas on optimizing the firm's online presence. In addition to imparting technical skills, Gen Y mentors provide Boomer mentees with insights into the values, consumer behaviors, and communication styles of the younger generation.

Time Warner enjoys the immeasurable benefits of a more market-attuned leadership team. In a broader sense, however, programs like these pay off by proving that a company is part of a new breed of employer—one that respects educated workers' increasing desires for flexibility, personal growth, connectivity, and a chance to give back.

To address the limitations of the traditional approach, many organizations use 360-degree evaluation and feedback systems.[50] Here, superiors, direct reports, colleagues, and even internal and external customers rate a person's performance.[51] Managers rate themselves to have a personal benchmark. The 360-degree feedback system complements teamwork, employee involvement, and organizational flattening. As organizations continue to push responsibility downward, traditional top-down appraisal systems become insufficient.[52] For example, a manager who previously managed the performance of 3 supervisors might now be responsible for 10 and is less likely to have the in-depth knowledge needed to appraise and develop them adequately. Exhibit 4.4 provides a portion of GE's 360-degree system.

Evaluation systems must also ensure that a manager's success does not come at the cost of compromising the organization's core values. Such behavior generally leads to only short-term wins for both the manager and the organization. The organization typically suffers long-term losses in terms of morale, turnover, productivity, and so on. Accordingly, Merck's former chairman, Ray Gilmartin, told his employees, "If someone is achieving results but not demonstrating the core values of the company, at the expense of our people, that manager does not have much of a career here."

> **360-degree evaluation and feedback systems** superiors, direct reports, colleagues, and even external and internal customers rate a person's performance.

Retaining Human Capital

It has been said that talented employees are like "frogs in a wheelbarrow."[53] They can jump out at any time! By analogy, the organization can either try to force employees to stay in the firm or try to keep them from jumping out by creating incentives.[54] In other words, today's leaders can either provide the work environment and incentives to keep productive employees and management from wanting to bail out, or they can use legal means such as employment contracts and noncompete clauses.[55] Firms must prevent the transfer of valuable and sensitive information outside the organization. Failure to do so would be the neglect of a leader's fiduciary responsibility to shareholders. However, greater efforts should be directed at the former (e.g., good work environment and incentives), but, as we all know, the latter (e.g., employment contracts and noncompete clauses) have their place.[56]

Vision	• Has developed and communicated a clear, simple, customer-focused vision/direction for the organization.
	• Forward-thinking, stretches horizons, challenges imaginations.
	• Inspires and energizes others to commit to Vision. Captures minds. Leads by example.
	• As appropriate, updates Vision to reflect constant and accelerating change affecting the business.

Customer/Quality Focus

Integrity

Accountability/Commitment

Communication/Influence

Shared Ownership/Boundaryless

Team Builder/Empowerment

Knowledge/Expertise/Intellect

Initiative/Speed

Global Mind-Set

Source: Adapted from Slater, R. 1994. *Get Better or Get Beaten:* 152–155. Burr Ridge, IL: Irwin Professional Publishing.

Note: This evaluation system consists of 10 "characteristics"—Vision, Customer/Quality Focus, Integrity, and so on. Each of these characteristics has four "performance criteria." For illustrative purposes, the four performance criteria of "Vision" are included.

Identifying with an Organization's Mission and Values   People who identify with and are more committed to the core mission and values of the organization are less likely to stray or bolt to the competition. For example, take the perspective of Steve Jobs, Apple's widely admired CEO:[57]

> When I hire somebody really senior, competence is the ante. They have to be really smart. But the real issue for me is: Are they going to fall in love with Apple? Because if they fall in love with Apple, everything else will take care of itself. They'll want to do what's best for Apple, not what's best for them, what's best for Steve, or anyone else.

"Tribal loyalty" is another key factor that links people to the organization.[58] A tribe is not the organization as a whole (unless it is very small). Rather, it is teams, communities of practice, and other groups within an organization or occupation.

Brian Hall, CEO of Values Technology in Santa Cruz, California, documented a shift in people's emotional expectations from work. From the 1950s on, a "task first" relationship—"tell me what the job is, and let's get on with it"—dominated employee attitudes. Emotions and personal life were checked at the door. In the past few years, a "relationship-first" set of values has challenged the task orientation. Hall believes that it will become dominant. Employees want to share attitudes and beliefs as well as workspace.

Challenging Work and a Stimulating Environment   Arthur Schawlow, winner of the 1981 Nobel Prize in physics, was asked what made the difference between highly creative and less creative scientists. His reply: "The labor of love aspect is very important. The most successful scientists often are not the most talented.[59] But they are the ones impelled by curiosity. They've got to know what the answer is."[60] Such insights highlight the importance of intrinsic motivation: the motivation to work on something because it is exciting, satisfying, or personally challenging.[61]

One way firms keep highly mobile employees motivated and challenged is through opportunities that lower barriers to an employee's mobility within a company. For example, Shell Oil Company has created an "open sourcing" model for talent. Jobs are listed on Shell's intranet, and, with a two-month notice, employees can go to work on anything that interests them. Monsanto[62] has developed a similar approach. According to one executive:

> Because we don't have a lot of structure, people will flow toward where success and innovation are taking place. We have a free-market system where people can move, so you have an outflow of people in areas where not much progress is being made. Before, the HR function ran processes like management development and performance evaluation. Now it also facilitates this movement of people.

Financial and Nonfinancial Rewards and Incentives   Financial rewards are a vital organizational control mechanism (as we will discuss in Chapter 9). Money—whether in the form of salary, bonus, stock options, and so forth—can mean many different things to people. It might mean security, recognition, or a sense of freedom and independence.

Paying people more is seldom the most important factor in attracting and retaining human capital.[63] Most surveys show that money is not the most important reason why people take or leave jobs, and that money, in some surveys, is not even in the top 10. Consistent with these findings, Tandem Computers (part of Hewlett-Packard) typically doesn't tell people being recruited what their salaries would be. People who asked were told that their salaries were competitive. If they persisted along this line of questioning, they would not be offered a position. Why? Tandem realized a rather simple idea: People who come for money will leave for money.

Another nonfinancial reward is accommodating working families with children. Balancing demands of family and work is a problem at some point for virtually all employees.

Exhibit 4.5 describes strategies used by three leading-edge firms to retain their key employees—even during difficult economic times.

Start a Talent Agency: Yum Brands started a Talent Scout program to recruit outsiders. Selected top performers nominate at least 25 people, and they get cash when a recruit is hired. Global talent VP John Kurnick says 25 percent of the finance team's recent hires came from this program. Although it wasn't designed for retention, "it's been the most gratifying for the scout," says Kurnick, and it encourages the scout to stay with the company.

Change Up Bonus Time: Software maker Intuit moved its annual restricted stock grant up from July to February to address the economic uncertainties that the employees felt. Intuit's human resources team wanted the grant to make a big impact. Program manager Eileen Fagan claims: "It took one more worry off people's plates. It was a huge incentive for feeling good about the company."

Send Them Abroad—If It Fits: During recessionary times, global opportunities can energize top performers, says Ari Bousbib, former executive VP of United Technologies. During the downturn, he says, the company offered more expatriate assignments (for those whose family situations allowed it) as bonuses came under pressure.

Source: McGregor, J. & Dubey, R. 2010. Giving Back to Your Stars. *Fortune.* November 1: 53–54.

Exhibit 4.5
Retention Rules: How Three Companies Are Keeping Their Best during Tough Times

Enhancing Human Capital: The Role of Diversity in the Workforce

A combination of demographic trends and accelerating globalization of business has made the management of cultural differences a critical issue.[64] Workforces, which reflect demographic changes in the overall population, will be increasingly heterogeneous along dimensions such as gender, race, ethnicity, and nationality.[65] Demographic trends in the United States indicate a growth in Hispanic Americans from 6.9 million in 1960 to over 35 million in 2000, an expected increase to over 59 million by 2020 and 102 million by 2050. Similarly, the Asian-American population should grow to 20 million in 2020 from 12 million in 2000 and only 1.5 million in 1970. And the African-American population is becoming more ethnically heterogeneous. Census estimates project that in 2010 as many as 10 percent of Americans of African descent were immigrants from Africa or the Caribbean.[66]

Such demographic changes have implications not only for the labor pool but also for customer bases, which are also becoming more diverse.[67] This creates important organizational challenges and opportunities.

The effective management of diversity can enhance the social responsibility goals of an organization.[68] However, there are many other benefits as well. Six other areas where sound management of diverse workforces can improve an organization's effectiveness and competitive advantages are: (1) cost, (2) resource acquisition, (3) marketing, (4) creativity, (5) problem-solving, and (6) organizational flexibility.

- *Cost Argument.* As organizations become more diverse, firms effective in managing diversity will have a cost advantage over those that are not.
- *Resource Acquisition Argument.* Firms with excellent reputations as prospective employers for women and ethnic minorities will have an advantage in the competition for top talent. As labor pools shrink and change in composition, such advantages will become even more important.
- *Marketing Argument.* For multinational firms, the insight and cultural sensitivity that members with roots in other countries bring to marketing efforts will be very useful. A similar rationale applies to subpopulations within domestic operations.
- *Creativity Argument.* Less emphasis on conformity to norms of the past and a diversity of perspectives will improve the level of creativity.
- *Problem-Solving Argument.* Heterogeniety in decision-making and problem-solving groups typically produces better decisions because of a wider range of perspectives as well as more thorough analysis. Jim Schiro, former CEO of PriceWaterhouse Coopers, explains, "When you make a genuine commitment to diversity, you bring a greater diversity of ideas, approaches, and experiences and abilities that can be applied to client problems. After all, six people with different perspectives have a better shot at solving complex problems than sixty people who all think alike."[69]
- *Organizational Flexibility Argument.* With effective programs to enhance workplace diversity, systems become less determinant, less standardized, and therefore more fluid. Such fluidity should lead to greater flexibility to react to environmental changes. Reactions should be faster and less costly.

Consider how MTV Networks (part of Viacom) has benefited from a diverse workforce.[70]

One cross-cultural group discovered marketing opportunities in the similarities between North American country music and Latin American music, which use many of the same instruments, feature singers with similar vocal styles, and—in the U.S. Sunbelt—appeal to much the same audience. Other groups have influenced the multicultural content of Nickelodeon's children's programming. Says Tom Freston, MTV's former CEO, "Those teams are diverse by design to generate innovation. The probability that you will get a good, original, innovative idea with that type of chemistry is simply much higher."

The Vital Role of Social Capital

>LO4.3
The key role of
social capital
in leveraging
human capital
within and across
the firm.

Successful firms are well aware that the attraction, development, and retention of talent *is a necessary but not sufficient condition* for creating competitive advantages.[71] In the knowledge economy, it is not the stock of human capital that is important, but the extent to which it is combined and leveraged.[72] In a sense, developing and retaining human capital becomes less important as key players (talented professionals, in particular) take the role of "free agents" and bring with them the requisite skill in many cases. Rather, the development of social capital (that is, the friendships and working relationships among talented individuals) gains importance, because it helps tie knowledge workers to a given firm.[73] Knowledge workers often exhibit greater loyalties to their colleagues and their profession than their employing organization, which may be "an amorphous, distant, and sometimes threatening entity."[74] Thus, a firm must find ways to create "ties" among its knowledge workers.

Let's look at a hypothetical example. Two pharmaceutical firms are fortunate enough to hire Nobel Prize–winning scientists.[75] In one case, the scientist is offered a very attractive salary, outstanding facilities and equipment, and told to "go to it!" In the second case, the scientist is offered approximately the same salary, facilities, and equipment plus one additional ingredient: working in a laboratory with 10 highly skilled and enthusiastic scientists. Part of the job is to collaborate with these peers and jointly develop promising drug compounds. There is little doubt as to which scenario will lead to a higher probability of retaining the scientist. The interaction, sharing, and collaboration will create a situation in which the scientist will develop firm-specific ties and be less likely to "bolt" for a higher salary offer. Such ties are critical because knowledge-based resources tend to be more tacit in nature, as we mentioned early in this chapter. Therefore, they are much more difficult to protect against loss (i.e., the individual quitting the organization) than other types of capital, such as equipment, machinery, and land.

Another way to view this situation is in terms of the resource-based view of the firm that we discussed in Chapter 3. That is, competitive advantages tend to be harder for competitors to copy if they are based on "unique bundles" of resources.[76] So, if employees are working effectively in teams and sharing their knowledge and learning from each other, not only will they be more likely to add value to the firm, but they also will be less likely to leave the organization, because of the loyalties and social ties that they develop over time.

How Social Capital Helps Attract and Retain Talent

The importance of social ties among talented professionals creates a significant challenge (and opportunity) for organizations. In *The Wall Street Journal,* Bernard Wysocki described the increase in a type of "Pied Piper Effect," in which teams or networks of people are leaving one company for another.[77] The trend is to recruit job candidates at the crux of social relationships in organizations, particularly if they are seen as having the potential to bring with them valuable colleagues.[78] This is a process that is referred to as "hiring via personal networks." Let's look at one instance of this practice.

Gerald Eickhoff, founder of an electronic commerce company called Third Millennium Communications, tried for 15 years to hire Michael Reene. Why? Mr. Eickhoff says that he has "these Pied Piper skills." Mr. Reene was a star at Andersen Consulting in the 1980s and at IBM in the 1990s. He built his businesses and kept turning down overtures from Mr. Eickhoff.

However, in early 2000, he joined Third Millennium as chief executive officer, with a salary of just $120,000 but with a 20 percent stake in the firm. Since then, he has brought in a raft of former IBM colleagues and Andersen subordinates. One protégé from his time at Andersen, Mary Goode, was brought on board as executive vice president. She promptly tapped her own network and brought along former colleagues.

Wysocki considers the Pied Piper effect one of the underappreciated factors in the war for talent today. This is because one of the myths of the New Economy is rampant individualism, wherein individuals find jobs on the Internet career sites and go to work for complete strangers. Perhaps, instead of Me Inc., the truth is closer to We Inc.[79]

Another example of social relationships causing human capital mobility is the emigration of talent from an organization to form start-up ventures. Microsoft is perhaps the best-known example of this phenomenon.[80] Professionals frequently leave Microsoft en masse to form venture capital and technology start-ups, called "Baby Bills," built around teams of software developers. For example, Ignition Corporation, of Bellevue, Washington, was formed by Brad Silverberg, a former Microsoft senior vice president. Eight former Microsoft executives, among others, founded the company.

Social relationships can provide an important mechanism for obtaining both resources and information from individuals and organizations outside the boundary of a firm.[81] Strategy Spotlight 4.3 describes how alumni programs for recently laid-off employees benefit both the individuals and the firm.

Social Networks: Implications for Knowledge Management and Career Success

>LO4.4

The importance of social networks in knowledge management and in promoting career success.

Managers face many challenges driven by such factors as rapid changes in globalization and technology. Leading a successful company is more than a one-person job. As Tom Malone recently put it in *The Future of Work,* "As managers, we need to shift our thinking from command and control to coordinate and cultivate—the best way to gain power is sometimes to give it away."[82] The move away from top-down bureaucratic control to more open, decentralized network models makes it more difficult for managers to understand how work is actually getting done, who is interacting with whom both within and outside the organization, and the consequences of these interactions for the long-term health of the organization.[83] In short, coordination, cultivation, and collaboration are increasingly becoming the mode of work at every level.[84]

social network analysis analysis of the pattern of social interactions among individuals.

But how can this be done? **Social network analysis** depicts the pattern of interactions among individuals and helps to diagnose effective and ineffective patterns.[85] It helps identify groups or clusters of individuals that comprise the network, individuals who link the clusters, and other network members. It helps diagnose communication patterns and, consequently, communication effectiveness.[86] Such analysis of communication patterns is helpful because the configuration of group members' social ties within and outside the group affects the extent to which members connect to individuals who:

- convey needed resources,
- have the opportunity to exchange information and support,
- have the motivation to treat each other in positive ways, and,
- have the time to develop trusting relationships that might improve the groups' effectiveness.

However, such relationships don't "just happen."[87] Developing social capital requires interdependence among group members. Social capital erodes when people in the network become independent. And increased interactions between members aid in the development and maintenance of mutual obligations in a social network.[88] Social networks such as Facebook may facilitate increased interactions between members in a social network via Internet-based communications.

Let's take a brief look at a simplified network analysis to get a grasp of the key ideas. In Exhibit 4.6, the links are used to depict informal relationships among individuals involving

Don't Go Away Mad . . . Now You Are a Valued Alum!

Traditionally, when an employee is laid off, the relationship between the company and that person comes to a bitter end. Increasingly, leading-edge companies such as Dow Chemical and JPMorgan Chase are trying to maintain ties with their "alumni," even if they are moving on to other companies. What benefits do these efforts provide to the company and its ex-employees?

These alumni networks, which are often organized on Facebook or LinkedIn, offer their members valuable benefits such as free job ads and connections to others who might help them in finding new jobs or facilitating entrepreneurial opportunities. For the firm, these networks constitute a laboratory for learning. Former employees who have nice things to say about a company are essentially "brand ambassadors" who can help in future recruiting efforts. The companies can also track the discussions in the network to identify hot topics, companies, products, and technologies. Best of all, when the economy recovers, this is an enormous talent pool for recruiting workers who are already familiar with the company and socialized into its culture.

Source: Baker, S. 2009. You're Fired—But Stay in Touch. *BusinessWeek*. May 4: 53–55.

communication flows, personal support, and advice networks. There may be some individuals with literally no linkages, such as Fred. These individuals are typically labeled "isolates." However, most people do have some linkages with others.

To simplify, there are two primary types of mechanisms through which social capital will flow: *closure relationships* (depicted by Bill, Frank, George, and Susan) and *bridging relationships* (depicted by Mary). As we can see, in the former relationships one member is central to the communication flows in a group. In contrast, in the latter relationship, one person "bridges" or brings together groups that would have been otherwise unconnected.

Both closure and bridging relationships have important implications for the effective flow of information in organizations and for the management of knowledge. We will now briefly discuss each of these types of relationships. We will also address some of the implications that understanding social networks has for one's career success.

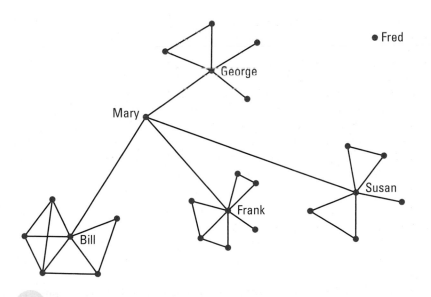

Exhibit 4.6 A Simplified Social Network

Closure   With **closure,** many members have relationships (or ties) with other members. As indicated in Exhibit 4.6, Bill's group would have a higher level of closure than Frank, Susan, or George's groups because more group members are connected to each other. Through closure, group members develop strong relationships with each other, high levels of trust, and greater solidarity. High levels of trust help to ensure that informal norms in the group are easily enforced and there is less "free riding." Social pressure will prevent people from withholding effort or shirking their responsibilities. In addition, people in the network are more willing to extend favors and "go the extra mile" on a colleague's behalf because they are confident that their efforts will be reciprocated by another member in their group. Another benefit of a network with closure is the high level of emotional support. This becomes particularly valuable when setbacks occur that may destroy morale or an unexpected tragedy happens that might cause the group to lose its focus. Social support helps the group to rebound from misfortune and get back on track.

But high levels of closure often come with a price. Groups that become too closed can become insular. They cut themselves off from the rest of the organization and fail to share what they are learning from people outside their group. Research shows that while managers need to encourage closure up to a point, if there is too much closure, they need to encourage people to open up their groups and infuse new ideas through bridging relationships.[89]

Bridging Relationships   The closure perspective rests on an assumption that there is a high level of similarity among group members. However, members can be quite heterogeneous with regard to their positions in either the formal or informal structures of the group or the organization. Such heterogeneity exists because of, for example, vertical boundaries (different levels in the hierarchy) and horizontal boundaries (different functional areas).

Bridging relationships, in contrast to closure, stresses the importance of ties connecting people. Employees who bridge disconnected people tend to receive timely, diverse information because of their access to a wide range of heterogeneous information flows. Such bridging relationships span a number of different types of boundaries.

The University of Chicago's Ron Burt originally coined the term **"structural holes"** to refer to the social gap between two groups. Structural holes are common in organizations. When they occur in business, managers typically refer to them as "silos" or "stovepipes." Sales and engineering are a classic example of two groups whose members traditionally interact with their peers rather than across groups.

A study that Burt conducted at Raytheon, a $25 billion U.S. electronics company and military contractor, provides further insight into the benefits of bridging.[90]

> Burt studied several hundred managers in Raytheon's supply chain group and asked them to write down ideas to improve the company's supply chain management. Then he asked two Raytheon executives to rate the ideas. The conclusion: *The best suggestions consistently came from managers who discussed ideas outside their regular work group.*
>
> Burt found that Raytheon managers were good at thinking of ideas but bad at developing them. Too often, Burt said, the managers discussed their ideas with colleagues already in their informal discussion network. Instead, he said, they should have had discussions outside their typical contacts, particularly with an informal boss, or someone with enough power to be an ally but not an actual supervisor.

Before we address how to overcome barriers to collaboration and the implications of social network theory for managers' career success, one might ask: Which is the more valuable mechanism to develop and nurture social capital—closure or bridging relationships? As with many aspects of strategic management, the answer becomes: "It all depends." So let's look at a few contingent issues.[91]

First, consider firms in competitive environments characterized by rapidly changing technologies and markets. Such firms should bridge relationships across networks because they need a wide variety of timely sources of information. Also, innovation is facilitated if there are multiple, interdisciplinary perspectives. On the other hand, firms competing in a stable environment would typically face less unpredictability. Thus, the cohesive ties associated with network closure would help to ensure the timely and effective implementation of strategies.

A second contingent factor would be the type of business strategies that a firm may choose to follow (a topic that we address next in Chapter 5). Managers with social networks characterized by closure would be in a preferred position if their firm is following an overall low cost strategy.[92] Here, there is a need for control and coordination to implement strategies that are rather constrained by pressures to reduce costs. Alternatively, the uncertainties generally associated with differentiation strategies (i.e., creating products that are perceived by customers as unique and highly valued) would require a broad range of information sources and inputs. Social networks characterized by bridging relationships across groups would access the diverse informational sources needed to deal with more complex, multifaceted strategies.

A caveat: In both contingencies that we have discussed—competitive environment and business strategy—closure and bridging relationships across groups are necessary. Our purpose is to address where one type should be more dominant.

Developing Social Capital: Overcoming Barriers to Collaboration Social capital within a group or organization develops through repeated interactions among its members and the resulting collaboration.[93] However, collaboration does not "just happen." People don't collaborate for various reasons. Effective collaboration requires overcoming four barriers:

- The not-invented-here barrier (people aren't willing to provide help)
- The hoarding barrier (people aren't willing to provide help)
- The search barrier (people are unable to find what they are looking for)
- The transfer barrier (people are unable to work with the people they don't know well)

All four barriers need to be low before effective collaboration can take place. Each one is enough to prevent people from collaborating well. The key is to identify which barriers are present in an organization and then to devise appropriate ways to overcome them.

Different barriers require different solutions. Motivational barriers require leaders to pull levers that make people more willing to collaborate. Ability barriers mean that leaders need to pull levers that enable motivated people to collaborate throughout the organization.

To be effective, leaders can choose a mix of three levers. First, when motivation is the problem, they can use the *unification lever,* wherein they craft compelling common goals, articulate a strong value of cross-company teamwork, and encourage collaboration in order to send strong signals to lift people's sights beyond their narrow interests toward a common goal.

Second, with the *people lever,* the emphasis isn't on getting people to collaborate more. Rather, it's on getting the right people to collaborate on the right projects. This means cultivating what may be called *T-shaped management:* people who simultaneously focus on the performance of their unit (the vertical part of the T) and across boundaries (the horizontal part of the T). People become able to collaborate when needed but are disciplined enough to say no when it's not required.

Third, by using the *network lever,* leaders can build nimble interpersonal networks across the company so that employees are better able to collaborate. Interpersonal networks are more effective than formal hierarchies. However, there is a dark side to networks: When people spend more time networking than getting work done, collaboration can adversely affect results.

unification lever method for making people more willing to collaborate by crafting compelling common goals articulating a strong value of cross-company teamwork, and encouraging collaboration in order to send strong signals to lift people's sights beyond their narrow interests towards a common goal.

network lever method for making people more willing to collaborate by building nimble interpersonal networks across the company.

T-shaped management people's dual focus on the performance of their unit (the vertical part of the T) and across boundaries (the horizontal part of the T).

people lever method for making people more willing to collaborate by getting the right people to work on the right projects.

strategy spotlight

Picasso versus van Gogh: Who Was More Successful and Why?

Vincent van Gogh and Pablo Picasso are two of the most iconoclastic—and famous—artists of modern times. Paintings by both of them have fetched over $100 million. And both of them were responsible for some of the most iconic images in the art world: Van Gogh's *Self-Portrait* (the one sans the earlobe) and *Starry Night* and Picasso's *The Old Guitarist* and *Guernica.* However, there is an important difference between van Gogh and Picasso. Van Gogh died penniless. Picasso's estate was estimated at $750 million when he died in 1973. What was the difference?

Van Gogh's primary connection to the art world was through his brother. Unfortunately, this connection didn't feed directly into the money that could have turned him into a living success. In contrast, Picasso's myriad connections provided him with access to commercial riches. As noted by Gregory Berns in his book *Iconoclast: A Neuroscientist Reveals How to Think Differently,* "Picasso's wide ranging social network, which included artists, writers, and politicians, meant that he was never more than a few people away from anyone of importance in the world."

In effect, van Gogh was a loner, and the charismatic Picasso was an active member of multiple social circles. In social networking terms, van Gogh was a solitary "node" who had few connections. Picasso, on the other hand, was a "hub" who embedded himself in a vast network

● Picasso was far more financially successful during his lifetime than van Gogh largely because of his extensive social network.

that stretched across various social lines. Where Picasso smoothly navigated multiple social circles, van Gogh had to struggle just to maintain connections with even those closest to him. Van Gogh inhabited an alien world, whereas Picasso was a social magnet. And because he knew so many people, the world was at Picasso's fingertips. From his perspective, the world was smaller.

Sources: Hayashi, A. M. 2008. Why Picasso Out Earned van Gogh. *MIT Sloan Management Review,* 50(1): 11–12; and Berns, G. 2008. *A Neuroscientist Reveals How to Think Differently.* Boston, MA: Harvard Business Press.

---

private information information that is not available from public sources, and is usually communicated in the context of personal relationships.

public information information that is available from public sources such as the internet.

Implications for Career Success   Let's go back in time in order to illustrate the value of social networks in one's career success. Consider two of the most celebrated artists of all time: Vincent van Gogh and Pablo Picasso. Strategy Spotlight 4.4 points out why these two artists enjoyed sharply contrasting levels of success during their lifetimes.

Effective social networks provide many advantages for the firm.[94] They can play a key role in an individual's career advancement and success. One's social network potentially can provide three unique advantages: private information, access to diverse skill sets, and power.[95] Managers see these advantages at work every day but might not consider how their networks regulate them.

Private Information   We make judgments, using both public and private information. Today, public information is available from many sources, including the Internet. However, since it is so accessible, public information offers less competitive advantage than it used to.

In contrast, private information from personal contacts can offer something not found in publicly available sources, such as the release date of a new product or knowledge about what a particular interviewer looks for in candidates. Private information can give managers an edge, though it is more subjective than public information since it cannot be easily verified by independent sources, such as Dunn & Bradstreet. Consequently the value of your private information to others—and the value of others' private information to you—depends on how much trust exists in the network of relationships.

Access to Diverse Skill Sets Linus Pauling, one of only two people to win a Nobel Prize in two different areas and considered one of the towering geniuses of the 20th century, attributed his creative success not to his immense brainpower or luck but to his diverse contacts. He said, "The best way to have a good idea is to have a lot of ideas."

While expertise has become more specialized during the past 15 years, organizational, product, and marketing issues have become more interdisciplinary. This means that success is tied to the ability to transcend natural skill limitations through others. Highly diverse network relationships, therefore, can help you develop more complete, creative, and unbiased perspectives on issues. Trading information or skills with people whose experiences differ from your own, provides you with unique, exceptionally valuable resources. It is common for people in relationships to share their problems. If you know enough people, you will begin to see how the problems that another person is struggling with can be solved by the solutions being developed by others. If you can bring together problems and solutions, it will greatly benefit your career.

Power Traditionally, a manager's power was embedded in a firm's hierarchy. But, when corporate organizations became flatter, more like pancakes than pyramids, that power was repositioned in the network's brokers (people who bridged multiple networks), who could adapt to changes in the organization, develop clients, and synthesize opposing points of view. Such brokers weren't necessarily at the top of the hierarchy or experts in their fields, but they linked specialists in the firm with trustworthy and informative relationships.[96]

Most personal networks are highly clustered; that is, an individual's friends are likely to be friends with one another as well. Most corporate networks are made up of several clusters that have few links between them. Brokers are especially powerful because they connect separate clusters, thus stimulating collaboration among otherwise independent specialists.

Before moving on, Strategy Spotlight 4.5 discusses an interesting research study. It points out how women may differ from men in how they develop their social networks.

The Potential Downside of Social Capital

We'd like to close our discussion of social capital by addressing some of its limitations. First, some firms have been adversely affected by very high levels of social capital because it may breed **"groupthink"**—a tendency not to question shared beliefs.[97] Such thinking may occur in networks with high levels of closure where there is little input from people outside of the network. In effect, too many warm and fuzzy feelings among group members prevent people from rigorously challenging each other. People are discouraged from engaging in the "creative abrasion" that Dorothy Leonard of Harvard University describes as a key source of innovation.[98] Two firms that were well known for their collegiality, strong sense of employee membership, and humane treatment—Digital Equipment (now part of Hewlett-Packard) and Polaroid—suffered greatly from market misjudgments and strategic errors. The aforementioned aspects of their culture contributed to their problems.

Second, if there are deep-rooted mindsets, there would be a tendency to develop dysfunctional human resource practices. That is, the organization (or group) would continue to

groupthink a tendency in an organization for individuals not to question shared beliefs.

Developing Social Capital: Do Women and Men Differ?

Several years ago, Boris Groysberg conducted a study in which he warned managers about the risks associated with hiring star performers away from companies. His research investigated more than 1,000 star stock analysts, and he found that when one of them switches companies, not only does the star's performance plunge, but also the market value of the star's new company declines. In addition, the players don't tend to stay with their new firms very long—despite the generous pay packages that lured them in the first place. So everyone loses out.

However, when Groysberg further analyzed the data, he gained some new insights. One group of analysts maintained their stardom after changing employers: women. Unlike their male counterparts, female stars who switched firms performed just as well, in aggregate, as those who stayed put.

Why the gender discrepancy? There were two explanations. *First, the best female analysts appear to have built their franchises on portable, external relationships with clients and companies they covered—rather than on relationships within their firms.* In contrast, male analysts

Source: Groysberg, B . 2008. How Star Women Build Portable Skills. *Harvard Business Review*, 86(2): 74–81.

built up greater firm- and team-specific human capital. That is, they invested more in internal networks and unique capabilities and resources of the firms where they worked.

Second, women took greater care when assessing a prospective employer. They evaluated their options more carefully and analyzed a wider range of factors than men did before deciding to uproot themselves from a firm where they had been successful. Female star analysts, it seems, take their work environment more seriously yet rely on it less than male stars do. And they tend to look for a firm that will allow them to keep building their successful franchise their own way.

There is a clear explanation as to why the female analysts spent more time developing their external networks. Most salespeople, traders, and investment bankers are men. And men tend to spend more time with other men. Not surprisingly, the star women in the study were generally thwarted in their efforts to integrate themselves into the existing power structure. Thus, they went to greater lengths to cultivate relationships with clients and contacts at the companies they covered. Their decision to maintain such an external focus rested on four main factors: uneasy in-house relationships, poor mentorships, neglect by colleagues, and a vulnerable position in the labor market.

hire, reward, and promote like-minded people who tend to further intensify organizational inertia and erode innovation. Such homogeneity would increase over time and decrease the effectiveness of decision-making processes.

Third, the socialization processes (orientation, training, etc.) can be expensive in terms of both financial resources and managerial commitment. Such investments can represent a significant opportunity cost that should be evaluated in terms of the intended benefits. If such expenses become excessive, profitability would be adversely affected.

Finally, individuals may use the contacts they develop to pursue their own interests and agendas that may be inconsistent with the organization's goals and objectives. Thus, they may distort or selectively use information to favor their preferred courses of action or withhold information in their own self-interest to enhance their power to the detriment of the common good. Drawing on our discussion of social networks, this is particularly true in an organization that has too many bridging relationships but not enough closure relationships. In high closure groups, it is easier to watch each other to ensure that illegal or unethical acts don't occur. By contrast, bridging relationships make it easier for a person to play one group or individual off on another, with no one being the wiser.[99] We will discuss some behavioral control mechanisms in Chapter 9 (rewards, control, boundaries) that reduce such dysfunctional behaviors and actions.[100]

Using Technology to Leverage Human Capital and Knowledge

Sharing knowledge and information throughout the organization can be a means of conserving resources, developing products and services, and creating new opportunities. In this section we will discuss how technology can be used to leverage human capital and knowledge within organizations as well as with customers and suppliers beyond their boundaries.

>LO4.5
The vital role of technology in leveraging knowledge and human capital.

Using Networks to Share Information

As we all know, e-mail is an effective means of communicating a wide variety of information. It is quick, easy, and almost costless. Of course, it can become a problem when employees use it extensively for personal reasons. And we all know how fast jokes or rumors can spread within and across organizations!

Below is an example of how a CEO curbed what he felt was excessive e-mail use in his firm.[101]

> Scott Dockter, CEO of PBD Worldwide Fulfillment Services in Alpharetta, Georgia, launched "no e-mail Friday." Why? He suspected that overdependence on e-mail at PBD, which offers services such as call center management and distribution, was hurting productivity and, perhaps, sales. Accordingly, he instructed his 275 employees to pick up the phone or meet in person each Friday, and reduce e-mail use the rest of the time.
>
> That was tough to digest, especially for the younger staffers. "We discovered a lot of introverts . . . who had drifted into a pattern of communicating by e-mail," says Dockter. "However, in less than four months, the simple directive resulted in quicker problem-solving, better teamwork, and, best of all, happier customers." "Our relationship with PBD is much stronger," says Cynthia Fitzpatrick of Crown Financial Ministries. "You can't get to know someone through e-mail."

E-mail can also cause embarrassment if one is not careful. Consider the plight of a potential CEO—as recalled by Marshall Goldsmith, a well-known executive coach:[102]

> I witnessed a series of e-mails between a potential CEO and a friend inside the company. The first e-mail to the friend provided an elaborate description of "why the current CEO is an idiot." The friend sent a reply. Several rounds of e-mails followed. Then the friend sent an e-mail containing a funny joke. The potential CEO decided that the current CEO would love this joke and forwarded it to him. You can guess what happened next. The CEO scrolled down the e-mail chain and found the "idiot" message. The heir apparent was gone in a week.

E-mail can, however, be a means for top executives to communicate information efficiently. For example, Martin Sorrell, chairman of WPP Group PLC, a $2.4 billion advertising and public relations firm, is a strong believer in the use of e-mail.[103] He e-mails all of his employees once a month to discuss how the company is doing, address specific issues, and offer his perspectives on hot issues, such as new business models for the Internet. He believes that it keeps people abreast of what he is working on.

Technology can also enable much more sophisticated forms of communication in addition to knowledge sharing. Buckman Laboratories is a $505 million specialty chemicals company based in Memphis, Tennessee, with approximately 1,500 employees in over 100 countries. Buckman has successfully used its global knowledge-sharing network—known as K'Netix—to enhance its competitive advantages:[104]

> Here's an example of how the network can be applied. One of Buckman's paper customers in Michigan realized that the peroxide it was adding to remove ink from old magazines

was no longer working. A Buckman sales manager presented this problem to the knowledge network. Within two days, salespeople from Belgium and Finland identified a likely cause: Bacteria in the paper slurry was producing an enzyme that broke down the peroxide. The sales manager recommended a chemical to control the bacteria, solving the problem. You can imagine how positive the customer felt about Buckman. And with the company and the customer co-creating knowledge, a new level of trust and value can emerge.

Electronic Teams: Using Technology to Enhance Collaboration

>LO4.6
Why "electronic" or "virtual" teams are critical in combining and leveraging knowledge in organizations and how they can be made more effective.

Technology enables professionals to work as part of electronic, or virtual, teams to enhance the speed and effectiveness with which products are developed. For example, Microsoft has concentrated much of its development on **electronic teams** (or e-teams) that are networked together.[105] This helps to accelerate design and testing of new software modules that use the Windows-based framework as their central architecture. Microsoft is able to foster specialized technical expertise while sharing knowledge rapidly throughout the firm. This helps the firm learn how its new technologies can be applied rapidly to new business ventures such as cable television, broadcasting, travel services, and financial services.

What are electronic teams (or e-teams)? There are two key differences between e-teams and more traditional teams:[106]

electronic teams a team of individuals that completes tasks primarily through e-mail communication.

- E-team members either work in geographically separated work places or they may work in the same space but at different times. E-teams may have members working in different spaces and time zones, as is the case with many multinational teams.
- Most of the interactions among members of e-teams occur through electronic communication channels such as fax machines and groupware tools such as e-mail, bulletin boards, chat, and videoconferencing.

E-teams have expanded exponentially in recent years.[107] Organizations face increasingly high levels of complex and dynamic change. E-teams are also effective in helping businesses cope with global challenges. Most e-teams perform very complex tasks and most knowledge-based teams are charged with developing new products, improving organizational processes, and satisfying challenging customer problems. For example, Eastman Kodak's e-teams design new products, Hewlett Packard's e-teams solve clients' computing problems, and Sun Microsystems' (part of oracle) e-teams generate new business models.

Advantages There are multiple advantages of e-teams.[108] In addition to the rather obvious use of technology to facilitate communications, the potential benefits parallel the other two major sections in this chapter—human capital and social capital.

First, e-teams are less restricted by the geographic constraints that are placed on face-to-face teams. Thus, e-teams have the potential to acquire a broader range of "human capital" or the skills and capacities that are necessary to complete complex assignments. So, e-team leaders can draw upon a greater pool of talent to address a wider range of problems since they are not constrained by geographic space. Once formed, e-teams can be more flexible in responding to unanticipated work challenges and opportunities because team members can be rotated out of projects when demands and contingencies alter the team's objectives.

Second, e-teams can be very effective in generating "social capital"—the quality of relationships and networks that form. Such capital is a key lubricant in work transactions and operations. Given the broader boundaries associated with e-teams, members and leaders generally have access to a wider range of social contacts than would be typically available in more traditional face-to-face teams. Such contacts are often connected to a broader scope of clients, customers, constituents, and other key stakeholders.

Challenges However, there are challenges associated with making e-teams effective. Successful action by both traditional teams and e-teams requires that:

- Members *identify* who among them can provide the most appropriate knowledge and resources, and,
- E-team leaders and key members know how to *combine* individual contributions in the most effective manner for a coordinated and appropriate response.

Group psychologists have termed such activities "identification and combination" activities and teams that fail to perform them face a "process loss."[109] Process losses prevent teams from reaching high levels of performance because of inefficient interaction dynamics among team members. Such poor dynamics require that some collective energy, time, and effort be devoted to dealing with team inefficiencies, thus diverting the team away from its objectives. For example, if a team member fails to communicate important information at critical phases of a project, other members may waste time and energy. This can lead to conflict and resentment as well as to decreased motivation to work hard to complete tasks.

The potential for process losses tends to be more prevalent in e-teams than in traditional teams because the geographical dispersion of members increases the complexity of establishing effective interaction and exchanges. Generally, teams suffer process loss because of low cohesion, low trust among members, a lack of appropriate norms or standard operating procedures, or a lack of shared understanding among team members about their tasks. With e-teams, members are more geographically or temporally dispersed, and the team becomes more susceptible to the risk factors that can create process loss. Such problems can be exacerbated when team members have less than ideal competencies and social skills. This can erode problem-solving capabilities as well as the effective functioning of the group as a social unit.

A variety of technologies, from e-mail and Internet groups to Skype (acquired by eBay in 2005) and Cisco's Umi TelePresence, have facilitated the formation and effective functioning of e-teams as well as a wide range of collaborations within companies. Strategy Spotlight 4.6 highlights Cisco's efforts to use technology to enable such communication. Such technologies greatly enhance the collaborative abilities of employees and managers within a company at a reasonable cost—despite the distances that separate them.

Codifying Knowledge for Competitive Advantage

There are two different kinds of knowledge. Tacit knowledge is embedded in personal experience and shared only with the consent and participation of the individual. Explicit (or codified) knowledge, on the other hand, is knowledge that can be documented, widely distributed, and easily replicated. One of the challenges of knowledge-intensive organizations is to capture and codify the knowledge and experience that, in effect, resides in the heads of its employees. Otherwise, they will have to constantly "reinvent the wheel," which is both expensive and inefficient. Also, the "new wheel" may not necessarily be superior to the "old wheel."[110]

Once a knowledge asset (e.g., a software code or processes) is developed and paid for, it can be reused many times at very low cost, assuming that it doesn't have to be substantially modified each time. Let's take the case of a consulting company, such as Accenture (formerly Andersen Consulting).[111] Since the knowledge of its consultants has been codified and stored in electronic repositories, it can be employed in many jobs by a huge number of consultants. Additionally, since the work has a high level of standardization (i.e., there are strong similarities across the numerous client engagements), there is a rather high ratio of consultants to partners. For example, the ratio of consultants to partners is roughly 30, which is quite high. As one might expect, there must be extensive training of the newly hired consultants for such an approach to work. The recruits are trained at Accenture's

Videoconferencing: Allowing Employees to Communicate Face-to-Face over Long Distances

Cisco Systems has recognized that collaboration is the biggest technological trend of the next decade, driving productivity gains of 5 to 10 percent per year. It has created a strong portfolio of collaboration technologies, including TelePresence; WebEx; phones that run over the Internet; devices that produce, distribute, and archive videos; and hardware that can carry, distribute, and manage communications traffic no matter the origin or destination.

Internally, the use of these technologies has helped make Cisco's workforce one of the most distributed, connected, and productive in the world. Employees have experienced—and driven—a cultural revolution of not only information-sharing, but also teamwork and transparency.

Sources: Copeland, M. V. 2010. The New Global Worker Gadget: Videophones. *Fortune*, November 15: 36; Sidhu, I. 2010. *Doing Both*. Boston: Harvard Business Press; and Baig, E. C. 2010. Umi TelePresence Brings Videoconferencing Home. *www.usatoday.com*. December 2: np.

In a recent year, for example, TelePresence usage has increased 10 times, while WebEx conferencing usage has soared by 25 times. In addition, video postings have grown by more than 11 times on the company's website.

Cisco recently launched a new videoconferencing product, Umi TelePresence, that is aimed at the consumer market. It costs $599 (for the camera, console, cables, and remote control that constitute the system) and comes with an unlimited calling plan that runs $25 a month. What makes the product more expensive is that you might have to purchase a second or third Umi for family members, simply because it takes at least "two to tango" when it comes to videoconferencing. However, corporations could also use such home systems to allow global employees to connect with headquarters during business hours. As noted by Srinath Narasimhan, CEO of Tata Communications, remote employees are loath to go to the office for a 3 A.M. call in a video "suite." However, with a home setup, these employees could stumble out of bed and into a meeting—as long as they remember to comb their hair first!

Center for Professional Education, a 150-acre campus in St. Charles, Illinois. Using the center's knowledge-management respository, the consultants work through many scenarios designed to improve business processes. In effect, the information technologies enable the consultants to be "implementers, not inventors."

Access Health, a call-in medical center, also uses technology to capture and share knowledge. When someone calls the center, a registered nurse uses the company's "clinical decision architecture" to assess the caller's symptoms, rule out possible conditions, and recommend a home remedy, doctor's visit, or trip to the emergency room. The company's knowledge repository contains algorithms of the symptoms of more than 500 illnesses. According to CEO Joseph Tallman, "We are not inventing a new way to cure disease. We are taking available knowledge and inventing processes to put it to better use." The software algorithms were very expensive to develop, but the investment has been repaid many times over. The first 300 algorithms that Access Health developed have each been used an average of 8,000 times a year. Further, the company's paying customers—insurance companies and provider groups—save money because many callers would have made expensive trips to the emergency room or the doctor's office had they not been diagnosed over the phone.

The user community can be a major source of knowledge creation for a firm. Strategy Spotlight 4.7 highlights how SAP, in an example of effective crowdsourcing, has been able to leverage the expertise and involvement of its users to develop new knowledge and transmit it to their entire user community.

Crowdsourcing: How SAP Taps Knowledge Well beyond Its Boundaries

Traditionally, organizations built and protected their knowledge stocks—proprietary resources that no one else could access. However, the more the business environment changes, the faster the value of what you know at any point in time diminishes. In today's world, success hinges on the ability to access a growing variety of knowledge flows in order to rapidly replenish the firm's knowledge stocks. For example, when an organization tries to improve cycle times in a manufacturing process, it finds far more value in problem solving shaped by the diverse experiences, perspectives, and learning of a tightly knit team (shared through knowledge flows) than in a training manual (knowledge stocks) alone.

Knowledge flows can help companies gain competitive advantage in an age of near-constant disruption. The

software company SAP, for example, routinely taps the more than 1.5 million participants in its Developer Network, which extends well beyond the boundaries of the firm. Those who post questions for the network community to address will receive a response in 17 minutes, on average, and 85 percent of all questions posted to date have been rated as "resolved." By providing a virtual platform for customers, developers, system integrators, and service vendors to create and exchange knowledge, SAP has significantly increased the productivity of all the participants in its ecosystem.

The site is open to everyone, regardless of whether you are an SAP customer, partner, or newcomer who needs to work with SAP technology. The site offers technical articles, Web-based training, code samples, evaluation systems, discussion forums, and excellent blogs for community experts.

Source: Hagel, J., III., Brown, J. S., & Davison, L. 2009. The Big Shift: Measuring the Forces of Change. *Harvard Business Review*, 87(4): 87; and Anonymous. undated. SAP Developer Network. *sap.sys-con.com*. np.

crowdsourcing

We close this section with a series of questions managers should consider in determining (1) how effective their organization is in attracting, developing, and retaining human capital and (2) how effective they are in leveraging human capital through social capital and technology. These questions, included in Exhibit 4.7, summarize some of the key issues addressed in this chapter.

Protecting the Intellectual Assets of the Organization: Intellectual Property and Dynamic Capabilities

> **>LO4.7**
> The challenge of protecting intellectual property and the importance of a firm's dynamic capabilities.

In today's dynamic and turbulent world, unpredictability and fast change dominate the business environment. Firms can use technology, attract human capital, or tap into research and design networks to get access to pretty much the same information as their competitors. So what would give firms a sustainable competitive advantage?[112] Protecting a firm's intellectual property requires a concerted effort on the part of the company. After all, employees become disgruntled and patents expire. The management of intellectual property (IP) involves, besides patents, contracts with confidentiality and noncompete clauses, copyrights, and the development of trademarks. Moreover, developing dynamic capabilities is the only avenue providing firms with the ability to reconfigure their knowledge and activities to achieve a sustainable competitive advantage.

Intellectual Property Rights

> **intellectual property rights** intangible property owned by a firm in the forms of patents, copyrights, trademarks, or trade secrets.

Intellectual property rights are more difficult to define and protect than property rights for physical assets (e.g., plant, equipment, and land). However, if intellectual property

Exhibit 4.7   Issues to Consider in Creating Value through Human Capital, Social Capital, and Technology

Human Capital

Recruiting "Top-Notch" Human Capital

- Does the organization assess attitude and "general makeup" instead of focusing primarily on skills and background in selecting employees at all levels?
- How important are creativity and problem-solving ability? Are they properly considered in hiring decisions?
- Do people throughout the organization engage in effective networking activities to obtain a broad pool of worthy potential employees? Is the organization creative in such endeavors?

Enhancing Human Capital through Employee Development

- Does the development and training process inculcate an "organizationwide" perspective?
- Is there widespread involvement, including top executives, in the preparation and delivery of training and development programs?
- Is the development of human capital effectively tracked and monitored?
- Are there effective programs for succession at all levels of the organization, especially at the top-most levels?
- Does the firm effectively evaluate its human capital? Is a 360-degree evaluation used? Why? Why not?
- Are mechanisms in place to assure that a manager's success does not come at the cost of compromising the organization's core values?

Retaining the Best Employees

- Are there appropriate financial rewards to motivate employees at all levels?
- Do people throughout the organization strongly identify with the organization's mission?
- Are employees provided with a stimulating and challenging work environment that fosters professional growth?
- Are valued amenities provided (e.g., flex time, child-care facilities, telecommuting) that are appropriate given the organization's mission, strategy, and how work is accomplished?
- Is the organization continually devising strategies and mechanisms to retain top performers?

Social Capital

- Are there positive personal and professional relationships among employees?
- Is the organization benefiting (or being penalized) by hiring (or by voluntary turnover) en masse?
- Does an environment of caring and encouragement rather than competition enhance team performance?
- Do the social networks within the organization have the appropriate levels of closure and bridging relationships?
- Does the organization minimize the adverse effects of excessive social capital, such as excessive costs and "groupthink"?

Technology

- Has the organization used technologies such as e-mail and networks to develop products and services?
- Does the organization effectively use technology to transfer best practices across the organization?
- Does the organization use technology to leverage human capital and knowledge both within the boundaries of the organization and among its suppliers and customers?
- Has the organization effectively used technology to codify knowledge for competitive advantage?
- Does the organization try to retain some of the knowledge of employees when they decide to leave the firm?

Source: Adapted from Dess, G. G., & Picken, J. C. 1999. *Beyond Productivity:* 63–64. New York: AMACON.

rights are not reliably protected by the state, there will be no incentive to develop new products and services. Property rights have been enshrined in constitutions and rules of law in many countries. In the information era, though, adjustments need to be made to accommodate the new realities of knowledge. Knowledge and information are fundamentally different assets from the physical ones that property rights have been designed to protect.

The protection of intellectual rights raises unique issues, compared to physical property rights. IP is characterized by significant development costs and very low marginal costs. Indeed, it may take a substantial investment to develop a software program, an idea, or a digital music tune. Once developed, though, their reproduction and distribution cost may be almost zero, especially if the Internet is used. Effective protection of intellectual property is necessary before any investor will finance such an undertaking. Appropriation of their returns is harder to police since possession and deployment are not as readily observable. Unlike physical assets, intellectual property can be stolen by simply broadcasting it. Recall Napster and MP3 as well as the debates about counterfeit software, music CDs, and DVDs coming from developing countries such as China. Part of the problem is that using an idea does not prevent others from simultaneously using it for their own benefit, which is typically impossible with physical assets. Moreover, new ideas are frequently built on old ideas and are not easily traceable.

Strategy Spotlight 4.8 describes the many legal battles fought by a Canadian firm, Research in Motion of Waterloo, the developer of the popular BlackBerry. This example illustrates the high stakes that ride on intellectual property rights.

Countries are attempting to pass new legislation to cope with developments in new pharmaceutical compounds, stem cell research, and biotechnology. However, a firm that is faced with this challenge today cannot wait for the legislation to catch up. New technological developments, software solutions, electronic games, online services, and other products and services contribute to our economic prosperity and the creation of wealth for those entrepreneurs who have the idea first and risk bringing it to the market.

Dynamic Capabilities

Dynamic capabilities entail the capacity to build and protect a competitive advantage.[113] This rests on knowledge, assets, competencies, and complementary assets and technologies as well as the ability to sense and seize new opportunities, generate new knowledge, and reconfigure existing assets and capabilities.[114] According to David Teece, an economist at the University of California at Berkeley, dynamic capabilities are related to the entrepreneurial side of the firm and are built within a firm through its environmental and technological "sensing" apparatus, its choices of organizational form, and its collective ability to strategize. Dynamic capabilities are about the ability of an organization to challenge the conventional wisdom within its industry and market, learn and innovate, adapt to the changing world, and continuously adopt new ways to serve the evolving needs of the market.[115]

Examples of dynamic capabilities include product development, strategic decision making, alliances, and acquisitions.[116] Some firms have clearly developed internal processes and routines that make them superior in such activities. For example, 3M and Apple are ahead of their competitors in product development. Cisco Systems has made numerous acquisitions over the years. They seem to have developed the capability to identify and evaluate potential acquisition candidates and seamlessly integrate them once the acquisition is completed. Other organizations can try to copy Cisco's practices. However, Cisco's combination of the resources of the acquired companies and their reconfiguration that Cisco has already achieved places them well ahead of their competitors. As markets become

dynamic capabilities a firm's capacity to build and protect a competitive advantage, which rests on knowledge, assets, competencies, complementary assets, and technologies. Dynamic capabilities include the ability to sense and seize new opportunities, generate new knowledge, and reconfigure existing assets and capabilities.

strategy spotlight

Research in Motion, Maker of the BlackBerry, Loses an Intellectual Property Lawsuit

Research in Motion (RIM) is a Waterloo, Ontario–based company that is best known for developing the Black-Berry, a wireless device that integrates the functionalities of a cell phone with the ability to receive e-mail messages. During its brief history, it has become one of the fastest growing companies in North America. Founded by Mike Lazaridis, a former University of Waterloo student in 1984, Research in Motion was a competent but obscure technology firm until 1999 when the first BlackBerry was released. Through the development of integrated hardware, software, and services that support multiple wireless network standards, the BlackBerry has enabled RIM to grow from less than $50 million in sales revenue in 1999 to $15 billion by 2010. Even more impressive, by early 2011 the company boasted a market capitalization in excess of $30 billion. RIM's commitment to their slogan "always on, always connected" has won them a legion of dedicated followers around the globe.

Interestingly, legal challenges have been the biggest obstacles that Research in Motion has faced in the eight years since the introduction of the first BlackBerry. In 2000, NTP, a pure patent-holding company, filed suit against RIM for violation of five of its patents and petitioned the court for an injunction on the sale and support of BlackBerry devices. The case dragged on for years, and RIM felt relatively secure that no injunction would be

● Research in Motion (RIM) has faced litigation over its highly successful BlackBerry.

issued. On February 24, 2006, things dramatically changed. U.S. District Court Judge James Spencer indicated that he was inclined to grant the injunction and that his ruling was imminent. Faced with the acute risk of an unfavorable decision, RIM settled only one week later for $612.5 million. It wound up paying a fortune for rights that were dubious at best—given that all five NTP patents had already been preliminarily invalidated by the U.S. Patent and Trademark Office and that two of them then received a final rejection.

Sources: Henkel, J. & Reitzig, M. 2008. Patent Sharks. *Harvard Business Review*, 86(6): 129–133; Hesseldahl, A. 2006. RIM's Latest Patent Problem. *BusinessWeek Online*, May 2: np; Anonymous. 2006. Settlement Reached in BlackBerry Patent Case. (The Associated Press) MSNBC.Com. March 3: np; Wolk, M . 2006. RIM Pays Up, Taking "One for the Team." MSNBC.Com. March 3; and *finance.yahoo.com*.

increasingly dynamic, traditional sources of long-term competitive advantage become less relevant. In such markets, all that a firm can strive for are a series of temporary advantages. Dynamic capabilities allow a firm to create this series of temporary advantages through new resource configurations.[117]

Reflecting on Career Implications . . .

- *Human Capital:* Does your organization effectively attract, develop, and retain talent? If not, you may have fewer career opportunities to enhance your human capital at your organization. Do you take advantage of your organization's human resource programs such as tuition reimbursement, mentoring, etc.
- *Human Capital:* Does your organization value diversity? What kinds of diversity seem to be encouraged (e.g., age-based or ethnicity-based)? If not, there may be limited perspectives on strategic and operational issues and a career at this organization may be less attractive to you.
- *Social Capital:* Does your organization have effective programs to build and develop social capital such that professionals develop strong "ties" to the organization? Alternatively, is social capital so strong that you see effects occur such as "groupthink"? From your perspective, how might you better leverage social capital towards pursuing other career opportunities?
- *Technology:* Does your organization provide and effectively use technology (e.g., groupware, knowledge management systems) to help you leverage your talents and expand your knowledge base?

Summary

Firms throughout the industrial world are recognizing that the knowledge worker is the key to success in the marketplace. However, we also recognize that human capital, although vital, is still only a necessary, but not a sufficient, condition for creating value. We began the first section of the chapter by addressing the importance of human capital and how it can be attracted, developed, and retained. Then we discussed the role of social capital and technology in leveraging human capital for competitive success. We pointed out that intellectual capital—the difference between a firm's market value and its book value—has increased significantly over the past few decades. This is particularly true for firms in knowledge-intensive industries, especially where there are relatively few tangible assets, such as software development.

The second section of the chapter addressed the attraction, development, and retention of human capital. We viewed these three activities as a "three-legged stool"—that is, it is difficult for firms to be successful if they ignore or are unsuccessful in any one of these activities. Among the issues we discussed in *attracting* human capital were "hiring for attitude, training for skill" and the value of using social networks to attract human capital. In particular, it is important to attract employees who can collaborate with others, given the importance of collective efforts such as teams and task forces. With regard to *developing* human capital, we discussed the need to encourage widespread involvement throughout the organization, monitor progress and track the development of human capital, and evaluate human capital. Among the issues that are widely practiced in evaluating human capital is the 360-degree evaluation system. Employees are evaluated by their superiors, peers, direct reports, and even internal and external customers. We also addressed the value of maintaining a diverse workforce. Finally, some mechanisms for retaining human capital are employees' identification with the organization's mission and values, providing challenging work and a stimulating environment, the importance of financial and nonfinancial rewards and incentives, and providing flexibility and amenities. A key issue here is that a firm should not overemphasize financial rewards. After all, if individuals join an organization for money, they also are likely to leave for money. With money as the primary motivator, there is little chance that employees will develop firm-specific ties to keep them with the organization.

The third section of the chapter discussed the importance of social capital in leveraging human capital. Social capital refers to the network of relationships that individuals have throughout the organization as well as with customers and suppliers. Such ties can be critical in obtaining both information and resources. With regard to recruiting, for example, we saw how some firms are able to hire en masse groups of individuals who are part of social networks. Social relationships can also be very important in the effective functioning of groups. Finally, we discussed some of the potential downsides of social capital. These include the expenses that firms may bear when promoting social and working relationships among individuals as well as the potential for "groupthink," wherein individuals are reluctant to express divergent (or opposing) views on an issue because of social pressures to conform. We also introduced the concept of social networks. The relative advantages of being central in a network versus bridging multiple networks was discussed. We addressed the key role that social networks can play in both improving knowledge management and promoting career success.

The fourth section addressed the role of technology in leveraging human capital. We discussed relatively simple means of using technology, such as e-mail and networks where individuals can collaborate by way of personal computers. We provided suggestions and guidelines on how electronic teams can be effectively managed. We also addressed more sophisticated uses of technology, such as sophisticated management systems. Here knowledge can be codified and reused at very low cost, as we saw in the examples of firms in the consulting, health care, and high-technology industries.

In the last section we discussed the increasing importance of protecting a firm's intellectual property. Although traditional approaches such as patents, copyrights, and trademarks are important, the development of dynamic capabilities may be the best protection in the long run.

Summary Review Questions

1. Explain the role of knowledge in today's competitive environment.

2. Why is it important for managers to recognize the interdependence in the attraction, development, and retention of talented professionals?

3. What are some of the potential downsides for firms that engage in a "war for talent"?

4. Discuss the need for managers to use social capital in leveraging their human capital both within and across their firm.

5. Discuss the key role of technology in leveraging knowledge and human capital.

Key Terms

knowledge
   economy, 125
intellectual capital, 126
human capital, 126
social capital, 126
explicit knowledge, 127
tacit knowledge, 127
social network
   analysis, 138
360-degree evaluation and
   feedback systems, 133
closure, 140
bridging
   relationships, 140

structural holes, 140
unification lever, 141
people lever, 141
T-shaped
   management, 141
networth lever, 141
private information, 142
public information, 142
groupthink, 143
electronic teams, 146
intellectual property
   rights, 149
dynamic
   capabilities, 151

Experiential Exercise

Pfizer, a leading health care firm with $68 billion in revenues, is often rated as one of *Fortune*'s "Most Admired Firms." It is also considered an excellent place to work and has generated high return to shareholders. Clearly, they value their human capital. Using the Internet and/or library resources, identify some of the actions/strategies Pfizer has taken to attract, develop, and retain human capital. What are their implications?

Activity	Actions/Strategies	Implications
Attracting human capital		
Developing human capital		
Retaining human capital		

Application Questions & Exercises

1. Look up successful firms in a high-technology industry as well as two successful firms in more traditional industries such as automobile manufacturing and retailing. Compare their market values and book values. What are some implications of these differences?

2. Select a firm for which you believe its social capital— both within the firm and among its suppliers and customers—is vital to its competitive advantage. Support your arguments.

3. Choose a company with which you are familiar. What are some of the ways in which it uses technology to leverage its human capital?

4. Using the Internet, look up a company with which you are familiar. What are some of the policies and procedures that it uses to enhance the firm's human and social capital?

Ethics Questions

1. Recall an example of a firm that recently faced an ethical crisis. How do you feel the crisis and management's handling of it affected the firm's human capital and social capital?

2. Based on your experiences or what you have learned in your previous classes, are you familiar with any companies that used unethical practices to attract talented professionals? What do you feel were the short-term and long-term consequences of such practices?

References

1. Farmbrough, R. 2010. List of the largest global technology companies: Part 1. *www.wikipedia.org.* November 1: np; and Arai, H. 2000. *Intellectual Property Policies for the Twenty-First Century: The Japanese Experience in Wealth Creation.* WIPO Publication No. 834 (E). We thank Pratik Kapadia for his valued contribution.

2. Parts of this chapter draw upon some of the ideas and examples from Dess, G. G. & Picken, J. C. 1999. *Beyond productivity.* New York: AMACOM.

3. An acknowledged trend: The world economic survey. 1996. *The Economist,* September 2(8): 25–28.

4. Quinn, J. B., Anderson, P., & Finkelstein, S. 1996. Leveraging intellect. *Academy of Management Executive,* 10(3): 7–27; and *https://www.cia.gov/library/publications/the=world=factbook/geos/us.html.*

5. Hamel, G. & Prahalad, C. K. 1996. Competing in the new economy: Managing out of bounds. *Strategic Management Journal,* 17: 238.

6. Stewart, T. A. 1997. *Intellectual capital: The new wealth of organizations.* New York: Doubleday/Currency.

7. Leif Edvisson and Michael S. Malone have a similar, more detailed definition of *intellectual capital:* "the combined knowledge, skill, innovativeness, and ability to meet the task at hand." They consider intellectual capital to equal human capital plus structural capital. *Structural capital* is defined as "the hardware, software, databases, organization structure, patents, trademarks, and everything else of organizational capability that supports those employees' productivity— in a word, everything left at the office when the employees go home." Edvisson, L. & Malone, M. S. 1997. *Intellectual capital: Realizing your company's true value by finding its hidden brainpower:* 10–14. New York: HarperBusiness.

8. Stewart, T. A. 2001. Accounting gets radical. *Fortune,* April 16: 184–194.

9. Adams, S. & Kichen, S. 2008. Ben Graham then and now. *Forbes,* November 10: 56.

10. An interesting discussion of Steve Jobs's impact on Apple's valuation is in: Lashinsky, A. 2009. Steve's leave—what does it really mean? *Fortune,* February 2: 96–102.

11. Anonyous. 2007. Intel opens first high volume 45 nm microprocessor manufacturing factory. *www.intel.com.* October 25: np.

12. Thomas Stewart has suggested this formula in his book *Intellectual capital.* He provides an insightful discussion on pages 224–225, including some of the limitations of this approach to measuring intellectual capital. We recognize, of course, that during the late 1990s and in early 2000, there were some excessive market valuations of high-technology and Internet firms. For an interesting discussion of the extraordinary market valuation of Yahoo!, an Internet company, refer to Perkins, A. B. 2001. The Internet bubble encapsulated: Yahoo! *Red Herring,* April 15: 17–18.

13. Roberts, P. W. & Dowling, G. R. 2002. Corporate reputation and sustained superior financial performance. *Strategic Management Journal,* 23(12): 1077–1095.

14. For a recent study on the relationships between human capital, learning, and sustainable competitive advantage, read Hatch, N. W. & Dyer, J. H. 2005. Human capital and learning as a source of sustainable competitive advantage. *Strategic Management Journal,* 25: 1155–1178.

15. One of the seminal contributions on knowledge management is Becker, G. S. 1993. *Human capital: A theoretical and empirical analysis with special reference to education* (3rd ed.). Chicago: University of Chicago Press.

16. For an excellent overview of the topic of social capital, read Baron, R. A. 2005. Social capital. In Hitt, M. A. & Ireland, R. D. (Eds.), *The Blackwell encyclopedia of management* (2nd ed.): 224–226. Malden, MA: Blackwell.

17. For an excellent discussion of social capital and its impact on organizational performance, refer to Nahapiet, J. & Ghoshal, S. 1998. Social capital, intellectual capital, and the organizational advantage. *Academy of Management Review,* 23: 242–266.

18. An interesting discussion of how knowledge management (patents) can enhance organizational performance can be found in Bogner, W. C. & Bansal, P. 2007. Knowledge management as the basis of sustained high performance. *Journal of Management Studies,* 44(1): 165–188.

19. Polanyi, M. 1967. *The tacit dimension.* Garden City, NY: Anchor Publishing.

20. Barney, J. B. 1991. Firm resources and sustained competitive advantage. *Journal of Management,* 17: 99–120.

21. For an interesting perspective of empirical research on how knowledge can adversely affect performance, read Haas, M. R. & Hansen, M. T. 2005. When using knowledge can hurt performance: The value of organizational capabilities in a management consulting company. *Strategic Management Journal,* 26(1): 1–24.

22. New insights on managing talent are provided in: Cappelli, P. 2008. Talent management for the twenty-first century. *Harvard Business Review,* 66(3): 74–81.

23. Some of the notable books on this topic include Edvisson & Malone, op. cit.; Stewart, op. cit.; and Nonaka, I. & Takeuchi, I. 1995. *The knowledge creating company.* New York: Oxford University Press.

24. Segalla, M. & Felton, N. 2010. Find the real power in your organization. *Harvard Business Review,* 88(5): 34–35.

25. Stewart, T. A. 2000. Taking risk to the marketplace. *Fortune,* March 6: 424.

26. Insights on the Generation X's perspective on the workplace are in: Erickson, T. J. 2008. Task, not time: Profile of a Gen Y job. *Harvard Business Review,* 86(2): 19.

27. Pfeffer, J. 2010. Building sustainable organizations: The human factor. *The Academy of Management Perspectives,* 24(1): 34–45.

28. Dutton, G. 1997. Are you technologically competent? *Management Review,* November: 54–58.

29. Some workplace implications for the aging workforce are addressed in: Strack, R., Baier, J., & Fahlander, A. 2008. Managing demographic risk. *Harvard Business Review,* 66(2): 119–128.

30. For a discussion of attracting, developing, and retaining top talent, refer to Goffee, R. & Jones, G. 2007. Leading clever people. *Harvard Business Review,* 85(3): 72–89.

31. Dess & Picken, op. cit.: 34.

32. Webber, A. M. 1998. Danger: Toxic company. *Fast Company,* November: 152–161.

33. Martin, J. & Schmidt, C. 2010. How to keep your top talent. *Harvard Business Review,* 88(5): 54–61.

34. Some interesting insights on why home-grown American talent is going abroad is found in: Saffo, P. 2009. A looming American diaspora. *Harvard Business Review,* 87(2): 27.

35. Morris, B. 1997. Key to success: People, people, people. *Fortune,* October 27: 232.

36. Davenport, T. H., Harris, J. & Shapiro, J. 2010. Competing on talent analytics. *Harvard Business Review,* 88(10): 62–69.

37. Ployhart, R. E. & Moliterno, T. P. 2011. Emergence of the human capital resource: A multilevel model. *Academy of Management Review,* 36(1): 127–150.

38. For insights on management development and firm performance in several countries, refer to: Mabey, C. 2008. Management development and firm performance in Germany, Norway, Spain, and the UK. *Journal of International Business Studies,* 39(8): 1327–1342.

39. Martin, J. 1998. So, you want to work for the best. . . . *Fortune,* January 12: 77.

40. Cardin, R. 1997. Make your own Bozo Filter. *Fast Company,* October–November: 56.

41. Gallagher, L. 2011. 100 best companies to work for *money.cnn.com.* January 20: np.

42. Martin, op. cit.; Henkoff, R. 1993. Companies that train best. *Fortune,* March 22: 53–60.

43. An interesting perspective on developing new talent rapidly when they join an organization can be found in Rollag, K., Parise, S., & Cross, R. 2005. Getting new hires up to speed quickly. *MIT Sloan Management Review,* 46(2): 35–41.

44. Stewart, T. A. 1998. Gray flannel suit? moi? *Fortune,* March 18: 80–82.

45. An interesting perspective on how Cisco Systems develops its talent can be found in Chatman, J., O'Reilly, C., & Chang, V. 2005. Cisco Systems: Developing a human capital strategy. *California Management Review,* 47(2): 137–166.

46. Anonymous. 2011. Schumpeter: The tussle for talent. *The Economist.* January 8: 68.

47. This section is based on Leonard, D. A. & Swap, W. 2004. Deep smarts. *Harvard Business Review,* 82(9): 88–97.

48. Useful insights on coaching can be found in: Coutu, D. & Kauffman, C. 2009. What coaches can do for you? *Harvard Business Review,* 67(1): 91–97.

49. For an innovative perspective on the appropriateness of alternate approaches to evaluation and rewards, refer to Seijts, G. H. & Lathan, G. P. 2005. Learning versus performance goals: When should each be used? *Academy of Management Executive,* 19(1): 124–132.

50. The discussion of the 360-degree feedback system draws on the article UPS. 1997. 360-degree feedback: Coming from all sides. *Vision* (a UPS Corporation internal company publication), March: 3; Slater, R. 1994. *Get better or get beaten: Thirty-one leadership secrets from Jack Welch.* Burr Ridge, IL: Irwin; Nexon, M. 1997. General Electric: The secrets of the finest company in the world.

L'Expansion, July 23: 18–30; and Smith, D. 1996. Bold new directions for human resources. *Merck World* (internal company publication), October: 8.

51. Interesting insights on 360-degree evaluation systems are discussed in: Barwise, P. & Meehan, Sean. 2008. So you think you're a good listener. *Harvard Business Review,* 66(4): 22–23.

52. Insights into the use of 360-degree evaluation are in: Kaplan, R. E. & Kaiser, R. B. 2009. Stop overdoing your strengths. *Harvard Business Review,* 87(2): 100–103.

53. Kets de Vries, M. F. R. 1998. Charisma in action: The transformational abilities of Virgin's Richard Branson and ABB's Percy Barnevik. *Organizational Dynamics,* Winter: 20.

54. For an interesting discussion on how organizational culture has helped Zappos become number one in *Fortune's* 2009 survey of the best companies to work for, see: O'Brien, J. M. 2009. Zappos knows how to kick it. *Fortune,* February 2: 54–58.

55. We have only to consider the most celebrated case of industrial espionage in recent years, wherein José Ignacio Lopez was indicted in a German court for stealing sensitive product planning documents from his former employer, General Motors, and sharing them with his executive colleagues at Volkswagen. The lawsuit was dismissed by the German courts, but Lopez and his colleagues were investigated by the U.S. Justice Department. Also consider the recent litigation involving noncompete employment contracts and confidentiality clauses of *International Paper v. Louisiana-Pacific, Campbell Soup v. H. J. Heinz Co.,* and *PepsiCo v. Quaker Oats's Gatorade.* In addition to retaining valuable human resources and often their valuable network of customers, firms must also protect proprietary information and knowledge. For interesting insights, refer to Carley, W. M. 1998. CEO gets hard lesson in how not to keep his lieutenants. *The Wall Street Journal,* February 11: A1, A10; and Lenzner, R.

& Shook, C. 1998. Whose Rolodex is it, anyway? *Forbes,* February 23: 100–103.

56. For an insightful discussion of retention of knowledge workers in today's economy, read Davenport, T. H. 2005. *The care and feeding of the knowledge worker.* Boston, MA: Harvard Business School Press.

57. Fisher, A. 2008. America's most admired companies. *Fortune,* March 17: 74.

58. Stewart, T. A. 2001. *The wealth of knowledge.* New York: Currency.

59. For insights on fulfilling one's potential, refer to: Kaplan, R. S. 2008. Reaching your potential. *Harvard Business Review,* 66(7/8): 45–57.

60. Amabile, T. M. 1997. Motivating creativity in organizations: On doing what you love and loving what you do. *California Management Review,* Fall: 39–58.

61. For an insightful perspective on alternate types of employee–employer relationships, read Erickson, T. J. & Gratton, L. 2007. What it means to work here. *Harvard Business Review,* 85(3): 104–112.

62. Monsanto has been part of Pharmacia since 2002. *Hoover's Handbook of Am. Bus.* 2004: 562.

63. Pfeffer, J. 2001. Fighting the war for talent is hazardous to your organization's health *Organizational Dynamics,* 29(4): 248–259.

64. Cox, T. L. 1991. The multinational organization. *Academy of Management Executive,* 5(2): 34–47. Without doubt, a great deal has been written on the topic of creating and maintaining an effective diverse workforce. Some excellent, recent books include: Harvey, C. P. & Allard, M. J. 2005. *Understanding and managing diversity: Readings, cases, and exercises.* (3rd ed.). Upper Saddle River, NJ: Pearson Prentice-Hall; Miller, F. A. & Katz, J. H. 2002. *The inclusion breakthrough: Unleashing the real power of diversity.* San Francisco: Berrett Koehler; and Williams, M. A. 2001. *The 10 lenses: Your guide to living and working in a multicultural world.* Sterling, VA: Capital Books.

65. For an interesting perspective on benefits and downsides of diversity in global consulting firms, refer to: Mors, M. L. 2010. Innovation in a global consulting firm: When the problem is too much diversity. *Strategic Management Journal,* 31(8): 841–872.

66. www.rand.org/publications/RB/RB/5050. U. S. Census Bureau. 1970, 1980, 1990, and 2000 decennial censuses. Population projections, July 1, 2000, to July 1, 2050.

67. Hewlett, S. A. & Rashid, R. 2010. The battle for female talent in emerging markets. *Harvard Business Review,* 88(5): 101–107.

68. This section, including the six potential benefits of a diverse workforce, draws on Cox, T. H. & Blake, S. 1991. Managing cultural diversity: Implications for organizational competitiveness. *Academy of Management Executive,* 5(3): 45–56.

69. www.pwcglobal.com/us/eng/careers/diversity/index.html.

70. Johansson, F. 2005. Masters of the multicultural. *Harvard Business Review,* 83(10): 18–19.

71. This discussion draws on Dess, G. G. & Lumpkin, G. T. 2001. Emerging issues in strategy process research. In Hitt, M. A., Freeman, R. E. & Harrison, J. S. (Eds.). *Handbook of strategic management:* 3–34 Malden, MA: Blackwell.

72. Wong, S.-S. & Boh, W. F. 2010. Leveraging the ties of others to build a reputation for trustworthiness among peers. *Academy of Management Journal,* 53(1): 129–148.

73. Adler, P. S. & Kwon, S. W. 2002. Social capital: Prospects for a new concept. *Academy of Management Review,* 27(1): 17–40.

74. Capelli, P. 2000. A market-driven approach to retaining talent. *Harvard Business Review,* 78(1): 103–113.

75. This hypothetical example draws on Peteraf, M. 1993. The cornerstones of competitive advantage. *Strategic Management Journal,* 14: 179–191.

76. Wernerfelt, B. 1984. A resource-based view of the firm. *Strategic Management Journal,* 5: 171–180.

77. Wysocki, B., Jr. 2000. Yet another hazard of the new economy: The Pied

Piper Effect. *The Wall Street Journal,* March 20: A1–A16.

78. Ideas on how managers can more effectively use their social network are addressed in: McGrath, C. & Zell, D. 2009. Profiles of trust: Who to turn to, and for what. *MIT Sloan Management Review,* 50(2): 75–80.

79. Ibid.

80. Buckman, R. C. 2000. Tech defectors from Microsoft resettle together. *The Wall Street Journal,* October: B1–B6.

81. An insightful discussion of the interorganizational aspects of social capital can be found in Dyer, J. H. & Singh, H. 1998. The relational view: Cooperative strategy and sources of interorganizational competitive advantage. *Academy of Management Review,* 23: 66–79.

82. A study of the relationship between social networks and performance in China is found in: Li, J. J., Poppo, L., & Zhou, K. Z. 2008. Do managerial ties in China always produce value? Competition, uncertainty, and domestic vs. foreign firms. *Strategic Management Journal,* 29(4): 383–400.

83. Aime, F., Johnson, S., Ridge, J. W. & Hill, A. D. 2010. The routine may be stable but the advantage is not: Competitive implications of key employee mobility. *Strategic Management Journal,* 31(1): 75–87.

84. Hoppe, B. 2005. Structural holes, Part one. *connectedness.blogspot.com.* January 18: np.

85. There has been a tremendous amount of theory building and empirical research in recent years in the area of social network analysis. Unquestionably, two of the major contributors to this domain have been Ronald Burt and J. S. Coleman. For excellent background discussions, refer to: Burt, R. S. 1992. *Structural holes: The social structure of competition.* Cambridge, MA: Harvard University Press; Coleman, J. S. 1990. *Foundations of social theory.* Cambridge, MA: Harvard University Press; and Coleman, J. S. 1988. Social capital in the creation of human capital. *American Journal of Sociology.* 94: S95–S120. For a more recent review and integration of current thought on

social network theory, consider: Burt, R. S. 2005. *Brokerage & closure: An introduction to social capital.* Oxford Press: New York.

86. Our discussion draws on the concepts developed by Burt, 1992, op. cit.; Coleman, 1990, op. cit.; Coleman, 1988, op. cit.; and Oh, H., Chung, M. & Labianca, G. 2004. Group social capital and group effectiveness: The role of informal socializing ties. *Academy of Management Journal,* 47(6): 860–875. We would like to thank Joe Labianca (University of Kentucky) for his helpful feedback and ideas in our discussion of social networks.

87. Arregle, J. L., Hitt, M. A., Sirmon, D. G., & Very, P. 2007. The development of organizational social capital: Attributes of family firms. *Journal of Management Studies,* 44(1): 73–95.

88. A novel perspective on social networks is in: Pentland, A. 2009. How social networks network best. *Harvard Business Review,* 87(2): 37.

89. Oh et al., op. cit.

90. Hoppe, op. cit.

91. The discussion of these two contingent factors draws on Dess, G. G. & Shaw, J. D. 2001. Voluntary turnover, social capital, and organizational performance. *Academy of Management Review,* 26(3): 446–456.

92. The business-level strategies of overall low cost and differentiation draws upon Michael E. Porter's classic work and will be discussed in more detail in Chapter 5. Source: Porter, M. E. 1985. *Competitive advantage.* Free Press: New York.

93. This section draws on: Hansen, M. T. 2009. *Collaboration: How leaders avoid the traps, create unity, and reap big results.* Boston, MA: Harvard Business Press.

94. Perspectives on how to use and develop decision networks are discussed in: Cross, R., Thomas, R. J., & Light, D. A. 2009. How "who you know" affects what you decide. *MIT Sloan Management Review,* 50(2): 35–42.

95. Our discussion of the three advantages of social networks draws on Uzzi, B. & Dunlap. S. 2005. How to

build your network. *Harvard Business Review,* 83(12): 53–60. For a recent, excellent review on the research exploring the relationship between social capital and managerial performance, read Moran, P. 2005. Structural vs. relational embeddedness: Social capital and managerial performance. *Strategic Management Journal,* 26(12): 1129–1151.

96. A perspective on personal influence is in: Christakis, N. A. 2009. The dynamics of personal influence. *Harvard Business Review,* 87(2): 31.

97. Prusak, L. & Cohen, D. 2001. How to invest in social capital. *Harvard Business Review,* 79(6): 86–93.

98. Leonard, D. & Straus, S. 1997. Putting your company's whole brain to work. *Harvard Business Review,* 75(4): 110–122.

99. For an excellent discussion of public (i.e., the organization) versus private (i.e., the individual manager) benefits of social capital, refer to Leana, C. R. & Van Buren, H. J. 1999. Organizational social capital and employment practices. *Academy of Management Review,* 24(3): 538–555.

100. The authors would like to thank Joe Labianca, University of Kentucky, and John Lin, University of Texas at Dallas, for their very helpful input in our discussion of social network theory and its practical implications.

101. Brady, D. 2006. !#?@ the e-mail. Can we talk?. *BusinessWeek,* December 4: 109.

102. Goldsmith, M. 2009. How not to lose the top job. *Harvard Business Review,* 87(1): 74.

103. Taylor, W. C. 1999. Whatever happened to globalization? *Fast Company,* December: 228–236.

104. Prahalad, C. K. & Ramaswamy, V. 2004. *The future of competition: Co-creating value with customers.* Boston: Harvard Business School Press.

105. Lei, D., Slocum, J., & Pitts, R. A. 1999. Designing organizations for competitive advantage: The power of unlearning and learning. *Organizational Dynamics,* Winter: 24–38.

106. This section draws upon Zaccaro, S. J. & Bader, P. 2002. E-Leadership and

the challenges of leading e-teams: Minimizing the bad and maximizing the good. *Organizational Dynamics,* 31(4): 377–387.

107. Kirkman, B. L., Rosen, B., Tesluk, P. E., & Gibson, C. B. 2004. The impact of team empowerment on virtual team performance: The moderating role of face-to-face interaction. *Academy of Management Journal,* 47(2): 175–192.

108. The discussion of the advantages and challenges associated with e-teams draws on Zacarro & Bader, op. cit.

109. For a recent study exploring the relationship between team empowerment, face-to-face interaction, and performance in virtual teams, read Kirkman, Rosen, Tesluk, & Gibson, op. cit.

110. For an innovative study on how firms share knowledge with competitors and the performance implications, read Spencer, J. W. 2003. Firms' knowledge sharing strategies in the global innovation system: Empirical evidence from the flat panel display industry. *Strategic Management Journal,* 24(3): 217–235.

111. The examples of Andersen Consulting and Access Health draw upon Hansen, M. T., Nohria, N., & Tierney, T. 1999. What's your strategy for managing knowledge? *Harvard Business Review,* 77(2): 106–118.

112. This discussion draws on Conley, J. G. 2005. *Intellectual capital management,* Kellogg School of Management and Schulich School of Business, York University, Toronto, KS 2003; Conley, J. G. & Szobocsan, J. 2001. Snow White shows the way. *Managing Intellectual Property,* June: 15–25; Greenspan, A. 2004. Intellectual property rights, The Federal Reserve Board, Remarks by the chairman, February 27; and Teece, D. J. 1998. Capturing value from knowledge assets, *California Management Review,* 40(3): 54–79. The authors would like to thank Professor Theo Peridis, York University, for his contribution to this section.

113. E. Danneels. 2011. Trying to become a different type of company: Dynamic capability at Smith Corona. *Strategic Management Journal,* 32(1): 1–31.

114. A study of the relationship between dynamic capabilities and related diversification is: Doving, E. & Gooderham, P. N. 2008. *Strategic Management Journal,* 29(8): 841–858.

115. A perspective on strategy in turbulent markets is in: Sull, D. 2009. How to thrive in turbulent markets. *Harvard Business Review,* 87(2): 78–88.

116. Lee, G. K. 2008. Relevance of organizational capabilities and its dynamics: What to learn from entrants' product portfolios about the determinants of entry timing. *Strategic Management Journal,* 29(12): 1257–1280.

117. Eisenhardt, K. M. & Martin, J. E. 2000. Dynamic capabilities: What are they? *Strategic Management Journal,* 21: 1105–1121.

chapter FIVE

Business-Level Strategy:

Creating and Sustaining Competitive Advantages

After reading this chapter, you should have a good understanding of:

LO5.1 The central role of competitive advantage in the study of strategic management, and the three generic strategies: overall cost leadership, differentiation, and focus.

LO5.2 How the successful attainment of generic strategies can improve a firm's relative power vis-à-vis the five forces that determine an industry's average profitability.

LO5.3 The pitfalls managers must avoid in striving to attain generic strategies.

LO5.4 How firms can effectively combine the generic strategies of overall cost leadership and differentiation.

LO5.5 What factors determine the sustainability of a firm's competitive advantage.

LO5.6 How Internet-enabled business models are being used to improve strategic positioning.

LO5.7 The importance of considering the industry life cycle to determine a firm's business-level strategy and its relative emphasis on functional area strategies and value-creating activities.

LO5.8 The need for turnaround strategies that enable a firm to reposition its competitive position in an industry.

LEARNING OBJECTIVES

How firms compete with each other and how they attain and sustain competitive advantages go to the heart of strategic management. In short, the key issue becomes: Why do some firms outperform others and enjoy such advantages over time? This subject, business-level strategy, is the focus of Chapter 5.

The first part of the chapter draws on Michael Porter's framework of generic strategies. He identifies three strategies—overall cost leadership, differentiation, and focus—that firms may apply to outperform their rivals in an industry. We begin by describing each of these strategies and providing examples of firms that have successfully attained them as a means of outperforming competitors in their industry. Next, we address how these strategies help a firm develop a favorable position vis-à-vis the "five forces," suggest some of the pitfalls that managers must avoid when pursuing these generic strategies, and discuss the conditions under which firms may effectively combine generic strategies to outperform rivals.

The second section discusses the factors that determine the sustainability of competitive advantages. Using an example from the manufacturing sector, we discuss whether or not a firm's competitive advantages may be sustained over a long period of time.

The third section addresses how competitive strategies should be revised and redeployed in light of the shifts in industry and competitive forces caused by Internet and digital strategies. Here, combination strategies are the most solid because they integrate the new capabilities with sound principles.

The fourth and final section discusses a vital consideration in the effective use of business-level strategies: industry life cycles. The four stages of the industry life cycle—introduction, growth, maturity, and decline—are indicative of an evolving management process that affects factors such as the market growth rate and the intensity of competition. Accordingly, the stages of an industry's life cycle are an important contingency that managers should take into account when making decisions concerning the optimal overall business-level strategies and the relative emphasis to place on functional capabilities and value-creating activities. At times, firms are faced with performance declines and must find ways to revitalize their competitive positions. The actions followed to do so are referred to as turnaround strategies, which may be needed at any stage of the industry life cycle. However, they occur more frequently during the maturity and decline stages.

Learning from Mistakes

Recently, a battle over strategy divided top management and franchise owners at KFC.[1] Many franchise owners became upset with KFC's new strategy that moved away from its Southern fried heritage and moved toward promoting grilled chicken and sandwiches. In early 2009, CEO Roger Eaton introduced grilled chicken in a move to target health-conscious consumers in today's changing society. However, many franchise owners were disappointed with this strategy. Why? What went wrong?

On January 2010, the KFC National Council and Advertising Cooperative (which represents all U.S. franchises) sued KFC to gain control of their own ad strategy. This "civil war" erupted when the company introduced grilled chicken with the slogan "Unthink KFC." To make matters worse, after a year in the market, reports stated that grilled chicken accounted for only about 16 percent of all "on the bone" chicken sold. Also, an internal survey of 642 franchisees showed almost 50 percent of the stores' grilled chicken was thrown away!

One glaring example of miscommunication regarding business strategy between management and franchise owners occurred when KFC launched a grilled chicken giveaway on *Oprah,* a wildly popular television program, in May 2009. Management told franchisees to expect a couple hundred customers to redeem online coupons at each store. However, thousands showed up expecting free grilled chicken. One franchise owner said, "The cost to the franchisee was much larger than they said," and that the promotion cost her almost $15,000! This started a continued downfall in trust between management and owners. KFC canceled the promotion, and CEO Eaton apologized to customers in an online video.

Disagreements between KFC management and franchise owners over strategy led to decreased sales and store closings. KFC's franchisees were upset with the decision to push grilled chicken and claimed that it hurts the brand. They sued KFC and now do a lot of their own advertising to promote fried chicken at their stores.

business-level strategy a strategy designed for a firm or a division of a firm that competes within a single business.

generic strategies an analysis of business strategy into basic types based on breadth of target market (industrywide versus narrow market segment) and type of competitive advantage (low cost versus uniqueness).

In order to create and sustain a competitive advantage, companies such as KFC should analyze the value chains of their customers and suppliers to see where they can add value. They should not focus only on their internal operations. By not listening to and consulting with franchise owners, KFC has ignored and angered a large part of their extended value chain. The battle over ad strategy within the company has hurt the brand and eroded KFC's competitive advantage.

Types of Competitive Advantage and Sustainability

> **>LO5.1**
>
> The central role of competitive advantage in the study of strategic management, and the three generic strategies: overall cost leadership, differentiation, and focus.

Michael Porter presented three generic strategies that a firm can use to overcome the five forces and achieve competitive advantage.[2] Each of Porter's generic strategies has the potential to allow a firm to outperform rivals in their industry. The first, *overall cost leadership,* is based on creating a low-cost-position. Here, a firm must manage the relationships throughout the value chain and lower costs throughout the entire chain. Second, *differentiation* requires a firm to create products and/or services that are unique and valued. Here, the primary emphasis is on "nonprice" attributes for which customers will gladly pay a premium.[3] Third, a *focus* strategy directs attention (or "focus") toward narrow product lines, buyer segments, or targeted geographic markets and they must attain advantages either through differentiation or cost leadership.[4] Whereas the overall cost leadership and differentiation strategies strive to attain advantages industrywide, focusers have a narrow target market in mind. Exhibit 5.1 illustrates these three strategies on two dimensions: competitive advantage and strategic target.

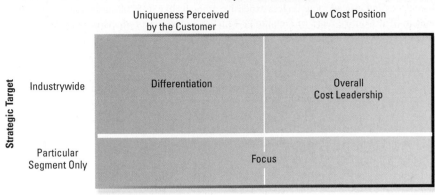

Exhibit 5.1 **Three Generic Strategies**

Source: Adapted and reprinted with the permission of The Free Press, a division of Simon & Schuster Inc. from *Competitive Strategy: Techniques for Analyzing Industries and Competitors* Michael E. Porter. Copyright © 1980, 1998 by The Free Press. All rights reserved.

Both casual observation and research support the notion that firms that identify with one or more of the forms of competitive advantage outperform those that do not.[5] There has been a rich history of strategic management research addressing this topic. One study analyzed 1,789 strategic business units and found that businesses combining multiple forms of competitive advantage (differentiation and overall cost leadership) outperformed businesses that used only a single form. The lowest performers were those that did not identify with any type of advantage. They were classified as "stuck in the middle." Results of this study are presented in Exhibit 5.2.[6]

For an example of the dangers of being "stuck in the middle," consider Coach and Tiffany—two brands in the "affordable luxury" category.[7] Such brands target middle-class customers for whom a $300 bag is a splurge. After sales and stock declines, they are migrating away from the middle—and going either higher or lower:

> In early 2008, Coach said that it would turn 40 of its nearly 300 stores into a more upscale format that will offer higher-end bags and concierge services. Tiffany, on the other hand, took

Exhibit 5.2 **Competitive Advantage and Business Performance**

	Competitive Advantage					
	Differentiation and Cost	Differentiation	Cost	Differentiation and Focus	Cost and Focus	Stuck in the Middle
Performance						
Return on investment (%)	35.5	32.9	30.2	17.0	23.7	17.8
Sales growth (%)	15.1	13.5	13.5	16.4	17.5	12.2
Gain in market share (%)	5.3	5.3	5.5	6.1	6.3	4.4
Sample size	123	160	100	141	86	105

the opposite tack. A new store opening in California will not sell any of its $148,000 diamond necklaces and instead focus on less expensive products like its $200-and-under silver jewelry. Claims Pat Conroy, head of Deloitte & Touche's consumer products sector: "Being in the middle is not a good place to be. You get assaulted from everyone."

overall cost leadership a firm's generic strategy based on appeal to the industrywide market using a competitive advantage based on low cost.

Overall Cost Leadership

The first generic strategy is overall cost leadership. Overall cost leadership requires a tight set of interrelated tactics that include:

- Aggressive construction of efficient-scale facilities.
- Vigorous pursuit of cost reductions from experience.
- Tight cost and overhead control.

Exhibit 5.3 Value-Chain Activities: Examples of Overall Cost Leadership

Support Activities

Firm Infrastructure

- Few management layers to reduce overhead costs.
- Standardized accounting practices to minimize personnel required.

Human Resource Management

- Minimize costs associated with employee turnover through effective policies.
- Effective orientation and training programs to maximize employee productivity.

Technology Development

- Effective use of automated technology to reduce scrappage rates.
- Expertise in process engineering to reduce manufacturing costs.

Procurement

- Effective policy guidelines to ensure low-cost raw materials (with acceptable quality levels).
- Shared purchasing operations with other business units.

Primary Activities

Inbound Logistics

- Effective layout of receiving dock operations.

Operations

- Effective use of quality control inspectors to minimize rework.

Outbound Logistics

- Effective utilization of delivery fleets

Marketing and Sales

- Purchase of media in large blocks.
- Sales force utilization is maximized by territory management.

Service

- Thorough service repair guidelines to minimize repeat maintenance calls.
- Use of single type of vehicle to minimize repair costs.

Source: Adapted from: Porter, M.E. 1985. *Competitive Advantage: Creating and Sustaining Superior Performance*. New York: Free Press.

The Experience Curve

The experience curve, developed by the Boston Consulting Group in 1968, is a way of looking at efficiencies developed through a firm's cumulative experience. In its basic form, the experience curve relates production costs to production output. As output doubles, costs decline by 10 percent to 30 percent. For example, if it costs $1 per unit to produce 100 units, the per unit cost will decline to between 70 to 90 cents as output increases to 200 units.

What factors account for this increased efficiency? First, the success of an experience curve strategy depends on the industry life cycle for the product. Early stages of a product's life cycle are typically characterized by rapid gains in technological advances in production efficiency. Most experience curve gains come early in the product life cycle.

Second, the inherent technology of the product offers opportunities for enhancement through gained experience. High-tech products give the best opportunity for gains in production efficiencies. As technology is developed, "value engineering" of innovative production processes is implemented, driving down the per unit costs of production.

Third, a product's sensitivity to price strongly affects a firm's ability to exploit the experience curve. Cutting the price of a product with high demand elasticity—where demand increases when price decreases—rapidly creates consumer purchases of the new product. By cutting prices, a firm can increase demand for its product. The increased demand in turn increases product manufacture, thus increasing the firm's experience in the manufacturing process. So by decreasing price and increasing demand, a firm gains manufacturing experience in that particular product, which drives down per unit production costs.

Fourth, the competitive landscape factors into whether or not a firm might benefit from an experience curve strategy. If other competitors are well positioned in the market,

Sources: Ghemawat, P. 1985. Building Strategy on the Experience Curve. *Harvard Business Review*, March–April: 143–149; Porter, M. E. 1996. *On Competition*. Boston: Harvard Business Review Press; and Oster, S. M. 1994. *Modern Competitive Analysis* (2nd ed.). New York: Oxford University Press.

have strong capital resources, and are known to promote their product lines aggressively to gain market share, an experience curve strategy may lead to nothing more than a price war between two or more strong competitors. But if a company is the first to market with the product and has good financial backing, an experience curve strategy may be successful.

In an article in the *Harvard Business Review,* Pankaj Ghemawat recommended answering several questions when considering an experience curve strategy.

- Does my industry exhibit a significant experience curve?
- Have I defined the industry broadly enough to take into account interrelated experience?
- What is the precise source of cost reduction?
- Can my company keep cost reductions proprietary?
- Is demand sufficiently stable to justify using the experience curve?
- Is cumulated output doubling fast enough for the experience curve to provide much strategic leverage?
- Do the returns from an experience curve strategy warrant the risks of technological obsolescence?
- Is demand price-sensitive?
- Are there well-financed competitors who are already following an experience curve strategy or are likely to adopt one if my company does?

Michael Porter suggested, however, that the experience curve is not useful in all situations. Whether or not to base strategy on the experience curve depends on what specifically causes the decline in costs. For example, if costs drop from efficient production facilities and not necessarily from experience, the experience curve is not helpful. But as Sharon Oster pointed out in her book on competitive analysis, the experience curve can help managers analyze costs when efficient learning, rather than efficient machinery, is the source of cost savings.

- Avoidance of marginal customer accounts.
- Cost minimization in all activities in the firm's value chain, such as R&D, service, sales force, and advertising.

Exhibit 5.3 draws on the value-chain concept (see Chapter 3) to provide examples of how a firm can attain an overall cost leadership strategy in its primary and support activities.

Key to an overall cost leadership strategy is the **experience curve,** which refers to how business "learns" to lower costs as it gains experience with production processes. With experience, unit costs of production decline as output increases in most industries. The experience curve concept is discussed in Strategy Spotlight 5.1 and Exhibit 5.4.

experience curve
the decline in unit costs of production as cumulative output increases.

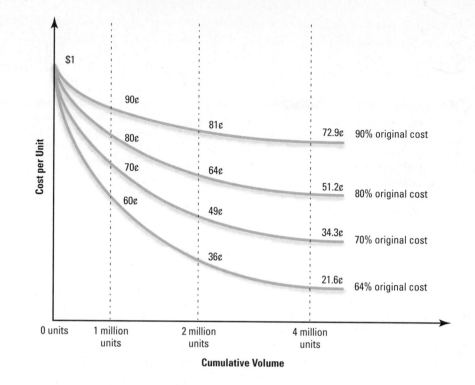

Exhibit 5.4 Comparing Experience Curve Effects

Cost per Unit

$1

90¢

81¢

72.9¢   90% original cost

80¢

70¢

64¢

51.2¢   80% original cost

60¢

49¢

34.3¢   70% original cost

36¢

21.6¢   64% original cost

0 units   1 million units   2 million units   4 million units

Cumulative Volume

competitive parity a firm's achievement of similarity, or being "on par," with competitors with respect to low cost, differentiation, or other strategic product characteristic.

To generate above-average performance, a firm following an overall cost leadership position must attain **competitive parity** on the basis of differentiation relative to competitors.[8] In other words, a firm achieving parity is similar to its competitors, or "on par," with respect to differentiated products.[9] Competitive parity on the basis of differentiation permits a cost leader to translate cost advantages directly into higher profits than competitors. Thus, the cost leader earns above-average returns.[10]

The failure to attain parity on the basis of differentiation can be illustrated with an example from the automobile industry—the ill-fated Yugo. Below is an excerpt from a speech by J. W. Marriott, Jr., Chairman of the Marriott Corporation:[11]

> . . . money is a big thing. But it's not the only thing. In the 1980s, a new automobile reached North America from behind the Iron Curtain. It was called the Yugo, and its main attraction was price. About $3,000 each. But the only way they caught on was as the butt of jokes. Remember the guy who told his mechanic, "I want a gas cap for my Yugo." "OK," the mechanic replied, "that sounds like a fair trade."

Yugo was offering a lousy value proposition. The cars literally fell apart before your eyes. And the lesson was simple. Price is just one component of value. No matter how good the price, the most cost-sensitive consumer won't buy a bad product.

Next, we discuss some examples of how firms enhance cost leadership position.

While other managed care providers were having a string of weak years, WellPoint, based in Thousand Oaks, California, has had a number of banner years and recently enjoyed an annual profit growth of over 42 percent to $4.8 billion over the past three years.[12] Chairman Leonard Schaeffer credits the company's focus on innovation for both expanding revenues and cutting costs. For example, WellPoint asked the Food and Drug Administration (FDA) to make the allergy drug Claritin available over the counter. Surprisingly, this may be the first time that an insurer has approached the FDA with such a request. Schaeffer claimed, "They were kind of stunned," but the FDA agreed to consider it. It was a smart move for WellPoint. If approved as an over-the-counter drug, Claritin would reduce patient

Ryanair: A Highly Effective Overall Cost Leadership Strategy

Michael O'Leary, CEO of Ryanair Holdings PLC, makes no apologies for his penny-pinching. Want to check luggage? You'll pay up to $9.50 per bag for the privilege. Expecting free drinks and snacks? You'll be disappointed. Even a bottle of water will cost you $3.40. And it is not just the passengers who are affected. Flight crews buy their own uniforms, and staff at Ryanair's Spartan Dublin Airport headquarters must supply their own pens. After a customer sued Ryanair for charging $34 for the use of a wheelchair, the company added a 63 cent "wheelchair levy" to every ticket!

Low-fare U.S. carriers have taken the opposite approach of Ryanair by adding perks such as leather seats, live television, and business class. "All of the low-cost carriers' costs have gotten a little out of control," says Tim Sieber, general manager of The Boyd Group, an Evergreen (Colorado) aviation consultant. Clearly Ryanair hasn't followed its industry peers.

Ryanair has been extremely successful. It recently became the first airline in Europe to carry more than 7 million passengers in one month. As of late 2010, the company had a market capitalization of $7.2 billion, dwarfing competitors easyJet ($2.3 billion) and Ireland's legacy airline, Aer Lingus ($612 million), but it is still a bit short of Southwest ($8.29 billion) and Delta ($8.22 billion). Over the past decade, at a time when the global airline industry collectively lost nearly $50 billion, Ryanair turned healthy net profits in 9 out of the 10 years—earning $431 million in the most recent year. In the process, O'Leary has become one of Ireland's wealthiest citizens—the value of his Ryanair shares is nearly $300 million.

What is O'Leary's secret? He thinks like a retailer and charges for every little thing. Imagine the seat as a cell

Sources: Gillete, F. 2010. The Duke of Discomfort. *Bloomberg, BusinessWeek* September 12: 58–61; Ryanair Annual Report, 2008; Capell, K. 2006. Walmart with Wings. *BusinessWeek.* November 27: 44–45; Kumar, N. 2006. Strategies to Fight Low-Cost Rivals. *Harvard Business Review,* 84(12): 104–113; and *Ryanair Annual Report,* 2006.

phone: It comes free, or nearly free, but its owner winds up spending money on all sorts of services.

However, what O'Leary loses in seat revenue he more than makes up by turning both his planes and the Ryanair website into stores brimming with irresistible goodies, even as he charges for such "perks" as priority boarding and assigned seating.

Sounds outrageous? Probably so, but the strategy is clearly working. Although its average fare is $53, compared with $92 for Southwest Airlines, Ryanair's net margins are, at 18 percent—more than double the 7 percent achieved by Southwest. Says Nick van den Brul, an aviation analyst: "Ryanair is Walmart with wings." As O'Leary says, "You want luxury? Go somewhere else."

A few other Ryanair practices include:

- Flight attendants sell digital cameras ($137.50) and iPocket MP3 players ($165).

- The seats don't recline, seat-back pockets have been removed to cut cleaning time and speed turnaround of the planes, there's no entertainment, and seat-back trays will soon carry ads.

- Ryanair sells more than 98 percent of its tickets online. Its website offers insurance, hotels, car rentals, and more—even online bingo.

O'Leary is certainly a colorful person, and he has some "creative" or downright nutty ideas. Recently, he came up with the idea of replacing the last 10 rows with a standing cabin, outfitted with handrails, much like a New York City subway car, only without the benches and panhandlers. The increased capacity, he claims, would lower fares by 20 percent to 25 percent. He says: "In no plane ever operated by Ryanair will it be all standing. You will always have the choice of paying for the seat. The argument against it is that if there's ever a crash, people will be injured. If there's ever a crash, the people in the sit-down seats will be injured, too."

visits to the doctor and eliminate the need for prescriptions—two reimbursable expenses for which WellPoint would otherwise be responsible.

Stephen Sanger, CEO of General Mills, recently came up with an idea that helped his firm cut costs.[13] To improve productivity, he sent technicians to watch pit crews during a NASCAR race. That experience inspired the techies to figure out how to reduce the time it takes to switch a plant line from five hours to 20 minutes. This provided an important lesson: Many interesting benchmarking examples can take place far outside of an industry. Often, process improvements involve identifying the best practices in other industries and adapting them for implementation in your own firm. After all, when firms benchmark competitors in their own industry, the end result is often copying and playing catch-up.[14]

A business that strives for a low-cost advantage must attain an absolute cost advantage relative to its rivals.[15] This is typically accomplished by offering a no-frills product or service to a broad target market using standardization to derive the greatest benefits from economies of scale and experience. However, such a strategy may fail if a firm is unable to attain parity on important dimensions of differentiation such as quick responses to customer requests for services or design changes. Strategy Spotlight 5.2 discusses Ryanair—a firm that has developed a very unique overall cost leadership strategy. One might say that it "one upped" Southwest Airlines!

>LO5.2

How the successful attainment of generic strategies can improve a firm's relative power vis-à-vis the five forces that determine an industry's average profitability.

Overall Cost Leadership: Improving Competitive Position vis-à-vis the Five Forces An overall low-cost position enables a firm to achieve above-average returns despite strong competition. It protects a firm against rivalry from competitors, because lower costs allow a firm to earn returns even if its competitors eroded their profits through intense rivalry. A low-cost position also protects firms against powerful buyers. Buyers can exert power to drive down prices only to the level of the next most efficient producer. Also, a low-cost position provides more flexibility to cope with demands from powerful suppliers for input cost increases. The factors that lead to a low-cost position also provide substantial entry barriers from economies of scale and cost advantages. Finally, a low-cost position puts the firm in a favorable position with respect to substitute products introduced by new and existing competitors.[16]

A few examples will illustrate these points. Ryanair's close attention to costs helps to protect them from buyer power and intense rivalry from competitors. Thus, they are able to drive down costs and enjoy relatively high power over their customers. By increasing productivity and lowering unit costs, General Mills (and its competitors in that industry) enjoy greater scale economies and erect higher entry barriers for others. Finally, as competitors such as WellPoint lower costs through means such as petitioning the FDA to make certain drugs available over the counter, they become less vulnerable to substitutes such as Internet-based competitors.

>LO5.3

The pitfalls managers must avoid in striving to attain generic strategies.

Potential Pitfalls of Overall Cost Leadership Strategies Potential pitfalls of overall cost leadership strategy include:

- *Too much focus on one or a few value-chain activities.* Would you consider a person to be astute if he cancelled his newspaper subscription and quit eating out to save money, but then "maxed out" several credit cards, requiring him to pay hundreds of dollars a month in interest charges? Of course not. Similarly, firms need to pay attention to all activities in the value chain.[17] Too often managers make big cuts in operating expenses, but don't question year-to-year spending on capital projects. Or managers may decide to cut selling and marketing expenses but ignore manufacturing expenses. Managers should explore *all* value-chain activities, including relationships among them, as candidates for cost reductions.

- *All rivals share a common input or raw material.* Here, firms are vulnerable to price increases in the factors of production. Since they're competing on costs, they are less able to pass on price increases, because customers can take their business to rivals who have lower prices. For example, consider manufacturing firms based in China which rely on a common input—low labor costs. Due to demographic factors, the supply of workers 16 to 24 years old has peaked and will drop by a third in the next 12 years, thanks to stringent family-planning policies that have sharply reduced China's population growth.[18] In one city, many factories are operating with vacancies of 15 to 20 percent, compelling some supervisors to cruise the streets in a desperate hiring quest during crunch times. Needless to say, there are strong demands for better working conditions and higher wages.

- *The strategy is imitated too easily.* One of the common pitfalls of a cost-leadership strategy is that a firm's strategy may consist of value-creating activities that are easy to imitate.[19] Such was the case with online brokers in recent years.[20] As of early 2001, there were about 140 online brokers, hardly symbolic of an industry where imitation is extremely difficult. But according to Henry McVey, financial services analyst at Morgan Stanley, "We think you need five to ten" online brokers.

What are some of the dynamics? First, although online brokers were geared up to handle 1.2 million trades a day, volume had shrunk to about 834,000—a 30 percent drop. Thus, competition for business intensified. Second, when the stock market is down, many investors trust their instincts less and seek professional guidance from brokerages that offer differentiated services. Eric Rajendra of A. T. Kearney, an international consulting company, claimed, "The current (online broker) model is inadequate for the pressures the industry is facing now."

- *A lack of parity on differentiation.* As noted earlier, firms striving to attain cost leadership advantages must obtain a level of parity on differentiation.[21] Firms providing online degree programs may offer low prices. However, they may not be successful unless they can offer instruction that is perceived as comparable to traditional providers. For them, parity can be achieved on differentiation dimensions such as reputation and quality and through signaling mechanisms such as accreditation agencies.

- *Erosion of cost advantages when the pricing information available to customers increases.* This is becoming a more significant challenge as the Internet dramatically increases both the quantity and volume of information available to consumers about pricing and cost structures. Life insurance firms offering whole life insurance provide an interesting example.[22] One study found that for each 10 percent increase in consumer use of the Internet, there is a corresponding reduction in insurance prices to consumers of 3 to 5 percent. Recently, the nationwide savings (or, alternatively, reduced revenues to providers) was between $115 and $125 million annually.

Differentiation

As the name implies, a **differentiation strategy** consists of creating differences in the firm's product or service offering by creating something that is perceived *industrywide* as unique and valued by customers.[23] Differentiation can take many forms:

- Prestige or brand image (Adam's Mark hotels, BMW automobiles).[24]
- Technology (Martin guitars, Marantz stereo components, North Face camping equipment).
- Innovation (Medtronic medical equipment, Apple's iPods).
- Features (Cannondale mountain bikes, Honda Goldwing motorcycles).
- Customer service (Nordstrom department stores, Sears lawn equipment retailing).
- Dealer network (Lexus automobiles, Caterpillar earthmoving equipment).

differentiation strategy a firm's generic strategy based on creating differences in the firm's product or service offering by creating something that is perceived *industrywide* as unique and valued by customers.

● Caterpillar is well known for its outstanding dealer network.

Exhibit 5.5
**Value-Chain Activities:
Examples of
Differentiation**

Support Activities
Firm Infrastructure
• Superior MIS—To integrate value-creating activities to improve quality.
• Facilities that promote firm image.
• Widely respected CEO enhances firm reputation.
Human Resource Management
• Programs to attract talented engineers and scientists.
• Provide training and incentives to ensure a strong customer service orientation.
Technology Development
• Superior material handling and sorting technology.
• Excellent applications engineering support.
Procurement
• Purchase of high-quality components to enhance product image.
• Use of most prestigious outlets.
Primary Activities
Inbound Logistics
• Superior material handling operations to minimize damage.
• Quick transfer of inputs to manufacturing process.
Operations
• Flexibility and speed in responding to changes in manufacturing specifications.
• Low defect rates to improve quality.
Outbound Logistics
• Accurate and responsive order processing.
• Effective product replenishment to reduce customer inventory.
Marketing and Sales
• Creative and innovative advertising programs.
• Fostering of personal relationship with key customers.
Service
• Rapid response to customer service requests.
• Complete inventory of replacement parts and supplies.

Source: Adapted from Porter, M.E. 1985. *Competitive Advantage: Creating and Sustaining Superior Performance.* New York: Free Press.

Exhibit 5.5 draws on the concept of the value chain as an example of how firms may differentiate themselves in primary and support activities.

Firms may differentiate themselves along several different dimensions at once.[25] For example, BMW is known for its high prestige, superior engineering, and high-quality automobiles. And Harley-Davidson differentiates on image and dealer services.[26]

Firms achieve and sustain differentiation advantages and attain above-average performance when their price premiums exceed the extra costs incurred in being unique.[27]

For example, both BMW and Harley-Davidson must increase consumer costs to offset added marketing expenses. Thus, a differentiator will always seek out ways of distinguishing itself from similar competitors to justify price premiums greater than the costs incurred by differentiating.[28] Clearly, a differentiator cannot ignore costs. After all, its premium prices would be eroded by a markedly inferior cost position. Therefore, it must attain a level of cost *parity* relative to competitors. Differentiators can do this by reducing costs in all areas that do not affect differentiation. Porsche, for example, invests heavily in engine design—an area in which its customers demand excellence—but it is less concerned and spends fewer resources in the design of the instrument panel or the arrangement of switches on the radio.[29]

Many companies successfully follow a differentiation strategy.[30] For example, FedEx's CEO and founder, Fred Smith, claims that the key to his firm's success is innovation.[31] He contends his management team didn't understand their real goal when they started the firm in 1971: "We thought that we were selling the transportation of goods; in fact, we were selling peace of mind." They now provide drivers with a handheld computer and a transmitting device so that customers can track their packages from their desktop PCs.

Lexus, a division of Toyota, provides an example of how a firm can strengthen its differentiation strategy by *achieving integration at multiple points along the value chain.*[32] Although the luxury car line was not introduced until the late 1980s, by the early 1990s the cars had already soared to the top of J. D. Power & Associates' customer satisfaction ratings.

> In the spirit of benchmarking, one of Lexus's competitors hired Custom Research Inc. (CRI), a marketing research firm, to find out why Lexus owners were so satisfied. CRI conducted a series of focus groups in which Lexus drivers eagerly offered anecdotes about the special care they experienced from their dealers. It became clear that, although Lexus was manufacturing cars with few mechanical defects, it was the extra care shown by the sales and service staff that resulted in satisfied customers. Such pampering is reflected in the feedback from one customer who claimed she never had a problem with her Lexus. However, upon further probing, she said, "Well, I suppose you could call the four times they had to replace the windshield a 'problem.' But frankly, they took care of it so well and always gave me a loaner car, so I never really considered it a problem until you mentioned it now." An insight gained in CRI's research is that perceptions of product quality (design, engineering, and manufacturing) can be strongly influenced by downstream activities in the value chain (marketing and sales, service).

Strategy Spotlight 5.3 addresses how Netflix, the successful Internet movie rental company, uses crowdsourcing to enhance its differentiation.

Differentiation: Improving Competitive Position vis-à-vis the Five Forces

Differentiation provides protection against rivalry since brand loyalty lowers customer sensitivity to price and raises customer switching costs.[33] By increasing a firm's margins, differentiation also avoids the need for a low-cost position. Higher entry barriers result because of customer loyalty and the firm's ability to provide uniqueness in its products or services.[34] Differentiation also provides higher margins that enable a firm to deal with supplier power. And it reduces buyer power, because buyers lack comparable alternatives and are therefore less price sensitive.[35] Supplier power is also decreased because there is a certain amount of prestige associated with being the supplier to a producer of highly differentiated products and services. Last, differentiation enhances customer loyalty, thus reducing the threat from substitutes.[36]

Our examples illustrate these points. Lexus has enjoyed enhanced power over buyers because its top J. D. Power ranking makes buyers more willing to pay a premium price. This lessens rivalry, since buyers become less price-sensitive. The prestige associated with its brand name also lowers supplier power since margins are high. Suppliers would probably desire to be associated with prestige brands, thus lessening their incentives to drive up prices. Finally, the loyalty and "peace of mind" associated with a service provider such as FedEx makes such firms less vulnerable to rivalry or substitute products and services.

strategy spotlight

Crowdsourcing: How Netflix Boosts Its Differentiation

5.3

Netflix is well-known for its inviting online presentation and efficient distribution system. However, this highly successful movie-rental company prides itself on its capability to offer subscribers a compact list of films that they are likely to enjoy watching. And it must be working: Netflix sends 35,000 titles a day to its 7.5 million subscribers.

"Imagine that our website was a brick-and-mortar store," says Netflix vice president, James Bennett. "When people walk through the door, they see DVDs rearrange themselves. The movies that might interest them fly onto the shelves, and all the rest go to the back room."

The movies, of course, don't do the rearranging—that is done by the customers themselves, with an assist from a computer program called Cinematch, which Netflix developed in 2000. Customers are invited to rate each film they watch on a 1 to 5 scale. Cinematch analyzes these ratings, searches through 80,000 titles in inventory, and determines the list of films tailored to the taste of each of the firm's subscribers. By enticing them to rate films, Netflix achieves the latest in business innovation—getting customers to serve themselves.

Netflix is not unique in their use of so-called recommenders. Consider other online retailers such as Amazon, Apple, eBay, and Overstock. All of these rely on their customers for a helping hand in predicting what products the customers will prefer—whether the product is bedding, books, CDs, or DVDs. Customer ratings are used to rank corporate service providers as well.

For all these companies, the recommender system provides more than a chance to create an extra service. It helps them to establish a stronger connection with their customers. And studies have shown that it can substantially increase online sales.

Sources: Copeland, M.V. 2009. Tapping Tech's Beautiful Minds. *Fortune* October 12: 35–36; Libert, B. & Spector, J. 2008. *We Are Smarter Than Me.* Philadelphia: Wharton Publishing; and Howe, J. 2008. *Crowdsourcing.* New York: Crown Business.

The extent of Netflix's commitment to personalized movie recommendations was made clear in 2006 when it offered a $1 million prize to anyone who could build a system that was at least 10 percent better than Cinematch. In late 2009, it awarded the prize to a seven-person team of computer scientists, mathematicians, and statisticians who were from New Jersey, Israel, Quebec, and Austria. They built a system that was 20 percent better than Cinematch.

● Netflix generated a lot of favorable publicity with its $1 million prize competition.

Netflix has also developed another crowdsourcing feature called Friends. Here, subscribers see each other's list of films watched and compare the ratings they have awarded the films—in exchange for suggestions on other films to watch.

crowdsourcing

Potential Pitfalls of Differentiation Strategies   Potential pitfalls of a differentiation strategy include:

- ***Uniqueness that is not valuable.*** A differentiation strategy must provide unique bundles of products and/or services that customers value highly. It's not enough just to be "different." An example is Gibson's Dobro bass guitar. Gibson came up with a unique idea: Design and build an acoustic bass guitar with sufficient sound volume so that amplification wasn't necessary. The problem with other acoustic bass guitars was that they did not project enough volume because of the low-frequency bass notes. By adding a resonator plate on the body of the traditional acoustic bass, Gibson increased the sound volume. Gibson believed this product would serve a particular niche market—bluegrass and folk artists who played in small group "jams" with other acoustic musicians. Unfortunately, Gibson soon discovered that its targeted market was content with their existing options: an upright bass amplified with a microphone or an acoustic electric guitar. Thus, Gibson developed a unique product, but it was not perceived as valuable by its potential customers.[37]

- **Too much differentiation.** Firms may strive for quality or service that is higher than customers desire.[38] Thus, they become vulnerable to competitors who provide an appropriate level of quality at a lower price. For example, consider the expensive Mercedes-Benz S-Class, which ranges in price between $93,650 and $138,000 for the 2011 models.[39] *Consumer Reports* described it as "sumptuous," "quiet and luxurious," and a "delight to drive." The magazine also considered it to be the least reliable sedan available in the United States. According to David Champion, who runs their testing program, the problems are electronic. "The engineers have gone a little wild," he says. "They've put every bell and whistle that they think of, and sometimes they don't have the attention to detail to make these systems work." Some features include: a computer-driven suspension that reduces body roll as the vehicle whips around a corner; cruise control that automatically slows the car down if it gets too close to another car; and seats that are adjustable 14 ways and that are ventilated by a system that uses eight fans.

- **Too high a price premium.** This pitfall is quite similar to too much differentiation. Customers may desire the product, but they are repelled by the price premium. For example, Duracell (a division of Gillette) recently charged too much for batteries.[40] The firm tried to sell consumers on its superior quality products, but the mass market wasn't convinced. Why? The price differential was simply too high. At a CVS drugstore just one block from Gillette's headquarters, a four-pack of Energizer AA batteries was on sale at $2.99 compared with a Duracell four-pack at $4.59. Duracell's market share dropped 2 percent in a recent two-year period, and its profits declined over 30 percent. Clearly, the price/performance proposition Duracell offered customers was not accepted.

- **Differentiation that is easily imitated.** As we noted in Chapter 3, resources that are easily imitated cannot lead to sustainable advantages. Similarly, firms may strive for, and even attain, a differentiation strategy that is successful for a time. However, the advantages are eroded through imitation. Consider Cereality's innovative differentiation strategy of stores which offer a wide variety of cereals and toppings for around $4.00.[41] As one would expect, once their idea proved successful, competitors entered the market because much of the initial risk had already been taken. Rivals include an Iowa City restaurant named the Cereal Cabinet, the Cereal Bowl in Miami, and Bowls: A Cereal Joint in Gainesville, Florida. Says David Roth, one of Cereality's founders: "With any good business idea, you're faced with people who see you've cracked the code and who try to cash in on it."

- **Dilution of brand identification through product-line extensions.** Firms may erode their quality brand image by adding products or services with lower prices and less quality. Although this can increase short-term revenues, it may be detrimental in the long run. Consider Gucci.[42] In the 1980s Gucci wanted to capitalize on its prestigious brand name by launching an aggressive strategy of revenue growth. It added a set of lower-priced canvas goods to its product line. It also pushed goods heavily into department stores and duty-free channels and allowed its name to appear on a host of licensed items such as watches, eyeglasses, and perfumes. In the short term, this strategy worked. Sales soared. However, the strategy carried a high price. Gucci's

Overall Cost Leadership:

- Too much focus on one or a few value-chain activities.
- All rivals share a common input or raw material.
- The strategy is imitated too easily.
- A lack of parity on differentiation.
- Erosion of cost advantages when the pricing information available to customers increases.

Differentiation:

- Uniqueness that is not valuable.
- Too much differentiation.
- The price premium is too high.
- Differentiation that is easily imitated.
- Dilution of brand identification through product-line extensions.
- Perceptions of differentiation may vary between buyers and sellers.

indiscriminate approach to expanding its products and channels tarnished its sterling brand. Sales of its high-end goods (with higher profit margins) fell, causing profits to decline.

- ***Perceptions of differentiation may vary between buyers and sellers.*** The issue here is that "beauty is in the eye of the beholder." Companies must realize that although they may perceive their products and services as differentiated, their customers may view them as commodities. Indeed, in today's marketplace, many products and services have been reduced to commodities.[43] Thus, a firm could overprice its offerings and lose margins altogether if it has to lower prices to reflect market realities.

Exhibit 5.6 summarizes the pitfalls of overall cost leadership and differentiation strategies. In addressing the pitfalls associated with these two generic strategies there is one common, underlying theme. Managers must be aware of the dangers associated with concentrating so much on one strategy that they fail to attain parity on the other.

Focus

focus strategy a firm's generic strategy based on appeal to a narrow market segment within an industry.

A **focus strategy** is based on the choice of a narrow competitive scope within an industry. A firm following this strategy selects a segment or group of segments and tailors its strategy to serve them. The essence of focus is the exploitation of a particular market niche. As you might expect, narrow focus itself (like merely "being different" as a differentiator) is simply not sufficient for above-average performance.

The focus strategy, as indicated in Exhibit 5.1, has two variants. In a cost focus, a firm strives to create a cost advantage in its target segment. In a differentiation focus, a firm seeks to differentiate in its target market. Both variants of the focus strategy rely on providing better service than broad-based competitors who are trying to serve the focuser's target segment. Cost focus exploits differences in cost behavior in some segments, while differentiation focus exploits the special needs of buyers in other segments.

Let's look at examples of two firms that have successfully implemented focus strategies. Network Appliance (NA) has developed a more cost-effective way to store and distribute computer files.[44] Its larger rival, EMC, makes mainframe-style products priced over $1 million that store files and accommodate Internet traffic. NA makes devices that cost under $200,000 for particular storage jobs such as caching (temporary storage) of Internet

If You Can't Afford an Extremely Expensive Car . . . You Can Rent One

If we assume that indulgence is best experienced in moderation, it should come as no surprise that the business of renting expensive sheet metal is soaring. Ken Kerzner, managing partner of Midway Car Rental in Los Angeles, has been renting high-end cars to business travelers, wealthy tourists, and movie moguls for 41 years.

He is having one of his best years. He claims that today's recession-weary customers are looking to try new things while avoiding the headaches and overhead of ownerships. His 2,000-vehicle fleet offers just about everything. It ranges from the Smart car ($89 a day) to the Ferrari California and Lamborghini Gallardo at $2,850 and $2,999 a day, respectively. Don't want to spring for these two super-high-end cars? You can get a Porsche Targa 4S for *only* $1,499 a day.

Kerzner does have some serious competition. Beverly Hills Rent-a-Car, with locations in Los Angeles and Las Vegas, offers an even wider range. Interested in renting the $1.7 million Bugatti Veyron with an astonishing 1,001 horse power? You can find it here.

Source: Callaway, S. 2010. Hot Rides for Rent. *Fortune.* September 6: 24.

---

content. Focusing on such narrow segments has certainly paid off for NA; it has posted a remarkable 20 straight quarters of revenue growth.

Paccar, an $8 billion Bellevue, Washington–based heavy-truck manufacturer, has chosen a differentiation focus strategy.[45] The firm targets one group of customers: owner-operators. These are the drivers who own their trucks and contract directly with shippers or serve as subcontractors to larger trucking companies.

Paccar has invested heavily to develop a variety of features with owner-operators in mind: luxurious sleeper cabins, plush leather seats, noise-insulated cabins, sleek exterior styling, and so forth. At Paccar's extensive network of dealers, prospective buyers use software to select among thousands of options to put their personal signature on their trucks. These customized trucks are built to order, not to stock, and are delivered in eight weeks. Not surprisingly, customers are happy to pay Paccar a 10 percent premium, and its Kenworth and Peterbilt brands are considered status symbols at truck stops.

Strategy Spotlight 5.4 illustrates that you can pay as much as you want for some products or services. Case in point: car rentals.

Focus: Improving Competitive Position vis-à-vis the Five Forces   Focus requires that a firm either have a low-cost position with its strategic target, high differentiation, or both. As we discussed with regard to cost and differentiation strategies, these positions provide defenses against each competitive force. Focus is also used to select niches that are least vulnerable to substitutes or where competitors are weakest.

Let's look at our examples to illustrate some of these points. First, Paccar experienced lower rivalry and greater bargaining power by providing products and services to a targeted market segment that was less price-sensitive. New rivals have difficulty attracting customers away from Paccar based only on lower prices. Similarly, the brand image and quality that this brand evoked heightened rivals' entry barriers. With regard to the strategy of cost focus, Network Appliances, the successful rival to EMC in the computer storage industry, was better able to absorb pricing increases from suppliers as a result of its lower cost structure, reducing supplier power.

Potential Pitfalls of Focus Strategies   Potential pitfalls of focus strategies include:

- ***Erosion of cost advantages within the narrow segment.*** The advantages of a cost focus strategy may be fleeting if the cost advantages are eroded over time. For example, Dell's pioneering direct selling model in the personal computer industry has been eroded by rivals such as Hewlett Packard as they gain experience with Dell's distribution method. Similarly, other firms have seen their profit margins drop as competitors enter their product segment.

- ***Even product and service offerings that are highly focused are subject to competition from new entrants and from imitation.*** Some firms adopting a focus strategy may enjoy temporary advantages because they select a small niche with few rivals. However, their advantages may be short-lived. A notable example is the multitude of dot-com firms that specialize in very narrow segments such as pet supplies, ethnic foods, and vintage automobile accessories. The entry barriers tend to be low, there is little buyer loyalty, and competition becomes intense. And since the marketing strategies and technologies employed by most rivals are largely nonproprietary, imitation is easy. Over time, revenues fall, profits margins are squeezed, and only the strongest players survive the shakeout.

- ***Focusers can become too focused to satisfy buyer needs.*** Some firms attempting to attain advantages through a focus strategy may have too narrow a product or service. Consider many retail firms. Hardware chains such as Ace and True Value are losing market share to rivals such as Lowe's and Home Depot that offer a full line of home and garden equipment and accessories. And given the enormous purchasing power of the national chains, it would be difficult for such specialty retailers to attain parity on costs.

Combination Strategies: Integrating Overall Low Cost and Differentiation

>LO5.4
How firms can effectively combine the generic strategies of overall cost leadership and differentiation.

Perhaps the primary benefit to firms that integrate low-cost and differentiation strategies is the difficulty for rivals to duplicate or imitate.[45] This strategy enables a firm to provide two types of value to customers: differentiated attributes (e.g., high quality, brand identification, reputation) and lower prices (because of the firm's lower costs in value-creating activities). The goal is thus to provide unique value to customers in an efficient manner.[46] Some firms are able to attain both types of advantages simultaneously.[47] For example, superior quality can lead to lower costs because of less need for rework in manufacturing, fewer warranty claims, a reduced need for customer service personnel to resolve customer complaints, and so forth. Thus, the benefits of combining advantages can be additive, instead of merely involving trade-offs. Next, we consider three approaches to combining overall low cost and differentiation.

combination strategies firms' integrations of various strategies to provide multiple types of value to customers.

Automated and Flexible Manufacturing Systems   Given the advances in manufacturing technologies such as CAD/CAM (computer aided design and computer aided manufacturing) as well as information technologies, many firms have been able to manufacture unique products in relatively small quantities at lower costs—a concept known as **mass customization.**[48]

mass customization a firm's ability to manufacture unique products in small quantities at low cost.

Let's consider Andersen Windows of Bayport, Minnesota—a $3 billion manufacturer of windows for the building industry.[49] Until about 20 years ago, Andersen was a mass producer, in small batches, of a variety of standard windows. However, to meet changing customer needs, Andersen kept adding to its product line. The result was catalogs of ever-increasing size and a bewildering set of choices for both homeowners and contractors. Over a 6-year period, the number of products tripled, price quotes took several hours, and the error rate increased. This not only damaged the company's reputation, but also added to its manufacturing expenses.

To bring about a major change, Andersen developed an interactive computer version of its paper catalogs that it sold to distributors and retailers. Salespersons can now customize each window to meet the customer's needs, check the design for structural soundness, and provide a price quote. The system is virtually error free, customers get exactly what

- At Nikeid.com, customers can design an athletic or casual shoe to their specifications online, selecting almost every element of the shoe from the material of the sole to the color of the shoelace.

- Eleuria sells custom perfumes. Each product is created in response to a user profile constructed from responses to a survey about habits and preferences. Eleuria then provides a sample at modest cost to verify fit.

- Lands' End offers customized shirts and pants. Consumers specify style parameters, measurements, and fabrics through the firm's website. These settings are saved so that returning users can easily order a duplicate item.

- Cannondale permits consumers to specify the parameters that define a road bike frame, including custom colors and inscriptions. The user specifies the parameters on the firm's website and then arranges for delivery through a dealer.

Source: Randall, T., Terwiesch, C. & Ulrich, K. T. 2005. Principles for User Design of Custom Products. *California Management Review*, 47(4): 68–85.

they want, and the time to develop the design and furnish a quotation has been cut by 75 percent. Each showroom computer is connected to the factory, and customers are assigned a code number that permits them to track the order. The manufacturing system has been developed to use some common finished parts, but it also allows considerable variation in the final products. Despite its huge investment, Andersen has been able to lower costs, enhance quality and variety, and improve its response time to customers.

Exhibit 5.7 provides other examples of how flexible production systems have enabled firms to successfully engage in mass customization for their customers:[50]

Exploiting the Profit Pool Concept for Competitive Advantage   A profit pool is defined as the total profits in an industry at all points along the industry's value chain.[51] Although the concept is relatively straightforward, the structure of the profit pool can be complex.[52] The potential pool of profits will be deeper in some segments of the value chain than in others, and the depths will vary within an individual segment. Segment profitability may vary widely by customer group, product category, geographic market, or distribution channel. Additionally, the pattern of profit concentration in an industry is very often different from the pattern of revenue generation.

> **profit pool** the total profits in an industry at all points along the industry's value chain

Consider the automobile industry profit pool in Exhibit 5.8. Here we see little relationship between the generation of revenues and capturing of profits. While manufacturing generates most of the revenue, this value activity is far smaller profitwise than other value activities such as financing and extended warranty operations. So while a car manufacturer may be under tremendous pressure to produce cars efficiently, much of the profit (at least proportionately) can be captured in the aforementioned downstream operations. Thus, a carmaker would be ill-advised to focus solely on manufacturing and leave downstream operations to others through outsourcing.

Coordinating the "Extended" Value Chain by Way of Information Technology Many firms have achieved success by integrating activities throughout the "extended value chain" by using information technology to link their own value chain with the value chains of their customers and suppliers. As noted in Chapter 3, this approach enables a firm to add value not only through its own value-creating activities, but also for its customers and suppliers.

Such a strategy often necessitates redefining the industry's value chain. A number of years ago, Walmart took a close look at its industry's value chain and decided to

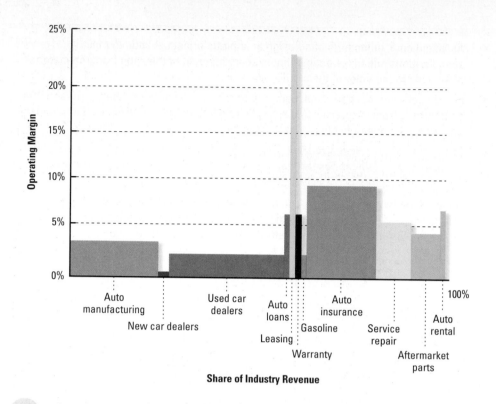

Exhibit 5.8 The U.S. Automobile Industry's Profit Pool

Source: Reprinted by permission of *Harvard Business Review,* Exhibit from "Profit Pools: A Fresh Look at Strategy," by O. Gadiesh and J. L. Gilbert, May–June 1999. Copyright © 1999 by the Harvard Business School Publishing Corporation; all rights reserved.

reframe the competitive challenge.[53] Although its competitors were primarily focused on retailing—merchandising and promotion—Walmart determined that it was not so much in the retailing industry as in the transportation logistics and communications industries. Here, linkages in the extended value chain became central. That became Walmart's chosen battleground. By redefining the rules of competition that played to its strengths, Walmart has attained competitive advantages and dominates its industry.

Integrated Overall Low-Cost and Differentiation Strategies: Improving Competitive Position vis-à-vis the Five Forces   Firms that successfully integrate both differentiation and cost advantages create an enviable position. For example, Walmart's integration of information systems, logistics, and transportation helps it to drive down costs and provide outstanding product selection. This dominant competitive position, serves to erect high entry barriers to potential competitors that have neither the financial nor physical resources to compete head-to-head. Walmart's size—over $400 billion in 2011 sales—provides the chain with enormous bargaining power over suppliers. Its low pricing and wide selection reduce the power of buyers (its customers), because there are relatively few competitors that can provide a comparable cost/value proposition. This reduces the possibility of intense head-to-head rivalry, such as protracted price wars. Finally, Walmart's overall value proposition makes potential substitute products (e.g., Internet competitors) a less viable threat.

Pitfalls of Integrated Overall Cost Leadership and Differentiation Strategies   The pitfalls of integrated overall cost leadership and differentiation include:

- *Firms that fail to attain both strategies may end up with neither and become "stuck in the middle."* A key issue in strategic management is the creation of competitive advantages that enable a firm to enjoy above-average returns. Some firms may become "stuck in the middle" if they try to attain both cost and differentiation advantages. An example that we are all familiar with would be the Big 3 U.S. automobile makers. They have been plagued by expensive "legacy costs" associated with pension and health care obligations—a central issue in 2008 federal bailout legislation. And they suffer from long-term customer perceptions of mediocre quality—inferior to their European and Japanese rivals. The troubling quality perceptions persist despite the fact that the Big 3 has attained approximate parity with their Japanese and European competitors in recent J. D. Power surveys.

- ***Underestimating the challenges and expenses associated with coordinating value-creating activities in the extended value chain.*** Integrating activities across a firm's value chain with the value chain of suppliers and customers involves a significant investment in financial and human resources. Firms must consider the expenses linked to technology investment, managerial time and commitment, and the involvement and investment required by the firm's customers and suppliers. The firm must be confident that it can generate a sufficient scale of operations and revenues to justify all associated expenses.

- ***Miscalculating sources of revenue and profit pools in the firm's industry.*** Firms may fail to accurately assess sources of revenue and profits in their value chain. This can occur for several reasons. For example, a manager may be biased due to his or her functional area background, work experiences, and educational background. If the manager's background is in engineering, he or she might perceive that proportionately greater revenue and margins were being created in manufacturing, product, and process design than a person whose background is in a "downstream" value chain activity such as marketing and sales. Or politics could make managers "fudge" the numbers to favor their area of operations. This would make them responsible for a greater proportion of the firm's profits, thus improving their bargaining position.

A related problem is directing an overwhelming amount of managerial time, attention, and resources to value-creating activities that produce the greatest margins—to the detriment of other important, albeit less profitable, activities. For example, a car manufacturer may focus too much on downstream activities, such as warranty fulfillment and financing operations, to the detriment of differentiation and cost of the cars themselves.

Can Competitive Strategies Be Sustained? Integrating and Applying Strategic Management Concepts

>LO5.5
What factors determine the sustainability of a firm's competitive advantage.

Thus far this chapter has addressed how firms can attain competitive advantages in the marketplace. We discussed the three generic strategies—overall cost leadership, differentiation, and focus—as well as combination strategies. Next we discussed the importance of linking value-chain activities (both those within the firm and those linkages between the firm's suppliers and customers) to attain such advantages. We also showed how successful competitive strategies enable firms to strengthen their position vis-à-vis the five forces of industry competition as well as how to avoid the pitfalls associated with the strategies.

Competitive advantages are, however, often short-lived. As we discussed in the beginning of Chapter 1, the composition of the firms that constitute the Fortune 500 list has experienced significant turnover in its membership over the years—reflecting the temporary nature of competitive advantages. And recall Dell's fall from grace (Chapter 3). Here was a firm whose advantages in the marketplace seemed unassailable in the early 2000s. In fact, it was *Fortune*'s "Most Admired Firm" in 2005. However, cracks began to appear in 2007, and its competitive position has recently been severely eroded by rivals such as Hewlett-Packard. In short, Dell focused so much on operational efficiency and perfecting its "direct model" that it failed to deliver innovations that an increasingly sophisticated market demanded. Also, Dell continues to face further pricing pressures as a result of the commoditization of the personal computer industry.[54]

Clearly, "nothing is forever" when it comes to competitive advantages. Rapid changes in technology, globalization, and actions by rivals from within—as well as outside—the industry can quickly erode a firm's advantages. It is becoming increasingly important to recognize that the duration of competitive advantages is declining, especially in technology intensive industries.[55] Even in industries which are normally viewed as "low tech," the increasing use of technology has suddenly made competitive advantages less sustainable.[56] Amazon's success in book retailing at the cost of Barnes & Noble, the former industry leader, as well as Blockbuster's struggle against Netflix in the video rental industry serve to illustrate how difficult it has become for industry leaders to sustain competitive advantages that they once thought would last forever.

In this section, we will discuss some factors that help determine whether a strategy is sustainable over a long period of time. We will draw on some strategic management concepts from the first five chapters. To illustrate our points, we will look at a company, Atlas Door, which created an innovative strategy in its industry and enjoyed superior performance for several years. Our discussion of Atlas Door draws on a *Harvard Business Review* article by George Stalk, Jr.[57] It was published some time ago (1988), which provides us the benefit of hindsight to make our points about the sustainability of competitive advantage. After all, the strategic management concepts we have been addressing in the text are quite timeless in their relevance to practice. A brief summary follows:

Atlas Door: A Case Example

Atlas Door, a U.S.-based company, has enjoyed remarkable success. It has grown at an average annual rate of 15 percent in an industry with an overall annual growth rate of less than 5 percent. Recently, its pre-tax earnings were 20 percent of sales—about five times the industry average. Atlas is debt free and by its 10th year, the company achieved the number one competitive position in its industry.

Atlas produces industrial doors—a product with almost infinite variety, involving limitless choices of width and height and material. Given the importance of product variety, inventory is almost useless in meeting customer orders. Instead, most doors can be manufactured only after the order has been placed.

How Did Atlas Door Create Its Competitive Advantages in the Marketplace? *First,* Atlas built just-in-time factories. Although simple in concept, they require extra tooling and machinery to reduce changeover times. Further, the manufacturing process must be organized by product and scheduled to start and complete with all of the parts available at the same time.

Second, Atlas reduced the time to receive and process an order. Traditionally, when customers, distributors, or salespeople called a door manufacturer with a request for price and delivery, they would have to wait more than one week for a response. In contrast, Atlas first streamlined and then automated its entire order-entry, engineering, pricing, and scheduling process. Atlas can price and schedule 95 percent of its incoming orders while the callers are still on the telephone. It can quickly engineer new special orders because it has preserved on computer the design and production data of all previous special orders—which drastically reduces the amount of reengineering necessary.

Third, Atlas tightly controlled logistics so that it always shipped only fully complete orders to construction sites. Orders require many components, and gathering all of them at the factory and making sure that they are with the correct order can be a time-consuming task. Of course, it is even more time-consuming to get the correct parts to the job site after the order has been shipped! Atlas developed a system to track the parts in production and the purchased parts for each order. This helped to ensure the arrival of all necessary parts at the shipping dock in time—a just-in-time logistics operation.

The Result?   When Atlas began operations, distributors had little interest in its product. The established distributors already carried the door line of a much larger competitor and saw little to no reason to switch suppliers except, perhaps, for a major price concession. But as a startup, Atlas was too small to compete on price alone. Instead, it positioned itself as the door supplier of last resort—the company people came to if the established supplier could not deliver or missed a key date.

Of course, with an average industry order fulfillment time of almost four months, some calls inevitably came to Atlas. And when it did get the call, Atlas commanded a higher price because of its faster delivery. Atlas not only got a higher price, but its effective integration of value-creating activities saved time and lowered costs. Thus, it enjoyed the best of both worlds.

In 10 short years, the company replaced the leading door suppliers in 80 percent of the distributors in the United States. With its strategic advantage, the company could be selective—becoming the supplier for only the strongest distributors.

Are Atlas Door's Competitive Advantages Sustainable?

We will now take both the "pro" and "con" position as to whether or not Atlas Door's competitive advantages will be sustainable for a very long time. It is important, of course, to assume that Atlas Door's strategy is unique in the industry, and the central issue becomes whether or not rivals will be able to easily imitate their strategy or create a viable substitute strategy.

"Pro" Position: The Strategy Is Highly Sustainable   Drawing on Chapter 2, it is quite evident that Atlas Door has attained a very favorable position vis-á-vis the five forces of industry competition. For example, it is able to exert power over its customers (distributors) because of its ability to deliver a quality product in a short period of time. Also, its dominance in the industry creates high entry barriers for new entrants. It is also quite evident that Atlas Door has been able to successfully integrate many value-chain activities within the firm—a fact that is integral to its just-in-time strategy. As noted in Chapter 3, such integration of activities provides a strong basis for sustainability, because rivals would have difficulty in imitating this strategy due to causal ambiguity and path dependency (i.e., it is difficult to build up in a short period of time the resources that Atlas Door has accumulated and developed as well as disentangle the causes of what the valuable resources are or how they can be re-created). Further, as noted in Chapter 4, Atlas Door benefits from the social capital that they have developed with a wide range of key stakeholders (Chapter 1) These would include customers, employees, and managers (a reasonable assumption, given how smoothly the internal operations flow and their long-term relationships with distributors). It would be very difficult for a rival to replace Atlas Door as the supplier of last resort—given the reputation that it has earned over time for "coming through in the clutch" on time-sensitive orders. Finally, we can conclude that Atlas Door has created competitive advantages in both overall low cost and differentiation (Chapter 5). Its strong linkages among value-chain activities—a requirement for its just-in-time operations—not only lowers costs but enables the company to respond quickly to customer orders. As noted in Exhibit 5.5 (page 170), many of the value-chain activities associated with a differentiation strategy reflect the element of speed or quick response.

"Con" Position: The Strategy Can Be Easily Imitated or Substituted   An argument could be made that much of Atlas Door's strategy relies on technologies that are rather well known and nonproprietary. Over time, a well-financed rival could imitate its strategy (via trial and error), achieve a tight integration among its value-creating activities, and implement a just-in-time manufacturing process. Because human capital is highly mobile (Chapter 4), a rival could hire away Atlas Door's talent, and these individuals could aid the rival in transferring Atlas Door's best practices. A new rival could also enter the industry with a large resource base, which might enable it to price its doors well under Atlas Door to build market share (but this would likely involve pricing below cost and would be a risky and nonsustainable strategy). Finally, a rival could potentially "leapfrog" the technologies and processes that Atlas Door has employed and achieve competitive superiority. With the benefit of hindsight, it could use the Internet to further speed up the linkages among its value-creating activities and the order entry processes with its customers and suppliers. (But even this could prove to be a temporary advantage, since rivals could relatively easily do the same thing.)

What Is the Verdict?   Both positions have merit. Over time, it would be rather easy to see how a new rival could achieve parity with Atlas Door—or even create a superior competitive position with new technologies or innovative processes. However, two factors make it extremely difficult for a rival to challenge Atlas Door in the short term: (1) the success that Atlas Door has enjoyed with its just-in-time scheduling and production systems—which involve the successful integration of many value-creating activities— helps the firm not only lower costs but also respond quickly to customer needs, and (2) the strong, positive reputational effects that it has earned with multiple stakeholders— especially its customers.

Finally, it is important to also understand that it is Atlas Door's ability to appropriate most of the profits generated by its competitive advantages that make it a highly successful company. As we discussed in Chapter 3, profits generated by resources can be appropriated by a number of stakeholders such as suppliers, customers, employees, or rivals. The structure of the industrial door industry makes such value appropriation difficult: the suppliers provide generic parts, no one buyer is big enough to dictate prices, the tacit nature of the knowledge makes imitation difficult, and individual employees may be easily replaceable. Still, even with the advantages that Atlas Door enjoys, they need to avoid becoming complacent or suffer the same fate as the dominant firm they replaced.

>LO5.6
How Internet-enabled business models are being used to improve strategic positioning.

How the Internet and Digital Technologies Affect the Competitive Strategies

Internet and digital technologies have swept across the economy and now have an impact on how nearly every company conducts its business. These changes have created new cost efficiencies and avenues for differentiation. However, the presence of these technologies is so widespread that it is questionable how any one firm can use them effectively in ways that genuinely set them apart from rivals. Thus, to stay competitive, firms must update their strategies to reflect the new possibilities and constraints that these phenomena represent. In this section, we address both the opportunities and the pitfalls that Internet and digital technologies offer to companies using overall cost leadership, differentiation, and focus strategies. We also briefly consider two major impacts that the Internet is having on business: lowering transaction costs and enabling mass customization.

Overall Cost Leadership

digital technologies information that is in numerical form, which facilitates its storage, transmission, analysis and manipulation.

The Internet and digital technologies create new opportunities for firms to achieve low-cost advantages by enabling them to manage costs and achieve greater efficiencies. Managing costs, and even changing the cost structures of certain industries, is a key feature of the digital economy. Most analysts agree that the Internet's ability to lower transaction costs has transformed business. Broadly speaking, *transaction costs* refer to all the various expenses associated with conducting business. It applies not just to buy/sell transactions

Exhibit 5.9 Internet-Enabled Low-Cost Leader Strategies

- Online bidding and order processing eliminate the need for sales calls and minimize sales-force expenses.

- Online purchase orders have made many transactions paperless, thus reducing the costs of procurement and paper.

- Direct access to progress reports and the ability of customers to periodically check work in progress minimize rework.

- Collaborative design efforts using Internet technologies that link designers, materials suppliers, and manufacturers reduce the costs and speed the process of new product development.

but to the costs of interacting with every part of a firm's value chain, within and outside the firm. Think about it. Hiring new employees, meeting with customers, ordering supplies, addressing government regulations—all of these exchanges have some costs associated with them. Because business can be conducted differently on the Internet, new ways of saving money are changing the competitive landscape.

Other factors also help to lower transaction costs. The process of disintermediation (in Chapter 2) has a similar effect. Each time intermediaries are used in a transaction, additional costs are added. Removing intermediaries lowers transaction costs. The Internet reduces the costs to search for a product or service, whether it is a retail outlet (as in the case of consumers) or a trade show (as in the case of business-to-business shoppers). Not only is the need for travel eliminated but so is the need to maintain a physical address, whether it's a permanent retail location or a temporary presence at a trade show.

Exhibit 5.9 identifies several types of cost leadership strategies that are made possible by Internet and digital technologies. These cost savings are available throughout a firm's value chain, in both primary and support activities.

disintermediation the process of bypassing buyer channel intermediaries such as wholesalers, distributors, and retailers.

Potential Internet-Related Pitfalls for Low-Cost Leaders One of the biggest threats to low-cost leaders is imitation. This problem is intensified for business done on the Internet. Most of the advantages associated with contacting customers directly, and even capabilities that are software driven (e.g., customized ordering systems or real-time access to the status of work in progress), can be duplicated quickly and without threat of infringement on proprietary information. Another pitfall relates to companies that become overly enamored with using the Internet for cost-cutting and thus jeopardize customer relations or neglect other cost centers.

Differentiation

For many companies, Internet and digital technologies have enhanced their ability to build brand, offer quality products and services, and achieve other differentiation advantages.[58] Among the most striking trends are new ways to interact with consumers. In particular, the Internet has created new ways of differentiating by enabling *mass customization,* which improves the response to customer wishes.

Mass customization has changed how companies go to market and has challenged some of the tried-and-true techniques of differentiation. Traditionally, companies reached customers using high-end catalogs, the showroom floor, personal sales calls and products using prestige packaging, celebrity endorsements, and charity sponsorships. All of these avenues are still available and may still be effective, depending on a firm's competitive environment. But many customers now judge the quality and uniqueness of a product or service by their ability to be involved in its planning and design, combined with speed of delivery and reliable results. Internet and digitally based capabilities are thus changing the

Exhibit 5.10 Internet-Enabled Differentiation Strategies

- Personalized online access provides customers with their own "site within a site" in which their prior orders, status of current orders, and requests for future orders are processed directly on the supplier's website.
- Online access to real-time sales and service information is being used to empower the sales force and continually update R&D and technology development efforts.
- Internet-based knowledge management systems that link all parts of the organization are shortening response times and accelerating organization learning.
- Quick online responses to service requests and rapid feedback to customer surveys and product promotions are enhancing marketing efforts.

way differentiators make exceptional products and achieve superior service. Such improvements are being made at a reasonable cost, allowing firms to achieve parity on the basis of overall cost leadership.

Exhibit 5.10 identifies differentiation activities that are made possible by Internet and digital technologies. Opportunities to differentiate are available in all parts of a company's value chain—both primary and support activities.

Potential Internet-Related Pitfalls for Differentiators   Traditional differentiation strategies such as building strong brand identity and prestige pricing have been undermined by Internet-enabled capabilities such as the ability to compare product features side-by-side or bid online for competing services. The sustainability of Internet-based gains from differentiation will deteriorate if companies offer differentiating features that customers don't want or create a sense of uniqueness that customers don't value. The result can be a failed value proposition—the value companies thought they were offering, does not translate into sales.

Focus

A focus strategy targets a narrow market segment with customized products and/or services. With focus strategies, the Internet offers new avenues in which to compete because they can access markets less expensively (low cost) and provide more services and features (differentiation). Some claim that the Internet has opened up a new world of opportunities for niche players who seek to access small markets in a highly specialized fashion.[59] Niche businesses are among the most active users of digital technologies and e-business solutions. According to the ClickZ.com division of Jupitermedia Corporation, 77 percent of small businesses agree that a website is essential for small business success. Small businesses also report that the Internet has helped them grow (58 percent), made them more profitable (51 percent), and helped reduce transaction costs (49 percent).[60] Clearly niche players and small businesses are using the Internet and digital technologies to create more viable focus strategies.

Many aspects of the Internet economy favor focus strategies because niche players and small firms have been able to extend their reach and effectively compete with larger competitors. For example, niche firms have been quicker than Fortune 1000 firms to adopt blogging as a way to create a community and gather customer feedback.[61] Effective use of blogs is an example of how focusers are using the new technology to provide the kinds of advantages that have been the hallmark of a focus strategy in the past—specialized knowledge, rapid response, and strong customer service. Thus, the Internet has provided many firms that pursue focus strategies with new tools for creating competitive advantages.

Exhibit 5.11 Internet-
Enabled Focus Strategies

- Permission marketing techniques are focusing sales efforts on specific customers who opt to receive advertising notices.
- Niche portals that target specific groups are providing advertisers with access to viewers with specialized interests.
- Virtual organizing and online "officing" are being used to minimize firm infrastructure requirements.
- Procurement technologies that use Internet software to match buyers and sellers are highlighting specialized buyers and drawing attention to smaller suppliers.

Exhibit 5.11 outlines several approaches to strategic focusing that are made possible by Internet and digital technologies. Both primary and support activities can be enhanced using the kind of singlemindedness that is characteristic of a focus strategy.

Potential Internet-Related Pitfalls for Focusers A key danger for focusers using the Internet relates to correctly assessing the size of the online marketplace. Focusers can misread the scope and interests of their target markets. This can cause them to focus on segments that are too narrow to be profitable or to lose their uniqueness in overly broad niches, making them vulnerable to imitators or new entrants.

What happens when an e-business focuser tries to overextend its niche? Efforts to appeal to a broader audience by carrying additional inventory, developing additional content, or offering additional services can cause it to lose the cost advantages associated with a limited product or service offering. Conversely, when focus strategies become too narrow, the e-business may have trouble generating enough activity to justify the expense of operating the website.

Are Combination Strategies the Key to E-Business Success?

Because of the changing dynamics presented by digital and Internet-based technologies, new strategic combinations that make the best use of the competitive strategies may hold the greatest promise.[62] Many experts agree that the net effect of the digital economy is *fewer* rather than more opportunities for sustainable advantages.[63] This means strategic thinking becomes more important.

More specifically, the Internet has provided all companies with greater tools for managing costs. So it may be that cost management and control will become more important management tools. In general, this may be good if it leads to an economy that makes more efficient use of its scarce resources. However, for individual companies, it may shave critical percentage points off profit margins and create a climate that makes it impossible to survive, much less achieve sustainable above-average profits.

Many differentiation advantages are also diminished by the Internet. The ability to comparison shop—to check product reviews and inspect different choices with a few clicks of the mouse—is depriving some companies, such as auto dealers, of the unique advantages that were the hallmark of their prior success. Differentiating is still an important strategy, of course. But how firms achieve it may change, and the best approach may be to combine differentiation with other competitive strategies.

Perhaps the greatest beneficiaries are the focusers who can use the Internet to capture a niche that previously may have been inaccessible. However, because the same factors that make it possible for a small niche player to be a contender may make that same niche attractive to a big company. That is, an incumbent firm that previously thought a niche

Liberty Mutual's Electronic Invoice System: Combining Low Cost and Differentiation Advantages

Boston-based Liberty Mutual Group is a leading global insurer and the sixth largest property and casualty insurer in the United States. Its largest line of business is personal automobile insurance. Liberty Mutual has $112.2 billion in assets and $33 billion in annual revenues—ranking the firm 71st on the Fortune 500 list of the largest corporations.

In 2000, Liberty Mutual became one of the first companies to experiment with electronic invoices. It set up a pilot program with a few law firms to submit its bills through a secured website. These firms, for the most part, handle claims litigation for Liberty, defending its policyholders in lawsuits. Its success with this program convinced Liberty that it could achieve significant cost savings and also pass along differentiating features to its customers and strategic partners. Liberty now processes nearly 400,000 electronic legal-services invoices a year— 70 percent of the total invoices that the firm receives.

As expected, the initial transition was quite expensive. The company invested nearly $1 million in the first four years. However, Liberty estimates that the electronic invoice program saves the company $750,000 a year in direct costs by streamlining the distribution, payment, storage, and retrieval of invoices. E-invoices enable Liberty to move from intake to payment with half the staff that it had taken to process paper invoices. The firm has also created new efficiencies by cutting costs resulting from data entry errors, late payments, and overpayments. As a relatively minor issue, Liberty saves more than $20,000 per year on postage, photocopying, archiving, and retrieval costs.

The legal invoices are organized by litigation phase or task—for example, taking a deposition or reporting a witness statement. Work is diced into tiny increments of

six minutes or less. A single invoice that covers a month of complex litigation, for example, can include well over 1,000 lines. However, by building and mining a database of law firm billing practices, Liberty is able to generate a highly granular report card about law firm activities and performance. The new knowledge generated by this system not only increases internal effectiveness but also allows Liberty to provide detailed feedback to clients and other external stakeholders.

Online invoicing has also helped speed up both processing and response time. Liberty can instantaneously see how firms deploy and bill for partners, paralegals, and other staff, how they compare with each other on rates, hours, and case outcomes; and whether, how, and how often they send duplicate invoices or charge for inappropriate services. The system also allows Liberty to instantly review all of the time billed for a particular attorney across many cases, enabling the firm to reconstruct the total time billed to Liberty during a single day. More than once they have found that attorneys have billed more than 24 hours in a day. Liberty is also able to easily expose prohibited formula billing patterns (wherein, for example, they are billed a set amount for a service instead of actual time spent). In two cases in which formula billing was used, Liberty found that there were more than $28,000 in suspected overcharges.

Liberty Mutual is in the process of developing a large database of law firms' billing practices on different types of cases. The database should eventually enable Liberty to evaluate a law firm's billing activities and compare them to the norms of all of its partner firms. With such intelligence, it will be a rather straightforward matter to rate each firm's cost effectiveness in handling certain types of cases and match firms with cases accordingly.

Liberty's decision to use electronic invoices was initially based on the potential for cost savings. But the differentiating advantages it has achieved in terms of rapid feedback, decreased response time, and a knowledge trove in databases that can be electronically mined has provided the company with a fruitful combination of Internet-based strategic advantages.

Sources: Coyle, M., & Angevine, R. 2007. Liberty Mutual Group reports fourth quarter 2006 results. February 26, *www.libertymutual.com*; Smunt, T. L., & Sutcliffe, C. L., 2004. There's Gold in Them Bills. *Harvard Business Review*, 82(9): 24–25; and *www.libertymutualgroup.com*.

market was not worth the effort may use Internet technologies to enter that segment for a lower cost than in the past. The larger firm can then bring its market power and resources to bear in a way that a smaller competitor cannot match.

A combination strategy challenges a company to carefully blend alternative strategic approaches and remain mindful of the impact of different decisions on the firm's value-creating processes and its extended value-chain activities. Strong leadership is needed to maintain a bird's-eye perspective on a company's overall approach and to coordinate the multiple dimensions of a combination strategy.

Strategy Spotlight 5.5 describes the efforts of Liberty Mutual, a company that used Internet and digital technologies to successfully combine both differentiation and overall low-cost advantages.

Industry Life Cycle Stages: Strategic Implications

The **industry life cycle** refers to the stages of introduction, growth, maturity, and decline that occur over the life of an industry. In considering the industry life cycle, it is useful to think in terms of broad product lines such as personal computers, photocopiers, or long-distance telephone service. Yet the industry life cycle concept can be explored from several levels, from the life cycle of an entire industry to the life cycle of a single variation or model of a specific product or service.

Why are industry life cycles important?[64] The emphasis on various generic strategies, functional areas, value-creating activities, and overall objectives varies over the course of an industry life cycle. Managers must become even more aware of their firm's strengths and weaknesses in many areas to attain competitive advantages. For example, firms depend on their research and development (R&D) activities in the introductory stage. R&D is the source of new products and features that everyone hopes will appeal to customers. Firms develop products and services to stimulate consumer demand. Later, during the maturity phase, the functions of the product have been defined, more competitors have entered the market, and competition is intense. Managers then place greater emphasis on production efficiencies and process (as opposed to the product) engineering in order to lower manufacturing costs. This helps to protect the firm's market position and to extend the product life cycle because the firm's lower costs can be passed on to consumers in the form of lower prices, and price-sensitive customers will find the product more appealing.

Exhibit 5.12 illustrates the four stages of the industry life cycle and how factors such as generic strategies, market growth rate, intensity of competition, and overall objectives change over time. Managers must strive to emphasize the key functional areas during each of the four stages and to attain a level of parity in all functional areas and value-creating activities. For example, although controlling production costs may be a primary concern during the maturity stage, managers should not totally ignore other functions such as marketing and R&D. If they do, they can become so focused on lowering costs that they miss market trends or fail to incorporate important product or process designs. Thus, the firm may attain low-cost products that have limited market appeal.

It is important to point out a caveat. While the life cycle idea is analogous to a living organism (i.e., birth, growth, maturity, and death), the comparison has limitations.[65] Products and services go through many cycles of innovation and renewal. Typically, only fad products have a single life cycle. Maturity stages of an industry can be "transformed" or followed by a stage of rapid growth if consumer tastes change, technological innovations take place, or new developments occur. The cereal industry is a good example. When medical research indicated that oat consumption reduced a person's cholesterol, sales of Quaker Oats increased dramatically.[66]

Strategies in the Introduction Stage

In the **introduction stage,** products are unfamiliar to consumers.[67] Market segments are not well defined, and product features are not clearly specified. The early development of an industry typically involves low sales growth, rapid technological change, operating losses, and the need for strong sources of cash to finance operations. Since there are few players and not much growth, competition tends to be limited.

---

industry life cycle
the stages of introduction, growth, maturity, and decline that typically occur over the life of an industry.

>LO5.7
The importance of considering the industry life cycle to determine a firm's business-level strategy and its relative emphasis on functional area strategies and value-creating activities.

introduction stage
the first stage of the industry life cycle, characterized by (1) new products that are not known to customers, (2) poorly defined market segments, (3) unspecified product features, (4) low sales growth, (5) rapid technological change, (6) operating losses, and (7) a need for financial support.

Exhibit 5.12 Stages of the Industry Life Cycle

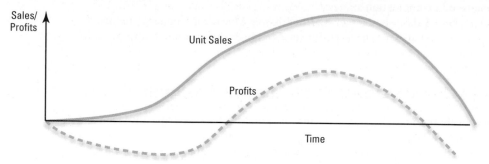

Stage Factor	Introduction	Growth	Maturity	Decline
Generic strategies	Differentiation	Differentiation	Differentiation Overall cost leadership	Overall cost leadership Focus
Market growth rate	Low	Very large	Low to moderate	Negative
Number of segments	Very few	Some	Many	Few
Intensity of competition	Low	Increasing	Very intense	Changing
Emphasis on product design	Very high	High	Low to moderate	Low
Emphasis on process design	Low	Low to moderate	High	Low
Major functional area(s) of concern	Research and development	Sales and marketing	Production	General management and finance
Overall objective	Increase market awareness	Create consumer demand	Defend market share and extend product life cycles	Consolidate, maintain, harvest, or exit

Success requires an emphasis on research and development and marketing activities to enhance awareness. The challenge becomes one of (1) developing the product and finding a way to get users to try it, and (2) generating enough exposure so the product emerges as the "standard" by which all other rivals' products are evaluated.

There's an advantage to being the "first mover" in a market.[68] It led to Coca-Cola's success in becoming the first soft-drink company to build a recognizable global brand and enabled Caterpillar to get a lock on overseas sales channels and service capabilities.

However, there can also be a benefit to being a "late mover." Target carefully considered its decision to delay its Internet strategy. Compared to its competitors Walmart and Kmart, Target was definitely an industry laggard. But things certainly turned out well:[69]

By waiting, Target gained a late mover advantage. The store was able to use competitors' mistakes as its own learning curve. This saved money, and customers didn't seem to mind the wait: When Target finally opened its website, it quickly captured market share from both Kmart and Walmart Internet shoppers. Forrester Research Internet analyst Stephen Zrike commented, "There's no question, in our mind, that Target has a far better understanding of how consumers buy online."

Examples of products currently in the introductory stages of the industry life cycle include electric vehicles, solar panels, and high-definition television (HDTV).

Strategies in the Growth Stage

The **growth stage** is characterized by strong increases in sales. Such potential attracts other rivals. In the growth stage, the primary key to success is to build consumer preferences for specific brands. This requires strong brand recognition, differentiated products, and the financial resources to support a variety of value-chain activities such as marketing and sales, and research and development. Whereas marketing and sales initiatives were mainly directed at spurring *aggregate* demand—that is, demand for all such products in the introduction stage—efforts in the growth stage are directed toward stimulating *selective* demand, in which a firm's product offerings are chosen instead of a rival's.

Revenues increase at an accelerating rate because (1) new consumers are trying the product and (2) a growing proportion of satisfied consumers are making repeat purchases.[70] In general, as a product moves through its life cycle, the proportion of repeat buyers to new purchasers increases. Conversely, new products and services often fail if there are relatively few repeat purchases. For example, Alberto-Culver introduced Mr. Culver's Sparklers, which were solid air fresheners that looked like stained glass. Although the product quickly went from the introductory to the growth stage, sales collapsed. Why? Unfortunately, there were few repeat purchasers because buyers treated them as inexpensive window decorations, left them there, and felt little need to purchase new ones. Examples of products currently in the growth stage include Internet servers and personal digital assistants (e.g., Palm Pilots).

growth stage the second stage of the product life cycle, characterized by (1) strong increases in sales; (2) growing competition; (3) developing brand recognition; and (4) a need for financing complementary value-chain activities such as marketing, sales, customer service, and research and development.

Strategies in the Maturity Stage

In the **maturity stage** aggregate industry demand softens. As markets become saturated, there are few new adopters. It's no longer possible to "grow around" the competition, so direct competition becomes predominant.[71] With few attractive prospects, marginal competitors exit the market. At the same time, rivalry among existing rivals intensifies because of fierce price competition at the same time that expenses associated with attracting new buyers are rising. Advantages based on efficient manufacturing operations and process engineering become more important for keeping costs low as customers become more price sensitive. It also becomes more difficult for firms to differentiate their offerings, because users have a greater understanding of products and services.

An article in *Fortune* magazine that addressed the intensity of rivalry in mature markets was aptly titled "A Game of Inches." It stated, "Battling for market share in a slowing industry can be a mighty dirty business. Just ask laundry soap archrivals Unilever and Procter & Gamble."[72] These two firms have been locked in a battle for market share since 1965. Why is the competition so intense? There is not much territory to gain and industry sales were flat. An analyst noted, "People aren't getting any dirtier." Thus, the only way to win is to take market share from the competition. To increase its share, Procter & Gamble (P&G) spends $100 million a year promoting its Tide brand on television, billboards, buses, magazines, and the Internet. But Unilever isn't standing still. Armed with an $80 million budget, it launched a soap tablet product named Wisk Dual Action Tablets. For example, it delivered samples of this product to 24 million U.S. homes in Sunday

maturity stage the third stage of the product life cycle, characterized by (1) slowing demand growth, (2) saturated markets, (3) direct competition, (4) price competition, and (5) strategic emphasis on efficient operations.

strategy spotlight

Reverse and Breakaway Positioning: How to Avoid Being Held Hostage to the Life-Cycle Curve

When firms adopt a reverse or breakaway positioning strategy, there is typically no pretense about what they are trying to accomplish. In essence, they subvert convention through unconventional promotions, prices, and attributes. That becomes a large part of their appeal—a cleverly positioned product offering. Next we discuss Commerce Bank's reverse positioning and Swatch's breakaway positioning.

Commerce Bank

While most banks offer dozens of checking and savings accounts and compete by trying to offer the highest interest rates, Commerce Bank takes a totally different approach. It pays among the lowest rates in its market. Further, it offers a very limited product line—just four checking accounts, for example. One would think that such a stingy approach would seem to scare off customers. However, Commerce Bank has been very successful. Between 1999 and 2005, it expanded from 120 to 373 branches and its total assets have soared from $5.6 billion to $39 billion.

How has it been so successful? It has stripped away all of what customers expect—lots of choices and peak interest rates and it has *reverse positioned* itself as "the most convenient bank in America." It's open seven days a week, including evenings until 8 p.m. You can get a debit card while you wait. And, when it rains, an escort with an umbrella will escort you to your car. Further, the bank offers free coffee, newspapers, and most of the branches

have free coin-counting machines that customers love (in one recent week, customers fed the machines a total of $28 million in loose change). Not too surprisingly, despite the inferior rates and few choices, new customers are flocking to the bank.

Swatch

Interestingly, the name "Swatch" is often misconstrued as a contraction of the words *Swiss watch*. However, Nicholas Hayek, Chairman, affirms that the original contraction was "Second Watch"—the new watch was introduced as a new concept of watches as casual, fun, and relatively disposable accessories. And therein lies Swatch's *breakaway positioning*.

When Swatch was launched in 1983, Swiss watches were marketed as a form of jewelry. They were serious, expensive, enduring, and discreetly promoted. Once a customer purchased one, it lasted a lifetime. Swatch changed all of that by defining its watches as playful fashion accessories which were showily promoted. They inspired impulse buying—customers would often purchase half a dozen in different designs. Their price—$40 when the brand was introduced—expanded Swatch's reach beyond its default category (watches as high-end jewelry) and moved it into the fashion accessory category, where it has different customers and competitors. Swatch was the official timekeeper of the 1996, 2000, and 2004 Summer Olympics.

Today, The Swatch Group is the largest watch company in the world. It has acquired many brands over the years including Omega, Longines, Calvin Klein, and Hamilton. Revenues have grown to $5.5 billion in 2009 and net income has increased to $753 million. These figures represent compound annual increases of 11 percent and 12 percent, respectively, over a four-year period.

Sources: Moon, Y. 2005. Break Free from the Product Life Cycle. *Harvard Business Review*, 83(5): 87–94; Commerce Bancorp, Inc. *www.hoovers.com*; Swatch. *en.wikipedia.org*; and *www.commercebank.com*.

reverse positioning a break in industry tendency to continuously augment products, characteristic of the product life cycle, by offering products with fewer product attributes and lower prices.

newspapers, followed by a series of TV ads. P&G launched a counteroffensive with Tide Rapid Action Tablets ads showed in side-by-side comparisons of the two products dropped into beakers of water. In the promotion, P&G claimed that its product is superior because it dissolves faster than Unilever's product.

Although this is only one example, many product classes and industries, including consumer products such as beer, automobiles, and televisions, are in maturity.

Firms do not need to be "held hostage" to the life-cycle curve. By positioning or repositioning their products in unexpected ways, firms can change how customers mentally categorize them. Thus, firms are able to rescue products floundering in the maturity phase of their life cycles and return them to the growth phase.

Two positioning strategies that managers can use to affect consumers' mental shifts are **reverse positioning,** which strips away "sacred" product attributes while adding new ones, and **breakaway positioning,** which associates the product with a radically different category.[73] We discuss each of these positioning strategies below and then provide an example of each in Strategy Spotlight 5.6.

Reverse Positioning   This assumes that although customers may desire more than the baseline product, they don't necessarily want an endless list of features. Such companies make the creative decision to step off the augmentation treadmill and shed product attributes that the rest of the industry considers sacred. Then, once a product is returned to its baseline state, the stripped-down product adds one or more carefully selected attributes that would usually be found only in a highly augmented product. Such an unconventional combination of attributes allows the product to assume a new competitive position within the category and move backward from maturity into a growth position on the life-cycle curve.

Breakaway Positioning   As noted above, with reverse positioning, a product establishes a unique position in its category but retains a clear category membership. However, with breakaway positioning, a product escapes its category by deliberately associating with a different one. Thus, managers leverage the new category's conventions to change both how products are consumed and with whom they compete. Instead of merely seeing the breakaway product as simply an alternative to others in its category, consumers perceive it as altogether different.

When a breakaway product is successful in leaving its category and joining a new one, it is able to redefine its competition. Similar to reverse positioning, this strategy permits the product to shift backward on the life-cycle curve, moving from the rather dismal maturity phase to a thriving growth opportunity.

Strategy Spotlight 5.6 provides examples of reverse and breakaway positioning.

breakaway positioning a break in industry tendency to incrementally improve products along specific dimensions, characteristic of the product life cycle, by offering products that are still in the industry but that are perceived by customers as being different.

Strategies in the Decline Stage

Although all decisions in the phases of an industry life cycle are important, they become particularly difficult in the **decline stage.** Firms must face up to the fundamental strategic choices of either exiting or staying and attempting to consolidate their position in the industry.[74]

The decline stage occurs when industry sales and profits begin to fall. Typically, changes in the business environment are at the root of an industry or product group entering this stage.[75] Changes in consumer tastes or a technological innovation can push a product into decline. Typewriters have entered into the decline stage because of the word processing capabilities of personal computers. Compact disks have forced cassette tapes into decline in the prerecorded music industry, and digital video disks (DVDs) are replacing compact disks. About 30 years earlier, of course, cassette tapes had led to the demise of long-playing records (LPs).

Products in the decline stage often consume a large share of management time and financial resources relative to their potential worth. Sales and profits decline. Also, competitors may start drastically cutting their prices to raise cash and remain solvent. The situation is further aggravated by the liquidation of assets, including inventory, of some of the competitors that have failed. This further intensifies price competition.

In the decline stage, a firm's strategic options become dependent on the actions of rivals. If many competitors leave the market, sales and profit opportunities increase. On the other hand, prospects are limited if all competitors remain.[76] If some competitors merge, their increased market power may erode the opportunities for the remaining players. Managers must carefully monitor the actions and intentions of competitors before deciding on a course of action.

Four basic strategies are available in the decline phase: *maintaining, harvesting, exiting, or consolidating.*[77]

decline stage the fourth stage of the product life cycle, characterized by (1) falling sales and profits, (2) increasing price competition, and (3) industry consolidation.

- *Maintaining* refers to keeping a product going without significantly reducing marketing support, technological development, or other investments, in the hope that competitors will eventually exit the market. Many offices, for example, still use typewriters for filling out forms and other purposes that cannot be completed on a PC. In some rural areas, rotary (or dial) telephones persist because of the older technology used in central switching offices. Thus, there may still be the potential for revenues and profits.

harvesting strategy a strategy of wringing as much profit as possible out of a business in the short to medium term by reducing costs.

- *Harvesting* involves obtaining as much profit as possible and requires that costs be reduced quickly. Managers should consider the firm's value-creating activities and cut associated budgets. Value-chain activities to consider are primary (e.g., operations, sales and marketing) and support (e.g., procurement, technology development). The objective is to wring out as much profit as possible.

- *Exiting the market* involves dropping the product from a firm's portfolio. Since a residual core of consumers exist, eliminating it should be carefully considered. If the firm's exit involves product markets that affect important relationships with other product markets in the corporation's overall portfolio, an exit could have repercussions for the whole corporation. For example, it may involve the loss of valuable brand names or human capital with a broad variety of expertise in many value-creating activities such as marketing, technology, and operations.

consolidation strategy a firm's acquiring or merging with other firms in an industry in order to enhance market power and gain valuable assets.

- *Consolidation* involves one firm acquiring at a reasonable price the best of the surviving firms in an industry. This enables firms to enhance market power and acquire valuable assets. One example of a consolidation strategy took place in the defense industry in the early 1990s. As the cliché suggests, "peace broke out" at the end of the Cold War and overall U.S. defense spending levels plummeted.[78] Many companies that make up the defense industry saw more than 50 percent of their market disappear. Only one-quarter of the 120,000 companies that once supplied the Department of Defense still serve in that capacity; the others have shut down their defense business or dissolved altogether. But one key player, Lockheed Martin, became a dominant rival by pursuing an aggressive strategy of consolidation. During the 1990s, it purchased 17 independent entities, including General Dynamics' tactical aircraft and space systems divisions, GE Aerospace, Goodyear Aerospace, and Honeywell ElectroOptics. These combinations enabled Lockheed Martin to emerge as the top provider to three governmental customers: the Department of Defense, the Department of Energy, and NASA.

Examples of products currently in the decline stage of the industry life cycle include automotive spark plugs (replaced by electronic fuel ignition), videocassette recorders (replaced by digital video disk recorders), and personal computer zip drives (replaced by compact disk read-write drives). And, as we mentioned previously, compact disks are being replaced by digital video disks (DVDs).

The introduction of new technologies and associated products does not always mean that old technologies quickly fade away. Research shows that in a number of cases, old technologies actually enjoy a very profitable "last gasp."[79] Examples include mainframe computers (versus minicomputers and PCs), coronary artery bypass graft surgery (versus angioplasty), and CISC (Complex Instruction Set Computing) architecture in computer processors versus RISC (Reduced Instruction Set Computing). In each case, the advent of new technology prompted predictions of the demise of the older technology, but each of these has proved to be resilient survivors. What accounts for their continued profitability and survival?

Retreating to more defensible ground is one strategy that firms specializing in technologies threatened with rapid obsolescence have followed. For example, while angioplasty may be appropriate for relatively healthier patients with blocked arteries, sicker, higher-risk patients seem to benefit more from coronary artery bypass graft surgery. This enabled the surgeons to concentrate on the more difficult cases and improve the technology itself. The advent of television unseated the radio as the major source of entertainment from American homes. However, the radio has survived and even thrived in venues where people are also engaged in other activities, such as driving.

Using the new to improve the old is a second approach. Carburetor manufacturers have improved the fuel efficiency of their product by incorporating electronic controls that were originally developed for electronic fuel injection systems. Similarly, CISC computer chip manufacturers have adopted many features from RISC chips.

Improving the price-performance trade-off is a third approach. IBM continues to make money selling mainframes long after their obituary was written. It retooled the technology using low-cost microprocessors and cut their prices drastically. Further, it invested and updated the software, enabling them to offer clients such as banks better performance and lower costs.

Clearly, "last gasps" may not necessarily translate into longer term gains, as the experience of the integrated steel mills suggests. When the first mini-mills appeared, integrated steel mills shifted to higher margin steel, but eventually mini-mills entered even the last strongholds of the integrated steel mills.

Turnaround Strategies

A **turnaround strategy** involves reversing performance decline and reinvigorating growth toward profitability.[80] A need for turnaround may occur at any stage in the life cycle but is more likely to occur during maturity or decline.

Most turnarounds require a firm to carefully analyze the external and internal environments.[81] The external analysis leads to identification of market segments or customer groups that may still find the product attractive.[82] Internal analysis results in actions aimed at reduced costs and higher efficiency. A firm needs to undertake a mix of both internally and externally oriented actions to effect a turnaround.[83] In effect, the cliché "you can't shrink yourself to greatness" applies.

A study of 260 mature businesses in need of a turnaround identified three strategies used by successful companies.[84]

- *Asset and cost surgery.* Very often, mature firms tend to have assets that do not produce any returns. These include real estate, buildings, etc. Outright sales or sale and leaseback free up considerable cash and improve returns. Investment in new plants and equipment can be deferred. Firms in turnaround situations try to aggressively cut administrative expenses and inventories and speed up collection of receivables. Costs also can be reduced by outsourcing production of various inputs for which market prices may be cheaper than in-house production costs.
- *Selective product and market pruning.* Most mature or declining firms have many product lines that are losing money or are only marginally profitable. One strategy is to discontinue such product lines and focus all resources on a few core profitable areas. For example, in the early 1980s, faced with possible bankruptcy, Chrysler Corporation sold off all its nonautomotive businesses as well as all its production facilities abroad. Focus on the North American market and identification of a profitable niche—namely, minivans—were keys to their eventual successful turnaround.
- *Piecemeal productivity improvements.* There are many ways in which a firm can eliminate costs and improve productivity. Although individually these are small gains, they cumulate over a period of time to substantial gains. Improving business processes by reengineering them, benchmarking specific activities against industry leaders, encouraging employee input to identify excess costs, increasing capacity utilization, and improving employee productivity lead to a significant overall gain.

Software maker Intuit is a case of a quick but well-implemented turnaround strategy. After stagnating and stumbling during the dot-com boom, Intuit, which is known for

turnaround strategy a strategy that reverses a firm's decline in performance and returns it to growth and profitability.

>LO5.8
The need for turnaround strategies that enable a firm to reposition its competitive position in an industry.

strategy spotlight

5.7

Alan Mulally: Leading Ford's Extraordinary Turnaround

Shortly after Alan Mulally took over as Ford's CEO in September 2006, he organized a weekly meeting with his senior managers and asked them how things were going. Fine, fine, fine were the responses from around the table. To this, an incredulous Mulally exclaimed: "We are forecasting a $17 billion loss and no one has any problems!" Clearly, there were cultural issues at play (such as denial and executive rivalry) but also very serious strategic and financial problems as well.

What a change a few years can make! Ford's profits for 2010 were $6.6 billion and the firm has enjoyed seven straight quarters of profitability. This is quite a sharp contrast from its $14.7 billion loss in 2008—a time when high gasoline prices, bloated operations, and uncompetitive labor costs combined with the deep recession to create a perfect storm.

How did Mulally turn Ford around? It took many tough strategic decisions—involving not just company executives but Ford staff and the United Auto Workers (UAW). It involved downsizing, creating greater efficiency, improving quality, selling off the European luxury brands, and mortgaging assets to raise money. Ford's leaders and the United Auto Workers (UAW) also made transformational changes to lower the company's cost structure—a critical component to the company's long-term competitiveness.

Let's take a closer look at Mulally's strategic actions. We have to begin with the plan to undertake a dramatic refinancing of the business by raising bank loans secured against the company's assets. One of his first tasks was to finalize Ford's recovery plan and sell it to the banks. This financing enabled Ford to be the only major American automaker that avoided government-sponsored bankruptcy. And, as noted by Mulally, "The response that we received because we did not ask for the precious taxpayer's money has been tremendous." In fact, Jim Farley, head of marketing for Ford worldwide, estimates that Ford's standing on its own feet has been worth $1 billion in favorable publicity for the company and has attracted appreciative Americans into its dealers' showrooms.

Second, he decided that the firm would concentrate resources on the Ford brand and sell off the Premier Automotive Group (PAG) businesses—even if it meant taking a loss. Mulally had ridiculed the idea that top management could focus on Jaguar before breakfast, attend to Volvo or Land Rover before lunch, and then consider Ford and its Lincoln offshoot in North America in the afternoon. Accordingly, in 2007, Aston Martin was sold

to private investors; Jaguar and Land Rover were sold to India's Tata Group in 2008; and a Chinese carmaker, Geely, bought Volvo in 2010. Further, the Mercury brand is being phased out.

Third, Mulally realized that in addition to fewer brands, Ford needed a much narrower range of cars, albeit higher quality ones, carrying its familiar blue oval logo in all segments of the market. At one point Ford's designers had to deal with 97 different models—that was cut to 36 and may go lower.

Fourth, along with rationalizing the product range, Mulally insisted on raising the aspiration level with regard to quality. Although Ford used to talk about claiming parity with Toyota's Camry, Mulally shifted the emphasis to trying to make each car that Ford sells "best in class." A number of new cars being created under the One Ford policy are coming from Europe. Quality has improved dramatically according to some of the industry's outside arbiters, such as J. D. Power.

Fifth, to ensure that regional stars such as the Focus could become global successes, 8 of Ford's 10 platforms (the floor pan and its underpinnings) are now global platforms. More shared platforms enables Ford to build different models more quickly and economically to account for regional tastes in cars and variations in regulations. For example, the various Fiesta-based cars may look different, but they share about two-thirds of their parts. Such actions are particularly important as Ford focuses (no pun intended) its efforts toward smaller, more fuel-efficient automobiles which traditionally have smaller margins. As noted by Lewis Booth, Ford's finance director, "Customers' tastes are converging. Fuel efficiency matters everywhere."

Sixth, Mulally had to make many painful restructuring decisions in order to match production to the number of cars that Ford could sell. Since 2006, Ford cut half of its shop-floor workforce in North America and a third of its office jobs. By the end of 2011, a total of 17 factories will have closed, and Ford's total employment will have fallen from 128,000 to 75,000. In addition, the number of dealers has been cut by a fifth. Helped by union concessions, Ford has shed about $14 billion in annual operational costs and now can compete with Japan's "transplant" factories in America.

Regarding Ford's successful transformation, Mulally claims: "We have earned the right now to make a complete family of best-in-class vehicles right here in the United States with U.S. workers and competing with the very best in the world. That's not only good for Ford and our customers and our stakeholders but that's good for the United States of America." Without doubt, such a statement a few years ago would have been dismissed as hyperbole.

Sources: Linn, A. 2010. For Ford's Mulally, big bets are paying off. *www.msnbc.com.* October 26: nd; Anonymous. 2010. Epiphany in Dearborn. *The Economist.* December 11: 83–85; Reagan, J. Ford Motor's extraordinary turnaround. December 10: np; and *www.finance.yahoo.com.*

its Quickbook and Turbotax software, hired Stephen M. Bennett, a 22-year GE veteran, in 1999. He immediately discontinued Intuit's online finance, insurance, and bill-paying operations that were losing money. Instead, he focused on software for small businesses that employ less than 250 people. He also instituted a performance-based reward system that greatly improved employee productivity. Within a few years, Intuit was once again making substantial profits and its stock was up 42 percent.[85]

Even when an industry is in overall decline, pockets of profitability remain. These are segments with customers who are relatively price insensitive. For example, the replacement demand for vacuum tubes affords its manufacturers an opportunity to earn above normal returns although the product itself is technologically obsolete. Surprisingly, within declining industries, there may still be segments that are either stable or growing. Although fountain pens ceased to be the writing instrument of choice a long time ago, the fountain pen industry has successfully reconceptualized the product as a high margin luxury item that signals accomplishment and success. In the final analysis, every business has the potential for rejuvenation. But it takes creativity, persistence, and most of all a clear strategy to translate that potential into reality.

Strategy Spotlight 5.7 discusses Ford's remarkable turnaround under the direction of CEO Alan Mulally.

Reflecting on Career Implications . . .

- **Types of Competitive Advantage:** Always be aware of your organization's business-level strategy. What do you do to help your firm either increase differentiation or lower costs? What are some ways that your role in the firm can help realize these outcomes?
- **Combining Sources of Competitive Advantage:** Are you engaged in activities that simultaneously help your organization increase differentiation and lower costs?
- **Industry Life Cycle:** If your firm is in the mature stage of the industry life cycle, can you think of ways to enhance your firm's level of differentiation in order to make customers less price sensitive to your organization's goods and services?
- **Industry Life Cycle:** If you sense that your career is maturing (or in the decline phase!), what actions can you take to restore career growth and momentum (e.g., training, mentoring, professional networking)? Should you actively consider professional opportunities in other industries?

Summary

How and why firms outperform each other goes to the heart of strategic management. In this chapter, we identified three generic strategies and discussed how firms are able not only to attain advantages over competitors, but also to sustain such advantages over time. Why do some advantages become long-lasting while others are quickly imitated by competitors?

The three generic strategies—overall cost leadership, differentiation, and focus—form the core of this chapter. We began by providing a brief description of each

generic strategy (or competitive advantage) and furnished examples of firms that have successfully implemented these strategies. Successful generic strategies invariably enhance a firm's position vis-à-vis the five forces of that industry—a point that we stressed and illustrated with examples. However, as we pointed out, there are pitfalls to each of the generic strategies. Thus, the sustainability of a firm's advantage is always challenged because of imitation or substitution by new or existing rivals. Such competitor moves erode a firm's advantage over time.

We also discussed the viability of combining (or integrating) overall cost leadership and generic differentiation strategies. If successful, such integration can enable a firm to enjoy superior performance and improve its competitive position. However, this is challenging, and managers must be aware of the potential downside risks associated with such an initiative.

We addressed the challenges inherent in determining the sustainability of competitive advantages. Drawing on an example from a manufacturing industry, we discussed both the "pro" and "con" positions as to why competitive advantages are sustainable over a long period of time.

The way companies formulate and deploy strategies is changing because of the impact of the Internet and digital technologies in many industries. Further, Internet technologies are enabling the mass customization capabilities of greater numbers of competitors. Focus strategies are likely to increase in importance because the Internet provides highly targeted and lower-cost access to narrow or specialized markets. These strategies are not without their pitfalls, however, and firms need to understand the dangers as well as the potential benefits of Internet-based approaches.

The concept of the industry life cycle is a critical contingency that managers must take into account in striving to create and sustain competitive advantages. We identified the four stages of the industry life cycle—introduction, growth, maturity, and decline—and suggested how these stages can play a role in decisions that managers must make at the business level. These include overall strategies as well as the relative emphasis on functional areas and value—creating activities.

When a firm's performance severely erodes, turnaround strategies are needed to reverse its situation and enhance its competitive position. We have discussed three approaches—asset cost surgery, selective product and market pruning, and piecemeal productivity improvements.

Summary Review Questions

1. Explain why the concept of competitive advantage is central to the study of strategic management.
2. Briefly describe the three generic strategies—overall cost leadership, differentiation, and focus.
3. Explain the relationship between the three generic strategies and the five forces that determine the average profitability within an industry.
4. What are some of the ways in which a firm can attain a successful turnaround strategy?
5. Describe some of the pitfalls associated with each of the three generic strategies.

6. Can firms combine the generic strategies of overall cost leadership and differentiation? Why or why not?
7. Explain why the industry life cycle concept is an important factor in determining a firm's business-level strategy.

Key Terms

business-level strategy, 162
generic strategies, 162
overall cost leadership, 164
experience curve, 165
competitive parity, 166
differentiation strategy, 169
focus strategy, 174
combination strategies, 176
mass customization, 176
profit pool, 177
digital technologies, 182
disintermediation, 183
industry life cycle, 187
introduction stage, 187
growth stage, 189
maturity stage, 189
reverse positioning, 190
breakaway positioning, 191
decline stage, 191
consolidation strategy, 192
harvesting strategy, 192
turnaround strategy, 193

Experiential Exercise

What are some examples of primary and support activities that enable Nucor, a $19 billion steel manufacturer, to achieve a low-cost strategy? (Fill in table on the following page.)

Application Questions Exercises

1. Go to the Internet and look up *www.walmart.com.* How has this firm been able to combine overall cost leadership and differentiation strategies?
2. Choose a firm with which you are familiar in your local business community. Is the firm successful in following one (or more) generic strategies? Why or why not? What do you think are some of the challenges it faces in implementing these strategies in an effective manner?
3. Think of a firm that has attained a differentiation focus or cost focus strategy. Are their advantages sustainable? Why? Why not? (*Hint:* Consider its position vis-à-vis Porter's five forces.)
4. Think of a firm that successfully achieved a combination overall cost leadership and differentiation strategy. What can be learned from this example? Are these advantages sustainable? Why? Why not? (*Hint:* Consider its competitive position vis-à-vis Porter's five forces.)

Value-Chain Activity	Yes/No	How Does Nucor Create Value for the Customer?
Primary:		
Inbound logistics		
Operations		
Outbound logistics		
Marketing and sales		
Service		
Support:		
Procurement		
Technology development		
Human resource management		
General administration		

Ethics Questions

1. Can you think of a company that suffered ethical consequences as a result of an overemphasis on a cost leadership strategy? What do you think were the financial and nonfinancial implications?

2. In the introductory stage of the product life cycle, what are some of the unethical practices that managers could engage in to enhance their firm's market position? What could be some of the long-term implications of such actions?

References

1. Helm, B. 2010. At KFC, a battle among the chicken-hearted. *Bloomberg Businessweek,* August 16: 19; De Nies, Y. 2010. Kentucky fried fight. *www. abcnews.go.com.* August 17: np; and Morran, C. 2010. Squabble between KFC & franchisees over advertising goes to court. *www.consumerist.com.* September 20: np. We thank Jason Hirsch for his valued contributions.

2. For a recent perspective by Porter on competitive strategy, refer to Porter, M. E. 1996. What is strategy? *Harvard Business Review,* 74(6): 61–78.

3. For insights into how a start-up is using solar technology, see: Gimbel, B. 2009. Plastic power. *Fortune,* February 2: 34.

4. Useful insights on strategy in an economic downturn are in: Rhodes, D. & Stelter, D. 2009. Seize advantage in a downturn. *Harvard Business Review,* 87(2): 50–58.

5. Some useful ideas on maintaining competitive advantages can be found in Ma, H. & Karri, R. 2005. Leaders beware: Some sure ways to lose your competitive advantage. *Organizational Dynamics,* 343(1): 63–76.

6. Miller, A. & Dess, G. G. 1993. Assessing Porter's model in terms of its generalizability, accuracy, and simplicity. *Journal of Management Studies,* 30(4): 553–585.

7. Cendrowski, S. 2008. Extreme retailing. *Fortune,* March 31: 14.

8. For insights on how discounting can erode a firm's performance, read: Stibel, J. M. & Delgrosso, P. 2008. Discounts can be dangerous. *Harvard Business Review,* 66(12): 31.

9. For a scholarly discussion and analysis of the concept of competitive parity, refer to Powell, T. C. 2003. Varieties of competitive parity. *Strategic Management Journal,* 24(1): 61–86.

10. Rao, A. R., Bergen, M. E., & Davis, S. 2000. How to fight a price war. *Harvard Business Review,* 78(2): 107–120.

11. Marriot, J. W. Jr. Our competitive strength: Human capital. A speech given to the Detroit Economic Club on October 2, 2000.

12. Whalen, C. J., Pascual, A. M., Lowery, T., & Muller, J. 2001. The top 25 managers. *BusinessWeek,* January 8: 63.

13. Ibid.

14. For an interesting perspective on the need for creative strategies, refer to Hamel, G. & Prahalad, C. K. 1994. *Competing for the future.* Boston: Harvard Business School Press.

15. Interesting insights on Walmart's effective cost leadership strategy are found in: Palmeri, C. 2008. Wal-Mart is up for this downturn. *BusinessWeek,* November 6: 34.

16. An interesting perspective on the dangers of price discounting is: Mohammad, R. 2011. Ditch the discounts. *Harvard Business Review,* 89 (1/2): 23–25.

17. Dholakia, U. M. 2011. Why employees can wreck promotional offers. *Harvard Business Review,* 89(1/2): 28.

18. Jacobs, A. 2010. Workers in China voting with their feet. *International Herald Tribune.* July 13: 1, 14.

19. For a perspective on the sustainability of competitive advantages, refer to

Barney, J. 1995. Looking inside for competitive advantage. *Academy of Management Executive,* 9(4): 49–61.

20. Thornton, E., 2001, Why e-brokers are broker and broker. *BusinessWeek,* January 22: 94.

21. Mohammed, R. 2011. Ditch the discounts. *Harvard Business Review,* 89(1/2): 23–25.

22. Koretz, G. 2001. E-commerce: The buyer wins. *BusinessWeek,* January 8: 30.

23. For an "ultimate" in differentiated services, consider time shares in exotic automobiles such as Lamborghinis and Bentleys. Refer to: Stead, D. 2008. My Lamborghini—today, anyway. *BusinessWeek,* January 18:17.

24. For an interesting perspective on the value of corporate brands and how they may be leveraged, refer to Aaker, D. A. 2004, *California Management Review,* 46(3): 6–18.

25. A unique perspective on differentiation strategies is: Austin, R. D. 2008. High margins and the quest for aesthetic coherence. *Harvard Business Review,* 86(1): 18–19.

26. MacMillan, I. & McGrath, R. 1997. Discovering new points of differentiation. *Harvard Business Review,* 75(4): 133–145; Wise, R. & Baumgarter, P. 1999. Beating the clock: Corporate responses to rapid change in the PC industry. *California Management Review,* 42(1): 8–36.

27. For a discussion on quality in terms of a company's software and information systems, refer to Prahalad, C. K. & Krishnan, M. S. 1999. The new meaning of quality in the information age. *Harvard Business Review,* 77(5): 109–118.

28. The role of design in achieving differentiation is addressed in: Brown, T. 2008. Design thinking. *Harvard Business Review.* 86(6): 84–92.

29. Taylor, A., III. 2001. Can you believe Porsche is putting its badge on this car? *Fortune,* February 19: 168–172.

30. Ward, S., Light, L., & Goldstine, J. 1999. What high-tech managers need to know about brands. *Harvard Business Review,* 77(4): 85–95.

31. Rosenfeld, J. 2000. Unit of one. *Fast Company,* April: 98.

32. Markides, C. 1997. Strategic innovation. *Sloan Management Review,* 38(3): 9–23.

33. Bonnabeau, E., Bodick, N., & Armstrong, R. W. 2008. A more rational approach to new-product development. *Harvard Business Review.* 66(3): 96–102.

34. Insights on Google's innovation are in: Iyer, B. & Davenport, T. H. 2008. Reverse engineering Google's innovation machine. *Harvard Business Review.* 66(4): 58–68.

35. A discussion of how a firm used technology to create product differentiation is in: Mehta, S. N. 2009. Under Armor reboots. *Fortune.* February 2: 29–33 (5)

36. Bertini, M. & Wathieu, L. 2010. How to stop customers from fixating on price. *Harvard Business Review,* 88(5): 84–91.

37. The authors would like to thank Scott Droege, a faculty member at Western Kentucky University, for providing this example.

38. Dixon, M., Freeman, K. & Toman, N. 2010. Stop trying to delight your customers. *Harvard Business Review,* 88(7/8).

39. Flint, J. 2004. Stop the nerds. *Forbes,* July 5: 80; and, Fahey, E. 2004. Over-engineering 101. *Forbes,* December 13: 62.

40. Symonds, W. C. 2000. Can Gillette regain its voltage? *BusinessWeek,* October 16: 102–104.

41. Caplan, J. 2006. In a real crunch. *Inside Business,* July: A37–A38.

42. Gadiesh, O. & Gilbert, J. L. 1998. Profit pools: A fresh look at strategy. *Harvard Business Review,* 76(3): 139–158.

43. Colvin, G. 2000. Beware: You could soon be selling soybeans. *Fortune,* November 13: 80.

44. Whalen et al., op. cit.: 63. Porter, M. E. 2008. The five competitive forces that shape strategy. *Harvard Business Review,* 86(1): 78–97; and *www. finance.yahoo.com.*

45. Hall, W. K. 1980. Survival strategies in a hostile environment, *Harvard Business Review,* 58: 75–87; on the paint and allied products industry, see Dess, G. G. & Davis, P. S. 1984. Porter's (1980) generic strategies as determinants of strategic group membership and organizational performance. *Academy of Management Journal,* 27: 467–488; for the Korean electronics industry, see Kim, L. & Lim, Y. 1988. Environment, generic strategies, and performance in a rapidly developing country: A taxonomic approach. *Academy of Management Journal,* 31: 802–827; Wright, P., Hotard, D., Kroll, M., Chan, P., & Tanner, J. 1990. Performance and multiple strategies in a firm: Evidence from the apparel industry. In Dean, B. V. & Cassidy, J. C. (Eds.). *Strategic management: Methods and studies:* 93–110. Amsterdam: Elsevier-North Holland; and Wright, P., Kroll, M., Tu, H., & Helms, M. 1991. Generic strategies and business performance: An empirical study of the screw machine products industry. *British Journal of Management,* 2: 1–9.

46. Gilmore, J. H. & Pine, B. J., II. 1997. The four faces of customization. *Harvard Business Review,* 75(1): 91–101.

47. Heracleous, L. & Wirtz, J. 2010. Singapore Airlines' balancing act. *Harvard Business Review,* 88(7/8): 145–149.

48. Gilmore & Pine, op. cit. For interesting insights on mass customization, refer to Cattani, K., Dahan, E., & Schmidt, G. 2005. Offshoring versus "spackling." *MIT Sloan Management Review,* 46(3): 6–7.

49. Goodstein, L. D. & Butz, H. E. 1998. Customer value: The linchpin of organizational change. *Organizational Dynamics,* Summer: 21–34.

50. Randall, T., Terwiesch, C., & Ulrich, K. T. 2005. Principles for user design of customized products. *California Management Review,* 47(4): 68–85.

51. Gadiesh & Gilbert, op. cit.: 139–158.

52. Insights on the profit pool concept are addressed in: Reinartz, W. & Ulaga, W. 2008. How to sell services more profitably. *Harvard Business Review,* 66(5): 90–96.

53. This example draws on Dess & Picken. 1997. op. cit.

54. A rigorous and thorough discussion of the threats faced by industries due to the commoditization of products and services and what strategic actions firm should consider is found

in: D'Aveni, R. A. 2010. *Beating the commodity trap.* Boston: Harvard Business Press.

55. For an insightful, recent discussion on the difficulties and challenges associated with creating advantages that are sustainable for any reasonable period of time and suggested strategies, refer to: D'Aveni, R. A., Dagnino, G. B. & Smith, K. G. 2010. The age of temporary advantage. *Strategic Management Journal.* 31(13): 1371–1385. This is the lead article in a special issue of this journal that provides many ideas that are useful to both academics and practicing managers. For an additional examination of declining advantage in technologically intensive industries, see: Vaaler, P. M. & McNamara, G. 2010. Are technology-intensive industries more dynamically competitive? No and yes. *Organization Science.* 21: 271–289.

56. Rita McGrath provides some interesting ideas on possible strategies for firms facing highly uncertain competitive environments: McGrath, R. G. 2011. When your business model is in trouble. *Harvard Business Review,* 89(1/2); 96–98.

57. The Atlas Door example draws on: Stalk, G., Jr. 1988. Time—the next source of competitive advantage. *Harvard Business Review,* 66(4): 41–51.

58. Edelman, D. C. 2010. Branding in the digital age. *Harvard Business Review.* 88(12): 62–69.

59. Seybold, P. 2000. Niches bring riches. *Business 2.0,* June 13: 135.

60. Greenspan, R. 2004. Net drives profits to small biz. ClickZ.com, March 25, *www.clickz.com.* Greenspan, R. 2002. Small biz benefits from Internet tools. ClickZ.com, March 28, *www.clickz.com.*

61. Burns, E. 2006. Executives slow to see value of corporate blogging. ClickZ.com, May 9, *www.clickz.com.*

62. Empirical support for the use of combination strategies in an e-business context can be found in Kim, E., Nam, D., & Stimpert, J. L. 2004. The applicability of Porter's generic strategies in the Digital Age: Assumptions,

conjectures, and suggestions. *Journal of Management,* 30(5): 569–589.

63. Porter, M. E. 2001. Strategy and the Internet. *Harvard Business Review,* 79: 63–78.

64. For an interesting perspective on the influence of the product life cycle and rate of technological change on competitive strategy, refer to Lei, D. & Slocum, J. W. Jr. 2005. Strategic and organizational requirements for competitive advantage. *Academy of Management Executive,* 19(1): 31–45.

65. Dickson, P. R. 1994. *Marketing management:* 293. Fort Worth, TX: Dryden Press; Day, G. S. 1981. The product life cycle: Analysis and application. *Journal of Marketing Research,* 45: 60–67.

66. Bearden, W. O., Ingram, T. N., & LaForge, R. W. 1995. *Marketing principles and practices.* Burr Ridge, IL: Irwin.

67. MacMillan, I. C. 1985. Preemptive strategies. In Guth, W. D. (Ed.). *Handbook of business strategy:* 9-1–9-22. Boston: Warren, Gorham & Lamont; Pearce, J. A. & Robinson, R. B. 2000. *Strategic management* (7th ed.). New York: McGraw-Hill; Dickson, op. cit.: 295–296.

68. Bartlett, C. A. & Ghoshal, S. 2000. Going global: Lessons for late movers. *Harvard Business Review,* 78(2): 132–142.

69. Neuborne, E. 2000. E-tailers hit the relaunch key. *BusinessWeek,* October 17: 62.

70. Berkowitz, E. N., Kerin, R. A., & Hartley, S. W. 2000. *Marketing* (6th ed.). New York: McGraw-Hill.

71. MacMillan, op. cit.

72. Brooker, K. 2001. A game of inches. *Fortune,* February 5: 98–100.

73. Our discussion of reverse and breakaway positioning draws on Moon, Y. 2005. Break free from the product life cycle. *Harvard Business Review,* 83(5): 87–94. This article also discusses stealth positioning as a means of overcoming consumer resistance and advancing a product from the introduction to the growth phase.

74. MacMillan, op. cit.

75. Berkowitz et al., op. cit.

76. Bearden et al., op. cit.

77. The discussion of these four strategies draws on MacMillan, op. cit.; Berkowitz et al., op. cit.; and Bearden et al., op. cit.

78. Augustine, N. R. 1997. Reshaping an industry: Lockheed Martin's survival story. *Harvard Business Review,* 75(3): 83–94.

79. Snow, D. C. 2008. Beware of old technologies' last gasps. *Harvard Business Review,* January: 17–18. Lohr, S. 2008. Why old technologies are still kicking. *New York Times,* March 23: np; and McGrath, R. G. 2008. Innovation and the last gasps of dying technologies. ritamcgrath.com, March 18: np.

80. Coyne, K. P., Coyne, S. T. & Coyne, E. J. Sr. 2010. When you've got to cut costs—now. *Harvard Business Review,* 88(5): 74–83.

81. A study that draws on the resource-based view of the firm to investigate successful turnaround strategies is: Morrow, J. S., Sirmon, D. G., Hitt, M. A., & Holcomb, T. R. 2007. *Strategic Management Journal,* 28(3): 271–284.

82. For a study investigating the relationship between organizational restructuring and acquisition performance, refer to: Barkema, H. G. & Schijven, M. Toward unlocking the full potential of acquisitions: The role of organizational restructuring. *Academy of Management Journal,* 51(4): 696–722.

83. For some useful ideas on effective turnarounds and handling downsizings, refer to Marks, M. S. & De Meuse, K. P. 2005. Resizing the organization: Maximizing the gain while minimizing the pain of layoffs, divestitures and closings. *Organizational Dynamics,* 34(1): 19–36.

84. Hambrick, D. C. & Schecter, S. M. 1983. Turnaround strategies for mature industrial product business units. *Academy of Management Journal,* 26(2): 231–248.

85. Mullaney, T. J. 2002. The wizard of Intuit. *BusinessWeek,* October 28: 60–63.

chapter SIX

Corporate-Level Strategy:

Creating Value through Diversification

After reading this chapter, you should have a good understanding of:

LO6.1 The reasons for the failure of many diversification efforts.

LO6.2 How managers can create value through diversification initiatives.

LO6.3 How corporations can use related diversification to achieve synergistic benefits through economies of scope and market power.

LO6.4 How corporations can use unrelated diversification to attain synergistic benefits through corporate restructuring, parenting, and portfolio analysis.

LO6.5 The various means of engaging in diversification—mergers and acquisitions, joint ventures/strategic alliances, and internal development.

LO6.6 Managerial behaviors that can erode the creation of value.

LEARNING OBJECTIVES

Corporate-level strategy addresses two related issues: (1) what businesses should a corporation compete in, and (2) how can these businesses be managed so they create "synergy"—that is, more value by working together than if they were freestanding units? As we will see, these questions present a key challenge for today's managers. Many diversification efforts fail or, in many cases, provide only marginal returns to shareholders. Thus, determining how to create value through entering new markets, introducing new products, or developing new technologies is a vital issue in strategic management.

We begin by discussing why diversification initiatives, in general, have not yielded the anticipated benefits. Then, in the next three sections of the chapter, we explore the two key alternative approaches: related and unrelated diversification. With related diversification, corporations strive to enter product markets that share some resources and capabilities with their existing business units or increase their market power. Here we suggest four means of creating value: leveraging core competencies, sharing activities, pooled negotiating power, and vertical integration. With unrelated diversification, there are few similarities in the resources and capabilities among the firm's business units, but value can be created in multiple ways. These include restructuring, corporate parenting, and portfolio analysis approaches. Whereas the synergies to be realized with related diversification come from *horizontal relationships* among the business units, the synergies from unrelated diversification are derived from *hierarchical relationships* between the corporate office and the business units.

The last two sections address (1) the various means that corporations can use to achieve diversification and (2) managerial behaviors (e.g., self-interest) that serve to erode shareholder value. We address mergers and acquisitions (M&A), divestitures, joint ventures/strategic alliances, and internal development. Each of these involves the evaluation of important trade-offs. Detrimental managerial behaviors, often guided by a manager's self-interest, are "growth for growth's sake," egotism, and antitakeover tactics. Some of these behaviors raise ethical issues because managers, in some cases, are not acting in the best interests of a firm's shareholders.●

Learning from Mistakes

Internet company AOL purchased the social networking firm Bebo in early 2008 for $850 million. In June 2010, it sold Bebo for the fire-sale price of $10 million. What went wrong?[1]

AOL was one of the biggest stars of the dotcom era, but its traditional business, dial-up Internet services, has steadily declined since its peak in 2001. The company tried to reinvent itself in 2008 by entering the social networking market by acquiring Bebo; the acquisition came shortly before AOL demerged from Time Warner in 2009. But in the words of Jeff Bewkes, Time Warner CEO at the time, from the get-go Bebo was seen as the "riskiest acquisition" the company made that year.

AOL's original rationale in purchasing Bebo was to tap into the phenomenon of online social networking by acquiring a presence in the rapidly growing community. The deal was part of AOL's strategy to shift from a subscription-based service for Internet connectivity to one focused on generating ad revenue by providing online media. The acquisition of Bebo pulled AOL away from their core strength of providing Internet service and placed the company in direct competition with social networking firms, such as Facebook. Unfortunately, Bebo proved to be an ineffective means of entering the online media industry.

In 2008, Bebo was a thriving, mainly European online social network community that was popular among teens, with about 40 million users. AOL's purchase of Bebo was intended to further the community's expansion into the U.S. market. Quite the opposite happened. In May of 2007, the firm had almost 9 million unique U.S. visitors, and a year later this number dropped to only 5 million unique visitors. (This was in contrast with their largest competitor in the social networking market, Facebook, who had 130.4 million unique U.S. visitors, showing continuous strong growth.)

One of the few actors that actually profited from Bebo was its founder, Michael Birch, who made $300 million from Bebo's original sale to AOL. According to Rory Cellan-Jones, BBC technology correspondent, AOL's decision to purchase Bebo was "one of the worst deals ever made in the dotcom era."

The acquisition was just one of a series of poor decisions that forced AOL to remove Randy Falco, the reigning CEO when the Bebo acquisition was made. They replaced him with Tim Armstrong, the one who divested it, in an effort to change strategies and bring the company back to profitability. According to Jim Clark, senior technology analyst at Mintel, the problems faced by AOL in integrating Bebo were a combination of paying too much in the first place as well as a lack of enough investment to make it profitable.*

* To make matters worse, in July 2010, AOL also sold ICQ instant messenger for $187.5 million, having purchased it for $400 million in 1998. The sales of Bebo and ICQ led to write-downs of $1.4 billion in the second quarter of 2010 and to a posted loss of $1.06 billion for the quarter.

> **>LO6.1**
> The reasons for the failure of many diversification efforts.

corporate-level strategy a strategy that focuses on gaining long-term revenue, profits, and market value through managing operations in multiple businesses.

AOL's experience with acquisitions is more the rule than the exception. Research shows that the vast majority of acquisitions result in value destruction rather than value creation. Many large multinational firms have also failed to effectively integrate their acquisitions, paid too high a premium for the target's common stock, or were unable to understand how the acquired firm's assets would fit with their own lines of business.[2] And, at times, top executives may not have acted in the best interests of shareholders. That is, the motive for the acquisition may have been to enhance the executives' power and prestige rather than to improve shareholder returns. At times, the only other people who may have benefited were the shareholders of the *acquired* firms—or the investment bankers who advise the acquiring firm, because they collect huge fees upfront regardless of what happens afterward![3]

Consider, for example, Pfizer's announcement on January 26, 2009, that it was acquiring Wyeth for $68 billion in cash and stock—which represented a 15 percent premium.[4] How did the market react? In rather typical fashion, Wyeth's stock went up 2 percent;

Pfizer's went down 9 percent. And, interestingly, the shares of Crucell, a Dutch biotech company, sank 10 percent after Wyeth pulled out of talks to buy it.

There have been several studies that were conducted over a variety of time periods that show how disappointing acquisitions have typically turned out. For example:

- A study evaluated the stock market reaction of 600 acquisitions over the period between 1975 and 1991. The results indicated that the acquiring firms suffered an average 4 percent drop in market value (after adjusting for market movements) in the three months following the acquisitions announcement.[5]
- In a study by Solomon Smith Barney of U.S. companies acquired since 1997 in deals for $15 billion or more, the stocks of the acquiring firms have, on average, underperformed the S&P stock index by 14 percentage points and underperformed their peer group by 4 percentage points after the deals were announced.[6]
- A study investigated 270 mergers that took place between 2000 and 2003 in multiple countries and regions. It found that after a merger, sales growth decreased by 6 percent, earnings growth dropped 9.4 percent, and market valuations declined 2.5 percent (figures are adjusted for industry trends and refer to three years pre- or postmerger).[7]
- A study that investigated 86 completed takeover bids that took place between 1993 and 2008 noted a negative return of 2 percent per month in long-term performance for the 3-year postacquisition period.[8]

Exhibit 6.1 lists some well-known examples of failed acquisitions and mergers. Recently there have been several acquisitions—often at fire sale prices—by financial services firms during the global financial crisis in 2008. For example, Bank of America bought

Exhibit 6.1
Some Well-Known M&A Blunders

Here are examples of some very expensive blunders:

- Sprint and Nextel merged in 2005. On January 31, 2008, the firm said it would take a merger related charge of $31 billion. And, as of late January, 2011, the stock has lost over 85 percent of its value since the merger.
- AOL paid $114 billion to acquire Time Warner in 2001. Over the next two years, AOL Time Warner lost $150 billion in market valuation.
- Conseco paid $5.8 billion to buy Green Tree, a mobile home mortgage lender, in 1998 though the company's net worth was not even $1 billion. In the next two years, Conseco lost 90 percent of its market value!
- Daimler Benz paid $36 billion to acquire Chrysler in 1998. After years of losses, it sold 80.1 percent of the unit to Cerberus Capital Management for $7.4 billion in 2007. And, as of 2009, Cerberus was trying to unload the unit.
- Quaker Oats' acquisition of the once high-flying Snapple for $1.8 billion in 1994 was followed by its divestment for $300 million three years later.
- AT&T bought computer equipment maker NCR for $7.4 billion in 1991, only to spin it off for $3.4 billion six years later.
- Sony acquired Columbia Pictures in 1989 for $4.8 billion although it had no competencies in movie production. Five years later, Sony was forced to take a $2.7 billion write-off on the acquisition.

Source: Ante, S.E. 2008. Sprint's Wake-Up Call. *Businessweek.com.* February 21: np; Gupta, P. 2008. Daimler May Sell Remaining Chrysler Stake. *www.reuters.com,* September 24: np; and Tully, S. 2006. The (Second) Worst Deal Ever. *Fortune,* October 16: 102–119.

Merrill Lynch, Wells Fargo purchased Wachovia, and JPMorgan acquired Washington Mutual. Only time will tell how well these turn out over the next few years.

Many acquisitions ultimately result in divestiture—an admission that things didn't work out as planned. In fact, some years ago, a writer for *Fortune* magazine lamented, "Studies show that 33 percent to 50 percent of acquisitions are later divested, giving corporate marriages a divorce rate roughly comparable to that of men and women."[9]

Admittedly, we have been rather pessimistic so far.[10] Clearly, many diversification efforts have worked out very well—whether through mergers and acquisitions, strategic alliances and joint ventures, or internal development. We will discuss many success stories throughout this chapter. Next, we will discuss the primary rationales for diversification.

Making Diversification Work: An Overview

>LO6.2
How managers can create value through diversification initiatives.

Clearly, not all diversification moves, including those involving mergers and acquisitions, erode performance. For example, acquisitions in the oil industry, such as British Petroleum's purchases of Amoco and Arco, are performing well as is the Exxon-Mobil merger. In the automobile industry, the Renault-Nissan alliance, under CEO Carlos Ghosn's leadership, has led to a quadrupling of its collective market capitalization—from $20.4 billion to $84.9 billion—by the end of 2006.[11] Many leading high-tech firms such as Microsoft, Cisco Systems, and Intel have dramatically enhanced their revenues, profits, and market values through a wide variety of diversification initiatives, including acquisitions, strategic alliances, and joint ventures, as well as internal development.*

So the question becomes: Why do some diversification efforts pay off and others produce poor results? This chapter addresses two related issues: (1) What businesses should a corporation compete in? and (2) How should these businesses be managed to jointly create more value than if they were freestanding units?

diversification the process of firms expanding their operations by entering new businesses.

Diversification initiatives—whether through mergers and acquisitions, strategic alliances and joint ventures, or internal development—must be justified by the creation of value for shareholders.[12] But this is not always the case.[13] Acquiring firms typically pay high premiums when they acquire a target firm. For example, in 2006 Freeport-McMoran paid a 30 percent premium to acquire Phelps Dodge in order to create the largest metals and mining concern in the U.S. In contrast, you and I, as private investors, can diversify our portfolio of stocks very cheaply. With an intensely competitive online brokerage industry, we can acquire hundreds (or thousands) of shares for a transaction fee of as little as $10.00 or less—a far cry from the 30 to 40 percent (or higher) premiums that corporations typically must pay to acquire companies.

Given the seemingly high inherent downside risks and uncertainties, one might ask: Why should companies even bother with diversification initiatives? The answer, in a word, is *synergy,* derived from the Greek word *synergos,* which means "working together." This can have two different, but not mutually exclusive, meanings.

First, a firm may diversify into *related* businesses. Here, the primary potential benefits to be derived come from *horizontal relationships;* that is, businesses sharing intangible resources (e.g., core competencies such as marketing) and tangible resources (e.g., production facilities, distribution channels).[14] Firms can also enhance their market power via

---

* Many high-tech firms, such as Motorola, IBM, Qualcomm, and Intel have also diversified through company-owned venture capital arms. Intel Capital, for example, has invested $4 billion in 1,000 companies over 15 years. Some 160 of those companies have been sold to other firms, while another 150 of them have been publicly listed. In 2006, Intel Capital's investments added $214 million to the parent company's net income. For an insightful discussion of how Apple might benefit from a venture capital initiative, refer to Hesseldahl, A. 2007. What to Do with Apple's Cash. *BusinessWeek,* March 19: 80.

pooled negotiating power and vertical integration. For example, Procter & Gamble enjoys many synergies from having businesses that share distribution resources.

Second, a corporation may diversify into *unrelated* businesses.[15] Here, the primary potential benefits are derived largely from *hierarchical relationships;* that is, value creation derived from the corporate office. Examples of the latter would include leveraging some of the support activities in the value chain that we discussed in Chapter 3, such as information systems or human resource practices. Cooper Industries has followed a successful strategy of unrelated diversification. There are few similarities in the products it makes or the industries in which it competes. However, the corporate office adds value through such activities as superb human resource practices and budgeting systems.

Please note that such benefits derived from horizontal (related diversification) and hierarchical (unrelated diversification) relationships are not mutually exclusive. Many firms that diversify into related areas benefit from information technology expertise in the corporate office. Similarly, unrelated diversifiers often benefit from the "best practices" of sister businesses even though their products, markets, and technologies may differ dramatically.

Exhibit 6.2 provides an overview of how we will address the various means by which firms create value through both related and unrelated diversification and also include a summary of some examples that we will address in this chapter.[16]

Exhibit 6.2
Creating Value through Related and Unrelated Diversification

Related Diversification: Economies of Scope

Leveraging core competencies

- 3M leverages its competencies in adhesives technologies to many industries, including automotive, construction, and telecommunications.

Sharing activities

- McKesson, a large distribution company, sells many product lines, such as pharmaceuticals and liquor, through its superwarehouses.

Related Diversification: Market Power

Pooled negotiating power

- The Times Mirror Company increases its power over customers by providing "one-stop shopping" for advertisers to reach customers through multiple media— television and newspapers—in several huge markets such as New York and Chicago.

Vertical integration

- Shaw Industries, a giant carpet manufacturer, increases its control over raw materials by producing much of its own polypropylene fiber, a key input to its manufacturing process.

Unrelated Diversification: Parenting, Restructuring, and Financial Synergies

Corporate restructuring and parenting

- The corporate office of Cooper Industries adds value to its acquired businesses by performing such activities as auditing their manufacturing operations, improving their accounting activities, and centralizing union negotiations.

Portfolio management

- Novartis, formerly Ciba-Geigy, uses portfolio management to improve many key activities, including resource allocation and reward and evaluation systems.

Related Diversification: Economies of Scope and Revenue Enhancement

related diversification a firm entering a different business in which it can benefit from leveraging core competencies, sharing activities, or building market power.

Related diversification enables a firm to benefit from horizontal relationships across different businesses in the diversified corporation by leveraging core competencies and sharing activities (e.g., production and distribution facilities). This enables a corporation to benefit from economies of scope. **Economies of scope** refers to cost savings from leveraging core competencies or sharing related activities among businesses in the corporation. A firm can also enjoy greater revenues if two businesses attain higher levels of sales growth combined than either company could attain independently.

economies of scope cost savings from leveraging core competencies or sharing related activities among businesses in a corporation.

For example, a sporting goods store with one or several locations may acquire retail stores carrying other product lines. This enables it to leverage, or reuse, many of its key resources—favorable reputation, expert staff and management skills, efficient purchasing operations—the basis of its competitive advantage(s), over a larger number of stores.[17]

Leveraging Core Competencies

>LO6.3
How corporations can use related diversification to achieve synergistic benefits through economies of scope and market power.

The concept of core competencies can be illustrated by the imagery of the diversified corporation as a tree.[18] The trunk and major limbs represent core products; the smaller branches are business units; and the leaves, flowers, and fruit are end products. The core competencies are represented by the root system, which provides nourishment, sustenance, and stability. Managers often misread the strength of competitors by looking only at their end products, just as we can fail to appreciate the strength of a tree by looking only at its leaves. Core competencies may also be viewed as the "glue" that binds existing businesses together or as the engine that fuels new business growth.

core competencies a firm's strategic resources that reflect the collective learning in the organization.

Core competencies reflect the collective learning in organizations—how to coordinate diverse production skills, integrate multiple streams of technologies, and market diverse products and services.[19] The knowledge necessary to put a radio on a chip does not in itself assure a company of the skill needed to produce a miniature radio approximately the size of a business card. To accomplish this, Casio, a giant electronic products producer, must synthesize know-how in miniaturization, microprocessor design, material science, and ultrathin precision castings. These are the same skills that it applies in its miniature card calculators, pocket TVs, and digital watches.

For a core competence to create value and provide a viable basis for synergy among the businesses in a corporation, it must meet three criteria.[20]

- *The core competence must enhance competitive advantage(s) by creating superior customer value.* Every value-chain activity has the potential to provide a viable basis for building on a core competence.[21] At Gillette, for example, scientists developed the Fusion and Mach 3 after the introduction of the tremendously successful Sensor System because of a thorough understanding of several phenomena that underlie shaving. These include the physiology of facial hair and skin, the metallurgy of blade strength and sharpness, the dynamics of a cartridge moving across skin, and the physics of a razor blade severing hair. Such innovations are possible only with

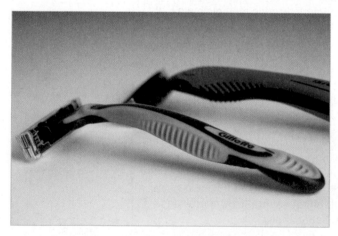

● Gillette's expertise in multiple competencies helps them develop superior shaving products.

Procter & Gamble Leverages Its Core Competence in Marketing and (Believe It or Not!) Franchising

Procter & Gamble, long dominant in detergents to wash clothes, wants to also dry clean them. The world's biggest consumer products company plans to roll out franchised Tide Dry Cleaners across America. P&G wants to put its brands to work selling services to boost U.S. revenue for its products.

Some think that their strategy could be a huge hit. For example, Andrew Cherng, founder of Panda Restaurant Group, which operates Chinese fast-food outlets in U.S. malls, plans to open around 150 Tide-branded dry cleaners over the next four years. He claims: "I wasn't around when McDonald's was taking franchisees. I'm not going to miss this one."

In 2007, the firm launched Mr. Clean Car Wash. Nine franchises are now in operation. The following year, P&G opened three test Tide Dry Cleaners in Kansas City. Having fine-tuned the concept, the firm is now going national. According to Michael Stone, P&G is moving into services

"that are virtually unbranded. One would think consumers would trust a Tide Dry Cleaners because they know P&G is behind it."

With more than 800,000 Facebook fans and legions of customers, P&G hopes that the Tide brand will draw people into franchise stores and that superior service—which includes drive-through service, 24-hour pickup, and cleaning methods it markets as environmentally safe—will keep them coming back. "The power of our brands represents disruptive innovation in these industries," claims Nathan Estruth, vice president for FutureWorks, P&G's entrepreneurial arm. "Imagine getting to start my new business with the power of Tide."

But . . . it won't be easy. Competition is fierce, and customers can be prickly: Woe to the dry cleaner that ruins a favorite suit or dress—even if it was cheaply made and decades old. Sanjiv Mehra, who headed Unilever's attempt to break into the dry-cleaning business about a decade ago, says that the key to success is in figuring out a way to do it cheaper or much better than the mom-and-pop stores that dominate the industry. At the end of the day, Unilever realized that it couldn't do either. He claims: "It comes back to, are you fundamentally changing the economics of the business?" adding that P&G's marketing muscle could turn out to be the difference. "That's where they will make a lot of money if they do it right."

Sources: Coleman-Lochner, L. & Clothier, M. 2010. P&G Puts Its Big Brands to Work in Franchises. *Bloomberg Businessweek.* September 6–12: 20; and Martin, A. 2010. Smelling an Opportunity. *www.nytimes.com.* December 8: np.

an understanding of such phenomena and the ability to combine such technologies into innovative products. Customers are willing to pay more for such technologically differentiated products.

- *Different businesses in the corporation must be similar in at least one important way related to the core competence.* It is not essential that the products or services themselves be similar. Rather, at least one element in the value chain must require similar skills in creating competitive advantage if the corporation is to capitalize on its core competence. At first glance you might think that cars and clothes have little in common. However, Strategy Spotlight 6.1 discusses how Procter & Gamble is leveraging its newfound competence in franchising to create a new revenue stream.

- *The core competencies must be difficult for competitors to imitate or find substitutes for.* As we discussed in Chapter 5, competitive advantages will not be sustainable if the competition can easily imitate or substitute them. Similarly, if the skills associated with a firm's core competencies are easily imitated or replicated, they are not a sound basis for sustainable advantages. Consider Sharp Corporation, a consumer electronics giant with 2010 revenues of $30 billion.[22] It has a set of specialized core competencies in optoelectronics technologies that are difficult to replicate and contribute to its competitive advantages in its core businesses. Its most successful technology has been liquid crystal displays (LCDs) that are critical components in nearly all of Sharp's products. Its expertise in this technology enabled Sharp to succeed in videocassette recorders (VCRs) with its innovative LCD viewfinder and led to the creation of its Wizard, a personal electronic organizer.

Steve Jobs provides insights on the importance of a firm's core competence. The Apple CEO is widely considered one of the world's most respected business leaders:[23]

> One of our biggest insights (years ago) was that we didn't want to get into any business where we didn't own or control the primary technology, because you'll get your head handed to you. We realized that for almost all future consumer electronics, the primary technology was going to be software. And we were pretty good at software. We could do the operating system software. We could write applications like iTunes on the Mac or even PC. And we could write the back-end software that runs on a cloud like iTunes. So we could write all these different kinds of software and tweed it all together and make it work seamlessly. And you ask yourself: What other companies can do that? It's a pretty short list.

Sharing Activities

As we saw above, leveraging core competencies involves transferring accumulated skills and expertise across business units in a corporation. Corporations also can achieve synergy by **sharing activities** across their business units. These include value-creating activities such as common manufacturing facilities, distribution channels, and sales forces. As we will see, sharing activities can potentially provide two primary payoffs: cost savings and revenue enhancements.

sharing activities having activities of two or more businesses' value chains done by one of the businesses.

Deriving Cost Savings   Typically, this is the most common type of synergy and the easiest to estimate. Peter Shaw, head of mergers and acquisitions at the British chemical and pharmaceutical company ICI, refers to cost savings as "hard synergies" and contends that the level of certainty of their achievement is quite high. Cost savings come from many sources, including the elimination of jobs, facilities, and related expenses that are no longer needed when functions are consolidated, or from economies of scale in purchasing. Cost savings are generally highest when one company acquires another from the same industry in the same country. Shaw Industries, recently acquired by Berkshire Hathaway, is the nation's largest carpet producer. Over the years, it has dominated the competition through a strategy of acquisition which has enabled Shaw, among other things, to consolidate its manufacturing operations in a few, highly efficient plants and to lower costs through higher capacity utilization.

Sharing activities inevitably involve costs that the benefits must outweigh such as the greater coordination required to manage a shared activity. Even more important is the need to compromise on the design or performance of an activity so that it can be shared. For example, a salesperson handling the products of two business units must operate in a way that is usually not what either unit would choose if it were independent. If the compromise erodes the unit's effectiveness, then sharing may reduce rather than enhance competitive advantage.

Enhancing Revenue and Differentiation   Often an acquiring firm and its target may achieve a higher level of sales growth together than either company could on its own. Shortly after Gillette acquired Duracell, it confirmed its expectation that selling Duracell batteries through Gillette's existing channels for personal care products would increase sales, particularly internationally. Gillette sold Duracell products in 25 new markets in the first year after the acquisition and substantially increased sales in established international markets. Also, a target company's distribution channel can be used to escalate the sales of the acquiring company's product. Such was the case when Gillette acquired Parker Pen. Gillette estimated that it could gain an additional $25 million in sales of its own Waterman pens by taking advantage of Parker's distribution channels.

Firms also can enhance the effectiveness of their differentiation strategies by means of sharing activities among business units. A shared order-processing system, for example, may permit new features and services that a buyer will value. Also, sharing can reduce the cost of differentiation. For instance, a shared service network may make more advanced, remote service technology economically feasible. To illustrate the potential for enhanced differentiation through sharing, consider $7 billion VF Corporation—producer of such well-known brands as Lee, Wrangler, Vanity Fair, and Jantzen.

> VF's acquisition of Nutmeg Industries and H. H. Cutler provided it with several large customers that it didn't have before, increasing its plant utilization and productivity. But more importantly, Nutmeg designs and makes licensed apparel for sports teams and organizations, while Cutler manufactures licensed brand-name children's apparel, including Walt Disney kids' wear. Such brand labeling enhances the differentiation of VF's apparel products. According to VF President Mackey McDonald, "What we're doing is looking at value-added knitwear, taking our basic fleece from Basset-Walker [one of its divisions], embellishing it through Cutler and Nutmeg, and selling it as a value-added product." Additionally, Cutler's advanced high-speed printing technologies will enable VF to be more proactive in anticipating trends in the fashion-driven fleece market. Claims McDonald, "Rather than printing first and then trying to guess what the customer wants, we can see what's happening in the marketplace and then print it up."[24]

As a cautionary note, managers must keep in mind that sharing activities among businesses in a corporation can have a negative effect on a given business's differentiation. For example, with the merger of Chrysler and Daimler-Benz, many consumers may lower their perceptions of Mercedes's quality and prestige because they felt that common production components and processes were being used across the two divisions. And Ford's Jaguar division was adversely affected as consumers came to understand that it shared many components with its sister divisions at Ford, including Lincoln. Perhaps, it is not too surprising that both Chrysler and Jaguar were divested by their parent corporations.

Related Diversification: Market Power

We now discuss how companies achieve related diversification through **market power.** We also address the two principal means by which firms achieve synergy through market power: *pooled negotiating power* and *vertical integration*. Managers do, however, have limits on their ability to use market power for diversification, because government regulations can sometimes restrict the ability of a business to gain very large shares of a particular market. Consider GE's attempt to acquire Honeywell:

market power firms' abilities to profit through restricting or controlling supply to a market or coordinating with other firms to reduce investment.

> When General Electric announced a $41 billion bid for Honeywell, the European Union stepped in. GE's market clout would have expanded significantly with the deal: GE would supply over one-half the parts needed to build several aircraft engines. The commission's concern, causing them to reject the acquisition, was that GE could use its increased market power to dominate the aircraft engine parts market and crowd out rivals.[25] Thus, while managers need to be aware of the strategic advantages of market power, they must at the same time be aware of regulations and legislation.

Pooled Negotiating Power

Similar businesses working together or the affiliation of a business with a strong parent can strengthen an organization's bargaining position relative to suppliers and customers and enhance its position vis-à-vis competitors. Compare, for example, the position of an independent food manufacturer with the same business within Nestlé. Being part of Nestlé provides the business with significant clout—greater bargaining power with suppliers and customers—since it is part of a firm that makes large purchases from suppliers

pooled negotiating power the improvement in bargaining position relative to suppliers and customers.

and provides a wide variety of products. Access to the parent's deep pockets increases the business's strength, and the Nestlé unit enjoys greater protection from substitutes and new entrants. Not only would rivals perceive the unit as a more formidable opponent, but the unit's association with Nestlé would also provide greater visibility and improved image.

Consolidating an industry can also increase a firm's market power.[26] This is clearly an emerging trend in the multimedia industry.[27] All of these mergers and acquisitions have a common goal: to control and leverage as many news and entertainment channels as possible.

When acquiring related businesses, a firm's potential for pooled negotiating power vis-à-vis its customers and suppliers can be very enticing. However, managers must carefully evaluate how the combined businesses may affect relationships with actual and potential customers, suppliers, and competitors. For example, when PepsiCo diversified into the fast-food industry with its acquisitions of Kentucky Fried Chicken, Taco Bell, and Pizza Hut (now part of Yum! Brands), it clearly benefited from its position over these units that served as a captive market for its soft-drink products. However, many competitors, such as McDonald's, have refused to consider PepsiCo as a supplier of its own soft-drink needs because of competition with Pepsi's divisions in the fast-food industry. Simply put, McDonald's did not want to subsidize the enemy! Thus, although acquiring related businesses can enhance a corporation's bargaining power, it must be aware of the potential for retaliation.

Strategy Spotlight 6.2 discusses how 3M's actions to increase its market power led to a lawsuit (which 3M lost) by a competitor.

Vertical Integration

vertical integration an expansion or extension of the firm by integrating preceding or successive production processes.

Vertical integration occurs when a firm becomes its own supplier or distributor. That is, it represents an expansion or extension of the firm by integrating preceding or successive production processes.[28] The firm incorporates more processes toward the original source of raw materials (backward integration) or toward the ultimate consumer (forward integration). For example, a car manufacturer might supply its own parts or make its own engines to secure sources of supply or control its own system of dealerships to ensure retail outlets for its products. Similarly, an oil refinery might secure land leases and develop its own drilling capacity to ensure a constant supply of crude oil. Or it could expand into retail operations by owning or licensing gasoline stations to guarantee customers for its petroleum products.

Clearly, vertical integration can be a viable strategy for many firms. Strategy Spotlight 6.3 discusses Shaw Industries, a carpet manufacturer that has attained a dominant position in the industry via a strategy of vertical integration. Shaw has successfully implemented strategies of both forward and backward integration. Exhibit 6.3 depicts the stages of Shaw's vertical integration.

Benefits and Risks of Vertical Integration   Vertical integration is a means for an organization to reduce its dependence on suppliers or its channels of distribution to end users. However, the benefits associated with vertical integration—backward or forward—must be carefully weighed against the risks.[29]

The *benefits* of vertical integration include (1) a secure supply of raw materials or distribution channels that cannot be "held hostage" to external markets where costs can fluctuate over time, (2) protection and control over assets and services required to produce and deliver valuable products and services, (3) access to new business opportunities and new forms of technologies, and (4) simplified procurement and administrative procedures since key activities are brought inside the firm, eliminating the need to deal with a wide variety of suppliers and distributors.

Winnebago, the leader in the market for drivable recreational vehicles with a 19.3 percent market share, illustrates some of vertical integration's benefits.[30] The word

How 3M's Efforts to Increase Its Market Power Backfired

In the spring and summer of 2006, 3M found itself in court facing three class-action lawsuits launched by consumers and retailers of transparent and invisible adhesive tape (often generically known as "Scotch tape"). The suits all alleged that 3M had unlawfully bullied its way into a monopoly position in the tape market and that, as a result, consumers had been deprived of their rightful amount of choice and often paid up to 40 percent too much for their tape.

One rival that was particularly interested in these cases is LaPage's Inc. of North York, Ontario—3M's only significant competitor in the home and office adhesive tape market. LaPage's has everything to gain from court penalties against 3M's selling practices. This includes greater access to the lucrative North American market. The Canadian company started 3M's legal travails in the first place: all of the current class-action suits were initiated by LePage's.

Back in 1997, LePage's (then based in Pittsburgh) filed a complaint in the Pennsylvania District Court against 3M's practice of selling its various tape products using what was called "bundled rebates." LePage's argued that it violated the Sherman Act, the century-old U.S. legislation that limited monopoly power. 3M's bundled rebate program offered significant rebates—sometimes in the millions of dollars—to retailers as a reward for selling targeted amounts of six product lines. LePage's claimed that such selling targets were so large that retailers could only meet them by excluding competing products—in this case LePage's tape—from store shelves. For example, LePage's argued that Kmart, which had constituted 10% of LePage's sales dropped the account when 3M started offering the discount chain $1 million in rebates in return for selling more than $15 million worth of 3M products each year. Further, LePage's offered its own conspiracy theory: 3M introduced rebates not simply to grow its sales, but to eliminate LePage's—its only significant competitor.

A jury awarded LePage's $68.5 million in damages (the amount after trebling)—almost 15 percent of the 3M Consumer and Office Business unit's operating income in 2000. The Court of Appeals for the Third Circuit rejected 3M's appeal and upheld the judgment. It concluded that rebate bundling, even if above cost, may exclude equally efficient competitors from offering product (in this case, tape). In the ruling, Judge Dolores K. Sloviter wrote that "they may foreclose portions of the market to a potential competitor who does not manufacture an equally diverse group of products and who therefore cannot make a comparable offer." Therefore, the bundled rebates were judged to be an exploitation of 3M's monopoly power.

Sources: Bush, D. & Gelb, B. D. 2005. When Marketing Practices Raise Antitrust Concerns. *MIT Sloan Management Review*, 46(4): 73–81; Campbell, C. 2006. Tale of the Tape. *Canadian Business*. April 24: 39–40; and Bergstrom, B. 2003. $68M Jury Award Upheld against 3M in Antitrust Case. *The Associated Press:* March 26.

ethics

Winnebago means "big RV" to most Americans. And the firm has a sterling reputation for great quality. The firm's huge northern Iowa factories do everything from extruding aluminum for body parts to molding plastics for water and holding tanks to dashboards. Such vertical integration at the factory may appear to be outdated and expensive, but it

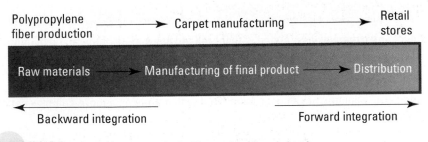

Exhibit 6.3 Simplified Stages of Vertical Integration: Shaw Industries

Vertical Integration at Shaw Industries

Shaw Industries (now part of Berkshire Hathaway) is an example of a firm that has followed a very successful strategy of vertical integration. By relentlessly pursuing both backward and forward integration, Shaw has become the dominant manufacturer of carpeting products in the United States. According to CEO Robert Shaw, "We want to be involved with as much of the process of making and selling carpets as practical. That way, we're in charge of costs." For example, Shaw acquired Amoco's polypropylene fiber manufacturing facilities in Alabama and Georgia. These new plants provide carpet fibers for internal use and for sale to other manufacturers. With this backward integration, fully one-quarter of Shaw's carpet fiber needs are now met in-house. In early 1996 Shaw began to integrate forward, acquiring seven floor-covering retailers in a move that suggested a strategy to consolidate the fragmented industry and increase its influence over retail pricing. Exhibit 6.3 provides a simplified depiction of the stages of vertical integration for Shaw Industries.

Sources: White, J. 2003. Shaw to home in on more with Georgia Tufters deal. *HFN: The Weekly Newspaper for the Home Furnishing Network*, May 5: 32; Shaw Industries. 1993, 2000. Annual reports; and Server, A. 1994. How to escape a price war. *Fortune*, June 13: 88.

guarantees excellent quality. The Recreational Vehicle Dealer Association started giving a quality award in 1996, and Winnebago has won it every year.

The *risks* of vertical integration include (1) the costs and expenses associated with increased overhead and capital expenditures to provide facilities, raw material inputs, and distribution channels inside the organization; (2) a loss of flexibility resulting from the inability to respond quickly to changes in the external environment because of the huge investments in vertical integration activities that generally cannot be easily deployed elsewhere; (3) problems associated with unbalanced capacities or unfilled demand along the value chain; and (4) additional administrative costs associated with managing a more complex set of activities. Exhibit 6.4 summarizes the benefits and risks of vertical integration.

In making vertical integration decisions, five issues should be considered.[31]

Exhibit 6.4
Benefits and Risks of Vertical Integration

Benefits
• A secure source of raw materials or distribution channels.
• Protection of and control over valuable assets.
• Access to new business opportunities.
• Simplified procurement and administrative procedures.

Risks
• Costs and expenses associated with increased overhead and capital expenditures.
• Loss of flexibility resulting from large investments.
• Problems associated with unbalanced capacities along the value chain.
• Additional administrative costs associated with managing a more complex set of activities.

1. *Is the company satisfied with the quality of the value that its present suppliers and distributors are providing?* If the performance of organizations in the vertical chain—both suppliers and distributors—is satisfactory, it may not, in general, be appropriate for a company to perform these activities themselves. Nike and Reebok have outsourced the manufacture of their shoes to countries such as China and Indonesia where labor costs are low. Since the strengths of these companies are typically in design and marketing, it would be advisable to continue to outsource production operations and continue to focus on where they can add the most value.

2. *Are there activities in the industry value chain presently being outsourced or performed independently by others that are a viable source of future profits?* Even if a firm is outsourcing value-chain activities to companies that are doing a credible job, it may be missing out on substantial profit opportunities. To illustrate, consider the automobile industry's profit pool. As you may recall from Chapter 5, there is much more potential profit in many downstream activities (e.g., leasing, warranty, insurance, and service) than in the manufacture of automobiles. Not surprisingly, carmakers such as Toyota and Honda are undertaking forward integration strategies to become bigger players in these high-profit activities.

3. *Is there a high level of stability in the demand for the organization's products?* High demand or sales volatility are not conducive to vertical integration. With the high level of fixed costs in plant and equipment as well as operating costs that accompany endeavors toward vertical integration, widely fluctuating sales demand can either strain resources (in times of high demand) or result in unused capacity (in times of low demand). The cycles of "boom and bust" in the automobile industry are a key reason why the manufacturers have increased the amount of outsourced inputs.

4. *Does the company have the necessary competencies to execute the vertical integration strategies?* As many companies would attest, successfully executing strategies of vertical integration can be very difficult. For example, Unocal, a major petroleum refiner, which once owned retail gas stations, was slow to capture the potential grocery and merchandise side of the business that might have resulted from customer traffic to its service stations. Unocal lacked the competencies to develop a separate retail organization and culture. The company eventually sold the assets and brand.

5. *Will the vertical integration initiative have potential negative impacts on the firm's stakeholders?* Managers must carefully consider the impact that vertical integration may have on existing and future customers, suppliers, and competitors. After Lockheed Martin, a dominant defense contractor, acquired Loral Corporation, an electronics supplier, for $9.1 billion, it had an unpleasant and unanticipated surprise. Loral, as a captive supplier of Lockheed, is now viewed as a rival by many of its previous customers. Thus, before Lockheed Martin can realize any net synergies from this acquisition, it must make up for the substantial business that it has lost.

Analyzing Vertical Integration: The Transaction Cost Perspective   Another approach that has proved very useful in understanding vertical integration is the **transaction cost perspective**.[32] According to this perspective, every market transaction involves some *transaction costs*. First, a decision to purchase an input from an outside source leads to *search* costs (i.e., the cost to find where it is available, the level of quality, etc.). Second, there are costs associated with *negotiating*. Third, a *contract* needs to be written spelling out future possible contingencies. Fourth, parties in a contract have to *monitor* each other. Finally, if a party does not comply with the terms of the contract, there are *enforcement* costs. Transaction costs are thus the sum of search costs, negotiation costs, contracting costs, monitoring costs, and enforcement costs. These transaction costs can be avoided by internalizing the activity, in other words, by producing the input in-house.

transaction cost perspective a perspective that the choice of a transaction's governance structure, such as vertical integration or market transaction, is influenced by transaction costs, including search, negotiating, contracting, monitoring, and enforcement costs, associated with each choice.

A related problem with purchasing a specialized input from outside is the issue of *transaction-specific investments.* For example, when an automobile company needs an input specifically designed for a particular car model, the supplier may be unwilling to make the investments in plant and machinery necessary to produce that component for two reasons. First, the investment may take many years to recover but there is no guarantee the automobile company will continue to buy from them after the contract expires, typically in one year. Second, once the investment is made, the supplier has no bargaining power. That is, the buyer knows that the supplier has no option but to supply at ever-lower prices because the investments were so specific that they cannot be used to produce alternative products. In such circumstances, again, vertical integration may be the only option.

Vertical integration, however, gives rise to a different set of costs. These costs are referred to as *administrative costs.* Coordinating different stages of the value chain now internalized within the firm causes administrative costs to go up. Decisions about vertical integration are, therefore, based on a comparison of transaction costs and administrative costs. If transaction costs are lower than administrative costs, it is best to resort to market transactions and avoid vertical integration. For example, McDonald's may be the world's biggest buyer of beef, but they do not raise cattle. The market for beef has low transaction costs and requires no transaction-specific investments. On the other hand, if transaction costs are higher than administrative costs, vertical integration becomes an attractive strategy. Most automobile manufacturers produce their own engines because the market for engines involves high transaction costs and transaction-specific investments.

>LO6.4
How corporations can use unrelated diversification to attain synergistic benefits through corporate restructuring, parenting, and portfolio analysis.

Unrelated Diversification: Financial Synergies and Parenting

With unrelated diversification, unlike related diversification, few benefits are derived from *horizontal relationships*—that is, the leveraging of core competencies or the sharing of activities across business units within a corporation. Instead, potential benefits can be gained from *vertical (or hierarchical) relationships*—the creation of synergies from the interaction of the corporate office with the individual business units. There are two main sources of such synergies. First, the corporate office can contribute to "parenting" and restructuring of (often acquired) businesses. Second, the corporate office can add value by viewing the entire corporation as a family or "portfolio" of businesses and allocating resources to optimize corporate goals of profitability, cash flow, and growth. Additionally, the corporate office enhances value by establishing appropriate human resource practices and financial controls for each of its business units.

unrelated diversification a firm entering a different business that has little horizontal interaction with other businesses of a firm.

parenting advantage the positive contributions of the corporate office to a new business as a result of expertise and support provided and not as a result of substantial changes in assets, capital structure, or management.

Corporate Parenting and Restructuring

We have discussed how firms can add value through related diversification by exploring sources of synergy *across* business units. Now, we discuss how value can be created *within* business units as a result of the expertise and support provided by the corporate office.

Parenting   The positive contributions of the corporate office are called the **"parenting advantage."**[33] Many firms have successfully diversified their holdings without strong evidence of the more traditional sources of synergy (i.e., horizontally across business units). Diversified public corporations such as BTR, Emerson Electric, and Hanson and leveraged buyout firms such as Kohlberg, Kravis, Roberts & Company, and Clayton, Dublilier & Rice are a few examples.[34] These parent companies create value through management expertise. How? They improve plans and budgets and provide especially competent central functions such as legal, financial, human resource management, procurement, and the like. They also help subsidiaries make wise choices in their own acquisitions, divestitures, and new internal development decisions. Such contributions often help business units to substantially increase their revenues and profits. Consider Texas-based Cooper Industries' acquisition of Champion International, the spark plug company, as an example of corporate parenting:[35]

> Cooper applies a distinctive parenting approach designed to help its businesses improve their manufacturing performance. New acquisitions are "Cooperized"—Cooper audits their manufacturing operations; improves their cost accounting systems; makes their planning, budgeting, and human resource systems conform with its systems; and centralizes union negotiations. Excess cash is squeezed out through tighter controls and reinvested in productivity enhancements, which improve overall operating efficiency. As one manager observed, "When you get acquired by Cooper, one of the first things that happens is a truckload of policy manuals arrives at your door." Such active parenting has been effective in enhancing the competitive advantages of many kinds of manufacturing businesses.

Restructuring   **Restructuring** is another means by which the corporate office can add value to a business.[36] The central idea can be captured in the real estate phrase "buy low and sell high." Here, the corporate office tries to find either poorly performing firms with unrealized potential or firms in industries on the threshold of significant, positive change. The parent intervenes, often selling off parts of the business; changing the management; reducing payroll and unnecessary sources of expenses; changing strategies; and infusing the company with new technologies, processes, reward systems, and so forth. When the restructuring is complete, the firm can either "sell high" and capture the added value or keep the business and enjoy financial and competitive benefits.[37]

Loews Corporation, a conglomerate with $15 billion in revenues competes in such industries as oil and gas, tobacco, watches, insurance, and hotels. It provides an exemplary example of how firms can successfully "buy low and sell high" as part of their corporate strategy.[38]

> Energy accounts for 33 percent of Loews' $30 billion in total assets. In the 1980s it bought six oil tankers for only $5 million each during a sharp slide in oil prices. The downside was limited. After all these huge hulks could easily have been sold as scrap steel. However, that didn't have to happen. Eight years after Loews purchased the tankers, they sold them for $50 million each.
>
> Loews was also extremely successful with its next energy play—drilling equipment. Although wildcatting for oil is very risky, selling services to wildcatters is not, especially if the assets are bought during a down cycle. Loews did just that. It purchased 10 offshore drilling rigs for $50 million in 1989 and formed Diamond Offshore Drilling. In 1995 Loews received $338 million after taking a 30 percent piece of this operation public!

For the restructuring strategy to work, the corporate management must have both the insight to detect undervalued companies (otherwise the cost of acquisition would be too high) or businesses competing in industries with a high potential for transformation.[39] Additionally, of course, they must have the requisite skills and resources to turn the businesses around, even if they may be in new and unfamiliar industries.

Restructuring can involve changes in assets, capital structure, or management.

- *Asset restructuring* involves the sale of unproductive assets, or even whole lines of businesses, that are peripheral. In some cases, it may even involve acquisitions that strengthen the core business.
- *Capital restructuring* involves changing the debt-equity mix, or the mix between different classes of debt or equity. Although the substitution of equity with debt is more common in buyout situations, occasionally the parent may provide additional equity capital.
- *Management restructuring* typically involves changes in the composition of the top management team, organizational structure, and reporting relationships. Tight

restructuring the intervention of the corporate office in a new business that substantially changes the assets, capital structure, and/or management, including selling off parts of the business, changing the management, reducing payroll and unnecessary sources of expenses, changing strategies, and infusing the new business with new technologies, processes, and reward systems.

financial control, rewards based strictly on meeting short- to medium-term performance goals, and reduction in the number of middle-level managers are common steps in management restructuring. In some cases, parental intervention may even result in changes in strategy as well as infusion of new technologies and processes.

Hanson, plc, a British conglomerate, made numerous such acquisitions in the United States in the 1980s, often selling these firms at significant profits after a few years of successful restructuring efforts. Hanson's acquisition and subsequent restructuring of the SCM group is a classic example of the restructuring strategy. Hanson acquired SCM, a diversified manufacturer of industrial and consumer products (including Smith-Corona typewriters, Glidden paints, and Durkee Famous Foods), for $930 million in 1986 after a bitter takeover battle. In the next few months, Hanson sold SCM's paper and pulp operations for $160 million, the chemical division for $30 million, Glidden paints for $580 million, and Durkee Famous Foods for $120 million, virtually recovering the entire original investment. In addition, Hanson also sold the SCM headquarters in New York for $36 million and reduced the headquarters staff by 250. They still retained several profitable divisions, including the titanium dioxide operations and managed them with tight financial controls that led to increased returns.[40]

Exhibit 6.5 summarizes the three primary types of restructuring activities.

Portfolio Management

During the 1970s and early 1980s, several leading consulting firms developed the concept of **portfolio management** to achieve a better understanding of the competitive position of an overall portfolio (or family) of businesses, to suggest strategic alternatives for each of the businesses, and to identify priorities for the allocation of resources. Several studies have reported widespread use of these techniques among American firms.[41]

portfolio management a method of (a) assessing the competitive position of a portfolio of businesses within a corporation, (b) suggesting strategic alternatives for each business, and (c) identifying priorities for the allocation of resources across the businesses.

Description and Potential Benefits   The key purpose of portfolio models is to assist a firm in achieving a balanced portfolio of businesses.[42] This consists of businesses whose profitability, growth, and cash flow characteristics complement each other and adds up to a satisfactory overall corporate performance. Imbalance, for example, could be caused either by excessive cash generation with too few growth opportunities or by insufficient cash generation to fund the growth requirements in the portfolio. Monsanto, for example, used portfolio planning to restructure its portfolio, divesting low-growth commodity chemicals businesses and acquiring businesses in higher-growth industries such as biotechnology.

The Boston Consulting Group's (BCG) growth/share matrix is among the best known of these approaches.[43] In the BCG approach, each of the firm's strategic business units (SBUs) is plotted on a two-dimensional grid in which the axes are relative market share and industry growth rate. The grid is broken into four quadrants. Exhibit 6.6 depicts the BCG matrix. Following are a few clarifications:

1. Each circle represents one of the corporation's business units. The size of the circle represents the relative size of the business unit in terms of revenues.

Exhibit 6.5
The Three Primary Types of Restructuring Activities

Asset Restructuring: The sale of unproductive assets, or even whole lines of businesses, that are peripheral.

Capital Restructuring: Changing the debt-equity mix, or the mix between different classes of debt or equity.

Management Restructuring: Changes in the composition of the top management team, organization structure, and reporting relationships.

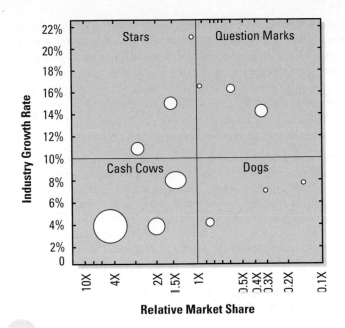

Exhibit 6.6 The Boston Consulting Group (BCG) Portfolio Matrix

2. Relative market share, measured by the ratio of the business unit's size to that of its largest competitor, is plotted along the horizontal axis.
3. Market share is central to the BCG matrix. This is because high relative market share leads to unit cost reduction due to experience and learning curve effects and, consequently, superior competitive position.

Each of the four quadrants of the grid has different implications for the SBUs that fall into the category:

*   **Stars** are SBUs competing in high-growth industries with relatively high market shares. These firms have long-term growth potential and should continue to receive substantial investment funding.
*   **Question Marks** are SBUs competing in high-growth industries but having relatively weak market shares. Resources should be invested in them to enhance their competitive positions.
*   **Cash Cows** are SBUs with high market shares in low-growth industries. These units have limited long-run potential but represent a source of current cash flows to fund investments in "stars" and "question marks."
*   **Dogs** are SBUs with weak market shares in low-growth industries. Because they have weak positions and limited potential, most analysts recommend that they be divested.

In using portfolio strategy approaches, a corporation tries to create shareholder value in a number of ways.[44] First, portfolio analysis provides a snapshot of the businesses in a corporation's portfolio. Therefore, the corporation is in a better position to allocate resources among the business units according to prescribed criteria (e.g., use cash flows from the "cash cows" to fund promising "stars"). Second, the expertise and analytical resources in the corporate office provide guidance in determining what firms may be attractive (or unattractive) acquisitions. Third, the corporate office is able to provide financial resources to the business units on favorable terms that reflect the corporation's overall ability to raise funds. Fourth, the corporate office can provide high-quality review and coaching for the individual businesses. Fifth, portfolio analysis provides a basis for developing strategic goals and reward/evaluation systems for business managers. For example, managers of cash cows would have lower targets for revenue growth than managers of stars, but the former would have higher threshold levels of profit targets on proposed projects than the managers of star businesses. Compensation systems would also reflect such realities. Cash cows understandably would be rewarded more on the basis of cash that their businesses generate than would managers of star businesses. Similarly, managers of star businesses would be held to higher standards for revenue growth than managers of cash cow businesses.

To see how companies can benefit from portfolio approaches, consider Ciba-Geigy.

> In 1994 Ciba-Geigy adopted portfolio planning approaches to help it manage its business units, which competed in a wide variety of industries, including chemicals, dyes, pharmaceuticals, crop protection, and animal health.[45] It placed each business unit in a category corresponding to the BCG matrix. The business unit's goals, compensation programs, personnel selection, and resource allocation were strongly associated with the category within which the business was placed. For example, business units classified as "cash cows" had much higher hurdles for obtaining financial resources (from the corporate office) for expansion than "question marks" since the latter were businesses for which Ciba-Geigy had high hopes for accelerated future growth and profitability. Additionally, the compensation of a business unit manager in a cash cow would be strongly associated with its success in generating cash to fund other businesses, whereas a manager of a question mark business would be rewarded on his or her ability to increase revenue growth and market share. The portfolio planning approaches appear to be working. In 2010, Ciba-Geigy's (now Novartis) revenues and net income stood at $45 billion and $8.5 billion, respectively. This represents a 110 percent increase in revenues and a most impressive 49 percent growth in net income over a six-year period.

Limitations   Despite the potential benefits of portfolio models, there are also some notable downsides. First, they compare SBUs on only two dimensions, making the implicit but erroneous assumption that (1) those are the only factors that really matter and (2) every unit can be accurately compared on that basis. Second, the approach views each SBU as a stand-alone entity, ignoring common core business practices and value-creating activities that may hold promise for synergies across business units. Third, unless care is exercised, the process becomes largely mechanical, substituting an oversimplified graphical model for the important contributions of the CEO's (and other corporate managers') experience and judgment. Fourth, the reliance on "strict rules" regarding resource allocation across SBUs can be detrimental to a firm's long-term viability. For example, according to one study, over one-half of all the businesses that should have been cash users (based on the BCG matrix) were instead cash providers.[46] Finally, while colorful and easy to comprehend, the imagery of the BCG matrix can lead to some troublesome and overly simplistic prescriptions. According to one author:

> The dairying analogy is appropriate (for some cash cows), so long as we resist the urge to oversimplify it. On the farm, even the best-producing cows eventually begin to dry up. The farmer's solution to this is euphemistically called "freshening" the cow: The farmer arranges a date for the cow with a bull, she has a calf, the milk begins flowing again. Cloistering the cow—isolating her from everything but the feed trough and the milking machines—assures that she will go dry.[47]

To see what can go wrong, consider Cabot Corporation.

> Cabot Corporation supplies carbon black for the rubber, electronics, and plastics industries. Following the BCG matrix, Cabot moved away from its cash cow, carbon black, and diversified into stars such as ceramics and semiconductors in a seemingly overaggressive effort to create more revenue growth for the corporation. Predictably, Cabot's return on assets declined as the firm shifted away from its core competence to unrelated areas. The portfolio model failed by pointing the company in the wrong direction in an effort to spur growth—away from their core business. Recognizing its mistake, Cabot Corporation

returned to its mainstay carbon black manufacturing and divested unrelated businesses. Today the company is a leader in its field with $3 billion in 2010 revenues.[48]

Exhibit 6.7 summarizes the limitations of portfolio model analysis.

Caveat: Is Risk Reduction a Viable Goal of Diversification?

One of the purposes of diversification is to reduce the risk that is inherent in a firm's variability in revenues and profits over time. That is, if a firm enters new products or markets that are affected differently by seasonal or economic cycles, its performance over time will be more stable. For example, a firm manufacturing lawn mowers may diversify into snow blowers to even out its annual sales. Or a firm manufacturing a luxury line of household furniture may introduce a lower-priced line since affluent and lower-income customers are affected differently by economic cycles.

At first glance the above reasoning may make sense, but there are some problems with it. First, a firm's stockholders can diversify their portfolios at a much lower cost than a corporation, and they don't have to worry about integrating the acquisition into their portfolio. Second, economic cycles as well as their impact on a given industry (or firm) are difficult to predict with any degree of accuracy.

Notwithstanding the above, some firms have benefited from diversification by lowering the variability (or risk) in their performance over time. Consider Emerson Electronic.[49]

Emerson Electronic is a $21 billion manufacturer that produces a wide variety of products, including measurement devices for heavy industry, temperature controls for heating

Exhibit 6.7
Benefits and Limitations of Portfolio Models

Benefits
• The corporation is in a better position to allocate resources to businesses according to explicit criteria.
• The corporate office can provide guidance on what firms may be attractive acquisitions.
• The corporate office can provide financial resources to businesses on favorable terms (that reflect the corporation's ability to raise funds).
• The corporate office can provide high-quality review and coaching for the individual businesses.
• It provides a basis for developing strategic goals and evaluation/reward systems for businesses.

Limitations
• They are overly simplistic, consisting of only two dimensions (growth and market share).
• They view each business as separate, ignoring potential synergies across businesses.
• The process may become overly largely mechanical, minimizing the potential value of managers' judgment and experience.
• The reliance on strict rules for resource allocation across SBUs can be detrimental to a firm's long-term viability.
• The imagery (e.g., cash cows, dogs) while colorful, may lead to troublesome and overly simplistic prescriptions.

and ventilation systems, and power tools sold at Home Depot. Recently, many analysts questioned Emerson's purchase of companies that sell power systems to the volatile tele-communications industry. Why? This industry is expected to experience, at best, minimal growth. However, CEO David Farr maintained that such assets could be acquired inexpensively because of the aggregate decline in demand in this industry. Additionally, he argued that the other business units, such as the sales of valves and regulators to the now-booming oil and natural gas companies, were able to pick up the slack. Therefore, while net profits in the electrical equipment sector (Emerson's core business) sharply decreased, Emerson's overall corporate profits increased 1.7 percent.

Risk reduction in and of itself is rarely viable as a means to create shareholder value. It must be undertaken with a view of a firm's overall diversification strategy.

The Means to Achieve Diversification

>LO6.5
The various means of engaging in diversification— mergers and acquisitions, joint ventures/strategic alliances, and internal development.

We have addressed the types of diversification (e.g., related and unrelated) that a firm may undertake to achieve synergies and create value for its shareholders. Now, we address the means by which a firm can go about achieving these desired benefits.

There are three basic means. First, through acquisitions or mergers, corporations can directly acquire a firm's assets and competencies. Although the terms *mergers* and *acquisitions* are used quite interchangeably, there are some key differences. With **acquisitions,** one firm buys another either through a stock purchase, cash, or the issuance of debt.[50] **Mergers,** on the other hand, entail a combination or consolidation of two firms to form a new legal entity. Mergers are relatively rare and entail a transaction among two firms on a relatively equal basis. Despite such differences, we consider both mergers and acquisitions to be quite similar in terms of their implications for a firm's corporate-level strategy.[51]

Second, corporations may agree to pool the resources of other companies with their resource base, commonly known as a joint venture or strategic alliance. Although these two forms of partnerships are similar in many ways, there is an important difference. Joint ventures involve the formation of a third-party legal entity where the two (or more) firms each contribute equity, whereas strategic alliances do not.

Third, corporations may diversify into new products, markets, and technologies through internal development. Called corporate entrepreneurship, it involves the leveraging and combining of a firm's own resources and competencies to create synergies and enhance shareholder value. We address this subject in greater length in Chapter 12.

acquisitions the incorporation of one firm into another through purchase.

mergers the combining of two or more firms into one new legal entity.

Mergers and Acquisitions

The rate of mergers and acquisitions (M&A) had dropped off beginning in 2001. This trend was largely a result of a recession, corporate scandals, and a declining stock market. However, the situation has changed dramatically. Over the past several years, several large mergers and acquisitions were announced. These include:[52]

- Kraft's acquisition of Cadbury for $19.4 billion.
- In Bev's acquisition of Anheuser-Busch for $52 billion.
- Pfizer's acquisition of Wyeth for $68 billion.
- Mittal Steel's acquisition of Arcelor for $33 billion.
- BellSouth's acquisition of AT&T for $86.0 billion.
- Sprint's merger with Nextel for $39 billion.
- Boston Scientific's $27 billion acquisition of medical device maker Guidant.
- Procter & Gamble's purchase of Gillette for $54 billion.
- Kmart Holding Corp.'s acquisition of Sears, Roebuck & Co. for $11 billion.

Exhibit 6.8 illustrates the dramatic increase in worldwide M&A activity in the U.S. up until 2008, when the global recession began. Several factors help to explain the rapid rise between 2002 and 2007. First, there was the robust economy and the increasing corporate profits that had boosted stock prices and cash. For example, the S&P 500 stock index companies, including financial companies, had a record of over $2 trillion in cash and other short-term assets.

Second, the weak U.S. dollar made U.S. assets less expensive relative to other countries. That is, from the perspective of a foreign acquirer, compared to any other period in recent memory, U.S. companies were "cheap." For example, a Euro, which was worth only 80 cents in 1999, was worth $1.35 by mid-2007. This made U.S. companies a relative bargain for a European acquirer.

Third, stricter governance standards were requiring poorly performing CEOs and boards of directors to consider unsolicited offers. In essence, top executives and board members were less likely to be protected by antitakeover mechanisms such as greenmail, poison pills, and golden parachutes (discussed at the end of the chapter).

2009 was a bad year for M&A activities due to the global recession. However, with the economy improving in 2010, the pace picked up again. The total value for M&A activity in 2010 was $2.8 trillion—a 17 percent increase over the previous year. Further, in the United States, companies sought approval on 1,166 M&A transactions in 2010 compared to only 716 in 2009—reflecting a 63 percent increase. (U.S. merger approval is required by the Federal Trade Commission for any deal valued at $63 million or more.)[53] According to Andrew Gavil, an antitrust law professor, "Merger activity is often associated with optimism, willingness to spend cash on hand, availability of credit and general levels of economic activity," though it may also indicate how difficult the recovery has been for some businesses (that is, assets can be acquired quite cheaply).

Motives and Benefits   Growth through mergers and acquisitions has played a critical role in the success of many corporations in a wide variety of high-technology and knowledge-intensive industries. Here, market and technology changes can occur very quickly and unpredictably.[54] Speed—speed to market, speed to positioning, and speed to becoming a viable company—is critical in such industries. For example, Alex Mandl, then

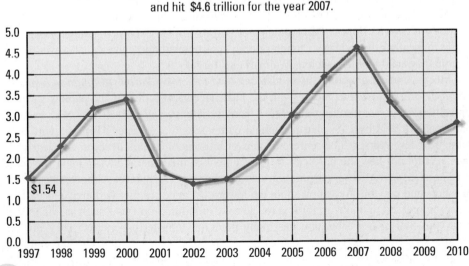

Global Value of Mergers and Acquisitions

Global mergers and acquisitions soared past their previous record and hit $4.6 trillion for the year 2007.

Exhibit 6.8 Global Value of Mergers and Acquisitions

Source: Bloomberg; Dealogic; personal communication with Meredith Leonard at Dealogic on January 27, 2009; and personal communication with Natalie Logan at Dealogic on January 27, 2011.

AT&T's president, was responsible for the acquisition of McCaw Cellular. Although many industry experts felt the price was too steep, he believed that cellular technology was a critical asset for the telecommunications business. Mandl claimed, "The plain fact is that acquiring is much faster than building."[55]

Mergers and acquisitions also can be a means of *obtaining valuable resources that can help an organization expand its product offerings and services.* For example, Cisco Systems, a dominant player in networking equipment, acquired more than 70 companies over a recent seven-year period.[56] This provides Cisco with access to the latest in networking equipment. Then it uses its excellent sales force to market the new technology to its corporate customers. Cisco also provides strong incentives to the staff of acquired companies to stay on. To realize the greatest value from its acquisitions, Cisco also has learned to integrate acquired companies efficiently and effectively.[57]

Mergers and acquisitions also can *provide the opportunity for firms to attain the three bases of synergy—leveraging core competencies, sharing activities, and building market power.* Consider Procter & Gamble's $57 billion acquisition of Gillette.[58] First, it helps Procter & Gamble to leverage its core competencies in marketing and product positioning in the area of grooming and personal care brands. For example, P&G has experience in repositioning brands such as Old Spice in this market (which recently passed Gillette's Right Guard brand to become No. 1 in the deodorant market). Gillette has very strong brands in razors and blades. Thus, P&G's marketing expertise enhances its market position. Second, there are opportunities to share value-creating activities. Gillette will benefit from P&G's stronger distribution network in developing countries where the potential growth rate for the industry's products remains higher than in the United States, Europe, or Japan. Consider the insight of A. F. Lafley, P&G's former CEO:

> When I was in Asia in the 90s, we had already gone beyond the top 500 cities in China. Today, we're way down into the rural areas. So we add three, four, five Gillette brands, and we don't even have to add a salesperson.

Third, the addition of Gillette increases P&G's market power. In recent years, the growth of powerful global retailers such as Walmart, Carrefour, and Costco has eroded much of the consumer goods industry's pricing power. A central part of P&G's recent strategy has been to focus its resources on enhancing its core brands. Today, 16 of its brands (each with revenues of over $1 billion) account for $30 billion of the firm's $51.4 billion in total revenues. Gillette, with $10.5 billion in total revenues, adds five brands which also have revenues of over $1 billion. P&G anticipates that its growing stable of "superbrands" will help it to weather the industry's tough pricing environment and enhance its power relative to large, powerful retailers such as Walmart and Target.

Merger and acquisition activity also can *lead to consolidation within an industry and can force other players to merge.*[59] In the pharmaceutical industry, the patents for many top-selling drugs are expiring and M&A activity is expected to heat up.[60] For example, many patents held by U.S. pharmaceutical companies (e.g., Pfizer's Lipitor) will expire in the next few years, which represents tens of billions of dollars in revenue. Clearly, this is an example of how the political—legal segment of the general environment (discussed in Chapter 2) can affect a corporation's strategy and performance. Although health care providers and patients are happy about the lower-cost generics that will arrive, drug firms are being pressed to make up for lost revenues. Combining top firms such as Glaxo Wellcome and SmithKline Beecham has many potential long-term benefits. They not only promise significant postmerger cost savings, but also the increased size of the combined companies brings greater research and development possibilities.

Corporations can also *enter new market segments by way of acquisitions.* Although Charles Schwab & Co. is best known for providing discount trading services for middle

America, it clearly is interested in other target markets.[61] In late 2000 Schwab surprised its rivals by paying $2.7 billion to acquire (divested in 2006) U.S. Trust Corporation, a 147-year-old financial services institution that is a top estate planner for the wealthy. However, Schwab is not ignoring its core market. The firm also purchased Cybercorp Inc., a Texas brokerage company, for $488 million. That firm offers active online traders sophisticated quotes and stock-screening tools. Exhibit 6.9 summarizes the benefits of mergers and acquisitions.

Potential Limitations   As noted in the previous section, mergers and acquisitions provide a firm with many potential benefits. However, at the same time, there are many potential drawbacks or limitations to such corporate activity.[62]

First, *the takeover premium that is paid for an acquisition typically is very high.* Two times out of three, the stock price of the acquiring company falls once the deal is made public. Since the acquiring firm often pays a 30 percent or higher premium for the target company, the acquirer must create synergies and scale economies that result in sales and market gains exceeding the premium price. Firms paying higher premiums set the performance hurdle even higher. For example, Household International paid an 82 percent premium to buy Beneficial, and Conseco paid an 83 percent premium to acquire Green Tree Financial. Historically, paying a high premium over the stock price has been a poor strategy.

Second, *competing firms often can imitate any advantages realized or copy synergies that result from the M&A.*[63] Thus, a firm can often see its advantages quickly erode. Unless the advantages are sustainable and difficult to copy, investors will not be willing to pay a high premium for the stock. Similarly, the time value of money must be factored into the stock price. M&A costs are paid up front. Conversely, firms pay for R&D, ongoing marketing, and capacity expansion over time. This stretches out the payments needed to gain new competencies. The M&A argument is that a large initial investment is worthwhile because it creates long-term advantages. However, stock analysts want to see immediate results from such a large cash outlay. If the acquired firm does not produce results quickly, investors often divest the stock, driving the price down.

Third, *managers' credibility and ego can sometimes get in the way of sound business decisions.* If the M&A does not perform as planned, managers who pushed for the deal find their reputation tarnished. This can lead them to protect their credibility by funneling more money, or escalating their commitment, into an inevitably doomed operation. Further, when a merger fails and a firm tries to unload the acquisition, they often must sell at a huge discount. These problems further compound the costs and erode the stock price.

Fourth, *there can be many cultural issues that may doom the intended benefits from M&A endeavors.* Consider, the insights of Joanne Lawrence, who played an important role in the merger between SmithKline and the Beecham Group.[64]

> The key to a strategic merger is to create a new culture. This was a mammoth challenge during the SmithKline Beecham merger. We were working at so many different cultural

- Obtain valuable resources that can help an organization expand its product offerings.
- Provide the opportunity for firms to attain three bases of synergy: leveraging core competencies, sharing activities, and building market power.
- Lead to consolidation within an industry and force other players to merge.
- Enter new market segments.

Exhibit 6.9
Benefits of Mergers and Acquisitions

Effectively Managing the Human Side of Acquisitions

When managing the human side of the merger and acquisition (M&A) process, firms face issues such as anxiety, employee shock, and protests. How companies manage such issues will reduce the volume of customer defections, supplier unrest, and government disapproval—as well as increase employee commitment.

In the follow-up to the P&G and Gillette merger, headhunters started targeting Gillette talent. P&G faced government disapproval and investigations in Gillette's home state of Massachusetts, as well as potential problems in India—where it intended to reduce the number of distributors. However, P&G was able to keep 90 percent of Gillette employees who were offered jobs, which is much higher than the average in M&A situations.

P&G enlisted all Gillette employees in an active effort to keep customers, suppliers, and distributors happy, even employees who would eventually be let go. Former Gillette Chairman Jim Kilts said, "A lot of people who left were going to retire and leave anyway in the short term. And I think we seeded the company with some great talent down in the organization, so time will tell." In the instances when processes used by Gillette were deemed more efficient than P&G's, they were adopted. Overall, the company achieved its cost and revenue targets from the first year following the merger.

The best may be yet to come, as the company was able to make aggressive moves in key markets such as Brazil and India. In addition, there was a growing investment and expertise in sports marketing and faster internal decision making.

Source: Kanter, R. M. 2009. Mergers That Stick. *Harvard Business Review,* 87(10): 121–125; and Neff. J. 2010. Why P&G's $57 Billion Bet on Gillette Hasn't Paid Off Big—Yet. *www.adage.com.* February 15: np.

levels, it was dizzying. We had two national cultures to blend—American and British—that compounded the challenge of selling the merger in two different markets with two different shareholder bases. There were also two different business cultures: One was very strong, scientific, and academic; the other was much more commercially oriented. And then we had to consider within both companies the individual businesses, each of which has its own little culture.

Exhibit 6.10 summarizes the limitations of mergers and acquisitions.

Strategy Spotlight 6.4 addresses the human side of M&A activity—how they may be successfully managed.

Divestment: The Other Side of the "M&A Coin" When firms acquire other businesses, it typically generates quite a bit of "press" in business publications such as *The Wall Street Journal, BusinessWeek,* and *Fortune.* It makes for exciting news, and one thing is for sure—large acquiring firms automatically improve their standing in the Fortune 500 rankings (since it is based solely on total revenues). However, managers must also carefully consider the strategic implications of exiting businesses.

Exhibit 6.10
Limitations of Mergers and Acquisitions

- Takeover premiums paid for acquisitions are typically very high.
- Competing firms often can imitate any advantages or copy synergies that result from the merger or acquisition.
- Managers' egos sometimes get in the way of sound business decisions.
- Cultural issues may doom the intended benefits from M&A endeavors.

Why Did Tyco International Sell a Majority Stake in One of Its Businesses?

Tyco International, with $17 billion in revenues, is the world's largest maker of security systems. On November 9, 2010, Tyco announced that it had agreed to sell a majority stake in its electrical and metal products unit to buy-out firm Clayton Dubilier & Rice (CD&R) for $720 million. By taking this action, it withdrew its plans to spin off the division.

The proceeds from the sale of Tyco's 51 percent stake will help the firm accelerate its share buyback

program, which it had announced two months earlier. The unit, which had $1.4 billion in 2009 revenues, will operate as a standalone entity called Atkore International. It makes products such as metal-clad electrical cables and barbed razor ribbon. Tyco felt that it could profit more by selling the remaining 49 percent when markets improve.

The acquisition is very attractive to CD&R. According to Nathan K. Sleeper, a CD&R partner, "As a manufacturer and distributor of industrial products, Atkore is a leader in a market that CD&R knows very well. We look forward to working with the Atkore management team to build on the core strengths of the business—including an outstanding reputation, well-recognized brands, long-term customer relationships, and significant scale advantages—to create an even more successful independent enterprise."

Sources: Winter, C. 2010. Tyco International. Biding Time in Hope of Better Markets. *Bloomberg Businessweek.* November 15–22: 34; and Franco, T. C. 2010. Clayton, Dubilier & Rice to Acquire Tyco International's Electrical and Metal Products Business to Be Renamed Atkore International. *www. prnewswire.com.* November 9: np.

Divestments, the exit of a business from a firm's portfolio, are quite common. One study found that large, prestigious U.S. companies divested more acquisitions than they had kept.[65] Well-known divestitures in business history include (1) Novell's purchase of WordPerfect for stock valued at $1.4 billion and later sold to Corel for $124 million, and (2) Quaker Oats' unloading of the Snapple Beverage Company to Triarc for only $300 million in 1997—three years after it had bought it for $1.8 billion!

> **divestment** the exit of a business from a firm's portfolio.

Divesting a business can accomplish many different objectives.* As the examples above demonstrate, it can be used to help a firm reverse an earlier acquisition that didn't work out as planned. Often, this is simply to help "cut their losses." Other objectives include: (1) enabling managers to focus their efforts more directly on the firm's core businesses,[66] (2) providing the firm with more resources to spend on more attractive alternatives, and (3) raising cash to help fund existing businesses. Strategy Spotlight 6.5 discusses another reason for a divestiture. Here, Tyco International sold part of one of its businesses to raise cash for its share buyback.

Divesting can enhance a firm's competitive position only to the extent that it reduces its tangible (e.g., maintenance, investments, etc.) or intangible (e.g., opportunity costs, managerial attention) costs without sacrificing a current competitive

---

* Firms can divest their businesses in a number of ways. Sell-offs, spin-offs, equity carve-outs, asset sales/ dissolution, and split-ups are some such modes of divestment. In a sell-off, the divesting firm privately negotiates with a third party to divest a unit/subsidiary for cash/stock. In a spin-off, a parent company distributes shares of the unit/subsidiary being divested pro-rata to its existing shareholders and a new company is formed. Equity carve-outs are similar to spin-offs except that shares in the unit/subsidiary being divested are offered to new shareholders. Dissolution involves sale of redundant assets, not necessarily as an entire unit/subsidiary as in sell-offs but a few bits at a time. A split-up, on the other hand, is an instance of divestiture where the parent company is split into two or more new companies and the parent ceases to exist. Shares in the parent company are exchanged for shares in new companies and the exact distribution varies case by case.

advantage or the seeds of future advantages.[67] To be effective, divesting requires a thorough understanding of a business unit's current ability and future potential to contribute to a firm's value creation. However, since such decisions involve a great deal of uncertainty, it is very difficult to make such evaluations. In addition, because of managerial self-interests and organizational inertia, firms often delay divestments of underperforming businesses.

Successful divestment involves establishing objective criteria for determining divestment candidates.[68] Clearly, firms should not panic and sell for a song in bad times. Private equity firms and conglomerates naturally place great emphasis on value when it comes to assessing which business units to keep. In identifying which assets to sell, the management committee of $10 billion Textron, for example, applies three tests of value to the firm's diverse portfolio—which is composed of some 12 divisions and 72 strategic business units (SBUs). For Textron to retain a business unit:

- The unit's long-term fundamentals must be sound. The team gauges this by assessing the attractiveness of each SBU's market and the unit's competitive strength within that market.
- Textron must be able to grow the unit's intrinsic value by 15 percent or more annually. The team applies this screen by carefully analyzing each SBU's business plan each year and challenging its divisional management teams to assess the value-growth potential of each business objectively.
- The unit's revenues must reach a certain threshold. Textron seeks to hold a portfolio of relevant businesses, each with at least $1 billion in revenue. Businesses that are not generating $1 billion or more in sales—and are not likely to reach this watershed within the foreseeable future—are targets for divestiture.

Strategic Alliances and Joint Ventures

strategic alliance a cooperative relationship between two or more firms.

A **strategic alliance** is a cooperative relationship between two (or more) firms.[69] Alliances may be either informal or formal—that is, involving a written contract. **Joint ventures** represent a special case of alliances, wherein two (or more) firms contribute equity to form a new legal entity.

Strategic alliances and joint ventures are assuming an increasingly prominent role in the strategy of leading firms, both large and small.[70] Such cooperative relationships have many potential advantages.[71] Among these are entering new markets, reducing manufacturing (or other) costs in the value chain, and developing and diffusing new technologies.[72]

joint ventures new entities formed within a strategic alliance in which two or more firms, the parents, contribute equity to form the new legal entity.

Entering New Markets   Often a company that has a successful product or service wants to introduce it into a new market. However, it may not have the financial resources or the requisite marketing expertise because it does not understand customer needs, know how to promote the product, or have access to the proper distribution channels.[73]

The partnerships formed between Time-Warner, Inc., and three African American–owned cable companies in New York City are examples of joint ventures created to serve a domestic market. Time-Warner built a 185,000-home cable system in the city and asked the three cable companies to operate it. Time-Warner supplied the product, and the cable companies supplied the knowledge of the community and the know-how to market the cable system. Joining with the local companies enabled Time-Warner to win the acceptance of the cable customers and to benefit from an improved image in the black community.

Strategy Spotlight 6.6 discusses how a strategic alliance between two firms will help them crowdsource creative concepts.

Crowdsourcing: How a Strategic Alliance Will Benefit Both Parties

MRM Worldwide, a New York–based advertising firm, has entered into a strategic alliance with Aniboom, a "virtual" animation company. The alliance is designed to bring MRM's clients quicker and more cost-efficient animation services.

Aniboom, an Israeli company with offices in New York and San Francisco, was founded in 2006 by Uri Shinar, the former CEO of Israeli broadcaster Kesheet. It is a web-based platform that connects 8,000 animators in 70 countries around the world with clients in the TV, film, music, and video game sectors. Prospective clients submit Request for Proposals (RFPs) via the platform, and animators all over the world can respond. MRM global Chief Creative Officer Oren Frank believes that agencies are more likely to rely on this crowdsourcing approach in the future as clients seek more efficient ways of doing business.

MRM's plans are to have animators compete for work: "MRMs clients can launch a content creation competition in the Aniboom community for advertising solutions and have the community at large or a panel of judges select the top finalists and ultimate winner of the assignment. Or the competition could be private, with only the final results exhibited to the public."

Such competitions are part of a group of highly volatile trends that have become increasingly popular. They breed competition and bolster the idea that capitalism weeds out the weak links. It also becomes harder (or more unappealing) for established industries to bid on business that's sought through these methods, because costs can outweigh profits. However, there is one thing that it has done: The playing field has been leveled somewhat for new players. May the best _____ win!

Sources: Van Hoven, M. 2009. Strategic Alliances: MRM and Aniboom Team Up, Crowdsource. *www.mediabistro.com.* August 31: np; and McClellan, S. 2009. MRM, Aniboom Team Up. *www.adweek.com.* August 31: np.

crowdsourcing

Reducing Manufacturing (or Other) Costs in the Value Chain   Strategic alliances (or joint ventures) often enable firms to pool capital, value-creating activities, or facilities in order to reduce costs. For example, Molson Companies and Carling O'Keefe Breweries in Canada formed a joint venture to merge their brewing operations. Although Molson had a modern and efficient brewery in Montreal, Carling's was outdated. However, Carling had the better facilities in Toronto. In addition, Molson's Toronto brewery was located on the waterfront and had substantial real estate value. Overall, the synergies gained by using their combined facilities more efficiently added $150 million of pretax earnings during the initial year of the venture. Economies of scale were realized and facilities were better utilized.

Developing and Diffusing New Technologies   Strategic alliances also may be used to build jointly on the technological expertise of two or more companies. This may enable then to develop products technologically beyond the capability of the companies acting independently.[74]

STMicroelectronics (ST) is a high-tech company based in Geneva, Switzerland, that has thrived—largely due to the success of its strategic alliances.[75] The firm develops and manufactures computer chips for a variety of applications such as mobile phones, set-top boxes, smart cards, and flash memories. In 1995 it teamed up with Hewlett-Packard to develop powerful new processors for various digital applications that are now nearing completion. Another example was its strategic alliance with Nokia to develop a chip that would give Nokia's phones a longer battery life. Here, ST produced a chip that tripled standby time to 60 hours—a breakthough that gave Nokia a huge advantage in the marketplace.

The firm's CEO, Pasquale Pistorio, was among the first in the industry to form R&D alliances with other companies. Now ST's top 12 customers, including HP, Nokia, and Nortel, account for 45 percent of revenues. According to Pistorio, "Alliances are in our DNA." Such relationships help ST keep better-than-average growth rates, even in difficult times. That's because close partners are less likely to defect to other suppliers.

Potential Downsides   Despite their promise, many alliances and joint ventures fail to meet expectations for a variety of reasons.[76] First, without the proper partner, a firm should never consider undertaking an alliance, even for the best of reasons.[77] Each partner should bring the desired complementary strengths to the partnership. Ideally, the strengths contributed by the partners are unique; thus synergies created can be more easily sustained and defended over the longer term. The goal must be to develop synergies between the contributions of the partners, resulting in a win–win situation. Moreover, the partners must be compatible and willing to trust each other.[78] Unfortunately, often little attention is given to nurturing the close working relationships and interpersonal connections that bring together the partnering organizations.[79]

Internal Development

internal development entering a new business through investment in new facilities, often called corporate enterpreneurship and new venture development.

Firms can also diversify by means of corporate entrepreneurship and new venture development. **In today's economy, internal development is such an important means by which companies expand their businesses that we have devoted a whole chapter to it (see Chapter 12).** Sony and the Minnesota Mining & Manufacturing Co. (3M), for example, are known for their dedication to innovation, R&D, and cutting-edge technologies. For example, 3M has developed its entire corporate culture to support its ongoing policy of generating at least 25 percent of total sales from products created within the most recent four-year period. During the 1990s, 3M exceeded this goal by achieving about 30 percent of sales per year from new internally developed products.

Zingerman's, a gourmet deli, has created a new business based on their core competence in human resource management. We discuss this new internal venture in Strategy Spotlight 6.7

Compared to mergers and acquisitions, firms that engage in internal development capture the value created by their own innovative activities without having to "share the wealth" with alliance partners or face the difficulties associated with combining activities across the value chains of several firms or merging corporate cultures.[80] Also, firms can often develop new products or services at a relatively lower cost and thus rely on their own resources rather than turning to external funding.[81]

>LO6.6
Managerial behaviors that can erode the creation of value.

There are also potential disadvantages. It may be time consuming; thus, firms may forfeit the benefits of speed that growth through mergers or acquisitions can provide. This may be especially important among high-tech or knowledge-based organizations in fast-paced environments where being an early mover is critical. Thus, firms that choose to diversify through internal development must develop capabilities that allow them to move quickly from initial opportunity recognition to market introduction.

How Managerial Motives Can Erode Value Creation

managerial motives managers acting in their own self-interest rather than to maximize long-term shareholder value.

Thus far in the chapter, we have implicitly assumed that CEOs and top executives are "rational beings"; that is, they act in the best interests of shareholders to maximize long-term shareholder value. In the real world, however, they may often act in their own self-interest. We now address some managerial motives that can serve to erode, rather than

A Gourmet Deli Firm Leverages Its Core Competence and Creates a New Business

In 1982, when Ari Weinzweig and Paul Saginaw opened Zingerman's Delicatessen in Ann Arbor, Michigan, their goal was to offer a world-class corned-beef sandwich. By 2003, Zingerman's was named "The Coolest Small Company in America" by *Inc.* magazine. Today, the Zingerman's Community of Businesses—including seven businesses—employs more than 500 people and generates annual sales of more than $35 million.

In 1994, the firm created a training arm, ZingTrain, to develop and deliver seminars on how to hire, fire, and inspire people. The program, mainly targeted at managers and small-business owners, promises "tips, tools, and techniques" to be more effective at every step—from hiring to the exit interview. At one session, the 15 participants included four managers from a pizza chain, a furniture store owner, two nonprofit executives, a co-owner of an Italian ice-cart business, and a journalist

Source: Kanter, R. M. 2009. Mergers That Stick. *Harvard Business Review.* 87(10): 121–125; O'Brien, C. 2008. ZingTrain Keeps Retail Workers on the Right Track. *newhope360.com.* October 1: np; and www.zingtrain.com.

● Zingerman's, a delicatessen, leveraged its core competence in human resource management to create training programs.

During the session, the leaders drew on Zingerman's culture, discussing the "compact" in which employees take responsibility for their training's effectiveness. There were also tips for writing a great job description.

---

enhance, value creation. These include "growth for growth's sake," excessive egotism, and the creation of a wide variety of antitakeover tactics.

Growth for Growth's Sake

There are huge incentives for executives to increase the size of their firm. And these are not consistent with increasing shareholder wealth. Top managers, including the CEO, of larger firms typically enjoy more prestige, higher rankings for their firms on the Fortune 500 list (based on revenues, *not* profits), greater incomes, more job security, and so on. There is also the excitement and associated recognition of making a major acquisition. As noted by Harvard's Michael Porter, "There's a tremendous allure to mergers and acquisitions. It's the big play, the dramatic gesture. With one stroke of the pen you can add billions to size, get a front-page story, and create excitement in markets."[82]

In recent years many high-tech firms have suffered from the negative impact of their uncontrolled growth. Consider, for example, Priceline.com's ill-fated venture into an online service to offer groceries and gasoline.[83] A myriad of problems—perhaps most importantly, a lack of participation by manufacturers—caused the firm to lose more than $5 million a *week* prior to abandoning these ventures. Such initiatives are often little more than desperate moves by top managers to satisfy investor demands for accelerating revenues. Unfortunately, the increased revenues often fail to materialize into a corresponding hike in earnings.

growth for growth's sake managers' actions to grow the size of their firms not to increase long-term profitability but to serve managerial self-interest.

Cornelius Vanderbilt: Going to Great Lengths to Correct a Wrong

Cornelius Vanderbilt's legendary ruthlessness set a bar for many titans to come. Back in 1853, the commodore took his first vacation, an extended voyage to Europe aboard his yacht. He was in for a big surprise when he returned.

Source: McGregor, J. 2007. Sweet Revenge. *Business Week*, January 22: 64–70.

Two of his associates had taken the power of attorney that he had left them and sold his interest in his steamship concern, Accessory Transit Company, to themselves.

"Gentlemen," he wrote, in a classic battle cry, "you have undertaken to cheat me. I won't sue you for the law is too slow. I'll ruin you." He converted his yacht to a passenger ship to compete with them and added other vessels. He started a new line, appropriately named *Opposition*. Before long, he bought his way back in and regained control of the company.

At times, executives' overemphasis on growth can result in a plethora of ethical lapses, which can have disastrous outcomes for their companies. A good example (of bad practice) is Joseph Bernardino's leadership at Andersen Worldwide. Bernardino had a chance early on to take a hard line on ethics and quality in the wake of earlier scandals at clients such as Waste Management and Sunbeam. Instead, according to former executives, he put too much emphasis on revenue growth. Consequently, the firm's reputation quickly eroded when it audited and signed off on the highly flawed financial statements of such infamous firms as Enron, Global Crossing, and WorldCom. Bernardino ultimately resigned in disgrace in March 2002, and his firm was dissolved later that year.[84]

egotism managers' actions to shape their firms' strategies to serve their selfish interests rather than to maximize long-term shareholder value.

Egotism

A healthy ego helps make a leader confident, clearheaded, and able to cope with change. CEOs, by their very nature, are intensely competitive people in the office as well as on the tennis court or golf course. But, sometimes when pride is at stake, individuals will go to great lengths to win. Such behaviour, of course, is not a new phenomenon. We discuss the case of Cornelius Vanderbilt, one of the original Americans moguls, in Strategy Spotlight 6.8

Egos can get in the way of a "synergistic" corporate marriage. Few executives (or lower-level managers) are exempt from the potential downside of excessive egos. Consider, for example, the reflections of General Electric's former CEO Jack Welch, considered by many to be the world's most admired executive. He admitted to a regrettable decision: "My hubris got in the way in the Kidder Peabody deal. [He was referring to GE's buyout of the soon-to-be-troubled Wall Street firm.] I got wise advice from Walter Wriston and other directors who said, 'Jack, don't do this.' But I was bully enough and on a run to do it. And I got whacked right in the head."[85] In addition to poor financial results, Kidder Peabody was wracked by a widely publicized trading scandal that tarnished the reputations of both GE and Kidder Peabody. Welch ended up selling Kidder in 1994.

The business press has included many stories of how egotism and greed have infiltrated organizations.[86] Some incidents are considered rather astonishing, such as Tyco's former (and now convicted) CEO Dennis Kozlowski's well-chronicled purchase of a $6,000 shower curtain and vodka-spewing, full-size replica of Michaelangelo's David.[87]

How Antitakeover Measures May Benefit Multiple Stakeholders, Not Just Management

Antitakeover defenses represent a gray area, because management can often legitimately argue that such actions are not there solely to benefit themselves. Rather, they can benefit other stakeholders, such as employees, customers, and the community.

In the late 1980s, takeovers were very popular. The Dayton Hudson Corporation (now Target) even appealed to the Minnesota legislature to pass an antitakeover bill to help Dayton Hudson in its struggle with Hafts—the former owners of Dart, a drug store chain on the East Coast. History had shown that the Dayton Hudson management in place at the time was much better able to manage Dayton Hudson in the long run. In addition to Minnesota, many states now have laws that allow firms to take the interests of all stakeholders into account when considering a takeover bid.

In the summer of 2003, Oracle launched a hostile bid for PeopleSoft. Many charged that the tactics of Oracle CEO Larry Ellison had been unfair, and many of

PeopleSoft's customers took its side, indicating that Oracle ownership would not be of benefit to them. PeopleSoft was concerned that Oracle was merely seeking to buy PeopleSoft for its lucrative base of application software and was not interested in supporting the company's products. Oracle, on the other hand, sued PeopleSoft in an attempt to have the latter's so-called poison pill takeover defense removed.

In December 2004, Oracle struck a deal to buy PeopleSoft—ending a bitter 18-month hostile takeover battle. Oracle's $10.3 billion acquisition valued the firm at $26.50 a share—an increase of 66 percent over its initial offer of $16 a share. Noted analyst John DiFucci: "This is a financial acquisition primarily. Oracle is buying PeopleSoft for its maintenance stream." And, worth noting, PeopleSoft executives, including CEO and company founder David Duffield, did not join Oracle during the conference call announcing the acquisition. Oracle dropped its suit against PeopleSoft in which the former charged that PeopleSoft's "poison pill" takeover defense should be dismissed.

On moral grounds, some antitakeover defenses are not undertaken to entrench and protect management, but often they are. When such defenses are used simply to keep management in power, they are wrong. However, when they are used to defend the long-term financial health of the company and to protect broader stakeholder interests, they will be morally permissible.

Sources: Bowie, N. E. & Werhane, P. H. 2005. *Management Ethics*. Malden, MA: Blackwell Publishing; and La Monica, P. R. 2004. Finally, Oracle to Buy PeopleSoft. *CNNMoney.com*, December 13: np.

Other well-known examples of power grabs and extraordinary consumption of compensation and perks include executives at Enron, the Rigas family who were convicted of defrauding Adelphia of roughly $1 billion, former CEO Bernie Ebbers's $408 million loan from WorldCom, and so on.

A more recent example of excess and greed was exhibited by John Thain.[88] On January 22, 2009, he was ousted as head of Merrill Lynch by Bank of America's CEO, Ken Lewis:

> Thain embarrassingly doled out $4 billion in discretionary year-end bonuses to favored employees just before Bank of America's rescue purchase of failing Merrill. The bonuses amounted to about 10 percent of Merrill's 2008 losses.
>
> Obviously, John Thain believed that he was entitled. When he took over ailing Merrill in early 2008, he began planning major cuts, but he also ordered that his office be redecorated. He spent $1.22 million of company funds to make it "livable," which, in part, included $87,000 for a rug, $87,000 for a pair of guest chairs, $68,000 for a 19th-century credenza, and (what really got the attention of the press) $35,000 for a "commode with legs."

antitakeover tactics managers' actions to avoid losing wealth or power as a result of a hostile takeover

He later agreed to repay the decorating costs. However, one might still ask: What kind of person treats other people's money like this? And who needs a commode that costs as much as a new Lexus? Finally, a comment by Bob O'Brien, stock editor at Barrons.com clearly applies: "The sense of entitlement that's been engendered in this group of people has clearly not been beaten out of them by the brutal performance of the financial sector over the course of the last year."

Antitakeover Tactics

greenmail a payment by a firm to a hostile party for the firm's stock at a premium, made when the firm's management feels that the hostile party is about to make a tender offer.

Unfriendly or hostile takeovers can occur when a company's stock becomes undervalued. A competing organization can buy the outstanding stock of a takeover candidate in sufficient quantity to become a large shareholder. Then it makes a tender offer to gain full control of the company. If the shareholders accept the offer, the hostile firm buys the target company and either fires the target firm's management team or strips them of their power. Thus, antitakeover tactics are common, including greenmail, golden parachutes, and poison pills.[89]

The first, **greenmail,** is an effort by the target firm to prevent an impending takeover. When a hostile firm buys a large block of outstanding target company stock and the target firm's management feels that a tender offer is impending, they offer to buy the stock back from the hostile company at a higher price than the unfriendly company paid for it. Although this often prevents a hostile takeover, the same price is not offered to preexisting shareholders. However, it protects the jobs of the target firm's management.

golden parachute a prearranged contract with managers specifying that, in the event of a hostile takeover, the target firm's managers will be paid a significant severance package.

Second, a **golden parachute** is a prearranged contract with managers specifying that, in the event of a hostile takeover, the target firm's managers will be paid a significant severance package. Although top managers lose their jobs, the golden parachute provisions protect their income.

poison pill used by a company to give shareholders certain rights in the event of takeover by another firm.

Third, **poison pills** are used by a company to give shareholders certain rights in the event of a takeover by another firm. They are also known as shareholder rights plans.

Clearly, antitakeover tactics can often raise some interesting ethical—and legal—issues. Strategy Spotlight 6.9 addresses how antitakeover measures can benefit multiple stakeholders—not just management.

Reflecting on Career Implications . . .

- *Corporate-Level Strategy:* Be aware of your firm's corporate-level strategy. Can you come up with an initiative that will create value both within and across business units?
- *Core Competencies:* What do you see as your core competencies? How can you leverage them both within your business unit as well as across other business units?
- *Sharing Infrastructures:* What infrastructure activities and resources (e.g., information systems, legal) are available in the corporate office that would help you add value for your business unit—or other business units?
- *Diversification:* From your career perspective, what actions can you take to diversify your employment risk (e.g., coursework at a local university, obtain professional certification such as a C.P.A., networking through professional affiliation, etc.)? For example, in periods of retrenchment, such actions will provide you with a greater number of career options.

Summary

A key challenge for today's managers is to create "synergy" when engaging in diversification activities. As we discussed in this chapter, corporate managers do not, in general, have a very good track record in creating value in such endeavors when it comes to mergers and acquisitions. Among the factors that serve to erode shareholder values are paying an excessive premium for the target firm, failing to integrate the activities of the newly acquired businesses into the corporate family, and undertaking diversification initiatives that are too easily imitated by the competition.

We addressed two major types of corporate-level strategy: related and unrelated diversification. With *related diversification* the corporation strives to enter into areas in which key resources and capabilities of the corporation can be shared or leveraged. Synergies come from horizontal relationships between business units. Cost savings and enhanced revenues can be derived from two major sources. First, economies of scope can be achieved from the leveraging of core competencies and the sharing of activities. Second, market power can be attained from greater, or pooled, negotiating power and from vertical integration.

When firms undergo *unrelated diversification* they enter product markets that are dissimilar to their present businesses. Thus, there is generally little opportunity to either leverage core competencies or share activities across business units. Here, synergies are created from vertical relationships between the corporate office and the individual business units. With unrelated diversification, the primary ways to create value are corporate restructuring and parenting, as well as the use of portfolio analysis techniques.

Corporations have three primary means of diversifying their product markets—mergers and acquisitions, joint ventures/strategic alliances, and internal development. There are key trade-offs associated with each of these. For example, mergers and acquisitions are typically the quickest means to enter new markets and provide the corporation with a high level of control over the acquired business. However, with the expensive premiums that often need to be paid to the shareholders of the target firm and the challenges associated with integrating acquisitions, they can also be quite expensive. Not surprisingly, many poorly performing acquisitions are subsequently divested. At times, however, divestitures can help firms refocus their efforts and generate resources. Strategic alliances and joint ventures between two or more firms, on the other hand, may be a means of reducing risk since they involve the sharing and combining of resources. But such joint initiatives also provide a firm with less control (than it would have with an acquisition) since governance is shared between two independent entities. Also, there is a limit to the potential upside for each partner because returns must be shared as well. Finally, with internal development, a firm is able to capture all of the value from its initiatives (as opposed to sharing it with a merger or alliance partner). However, diversification by means of internal development can be very time-consuming—a disadvantage that becomes even more important in fast-paced competitive environments.

Finally, some managerial behaviors may serve to erode shareholder returns. Among these are "growth for growth's sake," egotism, and antitakeover tactics. As we discussed, some of these issues—particularly antitakeover tactics—raise ethical considerations because the managers of the firm are not acting in the best interests of the shareholders.

Summary Review Questions

1. Discuss how managers can create value for their firm through diversification efforts.

2. What are some of the reasons that many diversification efforts fail to achieve desired outcomes?

3. How can companies benefit from related diversification? Unrelated diversification? What are some of the key concepts that can explain such success?

4. What are some of the important ways in which a firm can restructure a business?

5. Discuss some of the various means that firms can use to diversify. What are the pros and cons associated with each of these?

6. Discuss some of the actions that managers may engage in to erode shareholder value.

Key Terms

corporate-level
  strategy, 202
diversification, 204
related diversification, 206
economies of scope, 206
core competencies, 206
sharing activities, 208
market power, 209
pooled negotiating
  power, 209
vertical integration, 210
transaction cost
  perspective, 213

unrelated
  diversification, 214
parenting advantage, 214
restructuring, 215
portfolio
  management, 216
acquisitions, 220
mergers, 220
divestment, 225
strategic alliance, 226
joint ventures, 226
internal
  development, 228

diversification (e.g., leveraging core competencies, sharing infrastructures)?

Application Questions & Exercises

1. What were some of the largest mergers and acquisitions over the last two years? What was the rationale for these actions? Do you think they will be successful? Explain.

2. Discuss some examples from business practice in which an executive's actions appear to be in his or her self-interest rather than the corporation's well-being.

3. Discuss some of the challenges that managers must overcome in making strategic alliances successful. What are some strategic alliances with which you are familiar? Were they successful or not? Explain.

4. Use the Internet and select a company that has recently undertaken diversification into new product markets. What do you feel were some of the reasons for this

Ethics Questions

1. In recent years there has been a rash of corporate downsizing and layoffs. Do you feel that such actions raise ethical considerations? Why or why not?

2. What are some of the ethical issues that arise when managers act in a manner that is counter to their firm's best interests? What are the long-term implications for both the firms and the managers themselves?

Experiential Exercise

Time Warner (formerly AOL Time Warner) is a firm that follows a strategy of related diversification. Evaluate its success (or lack thereof) with regard to how well it has: (1) built on core competencies, (2) shared infrastructures, and (3) increased market power. (Fill answers in table below.)

Rationale for Related Diversification	Successful/Unsuccessful?	Why?
1. Build on core competencies		
2. Share infrastructures		
3. Increase market power		

References

1. Anonymous. 2010. Bebo sold by AOL after just two years. www.bbc.co.uk. June 17: np; Anonymous. 2010. AOL plans to sell or shut down Bebo. www.bbc.co.uk. April 7: np; Pimentel, B. 2008. AOL to buy Bebo for $850. www.marketwatch.com. October 25: np; Sarno, D. 2010. AOL posts loss but stock rises. Los Angeles Times, August 5: 3; Quinn, J. 2005. AOL losses top $1bn after write-downs. The Daily Telegraph. August 5: 3; Shearman, S. 2010. Returning to the fray. Marketing. October 13: 19; Steel, E. & Worthen, B. 2010 With Bebo a no-go, AOL will unload the social site. The Wall Street Journal, June 17: B1; and Whitney, L. 2010. AOL sells off Bebo at last. www.news.cnet.com. October 25: np. We thank Ciprian Stan for his valued contribution.

2. Insights on measuring M&A performance are addressed in: Zollo, M. & Meier, D. 2008. What is M&A performance? BusinessWeek, 22(3): 55–77.

3. Insights on how and why firms may overpay for acquisitions are addressed in: Malhotra, D., Ku, G., & Murnighan, J. K. 2008. When winning is everything. Harvard Business Review, 66(5); 78–86.

4. Pfizer deal helps lift stocks. 2009. online.wsy.com, January 26: np.

5. Dr. G. William Schwert, University of Rochester study cited in Pare, T. P. 1994. The new merger boom. Fortune. November 28: 96.

6. Lipin, S. & Deogun, N. 2000. Big mergers of the 1990's prove disappointing to shareholders. The Wall Street Journal. October 30: C1.

7. Rothenbuecher, J. & Schrottke, J. 2008. To get value from a merger, grow sales. *Harvard Business Review,* 86(5): 24–25; and Rothenbuecher, J. 2008. Personal communication, October 1.

8. Kyriazis, D. 2010. The long-term post acquisition performance of Greek acquiring firms. *International Research Journal of Finance and Economics.* 43: 69–79.

9. Pare, T. P. 1994. The new merger boom. *Fortune,* November 28: 96.

10. A discussion of the effects of director experience and acquisition performance is in: McDonald, M. L. & Westphal, J. D. 2008. What do they know? The effects of outside director acquisition experience on firm acquisition performance. *Strategic Management Journal,* 29(11): 1155–1177.

11. Ghosn, C. 2006. Inside the alliance: The win–win nature of a unique business mode. *Address to the Detroit Economic Club,* November 16.

12. For a study that investigates several predictors of corporate diversification, read: Wiersema, M. F. & Bowen, H. P. 2008. Corporate diversification: The impact of foreign competition, industry globalization, and product diversification. *Strategic Management Journal,* 29(2): 114–132.

13. Kumar, M. V. S. 2011. Are joint ventures positive sum games? The relative effects of cooperative and non-cooperative behavior. *Strategic Management Journal,* 32(1): 32–54.

14. Makri, M., Hitt, M. A., & Lane, P. J. 2010. Complementary technologies, knowledge relatedness, and invention outcomes in high technology mergers and acquisitions. *Strategic Management Journal,* 31(6): 602–628.

15. A discussion of Tyco's unrelated diversification strategy is in: Hindo, B. 2008. Solving Tyco's identity crisis. *BusinessWeek,* February 18: 62.

16. Our framework draws upon a variety of sources, including Goold, M. & Campbell, A. 1998. Desperately seeking synergy. *Harvard Business Review,* 76(5): 131–143; Porter, M. E. 1987. From advantage to corporate strategy. *Harvard Business Review,* 65(3): 43–59; and Hitt, M. A., Ireland, R. D., & Hoskisson, R. E. 2001. *Strategic management: competitiveness and globalization* (4th ed.). Cincinnati, OH: South-Western.

17. Collis, D. J. & Montgomery, C. A. 1987. *Corporate strategy: Resources and the scope of the firm.* New York: McGraw-Hill.

18. This imagery of the corporation as a tree and related discussion draws on Prahalad, C. K. & Hamel, G. 1990. The core competence of the corporation. *Harvard Business Review,* 68(3): 79–91. Parts of this section also draw on Picken, J. C. & Dess, G. G. 1997. *Mission critical:* chap. 5. Burr Ridge, IL: Irwin Professional Publishing.

19. Graebner, M. E., Eisenhardt, K. M. & Roundy, P. T. 2010. Success and failure in technology acquisitions: Lessons for buyers and sellers. *The Academy of Management Perspectives,* 24(3): 73–92.

20. This section draws on Prahalad & Hamel, op. cit.; and Porter, op. cit.

21. A recent study that investigates the relationship between a firm's technology resources, diversification, and performance can be found in Miller, D. J. 2004. Firms' technological resources and the performance effects of diversification. A longitudinal study. *Strategic Management Journal,* 25: 1097–1119.

22. Collis & Montgomery, op. cit.

23. Fisher, A. 2008. America's most admired companies. *Fortune,* March 17: 74.

24. Henricks, M. 1994. VF seeks global brand dominance. *Apparel Industry Magazine,* August: 21–40; VF Corporation. 1993. First quarter corporate summary report. *1993 VF Annual Report.*

25. Hill, A. & Hargreaves, D. 2001. Turbulent times for GE-Honeywell deal. *Financial Times,* February 28: 26.

26. An interesting discussion of a merger in the Russian mining industry is in: Bush, J. 2008. Welding a new metals giant. *BusinessWeek,* July 14 & 21: 56.

27. Lowry, T. 2001. Media. *BusinessWeek,* January 8: 100–101.

28. This section draws on Hrebiniak, L. G. & Joyce, W. F. 1984. *Implementing strategy.* New York: MacMillan; and Oster, S. M. 1994. *Modern competitive analysis.* New York: Oxford University Press.

29. The discussion of the benefits and costs of vertical integration draws on Hax, A. C. & Majluf, N. S. 1991. *The strategy concept and process: A pragmatic approach:* 139. Englewood Cliffs, NJ: Prentice Hall.

30. Fahey, J. 2005. Gray winds. *Forbes.* January 10: 143.

31. This discussion draws on Oster, op. cit.; and Harrigan, K. 1986. Matching vertical integration strategies to competitive conditions. *Strategic Management Journal,* 7(6): 535–556.

32. For a scholarly explanation on how transaction costs determine the boundaries of a firm, see Oliver E. Williamson's pioneering books *Markets and Hierarchies: Analysis and Antitrust Implications* (New York: Free Press, 1975) and *The Economic Institutions of Capitalism* (New York: Free Press, 1985).

33. Campbell, A., Goold, M., & Alexander, M. 1995. Corporate strategy: The quest for parenting advantage. *Harvard Business Review,* 73(2): 120–132; and Picken & Dess, op. cit.

34. Anslinger, P. A. & Copeland, T. E. 1996. Growth through acquisition: A fresh look. *Harvard Business Review,* 74(1): 126–133.

35. Campbell et al., op. cit.

36. This section draws on Porter, op. cit.; and Hambrick, D. C. 1985. Turnaround strategies. In Guth, W. D. (Ed.). *Handbook of business strategy:* 10-1–10-32. Boston: Warren, Gorham & Lamont.

37. There is an important delineation between companies that are operated for a long-term profit and those that are bought and sold for short-term gains. The latter are sometimes referred to as "holding companies" and are generally more concerned about financial issues than strategic issues.

38. Lenzner, R. 2007. High on Loews. *Forbes,* February 26: 98–102.

39. Casico. W. F. 2002. Strategies for responsible restructuring. *Academy of Management Executive,* 16(3): 80–91; and Singh, H. 1993. Challenges in

researching corporate restructuring. *Journal of Management Studies,* 30(1): 147–172.

40. Cusack, M. 1987. *Hanson Trust: A review of the company and its prospects.* London: Hoare Govett.

41. Hax & Majluf, op. cit. By 1979, 45 percent of Fortune 500 companies employed some form of portfolio analysis, according to Haspelagh, P. 1982. Portfolio planning: Uses and limits. *Harvard Busines Review,* 60: 58–73. A later study conducted in 1993 found that over 40 percent of the respondents used portfolio analysis techniques, but the level of usage was expected to increase to more than 60 percent in the near future: Rigby, D. K. 1994. Managing the management tools. *Planning Review,* September–October: 20–24.

42. Goold, M. & Luchs, K. 1993. Why diversify? Four decades of management thinking. *Academy of Management Executive,* 7(3): 7–25.

43. Other approaches include the industry attractiveness–business strength matrix developed jointly by General Electric and McKinsey and Company, the life-cycle matrix developed by Arthur D. Little, and the profitability matrix proposed by Marakon. For an extensive review, refer to Hax & Majluf, op. cit.: 182–194.

44. Porter, op. cit.: 49–52.

45. Collis, D. J. 1995. Portfolio planning at Ciba-Geigy and the Newport investment proposal. Harvard Business School Case No. 9-795-040. Novartis AG was created in 1996 by the merger of Ciba-Geigy and Sandoz.

46. Buzzell, R. D. & Gale, B. T. 1987. *The PIMS principles: Linking strategy to performance.* New York: Free Press; and Miller, A. & Dess, G. G. 1996. *Strategic management,* (2nd ed.). New York: McGraw-Hill.

47. Seeger, J. 1984. Reversing the images of BCG's growth share matrix. *Strategic Management Journal,* 5(1): 93–97.

48. Picken & Dess, op. cit.; Cabot Corporation. 2001. 10-Q filing, Securities and Exchange Commission, May 14.

49. Koudsi, S. 2001. Remedies for an economic hangover. *Fortune,* June 25: 130–139.

50. Insights on the performance of serial acquirers is found in: Laamanen, T. & Keil, T. 2008. Performance of serial acquirers: Toward an acquisition program perspective. *Strategic Management Journal,* 29(6): 663–672.

51. Some insights from Lazard's CEO on mergers and acquisitions are addressed in: Stewart, T. A. & Morse, G. 2008. Giving great advice. *Harvard Business Review,* 66(1): 106–113.

52. Coy, P., Thornton, E., Arndt, M., & Grow, B. 2005. Shake, rattle, and merge. *BusinessWeek,* January 10: 32–35; and Anonymous. 2005. Love is in the air. *Economist,* February 5: 9.

53. Silva, M. & Rovella, D. E. 2011. Intel is model to fight unfair competition, FTC chairman says. www.bloomberg.com. January 11: np.

54. For an interesting study of the relationship between mergers and a firm's product-market strategies, refer to Krisnan, R. A., Joshi, S., & Krishnan, H. 2004. The influence of mergers on firms' product-mix strategies. *Strategic Management Journal,* 25: 587–611.

55. Carey, D., moderator. 2000. A CEO roundtable on making mergers succeed. *Harvard Business Review,* 78(3): 146.

56. Shinal, J. 2001. Can Mike Volpi make Cisco sizzle again? *BusinessWeek,* February 26: 102–104; Kambil, A., Eselius, E. D., & Monteiro, K. A. 2000. Fast venturing: The quick way to start Web businesses. *Sloan Management Review,* 41(4): 55–67; and Elstrom, P. 2001. Sorry, Cisco: The old answers won't work. *BusinessWeek,* April 30: 39.

57. Like many high-tech firms during the economic slump that began in mid-2000, Cisco Systems experienced declining performance. On April 16, 2001, it announced that its revenues for the quarter closing April 30 would drop 5 percent from a year earlier—and a stunning 30 percent from the previous three months—to about $4.7 billion. Furthermore, Cisco announced that it would lay off 8,500 employees and take an enormous $2.5 billion charge to write down

inventory. By late October 2002, its stock was trading at around $10, down significantly from its 52-week high of $70. Elstrom, op. cit.: 39.

58. Coy, P., Thornton, E., Arndt, M., & Grow, B. 2005, Shake, rattle, and merge. *BusinessWeek,* January 10: 32–35; and, Anonymous. 2005. The rise of the superbrands. *Economist.* February 5: 63–65; and, Sellers, P. 2005. It was a no-brainer. *Fortune,* February 21: 96–102.

59. For a discussion of the trend toward consolidation of the steel industry and how Lakshmi Mittal is becoming a dominant player, read Reed, S. & Arndt, M. 2004. The Raja of steel. *BusinessWeek,* December 20: 50–52.

60. Barrett, A. 2001. Drugs. *BusinessWeek,* January 8: 112–113.

61. Whalen, C. J., Pascual, A. M., Lowery, T., & Muller, J. 2001. The top 25 managers. *BusinessWeek,* January 8: 63.

62. This discussion draws upon Rappaport, A. & Sirower, M. L. 1999. Stock or cash? The trade-offs for buyers and sellers in mergers and acquisitions. *Harvard Business Review,* 77(6): 147–158; and Lipin, S. & Deogun, N. 2000. Big mergers of 90s prove disappointing to shareholders. *The Wall Street Journal,* October 30: C1.

63. The downside of mergers in the airline industry is found in: Gimbel, B. 2008. Why airline mergers don't fly. *BusinessWeek,* March 17: 26.

64. Mouio, A. (Ed.). 1998. Unit of one. *Fast Company,* September: 82.

65. Porter, M. E. 1987. From competitive advantage to corporate strategy. *Harvard Business Review,* 65(3): 43.

66. The divestiture of a business which is undertaken in order to enable managers to better focus on its core business has been termed "downscoping." Refer to Hitt, M. A., Harrison, J. S., & Ireland, R. D. 2001. *Mergers and acquisitions: A guide to creating value for stakeholders.* Oxford Press: New York.

67. Sirmon, D. G., Hitt, M. A., & Ireland, R. D. 2007. Managing firm resources in dynamic environments to create value: Looking inside the black box. *Academy of Management Review,* 32(1): 273–292.

68. This discussion draws on: Mankins, M. C., Harding, D., & Weddigne, R-M. 2008. How the best divest. *Harvard Business Review,* 86(1): 92–99.

69. A study that investigates alliance performance is: Lunnan, R. & Haugland, S. A. 2008. Predicting and measuring alliance performance: A multidimensional analysis. *Strategic Management Journal,* 29(5): 545–556.

70. For scholarly perspectives on the role of learning in creating value in strategic alliances, refer to Anard, B. N. & Khanna, T. 2000. Do firms learn to create value? *Strategic Management Journal,* 12(3): 295–317; and Vermeulen, F. & Barkema, H. P. 2001. Learning through acquisitions. *Academy of Management Journal,* 44(3): 457–476.

71. For a detailed discussion of transaction cost economics in strategic alliances, read Reuer, J. J. & Arno, A. 2007. Strategic alliance contracts: Dimensions and determinants of contractual complexity. *Strategic Management Journal,* 28(3): 313–330.

72. This section draws on Hutt, M. D., Stafford, E. R., Walker, B. A., & Reingen, P. H. 2000. Case study: Defining the strategic alliance. *Sloan Management Review,* 41(2): 51–62; and Walters, B. A., Peters, S., & Dess, G. G. 1994. Strategic alliances and joint ventures: Making them work. *Business Horizons,* 4: 5–10.

73. A study that investigates strategic alliances and networks is: Tiwana, A. 2008. Do bridging ties complement strong ties? An empirical examination of alliance ambidexterity. *Strategic Management Journal,* 29(3): 251–272.

74. Phelps, C. 2010. A longitudinal study of the influence of alliance network structure and composition on firm exploratory innovation. *Academy of Management Journal,* 53(4): 890–913.

75. Edmondson, G. & Reinhardt, A. 2001. From niche player to Goliath. *BusinessWeek,* March 12: 94–96.

76. For an institutional theory perspective on strategic alliances, read: Dacin, M. T., Oliver, C., & Roy, J. P. 2007. The legitimacy of strategic alliances: An institutional perspective. *Strategic Management Journal,* 28(2): 169–187.

77. A study investigating factors that determine partner selection in strategic alliances is found in: Shah, R. H. & Swaminathan, V. 2008. *Strategic Management Journal,* 29(5): 471–494.

78. Arino, A. & Ring, P. S. 2010. The role of fairness in alliance formation. *Strategic Management Journal,* 31(6): 1054–1087.

79. Greve, H. R., Baum, J. A. C., Mitsuhashi, H. & Rowley, T. J. 2010. Built to last but falling apart: Cohesion, friction, and withdrawal from interfirm alliances. *Academy of Management Journal,* 53(4): 302–322.

80. For an insightful perspective on how to manage conflict between innovation and ongoing operations in an organization, read: Govindarajan, V. & Trimble, C. 2010. *The other side of innovation: Solving the execution challenge.* Boston, MA: Harvard Business School Press.

81. Dunlap-Hinkler, D., Kotabe, M. & Mudambi, R. 2010. A story of breakthrough versus incremental innovation: Corporate entrepreneurship in the global pharmaceutical industry. *Strategic Entrepreneurship Journal.* 4(2): 106–127.

82. Porter, op. cit.: 43–59.

83. Angwin, J. S. & Wingfield, N. 2000. How Jay Walker built WebHouse on a theory that he couldn't prove. *The Wall Street Journal,* October 16: A1, A8.

84. The fallen. 2003. *BusinessWeek,* January 13: 80–82.

85. The Jack Welch example draws upon Sellers, P. 2001. Get over yourself. *Fortune,* April 30: 76–88.

86. Li, J. & Tang, Y. 2010. CEO hubris and firm risk taking in China: The moderating role of managerial discretion. *Academy of Management Journal,* 53(1): 45–68.

87. Polek, D. 2002. The rise and fall of Dennis Kozlowski. *BusinessWeek,* December 23: 64–77.

88. John Thain and his golden commode. 2009. Editorial. Dallasnews.com, January 26: np; Task, A. 2009. Wall Street's $18.4B bonus: The sense of entitlement has not been beaten out. finance.yahoo.com, January 29: np; and Exit Thain. 2009. Newsfinancialcareers.com, January 22: np.

89. This section draws on Weston, J. F., Besley, S., & Brigham, E. F. 1996. *Essentials of managerial finance* (11th ed.): 18–20. Fort Worth, TX: Dryden Press, Harcourt Brace.

chapter SEVEN

International Strategy:

Creating Value in Global Markets

After reading this chapter, you should have a good understanding of:

LO7.1   The importance of international expansion as a viable diversification strategy.

LO7.2   The sources of national advantage; that is, why an industry in a given country is more (or less) successful than the same industry in another country.

LO7.3   The motivations (or benefits) and the risks associated with international expansion, including the emerging trend for greater offshoring and outsourcing activity.

LO7.4   The two opposing forces—cost reduction and adaptation to local markets—that firms face when entering international markets.

LO7.5   The advantages and disadvantages associated with each of the four basic strategies: international, global, multidomestic, and transnational.

LO7.6   The difference between regional companies and truly global companies.

LO7.7   The four basic types of entry strategies and the relative benefits and risks associated with each of them.

LEARNING OBJECTIVES

The global marketplace provides many opportunities for firms to increase their revenue base and their profitability. Furthermore, in today's knowledge-intensive economy, there is the potential to create advantages by leveraging firm knowledge when crossing national boundaries to do business. At the same time, however, there are pitfalls and risks that firms must avoid in order to be successful. In this chapter we will provide insights on how to be successful and create value when diversifying into global markets.

After some introductory comments on the global economy, we address the question: What explains the level of success of a given industry in a given country? To provide a framework for analysis, we draw on Michael Porter's "diamond of national advantage," in which he identified four factors that help to explain performance differences.

In the second section of the chapter, we shift our focus to the level of the firm and discuss some of the major motivations and risks associated with international expansion. Recognizing such potential benefits and risks enables managers to better assess the growth and profit potential in a given country. We also address important issues associated with a topic of growing interest in the international marketplace—offshoring and outsourcing.

Next, in the third section the largest in this chapter we address how firms can attain competitive advantages in the global marketplace. We discuss two opposing forces firms face when entering foreign markets: cost reduction and local adaptation. Depending on the intensity of each of these forces, they should select among four basic strategies: international, global, multidomestic, and transnational. We discuss both the strengths and limitations of each of these strategies. We also present a recent perspective which posits that even the largest multinational firms are more regional than global even today.

The final section addresses the four categories of entry strategies that firms may choose in entering foreign markets. These strategies vary along a continuum from low investment, low control (exporting) to high investment, high control (wholly owned subsidiaries and greenfield ventures). We discuss the pros and cons associated with each.●

Learning from Mistakes

Carrefour is Europe's top retailer and ranks second in the world (behind Walmart). However, in late 2010, it decided to close up shop in much of Southeast Asia.[1] Its 44 stores in Thailand, 23 in Malaysia, and 2 in Singapore are up for sale. Potential buyers include Britain's Tesco, Japan's Aeon, and France's Casino.

Unfortunately, Carrefour's retreat may be ill-timed. Compared to Europe, the Southeast Asian economy is very strong. Thailand's modern retail sector is growing rapidly despite the country's political turmoil. Ditto for Malaysia. What went wrong?

Carrefour was one of the first foreign grocers to open shops in the region in the 1990s. However, Tesco, which arrived later, was far savvier in figuring out what consumers wanted. For example, when it found out that Thai shoppers traveled for miles to its "big-box" stores, it opened much smaller stores in rural towns. Carrefour, on the other hand, focused on Bangkok's big spenders and stuck to its hypermarket format. Toby Desforges, a marketing consultant, called this a "take it or leave it" approach. Unfortunately, Thai shoppers left it.

Another factor in Tesco's success in these markets was its choice of local partners. For example, in Thailand, it joined forces with CP Group, an agri-conglomerate, before going it alone. And its Malaysian partner, Sime Darby, was able to help it find properties that were suitable for its hypermarkets. Tesco also acquired eight stores in Malaysia from a rival in 2007. In contrast, Carrefour decided to go it alone in both markets and found itself boxed in by rivals.

Carrefour has operations in about 30 countries (twice as many as Tesco) and it may have overreached. In 2009, it pulled the plug on Russia—only months after opening its first store there. Tesco's outgoing chief executive, Sir Terry Leahy, felt that its rival entered emerging markets without a clear roadmap. He asserts, "Lots of retailers have begun international expansion, hit a problem, then retreated and lost market share." In the end, Carrefour ranked a distant fourth in Thailand and Malaysia; Tesco was first in both countries. Globally speaking, Carrefour still outranks Tesco in total revenues. But Tesco is more profitable.

In this chapter we discuss how firms create value and achieve competitive advantage in the global marketplace. Multinational firms are constantly faced with the dilemma of choosing between local adaptation—in product offerings, locations, advertising, and pricing—and global integration. We discuss how firms can avoid pitfalls such as those experienced by Carrefour in Southeast Asia. In addition, we address factors that can influence a nation's success in a particular industry. In our view, this is an important context in determining how well firms might eventually do when they compete beyond their nation's boundaries.

> **>LO7.1**
> The importance of international expansion as a viable diversification strategy.

The Global Economy: A Brief Overview

Managers face many opportunities and risks when they diversify abroad.[2] The trade among nations has increased dramatically in recent years and it is estimated that by 2015, the trade *across* nations will exceed the trade within nations. In a variety of industries such as semiconductors, automobiles, commercial aircraft, telecommunications, computers, and consumer electronics, it is almost impossible to survive unless firms scan the world for competitors, customers, human resources, suppliers, and technology.[3]

GE's wind energy business benefits by tapping into talent around the world. The firm has built research centers in China, Germany, India, and the U.S. "We did it," says CEO Jeffrey Immelt, "to access the best brains everywhere in the world." All four centers have played a key role in GE's development of huge 92-ton turbines:[4]

- Chinese researchers in Shanghai designed the microprocessors that control the pitch of the blade.

- Mechanical engineers from India (Bangalore) devised mathematical models to maximize the efficiency of materials in the turbine.
- Power-systems experts in the U.S. (Niskayuna, New York), which has researchers from 55 countries, do the design work.
- Technicians in Munich, Germany, have created a "smart" turbine that can calculate wind speeds and signal sensors in other turbines to produce maximum electricity.

The rise of **globalization**—meaning the rise of market capitalism around the world—has undeniably contributed to the economic boom in America's New Economy, where knowledge is the key source of competitive advantage and value creation.[5] It is estimated that it has brought phone service to about 300 million households in developing nations and a transfer of nearly $2 trillion from rich countries to poor countries through equity, bond investments, and commercial loans.[6]

There have been extremes in the effect of global capitalism on national economies and poverty levels around the world.[7] The economies of East Asia have attained rapid growth, but there has been comparatively little progress in other areas of the world.[8] For example, income in Latin America grew by only 6 percent in the past two decades when the continent was opening up to global capitalism. Average incomes in sub-Saharan Africa and the old Eastern European bloc have actually declined. The World Bank estimates that the number of people living on $1 per day has *increased* to 1.3 billion over the past decade.

Such disparities in wealth among nations raise an important question: Why do some countries and their citizens enjoy the fruits of global capitalism while others are mired in poverty? Or why do some governments make the best use of inflows of foreign investment and know-how and others do not? There are many explanations. Among these are the need of governments to have track records of business-friendly policies to attract multinationals and local entrepreneurs to train workers, invest in modern technology, and nurture local suppliers and managers. Also, it means carefully managing the broader economic factors in an economy, such as interest rates, inflation, and unemployment, as well as a good legal system that protects property rights, strong educational systems, and a society where prosperity is widely shared.

The above policies are the type that East Asia—in locations such as Hong Kong, Taiwan, South Korea, and Singapore—has employed to evolve from the sweatshop economies of the 1960s and 1970s to industrial powers today. On the other hand, many countries have moved in the other direction. For example, in Guatemala only 52.0 percent of males complete fifth grade and an astonishing 39.8 percent of the population subsists on less than $1 per day.[9] (By comparison, the corresponding numbers for South Korea are 98 percent and less than 2 percent, respectively.)

Strategy Spotlight 7.1 provides an interesting perspective on global trade—marketing to the "bottom of the pyramid."[10] This refers to the practice of a multinational firm targeting its goods and services to the nearly 5 billion poor people in the world who inhabit developing countries. Collectively, this represents a very large market with $14 trillion in purchasing power.

Next, we will address in more detail the question of why some nations and their industries are more competitive.[11] This establishes an important context or setting for the remainder of the chapter. After we discuss why some *nations and their industries* outperform others, we will be better able to address the various strategies that *firms* can take to create competitive advantage when they expand internationally.

Factors Affecting a Nation's Competitiveness

Michael Porter of Harvard University conducted a four-year study in which he and a team of 30 researchers looked at the patterns of competitive success in 10 leading trading

globalization has two meanings. One is the increase in international exchange, including trade in goods and services as well as exchange of money, ideas, and information. Two is the growing similarity of laws, rules, norms, values, and ideas across countries.

Diamond of national advantage a framework for explaining why countries foster successful multinational corporations, consisting of four factors—factor endowments; demand conditions; related and supporting industries; and firm strategy, structure, and rivalry.

strategy spotlight

Marketing to the "Bottom of the Pyramid"

Many executives wrongly believe that profitable opportunities to sell consumer goods exist only in countries where income levels are high. Even when they expand internationally, they often tend to limit their marketing to only the affluent segments within the developing countries. Such narrow conceptualizations of the market cause them to ignore the vast opportunities that exist at "the bottom of the pyramid," according to University of Michigan professor C. K. Prahalad. The *bottom of the pyramid* refers to the nearly 5 billion poor people who inhabit the developing countries. Surprisingly, they represent $14 trillion in purchasing power! And they are looking for products and services that can improve the quality of their lives such as clean energy, personal-care products, lighting, and medicines. Multinationals are missing out on growth opportunities if they ignore this vast segment of the market.

Unilever, the Anglo-Dutch maker of such brands as Dove, Lipton, and Vaseline, built a following among the world's poorest consumers by upending some of the basic rules of marketing. Instead of focusing on value for money, it shrunk packages to set a price even consumers living on $2 a day could afford. It helped people make money to buy its products. "It's not about doing good," but about tapping new markets, says Chief Executive Patrick Cescau.

Sources: Reingold, J. 2011. Can P&G Make Money in Places Where People Earn $2-A-Day? *Fortune*, January 17: 86–91; McGregor, J. 2008. The World's Most Influential Companies. *BusinessWeek*, December 22: 43–53; Miller, C. C. 2006. Easy Money. *Forbes*, November 27: 134–138; and Prahalad, C. K. 2005. *The Fortune at the Bottom of the Pyramid: Eradicating Poverty through Profits.* Philadelphia: Wharton School Publishing.

The strategy was forged about 25 years ago when Indian subsidiary Hindustan Lever (HL) found its products out of reach for millions of Indians. HL came up with a strategy to lower the price while making a profit: single-use packets for everything from shampoo to laundry detergent, costing pennies a pack. A bargain? Maybe not. But it put marquee brands within reach.

It has trained rural women to sell products to their neighbors. "What Unilever does well is get inside these communities, understand their needs, and adapt its business model accordingly," notes a professor at Barcelona's IESE Business School.

Similarly, Procter & Gamble, with $79 billion in annual revenues, has launched a skunkworks. It is staffed mostly by technical staff, rather than market researchers, to approach the $2-a-day consumer from a new perspective. Rather than try to invent products first or rely on market research alone, the group spends days or weeks in the field, visiting homes in Brazil, China, India, and elsewhere. It's the same approach the company uses in developed markets but requires much more effort, without the obvious potential payoff from consumers with disposable income. According to Robert McDonald, P&G's CEO and Chairman: "Our innovation strategy is not just diluting the top-tier product for the lower-end consumer. You have to discretely innovate for every one of those consumers on that economic curve, and if you don't do that, you'll fail."

No one is helped by viewing the poor as the wretched of the earth. Instead, they are the latest frontier of opportunity for those who can meet their needs. A vast market that is barely tapped, the bottom of the pyramid offers enormous opportunities.

---

factor endowments (national advantage) a nation's position in factors of production.

demand conditions (national advantage) the nature of home-market demand for the industry's product or service.

nations. He concluded that there are four broad attributes of nations that individually, and as a system, constitute what is termed "the diamond of national advantage." In effect, these attributes jointly determine the playing field that each nation establishes and operates for its industries. These factors are:

- *Factor endowments.* The nation's position in factors of production, such as skilled labor or infrastructure, necessary to compete in a given industry.
- *Demand conditions.* The nature of home-market demand for the industry's product or service.
- *Related and supporting industries.* The presence or absence in the nation of supplier industries and other related industries that are internationally competitive.
- *Firm strategy, structure, and rivalry.* The conditions in the nation governing how companies are created, organized, and managed, as well as the nature of domestic rivalry.

Factor Endowments[12,13]

Classical economics suggests that factors of production such as land, labor, and capital are the building blocks that create usable consumer goods and services.[14] However, companies in advanced nations seeking competitive advantage over firms in other nations *create* many of the factors of production. For example, a country or industry dependent on scientific innovation must have a skilled human resource pool to draw upon. This resource pool is not inherited; it is created through investment in industry-specific knowledge and talent. The supporting infrastructure of a country—that is, its transportation and communication systems as well as its banking system—are also critical.

Factors of production must be developed that are industry and firm specific. In addition, the pool of resources is less important than the speed and efficiency with which these resources are deployed. Thus, firm-specific knowledge and skills created within a country that are rare, valuable, difficult to imitate, and rapidly and efficiently deployed are the factors of production that ultimately lead to a nation's competitive advantage.

For example, the island nation of Japan has little land mass, making the warehouse space needed to store inventory prohibitively expensive. But by pioneering just-in-time inventory management, Japanese companies managed to create a resource from which they gained advantage over companies in other nations that spent large sums to warehouse inventory.

>LO7.2
The sources of national advantage; that is, why an industry in a given country is more (or less) successful than the same industry in another country.

Demand Conditions

Demand conditions refer to the demands that consumers place on an industry for goods and services. Consumers who demand highly specific, sophisticated products and services force firms to create innovative, advanced products and services to meet the demand. This consumer pressure presents challenges to a country's industries. But in response to these challenges, improvements to existing goods and services often result, creating conditions necessary for competitive advantage over firms in other countries.

Countries with demanding consumers drive firms in that country to meet high standards, upgrade existing products and services, and create innovative products and services. The conditions of consumer demand influence how firms view a market. This, in turn, helps a nation's industries to better anticipate future global demand conditions and proactively respond to product and service requirements.

Denmark, for instance, is known for its environmental awareness. Demand from consumers for environmentally safe products has spurred Danish manufacturers to become leaders in water pollution control equipment—products it successfully exported.

Related and Supporting Industries

Related and supporting industries enable firms to manage inputs more effectively. For example, countries with a strong supplier base benefit by adding efficiency to downstream activities. A competitive supplier base helps a firm obtain inputs using cost-effective, timely methods, thus reducing manufacturing costs. Also, close working relationships with suppliers provide the potential to develop competitive advantages through joint research and development and the ongoing exchange of knowledge.

Related industries offer similar opportunities through joint efforts among firms. In addition, related industries create the probability that new companies will enter the market, increasing competition and forcing existing firms to become more competitive through efforts such as cost control, product innovation, and novel approaches to distribution. Combined, these give the home country's industries a source of competitive advantage.

In the Italian footwear industry the supporting industries enhance national competitive advantage. In Italy, shoe manufacturers are geographically located near their suppliers. The manufacturers have ongoing interactions with leather suppliers and learn about new

related and supporting industries (national advantage) the presence, absence, and quality in the nation of supplier industries and other related industries that supply services, support, or technology to firms in the industry value chain.

textures, colors, and manufacturing techniques while a shoe is still in the prototype stage. The manufacturers are able to project future demand and gear their factories for new products long before companies in other nations become aware of the new styles.

Firm Strategy, Structure, and Rivalry

firm strategy, structure, and rivalry (national advantage) the conditions in the nation governing how companies are created, organized, and managed, as well as the nature of domestic rivalry.

Rivalry is particularly intense in nations with conditions of strong consumer demand, strong supplier bases, and high new entrant potential from related industries. This competitive rivalry in turn increases the efficiency with which firms develop, market, and distribute products and services within the home country. Domestic rivalry thus provides a strong impetus for firms to innovate and find new sources of competitive advantage.

This intense rivalry forces firms to look outside their national boundaries for new markets, setting up the conditions necessary for global competitiveness. Among all the points on Porter's diamond of national advantage, domestic rivalry is perhaps the strongest indicator of global competitive success. Firms that have experienced intense domestic competition are more likely to have designed strategies and structures that allow them to successfully compete in world markets.

In the U.S., for example, intense rivalry has spurred companies such as Dell Computer to find innovative ways to produce and distribute its products. This is largely a result of competition from IBM and Hewlett-Packard.

Strategy Spotlight 7.2 discusses India's software industry. It provides an integrative example of how Porter's "diamond" can help to explain the relative degree of success of an industry in a given country. Exhibit 7.1 illustrates India's "software diamond."

Concluding Comment on Factors Affecting a Nation's Competitiveness

Porter drew his conclusions based on case histories of firms in more than 100 industries. Despite the differences in strategies employed by successful global competitors, a common theme emerged: Firms that succeeded in global markets had first succeeded in intensely competitive home markets. We can conclude that competitive advantage for global firms typically grows out of relentless, continuing improvement, and innovation.[15]

International Expansion: A Company's Motivations and Risks

>LO7.3
The motivations (or benefits) and the risks associated with international expansion, including the emerging trend for greater offshoring and outsourcing activity.

Motivations for International Expansion

Increase Market Size   There are many motivations for a company to pursue international expansion. The most obvious one is to *increase the size of potential markets* for a firm's products and services.[16] By early 2009, the world's population exceeded 6.9 billion, with the U.S. representing less than 5 percent. Exhibit 7.2 lists the population of the U.S. compared to other major markets abroad.

Many multinational firms are intensifying their efforts to market their products and services to countries such as India and China as the ranks of their middle class have increased over the past decade. These include Procter & Gamble's success in achieving a 50 percent share in China's shampoo market as well as PepsiCo's impressive inroads in the Indian soft-drink market.[17] Let's take a brief look at China's emerging middle class:[18]

multinational firms firms that manage operations in more than one country.

- China's middle class has finally attained a critical mass—between 35 million and 200 million people, depending on what definition is used. The larger number is preferred by Fan Gong, director of China's National Economic Research Institute, who fixes the lower boundary of "middle" as a family income of $10,000.

India and the Diamond of National Advantage

Consider the following facts:

- SAP, the German software company, has developed new applications for notebook PCs at its 500-engineer Bangalore facility.

- General Electric plans to invest $100 million and hire 2,600 scientists to create the world's largest research and development lab in Bangalore, India.

- Microsoft plans to invest $400 million in new research partnerships in India.

- Over one-fifth of Fortune 1000 companies outsource their software requirements to firms in India.

- Indian software exports have soared from $5.9 billion in 2000 to $23.6 billion in 2005 to a predicted $68 to $70 billion by 2012.

- For the past decade, the Indian software industry has grown at a 25 percent annual rate.

- More than 800 firms in India are involved in software services as their primary activity.

- Software and information technology firms in India employed 2.3 million people in 2010.

- The information technology industry accounted for 6 percent of India's Gross Domestic Product (GDP) in 2010—up from only 4.8 percent in 2007.

Sources: Sachitanand, R. 2010. The New Face of IT. *Business Today*, 19:62; Anonymous. 2010. Training to Lead. *www.Dqindia.com*. October 5: np; Nagaraju, B.2011. India's Software Exports Seen Up 16–18 pct.in Fy12. *www.reuters.com*, February 2: np; Ghemawat, P. & Hout, T. 2008. Tomorrow's Global Giants. *Harvard Business Review*, 86(11): 80–88; Mathur, S. K. 2007. Indian IT Industry: A Performance Analysis and a Model for Possible Adoption. *ideas.repec.org*, January 1: np; Kripalani, M. 2002. Calling Bangalore: Multinationals Are Making It a Hub for High-Tech Research *BusinessWeek*, November 25: 52–54; Kapur, D. & Ramamurti, R. 2001. India's Emerging Competitive Advantage in Services. 2001. *Academy of Management Executive*, 15(2): 20–33; World Bank. *World Development Report*: 6. New York: Oxford University Press. Reuters. 2001. Oracle in India Push, Taps Software Talent. *Washington Post Online*, July 5.

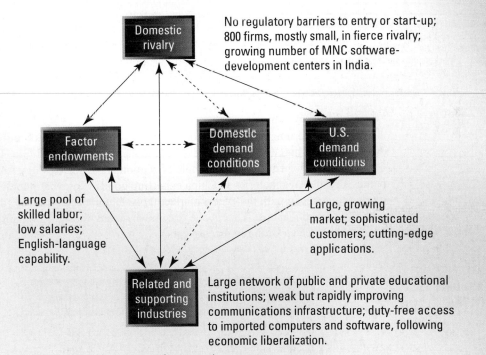

Note: Dashed lines represent weaker interactions.

Exhibit 7.1 India's Diamond in Software

Source: From Kampur D. and Ramamurti R., "India's Emerging Competition Advantage in Services," *Academy of Management Executive: The Thinking Manager's Source.* Copyright © 2001 by Academy of Management. Reproduced with permission of Academy of Management via Copyright Clearance Center.

(continued)

(continued)

What is causing such global interest in India's software services industry? Porter's diamond of national advantage helps clarify this question. See Exhibit 7.1.

First, *factor endowments* are conducive to the rise of India's software industry. Through investment in human resource development with a focus on industry-specific knowledge, India's universities and software firms have literally created this essential factor of production. For example, India produces the second largest annual output of scientists and engineers in the world, behind only the United States. In a knowledge-intensive industry such as software, development of human resources is fundamental to both domestic and global success.

Second, *demand conditions* require that software firms stay on the cutting edge of technological innovation. India has already moved toward globalization of its software industry; consumer demand conditions in developed nations such as Germany, Denmark, parts of Southeast Asia, and the United States created the consumer demand necessary to propel India's software makers toward sophisticated software solutions.*

Third, India has the *supplier base as well as the related industries* needed to drive competitive rivalry and

enhance competitiveness. In particular, information technology (IT) hardware prices declined rapidly in the 1990s. Furthermore, rapid technological change in IT hardware meant that latecomers like India were not locked into older-generation technologies. Thus, both the IT hardware and software industries could "leapfrog" older technologies. In addition, relationships among knowledge workers in these IT hardware and software industries offer the social structure for ongoing knowledge exchange, promoting further enhancement of existing products. Further infrastructure improvements are occurring rapidly.

Fourth, with over 800 firms in the software services industry in India, *intense rivalry forces firms to develop competitive strategies and structures.* Although firms like TCS, Infosys, and Wipro have become large, they were quite small less than a decade ago. And dozens of small and midsized companies are aspiring to catch up. This intense rivalry is one of the primary factors driving Indian software firms to develop overseas distribution channels, as predicted by Porter's diamond of national advantage.

It is interesting to note that the cost advantage of Indian firms may be eroding. For example, TCS's engineers' compensation has soared 13 percent in 2010. Other Asian companies are trying to steal its customers, and it is working hard to better understand overseas customers. Further, IBM and Accenture are aggressively building up their Indian operations, hiring tens of thousands of sought-after Indians by paying them more, thereby lowering their costs while raising those of TCS.

---

* Although India's success cannot be explained in terms of its home market demand (according to Porter's model), the nature of the industry enables software to be transferred among different locations simultaneously by way of communications links. Thus, competitiveness of markets outside India can be enhanced without a physical presence in those markets.

- The central government's emphasis on science and technology has boosted the rapid development of higher education, which is the incubator of the middle class.
- China may be viewed as a new example of economies of scale. Many American companies already have factories in China exporting goods. Now that there is a domestic market to go along with the export market, those factories can increase their output with little additional cost. That is one reason why many foreign companies' profits in China have been so strong in recent years.

Exhibit 7.2
Populations of Selected Nations and the World

Country	February 2011 (in est. millions)
China	1,334
India	1,182
United States	312
Japan	127
Germany	82
World Total	6,877

Source: *www.geohive.com/global/pop_data2.php.*

How Walmart Profits from Arbitrage

With sales of over $405 billion and net income of $14.8 billion, Walmart is considered one of the most successful companies in the world. In recent years, Walmart has embarked upon an ambitious international expansion agenda, opening stores in countries such as Mexico, China, Japan, and England. Walmart today has 4,122 stores outside the United States. Together they account for $100 billion in sales and $5 billion in operating income.

Walmart's above average industry profitability has been attributed to various factors, such as their superior logistics, strict control over overhead costs, and effective use of information systems. What is often lost sight of is that their "everyday low pricing" strategy cannot work successfully unless they are able to procure the thousands of items they carry in each of their stores at the lowest possible prices. This is where their expertise in arbitraging plays a critical role. In 2004, Walmart bought $18 billion worth of goods directly from China. By 2006, this had grown to $26.7 billion. If one considers indirect imports through their other suppliers as well, Walmart's total imports from China could be anywhere between $50 billion and $70 billion each year. At a conservative estimate, this represents cost savings of approximately $16 billion to $23 billion! (These savings represent how much more these goods would have likely cost Walmart had the firm purchased them from the United States.) Clearly, the core of Walmart's international strategy is not their international store expansion strategy but their pursuit of worldwide arbitrage opportunities.

Sources: 2010 Walmart Annual Report; Ghemawat, P. 2007. *Redefining Global Strategy.* Boston: Harvard Business School Press; Scott, R.E. 2007. The WalMart Effect. *epi.org,* June 26: np; and Basker, E. & Pham, V.H. 2008. WalMart as Catalyst to U.S.-China Trade. *ssrn.com;* np.

Expanding a firm's global presence also automatically increases its scale of operations, providing it with a larger revenue and asset base.[19] As we noted in Chapter 5 in discussing overall cost leadership strategies, such an increase in revenues and asset base potentially enables a firm to *attain economies of scale.* This provides multiple benefits. One advantage is the spreading of fixed costs such as R&D over a larger volume of production. Examples include the sale of Boeing's commercial aircraft and Microsoft's operating systems in many foreign countries.

Filmmaking is another industry in which international sales can help amortize huge developmental costs.[20] For example, Tom Cruise found foreign buyers for his "Valkyrie" in 2008 and the film ultimately got about 59 percent of its $200 million in ticket sales abroad. And Sylvester Stallone's latest *Rambo* opened the same year and picked up $70 million, or 62 percent of its $113 million in total ticket sales from international markets.

Take Advantage of Arbitrage *Taking advantage of arbitrage opportunities* is a second advantage of international expansion. In its simplest form, arbitrage involves buying something from where it is cheap and selling it somewhere where it commands a higher price. A big part of Walmart's success can be attributed to the company's expertise in arbitrage (see Strategy Spotlight 7.3). The possibilities for arbitrage are not necessarily confined to simple trading opportunities. It can be applied to virtually any factor of production and every stage of the value chain. For example, a firm may locate its call centers in India, its manufacturing plants in China, and its R&D in Europe, where the specific types of talented personnel may be available at the lowest possible price. In today's integrated global financial markets, a firm can borrow anywhere in the world where capital is cheap and use it to fund a project in a country where capital is expensive. Such arbitrage opportunities are even more attractive to global corporations because their larger size enables them to buy in huge volume, thus increasing their bargaining power with suppliers.

arbitrage opportunities an opportunity to profit by buying and selling the same good in different markets.

Extend a Product's Life Cycle *Extending the life cycle of a product* that is in its maturity stage in a firm's home country but that has greater demand potential elsewhere is another benefit of international expansion. As we noted in Chapter 5, products (and industries) generally go through a four-stage life cycle of introduction, growth, maturity, and decline. In recent decades, U.S. soft-drink producers such as Coca-Cola and PepsiCo have aggressively pursued international markets to attain levels of growth that simply would not be available in the United States. Similarly, personal computer manufacturers such as Dell and Hewlett-Packard have sought out foreign markets to offset the growing saturation in the U.S. market.

Optimize the Location of Value-Chain Activities *Optimizing the physical location for every activity in its value chain* is another benefit. Recall from our discussions in Chapters 3 and 5 that the value chain represents the various activities in which all firms must engage to produce products and services. They include primary activities, such as inbound logistics, operations, and marketing, as well as support activities, such as procurement, R&D, and human resource management. All firms have to make critical decisions as to where each activity will take place.[21] Optimizing the location for every activity in the value chain can yield one or more of three strategic advantages: performance enhancement, cost reduction, and risk reduction. We will now discuss each of these.

Performance Enhancement Microsoft's decision to establish a corporate research laboratory in Cambridge, England, is an example of a location decision that was guided mainly by the goal of building and sustaining world-class excellence in selected value-creating activities.[22] This strategic decision provided Microsoft with access to outstanding technical and professional talent. Location decisions can affect the quality with which any activity is performed in terms of the availability of needed talent, speed of learning, and the quality of external and internal coordination.

Cost Reduction Two location decisions founded largely on cost-reduction considerations are (1) Nike's decision to source the manufacture of athletic shoes from Asian countries such as China, Vietnam, and Indonesia, and (2) the decision of many multinational companies to set up production operations just south of the U.S.–Mexico border to access lower-cost labor. These operations are called *maquiladoras*. Such location decisions can affect the cost structure in terms of local manpower and other resources, transportation and logistics, and government incentives and the local tax structure.

Performance enhancement and cost-reduction benefits parallel the business-level strategies (discussed in Chapter 5) of differentiation and overall cost leadership. They can at times be attained simultaneously. Consider our example in the previous section on the Indian software industry. When Oracle set up a development operation in that country, the company benefited both from lower labor costs and operational expenses as well as from performance enhancements realized through the hiring of superbly talented professionals.

Risk Reduction Given the erratic swings in the exchange ratios between the U.S. dollar and the Japanese yen (in relation to each other and to other major currencies), an important basis for cost competition between Ford and Toyota has been their relative ingenuity at managing currency risks. One way for such rivals to manage currency risks has been to spread the high-cost elements of their manufacturing operations across a few select and carefully chosen locations around the world. Location decisions such as these can affect the overall risk profile of the firm with respect to currency, economic, and political risks.[23]

> **reverse innovation**
> new products developed by developed country multination firms for emerging markets that have adequate functionality at a low cost.

Explore Reverse Innovation Finally, *exploring possibilities for reverse innovation* has become a major motivation for international expansion. Many leading companies are discovering that developing products specifically for emerging markets can pay off in a big way. In the past, multinational companies typically developed products for their rich home markets and then tried to sell them in developing countries with minor adaptations.

However, as growth slows in rich nations and demand grows rapidly in developing countries such as India and China, this approach becomes increasingly inadequate. Instead, companies like GE have committed significant resources to developing products that meet the needs of developing nations, products that deliver adequate functionality at a fraction of the cost. Interestingly, these products have subsequently found considerable success in value segments in wealthy countries as well. Hence, this process is referred to as reverse innovation, a new motivation for international expansion.

As $3,000 cars, $300 computers, and $30 mobile phones bring what were previously considered as luxuries within the reach of the middle class of emerging markets, it is important to understand the motivations and implications of reverse innovation. *First,* it is impossible to sell first-world versions of products with minor adaptations in countries where average income per person is between $1,000 and $4,000, as is the case in most developing countries. To sell in these markets, entirely new products must be designed and developed by local technical talent and manufactured with local components. *Second,* although these countries are relatively poor, they are growing rapidly. For example, the Indian and Chinese economies are growing at double digit rates, and Brazil has achieved full employment. *Third,* if the innovation does not come from first-world multinationals, there are any number of local firms that are ready to grab the market with low-cost products. *Fourth,* as the consumers and governments of many first-world countries are rediscovering the virtues of frugality and are trying to cut down expenses, these products and services originally developed for the first world may gain significant market shares in developing countries as well.

Strategy Spotlight 7.4 describes several examples of reverse innovation.

Potential Risks of International Expansion

When a company expands its international operations, it does so to increase its profits or revenues. As with any other investment, however, there are also potential risks.[24] To help companies assess the risk of entering foreign markets, rating systems have been developed to evaluate political, economic, as well as financial and credit risks.[25] *Euromoney* magazine publishes a semiannual "Country Risk Rating" that evaluates political, economic, and other risks that entrants potentially face.[26] Exhibit 7.3 depicts a sample of country risk ratings, published by the World Bank, from the 170 countries that *Euromoney* evaluates. Note that the lower the score, the higher the country's expected level of risk.[27]

Next we will discuss the four main types of risk: political risk, economic risk, currency risk, and management risk.

Political and Economic Risk   Generally speaking, the business climate in the United States is very favorable. However, some countries around the globe may be hazardous to the health of corporate initiatives because of **political risk.**[28] Forces such as social unrest, military turmoil, demonstrations, and even violent conflict and terrorism can pose serious threats.[29] Consider, for example, the ongoing tension and violence in the Middle East between Israelis and Palestinians, and the social and political unrest in Indonesia.[30] Such conditions increase the likelihood of destruction of property and disruption of operations as well as nonpayment for goods and services. Thus, countries that are viewed as high risk are less attractive for most types of business.[31]

Another source of political risk in many countries is the absence of the rule of law. The absence of rules or the lack of uniform enforcement of existing rules leads to what might often seem to be arbitrary and inconsistent decisions by government officials. This can make it difficult for foreign firms to conduct business.

Consider Libya. The country is noted for its capricious government under the leadership of its ruler, Muammar Qaddafi, who has been in power for over 40 years. Here, business people often incur significant political risks. Let's look at a few examples:[32]

political risk potential threat to a firm's operations in a country due to ineffectiveness of the domestic political system.

rule of law a characteristic of legal systems where behavior is governed by rules that are uniformly enforced.

Reverse Innovation: How Developing Countries Are Becoming Hotbeds of Innovation

GE Healthcare's largest R&D facility is surprisingly located in Bangalore, India, thousands of miles away from its home country. Here, customers can hardly afford the sky-high prices of GE's medical devices. At 50,000 square feet and employing about 1,000 researchers and engineers, this facility recently developed a portable electrocardio-gram that weighs only about two pounds, runs on batter-ies, and can do an electrocardiogram for 20 cents! Over the next six years, GE plans to spend $3 billion to create at least 100 healthcare innovations that would significantly lower costs, improve quality, increase access, and con-quer the medical devices market in developing countries. Increasingly, many developing countries are becoming hotbeds of a new type of innovation often referred to as "reverse innovation" or "frugal innovation." Let us look at a few other examples of reverse innovation by GE as well as other companies:

- In the 1990s, GE attempted to sell ultrasound machines costing about $100,000 to high-end Chi-nese hospital imaging centers. But these expensive, bulky devices were poorly received by Chinese cus-tomers. Responding to this failure, a local GE team developed a cheap, portable ultrasound machine using a laptop computer enhanced with a probe which sold at a price between $30,000 and $40,000. By 2007, they were able to bring the price down to just $15,000. Today, these machines have found a worldwide market—both in developing economies as well as in the United States, where ambulance squads and emergency rooms are increasingly using them. Overall, sales of medical technology are exploding in China and India. China's market is expected to grow by 15 percent a year to 2015 and reach $43 billion by 2019. India's demand is growing at an even higher rate, 23 percent, and should top $10 billion by 2020.

- Moline, Illinois–based Deere & Co. opened a center in Pune, India, almost a decade ago with the inten-tion to penetrate the Indian market. Many observ-ers were skeptical about the ability of a company known for its heavy-duty farm equipment and big construction gear to succeed in a market where the majority of the farmers still used oxen-pulled plows. However, Deere saw potential and its engi-neers in Pune responded with four no-frills models. Though lacking first-world features like GPS and air conditioning, they were sturdy enough to handle the rigors of commercial farming. The tractors cost between $8400 and $11,600 in India. Subsequently, Deere targeted a segment of the home market that they had previously largely ignored—hobbyists as well as bargain hunters. These buyers do not care for advanced features but covet the same qualities as Indian farmers: affordability and maneuver-ability. Today, half of the no-frills models that Deere produces in India are exported to other countries. "These tractors are like Swiss Army knives. They get used for anything: mowing, transporting bales of hay, pushing dirt, and removing manure," claims Mike Alvin, a product manager at Deere.

- Narayana Hrudayalaya Hospital in Bangalore per-forms open heart surgeries at about $2000, which is a fraction of the $20,000 to $100,000 that it would cost in a U.S. hospital. How do they do it? By apply-ing mass-production techniques pioneered by Henry Ford in the auto industry. The hospital has 1000 beds, roughly eight times the size of an American hospital, and performs 600 operations a week. The large volume allows the hospital to benefit from both economies of scale (that reduce cost) and, even more importantly, experience curve effects that improve the success rate. Today the hospital has established video and Internet links with hospitals not only in India, but in countries in Africa as well as in Malaysia. As the need to contain healthcare costs becomes more pressing in developed countries like the United States, techniques pioneered by Naray-ana Hrudayalaya Hospital may find acceptance in these countries.

Sources: Anonymous. 2011. Frugal healing. *The Economist*. January 22: 73–74; Immelt, J. R., Govindarajan, V., & Trimble, C. 2009. How GE Is Disrupting Itself. *Harvard Business Review*, 87 (10): 56–64; Chandran, R. 2010. Profiting from Treating India's Poor. *International Herald Tribune*, July 6: 17; Anonymous. 2010. The World Turned Upside Down. *The Economist*, April 17: 3–17; Mero, J. 2008. John Deere's Farm Team. *Fortune*, April 14: 119–124; and Anonymous. 2008. No-Frills IndianTtractors Find Favor with U.S. Farmers. *www.theindian.com*, April 29: np.

Exhibit 7.3   A Sample of International Country Risk Ratings: September 2010

Rank	Country	Overall Score (100)	Political Risk (30)	Economic Performance (30)	Infrastructure (10)	Total of Debt and Credit Indicators (20)	Access to Bank Finance/Capital Markets (10)
1	Norway	93.33	28.19	26.89	8.25	20.00	10.00
2	Switzerland	90.22	26.80	24.99	8.44	20.00	10.00
3	Sweden	88.93	28.04	22.65	8.24	20.00	10.00
4	Denmark	88.80	27.90	22.81	8.09	20.00	10.00
5	Finland	88.55	27.99	22.40	8.16	20.00	10.00
6	Luxembourg	88.27	27.54	21.71	9.03	20.00	10.00
7	Canada	88.26	27.80	22.12	8.34	20.00	10.00
8	Netherlands	88.20	27.71	22.85	7.64	20.00	10.00
9	Hong Kong	87.18	25.25	24.87	8.10	18.96	10.00
10	Australia	86.18	27.10	21.43	7.86	19.79	10.00
17	United States	82.10	26.26	17.91	7.92	20.00	10.00
36	China	72.60	17.37	22.31	6.81	17.45	8.67
110	Nigeria	37.80	11.25	12.12	5.25	2.19	7.00
120	Nicaragua	34.53	10.71	9.96	1.00	9.86	3.00
127	Iran	32.97	12.25	14.81	5.24	0.00	0.67
151	Afghanistan	20.95	8.26	8.31	3.38	0.00	1.00

Source: Country Risk September 2010: Full Results. *www.euromoney.com.*

- An Egyptian grocer spent years building a thriving business in Libya. Unfortunately, he made the mistake of going home during a holiday. Abrupt changes to visa rules meant that he could no longer return.
- The new manager of a hotel in Tripoli, an expatriate, fired some staff and switched suppliers. This prompted someone to make a telephone call. A sudden snap health inspection of the hotel revealed a few canned goods beyond their sell-by date. The manager is now in prison!
- A small Canadian oil firm, Verenex, joined the rush into Libya and struck an exciting find. Early in 2009, a Chinese company offered to buy Verenex, nearly all of whose assets are in Libya, for close to $450 million. The Libyan government blocked the sale but promised to match the price. After months of wrangling in the oil ministry, Libya's sovereign wealth fund slashed its offer to barely $300 million. Faced with further trouble if they failed to sell, Verenex shareholders reluctantly agreed.

The laws, and the enforcement of laws, associated with the protection of intellectual property rights can be a major potential **economic risk** in entering new countries.[33] Microsoft, for example, has lost billions of dollars in potential revenue through piracy of its software products in many countries, including China. Other areas of the globe, such as the former Soviet Union and some eastern European nations, have piracy problems as well.[34] Firms rich in intellectual property have encountered financial losses as imitations of their products have grown due to a lack of law enforcement of intellectual property rights.[35]

economic risk potential threat to a firm's operations in a country due to economic policies and conditions, including property rights laws and enforcement of those laws.

Counterfeiting: A Worldwide Problem

Although counterfeiting used to be a luxury goods problem, people are now trying to counterfeit items that have a wider effect on the economy, such as pharmaceuticals and computer parts. A new study by the U.S. Department of Commerce shows that fake goods have been infiltrating the army. The number of counterfeit parts in military electronics systems more than doubled between 2005 and 2008, potentially damaging high-tech weapons.

Counterfeiting can have health and safety implications as well. The World Health Organization says that up to 10 percent of medicines worldwide are counterfeit—a deadly hazard that could be costing the pharmaceutical industry $46 billion a year. "You won't die from purchasing a pair of counterfeit blue jeans or a counterfeit golf club. You can die from taking counterfeit pharmaceutical products. And there's no doubt that people have died in China from bad medicine," says John Theirault, head of global security for American pharmaceutical giant Pfizer.

The International Anti-Counterfeiting Coalition (IACC), a Washington D.C.–based nonprofit organization, estimates that the true figure for counterfeit and pirated goods is close to $600 billion and makes up about 5–7 percent of world trade. Several factors have contributed to the increase in counterfeiting in recent years. The shift of much of the world's manufacturing to countries with poor protection of intellectual property rights has provided both technology and opportunity to make knock-offs. And the Internet and e-commerce sites like eBay have made it easier to distribute counterfeit goods. MarkMonitor, a firm that helps companies defend their brands online, estimates that sales of counterfeit goods via the Internet is about $135 billion.

The IACC provides some rather startling statistics relating to counterfeiting and its costs to business and society:

- Counterfeiting costs U.S. businesses $200 billion to $250 billion annually.

- Counterfeit merchandise is directly responsible for the loss of more than 750,000 American jobs.

- Since 1982, the global trade in illegitimate goods has increased from approximately $5.5 billion to $600 billion annually.

- U.S. companies suffer $9 billion in world trade losses due to international copyright piracy.

- Counterfeiting poses a threat to global health and safety.

The recent recession in the richer countries may have also given a boost to counterfeit goods. An anti-counterfeiting group has noticed a spike in knock-offs this recession, as consumers trade down from the real thing. Cost-cutting measures may have also made firms' supply chains more vulnerable to counterfeit parts. Lawsuits brought by companies are at an all-time high, says Kirsten Gilbert, a partner at a British law firm.

Source: Anonymous. 2010. Knock-offs Catch On. *The Economist*, March 6: 81–82; Balfour, F. 2005. Fake! *BusinessWeek*, February 7: 54–64; and Quinn, G. 2010. Counterfeiting Costs US Businesses $200 Billion Annually. *www.ipwatchdog.com*, August 30: np.

---

counterfeiting selling of trademarked goods without the consent of the trademark holder.

currency risk potential threat to a firm's operations in a country due to fluctuations in the local currency's exchange rate.

Strategy Spotlight 7.5 discusses a problem that is a severe threat to global trade—counterferting. Estimates are that counterfeiting accounts for between 5 to 7 percent of global merchandise trade—the equivalent of as much as $600 billion a year. And the potential corrosive effects include health and safety, not just economic, damage.[36]

Currency Risks Currency fluctuations can pose substantial risks. A company with operations in several countries must constantly monitor the exchange rate between its own currency and that of the host country to minimize **currency risks.** Even a small change in the exchange rate can result in a significant difference in the cost of production or net profit when doing business overseas. When the U.S. dollar appreciates against other currencies, for example, U.S. goods can be more expensive to consumers in foreign countries. At the same time, however, appreciation of the U.S. dollar can have negative implications for American companies that have branch operations overseas. The reason for this is that profits from abroad must be exchanged for dollars at a more expensive rate of exchange, reducing the amount of profit when measured in dollars. For example, consider an American firm doing business in Italy. If this firm had a 20 percent profit in euros at its Italian center of operations, this profit would be totally wiped out when converted into U.S. dollars if the euro had depreciated 20 percent against the U.S. dollar. (U.S. multinationals typically engage in sophisticated "hedging strategies" to minimize currency risk. The discussion of this is beyond the scope of this section.)

It is important to note that even when government intervention is well intended, the macroeconomic effects of such action can be very negative for multinational corporations. Such was the case in 1997 when Thailand suddenly chose to devalue its currency, the baht, after months of trying to support it at an artificially high level. This, in effect, made the baht nearly worthless compared to other currencies. And in 1998 Russia not only devalued its ruble but also elected not to honor its foreign debt obligations.

Below, we discuss how Israel's strong currency—the shekel—forced a firm to reevaluate its strategy.

> For years O.R.T. Technologies resisted moving any operations outside of Israel. However, when faced with a sharp rise in the value of the shekel, the maker of specialized software for managing gas stations froze all local hiring and decided to transfer some developmental work to Eastern Europe. Laments CEO Alex Milner, "I never thought I'd see the day when we would have to move R&D outside of Israel, but the strong shekel has forced us to do so."[37]

Management Risks   **Management risks** may be considered the challenges and risks that managers face when they must respond to the inevitable differences that they encounter in foreign markets. These take a variety of forms: culture, customs, language, income levels, customer preferences, distribution systems, and so on.[38] As we will note later in the chapter, even in the case of apparently standard products, some degree of local adaptation will become necessary.[39]

Differences in cultures across countries can also pose unique challenges for managers.[40] Cultural symbols can evoke deep feelings.[41] For example, in a series of advertisements aimed at Italian vacationers, Coca-Cola executives turned the Eiffel Tower, Empire State Building, and the Tower of Pisa into the familiar Coke bottle. So far, so good. However, when the white marble columns of the Parthenon that crowns the Acropolis in Athens

management risk potential threat to a firm's operations in a country due to the problems that managers have making decisions in the context of foreign markets.

were turned into Coke bottles, the Greeks became outraged. Why? Greeks refer to the Acropolis as the "holy rock," and a government official said the Parthenon is an "international symbol of excellence" and that "whoever insults the Parthenon insults international culture." Coca-Cola apologized. Below are some cultural tips for conducting business in HongKong:

- Handshakes when greeting and before leaving are customary.
- After the initial handshake, business cards are presented with both hands on the card. Carefully read the card before putting it away.
- In Hong Kong, Chinese people should be addressed by their professional title (or Mr., Mrs., Miss) followed by their surname.
- Appointments should be made as far in advance as possible.
- Punctuality is very important and demonstrates respect.

● Some of Hong Kong's customs are quite different from those of western countries.

- Negotiations in Hong Kong are normally very slow with much attention to detail. The same negotiating team should be kept throughout the proceedings.
- Tea will be served during the negotiations. Always accept and wait for the host to begin drinking before you partake.
- Be aware that "yes" may just be an indication that the person heard you rather than indicating agreement. A Hong Kong Chinese businessperson will have a difficult time saying "no" directly.

Below, we discuss a rather humorous example of how a local custom can affect operations at a manufacturing plant in Singapore.

Larry Henderson, plant manager, and John Lichthental, manager of human resources, were faced with a rather unique problem. They were assigned by Celanese Chemical Corp. to build a plant in Singapore, and the plant was completed in July. However, according to local custom, a plant should only be christened on "lucky" days. Unfortunately, the next lucky day was not until September 3.

The managers had to convince executives at Celanese's Dallas headquarters to delay the plant opening. As one might expect, it wasn't easy. But after many heated telephone conversations and flaming e-mails, the president agreed to open the new plant on a lucky day—September 3.[42]

Global Dispersion of Value Chains: Outsourcing and Offshoring

A major recent trend has been the dispersion of the value chains of multinational corporations across different countries; that is, the various activities that constitute the value chain of a firm are now spread across several countries and continents. Such dispersion of value occurs mainly through increasing offshoring and outsourcing.

A report issued by the World Trade Organization describes the production of a particular U.S. car as follows: "30 percent of the car's value goes to Korea for assembly, 17.5 percent to Japan for components and advanced technology, 7.5 percent to Germany for design, 4 percent to Taiwan and Singapore for minor parts, 2.5 percent to U.K. for advertising and marketing services, and 1.5 percent to Ireland and Barbados for data processing. This means that only 37 percent of the production value is generated in the U.S."[43] In today's economy, we are increasingly witnessing two interrelated trends: outsourcing and offshoring.

outsourcing using other firms to perform value-creating activities that were previously performed in-house.

Outsourcing occurs when a firm decides to utilize other firms to perform value-creating activities that were previously performed in-house.[44] It may be a new activity that the firm is perfectly capable of doing but chooses to have someone else perform for cost or quality reasons. Outsourcing can be to either a domestic or foreign firm.

offshoring shifting a value-creating activity from a domestic location to a foreign location.

Offshoring takes place when a firm decides to shift an activity that they were performing in a domestic location to a foreign location.[45] For example, both Microsoft and Intel now have R&D facilities in India, employing a large number of Indian scientists and engineers. Often, offshoring and outsourcing go together; that is, a firm may outsource an activity to a foreign supplier, thereby causing the work to be offshored as well.[46] Spending on offshore information technology will nearly triple between 2004 and 2010 to $60 billion, according to research firm Gartner.[47]

The recent explosion in the volume of outsourcing and offshoring is due to a variety of factors. Up until the 1960s, for most companies, the entire value chain was in one location. Further, the production took place close to where the customers were in order to keep transportation costs under control. In the case of service industries, it was generally believed that offshoring was not possible because the producer and consumer had to be present at the same place at the same time. After all, a haircut could not be performed if the barber and the client were separated!

For manufacturing industries, the rapid decline in transportation and coordination costs has enabled firms to disperse their value chains over different locations. For example, Nike's R&D takes place in the U.S., raw materials are procured from a multitude of countries, actual manufacturing takes place in China or Indonesia, advertising is produced in the U.S., and sales and service take place in practically all the countries. Each value-creating activity is performed in the location where the cost is the lowest or the quality is the best. Without finding optimal locations for each activity, Nike could not have attained its position as the world's largest shoe company.

The experience of the manufacturing sector was also repeated in the service sector by the mid-1990s. A trend that began with the outsourcing of low-level programming and data entry work to countries such as India and Ireland suddenly grew manyfold, encompassing a variety of white collar and professional activities ranging from call-centers to R&D. The cost of a long distance call from the U.S. to India has decreased from about $3 to $0.03 in the last 20 years, thereby making it possible to have call centers located in countries like India, where a combination of low labor costs and English proficiency presents an ideal mix of factor conditions.

Bangalore, India, in recent years, has emerged as a location where more and more U.S. tax returns are prepared. In India, U.S.–trained and licensed radiologists interpret chest X-rays and CT scans from U.S. hospitals for half the cost. The advantages from offshoring go beyond mere cost savings today. In many specialized occupations in science and engineering, there is a shortage of qualified professionals in developed countries, whereas countries, like India, China, and Singapore have what seems like an inexhaustible supply.[48]

For most of the 20th century, domestic companies catered to the needs of local populations. However, with the increasing homogenization of customer needs around the world and the institutionalization of free trade and investment as a global ideology (especially after the creation of the WTO), competition has become truly global. Each company has to keep its costs low in order to survive.[49] They also must find the best suppliers and the most skilled workers as well as locate each stage of the value chain in places where factor conditions are most conducive. Thus, outsourcing and offshoring are no longer mere options to consider, but an imperative for competitive survival.

While there is a compelling logic for companies to engage in offshoring, there can be many pitfalls. This has spurred many companies to outsource tech services to low-cost locations within the United States, instead of offshoring to foreign countries. We discuss this trend in Strategy Spotlight 7.6.

Achieving Competitive Advantage in Global Markets

We now discuss the two opposing forces that firms face when they expand into global markets: cost reduction and adaptation to local markets. Then we address the four basic types of international strategies that they may pursue: international, global, multidomestic, and transnational. The selection of one of these four types of strategies is largely dependent on a firm's relative pressure to address each of the two forces.

Two Opposing Pressures: Reducing Costs and Adapting to Local Markets

Many years ago, the famed marketing strategist Theodore Levitt advocated strategies that favored global products and brands. He suggested that firms should standardize all of their products and services for all of their worldwide markets. Such an approach would help a firm lower its overall costs by spreading its investments over as large a market as possible. Levitt's approach rested on three key assumptions:

>LO7.4
The two opposing forces—cost reduction and adaptation to local markets—that firms face when entering international markets.

A Small-Town Alternative to Offshoring Tech Services Work

These are great times for Cayuse Technologies, a 200-employee tech outsourcing firm. It is owned by the Confederated Tribes of the Umatilla Indian Reservation in northeast Oregon. In 2009 it had $7.7 million in revenues—seven times what it had in 2007, its first year in operation. And with its business from corporate clients like Accenture expected to soar next year, Cayuse plans to hire another 75 workers. Says Marc Benoist, the firm's general manager, "We still have capacity here at our facility, so we have plenty of room for growth."

Cayuse is one of many information technology companies in remote areas of the United States who position themselves as alternatives to offshore outsourcing. And the economics seem to make sense. On an hourly basis, these "rural outsourcers" charge much more than their overseas rivals. But when factors such as oversight and quality control of the offshore work are factored in, their rates are competitive. Their rates are also much lower than their domestic counterparts located in big cities, because they operate in areas that have lower living costs. "Their value proposition is, 'We cost less than the East or West Coast, and we're easier to deal with than India,'" says Mary Lacity, a professor at the University of Missouri at St. Louis, who studies outsourcing. Cayuse Technologies develops software, provides outsourcing of business processes, and serves as a contact for Accenture's clients, for example, processing and adjusting insurance claims. "It makes much more sense for Cayuse to perform those activities," according to Randall Willis, managing director of Accenture.

Sources: Lieber, N. 2010. 'Rural Outsourcers' vs. Bangalore. *Bloomberg Businessweek,* September 27–October 3: 52–53; Brickey, D. 2010. Rural Outsourcing Gains Favor; Cayuse Technologies as a Model. *www.eastoregonian.com,* October 13: np; and Alsever, J. 2010. Forget India, Outsource to Arkansas. *www.money.cnn.com,* July 8: np.

Consider the rationale behind Human Genome Sciences's (HGS) decision to use a rural outsourcing firm: HGS, a Rockville, Maryland biotech company with 900 employees, got bids from several outsourcers to handle the technical support for its back-office software. One of the bidders would have offshored the work to India. However, the idea of sending confidential company information overseas, outside the reach of the American intellectual property law, did not sit too well with David Evans, their IT director.

Instead, Evans hired Atlanta-based Rural Sourcing, Inc., and its team of software experts located in Jonesboro, Arkansas. HGS pays about $55 an hour for technical support from Rural Sourcing—a figure that is about 15 percent higher than the rates quoted by the Indian outsourcing firm that he considered. However, it is still about half of what it would cost for him to hire a software development firm located in the Washington, D.C., metro area.

Recently, IT research firm Gartner said in a report that while these firms make up a tiny portion of the market, they are an "attractive alternative" to offshore outsourcers because of language and other cultural factors. It is also easier for them to comply with U.S. data privacy regulations, according to the report.

Without a doubt, rural outsourcers won't replace the offshorers. After all, India has outsourcing revenues of about $50 billion, and that number is expected to triple by 2020, according to estimates by McKinsey & Company and an Indian trade group. In contrast, the rural outsourcing market is estimated to be less than $100 million. However, Lacity believes that this segment has growth potential—in part because of the efforts by federal policymakers to seek ways of creating jobs and as government outsourcing contracts increasingly require work to be done in the United States.

1. Customer needs and interests are becoming increasingly homogeneous worldwide.
2. People around the world are willing to sacrifice preferences in product features, functions, design, and the like for lower prices at high quality.
3. Substantial economies of scale in production and marketing can be achieved through supplying global markets.[50]

However, there is ample evidence to refute these assumptions.[51] Regarding the first assumption—the increasing worldwide homogeneity of customer needs and interests—consider the number of product markets, ranging from watches and handbags to soft drinks and fast foods. Companies have identified global customer segments and developed global products and brands targeted to those segments. Also, many other companies adapt lines to idiosyncratic country preferences and develop local brands targeted to local market segments. For example, Nestlé's line of pizzas marketed in the United Kingdom includes cheese with ham and pineapple topping on a French bread crust. Similarly, Coca-Cola in Japan markets Georgia (a tonic drink) as well as Classic Coke and Hi-C.

Consider the second assumption—the sacrifice of product attributes for lower prices. While there is invariably a price-sensitive segment in many product markets, there is no indication that this is increasing. In contrast, in many product and service markets—ranging from watches, personal computers, and household appliances, to banking and insurance—there is a growing interest in multiple product features, product quality, and service.

Finally, the third assumption is that significant economies of scale in production and marketing could be achieved for global products and services. Although standardization may lower manufacturing costs, such a perspective does not consider three critical and interrelated points. First, as we discussed in Chapter 5, technological developments in flexible factory automation enable economies of scale to be attained at lower levels of output and do not require production of a single standardized product. Second, the cost of production is only one component, and often not the critical one, in determining the total cost of a product. Third, a firm's strategy should not be product-driven. It should also consider other activities in the firm's value chain, such as marketing, sales, and distribution.

Based on the above, we would have a hard time arguing that it is wise to develop the same product or service for all markets throughout the world. While there are some exceptions, such as Harley-Davidson motorcycles and some of Coca-Cola's soft-drink products, managers must also strive to tailor their products to the culture of the country in which they are attempting to do business. Few would argue that "one size fits all" generally applies.

The opposing pressures that managers face place conflicting demands on firms as they strive to be competitive.[52] On the one hand, competitive pressures require that firms do what they can to *lower unit costs* so that consumers will not perceive their product and service offerings as too expensive. This may lead them to consider locating manufacturing facilities where labor costs are low and developing products that are highly standardized across multiple countries.

In addition to responding to pressures to lower costs, managers also must strive to be *responsive to local pressures* in order to tailor their products to the demand of the local market in which they do business. This requires differentiating their offerings and strategies from country to country to reflect consumer tastes and preferences and making changes to reflect differences in distribution channels, human resource practices, and governmental regulations. However, since the strategies and tactics to differentiate products and services to local markets can involve additional expenses, a firm's costs will tend to rise.

The two opposing pressures result in four different basic strategies that companies can use to compete in the global marketplace: international, global, multidomestic, and transnational. The strategy that a firm selects depends on the degree of pressure that it is facing for cost reductions and the importance of adapting to local markets. Exhibit 7.4 shows the conditions under which each of these strategies would be most appropriate.

It is important to note that we consider these four strategies to be "basic" or "pure"; that is, in practice, all firms will tend to have some elements of each strategy.

International Strategy

There are a small number of industries in which pressures for both local adaptation and lowering costs are rather low. An extreme example of such an industry is the "orphan" drug industry. These are medicines for diseases that are severe but affect only a small number of people. Diseases such as the Gaucher disease and Fabry disease fit into this category. Companies such as Genzyme and Oxford GlycoSciences are active in this segment of the drug

>LO7.5
The advantages and disadvantages associated with each of the four basic strategies: international, global, multidomestic, and transnational.

international strategy a strategy based on firms' diffusion and adaptation of the parent companies' knowledge and expertise to foreign markets, used in industries where the pressures for both local adaptation and lowering costs are low.

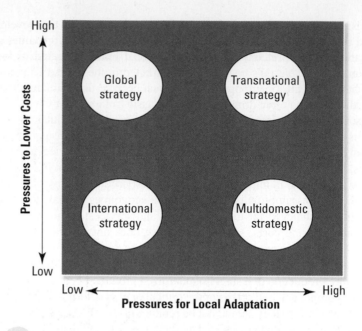

High

Pressures to Lower Costs

Low

| Global strategy | Transnational strategy |
| International strategy | Multidomestic strategy |

Low ← Pressures for Local Adaptation → High

Exhibit 7.4 Opposing Pressures and Four Strategies

industry. There is virtually no need to adapt their products to the local markets. And the pressures to reduce costs are low; even though only a few thousand patients are affected, the revenues and margins are significant, because patients are charged up to $100,000 per year. Legislation has made this industry even more attractive. The 1983 Orphan Drug Act provides various tax credits and exclusive marketing rights for any drug developed to treat a disease that afflicts fewer than 200,000 patients. Since 1983, more than 280 orphan drugs have been licensed and used to treat 14 million patients.[53]

An international strategy is based on diffusion and adaptation of the parent company's knowledge and expertise to foreign markets. Country units are allowed to make some minor adaptations to products and ideas coming from the head office, but they have far less independence and autonomy compared to multidomestic companies. The primary goal of the strategy is worldwide exploitation of the parent firm's knowledge and capabilities. All sources of core competencies are centralized.

The majority of large U.S. multinationals pursued the international strategy in the decades following World War II. These companies centralized R&D and product development but established manufacturing facilities as well as marketing organizations abroad. Companies such as McDonald's and Kellogg are examples of firms following such a strategy. Although these companies do make some local adaptations, they are of a very limited nature. With increasing pressures to reduce costs due to global competition, especially from low-cost countries, opportunities to successfully employ international strategy are becoming more limited. This strategy is most suitable in situations where a firm has distinctive competencies that local companies in foreign markets lack.

Risks and Challenges   Below, are some of the risks and challenges associated with an international strategy.

- Different activities in the value chain typically have different optimal locations. That is, R&D may be optimally located in a country with an abundant supply of scientists and engineers, whereas assembly may be better conducted in a low-cost location.

Nike, for example, designs its shoes in the United States, but all the manufacturing is done in countries like China or Thailand. The international strategy, with its tendency to concentrate most of its activities in one location, fails to take advantage of the benefits of an optimally distributed value chain.

- The lack of local responsiveness may result in the alienation of local customers. Worse still, the firm's inability to be receptive to new ideas and innovation from its foreign subsidiaries may lead to missed opportunities.

Exhibit 7.5 summarizes the strengths and weaknesses of international strategies in the global marketplace.

Global Strategy

As indicated in Exhibit 7.4, a firm whose emphasis is on lowering costs tends to follow a global strategy. Competitive strategy is centralized and controlled to a large extent by the corporate office. Since the primary emphasis is on controlling costs, the corporate office strives to achieve a strong level of coordination and integration across the various businesses.[54] Firms following a global strategy strive to offer standardized products and services as well as to locate manufacturing, R&D, and marketing activities in only a few locations.[55]

A global strategy emphasizes economies of scale due to the standardization of products and services, and the centralization of operations in a few locations. As such, one advantage may be that innovations that come about through efforts of either a business unit or the corporate office can be transferred more easily to other locations. Although costs may be lower, the firm following a global strategy may, in general, have to forgo opportunities for revenue growth since it does not invest extensive resources in adapting product offerings from one market to another.

A global strategy is most appropriate when there are strong pressures for reducing costs and comparatively weak pressures for adaptation to local markets. Economies of scale becomes an important consideration.[56] Advantages to increased volume may come from larger production plants or runs as well as from more efficient logistics and distribution networks. Worldwide volume is also especially important in supporting high levels of investment in research and development. As we would expect, many industries requiring high levels of R&D, such as pharmaceuticals, semiconductors, and jet aircraft, follow global strategies.

Another advantage of a global strategy is that it can enable a firm to create a standard level of quality throughout the world. Let's look at what Tom Siebel, former chairman of Siebel Systems (now part of Oracle), the $2 billion developer of e-business application software, has to say about global standardization.

> Our customers—global companies like IBM, Zurich Financial Services, and Citicorp—expect the same high level of service and quality, and the same licensing policies, no matter where we do business with them around the world. Our human resources and legal

global strategy a strategy based on firms' centralization and control by the corporate office, with the primary emphasis on controlling costs, and used in industries where the pressure for local adaptation is low and the pressure for lowering costs is high.

Strengths	Limitations
• Leverage and diffusion of a parent firm's knowledge and core competencies. • Lower costs because of less need to tailor products and services.	• Limited ability to adapt to local markets. • Inability to take advantage of new ideas and innovations occurring in local markets.

Exhibit 7.5
Strengths and Limitations of International Strategies in the Global Marketplace

departments help us create policies that respect local cultures and requirements worldwide, while at the same time maintaining the highest standards. We have one brand, one image, one set of corporate colors, and one set of messages, across every place on the planet. An organization needs central quality control to avoid surprises.[57]

Risks and Challenges There are, of course, some risks associated with a global strategy.[58]

- A firm can enjoy scale economies only by concentrating scale-sensitive resources and activities in one or few locations. Such concentration, however, becomes a "double-edged sword." For example, if a firm has only one manufacturing facility, it must export its output (e.g., components, subsystems, or finished products) to other markets, some of which may be a great distance from the operation. Thus, decisions about locating facilities must weigh the potential benefits from concentrating operations in a single location against the higher transportation and tariff costs that result from such concentration.
- The geographic concentration of any activity may also tend to isolate that activity from the targeted markets. Such isolation may be risky since it may hamper the facility's ability to quickly respond to changes in market conditions and needs.
- Concentrating an activity in a single location also makes the rest of the firm dependent on that location. Such dependency implies that, unless the location has world-class competencies, the firm's competitive position can be eroded if problems arise. A European Ford executive, reflecting on the firm's concentration of activities during a global integration program in the mid-1990s, lamented, "Now if you misjudge the market, you are wrong in 15 countries rather than only one."

Many firms have learned through experience that products that work in one market may not be well received in other markets. Strategy Spotlight 7.7 describes the very different receptions that Pura, a cleaner-burning gasoline from Shell, received in Thailand and the Netherlands.

Exhibit 7.6 summarizes the strengths and weaknesses of global strategies.

Multidomestic Strategy

multidomestic strategy a strategy based on firms' differentiating their products and services to adapt to local markets, used in industries where the pressure for local adaptation is high and the pressure for lowering costs is low.

According to Exhibit 7.4, a firm whose emphasis is on differentiating its product and service offerings to adapt to local markets follows a multidomestic strategy.[59] Decisions evolving from a multidomestic strategy tend to be decentralized to permit the firm to tailor its products and respond rapidly to changes in demand. This enables a firm to expand its market and to charge different prices in different markets. For firms following this strategy, differences in language, culture, income levels, customer preferences, and distribution systems are only a few of the many factors that must be considered. Even in the case of relatively standardized products, at least some level of local adaptation is often necessary. Consider, for example, Honda motorcycles.

> While Honda uses a common basic technology, it must develop different types of motorcycles for different regions of the world. For example, North Americans primarily use motorcycles for leisure and sports; thus aggressive looks and high horsepower are key. Southeast Asians provide a counterpoint. Here, motorcycles are a basic means of transportation. Thus, they require low cost and ease of maintenance. And in Australia and New Zealand, shepherds use motorcycles to herd sheep. Therefore, they demand low-speed torque, rather than high speed and horsepower.[60]

In addition to the products themselves, how they are packaged must sometimes be adapted to local market conditions. Some consumers in developing countries are likely to have packaging preferences very different from Western consumers. For example, single-serve packets, or sachets, are very popular in India.[61] They permit consumers to purchase

Why Shell's Innovative Gasoline Product Backfired in Holland

Not every consumer wants eco-friendly goods, and relatively few will pay more for them. However, every day more customers are including environmental factors in their buying decisions. But what "sells" in one place might not in another.

Consider, for example, Shell Oil's (part of the Royal Dutch/Shell Group) experience in marketing Pura, a new, cleaner-burning gasoline in two very different countries. According to Mark Weintraub, Shell's director of sustainable development strategy, the firm used a "sustainable development lens" to identify a need for cleaner fuels in Thailand. As is the case in much of Asia, the combination of dense cities and high traffic volume was damaging air quality in Bangkok and elsewhere. A cleaner-burning fuel such as Pura, which produced less sulfur and other harmful emissions, seemed like a winner.

In an example of superior eco-design, Shell developed just such a fuel by converting natural gas to a zero-sulfur liquid and then mixing it with regular diesel. Shell touted the blend as providing "more complete combustion to reduce smoke emissions and restore lost engine performance." Shell-Thailand Chairman Khun Vajrabhaya claimed, "Motorists should experience better performance of their vehicles within 2–3 tank-fulls of Shell Pura diesel. From our road tests on diesel-engine vehicles in both Thailand and the U.K., black smoke was satisfactorily reduced." Even though Shell charged a 7.5 cent a gallon premium, Pura gained market share and sales have been very strong. In short, the launch was a complete success.

Shell assumed that it could use the same pitch when it rolled out Pura in other countries. However, the launch in the Netherlands fell flat. Why? Shell later realized that emphasizing how cleaner-burning fuel protects a car's engine was not resonating in Holland. The message was more important in Thailand, where people are much more concerned about gasoline quality and the effect of impurities on engine performance and quality of life.

Clearly, the "green pitch" never went over well in Holland—even though the country is full of customers who say that they will buy green. It is just that the need to clean the local city air is not as pressing a concern as it is in Asia. Eventually, Shell relaunched Pura in Holland under the name V-Power and marketed it by stressing enhanced engine power.

Source: Esty, D. C., & Winston, A. S. 2009. *Green to Gold.* Hoboken, NJ: Wiley; Peckham, J. 2002. Shell Spots "Premium Diesel" Opportunity for GTL Blend. *Diesel Fuel News.* February 4: np; and www.showa-shell.co.jp.

---

only what they need, experiment with new products, and conserve cash. Products as varied as detergents, shampoos, pickles, and cough syrup are sold in sachets in India. It is estimated that they make up 20 to 30 percent of the total sold in their categories. In China, sachets are spreading as a marketing device for such items as shampoos. This reminds us of the importance of considering all activities in a firm's value chain (discussed in Chapters 3 and 5) in determining where local adaptations may be required.

Cultural differences may also require a firm to adapt its personnel practices when it expands internationally.[62] For example, some facets of Walmart stores have been easily

Exhibit 7.6
Strengths and Limitations of Global Strategies

Strengths	Limitations
• Strong integration across various businesses.	• Limited ability to adapt to local markets.
• Standardization leads to higher economies of scale, which lowers costs.	• Concentration of activities may increase dependence on a single facility.
• Helps create uniform standards of quality throughout the world.	• Single locations may lead to higher tariffs and transportation costs.

Dealing with Bribery Abroad

Most multinational firms experience difficult dilemmas when it comes to the question of adapting rules and guidelines, both formal and informal, while operating in foreign countries. A case in point is the Foreign Corrupt Practices Act of 1977, which makes it illegal for U.S. companies to bribe foreign officials to gain business or facilitate approvals and permissions. Unfortunately, in many parts of the world, bribery is a way of life, with large payoffs to government officials and politicians the norm to win government contracts. At a lower level, goods won't clear customs unless routine illegal, but well-accepted, payments, are made to officials. What is an American company to do in such situations?

Source: Begley, T. M., & Boyd, D. P. 2003. The Need for a Corporate Global Mind-Set. *MIT Sloan Management Review,* Winter: 25–32.

Intel follows a strict rule-based definition of bribery as "a thing of value given to someone with the intent of obtaining favorable treatment from the recipient." The company strictly prohibits payments to expedite a shipment through customs if the payment did not "follow applicable rules and regulations, and if the agent gives money or payment in kind to a government official for personal benefit." Texas Instruments, on the other hand, follows a middle approach. They require employees to "exercise good judgment" in questionable circumstances "by avoiding activities that could create even the appearance that our decisions could be compromised." And Analog Devices has set up a policy manager as a consultant to overseas operations. The policy manager does not make decisions for country managers. Instead, the policy manager helps country managers think through the issues and provides information on how the corporate office has handled similar situations in the past.

"exported" to foreign operations, while others have required some modifications.[63] When the retailer entered the German market in 1997, it took along the company "cheer"—Give me a W! Give me an A! Give me an L! Who's Number One? The Customer!—which suited German employees. However, Walmart's 10-Foot Rule, which requires employees to greet any customer within a 10-foot radius, was not so well received in Germany, where employees and shoppers alike weren't comfortable with the custom.

Strategy Spotlight 7.8 describes how U.S. multinationals have adapted to the problem of bribery in various countries while adhering to strict federal laws on corrupt practices abroad.

Risks and Challenges   As you might expect, there are some risks associated with a multidomestic strategy. Among these are the following:

- Typically, local adaptation of products and services will increase a company's cost structure. In many industries, competition is so intense that most firms can ill afford any competitive disadvantages on the dimension of cost. A key challenge of managers is to determine the trade-off between local adaptation and its cost structure. For example, cost considerations led Procter & Gamble to standardize its diaper design across all European

● Australia is geographically distant from the United States. However, it is much closer when other dimensions are considered, such as income levels, language, culture, and political/legal systems.

markets. This was done despite research data indicating that Italian mothers, unlike those in other countries, preferred diapers that covered the baby's navel. Later, however, P&G recognized that this feature was critical to these mothers, so the company decided to incorporate this feature for the Italian market despite its adverse cost implications.

- At times, local adaptations, even when well intentioned, may backfire. When the American restaurant chain TGI Fridays entered the South Korean market, it purposely incorporated many local dishes, such as kimchi (hot, spicy cabbage), in its menu. This responsiveness, however, was not well received. Company analysis of the weak market acceptance indicated that Korean customers anticipated a visit to TGI Fridays as a visit to America. Thus, finding Korean dishes was inconsistent with their expectations.

- The optimal degree of local adaptation evolves over time. In many industry segments, a variety of factors, such as the influence of global media, greater international travel, and declining income disparities across countries, may lead to increasing global standardization. On the other hand, in other industry segments, especially where the product or service can be delivered over the Internet (such as music), the need for even greater customization and local adaptation may increase over time. Firms must recalibrate the need for local adaptation on an ongoing basis; excessive adaptation extracts a price as surely as underadaptation.

Some films and TV programs may cross country boundaries rather successfully, while others are less successful. Let's consider an effort by Disney that fell far short:

> Remember *The Alamo*, not the nineteenth-century battle between Mexican forces and Texas rebels, but the 2004 movie? The film definitely met the big-budget criterion—it cost Disney nearly $100 million. It did not generate strong box-office receipts in English. But what was surprising was Disney's attempt to create crossover appeal to Latinos. These efforts included more balanced treatment of Anglos versus Mexicans, prominently featuring Tejano folk heroes in the film, and running a separate Spanish-language marketing effort. But such efforts were doomed to fail. Why? According to one authority, the Alamo is "such an open wound among American Hispanics."[64]

Exhibit 7.7 summarizes the strengths and limitations of multidomestic strategies.

Transnational Strategy

A *transnational strategy* strives to optimize the trade-offs associated with efficiency, local adaptation, and learning.[65] It seeks efficiency not for its own sake, but as a means to achieve global competitiveness.[66] It recognizes the importance of local responsiveness but as a tool for flexibility in international operations.[67] Innovations are regarded as an outcome of a larger process of organizational learning that includes the contributions of everyone in the firm.[68] Also, a core tenet of the transnational model is that a firm's assets and capabilities

transnational strategy a strategy based on firms' optimizing the trade-offs associated with efficiency, local adaptation, and learning, used in industries where the pressures for both local adaptation and lowering costs are high.

Strengths	Limitations
• Ability to adapt products and services to local market conditions.	• Decreased ability to realize cost savings through scale economies.
• Ability to detect potential opportunities for attractive niches in a given market, enhancing revenue.	• Greater difficulty in transferring knowledge across countries.
	• May lead to "overadaptation" as conditions change.

Exhibit 7.7
Strengths and Limitations of Multidomestic Strategies

are dispersed according to the most beneficial location for each activity. Thus, managers avoid the tendency to either concentrate activities in a central location (a global strategy) or disperse them across many locations to enhance adaptation (a multidomestic strategy). Peter Brabeck, Chairman of Nestlé, the giant food company, provides such a perspective.

> We believe strongly that there isn't a so-called global consumer, at least not when it comes to food and beverages. People have local tastes based on their unique cultures and traditions—a good candy bar in Brazil is not the same as a good candy bar in China. Therefore, decision making needs to be pushed down as low as possible in the organization, out close to the markets. Otherwise, how can you make good brand decisions? That said, decentralization has its limits. If you are too decentralized, you can become too complicated—you get too much complexity in your production system. The closer we come to the consumer, in branding, pricing, communication, and product adaptation, the more we decentralize. The more we are dealing with production, logistics, and supply-chain management, the more centralized decision making becomes. After all, we want to leverage Nestlé's size, not be hampered by it.[69]

The Nestlé example illustrates a common approach in determining whether or not to centralize or decentralize a value-chain activity. Typically, primary activities that are "downstream" (e.g., marketing and sales, and service), or closer to the customer, tend to require more decentralization in order to adapt to local market conditions. On the other hand, primary activities that are "upstream" (e.g., logistics and operations), or further away from the customer, tend to be centralized. This is because there is less need for adapting these activities to local markets and the firm can benefit from economies of scale. Additionally, many support activities, such as information systems and procurement, tend to be centralized in order to increase the potential for economies of scale.

A central philosophy of the transnational organization is enhanced adaptation to all competitive situations as well as flexibility by capitalizing on communication and knowledge flows throughout the organization.[70] A principal characteristic is the integration of unique contributions of all units into worldwide operations. Thus, a joint innovation by headquarters and by one of the overseas units can lead potentially to the development of relatively standardized and yet flexible products and services that are suitable for multiple markets.

Asea Brown Boveri (ABB) is a firm that successfully follows a transnational strategy. ABB, with its home bases in Sweden and Switzerland, illustrates the trend toward cross-national mergers that lead firms to consider multiple headquarters in the future. It is managed as a flexible network of units, and one of management's main functions is the facilitation of information and knowledge flows between units. ABB's subsidiaries have complete responsibility for product categories on a worldwide basis. Such a transnational strategy enables ABB to benefit from access to new markets and the opportunity to utilize and develop resources wherever they may be located.

Risks and Challenges   As with the other strategies, there are some unique risks and challenges associated with a transnational strategy.

- *The choice of a seemingly optimal location cannot guarantee that the quality and cost of factor inputs (i.e., labor, materials) will be optimal.* Managers must ensure that the relative advantage of a location is actually realized, not squandered because of weaknesses in productivity and the quality of internal operations. Ford Motor Co., for example, has benefited from having some of its manufacturing operations in Mexico. While some have argued that the benefits of lower wage rates will be partly offset by lower productivity, this does not always have to be the case. Since unemployment in Mexico is higher than in the United States, Ford can be more selective in its hiring practices for its Mexican operations. And, given the lower turnover among its Mexican employees, Ford can justify a high level of investment in training and development. Thus, the net result can be not only lower wage rates but also higher productivity than in the United States.

- *Although knowledge transfer can be a key source of competitive advantage, it does not take place "automatically."* For knowledge transfer to take place from one subsidiary to another, it is important for the source of the knowledge, the target units, and the corporate headquarters to recognize the potential value of such unique know-how. Given that there can be significant geographic, linguistic, and cultural distances that typically separate subsidiaries, the potential for knowledge transfer can become very difficult to realize. Firms must create mechanisms to systematically and routinely uncover the opportunities for knowledge transfer.

Exhibit 7.8 summarizes the relative advantages and disadvantages of transnational strategies.

Global or Regional? A Second Look at Globalization

>LO7.6
The difference between regional companies and truly global companies.

Thus far, we have suggested four possible strategies from which a firm must choose once it has decided to compete in the global marketplace. In recent years, many writers have asserted that the process of globalization has caused national borders to become increasingly irrelevant.[71] However, some scholars have recently questioned this perspective, and they have argued that it is unwise for companies to rush into full scale globalization.[72]

Before answering questions about the extent of firms' globalization, let's try to clarify what "globalization" means. Traditionally, a firm's globalization is measured in terms of its foreign sales as a percentage of total sales. However, this measure can be misleading. For example, consider a U.S. firm that has expanded its activities into Canada. Clearly, this initiative is qualitatively different from achieving the same sales volume in a distant country such as China. Similarly, if a Malaysian firm expands into Singapore or a German firm starts selling its products in Austria, this would represent an expansion into a geographically adjacent country. Such nearby countries would often share many common characteristics in terms of language, culture, infrastructure, and customer preferences. In other words, this is more a case of regionalization than globalization.

Extensive analysis of the distribution data of sales across different countries and regions led Alan Rugman and Alain Verbeke to conclude that there is a stronger case to be made in favor of regionalization than globalization. According to their study, a company would have to have at least 20 percent of its sales in each of the three major economic regions—North America, Europe, and Asia—to be considered a global firm. However, they found that only nine of the world's 500 largest firms met this standard! Even when they relaxed the criterion to 20 percent of sales each in at least two of the three regions, the number only increased to 25. *Thus, most companies are regional or, at best, biregional—not global—even today.* Exhibit 7.9 provides a listing of the large firms that met each of these two criteria.

regionalization
increasing international exchange of goods, services, money, people, ideas, and information; and the increasing similarity of culture, laws, rules, and norms within a region such as Europe, North America, or Asia.

Strengths	Limitations
• Ability to attain economies of scale. • Ability to adapt to local markets. • Ability to locate activities in optimal locations. • Ability to increase knowledge flows and learning.	• Unique challenges in determining optimal locations of activities to ensure cost and quality. • Unique managerial challenges in fostering knowledge transfer.

Exhibit 7.8
Strengths and Limitations of Transnational Strategies

Firms with at least 20 percent sales in Asia, Europe, and North America each but with less than 50 percent sales in any one region:

IBM	Nokia	Coca-Cola
Sony	Intel	Flextronics
Philips	Canon	LVMH

Firms with at least 20 percent sales in at least two of the three regions (Asia, Europe, North America) but with less than 50 percent sales in any one region:

BP Amoco	Alstom	Michelin
Toyota	Aventis	Kodak
Nissan	Daigeo	Electrolux
Unilever	Sun Microsystems	BAE
Motorola	Bridgestone	Alcan
GlaxoSmithKline	Roche	L'Oreal
EADS	3M	Lafarge
Bayer	Skanska	
Ericsson	McDonald's	

Firms with at least 50 percent of their sales in one of the three regions—other than their home region:

Daimler Chrysler	Santander	Sodexho Alliance
ING Group	Delhaize "Le Lion"	Manpower
Royal Ahold	Astra Zeneca	Wolseley
Honda	News Corporation	

Sources: Peng, M.W. 2010. *Global Strategy* 2nd ed. Mason, OH: Thomson Southwestern; and Rugman, A.M., & Verbeke, A. 2004. A Perspective on Regional and Global Strategies of Multinational Enterprises. *Journal of International Business Studies*, 35: 3–18.

In a world of instant communication, rapid transportation, and governments that are increasingly willing to open up their markets to trade and investment, why are so few firms "global"? The most obvious answer is that distance still matters. After all, it is easier to do business in a neighboring country than in a far away country, all else being equal. Distance, in the final analysis, may be viewed as a concept with many dimensions, not just a measure of geographical distance. For example, both Canada and Mexico are the same distance from the U.S. However, U.S. companies find it easier to expand operations into Canada than into Mexico. Why? Canada and the U.S. share many commonalities in terms of language, culture, economic development, legal and political systems, and infrastructure development. Thus, if we view distance as having many dimensions, the U.S. and Canada are very close, whereas there is greater distance between the U.S. and Mexico. Similarly, when we look at what we might call the "true" distance between the U.S. and China, the effects of geographic distance are multiplied by distance in terms of culture, language, religion, and legal and political systems between the two countries. On the other hand, although U.S. and Australia are geographically distant, the "true" distance is somewhat less when one considers distance along the other dimensions.

Another reason for regional expansion is the rise of the trading blocs. The European Union originally started in the 1950s as a regional trading bloc. However, recently it has

trading blocs groups of countries agreeing to increase trade between them by lowering trade barries.

achieved a large degree of economic and political integration in terms of common currency and common standards that many thought infeasible, if not impossible, only 20 years ago. The resulting economic benefits have led other regions also to consider similar moves. For example, the North American Free Trade Agreement (NAFTA) has the eventual abolition of all barriers to the free movement of goods and services among Canada, the U.S., and Mexico as its goal. Other regional trading blocks include MERCOSUR (consisting of Argentina, Brazil, Paraguay, and Uruguay) and the Association of Southeast Asian Nations (ASEAN) (consisting of about a dozen Southeast Asian countries).

Regional economic integration has progressed at a faster pace than global economic integration and the trade and investment patterns of the largest companies reflect this reality. After all, regions represent the outcomes of centuries of political and cultural history that results not only in commonalities but also mutual affinity. For example, stretching from Algeria and Morocco in the West to Oman and Yemen in the East, more than 30 countries share the Arabic language and the Muslim religion, making these countries a natural regional bloc. Similarly, the countries of South and Central America share the Spanish language (except Brazil), Catholic religion, and a shared history of Spanish colonialism. No wonder firms find it easier and less risky to expand within their region than to other regions.

Entry Modes of International Expansion

>LO7.7
The four basic types of entry strategies and the relative benefits and risks associated with each of them.

A firm has many options available to it when it decides to expand into international markets. Given the challenges associated with such entry, many firms first start on a small scale and then increase their level of investment and risk as they gain greater experience with the overseas market in question.[73]

Exhibit 7.10 illustrates a wide variety of modes of foreign entry, including exporting, licensing, franchising, joint ventures, strategic alliances, and wholly owned subsidiaries.[74] As the exhibit indicates, the various types of entry form a continuum ranging from exporting (low investment and risk, low control) to a wholly owned subsidiary (high investment and risk, high control).[75]

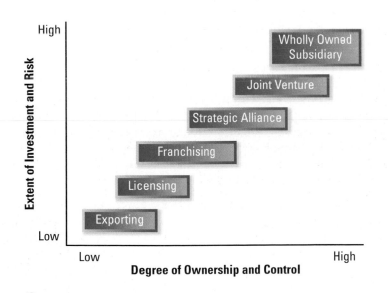

Exhibit 7.10 Entry Modes for International Expansion

There can be frustrations and setbacks as a firm evolves its international entry strategy from exporting to more expensive types, including wholly owned subsidiaries. For example, according to the CEO of a large U.S. specialty chemical company:

> In the end, we always do a better job with our own subsidiaries; sales improve, and we have greater control over the business. But we still need local distributors for entry, and we are still searching for strategies to get us through the transitions without battles over control and performance.[76]

Exporting

exporting
producing goods in one country to sell to residents of another country.

Exporting consists of producing goods in one country to sell in another.[77] This entry strategy enables a firm to invest the least amount of resources in terms of its product, its organization, and its overall corporate strategy. Many host countries dislike this entry strategy because it provides less local employment than other modes of entry.[78]

Multinationals often stumble onto a stepwise strategy for penetrating markets, beginning with the exporting of products. This often results in a series of unplanned actions to increase sales revenues. As the pattern recurs with entries into subsequent markets, this approach, named a "beachhead strategy," often becomes official policy.[79]

Benefits   Such an approach definitely has its advantages. After all, firms start from scratch in sales and distribution when they enter new markets. Because many foreign markets are nationally regulated and dominated by networks of local intermediaries, firms need to partner with local distributors to benefit from their valuable expertise and knowledge of their own markets. Multinationals, after all, recognize that they cannot master local business practices, meet regulatory requirements, hire and manage local personnel, or gain access to potential customers without some form of local partnership.

Multinationals also want to minimize their own risk. They do this by hiring local distributors and investing very little in the undertaking. In essence, the firm gives up control of strategic marketing decisions to the local partners—much more control than they would be willing to give up in their home market.

Risks and Limitations   Exporting is a relatively inexpensive way to enter foreign markets. However, it can still have significant downsides. In a study of 250 instances in which multinational firms used local distributors to implement their exporting entry strategy, the results were dismal. In the vast majority of the cases, the distributors were bought (to increase control) by the multinational firm or fired. In contrast, successful distributors shared two common characteristics:

- They carried product lines that complemented, rather than competed with, the multinational's products.
- They behaved as if they were business partners with the multinationals. They shared market information with the corporations, they initiated projects with distributors in neighboring countries, and they suggested initiatives in their own or nearby markets. Additionally, these distributors took on risk themselves by investing in areas such as training, information systems, and advertising and promotion in order to increase the business of their multinational partners.

The key point is the importance of developing collaborative, win–win relationships.

To ensure more control over operations without incurring significant risks, many firms have used licensing and franchising as a mode of entry. Let's now discuss these and their relative advantages and disadvantages.

Licensing and Franchising

licensing a contractual arrangement in which a company receives a royalty or fee in exchange for the right to use its trademark, patent, trade secret, or other valuable intellectual property.

Licensing and franchising are both forms of contractual arrangements. **Licensing** enables a company to receive a royalty or fee in exchange for the right to use its trademark, patent, trade secret, or other valuable item of intellectual property.[80]

Franchising contracts generally include a broader range of factors in an operation and have a longer time period during which the agreement is in effect. Franchising remains a primary form of American business. According to a recent survey, more than 400 U.S. franchisers have international exposure.[81] This is greater than the combined totals of the next four largest franchiser home countries—France, the United Kingdom, Mexico, and Austria.

Benefits   In international markets, an advantage of licensing is that the firm granting a license incurs little risk, since it does not have to invest any significant resources into the country itself. In turn, the licensee (the firm receiving the license) gains access to the trademark, patent, and so on, and is able to potentially create competitive advantages. In many cases, the country also benefits from the product being manufactured locally. For example, Yoplait yogurt is licensed by General Mills from Sodima, a French cooperative, for sale in the United States. The logos of college and professional athletic teams in the United States are another source of trademarks that generate significant royalty income domestically and internationally.

Franchising has the advantage of limiting the risk exposure that a firm has in overseas markets. At the same time, the firm is able to expand the revenue base of the company.

Risks and Limitations   The licensor gives up control of its product and forgoes potential revenues and profits. Furthermore, the licensee may eventually become so familiar with the patent and trade secrets that it may become a competitor; that is, the licensee may make some modifications to the product and manufacture and sell it independently of the licensor without having to pay a royalty fee. This potential situation is aggravated in countries that have relatively weak laws to protect intellectual property. Additionally, if the licensee selected by the multinational firm turns out to be a poor choice, the brand name and reputation of the product may be tarnished.[82]

With franchising, the multinational firm receives only a portion of the revenues, in the form of franchise fees. Had the firm set up the operation itself (e.g., a restaurant through direct investment), it would have had the entire revenue to itself.

Companies often desire a closer collaboration with other firms in order to increase revenue, reduce costs, and enhance their learning—often through the diffusion of technology. To achieve such objectives, they enter into strategic alliances or joint ventures, two entry modes we will discuss next.

> **franchising** a contractual arrangement in which a company receives a royalty or fee in exchange for the right to use its intellectual property; it usually involves a longer time period than licensing and includes other factors, such as monitoring of operations, training, and advertising.

Strategic Alliances and Joint Ventures

Joint ventures and strategic alliances have recently become increasingly popular.[83] These two forms of partnership differ in that joint ventures entail the creation of a third-party legal entity, whereas strategic alliances do not. In addition, strategic alliances generally focus on initiatives that are smaller in scope than joint ventures.[84]

Benefits   As we discussed in Chapter 6, these strategies have been effective in helping firms increase revenues and reduce costs as well as enhance learning and diffuse technologies.[85] These partnerships enable firms to share the risks as well as the potential revenues and profits. Also, by gaining exposure to new sources of knowledge and technologies, such partnerships can help firms develop core competencies that can lead to competitive advantages in the marketplace.[86] Finally, entering into partnerships with host country firms can provide very useful information on local market tastes, competitive conditions, legal matters, and cultural nuances.[87]

Strategic alliances can be between firms in totally different industries. Strategy Spotlight 7.9 discusses a collaboration between the Italian automaker Lamborghini and Callaway, the U.S. golf equipment manufacturer.

Lamborghini and Callaway Form a High-Tech Alliance

Lamborghini's Sesto Elemento concept car was the hit at the 2010 Paris Auto Show. It would not seem to have much in common with Callaway's new Diablo Octane and Octane Tour drivers. However, both are made using an ingenious new material called Forged Composite that the companies developed together. The material is much stronger than titanium but weighs only one-third as much.

The partnership between Lamborghini and Callaway began in 2008. Researchers from the two companies met at a materials science conference and found that they had much in common. Says Callaway's CEO George Fellows, "The collaboration has been great. The DNA of both companies, pushing for a technological edge in performance-oriented consumer products, is very similar." In short, both firms are engaged in developing lighter and stronger composite materials for their products. And most would agree that the markets that they serve are dissimilar enough to make full cooperation feasible.

Let's look at how each company has benefited from their joint development of Forged Composite.

The weight-savings in Callaway's new drivers, which deploy Forged Composite only in the crowns (the bottom half of the clubheads is still made of titanium), is only 10 grams. Although 10 grams might seem insignificant, such weight loss up top gives designers much more flexibility in how they distribute mass around the bottom. This helps to create more desirable ball flight characteristics and improve forgiveness on off-center hits.

For Lamborghini, Forged Composite enhances a car's power-to-weight ratio and acceleration capability. To illustrate, the Sesto Elemento can accelerate from zero to 60 miles per hour in an astonishing 2.5 seconds. This is almost a full second faster than the Italian automaker's speed champ—the $240,000 Superleggera. The difference is entirely due to weight, in part because both cars use the same 570-horsepower, four-wheel-drivetrain. But by building the chassis almost entirely of Forged Composite, engineers were able to reduce the curb weight by nearly a third—to an anorexic 2,072 pounds. "The power-to-weight ratio is more like a motorcycle's," claims Lamborghini's CEO Stephan Winkelmann. After further testing, he expects Forged Composite to begin working its way into production within a few years.

Source: Newport, J. P. 2010. Drive the Ball Like It's a Lamborghini, Maybe. *Wall Street Journal.* November 13–14: A14; *www.callaway.com*; and Anonymous. 2010. Automobili Lamborghini and Callaway Golf Form Strategic Partnership. *autonewscast.com*, September 30: np.

Risks and Limitations   Managers must be aware of the risks associated with strategic alliances and joint ventures and how they can be minimized.[88] First, there needs to be a clearly defined strategy that is strongly supported by the organizations that are party to the partnership. Otherwise, the firms may work at cross-purposes and not achieve any of their goals. Second, and closely allied to the first issue, there must be a clear understanding of capabilities and resources that will be central to the partnership. Without such clarification, there will be fewer opportunities for learning and developing competencies that could lead to competitive advantages. Third, trust is a vital element. Phasing in the relationship between alliance partners permits them to get to know each other better and develop trust. Without trust, one party may take advantage of the other by, for example, withholding its fair share of resources and gaining access to privileged information through unethical (or illegal) means. Fourth, cultural issues that can potentially lead to conflict and dysfunctional behaviors need to be addressed. An organization's culture is the set of values, beliefs, and attitudes that influence the behavior and goals of its employees.[89] Thus, recognizing cultural differences as well as striving to develop elements of a "common culture" for the partnership is vital. Without a unifying culture, it will become difficult to combine and leverage resources that are increasingly important in knowledge-intensive organizations (discussed in Chapter 4).[90]

Finally, the success of a firm's alliance should not be left to chance.[91] To improve their odds of success, many companies have carefully documented alliance-management knowledge by creating guidelines and manuals to help them manage specific aspects of the entire alliance life cycle (e.g., partner selection and alliance negotiation and contracting). For example, Lotus Corp. (part of IBM) created what it calls its "35 rules of thumb" to manage each phase of an alliance from formation to termination. Hewlett-Packard developed 60 different tools and templates, which it placed in a 300-page manual for guiding decision making. The manual included such tools as a template for making the business case for an alliance, a partner evaluation form, a negotiation template outlining the roles and responsibilities of different departments, a list of the ways to measure alliance performance, and an alliance termination checklist.

When a firm desires the highest level of control, it develops wholly owned subsidiaries. Although wholly owned subsidiaries can generate the greatest returns, they also have the highest levels of investment and risk. We will now discuss them.

Wholly Owned Subsidiaries

A **wholly owned subsidiary** is a business in which a multinational company owns 100 percent of the stock. Two ways a firm can establish a wholly owned subsidiary are to (1) acquire an existing company in the home country or (2) develop a totally new operation (often referred to as a "greenfield venture").

> **wholly owned subsidiary** a business in which a multinational company owns 100 percent of the stock.

Benefits Establishing a wholly owned subsidiary is the most expensive and risky of the various entry modes. However, it can also yield the highest returns. In addition, it provides the multinational company with the greatest degree of control of all activities, including manufacturing, marketing, distribution, and technology development.[92]

Wholly owned subsidiaries are most appropriate where a firm already has the appropriate knowledge and capabilities that it can leverage rather easily through multiple locations. Examples range from restaurants to semiconductor manufacturers. To lower costs, for example, Intel Corporation builds semiconductor plants throughout the world—all of which use virtually the same blueprint. Knowledge can be further leveraged by hiring managers and professionals from the firm's home country, often through hiring talent from competitors.

Risks and Limitations As noted, wholly owned subsidiaries are typically the most expensive and risky entry mode. With franchising, joint ventures, or strategic alliances, the risk is shared with the firm's partners. With wholly owned subsidiaries, the entire risk is assumed by the parent company. The risks associated with doing business in a new country (e.g., political, cultural, and legal) can be lessened by hiring local talent.

For example, Wendy's avoided committing two blunders in Germany by hiring locals to its advertising staff.[93] In one case, the firm wanted to promote its "old-fashioned" qualities. However, a literal translation would have resulted in the company promoting itself as "outdated." In another situation, Wendy's wanted to emphasize that its hamburgers could be prepared 256 ways. The problem? The German word that Wendy's wanted to use for "ways" usually meant "highways" or "roads." Although such errors may sometimes be entertaining to the public, it is certainly preferable to catch these mistakes before they confuse the consumer or embarrass the company.

We have addressed entry strategies as a progression from exporting through the creation of wholly owned subsidiaries. However, we must point out that many firms do not follow such an evolutionary approach. For example, because of political and regulatory reasons, Pepsi entered India through a joint venture with two Indian firms in 1998. As discussed in Strategy Spotlight 7.10, this provided Pepsi with a first-mover advantage within the Indian market, where it remains well ahead of its archrival, Coca-Cola.

Pepsi's First-Mover Advantage in India Has Paid Off

Pepsi (pronounced "Pay-psee") became a common synonym for cola in India's most widely spoken language after having the market to itself in the early 1990s. PepsiCo's linguistic advantage translates into higher sales for its namesake product. Although Atlanta-based Coke has larger total beverage sales in India because it owns several non-cola drink brands, Pepsi's 4.5 percent of the soft drink market outshines Coke's 2.6 percent, according to Euromonitor. That's a notable exception to much of the rest of the world, where Coke's cola soundly beats its main rival.

What explains Pepsi's success in India? Coke pulled out of the market in 1977 after new government regulations forced it to partner with an Indian company and share the drink's secret formula. In contrast, Pepsi formed a joint venture in 1988 with two Indian companies and introduced products under the Lehar brand. (Lehar Pepsi

Source: Srivastava, M. 2010. For India's Consumers, Pepsi Is the Real Thing. *Bloomberg Businessweek.* September 20–26: 26–27; Bhushan, R. 2010. Pepsi India Touches Eco Watershed, First Unit to Achieve Positive Water Balance. *www.indiatimes.com.* May 27: np; and *www.pepsicoindia.*

was introduced in 1990.) Coke then re-entered the market in 1993 after Indian regulations were changed to permit foreign brands to operate without Indian partners.

Coke's time out of India cost it dearly. "Pepsi got here sooner, and got to India just as it was starting to engage with the West and with Western products," said Lalita Desai, a linguist at Jadavpur University who studies how English words enter Indian languages. "And with no real international competition, 'Pepsi' became the catch-all for anything that was bottled, fizzy, and from abroad."

PepsiCo has also been very successful in promoting water conservation in India. Its Indian operation became the first of its global units (and probably the only one in the beverage industry) to conserve and replenish more water that it consumed in 2009. Its rival, Coca Cola, on the other hand, is facing a serious situation in India as it has been fined Rs 216 crore ($4.7 million) as compensation for groundwater pollution and depletion.

Today, PepsiCo is the fourth largest consumer products company in India. The firm also has invested more than $1 billion in India, created direct and indirect employment to 150,000 people in the country, and has 13 company-owned bottling plants, according to its website.

Reflecting on Career Implications . . .

- *International Strategy:* Be aware of your organization's international strategy. What percentage of the total firm activity is international? What skills are needed to enhance your company's international efforts? How can you get more involved in your organization's international strategy? For your career, what conditions in your home country might cause you to seek careers abroad?
- *Outsourcing and Offshoring:* What activities in your organization can/should be outsourced or offshored? Be aware that you are competing in the global marketplace for employment and professional advancement. Continually take inventory of your talents, skills, and competencies.
- *International Career Opportunities:* Work assignments in other countries can often provide a career boost. Be proactive in pursuing promising career opportunities in other countries. Anticipate how such opportunities will advance your short- and long-term career aspirations.
- *Management Risks:* Develop cultural sensitivity. This applies, of course, to individuals from different cultures in your home-based organization as well as in your overseas experience.

Summary

We live in a highly interconnected global community where many of the best opportunities for growth and profitability lie beyond the boundaries of a company's home country. Along with the opportunities, of course, there are many risks associated with diversification into global markets.

The first section of the chapter addressed the factors that determine a nation's competitiveness in a particular industry. The framework was developed by Professor Michael Porter of Harvard University and was based on a four-year study that explored the competitive success of 10 leading trading nations. The four factors, collectively termed the "diamond of national advantage," were factor conditions, demand characteristics, related and supporting industries, and firm strategy, structure, and rivalry.

The discussion of Porter's "diamond" helped, in essence, to set the broader context for exploring competitive advantage at the firm level. In the second section, we discussed the primary motivations and the potential risks associated with international expansion. The primary motivations included increasing the size of the potential market for the firm's products and services, achieving economies of scale, extending the life cycle of the firm's products, and optimizing the location for every activity in the value chain. On the other hand, the key risks included political and economic risks, currency risks, and management risks. Management risks are the challenges associated with responding to the inevitable differences that exist across countries such as customs, culture, language, customer preferences, and distribution systems. We also addressed some of the managerial challenges and opportunities associated with offshoring and outsourcing.

Next, we addressed how firms can go about attaining competitive advantage in global markets. We began by discussing the two opposing forces—cost reduction and adaptation to local markets—that managers must contend with when entering global markets. The relative importance of these two factors plays a major part in determining which of the four basic types of strategies to select: international, global, multidomestic, or transnational. The chapter covered the benefits and risks associated with each type of strategy. We also presented a recent perspective by Alan Rugman who argues that despite all the talk of globalization, most of the large multinationals are regional or at best biregional (in terms of geographical diversification of sales) rather than global.

The final section discussed the four types of entry strategies that managers may undertake when entering international markets. The key trade-off in each of these strategies is the level of investment or risk versus the level of control. In order of their progressively greater investment/risk and

control, the strategies range from exporting to licensing and franchising, to strategic alliances and joint ventures, to wholly owned subsidiaries. The relative benefits and risks associated with each of these strategies were addressed.

Summary Review Questions

1. What are some of the advantages and disadvantages associated with a firm's expansion into international markets?

2. What are the four factors described in Porter's diamond of national advantage? How do the four factors explain why some industries in a given country are more successful than others?

3. Explain the two opposing forces—cost reduction and adaptation to local markets—that firms must deal with when they go global.

4. There are four basic strategies—international, global, multidomestic, and transnational. What are the advantages and disadvantages associated with each?

5. What is the basis of Alan Rugman's argument that most multinationals are still more regional than global? What factors inhibit firms from becoming truly global?

6. Describe the basic entry strategies that firms have available when they enter international markets. What are the relative advantages and disadvantages of each?

Key Terms

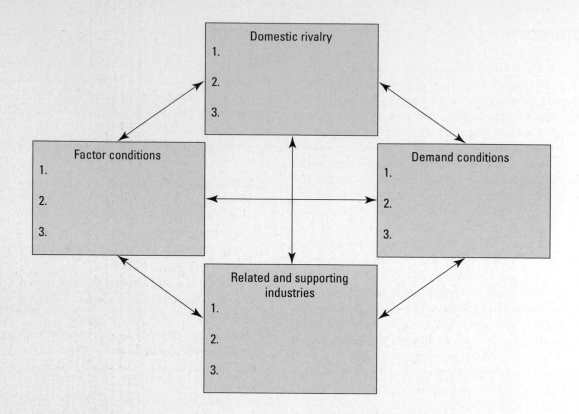

Domestic rivalry

1.

2.

3.

Factor conditions

1.

2.

3.

Demand conditions

1.

2.

3.

Related and supporting industries

1.

2.

3.

Experiential Exercise

The United States is considered a world leader in the motion picture industry. Using Porter's diamond framework for national competitiveness, explain the success of this industry.

Application Questions & Exercises

1. Data on the "competitiveness of nations" can be found at *www.imd.ch/wcy/ranking/*. This website provides a ranking on a 331 criteria for 59 countries. How might Porter's diamond of national advantage help to explain the rankings for some of these countries for certain industries that interest you?

2. The Internet has lowered the entry barriers for smaller firms that wish to diversify into international markets. Why is this so? Provide an example.

3. Many firms fail when they enter into strategic alliances with firms that link up with companies based in other countries. What are some reasons for this failure? Provide an example.

4. Many large U.S.–based management consulting companies such as McKinsey and Company and the BCG Group have been very successful in the international marketplace. How can Porter's diamond explain their success?

Ethics Questions

1. Over the past few decades, many American firms have relocated most or all of their operations from the United States to countries such as Mexico and China that pay lower wages. What are some of the ethical issues that such actions may raise?

2. Business practices and customs vary throughout the world. What are some of the ethical issues concerning payments that must be made in a foreign country to obtain business opportunities?

References

1. Anonymous. 2010. Exit Carrefour. *The Economist.* September 23: 77; Thomas, D. & Fuse, T. 2010. Retailers jump in for Carrefour SE Asia assets. *www.reuters.com.* September 1: np; and Chan, C. 2010. Carrefour said to list Tesco, Casino as potential unit buyers. *www.businessweek.com.* September 9: np.

2. For a recent discussion on globalization by one of international business's most respected authors, read Ohmae, K. 2005. *The next global stage: Challenges and opportunities in our borderless world.* Philadelphia: Wharton School Publishing.

3. Our discussion of globalization draws upon Engardio, P. & Belton, C. 2000. Global capitalism: Can it be made to work better? *BusinessWeek,* November 6: 72–98.

4. Sellers, P. 2005. Blowing in the wind. *Fortune,* July 25: 63.

5. An interesting and balanced discussion on the merits of multinationals to the U.S. economy is found in: Mandel, M. 2008. Multinationals: Are they good for America? *BusinessWeek,* March 10: 41–64.

6. Engardio & Belton, op. cit.

7. For insightful perspectives on strategy in emerging economies, refer to the article entitled: Strategy research in emerging economies: Challenging the conventional wisdom in the January 2005 issue of *Journal of Management Studies,* 42(1).

8. Black, J. S. & Morrison, A. J. 2010. A cautionary tale for emerging market giants. *Harvard Business Review,* 88(9): 99–105.

9. The above discussion draws on Clifford, M. L., Engardio, P., Malkin, E., Roberts, D., & Echikson, W. 2000. Up the ladder. *BusinessWeek,* November 6: 78–84.

10. A recent discussion of the "bottom of the pyramid" is: Akula, V. 2008. Business basics at the bottom of the pyramid. *Harvard Business Review,* 86(6): 53–59.

11. Some insights into how winners are evolving in emerging markets are addressed in: Ghemawat, P. & Hout, T. 2008. Tomorrow's global giants: Not the usual suspects. *Harvard Business Review,* 66(11): 80–88.

12. For another interesting discussion on a country perspective, refer to Makino, S. 1999. MITI Minister Kaora Yosano on reviving Japan's competitive advantages. *Academy of Management Executive,* 13(4): 8–28.

13. The following discussion draws heavily upon Porter, M. E. 1990. The competitive advantage of nations. *Harvard Business Review,* March–April: 73–93.

14. Landes, D. S. 1998. *The wealth and poverty of nations.* New York: W. W. Norton.

15. A recent study that investigates the relationship between international diversification and firm performance is Lu, J. W. & Beamish, P. W. 2004. International diversification and firm performance: The s-curve hypothesis. *Academy of Management Journal,* 47(4): 598–609.

16. Part of our discussion of the motivations and risks of international expansion draws upon Gregg, F. M. 1999. International strategy. In Helms, M. M. (Ed.). *Encyclopedia of management:* 434–438. Detroit: Gale Group.

17. These two examples are discussed, respectively, in Dawar, N. & Frost, T. 1999. Competing with giants. Survival strategies for local companies in emerging markets. *Harvard Business Review,* 77(2): 119–129; and Prahalad, C. K. & Lieberthal, K. 1998. The end of corporate imperialism. *Harvard Business Review,* 76(4): 68–79.

18. Meredith, R. 2004. Middle kingdom, middle class. *Forbes,* November 15: 188–192; and Anonymous. 2004. Middle class becomes rising power in China. *www.Chinadaily.com.* November 6.

19. Eyring, M. J., Johnson, M. W. & Nair, H. 2011. New business models in emerging markets. *Harvard Business Review,* 89 (1/2): 88–98.

20. Cieply, M. & Barnes, B. 2010. After rants, skepticism over Gibson bankability grows in non-U.S. markets. *International Herald Tribune,* July 23: 1.

21. This discussion draws upon Gupta, A. K. & Govindarajan, V. 2001. Converting global presence into global competitive advantage. *Academy of Management Executive,* 15(2): 45–56.

22. Stross, R. E. 1997. Mr. Gates builds his brain trust. *Fortune,* December 8: 84–98.

23. For a good summary of the benefits and risks of international expansion, refer to Bartlett, C. A. & Ghoshal, S. 1987. Managing across borders: New strategic responses. *Sloan Management Review,* 28(5): 45–53; and Brown, R. H. 1994. *Competing to win in a global economy.* Washington, DC: U.S. Department of Commerce.

24. For an interesting insight into rivalry in global markets, refer to MacMillan, I. C., van Putten, A. B., & McGrath, R. G. 2003. Global gamesmanship. *Harvard Business Review,* 81(5): 62–73.

25. It is important for firms to spread their foreign operations and outsourcing relationships with a broad, well-balanced mix of regions and countries to reduce risk and increase potential reward. For example, refer to Vestring, T., Rouse, T., & Reinert, U. 2005. Hedge your offshoring bets. *MIT Sloan Management Review,* 46(3): 27–29.

26. An interesting discussion of risks faced by Lukoil, Russia's largest oil firm is in: Gimbel, B. 2009. Russia's king of crude. *Fortune,* February 2: 88–92.

27. Some insights on how Africa has improved as a potential source of investment is in: Collier, P. & Warnholz, J-L. 2009. Now's the time to invest in Africa. *Harvard Business Review,* 87(2): 23.

28. For a discussion of some of the challenges associated with government corruption regarding entry strategies in foreign markets, read Rodriguez, P., Uhlenbruck, K., & Eden, L. 2005. Government corruption and entry strategies of multinationals. *Academy of Management Review,* 30(2): 383–396.

29. For a discussion of the political risks in China for United States companies,

refer to Garten, J. E. 1998. Opening the doors for business in China. *Harvard Business Review,* 76(3): 167–175.

30. Shari, M. 2001. Is a holy war brewing in Indonesia? *BusinessWeek,* October 15: 62.

31. Insights on how forensic economics can be used to investigate crimes and wrongdoing are in: Fisman, R. 2009. The rise of forensic economics. *Harvard Business Review,* 87(2): 26.

32. Anonymous. 2010. Libya: Why it is still stuck. *The Economist,* April 10: 49.

33. For an interesting perspective on the relationship between diversification and the development of a nation's institutional environment, read Chakrabarti, A., Singh, K., & Mahmood, I. 2007. Diversification and performance: Evidence from East Asian firms. *Strategic Management Journal,* 28(2): 101–120.

34. A study looking into corruption and foreign direct investment is: Brouthers, L. E., Gao, Y., & McNicol, J. P. 2008. *Strategic Management Journal,* 29(6): 673–680.

35. Gikkas, N. S. 1996. International licensing of intellectual property: The promise and the peril. *Journal of Technology Law & Policy,* 1(1): 1–26.

36. Insights into bribery in the international context are addressed in: Martin, K. D., Cullen, J. B., Johnson, J. L., & Parboteeah, P. 2008. Deciding to bribe: A cross-level analysis of firm and home country influences on bribery activity. *Academy of Management Journal,* 50(6): 1401–1422.

37. Sandler, N. 2008. Israel: Attack of the super-shekel. *BusinessWeek,* February 25: 38.

38. For an excellent theoretical discussion of how cultural factors can affect knowledge transfer across national boundaries, refer to Bhagat, R. S., Kedia, B. L., Harveston, P. D., & Triandis, H. C. 2002. Cultural variations in the cross-border transfer of organizational knowledge: An integrative framework. *Academy of Management Review,* 27(2): 204–221.

39. An interesting discussion on how local companies compete effectively with large multinationals is in: Bhatacharya, A. K. & Michael, D. C.

2008. *Harvard Business Review,* 66(3): 84–95.

40. To gain insights on the role of national and regional cultures on knowledge management models and frameworks, read Pauleen, D. J. & Murphy, P. 2005. In praise of cultural bias. *MIT Sloan Management Review,* 46(2): 21–22.

41. Berkowitz, E. N. 2000. *Marketing* (6th ed.). New York: McGraw-Hill.

42. Harvey, M. & Buckley, M. R. 2002. Assessing the "conventional wisdoms" of management for the 21st century organization. *Organization Dynamics,* 30 (4): 368–378.

43. World Trade Organization. *Annual Report 1998.* Geneva: World Trade Organization.

44. Lei, D. 2005. Outsourcing. In Hitt, M. A. & Ireland, R. D. (Eds.). *The Blackwell encyclopedia of management.* Entrepreneurship: 196–199. Malden, MA: Blackwell.

45. Future trends in offshoring are addressed in: Manning, S., Massini, S., & Lewin, A. Y. 2008. A dynamic perspective on next-generation offshoring: The global sourcing of science and engineering talent. *Academy of Management Perspectives,* 22(3): 35–54.

46. An interesting perspective on the controversial issue regarding the offshoring of airplane maintenance is in: Smith, G. & Bachman, J. 2008. Flying in for a tune-up overseas. *Business Week.* April 21: 26–27.

47. Dolan, K.A. 2006. Offshoring the offshorers. *Forbes.* April 17: 74–78.

48. The discussion above draws from Colvin, J. 2004. Think your job can't be sent to India? Just watch. *Fortune,* December 13: 80; Schwartz, N. D. 2004. Down and out in white collar America. *Fortune,* June 23: 321–325; Hagel, J. 2004. Outsourcing is not just about cost cutting. *The Wall Street Journal,* March 18: A3.

49. Insightful perspectives on the outsourcing of decision making are addressed in: Davenport, T. H. & Iyer, B. 2009. Should you outsource your brain? *Harvard Business Review.* 87 (2): 38. (7)

50. Levitt, T. 1983. The globalization of markets. *Harvard Business Review,* 61(3): 92–102.

51. Our discussion of these assumptions draws upon Douglas, S. P. & Wind, Y. 1987. The myth of globalization. *Columbia Journal of World Business,* Winter: 19–29.

52. Ghoshal, S. 1987. Global strategy: An organizing framework. *Strategic Management Journal,* 8: 425–440.

53. Huber, P. 2009. Who pays for a cancer drug? *Forbes,* January 12: 72.

54. For insights on global branding, refer to Aaker, D. A. & Joachimsthaler, E. 1999. The lure of global branding. *Harvard Business Review,* 77(6): 137–146.

55. For an interesting perspective on how small firms can compete in their home markets, refer to Dawar & Frost, op. cit.: 119–129.

56. Hout, T., Porter, M. E., & Rudden, E. 1982. How global companies win out. *Harvard Business Review,* 60(5): 98–107.

57. Fryer, B. 2001. Tom Siebel of Siebel Systems: High tech the old-fashioned way. *Harvard Business Review,* 79(3): 118–130.

58. The risks that are discussed for the global, multidomestic, and transnational strategies draw upon Gupta & Govindarajan, op. cit.

59. A discussion on how McDonald's adapts its products to overseas markets is in: Gumbel, P. 2008. Big Mac's local flavor. *Fortune,* May 5: 115–121.

60. Sigiura, H. 1990. How Honda localizes its global strategy. *Sloan Management Review,* 31: 77–82.

61. Prahalad & Lieberthal, op. cit.: 68–79. Their article also discusses how firms may have to reconsider their brand management, costs of market building, product design, and approaches to capital efficiency when entering foreign markets.

62. Hofstede, G. 1980. *Culture's consequences: International differences in work-related values.* Beverly Hills, CA: Sage; Hofstede, G. 1993. Cultural constraints in management theories. *Academy of Management Executive,* 7(1): 81–94; Kogut, B. & Singh, H. 1988. The effect of national culture on the choice of entry mode. *Journal of International Business Studies,* 19: 411–432; and

Usinier, J. C. 1996. *Marketing across cultures.* London: Prentice Hall.

63. McCune, J. C. 1999. Exporting corporate culture. *Management Review,* December: 53–56.

64. Ghemawat, P. 2007. *Redefining global strategy.* Boston: Harvard School Press.

65. Prahalad, C. K. & Doz, Y. L. 1987. *The multinational mission: Balancing local demands and global vision.* New York: Free Press.

66. For an insightful discussion on knowledge flows in multinational corporations, refer to: Yang, Q., Mudambi, R., & Meyer, K. E. 2008. Conventional and reverse knowledge flows in multinational corporations. *Journal of Management,* 34(5): 882–902.

67. Kidd, J. B. & Teramoto, Y. 1995. The learning organization: The case of Japanese RHQs in Europe. *Management International Review,* 35 (Special Issue): 39–56.

68. Gupta, A. K. & Govindarajan, V. 2000. Knowledge flows within multinational corporations. *Strategic Management Journal,* 21(4): 473–496.

69. Wetlaufer, S. 2001. The business case against revolution: An interview with Nestlé's Peter Brabeck. *Harvard Business Review,* 79(2): 112–121.

70. Nobel, R. & Birkinshaw, J. 1998. Innovation in multinational corporations: Control and communication patterns in international R&D operations. *Strategic Management Journal,* 19(5): 461–478.

71. Chan, C. M., Makino, S., & Isobe, T. 2010. Does subnational region matter? Foreign affiliate performance in the United States and China. *Strategic Management Journal,* 31 (11): 1226–1243.

72. This section draws upon Ghemawat, P. 2005. Regional strategies for global leadership. *Harvard Business Review.* 84(12): 98–108; Ghemawat, P. 2006. Apocalypse now? *Harvard Business Review.* 84(12): 32; Ghemawat, P. 2001. Distance still matters: The hard reality of global expansion. *Harvard Business Review,* 79(8): 137–147; Peng, M.W. 2006. *Global strategy:* 387. Mason, OH: Thomson Southwestern; and Rugman, A. M. & Verbeke, A. 2004. A perspective on regional and global strategies of multinational enterprises. *Journal of International Business Studies.* 35: 3–18.

73. For a rigorous analysis of performance implications of entry strategies, refer to Zahra, S. A., Ireland, R. D., & Hitt, M. A. 2000. International expansion by new venture firms: International diversity, modes of entry, technological learning, and performance. *Academy of Management Journal,* 43(6): 925–950.

74. Li, J. T. 1995. Foreign entry and survival: The effects of strategic choices on performance in international markets. *Strategic Management Journal,* 16: 333–351.

75. For a discussion of how home-country environments can affect diversification strategies, refer to Wan, W. P. & Hoskisson, R. E. 2003. Home country environments, corporate diversification strategies, and firm performance. *Academy of Management Journal,* 46(1): 27–45.

76. Arnold, D. 2000. Seven rules of international distribution. *Harvard Business Review,* 78(6): 131–137.

77. Sharma, A. 1998. Mode of entry and ex-post performance. *Strategic Management Journal,* 19(9): 879–900.

78. This section draws upon Arnold, op. cit.: 131–137; and Berkowitz, op. cit.

79. Salomon, R. & Jin, B. 2010. Do leading or lagging firms learn more from exporting? *Strategic Management Journal,* 31(6): 1088–1113.

80. Kline, D. 2003. Strategic licensing. *MIT Sloan Management Review.* 44(3): 89–93.

81. Martin, J. 1999. Franchising in the Middle East. *Management Review.* June: 38–42.

82. Arnold, op. cit.; and Berkowitz, op. cit.

83. An in-depth case study of alliance dynamics is found in: Faems, D., Janssens, M., Madhok, A., & Van Looy, B. 2008. Toward an integrative perspective on alliance governance: Connecting contract design, trust dynamics, and contract application. *Academy of Management Journal,* 51(6): 1053–1078.

84. Knowledge transfer in international joint ventures is addressed in: Inkpen, A. 2008. Knowledge transfer and international joint ventures. *Strategic Management Journal,* 29(4): 447–453.

85. Wen, S. H. & Chuang, C.-M. 2010. To teach or to compete? A strategic dilemma of knowledge owners in international alliances. *Asia Pacific Journal of Management,* 27(4): 697–726.

86. Manufacturer–supplier relationships can be very effective in global industries such as automobile manufacturing. Refer to Kotabe, M., Martin, X., & Domoto, H. 2003. Gaining from vertical partnerships: Knowledge transfer, relationship duration, and supplier performance improvement in the U.S. and Japanese automotive industries. *Strategic Management Journal,* 24(4): 293–316.

87. For a good discussion, refer to Merchant, H. & Schendel, D. 2000. How do international joint ventures create shareholder value? *Strategic Management Journal,* 21(7): 723–738.

88. This discussion draws upon Walters, B. A., Peters, S., & Dess, G. G. 1994. Strategic alliances and joint ventures: Making them work. *Business Horizons,* 37(4): 5–11.

89. Some insights on partnering in the global area are discussed in: MacCormack, A. & Forbath, T. 2008. *Harvard Business Review,* 66(1): 24, 26.

90. For a rigorous discussion of the importance of information access in international joint ventures, refer to Reuer, J. J. & Koza, M. P. 2000. Asymmetric information and joint venture performance: Theory and evidence for domestic and international joint ventures. *Strategic Management Journal,* 21(1): 81–88.

91. Dyer, J. H., Kale, P., & Singh, H. 2001. How to make strategic alliances work. *MIT Sloan Management Review,* 42(4): 37–43.

92. For a discussion of some of the challenges in managing subsidiaries, refer to O'Donnell, S. W. 2000. Managing foreign subsidiaries: Agents of headquarters, or an independent network? *Strategic Management Journal,* 21(5): 525–548.

93. Ricks, D. 2006. *Blunders in international business* (4th ed.). Malden, MA: Blackwell Publishing.

chapter EIGHT

Entrepreneurial Strategy and Competitive Dynamics

After reading this chapter, you should have a good understanding of:

LO8.1 The role of new ventures and small businesses in the U.S. economy.

LO8.2 The role of opportunities, resources, and entrepreneurs in successfully pursuing new ventures.

LO8.3 Three types of entry strategies—pioneering, imitative, and adaptive—commonly used to launch a new venture.

LO8.4 How the generic strategies of overall cost leadership, differentiation, and focus are used by new ventures and small businesses.

LO8.5 How competitive actions, such as the entry of new competitors into a marketplace, may launch a cycle of actions and reactions among close competitors.

LO8.6 The components of competitive dynamics analysis—new competitive action, threat analysis, motivation and capability to respond, types of competitive actions, and likelihood of competitive reaction.

LEARNING OBJECTIVES

New technologies, shifting social and demographic trends, and sudden changes in the business environment create opportunities for entrepreneurship. New ventures, which often emerge under such conditions, face unique strategic challenges if they are going to survive and grow. Young and small businesses, which are a major engine of growth in the U.S. economy because of their role in job creation and innovation, must rely on sound strategic principles to be successful.

This chapter addresses how new ventures and entrepreneurial firms can achieve competitive advantages. It also examines how entrepreneurial activity influences a firm's strategic priorities and intensifies the rivalry among an industry's close competitors.

In the first section, we discuss the role of opportunity recognition in the process of new venture creation. Three factors that are important in determining whether a value-creating opportunity should be pursued are highlighted—the nature of the opportunity, the resources available to undertake it, and the characteristics of the entrepreneur(s) pursuing it.

The second section addresses three different types of new entry strategies—pioneering, imitative, and adaptive. Then, the generic strategies (discussed in Chapter 5) as well as combination strategies are addressed in terms of how they apply to new ventures and entrepreneurial firms. Additionally, some of the pitfalls associated with each of these strategic approaches are presented.

In section three, we explain how new entrants and other competitors often set off a series of actions and reactions that affect the competitive dynamics of an industry. In determining how to react to a competitive action, firms must analyze whether they are seriously threatened by the action, how important it is for them to respond, and what resources they can muster to mount a response. They must also determine what type of action is appropriate—strategic or tactical—and whether their close competitors are likely to counterattack. Taken together, these actions often have a strong impact on the strategic choices and overall profitability of an industry ●.

Learning from Mistakes

The wildly successful eBay concept allowed individuals to sell to the world.[1] Not surprisingly, the business of intermediating such sales quickly took off. It was even portrayed in the movie *The 40-Year-Old Virgin.* iSold It was one of the champions of this model and quickly gained popularity, as it made eBay access easier for people who did not want the hassle of researching prices, posting online, and collecting money. The company began in December 2003 by helping customers sell their unwanted stuff on eBay—basically acting as an intermediary and charging a percentage of the sales price. More recently, however, the company stopped selling franchises and is retracting many of the franchises already sold, because of financial losses. How did the company go from a top franchise pick by *Entrepreneur* magazine in 2006 to the firm in full retreat that we see today?

In 2005 the idea of a store helping customers sell their unwanted things on eBay was very popular, resulting in 7,000 of these types of stores opening around the United States. In June 2006, *Entrepreneur* magazine named iSold It "Hotter than hot" and ranked the firm 30th among other fastest-growing franchises. What is more, in 2007 iSold It earned the top spot in *Entrepreneur*'s new franchise rankings, listing a start-up cost of $105,000 per location! At the time, it seemed that selling other people's stuff online and collecting a fee had endless potential.

The firm researched the potential sale price, wrote the product description, posted the ads on eBay, monitored the auction, responded to any e-mails, collected the proceeds from the sale, and finally mailed the purchaser the product. The firm did not guarantee that the product would sell and had selection standards about what they tried to sell—they have to put in the same amount of effort whether the product sells for $75 or $1,000. If the advertised product did not sell, the firm still paid eBay's listing fee.

iSold It's founders realized that the firm was growing at a rate above their capabilities, so they stepped aside and hired outside help. In 2004 Ken Sully, a former vice president of Mail Boxes Etc., came on board as the new CEO. Ken standardized the firm's operations and made it possible for a store to be installed and set up in 48 hours. iSold It's founders saw no end in sight for the firm's growth, stating in 2006, "We've created this brick-and-mortar interface to the Internet" and stating that their firm was in a position to capitalize on the growth of Internet trade. In fact, by June 2006 the firm had already sold 800 franchises.

Although iSold It knew that people could sell their own merchandise online, they overestimated their willingness to pay an intermediary 20–30 percent of the sales price for the convenience of listing their products and collecting the money. *Entrepreneur* magazine in January 2010 called the eBay drop-off store concept "ridiculous," as customers quickly learned how to sell their stuff by themselves. With low barriers to entry in this industry, many copycat firms quickly entered the market. In early 2007, iSold It stopped selling new franchises and is quickly losing the ones they sold.

By offering a service tied to the rapid growth of eBay, iSold It seemed to have identified an attractive opportunity. But the start-up's failure shows what can go wrong when—even though a good opportunity, sufficient resources, and an experienced entrepreneurial team are brought together—a business opportunity disappears as quickly as it appeared.

The iSold It case illustrates how important it is for new entrepreneurial entrants—whether they are start-ups or incumbents—to think and act strategically. Even with a strong resource base and good track record, entrepreneurs are unlikely to succeed if their business ideas are easily imitated or substituted for.

In this chapter we address entrepreneurial strategies. The previous three chapters have focused primarily on the business-level, corporate-level, and international strategies of incumbent firms. Here we ask: What about the strategies of those entering into a market or industry for the first time? Whether it's a fast-growing start-up such as iSold It or an existing company seeking growth opportunities, new entrants need effective strategies.

Companies wishing to launch new ventures must also be aware that, consistent with the five forces model in Chapter 2, new entrants are a threat to existing firms in an industry. Entry into a new market arena is intensely competitive from the perspective of incumbents in that arena. Therefore, new entrants can nearly always expect a competitive response from other companies in the industry it is entering. Knowledge of the competitive dynamics that are at work in the business environment is an aspect of entrepreneurial new entry that will be addressed later in this chapter.

Before moving on, it is important to highlight the role that entrepreneurial start-ups and small business play in entrepreneurial value creation. Young and small firms are responsible for more innovations and more new job creation than any other type of business.[2] Strategy Spotlight 8.1 addresses some of the reasons why small business and entrepreneurship are viewed favorably in the United States.

>LO8.1
The role of new ventures and small businesses in the U.S. economy.

Recognizing Entrepreneurial Opportunities

Defined broadly, **entrepreneurship** refers to new value creation. Even though entrepreneurial activity is usually associated with start-up companies, new value can be created in many different contexts including:

entrepreneurship
the creation of new value by an existing organization or new venture that involves the assumption of risk.

- Start-up ventures
- Major corporations
- Family-owned businesses
- Non profit organizations
- Established institutions

For an entrepreneurial venture to create new value, three factors must be present—an entrepreneurial opportunity, the resources to pursue the opportunity, and an entrepreneur or entrepreneurial team willing and able to undertake the opportunity.[3] The entrepreneurial strategy that an organization uses will depend on these three factors. Thus, beyond merely identifying a venture concept, the opportunity recognition process also involves organizing the key people and resources that are needed to go forward. Exhibit 8.3 depicts the three factors that are needed to successfully proceed—opportunity, resources, and entrepreneur(s). In the sections that follow, we address each of these factors.

>LO8.2
The role of opportunities, resources, and entrepreneurs in successfully pursuing new ventures.

Entrepreneurial Opportunities

The starting point for any new venture is the presence of an entrepreneurial opportunity. Where do opportunities come from? For new business start-ups, opportunities come from many sources—current or past work experiences, hobbies that grow into businesses or lead to inventions, suggestions by friends or family, or a chance event that makes an entrepreneur aware of an unmet need. For established firms, new business opportunities come from the needs of existing customers, suggestions by suppliers, or technological developments that lead to new advances.[4] For all firms, there is a major, overarching factor behind all viable opportunities that emerge in the business landscape: change. Change creates opportunities. Entrepreneurial firms make the most of changes brought about by new technology, sociocultural trends, and shifts in consumer demand.

How do changes in the external environment lead to new business creation? They spark creative new ideas and innovation. Businesspeople often have ideas for entrepreneurial ventures. However, not all such ideas are good ideas—that is, viable business opportunities. To determine which ideas are strong enough to become new ventures, entrepreneurs

strategy spotlight

8.1

The Contribution of Small Businesses to the U.S. Economy

In the late 1970s, MIT professor David Birch launched a study to explore the sources of business growth. "I wasn't really looking for anything in particular," says Birch. But the findings surprised him: Small businesses create the most jobs. Since then, Birch and others have shown that it's not just big companies that power the economy. Small

business and entrepreneurship have become a major component of new job creation.

Here are the facts:

- In the United States, there are approximately 5.9 million companies with fewer than 100 employees. Another 88,586 companies have 100 to 500 employees. In addition, approximately 17.0 million individuals are nonemployer sole proprietors.

- Small businesses create the majority of new jobs. According to recent data, small business created 65 percent of U.S. net new jobs in a recent 17-year period. A small percentage of the fastest growing entrepreneurial firms (5 to 15 percent) account for a majority of the new jobs created.

Sources: Small Business Administration. 2009. *The Small Business Economy.* Washington, DC: U.S. Government Printing Office; Small Business Administration. 2010. Small Business by the Numbers. *SBA Office of Advocacy,* June, *www.sba.gov/advo/; Inc.* 2001. Small Business 2001: Where We Are Now? May 29: 18–19; Minniti, M., & Bygrave, W. D. 2004. *Global Entrepreneurship Monitor—National Entrepreneurship Assessment: United States of America 2004, Executive Report.* Kansas City, MO: Kauffman Center for Entrepreneurial Leadership; and *Fortune.* 2001. The Heroes: A Portfolio. October 4: 74.

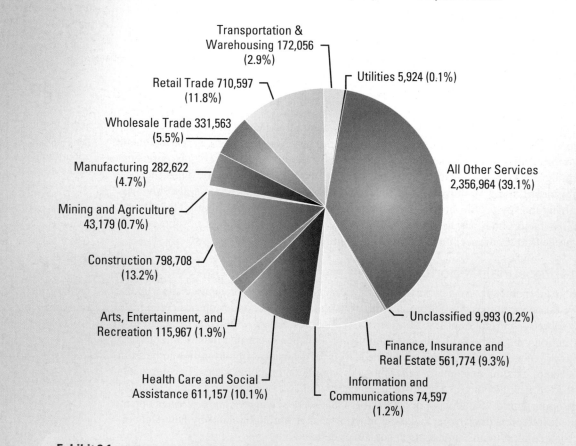

Exhibit 8.1 All U.S. Small Companies by Industry*

* Businesses with 500 or fewer employees in 2007.

Source: Small Business Administration's Office of Advocacy, based on data provided by the U.S. Census Bureau, statistics of U.S. businesses.

(continued)

(continued)

- Small businesses (fewer than 500 employees) employ more than half of the private sector workforce (59.9 million in 2007) and account for more than 50 percent of nonfarm private gross domestic product (GDP).

- Small firms produce 13 to 14 times more patents per employee than large patenting firms and employ 39 percent of high-tech workers (such as scientists and engineers). In addition, smaller entrepreneurial firms account for 55 percent of all innovations.

- Small businesses make up 97.5 percent of all U.S. exporters and accounted for 31 percent of known U.S. export value in 2008.

Exhibit 8.1 shows the number of small businesses in the United States and how they are distributed through different sectors of the economy.

There are also many types of small businesses. Exhibit 8.2 identifies three major categories that are often small and generally considered to be entrepreneurial—franchises, family businesses, and home-based businesses.

Type	Characteristics
Family Businesses	**Definition:** A family business, broadly defined, is a privately held firm in which family members have some degree of control over the strategic direction of the firm and intend for the business to remain within the family. **Scope:** According to the Family Firm Institute (FFI), family-owned businesses that meet the broad definition above comprise 80 to 90 percent of all business enterprises in the U.S., including 30 to 35 percent of the Fortune 500 companies. Further, 64 percent of the U.S. Gross Domestic Product (GDP) is generated by family-owned businesses.
Franchises	**Definition:** A franchise exists when a company that already has a successful product or service (franchisor) contracts with another business to be a dealer (franchisee) by using the franchisor's name, trademark and business system in exchange for a fee. The most common type is the Business Format Franchise in which the franchisor provides a complete plan, or format, for managing the business. **Scope:** According to the International Franchise Association (IFA), franchises were the cause of $863 billion in annual output in the U.S. in 2010. There are over 900,000 franchise establishments employing more than 9.5 million people.
Home-Based Businesses	**Definition:** A home-based business, also referred to as SOHO (Small Office/Home Office) consists of companies with 20 or fewer employees, including the self-employed, freelancers, telecommuters, or other independent professionals working from a home-based setting. **Scope:** According to the National Association of Home-Based Businesses (NAHBB), approximately 20 million businesses are home-based. The U.S. Commerce Department estimates that more than half of all small businesses are home-based.

Sources: *www.ffi.org; www.franchise.org;* and *www.workingsolo.com.*

Exhibit 8.2 **Types of Entrepreneurial Ventures**

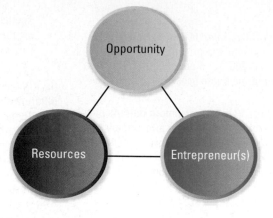

Exhibit 8.3 Opportunity Analysis Framework

Sources: Based on Timmons, J. A. & Spinelli, S. 2004. *New Venture Creation* (6th ed.). New York: McGraw-Hill/Irwin; and Bygrave, W. D. 1997. The Entrepreneurial Process. In W. D. Bygrave (Ed.), *The Portable MBA in Entrepreneurship* (2nd ed.). New York: Wiley.

opportunity recognition the process of discovering and evaluating changes in the business environment, such as a new technology, sociocultural trends, or shifts in consumer demand, that can be exploited.

must go through a process of identifying, selecting, and developing potential opportunities. This is the process of **opportunity recognition.**[5]

Opportunity recognition refers to more than just the "Eureka!" feeling that people sometimes experience at the moment they identify a new idea. Although such insights are often very important, the opportunity recognition process involves two phases of activity—discovery and evaluation—that lead to viable new venture opportunities.[6]

The discovery phase refers to the process of becoming aware of a new business concept.[7] Many entrepreneurs report that their idea for a new venture occurred to them in an instant, as a sort of "Aha!" experience—that is, they had some insight or epiphany, often based on their prior knowledge, that gave them an idea for a new business. The discovery of new opportunities is often spontaneous and unexpected. For example, Howard Schultz, CEO of Starbucks, was in Milan, Italy, when he suddenly realized that the coffee-and-conversation café model that was common in Europe would work in the U.S. as well. According to Schultz, he didn't need to do research to find out if Americans would pay $3 for a cup of coffee—he just *knew.* Starbucks was just a small business at the time but Schultz began literally shaking with excitement about growing it into a bigger business.[8] Strategy Spotlight 8.2 tells how three entrepreneurs in the struggling city of Detroit identified their business opportunities.

Opportunity discovery also may occur as the result of a deliberate search for new venture opportunities or creative solutions to business problems. Viable opportunities often emerge only after a concerted effort. It is very similar to a creative process, which may be unstructured and "chaotic" at first but eventually leads to a practical solution or business innovation. To stimulate the discovery of new opportunities, companies often encourage creativity, out-of-the-box thinking, and brainstorming.

Opportunity evaluation, which occurs after an opportunity has been identified, involves analyzing an opportunity to determine whether it is viable and strong enough to be developed into a full-fledged new venture. Ideas developed by new-product groups or in brainstorming sessions are tested by various methods, including talking to potential target customers and discussing operational requirements with production or logistics managers. A technique known as feasibility analysis is used to evaluate these and other critical

8.2

strategy spotlight

Entrepreneurial Vision to Revitalize Detroit

Detroit is the poorest major city in America. With an unemployment rate of 26 percent and a declining population, it would seem to be a nearly impossible place to start a new business. But challenging economic times are often the trigger for entrepreneurs to pursue their vision. Half the corporations listed on the *Fortune* 500 in 2010 were founded during challenging economic times, according to Dane Stangler, a senior analyst at the Kauffman Foundation. Individually and with the help of others, a range of entrepreneurs is striving to rejuvenate Detroit and realize their visions. Some of their businesses are the result of "Aha!" moments in which they envisioned bold new opportunities. Others are more modest traditional business ideas, but they all aim both to enrich the firms' founders and to improve the economic climate and the community of Detroit.

Daniel Gizaw, Founder of Danotek Motion Technologies

Rural Ethiopia is far from Detroit in more ways than one. Daniel Gizaw has taken the long journey from working on his father's farm in Ethiopia to founding a firm that produces products for the green energy business. He began by leaving home to study electrical engineering in Poland and Germany and later was part of the team designing the EV1, General Motor's first electric car. In order to follow his desire to pursue bold innovations and to exploit growing markets, he founded Danotek Motion Technologies, a firm that builds highly efficient turbines for the wind energy market as well as components for electric vehicles. To achieve his vision, he has recruited former colleagues, gotten support from Automation Alley (a consortium of business and government partners to improve the economic conditions of southeastern Michigan), and received governmental tax breaks to foster business growth. His firm plans to grow its business rapidly, keeping all its manufacturing in the greater Detroit area, as they create over 350 new jobs. Daniel's advice to would-be entrepreneurs is clear, "Don't limit yourself to the sector you are in. Look into growing industries and ask, 'What can I offer?'"

Glenn Oliver, Founder of H2bid.com

Though he is an attorney by training and never ran a business prior to starting H2bid, Glenn Oliver inherited an entrepreneurial interest from his grandfather, who owned an appliance repair and installation business. Living in a state that is surrounded by the Great Lakes and having served as a member of the Detroit Water and Sewerage Board of Commissioners, Oliver appreciated the value of water as a critical resource needed for economic development. Fresh water is a commodity increasingly demanded around the globe. Oliver saw opportunity here and has created H2bid.com, a marketplace where contractors and suppliers can bid on water supply projects around the world. While he thinks the business will be profitable, he also believes his start-up will benefit the Detroit area. As he concludes, "Entrepreneurship is the largest creator of wealth." Others in the area are noting the potential with this business. Oliver received recognition as a "Champion of the New Economy," an award sponsored by *DBusiness,* WJR radio, and Junior Achievement to recognize people whose businesses are helping to diversify Michigan's economy.

John Hantz, Founder of Hantz Farms

When many people drive through Detroit, they see a landscape of abandoned homes, empty commercial buildings, and vacant land. John Hantz sees opportunity. Already a successful entrepreneur, having founded Hantz Financial Services, a firm with 20 offices, 500 employees, and over $1.3 billion in assets under management, Hantz now has a new entrepreneurial vision. His vision grew out of his commuting across Detroit from his home to his office. Seeing all of the unused land and abandoned homes, he realized that he had to find a way to change the supply and demand relationship for land in Detroit. He sees urban farming as a partial solution to this issue. The farms he envisions are not the old style of farms growing crops in rows in large, open-air plots worked with large tractors. Instead, he plans to build compost-heated greenhouses and use hydroponic and aeroponic growing systems that don't rely on soil to grow crops. He is drawing on up to $30 million of his own financial resources to start the project and has tapped into expertise in the region, hiring Mike Score, an agricultural expert from Michigan State University to serve as president of the firm. He sees an economic opportunity here but also a chance to revitalize the area. His plan is to build small, visually attractive 300 to 1,000 acre farms or "pods" all across Detroit which will be surrounded by frontage property that could be developed for housing or commercial activity. Thus, he sees the farms as a way to reduce the supply of unused land while also stoking demand for redeveloped land surrounding the farms.

Although these businesses span a wide range of industries, they demonstrate that entrepreneurial vision often arises out an individual's experiences and can encompass both a business idea as well as a vehicle with which to improve conditions in a larger community.

Sources: Sohail, F. 2010. Alternative Energy: Creating Non-exportable Jobs. *Forbes.com*, June 30: np; Easton, N. 2010. If You Can Remake Yourself Here. *Fortune*, November 1: 59–63; Gray, S. 2010. Where Entrepreneurs Need Nerves of Steel. *Fortune*, October 18: 63–66; Saulny, S. 2010. Detroit Entrepreneurs Opt to Look Up. *The New York Times*, January 10: A18; Anonymous. 2010. Champions of the New Economy, *dBusiness*, May/June: np; Whitford, D. 2010. Can Farming Save Detroit? *Fortune*, January 18: 78–84.

success factors. This type of analysis often leads to the decision that a new venture project should be discontinued. If the venture concept continues to seem viable, a more formal business plan may be developed.[9]

Among the most important factors to evaluate is the market potential for the product or service. Established firms tend to operate in established markets. They have to adjust to market trends and to shifts in consumer demand, of course, but they usually have a customer base for which they are already filling a marketplace need. New ventures, in contrast, must first determine whether a market exists for the product or service they are contemplating. Thus, a critical element of opportunity recognition is assessing to what extent the opportunity is viable *in the marketplace*.

For an opportunity to be viable, it needs to have four qualities.[10]

- *Attractive.* The opportunity must be attractive in the marketplace; that is, there must be market demand for the new product or service.
- *Achievable.* The opportunity must be practical and physically possible.
- *Durable.* The opportunity must be attractive long enough for the development and deployment to be successful; that is, the window of opportunity must be open long enough for it to be worthwhile.
- *Value creating.* The opportunity must be potentially profitable; that is, the benefits must surpass the cost of development by a significant margin.

If a new business concept meets these criteria, two other factors must be considered before the opportunity is launched as a business: the resources available to undertake it, and the characteristics of the entrepreneur(s) pursuing it. In the next section, we address the issue of entrepreneurial resources; following that, we address the importance of entrepreneurial leaders and teams. But first, consider the opportunities that have been created by the recent surge in interest in environmental sustainability. Strategy Spotlight 8.3 discusses how an entrepreneurial firm is working to develop and sell a line of biodegradable plastics.

Entrepreneurial Resources

As Exhibit 8.3 indicates, resources are an essential component of a successful entrepreneurial launch. For start-ups, the most important resource is usually money because a new firm typically has to expend substantial sums just to start the business. However, financial resources are not the only kind of resource a new venture needs. Human capital and social capital are also important. Many firms also rely on government resources to help them thrive.[11]

Financial Resources Hand-in-hand with the importance of markets (and marketing) to new-venture creation, entrepreneurial firms must also have financing. In fact, the level of available financing is often a strong determinant of how the business is launched and its eventual success. Cash finances are, of course, highly important. But access to capital, such as a line of credit or favorable payment terms with a supplier, can also help a new venture succeed.

The types of financial resources that may be needed depend on two factors: the stage of venture development and the scale of the venture.[12] Entrepreneurial firms that are starting from scratch—start-ups—are at the earliest stage of development. Most start-ups also begin on a relatively small scale. The funding available to young and small firms tends to be quite limited. In fact, the majority of new firms are low-budget start-ups launched with personal savings and the contributions of family and friends.[13] Among firms included in the *Entrepreneur* list of the 100 fastest-growing new businesses in a recent year, 61 percent reported that their start-up funds came from personal savings.[14]

strategy spotlight

8.3

Green Plastics

Despite an increasing emphasis on recycling, only 7 percent of the plastic used by Americans is currently recycled. The remainder goes into landfills or ends up in lakes and oceans, where the plastic poisons fish that consume it. One vivid place to find the consequences of plastic use is in the middle of the ocean over a thousand miles off the California coast. It is the Great Pacific Garbage Patch, a collection of mostly plastic trash that has been estimated to be up to twice the size of France, formed as ocean currents pull plastic trash from coastal areas.

How do we reduce our reliance on nonbiodegradable plastics that clog our landfills and oceans? Metabolix, a small firm based in Cambridge, Massachusetts, is stepping up with an innovative solution—environmentally friendly biodegradable plastics. Plastic is typically made from petroleum, and the products made from petroleum-based plastic can take hundreds of years to decompose in landfills. Metabolix has developed a process to make plastics out of plant materials—the first 100 percent bioplastic product that is both biodegradable and durable enough to stand up to heat and use. The firm uses a genetically engineered microbe that consumes the sugar in corn, producing a plastic molecule called PHA. Plastic products made from PHA will decompose in water or soil in a few months. The products are so pure that consumers can toss them into their backyard compost piles and use the resulting mulch in their vegetable gardens or around their fruit trees.

Sources: Dumaine, B. 2010. Feel-Good Plastic. *Fortune*, May 3: 36; Ziegler, J. 2009. Metabolix Defies Skeptics with Plastic from Plants. *Bloomberg*, May 7: np; Anonymous. 2010. Metabolix: FDA Clears Bioplastic for Use with Food. *BusinessWeek Online*, May 12: np; Anonymous. 2009. Drowning in Plastic: The Great Pacific Garbage Patch Is Twice the Size of France. *telegraph.co.uk*, April 24: np.

To manufacture and sell the product, Metabolix has created a joint venture, Telles, with agribusiness giant Archer Daniels Midland (ADM). They sell the biodegradable plastic for around $2.50 a pound, about twice the cost of typical, petroleum-based plastic. Since they can't compete head to head on price with other plastics and want to maximize the ecological benefits of their product, Metabolix and ADM have initially focused on getting their plastic used in products that would not normally be recycled. Instead of trying to get their plastic, Mirel, used in plastic bottles, they have aimed their sales toward plastic gift cards, bags, forks and knives, container lids, and disposable pens. For example, one of the first products to use Mirel is a biodegradable Paper Mate pen. One of the benefits is that the pen uses so little plastic that the use of the higher cost bioplastic has a minimal effect on the overall cost of the pen.

Metabolix is aiming to improve the cost efficiency of their product to be able to compete with other plastics by developing genetically engineered nonfood crops, such as switchgrass and oilseeds, that will produce the PHA polymer within the plant and require less processing to extract into usable plastics. Their goal is to grow 160 million tons of plastic-producing plants to produce 15 million tons of bioplastic per year. This will reduce the need for petroleum and landfill space and, hopefully, begin to reduce the size of the Great Pacific Garbage Patch.

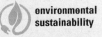 environmental sustainability

Although bank financing, public financing, and venture capital are important sources of small business finance, these types of financial support are typically available only after a company has started to conduct business and generate sales. Even "angel" investors—private individuals who provide equity investments for seed capital during the early stages of a new venture—favor companies that already have a winning business model and dominance in a market niche.[15] According to Cal Simmons, coauthor of *Every Business Needs an Angel*, "I would much rather talk to an entrepreneur who has already put his money and his effort into proving the concept."[16] Peer-to-peer lending is a rapidly increasing Internet-based source of funding for entrepreneurs. Strategy Spotlight 8.4 discusses Prosper.com, a peer-to-peer lending website that uses social affiliation to bring together entrepreneurs and potential lenders.

angel investors private individuals who provide equity investments for seed capital during the early stages of a new venture.

Prosper.com: Using the Power of the Social Group to Fund Entrepreneurs

Start-up entrepreneurs may need only a small amount of money to launch their ventures. However, if they have limited personal resources, they may never be able to turn their business ideas into operating enterprises. With lower credit limits and higher interest rates on credit cards and tougher standards for borrowers seeking bank loans, entrepreneurs are increasingly turning to other sources for seed capital. To fill this need, a new breed of lender has emerged online: peer-to-peer (P2P) lenders. This form of lending has taken off and was projected to involve over $5.8 billion in lending in 2010 according to the research firm Celent.

With P2P lending, borrowers seeking loans post descriptions of their business concepts, including the amount of funding they are seeking and personal information, such as their credit rating. Lenders, who are looking for opportunities to lend their money and make a decent return but who also often find satisfaction from helping out entrepreneurs, review business proposals and the borrowers' background information before making lending decisions. Depending on the rules of each P2P website, lenders either make a loan to borrowers at a preset interest rate or participate in an auction to "win" the opportunity to lend to the borrower. On the auction sites, lenders willing to lend at the lowest interest rates fund a borrower. Since the loans are unsecured, lenders are encouraged to spread their funds around, making small loans to a number of borrowers. As a result, a number of lenders typically provide small amounts of money that collectively meet the borrowing needs of an individual borrower.

One of the largest P2P lending websites is Prosper. com. Launched in 2006, Prosper reports that investors lending through their website have provided over $214 million in loans to entrepreneurs and that they have over one million members. The root idea for Prosper.com came from the experience of Lyna Lam, the wife of Prosper's founder Chris Larsen. Lyna's family came to the United States as refugees from Vietnam in the early 1980s. Once they settled in San Jose, California, they joined a Vietnamese Hui group, a group of individuals who make contributions to create a pool of money that one of the members can borrow to start or grow a business. Lyna Lam's family used money from the Hui to start a landscaping business.

Chris saw the group structure as a key strength of the Hui. Hui groups tend to be successful because members of the group offer advice to each other but also feel strong social pressure from the group to work hard to repay the money borrowed from the group. This addresses one of the key weaknesses of P2P lending—the lack of trust that someone the lender doesn't know and never interacted with directly will repay the loan. Like most other P2P lending sites, Prosper collects factual information on the borrower and the business idea, runs a credit check on the borrower, and offers them scores that range from AA (the best rating) to HR (high risk) or NC (no credit history). But they also give borrowers the opportunity to join a group. These groups are created and organized by a leader and bring together borrowers that share a common interest or identity, such as nationality, educational affiliation, religion, type of business, or hobby. Members of successful groups, those that have a strong repayment record, can attract more favorable interest terms from lenders. Thus, the group offers positive peer pressure to members to repay their loans. Members don't want to lose face by defaulting on their loan and tarnishing the group's reputation, resulting in financial consequences for all borrowers in the group. The group leader can also provide advice to the borrower and is rewarded when members of the group repay their loans. The system appears to work well, as 92 percent of loans were being repaid on schedule as of February 2010 according to Prosper.com's statistics.

Sources: Libert, B. & Spector, J. 2008. *How to Unleash the Power of Crowds in Your Business.* Philadelphia: Wharton School Publishing: 104–106; Dishman, L. 2009. Peer-to-Peer Lending Explained: Brother, Can You Spare $100? *Fast Company,* November 11: np; *www.prosper.com*; *www.wikipedia. org*; and *www.oneviet.com.*

crowdsourcing

Once a venture has established itself as a going concern, other sources of financing become readily available. Banks, for example, are more likely to provide later-stage financing to companies with a track record of sales or other cash-generating activity. Start-ups that involve large capital investments or extensive development costs—such as manufacturing or engineering firms trying to commercialize an innovative product—may have high cash requirements soon after they are founded. Others need financing only when they are on the brink of rapid growth. To obtain such funding, entrepreneurial firms often seek venture capital.

Venture capital is a form of private equity financing through which entrepreneurs raise money by selling shares in the new venture. In contrast to angel investors, who invest their own money, venture capital companies are organized to place the funds of private investors into lucrative business opportunities. Venture capitalists nearly always have high performance expectations from the companies they invest in, but they also provide important managerial advice and links to key contacts in an industry.[17]

venture capitalists companies organized to place their investors' finds in lucrative business opportunities.

Despite the importance of venture capital to many fast-growing firms, the majority of external funding for young and small firms comes from informal sources such as family and friends. Based on a Kaufmann Foundation survey of entrepreneurial firms, Exhibit 8.4 identifies the source of funding used by start-up businesses and by ongoing firms that are five years old. The survey shows that most start-up funding, about 70 percent, comes from either equity investments by the entrepreneur and the entrepreneur's family and friends or personal loans taken out by the entrepreneur. After five years of operation, the largest source of funding is from loans taken out by the business. At both stages, 5 percent or less of the funding comes from outside investors, such as angel investors or venture capitalists. In fact, very few firms ever receive venture-capital investments—only 7 of 2606 firms in the Kaufmann study received money from outside investors. But when they do, these firms receive a substantial level of investment—over $1 million on average in the survey—because they tend to be the firms that are the most innovative and have the greatest growth potential. Regardless of their source, financial resources are essential for entrepreneurial ventures.[18]

Human Capital   Bankers, venture capitalists, and angel investors agree that the most important asset an entrepreneurial firm can have is strong and skilled management.[19] According to Stephen Gaal, founding member of Walnut Venture Associates, venture investors do not invest in businesses; instead "We invest in people . . . very smart people with very high integrity." Managers need to have a strong base of experience and extensive domain knowledge, as well as an ability to make rapid decisions and change direction as shifting circumstances may require. In the case of start-ups, more is better. New ventures that are started by teams of three, four, or five entrepreneurs are more likely to succeed in the long run than are ventures launched by "lone wolf" entrepreneurs.[20]

Exhibit 8.4
Sources of Capital for Start-Up Firms

	Capital Invested in Their First Year	Percentage of Capital Invested in Their First Year	Capital Invested in Their Fifth Year	Percentage of Capital Invested in Their Fifth Year
Insider equity	$33,034	41.1	$13,914	17.9
Investor equity	$4,108	5.1	$3,108	4.0
Personal debt of owners	$23,353	29.1	$21,754	28.0
Business debt	$19,867	24.7	$39,009	50.1
Total average capital invested	$80,362		$77,785	

Source: From Robb, A., Reedy, E. J., Ballou, J., DesRoches, D., Potter, F., & Zhao, A. 2010. An Overview of the Kauffman Firm Survey. Reproduced with permission from the Ewing Marion Kauffman Foundation.

Social Capital New ventures founded by entrepreneurs who have extensive social contacts are more likely to succeed than are ventures started without the support of a social network.[21] Even though a venture may be new, if the founders have contacts who will vouch for them, they gain exposure and build legitimacy faster.[22] This support can come from several sources: prior jobs, industry organizations, and local business groups such as the chamber of commerce. These contacts can all contribute to a growing network that provides support for the entrepreneurial firm. Janina Pawlowski, co-founder of the online lending company E-Loan, attributes part of her success to the strong advisors she persuaded to serve on her board of directors, including Tim Koogle, former CEO of Yahoo![23]

Strategic alliances represent a type of social capital that can be especially important to young and small firms.[24] Strategy Spotlight 8.5 presents a few examples of alliances and some potential pitfalls of using alliances.[25]

Government Resources In the U.S., the federal government provides support for entrepreneurial firms in two key arenas—financing and government contracting. The Small Business Administration (SBA) has several loan guarantee programs designed to support the growth and development of entrepreneurial firms. The government itself does not typically lend money but underwrites loans made by banks to small businesses, thus reducing the risk associated with lending to firms with unproven records. The SBA also offers training, counseling, and support services through its local offices and Small Business Development Centers.[26] State and local governments also have hundreds of programs to provide funding, contracts, and other support for new ventures and small businesses. These programs are often designed to grow the economy of a region, as seen with Danotek Motion Technologies in Strategy Spotlight 8.2.

Another key area of support is in government contracting. Programs sponsored by the SBA and other government agencies ensure that small businesses have the opportunity to bid on contracts to provide goods and services to the government. Although working with the government sometimes has its drawbacks in terms of issues of regulation and time-consuming decision making, programs to support small businesses and entrepreneurial activity constitute an important resource for entrepreneurial firms.

Entrepreneurial Leadership

entrepreneurial leadership leadership appropriate for new ventures that requires courage, belief in ones convictions, and the energy to work hard even in difficult circumstances; and embody vision, dedication and drive, and commit to excellence.

Whether a venture is launched by an individual entrepreneur or an entrepreneurial team, effective leadership is needed. Launching a new venture requires a special kind of leadership.[27] It involves courage, belief in one's convictions, and the energy to work hard even in difficult circumstances. Yet these are the very challenges that motivate most business owners. Entrepreneurs put themselves to the test and get their satisfaction from acting independently, overcoming obstacles, and thriving financially. To do so, they must embody three characteristics of leadership—vision, dedication and drive, and commitment to excellence—and pass these on to all those who work with them:

- *Vision.* This may be an entrepreneur's most important asset. Entrepreneurs envision realities that do not yet exist. But without a vision, most entrepreneurs would never even get their venture off the ground. With vision, entrepreneurs are able to exercise a kind of transformational leadership that creates something new and, in some way, changes the world. Just having a vision, however, is not enough. To develop support, get financial backing, and attract employees, entrepreneurial leaders must share their vision with others.

- *Dedication and drive.* Dedication and drive are reflected in hard work. Drive involves internal motivation; dedication calls for an intellectual commitment that keeps an entrepreneur going even in the face of bad news or poor luck. They both require patience, stamina, and a willingness to work long hours. However, a business built on the heroic efforts of one person may suffer in the long run. That's why the

strategy spotlight

Strategic Alliances: A Key Entrepreneurial Resource

Strategic alliances provide a key avenue for growth by entrepreneurial firms. By partnering with other companies, young or small firms can expand or give the appearance of entering numerous markets and/or handling a range of operations. Here are several types of alliances that have been used to extend or strengthen entrepreneurial firms:

Technology Alliances

Tech-savvy entrepreneurial firms often benefit from forming alliances with older incumbents. The alliance allows the larger firm to enhance its technological capabilities and expands the revenue and reach of the smaller firm.

Manufacturing Alliances

The use of outsourcing and other manufacturing alliances by small firms has grown dramatically in recent years. Internet-enabled capabilities such as collaborating online about delivery and design specifications has greatly simplified doing business, even with foreign manufacturers.

Retail Alliances

Licensing agreements allow one company to sell the products and services of another in different markets, including overseas. Specialty products—the types sometimes made by entrepreneurial firms—often seem more exotic when sold in another country.

According to the National Federation of Independent Business (NFIB), nearly two-thirds of small businesses currently hold or have held some type of alliance. Strategic alliances among entrepreneurial firms can take many different forms. Exhibit 8.5 shows the different types of partnering that small businesses and small manufacturers in the NFIB study often use.

Although such alliances often sound good, there are also potential pitfalls. Lack of oversight and control is one danger of partnering with foreign firms. Problems with product quality, timely delivery, and receiving payments can also sour an alliance relationship if it is not carefully managed. With technology alliances, there is a risk that big firms may take advantage of the technological know-how of their entrepreneurial partners. However, even with these potential problems, strategic alliances provide a good means for entrepreneurial firms to develop and grow.

Sources: Copeland, M. V. & Tilin, A. 2005. Get Someone to Build It. *Business 2.0*, 6(5): 88–90 Misner, I. 2008. Use Small Actions to Get Big Results. *Entrepreneur*. www.entrepreneur.com, December 3. Monahan, J. 2005. All Systems Grow. *Entrepreneur*, March: 78–82; Prince, C. J. 2005. Foreign Affairs. *Entrepreneur*, March: 56; and, Weaver, K. M. & Dickson, P. 2004. Strategic Alliances. In W. J. Dennis, Jr. (Ed.), *NFIB National Small Business Poll*. Washington, DC: National Federation of Independent Business.

Type of Alliance and/or Long-Term Agreement*	Small Manufacturers	Small Businesses
Licensing	20.0%	32.5%
Export/Import	14.4%	7.3%
Franchise	5.0%	5.3%
Marketing	18.0%	25.2%
Distribution	20.1%	20.5%
Production	26.5%	11.3%
Product/Services R&D	12.2%	12.6%
Process R&D	6.7%	5.3%
Purchaser/Supplier	23.5%	13.9%
Outside Contracting	23.2%	28.5%

Source: From Weaver, K. M. & Dickson, P. 2004. Strategic Alliances. In W. J. Dennis, Jr. (Ed.), *NFIB National Small Business Poll*. Washington, DC: National Federation of Independent Business. Reprinted with permission.

* Columns add to over 100 percent because firms may use multiple alliances.

Exhibit 8.5 Use of Strategic Alliances by Small Businesses and Small Manufacturers

dedicated entrepreneur's enthusiasm is also important—like a magnet, it attracts others to the business to help with the work.[28]

- ***Commitment to excellence.*** Excellence requires entrepreneurs to commit to knowing the customer, providing quality goods and services, paying attention to details, and continuously learning. Entrepreneurs who achieve excellence are sensitive to how these factors work together. However, entrepreneurs may flounder if they think they are the only ones who can create excellent results. The most successful, by contrast, often report that they owe their success to hiring people smarter than themselves.

In his book *Good to Great,* Jim Collins makes another important point about entrepreneurial leadership: Ventures built on the charisma of a single person may have trouble growing "from good to great" once that person leaves.[29] Thus, the leadership that is needed to build a great organization is usually exercised by a team of dedicated people working together rather than a single leader. Another aspect of this team approach is attracting team members who fit with the company's culture, goals, and work ethic. Thus, for a venture's leadership to be a valuable resource and not a liability it must be cohesive in its vision, drive and dedication, and commitment to excellence.

Once an opportunity has been recognized, and an entrepreneurial team and resources have been assembled, a new venture must craft a strategy. Prior chapters have addressed the strategies of incumbent firms. In the next section, we highlight the types of strategies and strategic considerations faced by new entrants.

Entrepreneurial Strategy

entrepreneurial strategy a strategy that enables a skilled and dedicated entrepreneur, with a viable opportunity and access to sufficient resources, to successfully launch a new venture.

Successfully creating new ventures requires several ingredients. As indicated in Exhibit 8.3, three factors are necessary—a viable opportunity, sufficient resources, and a skilled and dedicated entrepreneur or entrepreneurial team. Once these elements are in place, the new venture needs a strategy. In this section, we consider several different strategic factors that are unique to new ventures and also how the generic strategies introduced in Chapter 5 can be applied to entrepreneurial firms. We also indicate how combination strategies might benefit entrepreneurial firms and address the potential pitfalls associated with launching new venture strategies.

To be successful, new ventures must evaluate industry conditions, the competitive environment, and market opportunities in order to position themselves strategically. However, a traditional strategic analysis may have to be altered somewhat to fit the entrepreneurial situation. For example, five-forces analysis (as discussed in Chapter 2) is typically used by established firms. It can also be applied to the analysis of new ventures to assess the impact of industry and competitive forces. But you may ask: How does a new entrant evaluate the threat of other new entrants?

First, the new entrant needs to examine barriers to entry. If the barriers are too high, the potential entrant may decide not to enter or to gather more resources before attempting to do so. Compared to an older firm with an established reputation and available resources, the barriers to entry may be insurmountable for an entrepreneurial start-up. Therefore, understanding the force of these barriers is critical in making a decision to launch.

A second factor that may be especially important to a young venture is the threat of retaliation by incumbents. In many cases, entrepreneurial ventures *are* the new entrants that pose a threat to incumbent firms. Therefore, in applying the five-forces model to new ventures, the threat of retaliation by established firms needs to be considered.

Part of any decision about what opportunity to pursue is a consideration of how a new entrant will actually enter a new market. The concept of entry strategies provides a useful means of addressing the types of choices that new ventures have.

Entry Strategies

One of the most challenging aspects of launching a new venture is finding a way to begin doing business that quickly generates cash flow, builds credibility, attracts good employees, and overcomes the liability of newness. The idea of an entry strategy or "entry wedge" describes several approaches that firms may take to get a foothold in a market.[30] Several factors will affect this decision.

>LO8.3
Three types of entry strategies—pioneering, imitative, and adaptive—commonly used to launch a new venture.

- Is the product/service high-tech or low-tech?
- What resources are available for the initial launch?
- What are the industry and competitive conditions?
- What is the overall market potential?
- Does the venture founder prefer to control the business or to grow it?

In some respects, any type of entry into a market for the first time may be considered entrepreneurial. But the entry strategy will vary depending on how risky and innovative the new business concept is.[31] New-entry strategies typically fall into one of three categories—pioneering new entry, imitative new entry, or adaptive new entry.[32]

Pioneering New Entry   New entrants with a radical new product or highly innovative service may change the way business is conducted in an industry. This kind of breakthrough—creating new ways to solve old problems or meeting customers' needs in a unique new way—is referred to as a **pioneering new entry.** If the product or service is unique enough, a pioneering new entrant may actually have little direct competition. The first personal computer was a pioneering product; there had never been anything quite like it and it revolutionized computing. The first Internet browser provided a type of pioneering service. These breakthroughs created whole new industries and changed the competitive landscape. And breakthrough innovations continue to inspire pioneering entrepreneurial efforts. Strategy Spotlight 8.6 discusses Pandora, a firm that pioneered a new way to broadcast music.

The pitfalls associated with a pioneering new entry are numerous. For one thing, there is a strong risk that the product or service will not be accepted by consumers. The history of entrepreneurship is littered with new ideas that never got off the launching pad. Take, for example, Smell-O-Vision, an invention designed to pump odors into movie theatres from the projection room at preestablished moments in a film. It was tried only once (for the film *Scent of a Mystery*) before it was declared a major flop. Innovative? Definitely. But hardly a good idea at the time.[33]

A pioneering new entry is disruptive to the status quo of an industry. It is likely based on a technological breakthrough. If it is successful, other competitors will rush in to copy it. This can create issues of sustainability for an entrepreneurial firm, especially if a larger company with greater resources introduces a similar product. For a new entrant to sustain its pioneering advantage, it may be necessary to protect its intellectual property, advertise heavily to build brand recognition, form alliances with businesses that will adopt its products or services, and offer exceptional customer service.

Imitative New Entry   Whereas pioneers are often inventors or tinkerers with new technology, imitators usually have a strong marketing orientation. They look for opportunities to capitalize on proven market successes. An **imitative new entry** strategy is used by entrepreneurs who see products or business concepts that have been successful in one market niche or physical locale and introduce the same basic product or service in another segment of the market.

Sometimes the key to success with an imitative strategy is to fill a market space where the need had previously been filled inadequately. Entrepreneurs are also prompted to be imitators when they realize that they have the resources or skills to do a job better than an existing competitor. This can actually be a serious problem for entrepreneurial start-ups if the imitator is an established company. Consider the example of Tesla Motors. Founded in

pioneering new entry a firm's entry into an industry with a radical new product or highly innovative service that changes the way business is conducted.

imitative new entry a firm's entry into an industry with products or services that capitalize on proven market successes and that usually has a strong marketing orientation.

Pandora Rocks the Music Business

Whether the music was transmitted over FM radio signals, streamed over the web, or from a satellite, the musical choices radio listeners had were fairly standardized until Pandora arrived. Radio stations determined their play list based on a combination of interest evident in music sales and listener surveys along with the format of their stations. Listeners in a given market could decide if they wanted to listen to a top 40, adult contemporary, country, or classic rock station, but they couldn't custom design a station to meet their eclectic musical tastes.

Tim Westergren completely changed the radio business when he created Pandora. In 1999 he developed the Music Genome Project—a system that analyzes music for its underlying traits, including melody, rhythm, lyrics, instrumentation, and many other traits. Each song is measured on approximately 400 musical "genes" and given a vector or list of attributes. The vectors of multiple songs can be compared to assess the "distance" between the two songs. Using the Music Genome Project, Westergren launched Pandora in 2000. Users input bands or songs

they like, and Pandora creates a customized station that plays music that meets the users' tastes. Users can then tweak the station by giving input on whether or not they like the songs Pandora plays for them.

Pandora radically changes the radio business in multiple ways. First, users create their own customized stations. Second, users can access their personal radio stations wherever they go through any Internet-connected device. Third, the playing of songs is driven by their musical traits, not how popular a band is. If an unsigned garage band has musical traits similar to Pearl Jam, their music will get play on a user's Pearl Jam station. This offers great exposure to aspiring musicians not available on commercial radio. It also offers an avenue for record labels to get exposure for newly signed bands that don't yet get air play on traditional radio.

Pandora has grown in 10 years from a boldly new idea to become the largest "radio" station in the world, with 65 million registered users. The next move is to dominate the location where Americans do most of their radio listening—their cars. Ford began offering a voice-activated Pandora system in their cars in early 2011. Other manufacturers are following suit. Pioneer is selling car stereos that support Pandora. In gaining control of music in cars, Pandora continues to rock the music business.

Sources: Copeland, M. V. 2010. Pandora's Founder Rocks the Music Business. *Fortune*, July 5: 27–28; Levy, A. 2010. Pandora's Next Frontier: Your Wheels. *BusinessWeek.com*, October 14: np; and *www.pandora.com*.

2003, Tesla designs and manufactures electric cars. The average cost of a gallon of gasoline was about $1.50 when Tesla was incorporated, and the demand for alternative-fuel cars was not strong. Thus, they initially faced limited competition in this niche of the automotive market. However, by the time their first Tesla Roadster was ready for sale in 2008, rising gasoline prices and concerns about auto emissions had dramatically increased interest in electric cars. Tesla's success in winning design awards and car orders increased the profile of the firm and, more generally, electric cars. The major automakers are responding with their own models in this market. The Chevy Volt and Nissan Leaf both came on the market in 2010. Ford will launch an electric version of the Ford Focus in 2011. Other major auto manufacturers are following suit. While Tesla's original vehicle is a high-performance car that faces no direct competition, their goal was to expand into the mainstream market with an electric-powered sedan. With the fast response by major competitors, it is not clear that Tesla will be able to continue to grow their business.[34]

Adaptive New Entry Most new entrants use a strategy somewhere between "pure" imitation and "pure" pioneering. That is, they offer a product or service that is somewhat new and sufficiently different to create new value for customers and capture market share. Such firms are adaptive in the sense that they are aware of marketplace conditions and conceive entry strategies to capitalize on current trends.

According to business creativity coach Tom Monahan, "Every new idea is merely a spin of an old idea. [Knowing that] takes the pressure off from thinking [you] have to be totally creative. You don't. Sometimes it's one slight twist to an old idea that makes all the difference."[35] An **adaptive new entry** approach does not involve "reinventing the wheel," nor is it merely imitative either. It involves taking an existing idea and adapting it to a particular situation. Exhibit 8.6 presents examples of four young companies that successfully modified or adapted existing products to create new value.

There are several pitfalls that might limit the success of an adaptive new entrant. First, the value proposition must be perceived as unique. Unless potential customers believe a new product or service does a superior job of meeting their needs, they will have little motivation to try it. Second, there is nothing to prevent a close competitor from mimicking the new firm's adaptation as a way to hold on to its customers. Third, once an adaptive entrant achieves initial success, the challenge is to keep the idea fresh. If the attractive features of the new business are copied, the entrepreneurial firm must find ways to adapt and improve the product or service offering.

Considering these choices, an entrepreneur or entrepreneurial team might ask, Which new entry strategy is best? The choice depends on many competitive, financial, and marketplace considerations. Nevertheless, research indicates that the greatest opportunities may stem from being willing to enter new markets rather than seeking growth only in existing markets. A recent study found that companies that ventured into arenas that were new to the world or new to the company earned total profits of 61 percent. In contrast, companies that made only incremental improvements, such as extending an existing product line, grew total profits by only 39 percent.[36]

adaptive new entry a firm's entry into an industry by offering a product or service that is somewhat new and sufficiently different to create value for customers by capitalizing on current market trends.

Exhibit 8.6   **Examples of Adaptive New Entrants**

Company Name	Product	Adaptation	Result
Under Armour, Inc. Founded in 1995	Undershirts and other athletic gear	Used moisture-wicking fabric to create better gear for sweaty sports.	Under Armour has 3,000 employees and 2010 sales in excess of $850 million.
Mint.com Founded in 2005	Comprehensive online money management	Created software that tells users what they are spending by aggregating financial information from online bank and credit card accounts.	Mint has over 4 million users and is tracking $200 billion in transactions.
Plum Organics Founded in 2005	Organic frozen baby food	Made convenient line of baby food using organic ingredients.	Added to Whole Foods product offering in 2006 and Babies 'R' Us in 2009.
Spanx Founded in 2000	Footless pantyhose and other undergarments for women	Combined nylon and Lycra® to create a new type of undergarment that is comfortable and eliminates panty lines.	Now produces over 200 products sold in 3,000 stores to over 6 million customers.

Sources: Bryan, M. 2007. Spanx Me, Baby! *www.observer.com*, December 10, np.; Carey, J. 2006. Perspiration Inspiration. *BusinessWeek*, June 5: 64; Palanjian, A. 2008. A Planner Plumbs for a Niche. *www.wsj.com*, September 30, np.; Worrell, D. 2008. Making Mint. *Entrepreneur*, September: 55; *www.mint.com*; *www.spanx.com*; *www.underarmour.com*; and Buss, D. 2010. The Mothers of Invention. *The Wall Street Journal*, February 8: R7.

These findings led W. Chan Kim and Renee Mauborgne in their new book *Blue Ocean Strategy* to conclude that companies that are willing to venture into market spaces where there is little or no competition—labeled "blue oceans"—will outperform those firms that limit growth to incremental improvements in competitively crowded industries—labeled "red oceans." Companies that identify and pursue blue ocean strategies follow somewhat different rules than those that are "bloodied" by the competitive practices in red oceans. Consider the following elements of a blue ocean strategy:

- *Create uncontested market space.* By seeking opportunities where they are not threatened by existing competitors, blue ocean firms can focus on customers rather than on competition.
- *Make the competition irrelevant.* Rather than using the competition as a benchmark, blue ocean firms cross industry boundaries to offer new and different products and services.
- *Create and capture new demand.* Rather than fighting over existing demand, blue ocean companies seek opportunities in uncharted territory.
- *Break the value/cost trade-off.* Blue ocean firms reject the idea that a trade-off between value and cost is inevitable and instead seek opportunities in areas that benefit both their cost structure and their value proposition to customers.
- *Pursue differentiation and low cost simultaneously.* By integrating the range of a firm's utility, price, and cost activities, blue ocean companies align their whole system to create sustainable strategies.

The essence of blue ocean strategy is not just to find an uncontested market, but to create one. Some blue oceans arise because new technologies create new possibilities, such as eBay's online auction business. Yet technological innovation is not a defining feature of a blue ocean strategy. Most blue oceans are created from within red oceans by companies that push beyond the existing industry boundaries. Any of the new entry strategies described earlier could be used to pursue a blue ocean strategy. Consider the example of Cirque du Soleil, which created a new market for circus entertainment by making traditional circus acts more like theatrical productions:

> By altering the industry boundaries that traditionally defined the circus concept, Cirque du Soleil created a new type of circus experience. Since the days of Ringling Bros. and Barnum & Bailey, the circus had consisted of animal acts, star performers, and Bozo-like clowns. Cirque questioned this formula and researched what audiences really wanted. It found that interest in animal acts was declining, in part because of public concerns over the treatment of circus animals. Because managing animals—and the celebrity trainers who performed with them—was costly, Cirque eliminated them.
>
> Instead, Cirque focused on three elements of the traditional circus tent event that still captivated audiences: acrobatic acts, clowns, and the tent itself. Elegant acrobatics became a central feature of its performances, and clown humor became more sophisticated and less slapstick. Cirque also preserved the image of the tent by creating exotic facades that captured the symbolic elements of the traditional tent. Finally, rather than displaying three different acts simultaneously, as in the classic three-ring circus, Cirque offers multiple productions with theatrical story lines, giving audiences a reason to go to the circus more often. Each production has a different theme and its own original musical score.
>
> Cirque's efforts to redefine the circus concept have paid off. Since 1984, Cirque's productions have been seen by over 90 million people in some 200 cities around the world.[37]

Once created, a blue ocean strategy is difficult to imitate. If customers flock to blue ocean creators, firms rapidly achieve economies of scale, learning advantages, and synergies across their organizational systems. Body Shop, for example chartered new territory by refusing to focus solely on beauty products. Traditional competitors such as Estee

Lauder and L'Oreal, whose brands are based on promises of eternal youth and beauty, found it difficult to imitate this approach without repudiating their current images.

These factors suggest that blue ocean strategies provide an avenue by which firms can pursue an entrepreneurial new entry. Such strategies are not without risks, however. A new entrant must decide not only the best way to enter into business but also what type of strategic positioning will work best as the business goes forward. Those strategic choices can be informed by the guidelines suggested for the generic strategies. We turn to that subject next.

Generic Strategies

Typically, a new entrant begins with a single business model that is equivalent in scope to a business-level strategy (Chapter 5). In this section we address how overall low cost, differentiation, and focus strategies can be used to achieve competitive advantages.

>LO8.4

How the generic strategies of overall cost leadership, differentiation, and focus are used by new ventures and small businesses.

Overall Cost Leadership   One of the ways entrepreneurial firms achieve success is by doing more with less. By holding down costs or making more efficient use of resources than larger competitors, new ventures are often able to offer lower prices and still be profitable. Thus, under the right circumstances, a low-cost leader strategy is a viable alternative for some new ventures. The way most companies achieve low-cost leadership, however, is typically different for young or small firms.

Recall from Chapter 5 that three of the features of a low-cost approach included operating at a large enough scale to spread costs over many units of production (economies of scale), making substantial capital investments in order to increase scale economies, and using knowledge gained from experience to make cost-saving improvements. These elements of a cost-leadership strategy may be unavailable to new ventures. Because new ventures are typically small, they usually don't have high economies of scale relative to competitors. Because they are usually cash strapped, they can't make large capital investments to increase their scale advantages. And because many are young, they often don't have a wealth of accumulated experience to draw on to achieve cost reductions.

Given these constraints, how can new ventures successfully deploy cost-leader strategies? Compared to large firms, new ventures often have simple organizational structures that make decision making both easier and faster. The smaller size also helps young firms change more quickly when upgrades in technology or feedback from the marketplace indicate that improvements are needed. They are also able to make decisions at the time they are founded that help them deal with the issue of controlling costs. For example, they may source materials from a supplier that provides them more cheaply or set up manufacturing facilities in another country where labor costs are especially low. Thus, new firms have several avenues for achieving low cost leadership. Strategy Spotlight 8.7 highlights the success of Vizio, Inc., a new entrant with an overall cost leadership strategy. Whatever methods young firms use to achieve a low-cost advantage, this has always been a way that entrepreneurial firms take business away from incumbents—by offering a comparable product or service at a lower price.

Differentiation   Both pioneering and adaptive entry strategies involve some degree of differentiation. That is, the new entry is based on being able to offer a differentiated value proposition. In the case of pioneers, the new venture is attempting to do something strikingly different, either by using a new technology or deploying resources in a way that radically alters the way business is conducted. Often, entrepreneurs do both.

Amazon founder Jeff Bezos set out to use Internet technology to revolutionize the way books are sold. He garnered the ire of other booksellers and the attention of the public by making bold claims about being the "earth's largest bookseller." As a bookseller, Bezos was not doing anything that had not been done before. But two key differentiating

strategy spotlight

Low-Cost Imitator Vizio, Inc., Takes Off

The popularity of flat-panel TVs has grown rapidly since they were first introduced in the late 1990s—by 2012, it is estimated 85 percent of U.S households will have one. When first introduced, major manufacturers such as Samsung, Sony, and Matsushita (maker of Panasonic) made heavy investments in R&D in a competition for technological leadership. As a result, the early flat-panel TVs were expensive. Even as technological advances drove prices down, the TVs were growing larger and flatter, and they continued to command premium prices. By 2002, 50-inch plasma TVs were still selling for $8,000–$10,000. But by then, panel technology had also become somewhat commoditized. That's when William Wang, a former marketer of computer monitors, realized he could use existing technologies to create a high quality TV. Wang discovered he could keep operations lean and outsource everything from tech support to R&D, so he founded Vizio, Inc.

In January 2003, Wang pitched Costco Wholesale Corp. on a 46-inch flat-panel plasma TV for $3,800—half the price of the competition. Although Costco executives laughed when Wang said he wanted to become the next

Sources: Lawton, C., Kane, Y. I., & Dean, J. 2008. U.S. Upstart Takes on TV Giants in Price War. *www.wsj.com*, April 15, np.; Taub, E. A. 2008. Flat-Panel TV Prices Plummet. *www.nytimes.com*, December 2, np.; Wilson, S. 2008. Picture It. *Entrepreneur*, July: 43; *www.wikipedia.com*; Kane, Y.I. 2011. Vizio Extends Battle Plan. *Wall Street Journal*, January 3: B3; and Edwards, C. 2010. How Vizio Beat Sony in High-def TV. *Bloomberg Businessweek*, April 26: 51–52. www.keloland.com

Sony, they decided to give him a chance. By March 2003, the TVs were being offered in over 300 of Costco's U.S. warehouse stores. Today, Vizio is one of Costco's largest suppliers of TVs.

Vizio's success is due not only to enlightened imitation and low-cost operations, but also to Wang's unique approach to financing growth. Although he initially mortgaged his home and borrowed from family and friends, when he needed additional funding, he targeted the manufacturing partners who were supplying him parts. In 2004, Taiwan-based contract manufacturer AmTran Technology Co. purchased an 8 percent stake in Vizio for $1 million; today, AmTran owns 23 percent of Vizio and supplies over 80 percent of its TVs. "Unlike many PC companies who try to make their money by squeezing the vendor," says Wang, "we try to work with our vendor."

Although Vizio has a long way to go to be the next Sony, it has made remarkable progress. Vizio shipped 19.9 percent of the LCD TVs sold in the third quarter of 2010, leading the number two firm, Samsung, which had 17.7 percent of the market. Vizio expected to sell 6 million TVs in 2010, generating over $2.5 billion in sales. Vizio is now turning its attention to smaller electronic devices. Vizio recently announced it will introduce a line of cellphones and tablet computers. In extending its low-cost business model to these markets, it is taking one more step to being a full-range competitor to Sony, Samsung, and other major consumer electronics firms.

---

features—doing it on the Internet and offering extraordinary customer service—have made Amazon a differentiated success.

There are several factors that make it more difficult for new ventures to be successful as differentiators. For one thing, the strategy is generally thought to be expensive to enact. Differentiation is often associated with strong brand identity, and establishing a brand is usually considered to be expensive because of the cost of advertising and promotion, paid endorsements, exceptional customer service, etc. Differentiation successes are sometimes built on superior innovation or use of technology. These are also factors where it may be challenging for young firms to excel relative to established competitors.

Nevertheless all of these areas—innovation, technology, customer service, distinctive branding—are also arenas where new ventures have sometimes made a name for themselves even though they must operate with limited resources and experience. To be successful, according to Garry Ridge, CEO of the WD-40 Company, "You need to have a great product, make the end user aware of it, and make it easy to buy."[38] It sounds simple, but it is a difficult challenge for new ventures with differentiation strategies.

Focus   Focus strategies are often associated with small businesses because there is a natural fit between the narrow scope of the strategy and the small size of the firm. A focus strategy may include elements of differentiation and overall cost leadership, as well as combinations of these approaches. But to be successful within a market niche, the key strategic requirement is to stay focused. Here's why:

Despite all the attention given to fast-growing new industries, most start-ups enter industries that are mature.[39] In mature industries, growth in demand tends to be slow and there are often many competitors. Therefore, if a start-up wants to get a piece of the action, it often has to take business away from an existing competitor. If a start-up enters a market with a broad or aggressive strategy, it is likely to evoke retaliation from a more powerful competitor. Young firms can often succeed best by finding a market niche where they can get a foothold and make small advances that erode the position of existing competitors.[40] From this position, they can build a name for themselves and grow.

Consider, for example, the "Miniature Editions" line of books launched by Running Press, a small Philadelphia publisher. The books are palm-sized minibooks positioned at bookstore cash registers as point-of-sale impulse items costing about $4.95. Beginning with just 10 titles in 1993, Running Press grew rapidly and within 10 years had sold over 20 million copies. Even though these books represent just a tiny fraction of total sales in the $23 billion publishing industry, they have been a mainstay for Running Press.[41] As the Running Press example indicates, many new ventures are successful even though their share of the market is quite small.

Combination Strategies

One of the best ways for young and small businesses to achieve success is by pursuing combination strategies. By combining the best features of low-cost, differentiation, and focus strategies, new ventures can often achieve something truly distinctive.

Entrepreneurial firms are often in a strong position to offer a combination strategy because they have the flexibility to approach situations uniquely. For example, holding down expenses can be difficult for big firms because each layer of bureaucracy adds to the cost of doing business across the boundaries of a large organization.[42]

A similar argument could be made about entrepreneurial firms that differentiate. Large firms often find it difficult to offer highly specialized products or superior customer services. Entrepreneurial firms, by contrast, can often create high-value products and services through their unique differentiating efforts. Strategy Spotlight 8.8 shows how two entrepreneurs found a recipt to sell a common product line to a niche market while both cutting costs and offering a high service level.

For nearly all new entrants, one of the major dangers is that a large firm with more resources will copy what they are doing. Well-established incumbents that observe the success of a new entrant's product or service will copy it and use their market power to overwhelm the smaller firm. The threat may be lessened for firms that use combination strategies. Because of the flexibility of entrepreneurial firms, they can often enact combination strategies in ways that the large firms cannot copy. This makes the new entrant's strategies much more sustainable.

Perhaps more threatening than large competitors are close competitors, because they have similar structural features that help them adjust quickly and be flexible in decision making. Here again, a carefully crafted and executed combination strategy may be the best way for an entrepreneurial firm to thrive in a competitive environment. Nevertheless, competition among rivals is a key determinant of new venture success. To address this, we turn next to the topic of competitive dynamics.

>LO8.5
How competitive actions, such as the entry of new competitors into a marketplace, may launch a cycle of actions and reactions among close competitors.

Competitive Dynamics

New entry into markets, whether by start-ups or by incumbent firms, nearly always threatens existing competitors. This is true in part because, except in very new markets, nearly

strategy spotlight

Diapers.com—Combining Focus, Low Cost, and Differentiation

Focusing on the needs of families with infants and toddlers, Marc Lore and Vinit Bharara turned a simple idea into a business worth $540 million in a matter of six years. Founded in January 2005, Diapers.com began by selling diapers out of a garage in Long Island, New York. Their business grew rapidly in geographic reach, products sold, and sales. But the firm's success relied on their ability to simultaneously focus on a particular market segment, offer a higher level of service, and maintain efficiency in operations. They now have a 30,000 square foot headquarters, over 500 employees, and over 600,000 square feet in warehouse space. In November 2010, at about the same time that they shipped their 500 millionth diaper, Diapers.com agreed to be acquired by Amazon.com for over a half billion dollars.

Diapers.com attracts customers by offering a high service level to busy parents who don't have the time to run out to Costco every time they need diapers and related baby care items. Over 70 percent of Diapers.com sales are to women, the majority of whom are in the 25–34 age range. Diapers.com sells 25,000 products, but they are

high-use products for baby care, such as diapers, wipes, shampoo, and formula. In focusing on this limited range of products, Diapers.com is able to differentiate itself by offering a high level of service. Their website is simpler to navigate than broad Internet retailers. If customers need the help of knowledgeable customer service agents, Diapers.com has a staff of 85 agents to handle their inquiries. Meeting the needs of their customers, whom they refer to as Moms, is key. As co-founder Marc Lore commented, "The concept is just if Mom calls and there's an issue, do whatever is necessary to make her happy and really wow her." Diapers.com also delivers quickly, with nearly 75 percent of their shipments being overnight deliveries and free shipping for any order over $49. This has resulted in a loyal set of customers whose word-of-mouth advertising draws in new customers to the firm. Their focus allows the firm to be extremely efficient. Their advertising is focused in magazines targeted toward parents. Operationally, they have developed sophisticated algorithms to maintain the minimum inventory needed to insure they can fill customer orders 95 percent of the time and have a highly automated warehouse that relies on robots manufactured by Kiva Systems to quickly and efficiently fill orders. They also rely on a computer algorithm to pick out the smallest box possible for an order to minimize shipping costs. They also use different shipping firms to ship to different regions, finding the lowest cost firm for that area. By meeting the needs of a narrow set of customers with a high service level and efficiency-oriented processes and resources, Diapers.com has excelled in a competitive, low-margin business.

Sources: Fowler, G. A. & Byron, L. 2010. Corporate News: Amazon to Buy Diapers.com Site. *The Wall Street Journal*, November 8: B4; Urstadt, B. 2010. Diapers vs. Goliath: Can Two Guys from Jersey Outsell Amazon? *Bloomberg Businessweek*, October 11: 62–68. Birchall, J. 2010. Amazon Aims to Woo Women with Quidsi Acquisition. *Financial Times*, November 9: 23; and Tiku, N. 2009. The Way I Work: Marc Lore of Diapers.com. *Inc. com*, September 1: np.

every market need is already being met, either directly or indirectly, by existing firms. As a result, the competitive actions of a new entrant are very likely to provoke a competitive response from companies that feel threatened. This, in turn, is likely to evoke a reaction to the response. As a result, a competitive dynamic—action and response—begins among the firms competing for the same customers in a given marketplace.

competitive dynamics intense rivalry, involving actions and responses, among similar competitors vying for the same customers in a marketplace.

Competitive dynamics—intense rivalry among similar competitors—has the potential to alter a company's strategy. New entrants may be forced to change their strategies or develop new ones to survive competitive challenges by incumbent rivals. New entry is among the most common reasons why a cycle of competitive actions and reactions gets started. It might also occur because of threatening actions among existing competitors, such as aggressive cost cutting. Thus, studying competitive dynamics helps explain why strategies evolve and reveals how, why, and when to respond to the actions of close competitors. Exhibit 8.7 identifies the factors that competitors need to consider when determining how to respond to a competitive act.

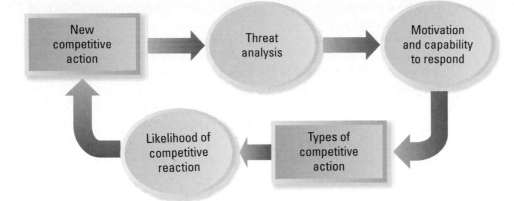

Exhibit 8.7 **Model of Competitive Dynamics**

Sources: Adapted from Chen, M. J. 1996. Competitor Analysis and Interfirm Rivalry: Toward a Theoretical Integration. *Academy of Management Review,* 21(1): 100–134; Ketchen, D. J., Snow, C. C., & Hoover, V. L. 2004. Research on competitive dynamics: Recent Accomplishments and Future Challenges. *Journal of Management,* 30(6): 779–804; and Smith, K. G., Ferrier, W. J., & Grimm, C. M. 2001. King of the Hill: Dethroning the Industry Leader. *Academy of Management Executive,* 15(2): 59–70.

New Competitive Action

Entry into a market by a new competitor is a good starting point to begin describing the cycle of actions and responses characteristic of a competitive dynamic process.[43] However, new entry is only one type of competitive action. Price cutting, imitating successful products, or expanding production capacity are other examples of competitive acts that might provoke competitors to react.

Why do companies launch new competitive actions? There are several reasons:

- Improve market position
- Capitalize on growing demand
- Expand production capacity
- Provide an innovative new solution
- Obtain first mover advantages

Underlying all of these reasons is a desire to strengthen financial outcomes, capture some of the extraordinary profits that industry leaders enjoy, and grow the business. Some companies are also motivated to launch competitive challenges because they want to build their reputation for innovativeness or efficiency. For example, Southwest Airlines, once an upstart airline with only a few routes, has become phenomenally successful and an industry leader. For years it went virtually unchallenged. But Southwest's costs have crept up, and now start-up airlines such as JetBlue are challenging the industry leader with their own low-cost strategies.[44] This is indicative of the competitive dynamic cycle. As former Intel Chairman Andy Grove stated, "Business success contains the seeds of its own destruction. The more successful you are, the more people want a chunk of your business and then another chunk and then another until there is nothing left."[45]

When a company enters into a market for the first time, it is an attack on existing competitors. As indicated earlier in the chapter, any of the entry strategies can be used to take competitive action. But competitive attacks come from many sources besides new entrants. Some of the most intense competition is among incumbent rivals intent on gaining strategic advantages. "Winners in business play rough and don't apologize for it," according to Boston Consulting Group authors George Stalk, Jr. and Rob Lachenauer in

>LO8.6

The components of competitive dynamics analysis—new competitive action, threat analysis, motivation and capability to respond, types of competitive actions, and likelihood of competitive reaction.

new competitive action acts that might provoke competitors to react, such as new market entry, price cutting, imitating successful products, and expanding production capacity.

their book *Hardball: Are You Playing to Play or Playing to Win?*[46] Exhibit 8.8 outlines their five strategies.

The likelihood that a competitor will launch an attack depends on many factors.[47] In the remaining sections, we discuss factors such as competitor analysis, market conditions, types of strategic actions, and the resource endowments and capabilities companies need to take competitive action.

Threat Analysis

Prior to actually observing a competitive action, companies may need to become aware of potential competitive threats. That is, companies need to have a keen sense of who their closest competitors are and the kinds of competitive actions they might be planning.[48] This may require some environmental scanning and monitoring of the sort described in Chapter 2. Awareness of the threats posed by industry rivals allows a firm to understand what type of competitive response, if any, may be necessary.

For example, Netflix founder and CEO Reed Hastings has faced numerous competitive threats since launching the online movie rental company in 1997. According to Hastings, however, not all potential threats need to be taken seriously:

> We have to recognize that now there are tens and maybe hundreds of start-ups who think that they are going to eat Netflix's lunch. The challenge for a management team is to figure out which are real threats and which aren't. . . . It's conventional to say, "only the paranoid survive" but that's not true. The paranoid die because the paranoid take all threats as serious and get very distracted.
>
> There are markets that aren't going to get very big, and then there are markets that are going to get big, but they're not directly in our path. In the first camp we have small companies like Movielink—a well-run company but not an attractive model for consumers, sort of a $4-download to watch a movie. We correctly guessed when it launched four years ago that this was not a threat and didn't react to it.
>
> The other case I brought up is markets that are going to be very large markets, but we're just not the natural leader. Advertising supported online video, whether that's at CBS. com or You Tube—great market, kind of next door to us. But we don't do advertising-supported video, we do subscription, so it would be a huge competence expansion for us. And it's not a threat to movies.

Being aware of competitors and cognizant of whatever threats they might pose is the first step in assessing the level of competitive threat. Once a new competitive action becomes apparent, companies must determine how threatening it is to their business. Competitive dynamics are likely to be most intense among companies that are competing for the same customers or who have highly similar sets of resources.[49] Two factors are used to assess whether or not companies are close competitors:

- **Market commonality**—Whether or not competitors are vying for the same customers and how many markets they share in common. For example, aircraft manufacturers Boeing and Airbus have a high degree of market commonality because they make very similar products and have many buyers in common.

- **Resource similarity**—The degree to which rivals draw on the same types of resources to compete. For example, the home pages of Google and Yahoo! may look very different, but behind the scenes, they both rely on the talent pool of high-caliber software engineers to create the cutting-edge innovations that help them compete.

When any two firms have both a high degree of market commonality and highly similar resource bases, a stronger competitive threat is present. Such a threat, however, may not lead to competitive action. On the one hand, a market rival may be hesitant to attack a company that it shares a high degree of market commonality with because it could lead to

Exhibit 8.8 Five "Hardball" Strategies

Strategy	Description	Examples
Devastate rivals' profit sanctuaries	Not all business segments generate the same level of profits for a company. Through focused attacks on a rival's most profitable segments, a company can generate maximum leverage with relatively smaller-scale attacks. Recognize, however, that companies closely guard the information needed to determine just what their profit sanctuaries are.	In 2005, Walmart began offering low-priced extended warranties on home electronics after learning that its rivals such as Best Buy derived most of their profits from extended warranties.
Plagiarize with pride	Just because a close competitor comes up with an idea first does not mean it cannot be successfully imitated. Second movers, in fact, can see how customers respond, make improvements, and launch a better version without all the market development costs. Successful imitation is harder than it may appear and requires the imitating firm to keep its ego in check.	Blockbuster copied the online DVD rental strategy of its rival Netflix. Not only does Blockbuster continue to struggle even after this imitation, but also Netflix sued Blockbuster for patent violations.
Deceive the competition	A good gambit sends the competition off in the wrong direction. This may cause the rivals to miss strategic shifts, spend money pursuing dead ends, or slow their responses. Any of these outcomes support the deceiving firms' competitive advantage. Companies must be sure not to cross ethical lines during these actions.	Boeing spent several years touting its plans for a new high-speed airliner. After it became clear the customer valued efficiency over speed, Boeing quietly shifted its focus. When Boeing announced its new 7e7 (now 787) Dreamliner, its competitor, Airbus Industries, was surprised and caught without an adequate response, which helped the 787 set new sales records.
Unleash massive and overwhelming force	While many hardball strategies are subtle and indirect, this one is not. This is a full-frontal attack where a firm commits significant resources to a major campaign to weaken rivals' positions in certain markets. Firms must be sure they have the mass and stamina required to win before they declare war against a rival.	Southwest Airlines took on US Airways in Baltimore and drove US Airways' market share from over 50 percent to 10 percent. Southwest followed this up by flying to Philadelphia and Pittsburgh as well—additional key markets for US Airways.
Raise competitors' costs	If a company has superior insight into the complex cost and profit structure of the industry, it can compete in a way that steers its rivals into relatively higher cost/lower profit arenas. This strategy uses deception to make the rivals think they are winning, when in fact they are not. Again, companies using this strategy must be confident that they understand the industry better than their rivals.	Ecolab, a company that sells cleaning supplies to businesses, encouraged a leading competitor, Diversity, to adopt a strategy to go after the low-volume, high-margin customers. What Ecolab knew that Diversity didn't is that the high servicing costs involved with this segment make the segment unprofitable—a situation Ecolab assured by bidding high enough to lose the contracts to Diversity but low enough to ensure the business lost money for Diversity.

Sources: Berner, R. 2005. Watch Out, Best Buy and Circuit City. *BusinessWeek,* November 10; Halkias, M. 2006. Blockbuster Strikes Back at Netflix Suit. *Dallas Morning News,* June 14; McCartney, S. 2007. Southwest Makes Inroads at Hubs. *The Wall Street Journal,* May 1, D3; Stalk, G. Jr. 2006. Curveball Strategies to Fool the Competition. *Harvard Business Review,* 84(9): 114–121; and Stalk, Jr., G. & Lachenauer, R. 2004. *Hardball: Are You Playing to Play or Playing to Win?* Cambridge, MA: Harvard Business School Press. Reprinted by permission of Harvard Business School Press from G. Stalk, Jr. and R. Lachenauer. Copyright 2004 by the Harvard Business School Publishing Corporation; all rights reserved.

an intense battle. On the other hand, once attacked, rivals with high market commonality will be much more motivated to launch a competitive response. This is especially true in cases where the shared market is an important part of a company's overall business.

How strong a response an attacked rival can mount will be determined by their strategic resource endowments. In general, the same set of conditions holds true with regard to resource similarity. Companies that have highly similar resource bases will be hesitant to launch an initial attack but pose a serious threat if required to mount a competitive response.[50] Greater strategic resources increase a firm's capability to respond.

Motivation and Capability to Respond

Once attacked, competitors are faced with deciding how to respond. Before deciding, however, they need to evaluate not only how they will respond, but also their reasons for responding and their capability to respond. Companies need to be clear about what problems a competitive response is expected to address and what types of problems it might create.[51] There are several factors to consider.

First, how serious is the impact of the competitive attack to which they are responding? For example, a large company with a strong reputation that is challenged by a small or unknown company may elect to simply keep an eye on the new competitor rather than quickly react or overreact. Part of the story of online retailer Amazon's early success is attributed to Barnes & Noble's overreaction to Amazon's claim that it was "earth's biggest bookstore." Because Barnes & Noble was already using the phrase "world's largest bookstore," it sued Amazon, but lost. The confrontation made it to the front pages of *The Wall Street Journal* and Amazon was on its way to becoming a household name.[52]

Companies planning to respond to a competitive challenge must also understand their motivation for responding. What is the intent of the competitive response? Is it merely to blunt the attack of the competitor or is it an opportunity to enhance its competitive position? Sometimes the most a company can hope for is to minimize the damage caused by a competitive action.

● *The Wall Street Journal* and *The New York Times* are engaged in an intense rivalry for market share.

A company that seeks to improve its competitive advantage may be motivated to launch an attack rather than merely respond to one. Strategy Spotlight 8.9 highlights how *The Wall Street Journal* saw an opportunity to improve its position by attaching a weakened *New York Times*. A company must also assess its capability to respond. What strategic resources can be deployed to fend off a competitive attack? Does the company have an array of internal strengths it can draw on, or is it operating from a position of weakness?

Consider, the role of firm age and size in calculating a company's ability to respond. Most entrepreneurial new ventures start out small. The smaller size makes them more nimble compared to large firms so they can respond quickly to competitive attacks. Because they are not well-known, start-ups also have the advantage of the element of surprise in how and when they attack. Innovative uses of technology, for example, allow small firms to deploy resources in unique ways.

Because they are young, however, start-ups may not have the financial resources needed to follow through with a competitive response.[53] In contrast, older and larger firms may have more resources and a repertoire of competitive techniques they can use in a counterattack. Large firms, however, tend to be slower to respond. Older firms tend to be predictable in their responses because they often lose touch with the competitive environment and rely on strategies and actions that have worked in the past.

strategy spotlight

The Wall Street Journal Challenges The New York Times

The newspaper business is an increasingly tough market. Circulation and advertising rates are dropping as news consumers move from traditional newspaper providers to online news services. In this difficult environment, newspapers both have increased motivation to take business from their remaining traditional competitors and reduced capability to respond to competitive attacks. These competing factors have resulted in an interesting competitive action in New York City. The Wall Street Journal (WSJ), a newspaper that has emphasized business and investing news since its inception in 1889, is taking on The New York Times (Times), a traditional city newspaper. The WSJ launched its Greater New York Edition in April 2010 to increase its base of affluent subscribers and female readers in the New York region, the core readers of the Times.

Why the Times, and why now? The WSJ has high motivation to act now. News Corp. purchased the WSJ in 2007 and brought with it an aggressive attitude that called for change at the WSJ. Rupert Murdoch, the chairman of News Corp., specifically stated at the time that he wanted to see the WSJ compete more directly with the Times. They are also motivated to act since the customers they are striving to attract make the WSJ more attractive to luxury product and service advertisers in the New York

area. Their new edition has signed on luxury advertisers Saks Fifth Avenue, Bloomingdales, Cathay Pacific Airlines, Broadway's Jersey Boys musical, and the American Ballet Theatre. They also have the capability to act because the WSJ is one of the few traditional news providers with a growing number of readers. They also have the backing of News Corp., a major global media firm. Thus, they have the financial resources necessary to launch and sustain a competitive action against the Times.

But it is a different situation at the Times. While motivated to respond to the WSJ's attack, they have limited resources to mount a major competitive response. They have experienced a significant decline in subscriptions, with the number of subscribers falling 8.5 percent in March 2010 compared to one year earlier. This has reduced the advertising rates they are able to charge. Also, the Times has limited cash resources. They are so strapped for cash that they were forced to borrow $250 million from Mexican industrialist Carlos Slim in 2009 at a 14 percent interest rate. When the WSJ launched their Greater New York Edition, the Times only had $36.5 million in cash on their balance sheet—not much of a war chest to take on News Corp. For Rupert Murdoch, the Times's struggles are a signal to attack and an opportunity to cripple and potentially destroy The New York Times. As media investment expert Richard Dorfman stated, "This could be a money-losing venture for the Journal, but a potential big winner for Rupert if he's able to throw the Times over the edge of the abyss."

Other local papers should be wary. There are reports that, if successful with their Greater New York Edition, The Wall Street Journal will consider launching similar ventures in other major markets, including San Francisco, Los Angeles, and Washington, D.C.

Sources: Anonymous. 2010. Is the Times Ready for a Newspaper War? Bloomberg Businessweek. April 26: 30–31; Bensinger, G. 2010. Wall Street Journal Circulation Gains as New Edition Debuts. Bloomberg Businessweek, April 26: np; Anonymous. 2010. Wall Street Journal Considers Other Local Markets if NY Edition a Success. Mediabuyerplanner.com, April 18: np; and Sreenivasan, S. 2010. The Wall Street Journal's Local Edition Launches. Dnainfo.com, April 26: np.

Other resources may also play a role in whether a company is equipped to retaliate. For example, one avenue of counterattack may be launching product enhancements or new product/service innovations. For that approach to be successful, it requires a company to have both the intellectual capital to put forward viable innovations and the teamwork skills to prepare a new product or service and get it to market. Resources such as cross-functional teams and the social capital that makes teamwork production effective and efficient represent the type of human capital resources that enhance a company's capability to respond.

Types of Competitive Actions

Once an organization determines whether it is willing and able to launch a competitive action, it must determine what type of action is appropriate. The actions taken will be determined by both its resource capabilities and its motivation for responding. There are also marketplace considerations. What types of actions are likely to be most effective given a company's internal strengths and weaknesses as well as market conditions?

strategy spotlight 8.10

AMD and Intel: The Multiple Dimensions of Competitive Dynamics

Few business battles are as intense or as intensely reported as the one between chipmakers Intel and Advanced Micro Devices (AMD). These two firms have fought an intense competitive battle for over two decades. They started out on a much different footing. They were both founded in the late 1960s in Silicon Valley and were partners in their early years. But their history changed in 1986 after Intel cancelled a licensing agreement with AMD to manufacture microprocessors and refused to turn over technical details. Since that time, Intel has dominated the microprocessor market with approximately 80 percent market share but has regularly faced competitive initiatives from AMD and has as regularly taken competitive initiatives against AMD. As Intel Executive Vice President Sean Maloney stated, "We intend to energetically compete for every single microprocessor opportunity."

Their battle points out how highly competitive firms can take their competitive attacks to multiple battlefields. They have fought product design battles. Time and time again, they have aimed to pioneer new generations of chips. They fought over who would launch the first 64-bit processors. They competed in introducing multiple-core chips. They competed in producing low-energy chips for laptops and notebooks. Currently, they are racing to launch chips that integrate graphics chip capabilities into the microprocessor. They have fought to build relationships with customers. According to governmental regulators, Intel locked in Dell and other PC manufacturers as exclusive customers by offering them rebates to use only Intel microprocessors. AMD fought back and won business supplying chips to Dell in 2006 and for Lenovo notebooks in 2009. They have developed aggressive marketing campaigns to promote their products. They have acquired other firms to pull in new technology to gain an advantage. For example, AMD bought ATI Technologies to gain access to graphics chip technology that they have integrated with the CPU in their latest generation of chips, the Fusion. They have fought legal battles. Both firms have sued each other over the right to technologies. Intel finally settled a multiyear legal battle with AMD for $1.25 billion in 2009.

This competitive battle shows how a long-standing competitive battle between firms can include a range of tactical and strategic actions as firms act to improve their own competitive position and unsettle the competitive position of their rival. This battle also demonstrates the potential benefits of high industry rivalry for consumers. The rivalry between AMD and Intel has led to tremendous improvements in microprocessor capabilities with declining prices over time. And there is no end in sight for these two pitched rivals.

Sources: Fortt, J. 2010. Intel vs. AMD Gets Interesting Again. *CNNmoney.com,* May 12: np; Clark, D. 2010. AMD Starts Shipping New Breed of Chips. *The Wall Street Journal,* November 10: B7; Vance, A. 2010. Dell's Trouble Kicking the Intel Habit. *New York Times,* July 23; Parloff, R. 2010. What the Dell Settlement Means for Intel. *Fortune.com,* July 27: np; and *www.wikipedia.org.*

strategic actions major commitments of distinctive and specific resources to strategic initiatives.

tactical actions refinements or extensions of strategies usually involving minor resource commitments.

Two broadly defined types of competitive action include strategic actions and tactical actions. **Strategic actions** represent major commitments of distinctive and specific resources. Examples include launching a breakthrough innovation, building a new production facility, or merging with another company. Such actions require significant planning and resources and, once initiated, are difficult to reverse.

Tactical actions include refinements or extensions of strategies. Examples of tactical actions include cutting prices, improving gaps in service, or strengthening marketing efforts. Such actions typically draw on general resources and can be implemented quickly. Exhibit 8.9 identifies several types of strategic and tactical competitive actions, and Strategy Spotlight 8.10 shows the range of actions that can occur in a rivalrous relationship.

Some competitive actions take the form of frontal assaults, that is, actions aimed directly at taking business from another company or capitalizing on industry weaknesses. This can be especially effective when firms use a low-cost strategy. The airline industry provides a good example of this head-on approach. When Southwest Airlines began its no-frills, no-meals, strategy in the late-1960s, it represented a direct assault on the major carriers of the day. In Europe, Ryanair has similarly directly challenged the traditional carriers with an overall cost leadership strategy.

Exhibit 8.9 **Strategic and Tactical Competitive Actions**

	Actions	Examples
Strategic Actions	• Entering new markets	• Make geographical expansions • Expand into neglected markets • Target rivals' markets • Target new demographics
	• New product introductions	• Imitate rivals' products • Address gaps in quality • Leverage new technologies • Leverage brand name with related products • Protect innovation with patents
	• Changing production capacity	• Create overcapacity • Tie up raw materials sources • Tie up preferred suppliers and distributors • Stimulate demand by limiting capacity
	• Mergers/Alliances	• Acquire/partner with competitors to reduce competition • Tie up key suppliers through alliances • Obtain new technology/intellectual property • Facilitate new market entry
Tactical Actions	• Price cutting (or increases)	• Maintain low price dominance • Offer discounts and rebates • Offer incentives (e.g., frequent flyer miles) • Enhance offering to move upscale
	• Product/service enhancements	• Address gaps in service • Expand warranties • Make incremetal product improvements
	• Increased marketing efforts	• Use guerilla marketing • Conduct selective attacks • Change product packaging • Use new marketing channels
	• New distribution channels	• Access suppliers directly • Access customers directly • Develop multiple points of contact with customers • Expand Internet presence

Sources: Chen, M. J. & Hambrick, D. 1995. Speed, Stealth, and Selective Attack: How Small Firms Differ from Large Firms in Competitive Behavior. *Academy of Management Journal,* 38: 453–482; Davies, M. 1992. Sales Promotions as a Competitive Strategy. *Management Decision,* 30(7): 5–10; Ferrier, W., Smith, K., & Grimm, C. 1999. The Role of Competitive Action in Market Share Erosion and Industry Dethronement: A Study of Industry Leaders and Challengers. *Academy of Management Journal,* 42(4): 372–388; and Garda, R. A. 1991. Use Tactical Pricing to Uncover Hidden Profits. *Journal of Business Strategy,* 12(5): 17–23.

Guerilla offensives and selective attacks provide an alternative for firms with fewer resources.[54] These draw attention to products or services by creating buzz or generating enough shock value to get some free publicity. TOMS shoes has found a way to generate interest in its products without a large advertising budget to match Nike. Their policy of donating one pair of shoes to those in need for every pair of shoes purchased by customers has generated a lot of buzz on the internet.[55] Over 700,000 people have given a "like" rating on TOMS's Facebook page.

● Intel and AMD have had a fierce rivalry over the years.

The policy has a real impact as well, with over 1,000,000 shoes donated as of September 2010.[56]

Some companies limit their competitive response to defensive actions. Such actions rarely improve a company's competitive advantage, but a credible defensive action can lower the risk of being attacked and deter new entry. This may be especially effective during periods such as an industry shake-up, when pricing levels or future demand for a product line become highly uncertain. At such times, tactics such as lowering prices on products that are easily duplicated, buying up the available supply of goods or raw materials, or negotiating exclusive agreements with buyers and/or suppliers can insulate a company from a more serious attack.

Several of the factors discussed earlier in the chapter, such as types of entry strategies and the use of cost leadership versus differentiation strategies, can guide the decision about what types of competitive actions to take. Before launching a given strategy, however, assessing the likely response of competitors is a vital step.[57]

Likelihood of Competitive Reaction

The final step before initiating a competitive response is to evaluate what a competitor's reaction is likely to be. The logic of competitive dynamics suggests that once competitive actions are initiated, it is likely they will be met with competitive responses.[58] The last step before mounting an attack is to evaluate how competitors are likely to respond. Evaluating potential competitive reactions helps companies plan for future counterattacks. It may also lead to a decision to hold off—that is, not to take any competitive action at all because of the possibility that a misguided or poorly planned response will generate a devastating competitive reaction.

How a competitor is likely to respond will depend on three factors: market dependence, competitor's resources, and the reputation of the firm that initiates the action (actor's reputation). The implications of each of these is described briefly in the following sections.

market dependence degree of concentration of a firm's business in a particular industry.

Market Dependence   If a company has a high concentration of its business in a particular industry, it has more at stake because it must depend on that industry's market for its sales. Single-industry businesses or those where one industry dominates are more likely to mount a competitive response. Young and small firms with a high degree of market dependence may be limited in how they respond due to resource constraints. JetBlue, itself an aggressive competitor, is unable to match some of the perks its bigger rivals can offer, such as first-class seats or international travel benefits.

Competitor's Resources   Previously, we examined the internal resource endowments that a company must evaluate when assessing its capability to respond. Here, it is the competitor's resources that need to be considered. For example, a small firm may be unable to mount a serious attack due to lack of resources. Also, as we saw in Strategy Spotlight 8.9, a large but poorly performing firm may lack the resources to respond to an attack. As a result, it is more likely to react to tactical actions such as incentive pricing or enhanced service offerings because they are less costly to attack than large-scale strategic actions. In contrast, a firm with financial "deep pockets" may be able to mount and sustain a costly counterattack.

Actor's Reputation   Whether a company should respond to a competitive challenge will also depend on who launched the attack against it. Compared to relatively smaller firms with less market power, competitors are more likely to respond to competitive moves by market leaders. Another consideration is how successful prior attacks have been. For example, price-cutting by the big automakers usually has the desired result—increased sales to price-sensitive buyers—at least in the short run. Given that history, when GM offers discounts or incentives, rivals Ford and Chrysler cannot afford to ignore the challenge and quickly follow suit.

Choosing Not to React: Forbearance and Co-opetition

The above discussion suggests that there may be many circumstances in which the best reaction is no reaction at all. This is known as **forbearance**—refraining from reacting at all as well as holding back from initiating an attack. The decision of whether a firm should respond or show forbearance is not always clear. In Strategy Spotlight 8.11, we see the NFL and the UFL facing such a decision.

forbearance a firm's choice of not reacting to a rival's new competitive action.

Related to forbearance is the concept of **co-opetition.** This is a term that was coined by network software company Novell's founder and former CEO Raymond Noorda to suggest that companies often benefit most from a combination of competing and cooperating.[59] Close competitors that differentiate themselves in the eyes of consumers may work together behind the scenes to achieve industrywide efficiencies.[60] For example, breweries in Sweden cooperate in recycling used bottles but still compete for customers on the basis of taste and variety. As long as the benefits of cooperating are enjoyed by all participants in a co-opetition system, the practice can aid companies in avoiding intense and damaging competition.[61]

co-opetition a firm's strategy of both cooperating and competing with rival firms.

Despite the potential benefits of co-opetition, companies need to guard against cooperating to such a great extent that their actions are perceived as collusion, a practice that has legal ramifications in the United States. Recently, Dell and other PC manufacturers have faced scrutiny due to their possible collusion with Intel.

Once a company has evaluated a competitor's likelihood of responding to a competitive challenge, it can decide what type of action is most appropriate. Competitive actions can take many forms: the entry of a start-up into a market for the first time, an attack by a lower-ranked incumbent on an industry leader, or the launch of a breakthrough innovation that disrupts the industry structure. Such actions forever change the competitive dynamics of a marketplace. Thus, the cycle of actions and reactions that occur in business every day is a vital aspect of entrepreneurial strategy that leads to continual new value creation and the ongoing advancement of economic well-being.

Reflecting on Career Implications . . .

- *Opportunity Recognition:* What ideas for new business activities are actively discussed in your work environment? Could you apply the four characteristics of an opportunity to determine whether they are viable opportunities?
- *Entrepreneurial New Entry:* Are there opportunities to launch new products or services that might add value to the organization? What are the best ways for you to bring these opportunities to the attention of key managers? Or, might this provide an opportunity for you to launch your own entrepreneurial venture?
- *Entrepreneurial Strategy:* Does your organization face competition from new ventures? If so, how are those young firms competing: Low cost? Differentiation? Focus? What could you do to help your company to address those competitive challenges?
- *Competitive Dynamics:* Is your organization "on the offense" with its close competitors or "playing defense"? What types of strategic and/or tactical actions have been taken by your close rivals recently to gain competitive advantages?

strategy spotlight

8.11

The UFL and the NFL: Cooperate or Compete?

If we look at the success and failure of professional football leagues from the past, the future for the United Football League (UFL) would not appear to be promising. Since the merger of the NFL with the AFL in the 1960s, several leagues trying to build a position in the American football market have failed. In the 1970s, it was the World Football League that rose and fell in a few years. In the 1980s, it was the United States Football league that followed the same pattern. In the 1990s, the Canadian Football League tried expanding south of the border, only to quickly retreat back north. The XFL lasted only a single year in 2001. Only the unique Arena Football League has lasted more than a few years, but its history has still been bumpy. The league went through bankruptcy in 2008 only to return in 2010.

The UFL is a new upstart football league trying to carve out a position in the professional football market. Unlike the Arena Football League, the UFL is playing a version of football that is almost identical to the NFL and plays during the traditional fall football season. The league began play in 2009 with four teams, expanded to five teams in 2010, and will play with either six or eight teams in 2011.

However, it is unclear at this point to what degree the UFL will compete with the NFL, and it is also unclear whether the NFL will act in a way to push the UFL out of the market or show forbearance and let them stay in the game. The UFL appears to be taking actions to avoid a direct confrontation with the NFL. They have placed their franchises in cities, such as Las Vegas, Omaha, and Orlando, that currently do not have NFL franchises. They also have not tried to compete with the NFL for players. They have made no effort to sign active NFL players. Instead, their rosters are a combination of former NFL players, such as JaMarcus Russell, hoping to revive their NFL careers and young players hoping to make an impression and move up to the NFL. However, the league appears reluctant to position themselves simply as a minor or developmental league for the NFL. They require the NFL to pay a $150,000 transfer fee to allow a UFL player to sign with an NFL team, limiting the willingness of NFL teams to sign UFL players. Also, they are looking to expand into markets that the NFL also sees as desirable. The UFL has announced an expansion into the Los Angeles market in either 2011 or 2012, but the NFL is working with potential owners interested in moving an NFL franchise into the LA market as well. The intentions of the NFL are also unclear. The NFL has not taken any direct actions against the UFL. But the NFL has also not pursued a cooperative relationship with the upstart league. According to ESPN, the UFL offered the NFL the opportunity to buy part of the league and set up consistent rules for players to move from one league to the other, but the NFL did not agree to make the investment. It may be that the NFL is focused on their unsettled labor contract with the players' union and, as a result, doesn't have the motivation to act either cooperatively or competitively with the UFL at this point in time.

Given the history of prior football leagues, the ability of the UFL to find a position where they don't directly compete with the NFL for ticket buyers, players, or TV placement would appear to be key to their viability. Thus, figuring out how to appear similar enough to the NFL to attract fans while also different enough to not trigger a competitive reaction by the NFL should be a primary factor driving the UFL's actions.

Sources: Mortensen, C. 2010. UFL Puts 30 Percent Offer on NFL's Table. *ESPN.com*, March 19: np; Cohan, W. D. 2010. Football's New Game in Town. *Fortune*, October 18: 111–112; and *www.wikipedia.org*.

Summary

New ventures and entrepreneurial firms that capitalize on marketplace opportunities make an important contribution to the U.S. economy. They are leaders in terms of implementing new technologies and introducing innovative products and services. Yet entrepreneurial firms face unique challenges if they are going to survive and grow.

To successfully launch new ventures or implement new technologies, three factors must be present: an entrepreneurial opportunity, the resources to pursue the opportunity, and an entrepreneur or entrepreneurial team willing and able to undertake the venture. Firms must develop a strong ability to recognize viable opportunities.

Opportunity recognition is a process of determining which venture ideas are, in fact, promising business opportunities.

In addition to strong opportunities, entrepreneurial firms need resources and entrepreneurial leadership to thrive. The resources that start-ups need include financial resources as well as human and social capital. Many firms also benefit from government programs that support new venture development and growth. New ventures thrive best when they are led by founders or owners who have vision, drive and dedication, and a commitment to excellence.

Once the necessary opportunities, resources, and entrepreneur skills are in place, new ventures still face numerous strategic challenges. Decisions about the strategic positioning of new entrants can benefit from conducting strategic analyses and evaluating the requirements of niche markets. Entry strategies used by new ventures take several forms, including pioneering new entry, imitative new entry, and adaptive new entry. Entrepreneurial firms can benefit from using overall low cost, differentiation, and focus strategies although each of these approaches has pitfalls that are unique to young and small firms. Entrepreneurial firms are also in a strong position to benefit from combination strategies.

The entry of a new company into a competitive arena is like a competitive attack on incumbents in that arena. Such actions often provoke a competitive response, which may, in turn, trigger a reaction to the response. As a result, a competitive dynamic—action and response—begins among close competitors. In deciding whether to attack or counterattack, companies must analyze the seriousness of the competitive threat, their ability to mount a competitive response, and the type of action—strategic or tactical—that the situation requires. At times, competitors find it is better not to respond at all or to find avenues to cooperate with, rather than challenge, close competitors.

Summary Review Questions

1. Explain how the combination of opportunities, resources, and entrepreneurs helps determine the character and strategic direction of an entrepreneurial firm.

2. What is the difference between discovery and evaluation in the process of opportunity recognition? Give an example of each.

3. Describe the three characteristics of entrepreneurial leadership: vision, dedication and drive, and commitment to excellence.

4. Briefly describe the three types of entrepreneurial entry strategies: pioneering, imitative, and adaptive.

5. Explain why entrepreneurial firms are often in a strong position to use combination strategies.

6. What does the term *competitive dynamics* mean?

7. Explain the difference between strategic actions and tactical actions and provide examples of each.

Key Terms

entrepreneurship, 281
opportunity recognition, 284
angel investors, 287
venture capitalists, 289
entrepreneurial leadership, 290
entrepreneurial strategy, 292
pioneering new entry, 293
imitative new entry, 293
adaptive new entry, 295

competitive dynamics, 300
new competitive action, 301
threat analysis, 302
market commonality, 302
resource similarity, 302
strategic actions, 306
tactical actions, 306
market dependence, 308
forbearance, 309
co-opetition, 309

Applications Questions & Answers

1. E-Loan and Lending Tree are two entrepreneurial firms that offer lending services over the Internet. Evaluate the features of these two companies and, for each company:

   a. Evaluate their characteristics and assess the extent to which they are comparable in terms of market commonality and resource similarity.

   b. Based on your analysis, what strategic and/or tactical actions might these companies take to improve their competitive position? Could E-Loan and Lending Tree improve their performance more through co-opetition rather than competition? Explain your rationale.

2. Using the Internet, research the Small Business Administration's website (*www.sba.gov*). What different types of financing are available to small firms? Besides financing, what other programs are available to support the growth and development of small businesses?

3. Think of an entrepreneurial firm that has been successfully launched in the last 10 years. What kind of entry strategy did it use—pioneering, imitative, or adaptive? Since the firm's initial entry, how has

Company	Market Commonality	Resource Similarity
E-Loan		
Lending Tree		

Company	Strategic Actions	Tectical Actions
E-Loan		
Lending Tree		

it used or combined overall low-cost, differentiation and/or focus strategies?

4. Select an entrepreneurial firm you are familiar with in your local community. Research the company and discuss how it has positioned itself relative to its close competitors. Does it have a unique strategic advantage? Disadvantage? Explain.

Ethics Questions

1. Imitation strategies are based on the idea of copying another firm's idea and using it for your own purposes. Is this unethical or simply a smart business practice? Discuss the ethical implications of this practice (if any).

2. Intense competition such as price wars are an accepted practice in the United States, but cooperation between companies has legal ramifications because of antitrust laws. Should price wars that drive small businesses or new entrants out of business be illegal? What ethical considerations are raised (if any)?

References

1. Anonymous. 2006. 2006 Fastest-growing franchise rankings. *Entrepreneur. http://entrepreneur.com*, October 2010: np; Anonymous, 2007. Rising stars. *Entrepreneur. http://entrepreneur.com*, October 2010: np; Edersheim Kalb, P. 2009 Cranky consumer: Hiring middlemen to sell stuff on eBay. *Wall Street Journal,* January 29: D2; Ohngren, K. 2010. Kaboom! A look back at the wacky franchise ideas that exploded (and imploded) in an instant. Meet you at the eBay store. *Entrepreneur,* January 38(1): 120–124; and Wilson, S. 2006. Hotter than hot. *Entrepreneur,* June 34(6): 72–81; April 35(4): 108–111. We thank Ciprian Stan for his valued contribution.

2. Small Business Administration. 2004. *The small business economy* Washington, D.C.: U.S. Government Printing Office.

3. Timmons, J. A. & Spinelli, S. 2004. *New venture creation* (6th ed.). New York: McGraw-Hill/Irwin; and Bygrave, W. D. 1997. The entrepreneurial process. In W. D. Bygrave

(Ed.), *The portable MBA in entrepreneurship*, 2nd ed. New York: Wiley.

4. Fromartz, S. 1998. How to get your first great idea. *Inc. Magazine*, April 1: 91–94; and, Vesper, K. H. 1990. *New venture strategies*, 2nd ed. Englewood Cliffs, NJ: Prentice-Hall.

5. For an interesting perspective on the nature of the opportunity recognition process, see Baron, R. A. 2006. Opportunity recognition as pattern recognition: How entrepreneurs "connect the dots" to identify new business opportunities. *Academy of Management Perspectives*, February: 104–119.

6. Gaglio, C. M. 1997. Opportunity identification: Review, critique and suggested research directions. In J. A. Katz, ed. *Advances in entrepreneurship, firm emergence and growth*, vol. 3. Greenwich, CT: JAI Press: 139–202; Lumpkin, G. T., Hills, G. E., & Shrader, R. C. 2004. Opportunity recognition. In Harold L. Welsch, (Ed.), *Entrepreneurship: The road ahead*, pp. 73–90. London: Routledge; and Long, W. & McMullan, W. E. 1984. Mapping the new venture opportunity identification process. *Frontiers of entrepreneurship research, 1984*. Wellesley, MA: Babson College: 567–90.

7. For an interesting discussion of different aspects of opportunity discovery, see Shepherd, D. A. & De Tienne, D. R. 2005. Prior knowledge, potential financial reward, and opportunity identification. *Entrepreneurship theory & practice*, 29(1): 91–112; and Gaglio, C. M. 2004. The role of mental simulations and counterfactual thinking in the opportunity identification process. *Entrepreneurship theory & practice*, 28(6): 533–552.

8. Stewart, T. A. 2002. How to think with your gut. *Business 2.0*, November: 99–104.

9. For more on the opportunity recognition process, see Smith, B. R., Matthews, C. H., & Schenkel, M. T. 2009. Differences in entrepreneurial opportunities: The role of tacitness and codification in opportunity identification. *Journal of Small Business Management*, 47(1): 38–57.

10. Timmons, J. A. 1997. Opportunity recognition. In W. D. Bygrave, ed.

The portable MBA in entrepreneurship, 2nd ed. New York: John Wiley: 26–54.

11. Social networking is also proving to be an increasingly important type of entrepreneurial resource. For an interesting discussion, see Aldrich, H. E. & Kim, P. H. 2007. Small worlds, infinite possibilities? How social networks affect entrepreneurial team formation and search. *Strategic Entrepreneurship Journal*, 1(1): 147–166.

12. Bhide, A. V. 2000. *The origin and evolution of new businesses*. New York: Oxford University Press.

13. Small Business 2001: Where are we now? 2001. *Inc. Magazine*, May 29: 18–19; and Zacharakis, A. L., Bygrave, W. D., & Shepherd, D. A. 2000. *Global entrepreneurship monitor—National entrepreneurship assessment: United States of America 2000 Executive Report*. Kansas City, MO: Kauffman Center for Entrepreneurial Leadership.

14. Cooper, S. 2003. Cash cows. *Entrepreneur*, June: 36.

15. Seglin, J. L. 1998. What angels want. *Inc. Magazine*, 20(7): 43–44.

16. Torres, N. L. 2002. Playing an angel. *Entrepreneur*, May: 130–138.

17. For an interesting discussion of how venture capital practices vary across different sectors of the economy, see Gaba, V. & Meyer, A. D. 2008. Crossing the organizational species barrier: How venture capital practices infiltrated the information technology sector. *Academy of Management Journal*, 51(5): 391–412.

18. For more on how different forms of organizing entrepreneurial firms as well as different stages of new firm growth and development affect financing, see Cassar, G. 2004. The financing of business start-ups. *Journal of Business Venturing*, 19(2): 261–283.

19. Kroll, M., Walters, B., & Wright, P. 2010. The impact of insider control and environment on post-IPO performance. *Academy of Management Journal*, 53: 693–725.

20. Eisenhardt, K. M. & Schoonhoven, C. B. 1990. Organizational growth: Linking founding team, strategy,

environment, and growth among U.S. semiconductor ventures, 1978–1988. *Administrative Science Quarterly*, 35: 504–529.

21. Dubini, P. & Aldrich, H. 1991. Personal and extended networks are central to the entrepreneurship process. *Journal of Business Venturing*, 6(5): 305–333.

22. For more on the role of social contacts in helping young firms build legitimacy, see Chrisman, J. J. & McMullan, W. E. 2004. Outside assistance as a knowledge resource for new venture survival. *Journal of Small Business Management*, 42(3): 229–244.

23. Vogel, C. 2000. Janina Pawlowski. *Working woman*, June: 70.

24. For a recent perspective on entrepreneurship and strategic alliances, see Rothaermel, F. T. & Deeds, D. L. 2006. Alliance types, alliance experience and alliance management capability in high-technology ventures. *Journal of Business Venturing*, 21(4): 429–460; and Lu, J. W. & Beamish, P. W. 2006. Partnering strategies and performance of SMEs' international joint ventures. *Journal of Business Venturing*, 21(4): 461–486.

25. For more on the role of alliances in creating competitive advantages, see Wiklund, J. & Shepherd, D. A. 2009. The effectiveness of alliances and acquisitions: The role of resource combination activities. *Entrepreneurship Theory & Practice*, 33(1): 193–212.

26. For more information, go to the Small Business Administration website at *www.sba.gov*.

27. Simsek, Z., Heavey, C., & Veiga, J. 2009. The Impact of CEO core self-evaluations on entrepreneurial orientation. *Strategic Management Journal*, 31: 110–119.

28. For an interesting study of the role of passion in entrepreneurial success, see Chen, X-P., Yao, X., & Kotha, S. 2009 Entrepreneur passion and preparedness in business plan presentations: A persuasion analysis of venture capitalists' funding decisions. *Academy of Management Journal*, 52(1): 101–120.

29. Collins, J. 2001. *Good to great*. New York: HarperCollins.

30. The idea of entry wedges was discussed by Vesper, K. 1990. *New venture*

strategies (2nd ed.). Englewood Cliffs, NJ: Prentice-Hall; and Drucker, P. F. 1985. *Innovation and entrepreneurship.* New York: HarperBusiness.

31. See Dowell, G. & Swaminathan, A. 2006. Entry timing, exploration, and firm survival in the early U.S. bicycle industry. *Strategic Management Journal,* 27: 1159–1182, for a recent study of the timing of entrepreneurial new entry.

32. Dunlap-Hinkler, D., Kotabe, M., & Mudambi, R. 2010. A story of breakthrough vs. incremental innovation: Corporate entrepreneurship in the global pharmaceutical industry. *Strategic Entrepreneurship Journal,* 4: 106–127.

33. Maiello, M. 2002. They almost changed the world. *Forbes,* December 22: 217–220.

34. Wilson, R. 2010. 7 electric cars you'll be able to buy very soon. *The Huffington Post,* November 17: np.

35. Williams, G. 2002. Looks like rain. *Entrepreneur,* September: 104–111.

36. Pedroza, G. M. 2002. Tech tutors. *Entrepreneur,* September: 120.

37. Kim, W. C., and Mauborgne, R. 2004. Blue ocean strategy. *Harvard Business Review,* October: 76–84; and *www.cirquedusoleil.com.*

38. Romanelli, E. 1989. Environments and strategies of organization startup: Effects on early survival. *Administrative Science Quarterly,* 34(3): 369–87.

39. Wallace, B. 2000. Brothers. *Philadelphia Magazine,* April: 66–75.

40. Buchanan, L. 2003. The innovation factor: A field guide to innovation. *Forbes,* April 21, *www.forbes.com.*

41. Kim, W. C. & Mauborgne, R. 2005. *Blue ocean strategy.* Boston: Harvard Business School Press.

42. For more on how unique organizational combinations can contribute to competitive advantages of entrepreneurial firms, see Steffens, P., Davidsson, P., & Fitzsimmons, J. Performance configurations over times: Implications for growth- and profit-oriented strategies. *Entrepreneurship Theory & Practice,* 33(1): 125–148.

43. Smith, K. G., Ferrier, W. J., & Grimm, C. M. 2001. King of the hill: Dethroning the industry leader. *Academy of Management Executive,* 15(2): 59–70.

44. Kumar, N. 2006. Strategies to fight low-cost rivals. *Harvard Business Review,* December: 104–112.

45. Grove, A. 1999. *Only the paranoid survive: How to exploit the crises points that challenge every company.* New York: Random House.

46. Stalk, Jr., G. & Lachenauer, R. 2004. *Hardball: Are you playing to play or playing to win?* Cambridge, MA: Harvard Business School Press.

47. Chen, M. J., Lin, H. C, & Michel, J. G. 2010. Navigating in a hypercompetitive environment: The roles of action aggressiveness and TMT integration. *Strategic Management Journal,* 31: 1410–1430.

48. Peteraf, M. A. & Bergen, M. A. 2003. Scanning competitive landscapes: A market-based and resource-based framework. *Strategic Management Journal,* 24: 1027–1045.

49. Chen, M. J. 1996. Competitor analysis and interfirm rivalry: Toward a theoretical integration. *Academy of Management Review,* 21(1): 100–134.

50. Chen, 1996, op.cit.

51. Chen, M. J., Su, K. H, & Tsai, W. 2007. Competitive tension: The awareness-motivation-capability perspective. *Academy of Management Journal,* 50(1): 101–118.

52. St. John, W. 1999. Barnes & Noble's Epiphany. *Wired, www.wired.com,* June.

53. Souder, D. & Shaver, J. M. 2010. Constraints and incentives for making long horizon corporate investments. *Strategic Management Journal,* 31: 1316–1336.

54. Chen, M. J. & Hambrick, D. 1995. Speed, stealth, and selective attack: How small firms differ from large firms in competitive behavior. *Academy of Management Journal,* 38: 453–482.

55. Fenner, L. 2009. TOMS shoes donates one pair of shoes for every pair purchased. *America.gov,* October 19: np.

56. *www.facebook.com/tomsshoes.*

57. For a discussion of how the strategic actions of Apple Computer contribute to changes in the competitive dynamics in both the cellular phone and music industries, see Burgelman, R. A. & Grove, A. S. 2008. Cross-boundary disruptors: Powerful interindustry entrepreneurial change agents. *Strategic Entrepreneurship Journal,* 1(1): 315–327,

58. Smith, K. G., Ferrier, W. J., & Ndofor, H. 2001. Competitive dynamics research: Critique and future directions. In M. A. Hitt, R. E. Freeman, & J. S. Harrison (Eds.), *The Blackwell handbook of strategic management,* pp. 315–361. Oxford, UK: Blackwell.

59. Gee, P. 2000. Co-opetition: The new market milieu. *Journal of Healthcare Management,* 45: 359–363.

60. Ketchen, D. J., Snow, C. C., & Hoover, V. L. 2004. Research on competitive dynamics: Recent accomplishments and future challenges. *Journal of Management,* 30(6): 779–804.

61. Khanna, T., Gulati, R., & Nohria, N. 2000. The economic modeling of strategy process: Clean models and dirty hands. *Strategic Management Journal,* 21: 781–790.

chapter **NINE**

Strategic Control and Corporate Governance

After reading this chapter, you should have a good understanding of:

LO9.1 The value of effective strategic control systems in strategy implementation.

LO9.2 The key difference between "traditional" and "contemporary" control systems.

LO9.3 The imperative for "contemporary" control systems in today's complex and rapidly changing competitive and general environments.

LO9.4 The benefits of having the proper balance among the three levers of behavioral control: culture; rewards and incentives; and, boundaries.

LO9.5 The three key participants in corporate governance: shareholders, management (led by the CEO), and the board of directors.

LO9.6 The role of corporate governance mechanisms in ensuring that the interests of managers are aligned with those of shareholders from both the United States and international perspectives.

LEARNING OBJECTIVES

O rganizations must have effective strategic controls if they are to successfully implement their strategies. This includes systems that exercise both informational control and behavioral control. Controls must be consistent with the strategy that the firm is following. In addition, a firm must promote sound corporate governance to ensure that the interests of managers and shareholders are aligned.

In the first section, we address the need to have effective informational control, contrasting two approaches to informational control. The first approach, which we call "traditional," is highly sequential. Goals and objectives are set, then implemented, and after a set period of time, performance is compared to the desired standards. In contrast, the second approach, termed "contemporary," is much more interactive. Here, the internal and external environments are continually monitored, and managers determine whether the strategy itself needs to be modified. Today the contemporary approach is required, given the rapidly changing conditions in virtually all industries.

Next, we discuss behavioral control. Here the firm must strive to maintain a proper balance between culture, rewards, and boundaries. We also argue that organizations that have strong, positive cultures and reward systems can rely less on boundaries, such as rules, regulations, and procedures. When individuals in the firm internalize goals and strategies, there is less need for monitoring behavior, and efforts are focused more on important organizational goals and objectives.

The third section addresses the role of corporate governance in ensuring that managerial and shareholder interests are aligned. We provide examples of both effective and ineffective corporate governance practices. We discuss three governance mechanisms for aligning managerial and shareholder interests: a committed and involved board of directors, shareholder activism, and effective managerial rewards and incentives. Public companies are also subject to external control. We discuss several external control mechanisms, such as the market for corporate control, auditors, banks and analysts, the media, and public activists. We close with a discussion of corporate governance from an international perspective.●

Learning from Mistakes

Chesapeake Energy had a terrible year in 2008. Its net income dropped about 50 percent from the previous year and its stock plummeted from 39 to 17 during the year—a loss of 56 percent.[1] Its board of directors, however, fared much better than its shareholders. In fact, its directors were among the highest paid corporate directors in 2008. For example, one of the eight "independent" directors, 80-year-old Breene Kerr, received $784,687 in total compensation. He's considered independent only because he is not a member of Chesapeake's management, but he just happens to be the cousin of the CEO, Aubrey McClendon. The other directors did almost as well, receiving an average of about $670,000 each. Let's take a look and see what possible reasons there may be for why the directors have been compensated so well.

CEO Aubrey McClendon aggressively bought Chesapeake's stock in July 2008, mostly on margin, at prices as high as $72 a share. Unfortunately, the stock began to sharply drop. In September, margin calls forced McClendon to sell almost all of his position at a price between $13.60 and $24 a share, depleting his net worth.

The board rushed to the rescue! It promptly awarded McClendon a $75 million "special bonus" for 2008. As if such enormous (and undeserved) compensation were not sufficient, the board felt it necessary to justify another use of corporate funds. In December 2008, the company purchased McClendon's extensive collection of antique historic maps of the American Southwest for $12.1 million.

But that is not all. At a cost of $3.5 million, the company became a founding sponsor of the Oklahoma City Thunder, a National Basketball Association franchise owned and operated by The Professional Basketball Club, LLC ("PBC"). McClendon had a 19.2 percent equity interest in the franchise.

The company's compensation committee did provide a rationale for McClendon's huge bonus: it stressed the board's wish to keep him as CEO. And McClendon reciprocated when asked why Chesapeake pays its directors so much, "We have a very large and complex company and we value our directors' time."

strategic control the process of monitoring and correcting a firm's strategy and performance.

We first explore two central aspects of **strategic control:**[2] (1) *informational control,* which is the ability to respond effectively to environmental change, and (2) *behavioral control,* which is the appropriate balance and alignment among a firm's culture, rewards, and boundaries. In the final section of this chapter, we focus on strategic control from a much broader perspective—what is referred to as *corporate governance.*[3] Here, we direct our attention to the need for a firm's shareholders (the owners) and their elected representatives (the board of directors) to ensure that the firm's executives (the management team) strive to fulfill their fiduciary duty of maximizing long-term shareholder value. As we just saw in the Chesapeake Energy example, clearly there was a breakdown in corporate governance. This gave the CEO seemingly unlimited power at the expense of the shareholders.

>LO9.1
The value of effective strategic control systems in strategy implementation.

Ensuring Informational Control: Responding Effectively to Environmental Change

We discuss two broad types of control systems: "traditional" and "contemporary." As both general and competitive environments become more unpredictable and complex, the need for contemporary systems increases.

A Traditional Approach to Strategic Control

The **traditional approach to strategic control** is sequential: (1) strategies are formulated and top management sets goals, (2) strategies are implemented, and (3) performance is measured against the predetermined goal set, as illustrated in Exhibit 9.1.

Control is based on a feedback loop from performance measurement to strategy formulation. This process typically involves lengthy time lags, often tied to a firm's annual planning cycle. Such traditional control systems, termed "single-loop" learning by Harvard's Chris Argyris, simply compare actual performance to a predetermined goal.[4] They are most appropriate when the environment is stable and relatively simple, goals and objectives can be measured with a high level of certainty, and there is little need for complex measures of performance. Sales quotas, operating budgets, production schedules, and similar quantitative control mechanisms are typical. The appropriateness of the business strategy or standards of performance is seldom questioned.[5]

James Brian Quinn of Dartmouth College has argued that grand designs with precise and carefully integrated plans seldom work.[6] Rather, most strategic change proceeds incrementally—one step at a time. Leaders should introduce some sense of direction, some logic in incremental steps.[7] Similarly, McGill University's Henry Mintzberg has written about leaders "crafting" a strategy.[8] Drawing on the parallel between the potter at her wheel and the strategist, Mintzberg pointed out that the potter begins work with some general idea of the artifact she wishes to create, but the details of design—even possibilities for a different design—emerge as the work progresses. For businesses facing complex and turbulent business environments, the craftsperson's method helps us deal with the uncertainty about how a design will work out in practice and allows for a creative element.

Mintzberg's argument, like Quinn's, questions the value of rigid planning and goal-setting processes. Fixed strategic goals also become dysfunctional for firms competing in highly unpredictable competitive environments. Strategies need to change frequently and opportunistically. An inflexible commitment to predetermined goals and milestones can prevent the very adaptability that is required of a good strategy.

Even organizations that have been extremely successful in the past can become complacent or fail to adapt their goals and strategies to the new conditions. An example of such a firm is General Motors (GM). For many decades, it was the leading firm in the automotive industry. As recently as 2006, it was recognized by Morgan Stanley as the top car producer. However, GM suffered from many underlying problems that were aggravated by the recent worldwide recession, which eroded demand for automobiles. In Strategy Spotlight 9.1, we address what may be considered one of their key underlying problems—a lack of informational control.

A Contemporary Approach to Strategic Control

Adapting to and anticipating both internal and external environmental change is an integral part of strategic control. The relationships between strategy formulation, implementation, and control are highly interactive, as suggested by Exhibit 9.2. It also illustrates two different types of strategic control: informational control and behavioral control. **Informational control** is primarily concerned with whether or not the organization is "doing the right

Exhibit 9.1 Traditional Approach to Strategic Control

strategy spotlight

What Did General Motors Do Wrong?

General Motors (GM), which was founded in 1908, had been ruling the automotive industry for more than half a century. GM provided a broad range of vehicles, reflecting the company's promise to offer "a car for every purse and purpose." As recently as 2007, their stock was trading above $40 a share. And then just few months after celebrating its 100th anniversary in 2008, GM filed for bankruptcy. On May 29, 2009, GM's stock closed at 75 cents a share, which was a historic low for the company. The government funded a $50 billion bailout to save GM and took a 60 percent ownership stake in the company when they exited bankruptcy in 2010.

GM's market dominance grew out of its abilities to mass manufacture, market, and distribute cars for all customer types. While their advantage initially was based on automotive design and manufacturing prowess, over time, GM became rigid and lost its feel for reading the American car market that it helped create. They were not manufacturing competitive vehicles and increasingly relied on volume and the profits from financing auto sales for their success. At the same time, GM faced increasing competition from Japanese automakers, but they were slow to respond to this competitive entry due to their bureaucratic culture and complacency driven by the profitability of their financing operations. The Japanese competitors developed competencies to design world-class vehicles and produced them more efficiently than GM. As a result, they lured away many of GM's customers. GM's management failed to respond to changes in customer needs and automotive technologies as well as the evolving competitive landscape.

GM did have vast numbers of loyal buyers, but lost many of them through a series of strategic and cultural missteps. Trying to balance the competing needs of seven major brands, GM often resorted to a practice (sarcastically) called "launch and leave"—spending billions upfront to bring vehicles to market, but then failing to keep supporting them with sustained advertising. They also failed to differentiate the brands. Originally, each brand was designed to meet the needs of a different customer segment. However, GM's brand identities became muddled as they sold essentially the same car for different brands. According to Jim Wangers, a retired advertising

● A 1957 Cadillac—a successful product that reflects General Motors' glory days.

executive, "Nobody gave any respect to this thing called image because it wasn't in the business plan. It was all about, 'When is this going to earn a profit?'"

Faced with a declining market position, GM executives did not address the need for changes. Instead, they fell prey to two common biases. First, they exhibited *attribution bias*. When their performance started to fall, they attributed their struggles to outside forces, such as the weak Japanese yen, unfair trade practices, and higher costs from their unionized workers. In short, they became expert at the art of explaining away their problems, attributing blame to everyone but themselves. Second, they exhibited *confirmation bias*—the tendency of managers to filter out information that does not match up with their preconceived notions. GM rewarded people who followed the old way of doing things, and those who challenged that thinking were marginalized—causing them to lose opportunities for promotion. So the smart thing for those seeking promotion within GM was to praise the CEO's wisdom and carry out his orders. This confirmation bias syndrome kept GM from viewing the threat from Japanese automakers as significant, contributed to its decision to pull its electric car off the market, and more recently led it to ignore the effect of higher gas prices and a collapse in credit markets on consumers' willingness to buy profitable gas guzzlers like the Hummer or tricked-out Escalades and SUVs. In falling prey to these biases, GM's management failed to recognize the need for change in response to changes in the market, in technology, and in customers' demands.

Sources: Maynard, M. 2009. After Many Stumbles, the Fall of a Giant. *The New York Times*. June 1: A1; Smith, A. 2009. GM Stock Falls below $1. *money.cnn.com*. May 29: np; Maynard, M. 2009. After 93 Years, GM Shares Go Out on a Low Note. *dealbook.nytimes.com*. May 29: np; Holstein, W. J. 2009. Who's to Blame for GM's Bankruptcy? *www.businessweek.com*. June 1: np; and Cohan, P. 2009. After 101 Years, Why GM Failed. *www.dailyfinance.com*. May 31: np.

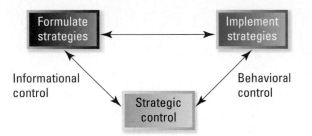

Exhibit 9.2 Contemporary Approach to Strategic Control

things." **Behavioral control,** on the other hand, asks if the organization is "doing things right" in the implementation of its strategy. Both the informational and behavioral components of strategic control are necessary, but not sufficient, conditions for success. What good is a well-conceived strategy that cannot be implemented? Or what use is an energetic and committed workforce if it is focused on the wrong strategic target?

John Weston is the former CEO of ADP Corporation, the largest payroll and tax-filing processor in the world. He captures the essence of contemporary control systems.

> At ADP, 39 plus 1 adds up to more than 40 plus 0. The 40-plus-0 employee is the harried worker who at 40 hours a week just tries to keep up with what's in the "in" basket. . . . Because he works with his head down, he takes zero hours to think about what he's doing, why he's doing it, and how he's doing it. . . . On the other hand, the 39-plus-1 employee takes at least 1 of those 40 hours to think about what he's doing and why he's doing it. That's why the other 39 hours are far more productive.[9]

Informational control deals with the internal environment as well as the external strategic context. It addresses the assumptions and premises that provide the foundation for an organization's strategy. Do the organization's goals and strategies still "fit" within the context of the current strategic environment? Depending on the type of business, such assumptions may relate to changes in technology, customer tastes, government regulation, and industry competition.

This involves two key issues. First, managers must scan and monitor the external environment, as we discussed in Chapter 2. Also, conditions can change in the internal environment of the firm, as we discussed in Chapter 3, requiring changes in the strategic direction of the firm. These may include, for example, the resignation of key executives or delays in the completion of major production facilities.

In the contemporary approach, information control is part of an ongoing process of organizational learning that continuously updates and challenges the assumptions that underlie the organization's strategy. In such "double-loop" learning, the organization's assumptions, premises, goals, and strategies are continuously monitored, tested, and reviewed. The benefits of continuous monitoring are evident—time lags are dramatically shortened, changes in the competitive environment are detected earlier, and the organization's ability to respond with speed and flexibility is enhanced.

Contemporary control systems must have four characteristics to be effective.[10]

1. Focus on constantly changing information that has potential strategic importance.
2. The information is important enough to demand frequent and regular attention from all levels of the organization.
3. The data and information generated are best interpreted and discussed in face-to-face meetings.
4. The control system is a key catalyst for an ongoing debate about underlying data, assumptions, and action plans.

An executive's decision to use the control system interactively—in other words, to invest the time and attention to review and evaluate new information—sends a clear signal

behavioral control a method of organizational control in which a firm influences the actions of employees through culture, rewards, and boundaries.

Google's Interactive Control System

Google has tried typical hierarchical control systems typically found in large firms. However, the firm reverted to its interactive control system within weeks. All of Google's roughly 5,000 product developers work in teams of three engineers. Larger projects simply assemble several teams of three workers. Within teams, there is a rotating "über-tech leader" depending on the project. Engineers tend to work in more than one team and do not need permission to switch teams. According to Shona Brown, VP for operations, "If at all possible, we want people to commit to things rather than be assigned to things." At Google "employees don't need a lot of signoffs to try something new, but they won't get much in the way of resources until they've accumulated some positive user feedback."

Google's executives regularly review projects with project leaders and analyze data about projects. Google uses some of its own web page ranking technology in the review of software and other business projects. Using their own employees as mini test markets, managers often solicit employee opinions and analyze usage patterns of new product features and technologies. This interactive control of corporate information allows Google to make faster decisions about its business, including:

- Compare performance of customer usage and feedback among all components of the Google business in real time.

- Quickly discover shortfalls before major problems arise.

Sources: Hamel, G. 2007. Break Free. *Fortune,* October 1, 156(7): 119–126; Iyer, B. and Davenport, T. 2008. Reverse Engineering Google's Innovation Machine. *Harvard Business Review,* April: 59–68; Pham, A. 2008. Google to End Virtual World, Lively, Launched by the Internet Giant Less Than Five Months Ago. *Los Angeles Times,* November 21: C3; and Helft, M. 2009. Google Ends Sale of Ads in Papers after 2 Years. *New York Times,* January 21: B3.

- Become aware of unexpected successes that have often led to innovations.

- Discontinue failing products and services in a timely manner to save the company money.

These manager meetings return significant rewards for Google. Innovations that have been implemented as a result of high information control include:

- Gmail, an e-mail system that utilizes Google's core search features to help users organize and find e-mail messages easily.

- Google News, a computer-generated news site that aggregates headlines from more than 4,500 English-language news sources worldwide, groups similar stories together, and displays them according to each reader's personalized interests.

- Google AdSense, a service that matches ads to a website's content and audience and operates on a revenue-sharing business model.

Google managers are able to quickly analyze user feedback and revenue data to discontinue projects that are not working out as originally intended. This information control allows managers to reallocate resources to more promising projects in a timely manner.

- Google Lively, a virtual world simulation, was launched and shut down after five months in 2008 after management determined that the service was not competitive.

- Google Print Ads, Google's automated method of selling ads through auctions to the newspaper industry, was terminated in early 2009 when managers analyzed the data and determined that the revenue stream was negligible compared to the costs of the program.

---

to the organization about what is important. The dialogue and debate that emerge from such an interactive process can often lead to new strategies and innovations. Strategy Spotlight 9.2 discusses how executives at Google use an interactive control process.

>LO9.4
The benefits of having the proper balance among the three levers of behavioral control: culture, rewards and incentives, and boundaries.

Attaining Behavioral Control: Balancing Culture, Rewards, and Boundaries

Behavioral control is focused on implementation—doing things right. Effectively implementing strategy requires manipulating three key control "levers": culture, rewards, and boundaries (see Exhibit 9.3). There are two compelling reasons for an increased emphasis on culture and rewards in a system of behavioral controls.[11]

First, the competitive environment is increasingly complex and unpredictable, demanding both flexibility and quick response to its challenges. As firms simultaneously downsize and face the need for increased coordination across organizational boundaries, a control system based primarily on rigid strategies, rules, and regulations is dysfunctional. The use of rewards and culture to align individual and organizational goals becomes increasingly important.

Second, the implicit long-term contract between the organization and its key employees has been eroded.[12] Today's younger managers have been conditioned to see themselves as "free agents" and view a career as a series of opportunistic challenges. As managers are advised to "specialize, market yourself, and have work, if not a job," the importance of culture and rewards in building organizational loyalty claims greater importance.

Each of the three levers—culture, rewards, and boundaries—must work in a balanced and consistent manner. Let's consider the role of each.

Building a Strong and Effective Culture

Organizational culture is a system of shared values (what is important) and beliefs (how things work) that shape a company's people, organizational structures, and control systems to produce behavioral norms (the way we do things around here).[13] How important is culture? Very. Over the years, numerous best sellers, such as *Theory Z, Corporate Cultures, In Search of Excellence,* and *Good to Great,*[14] have emphasized the powerful influence of culture on what goes on within organizations and how they perform.

Collins and Porras argued in *Built to Last* that the key factor in sustained exceptional performance is a cultlike culture.[15] You can't touch it or write it down, but it's there in every organization; its influence is pervasive; it can work for you or against you.[16] Effective leaders understand its importance and strive to shape and use it as one of their important levers of strategic control.[17]

> **organizational culture** a system of shared values and beliefs that shape a company's people, organizational structures, and control systems to produce behavioral norms.

The Role of Culture   Culture wears many different hats, each woven from the fabric of those values that sustain the organization's primary source of competitive advantage. Some examples are:

- Federal Express and Southwest Airlines focus on customer service.
- Lexus (a division of Toyota) and Hewlett-Packard emphasize product quality.
- Newell Rubbermaid and 3M place a high value on innovation.
- Nucor (steel) and Emerson Electric are concerned, above all, with operational efficiency.

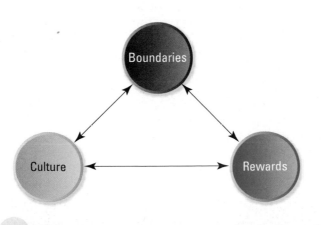

Exhibit 9.3 **Essential Elements of Behavioral Control**

Culture sets implicit boundaries—unwritten standards of acceptable behavior—in dress, ethical matters, and the way an organization conducts its business.[18] By creating a framework of shared values, culture encourages individual identification with the organization and its objectives. Culture acts as a means of reducing monitoring costs.[19]

Sustaining an Effective Culture   Powerful organizational cultures just don't happen overnight, and they don't remain in place without a strong commitment—both in terms of words and deeds—by leaders throughout the organization.[20] A viable and productive organizational culture can be strengthened and sustained. However, it cannot be "built" or "assembled"; instead, it must be cultivated, encouraged, and "fertilized."[21]

Storytelling is one way effective cultures are maintained. Many are familiar with the story of how Art Fry's failure to develop a strong adhesive led to 3M's enormously successful Post-it Notes. Perhaps less familiar is the story of Francis G. Okie.[22] In 1922 Okie came up with the idea of selling sandpaper to men as a replacement for razor blades. The idea obviously didn't pan out, but Okie was allowed to remain at 3M. Interestingly, the technology developed by Okie led 3M to develop its first blockbuster product: a waterproof sandpaper that became a staple of the automobile industry. Such stories foster the importance of risk taking, experimentation, freedom to fail, and innovation—all vital elements of 3M's culture.

Rallies or "pep talks" by top executives also serve to reinforce a firm's culture. The late Sam Walton was known for his pep rallies at local Walmart stores. Four times a year, the founders of Home Depot—former CEO Bernard Marcus and Arthur Blank—used to don orange aprons and stage Breakfast with Bernie and Arthur, a 6:30 a.m. pep rally, broadcast live over the firm's closed-circuit TV network to most of its 45,000 employees.[23]

Southwest Airlines' "Culture Committee" is a unique vehicle designed to perpetuate the company's highly successful culture. The following excerpt from an internal company publication describes its objectives:

> The goal of the Committee is simple—to ensure that our unique Corporate Culture stays alive. . . . Culture Committee members represent all regions and departments across our system and they are selected based upon their exemplary display of the "Positively Outrageous Service" that won us the first-ever Triple Crown; their continual exhibition of the "Southwest Spirit" to our Customers and to their fellow workers; and their high energy level, boundless enthusiasm, unique creativity, and constant demonstration of teamwork and love for their fellow workers.[24]

Motivating with Rewards and Incentives

Reward and incentive systems represent a powerful means of influencing an organization's culture, focusing efforts on high-priority tasks, and motivating individual and collective task performance.[25] Just as culture deals with influencing beliefs, behaviors, and attitudes of people within an organization, the **reward system**—by specifying who gets rewarded and why—is an effective motivator and control mechanism.[26] Consider how Starbucks uses its stock option plan as an incentive to motivate its employees.[27] By introducing a stock option plan called "bean stock" to managers, baristas, and other employees, Starbucks has turned every employee into a partner. Starbucks' managers began referring to all employees as *partners,* an appropriate title because all staff, including part-timers working at least 20 hours per week, were eligible for stock options after six months with the company. By turning employees into partners, Starbucks gave them a chance to share in the success of the company and make the connection between their contributions and the company's market value very clear. There was a pronounced effect on the attitudes and performance of employees because of the bean stock program. They began coming up with many innovative ideas about how to cut costs, increase sales, and create value.

The Potential Downside   Generally speaking, people in organizations act rationally, each motivated by their personal best interest.[28] However, the collective sum of individual

reward system
policies that specify who gets rewarded and why.

behaviors of an organization's employees does not always result in what is best for the organization; individual rationality is no guarantee of organizational rationality.

As corporations grow and evolve, they often develop different business units with multiple reward systems. They may differ based on industry contexts, business situations, stage of product life cycles, and so on. Subcultures within organizations may reflect differences among functional areas, products, services, and divisions. To the extent that reward systems reinforce such behavioral norms, attitudes, and belief systems, cohesiveness is reduced; important information is hoarded rather than shared, individuals begin working at cross-purposes, and they lose sight of overall goals.

Such conflicts are commonplace in many organizations. For example, sales and marketing personnel promise unrealistically quick delivery times to bring in business, much to the dismay of operations and logistics; overengineering by R&D creates headaches for manufacturing; and so on. Conflicts also arise across divisions when divisional profits become a key compensation criterion. As ill will and anger escalate, personal relationships and performance may suffer.

Creating Effective Reward and Incentive Programs To be effective, incentive and reward systems need to reinforce basic core values, enhance cohesion and commitment to goals and objectives, and meet with the organization's overall mission and purpose.[29]

At General Mills, to ensure a manager's interest in the overall performance of his or her unit, half of a manager's annual bonus is linked to business-unit results and half to individual performance.[30] For example, if a manager simply matches a rival manufacturer's performance, his or her salary is roughly 5 percent lower. However, if a manager's product ranks in the industry's top 10 percent in earnings growth and return on capital, the manager's total pay can rise to nearly 30 percent beyond the industry norm.

Effective reward and incentive systems share a number of common characteristics.[31] (see Exhibit 9.4). The perception that a plan is "fair and equitable" is critically important. The firm must have the flexibility to respond to changing requirements as its direction and objectives change. In recent years many companies have begun to place more emphasis on growth. Emerson Electric has shifted its emphasis from cost cutting to growth. To ensure that changes take hold, the management compensation formula has been changed from a largely bottom-line focus to one that emphasizes growth, new products, acquisitions, and international expansion. Discussions about profits are handled separately, and a culture of risk taking is encouraged.[32]

Setting Boundaries and Constraints

In an ideal world, a strong culture and effective rewards should be sufficient to ensure that all individuals and subunits work toward the common goals and objectives of the whole organization.[33] However, this is not usually the case. Counterproductive behavior can arise because of motivated self-interest, lack of a clear understanding of goals and objectives, or outright malfeasance. **Boundaries and constraints** can serve many useful purposes for organizations, including:

boundaries and constraints rules that specify behaviors that are acceptable and unacceptable.

- Objectives are clear, well understood, and broadly accepted.
- Rewards are clearly linked to performance and desired behaviors.
- Performance measures are clear and highly visible.
- Feedback is prompt, clear, and unambiguous.
- The compensation "system" is perceived as fair and equitable.
- The structure is flexible; it can adapt to changing circumstances.

Exhibit 9.4
Characteristics of Effective Reward and Evaluation Systems

- Focusing individual efforts on strategic priorities.
- Providing short-term objectives and action plans to channel efforts.
- Improving efficiency and effectiveness.
- Minimizing improper and unethical conduct.

Focusing Efforts on Strategic Priorities   Boundaries and constraints play a valuable role in focusing a company's strategic priorities. A well-known example of a strategic boundary is Jack Welch's (former CEO of General Electric) demand that any business in the corporate portfolio be ranked first or second in its industry. Similarly, Eli Lilly has reduced its research efforts to five broad areas of disease, down from eight or nine a decade ago.[34] This concentration of effort and resources provides the firm with greater strategic focus and the potential for stronger competitive advantages in the remaining areas.

Norman Augustine, Lockheed Martin's former chairman, provided four criteria for selecting candidates for diversification into "closely related" businesses.[35] They must (1) be high tech, (2) be systems-oriented, (3) deal with large customers (either corporations or government) as opposed to consumers, and (4) be in growth businesses. Augustine said, "We have found that if we can meet most of those standards, then we can move into adjacent markets and grow."

Boundaries also have a place in the nonprofit sector. For example, a British relief organization uses a system to monitor strategic boundaries by maintaining a list of companies whose contributions it will neither solicit nor accept. Such boundaries are essential for maintaining legitimacy with existing and potential benefactors.

Providing Short-Term Objectives and Action Plans   In Chapter 1 we discussed the importance of a firm having a vision, mission, and strategic objectives that are internally consistent and that provide strategic direction. In addition, short-term objectives and action plans provide similar benefits. That is, they represent boundaries that help to allocate resources in an optimal manner and to channel the efforts of employees at all levels throughout the organization.[36] To be effective, short-term objectives must have several attributes. They should:

- Be specific and measurable.
- Include a specific time horizon for their attainment.
- Be achievable, yet challenging enough to motivate managers who must strive to accomplish them.

Research has found that performance is enhanced when individuals are encouraged to attain specific, difficult, yet achievable, goals (as opposed to vague "do your best" goals).[37]

Short-term objectives must provide proper direction and also provide enough flexibility for the firm to keep pace with and anticipate changes in the external environment, new government regulations, a competitor introducing a substitute product, or changes in consumer taste. Unexpected events within a firm may require a firm to make important adjustments in both strategic and short-term objectives. The emergence of new industries can have a drastic effect on the demand for products and services in more traditional industries.

Action plans are critical to the implementation of chosen strategies. Unless action plans are specific, there may be little assurance that managers have thought through all of the resource requirements for implementing their strategies. In addition, unless plans are specific, managers may not understand what needs to be implemented or have a clear time frame for completion. This is essential for the scheduling of key activities that must be implemented. Finally, individual managers must be held accountable for the implementation. This helps to provide the necessary motivation and "sense of ownership" to implement action plans on a timely basis. Strategy Spotlight 9.3 illustrates how action

9.3

strategy spotlight

Developing Meaningful Action Plans: Aircraft Interior Products, Inc.

MSA Aircraft Interior Products, Inc., is a manufacturing firm based in San Antonio, Texas, that was founded in 1983 by Mike Spraggins and Robert Plenge. The firm fulfills a small but highly profitable niche in the aviation industry with two key products. The Accordia line consists of patented, lightweight, self-contained window-shade assemblies. MSA's interior cabin shells are state-of-the-art assemblies that include window panels, side panels, headliners, and suspension system structures. MSA's products have been installed on a variety of aircraft, such as the Gulfstream series; the Cessna Citation; and Boeing's 727, 737, 757, and 707.

Much of MSA's success can be attributed to carefully articulated action plans consistent with the firm's mission and objectives. During the past five years, MSA has increased its sales at an annual rate of 15 to 18 percent. It has also succeeded in adding many prestigious companies to its customer base. Below are excerpts from MSA's mission statement and objectives as well as the action plans to achieve a 20 percent annual increase in sales.

Mission Statement

- Be recognized as an innovative and reliable supplier of quality interior products for the high-end, personalized transportation segments of the aviation, marine, and automotive industries.

- Design, develop, and manufacture interior fixtures and components that provide exceptional value to

Source: For purposes of confidentiality, some of the information presented in this spotlight has been disguised. We would like to thank company management and Joseph Picken, consultant, for providing us with the information used in this application.

the customer through the development of innovative designs in a manner that permits decorative design flexibility while retaining the superior functionality, reliability, and maintainability of well-engineered, factory-produced products.

- Grow, be profitable, and provide a fair return, commensurate with the degree of risk, for owners and stockholders.

Objectives

1. Achieve sustained and profitable growth over the next three years:
   - 20 percent annual growth in revenues
   - 12 percent pretax profit margins
   - 18 percent return on shareholder's equity

2. Expand the company's revenues through the development and introduction of two or more new products capable of generating revenues in excess of $8 million a year by 2014.

3. Continue to aggressively expand market opportunities and applications for the Accordia line of window-shade assemblies, with the objective of sustaining or exceeding a 20 percent annual growth rate for at least the next three years.

Exhibit 9.5 details an "Action Plan" for Objective 3.

MSA's action plans are supported by detailed month-by-month budgets and strong financial incentives for its executives. Budgets are prepared by each individual department and include all revenue and cost items. Managers are motivated by their participation in a profit-sharing program, and the firm's two founders each receive a bonus equal to three percent of total sales.

Description	Primary Responsibility	Target Date
1. Develop and implement 2010 marketing plan, including specific plans for addressing Falcon 20 retrofit programs and expanded sales of cabin shells.	R. H. Plenge (V.P. Marketing)	December 15, 2011
2. Negotiate new supplier agreement with Gulfstream Aerospace.	M. Spraggins (President)	March 1, 2012
3. Continue and complete the development of the UltraSlim window and have a fully tested and documented design ready for production at a manufacturing cost of less than $900 per unit.	D. R. Pearson (V.P. Operations)	June 15, 2012
4. Develop a window design suitable for L-1011 and similar wide-body aircraft and have a fully tested and documented design ready for production at a manufacturing cost comparable to the current Boeing window.	D. R. Pearson (V.P. Operations)	September 15, 2012

Exhibit 9.5 Action Plan for Objective Number 3

plans fit into the mission statement and objectives of a small manufacturer of aircraft interior components. Exhibit 9.5 provides details of an action plan to fulfill one of the firm's objectives.

Improving Operational Efficiency and Effectiveness   Rule-based controls are most appropriate in organizations with the following characteristics:

- Environments are stable and predictable.
- Employees are largely unskilled and interchangeable.
- Consistency in product and service is critical.
- The risk of malfeasance is extremely high (e.g., in banking or casino operations).[38]

McDonald's Corp. has extensive rules and regulations that regulate the operation of its franchises.[39] Its policy manual states, "Cooks must turn, never flip, hamburgers. If they haven't been purchased, Big Macs must be discarded in 10 minutes after being cooked and French fries in 7 minutes. Cashiers must make eye contact with and smile at every customer."

Guidelines can also be effective in setting spending limits and the range of discretion for employees and managers, such as the $2,500 limit that hotelier Ritz-Carlton uses to empower employees to placate dissatisfied customers. Regulations also can be initiated to improve the use of an employee's time at work.[40] Computer Associates restricts the use of e-mail during the hours of 10 a.m. to noon and 2 p.m. to 4 p.m. each day.[41]

Minimizing Improper and Unethical Conduct   Guidelines can be useful in specifying proper relationships with a company's customers and suppliers.[42] Many companies have explicit rules regarding commercial practices, including the prohibition of any form of payment, bribe, or kickback. Cadbury Schweppes has followed a simple but effective step in controlling the use of bribes by specifying that all payments, no matter how unusual, are recorded on the company's books. Its former chairman, Sir Adrian Cadbury, contended that such a practice causes managers to pause and consider whether a payment is simply a bribe or a necessary and standard cost of doing business.[43]

Regulations backed up with strong sanctions can also help an organization avoid conducting business in an unethical manner. After the passing of the Sarbanes-Oxley Act (which provides for stiffer penalties for financial reporting misdeeds), many chief financial officers (CFOs) have taken steps to ensure ethical behavior in the preparation of financial statements. For example, Home Depot's CFO, Carol B. Tome, strengthened the firm's code of ethics and developed stricter guidelines. Now all 25 of her subordinates must sign personal statements that all of their financial statements are correct—just as she and her CEO, have to do now.[44]

● McDonald's relies on extensive rules and regulations to maintain efficient operations at its restaurants.

Behavioral Control in Organizations: Situational Factors

Here, the focus is on ensuring that the behavior of individuals at all levels of an organization is directed toward achieving organizational goals and objectives. The three fundamental types of control are culture, rewards and incentives, and boundaries and constraints. An organization may pursue one or a combination of them on the basis of a variety of internal and external factors.

Not all organizations place the same emphasis on each type of control.[45] In high-technology firms engaged in basic research, members may work under high levels of autonomy. An individual's performance is generally quite difficult to measure accurately because of the long lead times involved in R&D activities. Thus, internalized norms and values become very important.

When the measurement of an individual's output or performance is quite straightforward, control depends primarily on granting or withholding rewards. Frequently, a sales manager's compensation is in the form of a commission and bonus tied directly to his or her sales volume, which is relatively easy to determine. Here, behavior is influenced more strongly by the attractiveness of the compensation than by the norms and values implicit in the organization's culture. The measurability of output precludes the need for an elaborate system of rules to control behavior.[46]

Control in bureaucratic organizations is dependent on members following a highly formalized set of rules and regulations. Most activities are routine and the desired behavior can be specified in a detailed manner because there is generally little need for innovative or creative activity. Managing an assembly plant requires strict adherence to many rules as well as exacting sequences of assembly operations. In the public sector, the Department of Motor Vehicles in most states must follow clearly prescribed procedures when issuing or renewing driver licenses.

Exhibit 9.6 provides alternate approaches to behavioral control and some of the situational factors associated with them.

Evolving from Boundaries to Rewards and Culture

In most environments, organizations should strive to provide a system of rewards and incentives, coupled with a culture strong enough that boundaries become internalized. This reduces the need for external controls such as rules and regulations.

First, hire the right people—individuals who already identify with the organization's dominant values and have attributes consistent with them. We addressed this issue in Chapter 4; recall the "Bozo Filter" developed by Cooper Software (pages 129–130). Microsoft's David Pritchard is well aware of the consequences of failing to hire properly.

Exhibit 9.6
Organizational Control: Alternative Approaches

Approach	Some Situational Factors
Culture: A system of unwritten rules that forms an internalized influence over behavior.	• Often found in professional organizations. • Associated with high autonomy. • Norms are the basis for behavior.
Rules: Written and explicit guidelines that provide external constraints on behavior.	• Associated with standardized output. • Tasks are generally repetitive and routine. • Little need for innovation or creative activity.
Rewards: The use of performance-based incentive systems to motivate.	• Measurement of output and performance is rather straightforward. • Most appropriate in organizations pursuing unrelated diversification strategies. • Rewards may be used to reinforce other means of control.

If I hire a bunch of bozos, it will hurt us, because it takes time to get rid of them. They start infiltrating the organization and then they themselves start hiring people of lower quality. At Microsoft, we are always looking for people who are better than we are.

Second, training plays a key role. For example, in elite military units such as the Green Berets and Navy SEALs, the training regimen so thoroughly internalizes the culture that individuals, in effect, lose their identity. The group becomes the overriding concern and focal point of their energies. At firms such as FedEx, training not only builds skills, but also plays a significant role in building a strong culture on the foundation of each organization's dominant values.

Third, managerial role models are vital. Andy Grove, former CEO and co-founder of Intel, didn't need (or want) a large number of bureaucratic rules to determine who is responsible for what, who is supposed to talk to whom, and who gets to fly first class (no one does). He encouraged openness by not having many of the trappings of success—he worked in a cubicle like all the other professionals. Can you imagine any new manager asking whether or not he can fly first class? Grove's personal example eliminated such a need.

Fourth, reward systems must be clearly aligned with the organizational goals and objectives. Where do you think rules and regulations are more important in controlling behavior—Home Depot, with its generous bonus and stock option plan, or Walmart, which does not provide the same level of rewards and incentives?

The Role of Corporate Governance

>LO9.5

The three key participants in corporate governance: shareholders, management (led by the CEO), and the board of directors.

We now address the issue of strategic control in a broader perspective, typically referred to as "corporate governance." Here we focus on the need for both shareholders (the owners of the corporation) and their elected representatives, the board of directors, to actively ensure that management fulfills its overriding purpose of increasing long-term shareholder value.[47]

corporate governance the relationship among various participants in determining the direction and performance of corporations. The primary participants are (1) the shareholders, (2) the management, and (3) the board of directors.

Robert Monks and Nell Minow, two leading scholars in **corporate governance,** define it as "the relationship among various participants in determining the direction and performance of corporations. The primary participants are (1) the shareholders, (2) the management (led by the CEO), and (3) the board of directors."* Our discussion will center on how corporations can succeed (or fail) in aligning managerial motives with the interests of the shareholders and their elected representatives, the board of directors.[48] As you will recall from Chapter 1, we discussed the important role of boards of directors and provided some examples of effective and ineffective boards.[49]

Good corporate governance plays an important role in the investment decisions of major institutions, and a premium is often reflected in the price of securities of companies that practice it. The corporate governance premium is larger for firms in countries with sound corporate governance practices compared to countries with weaker corporate governance standards.[50]

Sound governance practices often lead to superior financial performance. However, this is not always the case. For example, practices such as independent directors (directors who are not part of the firm's management) and stock options are generally assumed to result in

---

*Management cannot ignore the demands of other important firm stakeholders such as creditors, suppliers, customers, employees, and government regulators. At times of financial duress, powerful creditors can exert strong and legitimate pressures on managerial decisions. In general, however, the attention to stakeholders other than the owners of the corporation must be addressed in a manner that is still consistent with maximizing long-term shareholder returns. For a seminal discussion on stakeholder management, refer to Freeman, R. E. 1984. *Strategic Management: A Stakeholder Approach.* Boston: Pitman.

The Relationship between Recommended Corporate Governance Practices and Firm Performance

A significant amount of research has examined the effect of corporate governance on firm performance. Some research has shown that implementing good corporate governance structures yields superior financial performance. Other research has not found a positive relationship between governance and performance. Results of a few of these studies are summarized below.

1. *A positive correlation between corporate governance and different measures of corporate performance.* Recent studies show that there is a strong positive correlation between effective corporate governance and different indicators of corporate performance such as growth, profitability, and customer satisfaction. Over a recent three-year period, the average return of large capitalized firms with the best governance practices was more than five times higher than the performance of firms in the bottom corporate governance quartile.

Sources: Dalton, D. R., Daily, C. M., Ellstrand, A. E., & Johnson, J. L., 1998. Meta-analytic reviews of board composition, leadership structure, and financial performance. *Strategic Management Journal,* 19(3): 269–290; Sanders, W. G. & Hambrick, D. C. 2007. Swinging for the fences: The effects of CEO stock options on company risk-taking and performance. *Academy of Management Journal,* 50(5): 1055–1078; Harris, J. & Bromiley, P. 2007. Incentives to cheat: The influence of executive compensation and firm performance on financial misrepresentation. *Organization Science,* 18(3): 350–367; Bauwhede, H. V. 2009. On the relation between corporate governance compliance and operating performance. *Accounting and Business Research,* 39(5): 497–513; Gill, A. 2001. Credit Lyonnais Securities (Asia). *Corporate governance in emerging markets: Saints and sinners,* April; and Low, C. K. 2002. *Corporate governance: An Asia-Pacific critique.* Hong Kong: Sweet & Maxwell Asia.

2. *Compliance with international best practices leads to superior performance.* Studies of European companies show that greater compliance with international corporate governance best practices concerning board structure and function has significant and positive relationships with return on assets (ROA). In 10 of 11 Asian and Latin American markets, companies in the top corporate governance quartile for their respective regions averaged 10 percent greater return on capital employed (ROCE) than their peers. In a study of 12 emerging markets, companies in the lowest corporate governance quartile had a much lower ROCE than their peers.

3. *Many recommended corporate governance practices do not have a positive relationship with firm performance.* In contrast to these studies, there is also a body of research suggesting that corporate governance practices do not have a positive influence on firm performance. With corporate boards, there is no evidence that including more external directors on the board of directors of U.S. corporations has led to substantially higher firm performance. Also, giving more stock options to CEOs to align their interests with stakeholders may lead them to take high-risk bets in firm investments that have a low probability to improve firm performance. Rather than making good decisions, CEOs may "swing for the fences" with these high-risk investments. Additionally, motivating CEOs with large numbers of stock options appears to increase the likelihood of unethical accounting violations by the firm as the CEO tries to increase the firm's stock price.

ethics

better performance. But in many cases, independent directors may not have the necessary expertise or involvement, and the granting of stock options to the CEO may lead to decisions and actions calculated to prop up share price only in the short term. Strategy Spotlight 9.4 presents some research evidence on governance practices and firm performance.

At the same time, few topics in the business press are generating as much interest (and disdain!) as corporate governance.

Some recent notable examples of flawed corporate governance include:[51]

- Satyam Computer Services, a leading Indian outsourcing company that serves more than a third of the Fortune 500 companies, significantly inflated its earnings and assets for years. The chairman, Ramalinga Raju, resigned and admitted he had cooked the books. Mr. Raju said he had overstated cash on hand by $1 billion and inflated profits and revenues in the September 2008 quarter. Satyam shares sank 78 percent, and the benchmark Sensex index lost 7.3 percent that day (January 7, 2009).

- Former Brocade CEO Gregory Reyes was sentenced to 21 months in prison and fined $15 million for his involvement in backdating stock option grants. Mr. Reyes was the first executive to go on trial and be convicted over the improper dating of stock-option awards, which dozens of companies have acknowledged since the practice came to light (January 17, 2008).
- In October 2010, Angelo Mozilo, the co-founder of Countrywide Financial, agreed to pay $67.5 million to the Securities and Exchange Commission (SEC) to settle fraud charges. He was charged with deceiving the home loan company's investors while reaping a personal windfall. He was accused of hiding risks about Countrywide's loan portfolio as the real estate market soured. Former Countrywide President David Sambol and former Chief Financial Officer Eric Sieracki were also charged with fraud, as they failed to disclose the true state of Countrywide's deteriorating mortgage portfolio. The SEC accused Mozilo of insider trading, alleging that he sold millions of dollars worth of Countrywide stock after he knew the company was doomed.
- Bernard L. Madoff, a former stock broker, investment advisor, and nonexecutive chairman of the NASDAQ stock market, was sentenced to 150 years of prison in June 2009 for a massive Ponzi scheme that defrauded thousands of investors of billions of dollars. Mr. Madoff pleaded guilty to 11 felony counts and admitted to managing the largest Ponzi scheme in history and concealing it from federal authorities and investors for more than a decade.

Because of the many lapses in corporate governance, we can see the benefits associated with effective practices.[52] However, corporate managers may behave in their own self-interest, often to the detriment of shareholders. Next we address the implications of the separation of ownership and management in the modern corporation, and some mechanisms that can be used to ensure consistency (or alignment) between the interests of shareholders and those of the managers to minimize potential conflicts.

The Modern Corporation:
The Separation of Owners (Shareholders) and Management

Some of the proposed definitions for a *corporation* include:

- "The business corporation is an instrument through which capital is assembled for the activities of producing and distributing goods and services and making investments. Accordingly, a basic premise of corporation law is that a business corporation should have as its objective the conduct of such activities with a view to enhancing the corporation's profit and the gains of the corporation's owners, that is, the shareholders." (Melvin Aron Eisenberg, *The Structure of Corporation Law*)
- "A body of persons granted a charter legally recognizing them as a separate entity having its own rights, privileges, and liabilities distinct from those of its members." (*American Heritage Dictionary*)
- "An ingenious device for obtaining individual profit without individual responsibility." (Ambrose Bierce, *The Devil's Dictionary*)[53]

corporation a mechanism created to allow different parties to contribute capital, expertise, and labor for the maximum benefit of each party.

All of these definitions have some validity and each one reflects a key feature of the corporate form of business organization—its ability to draw resources from a variety of groups and establish and maintain its own persona that is separate from all of them. As Henry Ford once said, "A great business is really too big to be human."

Simply put, a **corporation** is a mechanism created to allow different parties to contribute capital, expertise, and labor for the maximum benefit of each party.[54] The shareholders (investors) are able to participate in the profits of the enterprise without taking direct responsibility for the operations. The management can run the company without the responsibility of personally providing the funds. The shareholders have limited liability as well as rather limited involvement in the company's affairs. However, they reserve the right to elect directors who have the fiduciary obligation to protect their interests.

Over 70 years ago, Columbia University professors Adolf Berle and Gardiner C. Means addressed the divergence of the interests of the owners of the corporation from the professional managers who are hired to run it. They warned that widely dispersed ownership "released management from the overriding requirement that it serve stockholders." The separation of ownership from management has given rise to a set of ideas called "agency theory." Central to agency theory is the relationship between two primary players—the *principals* who are the owners of the firm (stockholders) and the *agents,* who are the people paid by principals to perform a job on their behalf (management). The stockholders elect and are represented by a board of directors that has a fiduciary responsibility to ensure that management acts in the best interests of stockholders to ensure long-term financial returns for the firm.

Agency theory is concerned with resolving two problems that can occur in agency relationships.[55] *The first is the agency problem that arises (1) when the goals of the principals and agents conflict, and (2) when it is difficult or expensive for the principal to verify what the agent is actually doing.*[56] The board of directors would be unable to confirm that the managers were actually acting in the shareholders' interests because managers are "insiders" with regard to the businesses they operate and thus are better informed than the principals. Thus, managers may act "opportunistically" in pursuing their own interests—to the detriment of the corporation.[57] Managers may spend corporate funds on expensive perquisites (e.g., company jets and expensive art), devote time and resources to pet projects (initiatives in which they have a personal interest but that have limited market potential), engage in power struggles (where they may fight over resources for their own betterment and to the detriment of the firm), and negate (or sabotage) attractive merger offers because they may result in increased employment risk.[58]

The second issue is the problem of risk sharing. This arises when the principal and the agent have different attitudes and preferences toward risk. The executives in a firm may favor additional diversification initiatives because, by their very nature, they increase the size of the firm and thus the level of executive compensation.[59] At the same time, such diversification initiatives may erode shareholder value because they fail to achieve some synergies that we discussed in Chapter 6 (e.g., building on core competencies, sharing activities, or enhancing market power). Agents (executives) may have a stronger preference toward diversification than shareholders because it reduces their personal level of risk from potential loss of employment. Executives who have large holdings of stock in their firms were more likely to have diversification strategies that were more consistent with shareholder interests—increasing long-term returns.[60]

At times, top-level managers engage in actions that reflect their self-interest rather than the interests of shareholders. We provide two examples below:[61]

- Micky M. Arison is chief executive of Carnival, the big cruise line. He is also chief executive and owner of the Miami Heat of the National Basketball Association. Carnival paid the Heat $675,000 for sponsorship, advertising, and season tickets. Although that may be a rather small sum—given Carnival's $2.2 billion in net income for the period—we could still ask whether the money would have been spent on something else if Arison didn't own the team.
- Alliance Semiconductor CEO N. Damodar Reddy has committed $20 million to Solar Ventures, a venture capital company run by his brother, C. N. Reddy. Other unnamed insiders purchased undisclosed stakes in Solar. However, Alliance won't disclose whether its CEO is one of them. To date, it has invested $12.5 million in

agency theory a theory of the relationship between principals and their agents, with emphasis on two problems: (1) the conflicting goals of principals and agents, along with the difficulty of principals to monitor the agents, and (2) the different attitudes and preferences toward risk of principals and agents.

Solar. Beth Young, senior research associate of the Corporate Library poses an interesting question: "Is Reddy using shareholder capital just to keep afloat his brother's fund and the insiders' investment?"

Governance Mechanisms: Aligning the Interests of Owners and Managers

>LO9.6
The role of corporate governance mechanisms in ensuring that the interests of managers are aligned with those of shareholders from both the United States and international perspectives.

As noted above, a key characteristic of the modern corporation is the separation of ownership from control. To minimize the potential for managers to act in their own self-interest, or "opportunistically," the owners can implement some governance mechanisms.[62] First, there are two primary means of monitoring the behavior of managers. These include (1) a committed and involved *board of directors* that acts in the best interests of the shareholders to create long-term value and (2) *shareholder activism,* wherein the owners view themselves as share*owners* instead of share*holders* and become actively engaged in the governance of the corporation. Finally, there are managerial incentives, sometimes called "contract-based outcomes," which consist of *reward and compensation agreements.* Here the goal is to carefully craft managerial incentive packages to align the interests of management with those of the stockholders.[63]

We close this section with a brief discussion of one of the most controversial issues in corporate governance—duality. Here, the question becomes: Should the CEO also be chairman of the board of directors? In many Fortune 500 firms, the same individual serves in both roles. However, in recent years, we have seen a trend toward separating these two positions. The key issue is what implications CEO duality has for firm governance and performance.

A Committed and Involved Board of Directors   The **board of directors** acts as a fulcrum between the owners and controllers of a corporation. They are the intermediaries who provide a balance between a small group of key managers in the firm based at the corporate headquarters and a sometimes vast group of shareholders.[64] In the United States, the law imposes on the board a strict and absolute fiduciary duty to ensure that a company is run consistent with the long-term interests of the owners—the shareholders. The reality, as we have seen, is somewhat more ambiguous.[65]

board of directors a group that has a fiduciary duty to ensure that the company is run consistently with the long-term interests of the owners, or shareholders, of a corporation and that acts as an intermediary between the shareholders and management.

The Business Roundtable, representing the largest U.S. corporations, describes the duties of the board as follows:

1.   Select, regularly evaluate, and, if necessary, replace the CEO. Determine management compensation. Review succession planning.
2.   Review and, where appropriate, approve the financial objectives, major strategies, and plans of the corporation.
3.   Provide advice and counsel to top management.
4.   Select and recommend to shareholders for election an appropriate slate of candidates for the board of directors; evaluate board processes and performance.
5.   Review the adequacy of the systems to comply with all applicable laws/regulations.[66]

Given these principles, what makes for a good board of directors?[67] According to the Business Roundtable, the most important quality is a board of directors who are active, critical participants in determining a company's strategies.[68] That does not mean board members should micromanage or circumvent the CEO. Rather, they should provide strong oversight going beyond simply approving the CEO's plans. A board's primary responsibilities are to ensure that strategic plans undergo rigorous scrutiny, evaluate managers against high performance standards, and take control of the succession process.[69]

Although boards in the past were often dismissed as CEO's rubber stamps, increasingly they are playing a more active role by forcing out CEOs who cannot deliver on performance.[70] According to the consulting firm Booz Allen Hamilton, the rate of CEO departures for performance reasons more than tripled, from 1.3 percent to 4.2 percent, between 1995 and 2002.[71] And today's CEOs are not immune to termination. In September 2010, Jonathan Klein, the president of the CNN/U.S. cable channel, was fired because CNN's ratings had suffered.[72] Don Blankenship, CEO of coal mining giant Massey Energy, resigned in December 2010 after a deadly explosion in Massey's Upper Big Branch mine in West Virginia, a mine that had received numerous citations for safety violations in the last few years. The blast was the worst mining disaster in the United States in 40 years and resulted in criminal as well as civil investigations and lawsuits. Tony Hayward, CEO of oil and energy company British Petroleum (BP), was forced to step down in October 2010 after the Deepwater Horizon oil spill in the Gulf of Mexico led to an environmental disaster and a $20 billion recovery fund financed by BP.

Interestingly, CEO turnover declined during the recent financial crisis—going from 12.7 percent in 2007 to only 9.4 percent in 2010. One likely reason: Boards were reluctant to change leadership during the recession, concerned that if a CEO departed, investors might think that the company was coming unglued. However, with the economy recovering, Peter Crist, chairman of an executive search firm, predicts a return to double-digit turnover at big companies. He says, "We are going into a 24-month cycle of CEO volatility." "Deliver or depart" will clearly become a stronger message from boards.

Increasing CEO turnover could, however, pose a major problem for many organizations. Why? It appears that boards of directors are not typically engaged in effective succession planning. For example, only 35 percent of 1,318 executives surveyed by Korn/Ferry International in December 2010 said their companies had a succession plan. And 61 percent of respondents to a survey (conducted by Heidrick & Struggles and Stanford University's Rock Center for Corporate Governance) claimed their companies had *no* viable internal candidates.

Another key component of top-ranked boards is director independence.[73] Governance experts believe that a majority of directors should be free of all ties to either the CEO or the company.[74] That means a minimum of "insiders" (past or present members of the management team) should serve on the board, and that directors and their firms should be barred from doing consulting, legal, or other work for the company.[75] Interlocking directorships—in which CEOs and other top managers serve on each other's boards—are not desirable. But perhaps the best guarantee that directors act in the best interests of shareholders is the simplest: Most good companies now insist that directors own significant stock in the company they oversee.[76]

Such guidelines are not always followed. At times, the practices of the boards of directors are the antithesis of such guidelines. Consider the Walt Disney Co. Over a five-year period, former CEO Michael Eisner pocketed an astonishing $531 million. He likely had very little resistance from his board of directors:

> Many investors view the Disney board as an anachronism. Among Disney's 16 directors is Eisner's personal attorney—who for several years was chairman of the company's compensation committee! There was also the architect who designed Eisner's Aspen home and his parents' apartment. Joining them are the principal of an elementary school once attended by his children and the president of a university to which Eisner donated $1 million. The board also includes the actor Sidney Poitier, seven current and former Disney executives, and an attorney who does business with Disney. Moreover, most of the outside directors own little or no Disney stock. "It is an egregiously bad board—a train wreck waiting to happen," warns Michael L. Useem, a management professor at the University of Pennsylvania's Wharton School.[77]

This example also shows that "outside directors" are only beneficial to strong corporate governance if they are vigilant in carrying out their responsibilities.[78] As humorously suggested by Warren Buffett, founder and chairman of Berkshire Hathaway: "The ratcheting up of compensation has been obscene. . . . There is a tendency to put cocker spaniels on compensation committees, not Doberman pinschers."[79]

Many firms do have exemplary board practices. Below we list some of the excellent practices at Intel Corp., the world's largest semiconductor chip manufacturer, with $35 billion in revenues:[80]

- **Mix of inside and outside directors.** The board believes that there should be a majority of independent directors on the board. However, the board is willing to have members of management, in addition to the CEO, as directors.
- **Board presentations and access to employees.** The board encourages management to schedule managers to be present at meetings who: (1) can provide additional insight into the items being discussed because of personal involvement in these areas, or (2) have future potential that management believes should be given exposure to the board.
- **Formal evaluation of officers.** The Compensation Committee conducts, and reviews with the outside directors, an annual evaluation to help determine the salary and executive bonus of all officers, including the chief executive officer.

Exhibit 9.7 shows how boards of directors can improve their practices.

Shareholder Activism　As a practical matter, there are so many owners of the largest American corporations that it makes little sense to refer to them as "owners" in the sense of

Exhibit 9.7　**Best Practice Ideas: The New Rules for Directors**

Issue	Suggestion
Pay	**Know the Math**
Companies will disclose full details of CEO payouts. Activist investors are already drawing up hit lists of companies where CEO paychecks are out of line with performance.	Before okaying any financial package, directors must make sure they can explain the numbers. They need to adopt the mindset of an activist investor and ask: What's the harshest criticism someone could make about this package?
Strategy	**Make It a Priority**
Boards have been so focused on compliance that duties like strategy and leadership oversight too often get ignored. Only 59 percent of directors in a recent study rated their board favorably on setting strategy	To avoid spending too much time on compliance issues, move strategy up to the beginning of the meeting. Annual one-, two- or three-day offsite meetings on strategy alone are becoming standard for good boards.
Financials	**Put in the Time**
Although 95 percent of directors in the recent study said they were doing a good job of monitoring financials, the number of earnings restatements hit a new high in 2006, after breaking records in 2004 and 2005.	Even nonfinancial board members need to monitor the numbers and keep a close eye on cash flows. Audit committee members should prepare to spend 300 hours a year on committee responsibilities.
Crisis Management	**Dig in**
Some 120 companies are under scrutiny for options backdating, and the 100 largest companies have replaced 56 CEOs in the past five years—nearly double the terminations in the prior five years.	The increased scrutiny on boards means that a perfunctory review will not suffice if a scandal strikes. Directors can no longer afford to defer to management in a crisis. They must roll up their sleeves and move into watchdog mode.

Source: From No Byrnes and J. Sassen, "Board of Hard Knocks," *BusinessWeek,* January 22, 2007, pp. 36–39. Used with permission of *Bloomberg BusinessWeek.* copyright © 2007. All rights reserved.

individuals becoming informed and involved in corporate affairs.[81] However, even an individual shareholder has several rights, including (1) the right to sell the stock, (2) the right to vote the proxy (which includes the election of board members), (3) the right to bring suit for damages if the corporation's directors or managers fail to meet their obligations, (4) the right to certain information from the company, and (5) certain residual rights following the company's liquidation (or its filing for reorganization under bankruptcy laws), once creditors and other claimants are paid off.[82]

Collectively, shareholders have the power to direct the course of corporations.[83] This may involve acts such as being party to shareholder action suits and demanding that key issues be brought up for proxy votes at annual board meetings.[84] The power of shareholders has intensified in recent years because of the increasing influence of large institutional investors such as mutual funds (e.g., T. Rowe Price and Fidelity Investments) and retirement systems such as TIAA-CREF (for university faculty members and school administrative staff).[85] Institutional investors hold approximately 50 percent of all listed corporate stock in the United States.[86]

Shareholder activism refers to actions by large shareholders, both institutions and individuals, to protect their interests when they feel that managerial actions diverge from shareholder value maximization.

Many institutional investors are aggressive in protecting and enhancing their investments. They are shifting from traders to owners. They are assuming the role of permanent shareholders and rigorously analyzing issues of corporate governance. In the process they are reinventing systems of corporate monitoring and accountability.[87]

Consider the proactive behavior of CalPERS, the California Public Employees' Retirement System, which manages over $200 billion in assets and is the third largest pension fund in the world. Every year CalPERS reviews the performance of U.S. companies in its stock portfolio and identifies those that are among the lowest long-term relative performers and have governance structures that do not ensure full accountability to company owners. This generates a long list of companies, each of which may potentially be publicly identified as a CalPERS "Focus Company"—corporations to which CalPERS directs specific suggested governance reforms. CalPERS meets with the directors of each of these companies to discuss performance and governance issues. The CalPERS Focus List contains those companies that continue to merit public and market attention at the end of the process.

The 2009 CalPERS Focus List named four companies for poor economic and governance practices: *Eli Lilly* of Indianapolis, Indiana; *Hill-Rom Holdings* of Batesville, Indiana; *Hospitality Properties Trust* of Newton, Massachusetts; and *IMS Health* of Norwalk, Connecticut.[88] In addition to the four firms performing below their peer group for the past five years, CalPERS has expressed the following specific concerns about these firms:

- Eli Lilly, the big drug manufacturer, continues to deny shareowners any opportunity to amend bylaws.
- Hill-Rom Holdings, a medical technology provider, refuses to remove its staggered board structure and to allow shareowners to amend its bylaws.
- Hospitality Properties Trust, a real estate investment fund in hotels and trade centers, refuses to terminate its "classified" board, where directors serve staggered terms rather than standing for election each year.
- IMS Health, a provider of intelligence to the pharmaceutical and health care industries, denies the right of shareowners to call a special meeting or act by written consent and to adopt annual nonbinding advisory votes on executive compensation practices.

While appearing punitive to company management, such aggressive activism has paid significant returns for CalPERS (and other stockholders of the "Focused" companies). A Wilshire Associates study of the "CalPERS Effect" of corporate governance examined the performance of 62 targets over a five-year period: while the stock of these companies

shareholder activism actions by large shareholders to protect their interests when they feel that managerial actions of a corporation diverge from shareholder value maximization.

trailed the Standard & Poor's Index by 89 percent in the five-year period before CalPERS acted, the same stocks outperformed the index by 23 percent in the following five years, adding approximately $150 million annually in additional returns to the fund.

Perhaps no discussion of shareholder activism would be complete without mention of Carl Icahn, a famed activist with a personal net worth of about $13 billion:

> The bogeyman I am now chasing is the structure of American corporations, which permit managements and boards to rule arbitrarily and too often receive egregious compensation even after doing a subpar job. Yet they remain accountable to no one.[89]

Managerial Rewards and Incentives   As we discussed earlier in the chapter, incentive systems must be designed to help a company achieve its goals.[90] From the perspective of governance, one of the most critical roles of the board of directors is to create incentives that align the interests of the CEO and top executives with the interests of owners of the corporation—long-term shareholder returns.[91] Shareholders rely on CEOs to adopt policies and strategies that maximize the value of their shares.[92] A combination of three basic policies may create the right monetary incentives for CEOs to maximize the value of their companies:[93]

1. Boards can require that the CEOs become substantial owners of company stock.
2. Salaries, bonuses, and stock options can be structured so as to provide rewards for superior performance and penalties for poor performance.
3. Threat of dismissal for poor performance can be a realistic outcome.

In recent years the granting of stock options has enabled top executives of publicly held corporations to earn enormous levels of compensation. In 2007, the average CEO in the Standard & Poor's 500 stock index took home 433 times the pay of the average worker—up from 40 times the average in 1980. The counterargument, that the ratio is down from the 514 multiple in 2000, doesn't get much traction.[94] It has been estimated that there could be as many as 50 or more companies with CEO pay packages over $150 million.[95]

Many boards have awarded huge option grants despite poor executive performance, and others have made performance goals easier to reach. In 2002 nearly 200 companies swapped or repriced options—all to enrich wealthy executives who are already among the country's richest people. However, stock options can be a valuable governance mechanism to align the CEO's interests with those of the shareholders. The extraordinarily high level of compensation can, at times, be grounded in sound governance principles.[96] For example, Howard Solomon, CEO of Forest Laboratories, received total compensation of $148.5 million in 2001.[97] This represented $823,000 in salary, $400,000 in bonus, and $147.3 million in stock options that were exercised. However, shareholders also did well, receiving gains of 40 percent. The firm has enjoyed spectacular growth over the past ten years, and Solomon has been CEO since 1977. Thus, huge income is attributed largely to gains that have built up over many years. As stated by compensation committee member Dan Goldwasser, "If a CEO is delivering substantial increases in shareholder value, . . . it's only appropriate that he be rewarded for it."

However, the "pay for performance" principle doesn't always hold.[98] In addition to the granting of stock options, boards of directors are often failing to fulfill their fiduciary responsibilities to shareholders when they lower the performance targets that executives need to meet in order to receive millions of dollars. At Ford, for example, its "profit" goal for 2007 was to *lose* $4.9 billion. Ford beat the target, however, and lost *only* $3.9 billion. CEO Alan Mulally was rewarded $12 million in compensation, including a $7 million bonus for exceeding the profit goal. Ford's stock price fell 10 percent in 2007.

TIAA-CREF has provided several principles of corporate governance with regard to executive compensation (see Exhibit 9.8).[99] These include the importance of aligning the rewards of all employees—rank and file as well as executives—to the long-term performance of the corporation; general guidelines on the role of cash compensation, stock, and "fringe benefits"; and the mission of a corporation's compensation committee.[100]

Stock-based compensation plans are a critical element of most compensation programs and can provide opportunities for managers whose efforts contribute to the creation of shareholder wealth. In evaluating the suitability of these plans, considerations of reasonableness, scale, linkage to performance, and fairness to shareholders and all employees also apply. TIAA-CREF, the largest pension system in the world, has set forth the following guidelines for stock-based compensation. Proper stock-based plans should:

- Allow for creation of executive wealth that is reasonable in view of the creation of shareholder wealth. Management should not prosper through stock while share-holders suffer.

- Have measurable and predictable outcomes that are directly linked to the company's performance.

- Be market oriented, within levels of comparability for similar positions in companies of similar size and business focus.

- Be straightforward and clearly described so that investors and employees can understand them.

- Be fully disclosed to the investing public and be approved by shareholders.

Source: *www.tiaa-cref.org/pubs.*

CEO Duality: Is It Good or Bad?

CEO duality is one of the most controversial issues in corporate governance. It refers to the dual leadership structure where the CEO acts simultaneously as the chair of the board of directors.[101] Scholars, consultants, and executives who are interested in determining the best way to manage a corporation are divided on the issue of the roles and responsibilities of a CEO. Two schools of thought represent the alternative positions:

Unity of Command Advocates of the unity of command perspective believe when one person holds both roles, he or she is able to act more efficiently and effectively. CEO duality provides firms with a clear focus on both objectives and operations as well as eliminates confusion and conflict between the CEO and the chairman. Thus, it enables smoother, more effective strategic decision making. Holding dual roles as CEO/chairman creates unity across a company's managers and board of directors and ultimately allows the CEO to serve the shareholders even better. Having leadership focused in a single individual also enhances a firm's responsiveness and ability to secure critical resources. This perspective maintains that separating the two jobs—that of a CEO and that of the chairperson of the board of directors—may produce all types of undesirable consequences. CEOs may find it harder to make quick decisions. Ego-driven chief executives and chairmen may squabble over who is ultimately in charge. The shortage of first-class business talent may mean that bosses find themselves second-guessed by people who know little about the business.[102] Companies like Coca-Cola, JPMorgan Chase, and Time Warner have refused to divide the CEO's and chairman's jobs and support this duality structure.

Agency Theory Supporters of agency theory argue that the positions of CEO and chairman should be separate. The case for separation is based on the simple principle of the separation of power. How can boards discharge their basic duty—monitoring the boss—if the boss is chairing its meetings and setting its agenda? How can a board act as a safeguard against corruption or incompetence when the possible source of that corruption and incompetence is sitting at the head of the table? CEO duality can create a conflict of interest that could negatively affect the interests of the shareholders.

Duality also complicates the issue of CEO succession. In some cases, a CEO/chairman may choose to retire as CEO but keep his or her role as the chairman. Although this splits up the roles, which appeases an agency perspective, it nonetheless puts the new CEO in a difficult position. The chairman is bound to question some of the new changes put in place, and the board as a whole might take sides with the chairman they trust and with whom they have a history. This conflict of interest would make it difficult for the new CEO to institute any changes, as the power and influence would still remain with the former CEO.[103]

Duality also serves to reinforce popular doubts about the legitimacy of the system as a whole and evokes images of bosses writing their own performance reviews and setting their own salaries. One of the first things that some of America's troubled banks, including Citigroup, Washington Mutual, Wachovia, and Wells Fargo, did when the financial crisis hit in 2007–2008 was to separate the two jobs. Firms like Siebel Systems, Disney, Oracle, and Microsoft have also decided to divide the roles between CEO and the chairman and eliminate duality.

The increasing pressures for effective corporate governance have led to a sharp decline in duality. Firms now routinely separate the jobs of chairman and chief executive. For example, in 2009, fewer than 12 percent of incoming CEOs were also made chairman—compared with 48 percent in 2002.

These same pressures have led to other changes in corporate governance practices. For example, the New York Stock Exchange and NASDAQ have demanded that companies should have a majority of independent directors. Also, CEOs are held accountable for their performance and tossed out if they fail to perform, with the average length of tenure dropping from 8.1 years in 2000 to 6.3 years in 2009. Finally, more than 90 percent of S&P 500 companies with CEOs who also serve as chairman of the board have appointed "lead" or "presiding" directors to act as a counterweight to a combined chairman and chief executive.

External Governance Control Mechanisms

Thus far, we've discussed internal governance mechanisms. Internal controls, however, are not always enough to ensure good governance. The separation of ownership and control that we discussed earlier requires multiple control mechanisms, some internal and some external, to ensure that managerial actions lead to shareholder value maximization. Further, society-at-large wants some assurance that this goal is met without harming other stakeholder groups. Now we discuss several **external governance control mechanisms** that have developed in most modern economies. These include the market for corporate control, auditors, governmental regulatory bodies, banks and analysts, media, and public activists.

external governance control mechanisms methods that ensure that managerial actions lead to shareholder value maximization and do not harm other stakeholder groups that are outside the control of the corporate governance system.

The Market for Corporate Control   Let us assume for a moment that internal control mechanisms in a company are failing. This means that the board is ineffective in monitoring managers and is not exercising the oversight required of them and that shareholders are passive and are not taking any actions to monitor or discipline managers. Under these circumstances managers may behave opportunistically.[104] Opportunistic behavior can take many forms. First, they can *shirk* their responsibilities. Shirking means that managers fail to exert themselves fully, as is required of them. Second, they can engage in *on the job consumption.* Examples of on the job consumption include private jets, club memberships, expensive artwork in the offices, and so on. Each of these represents consumption by managers that does not in any way increase shareholder value. Instead, they actually diminish shareholder value. Third, managers may engage in *excessive product-market diversification.*[105] As we discussed in Chapter 6, such diversification serves to reduce only the employment risk of the managers rather than the financial risk of the shareholders, who can more cheaply diversify their risk by owning a portfolio of investments. Is there any external mechanism to stop managers from shirking, consumption on the job, and excessive diversification?

The **market for corporate control** is one external mechanism that provides at least some partial solution to the problems described. If internal control mechanisms fail and the management is behaving opportunistically, the likely response of most shareholders will be to sell their stock rather than engage in activism.[106] As more stockholders vote with their feet, the value of the stock begins to decline. As the decline continues, at some point the market value of the firm becomes less than the book value. A corporate raider can take over the company for a price less than the book value of the assets of the company. The first thing that the raider may do on assuming control over the company will be to fire the underperforming management. The risk of being acquired by a hostile raider is often referred to as the **takeover constraint.** The takeover constraint deters management from engaging in opportunistic behavior.[107]

Although in theory the takeover constraint is supposed to limit managerial opportunism, in recent years its effectiveness has become diluted as a result of a number of defense tactics adopted by incumbent management (see Chapter 6). Foremost among them are poison pills, greenmail, and golden parachutes. Poison pills are provisions adopted by the company to reduce its worth to the acquirer. An example would be payment of a huge one-time dividend, typically financed by debt. Greenmail involves buying back the stock from the acquirer, usually at an attractive premium. Golden parachutes are employment contracts that cause the company to pay lucrative severance packages to top managers fired as a result of a takeover, often running to several million dollars.

Auditors Even when there are stringent disclosure requirements, there is no guarantee that the information disclosed will be accurate. Managers may deliberately disclose false information or withhold negative financial information as well as use accounting methods that distort results based on highly subjective interpretations. Therefore, all accounting statements are required to be audited and certified to be accurate by external auditors. These auditing firms are independent organizations staffed by certified professionals who verify the firm's books of accounts. Audits can unearth financial irregularities and ensure that financial reporting by the firm conforms to standard accounting practices.

Recent developments leading to the bankruptcy of firms such as Enron and World-Com and a spate of earnings restatements raise questions about the failure of the auditing firms to act as effective external control mechanisms. Why did an auditing firm like Arthur Andersen, with decades of good reputation in the auditing profession at stake, fail to raise red flags about accounting irregularities? First, auditors are appointed by the firm being audited. The desire to continue that business relationship sometimes makes them overlook financial irregularities. Second, most auditing firms also do consulting work and often have lucrative consulting contracts with the firms that they audit. Understandably, some of them tend not to ask too many difficult questions, because they fear jeopardizing the consulting business, which is often more profitable than the auditing work.

The recent restatement of earnings by Xerox is an example of the lack of independence of auditing firms. The SEC filed a lawsuit against KPMG, the world's third largest accounting firm, in January 2003 for allowing Xerox to inflate its revenues by $3 billion between 1997 and 2000. Of the $82 million that Xerox paid KPMG during those four years, only $26 million was for auditing. The rest was for consulting services. When one of the auditors objected to Xerox's practice of booking revenues for equipment leases earlier than it should have, Xerox asked KPMG to replace him. It did.[108]

Banks and Analysts Commercial and investment banks have lent money to corporations and therefore have to ensure that the borrowing firm's finances are in order and that the loan covenants are being followed. Stock analysts conduct ongoing in-depth studies of the firms that they follow and make recommendations to their clients to buy, hold, or

market for corporate control an external control mechanism in which shareholders dissatisfied with a firm's management sell their shares.

takeover constraint the risk to management of the firm being acquired by a hostile raider.

sell. Their rewards and reputation depend on the quality of these recommendations. Their access to information, knowledge of the industry and the firm, and the insights they gain from interactions with the management of the company enable them to alert the investing community of both positive and negative developments relating to a company.

It is generally observed that analyst recommendations are often more optimistic than warranted by facts. "Sell" recommendations tend to be exceptions rather than the norm. Many analysts failed to grasp the gravity of the problems surrounding failed companies such as Enron and Global Crossing till the very end. Part of the explanation may lie in the fact that most analysts work for firms that also have investment banking relationships with the companies they follow. Negative recommendations by analysts can displease the management, who may decide to take their investment banking business to a rival firm. Otherwise independent and competent analysts may be pressured to overlook negative information or tone down their criticism. A recent settlement between the Securities and Exchange Commission and the New York State Attorney General with 10 banks requires them to pay $1.4 billion in penalties and to fund independent research for investors.[109]

Regulatory Bodies   The extent of government regulation is often a function of the type of industry. Banks, utilities, and pharmaceuticals are subject to more regulatory oversight because of their importance to society. Public corporations are subject to more regulatory requirements than private corporations.[110]

All public corporations are required to disclose a substantial amount of financial information by bodies such as the Securities and Exchange Commission. These include quarterly and annual filings of financial performance, stock trading by insiders, and details of executive compensation packages. There are two primary reasons behind such requirements. First, markets can operate efficiently only when the investing public has faith in the market system. In the absence of disclosure requirements, the average investor suffers from a lack of reliable information and therefore may completely stay away from the capital market. This will negatively impact an economy's ability to grow. Second, disclosure of information such as insider trading protects the small investor to some extent from the negative consequences of information asymmetry. The insiders and large investors typically have more information than the small investor and can therefore use that information to buy or sell before the information becomes public knowledge.

The failure of a variety of external control mechanisms led the U.S. Congress to pass the Sarbanes-Oxley Act in 2002. This act calls for many stringent measures that would ensure better governance of U.S. corporations. Some of these measures include:[111]

- *Auditors* are barred from certain types of nonaudit work. They are not allowed to destroy records for five years. Lead partners auditing a client should be changed at least every five years.
- *CEOs* and *CFOs* must fully reveal off-balance-sheet finances and vouch for the accuracy of the information revealed.
- *Executives* must promptly reveal the sale of shares in firms they manage and are not allowed to sell when other employees cannot.
- *Corporate lawyers* must report to senior managers any violations of securities law lower down.

Strategy Spotlight 9.5 addresses one of the increased expenses that many companies now face in complying with the Sarbanes-Oxley Act—higher compensation for more involved and committed directors.

Media and Public Activists   The press is not usually recognized as an external control mechanism in the literature on corporate governance. There is no denying that in all developed capitalist economies, the financial press and media play an important indirect role in monitoring the management of public corporations. In the United States, business magazines such as *Bloomberg Businessweek* and *Fortune,* financial newspapers such as

The Impact of the 2002 Sarbanes-Oxley Act on Corporate Directors

The cost of outside directors has been rising. Not only are well-qualified directors in short supply but also the Sarbanes-Oxley Act has increased the demands of the job. According to compensation consultants Pearl Meyer & Partners, the typical director of a large corporation earned $216,000 in 2009, up from $129,667 in 2003. For some, total compensation, including cash payments, stock grants, and other perks, has climbed above seven figures. Even during the recession of 2008–2009, corporate directors' paychecks seemed to be soaring. For example, in 2008 Anthony P. Terracciano made $4.8 million as the chairman of student loan giant SLM and Jack P. Randall made $1.5 million from XTO Energy, an oil and natural gas producing company.

Directors can thank the Sarbanes-Oxley Act for the continuing generosity. The Act was created to protect shareholders by restricting the power of corporate executives. In the past, many boards had become little more than rubber stamps for everything from merger strategy to executive compensation. This led to disaster in cases such as Enron, WorldCom, and Tyco. Sarbanes-Oxley and other regulatory efforts sought to protect shareholders by empowering directors and making them more accountable.

Following the Sarbanes-Oxley Act, there were several years of 20 percent to 30 percent annual increases as director compensation rose to reflect the new realities of expanded responsibilities for directors as well as the increased demand for directors who met independence rules. The pay increases came at a time when the supply of new directors was declining due to the additional risks—real or perceived—of serving as a director.

One consequence of Sarbanes-Oxley is that many directors work harder. A decade ago a typical director attended four board meetings a year and spent about 100 hours a year on board tasks, according to the National Association of Corporate Directors. Now, directors attend an average of six board meetings a year, spend an average of 225 hours a year on board duties, and convene at other times for committee meetings. In fact, corporate directors can log as many as 400 hours a year when corporations are financially distressed or reorganizing.

Sources: Byrnes, N. 2010. The Gold-Plated Boardroom. *Bloomberg Businessweek*. February 22: 12–13; and Hilburn, W. 2010. Trends in Director Compensation. *www.businessweek.com*. October 19: np.

The Wall Street Journal and *Investors Business Daily*, as well as television networks like Financial News Network and CNBC are constantly reporting on companies. Public perceptions about a company's financial prospects and the quality of its management are greatly influenced by the media. Food Lion's reputation was sullied when ABC's *Prime Time Live* in 1992 charged the company with employee exploitation, false package dating, and unsanitary meat handling practices. Bethany McLean of *Fortune* magazine is often credited as the first to raise questions about Enron's long-term financial viability.[112]

Similarly, consumer groups and activist individuals often take a crusading role in exposing corporate malfeasance.[113] Well-known examples include Ralph Nader and Erin Brockovich, who played important roles in bringing to light the safety issues related to GM's Corvair and environmental pollution issues concerning Pacific Gas and Electric Company, respectively. Ralph Nader has created over 30 watchdog groups, including:[114]

- *Aviation Consumer Action Project.* Works to propose new rules to prevent flight delays, impose penalties for deceiving passengers about problems, and push for higher compensation for lost luggage.
- *Center for Auto Safety.* Helps consumers find plaintiff lawyers and agitate for vehicle recalls, increased highway safety standards, and lemon laws.
- *Center for Study of Responsive Law.* This is Nader's headquarters. Home of a consumer project on technology, this group sponsored seminars on Microsoft remedies and pushed for tougher Internet privacy rules. It also took on the drug industry over costs.
- *Pension Rights Center.* This center helped employees of IBM, General Electric, and other companies to organize themselves against cash-balance pension plans.

strategy spotlight

Two Examples of Powerful External Control Mechanisms

McDonald's

After years of fending off and ignoring critics, McDonald's has begun working with them. In 1999, People for the Ethical Treatment of Animals (PETA) launched its "McCruelty" campaign asking the company to take steps to alleviate the suffering of animals killed for its restaurants. Since then, PETA has switched tactics and is cooperating with the burger chain to modernize the company's animal welfare standards and make further improvements. Following pressure from PETA, McDonald's used its influence to force egg suppliers to improve the living conditions of hens and cease debeaking them. PETA has publicly lauded the company for its efforts. Recently, McDonald's also has required beef and pork processors to improve their handling of livestock prior to slaughter. The company conducts regular audits of the packing plants to determine whether the animals are being treated humanely and will suspend purchases from slaughterhouses that don't meet the company's standards. The company's overall image appears to have improved. According to the global consulting firm Reputation Institute, McDonald's score, on a scale of 100, has climbed 8 points to 63 since 2007—a dramatic improvement.

Sources: Kiley, D. & Helm, B. 2009. The Great Trust Offensive. *Bloomberg Businessweek*, September 28: 38–42; Brasher, P. 2010. McDonald's Orders Improvements in Treatment of Hens. *abcnews.com*, August 23: np; Glover, K. 2009. PETA vs. McDonald's: The Nicest Way to Kill a Chicken. *www.bnet.com*. February 20: np; *www.mccruelty.com*; Greenhouse, S. 2010. Pressured, Nike to Help Workers in Honduras. *The New York Times*, July 27: B1; Padgett, T. 2010. Just Pay It: Nike Creates Fund for Honduran Workers. *www.time.com*, July 27: np; and Bustillo, M. 2010. Nike to Pay Some $2 Million to Workers Fired by Subcontractors. *www.online.wsj.com*, July 26: np.

Nike

In January 2009, 1,800 laborers lost their jobs in Honduras when two local factories that made shirts for the U.S. sports-apparel giant Nike suddenly closed their doors and did not pay workers the $2 million in severance and other unemployment benefits they were due by law. Following pressure from U.S. universities and student groups, Nike announced that it was setting up a $1.5 million "workers' relief fund" to assist the workers. Nike also agreed to provide vocational training and finance health coverage for workers laid off by the two subcontractors.

The relief fund from Nike came after pressure by groups such as the Worker Rights Consortium, which informed Nike customers of the treatment of the workers. The Worker Rights Consortium also convinced scores of U.S. universities whose athletic programs and campus shops buy Nike shoes and clothes to threaten cancellation of those lucrative contracts unless Nike did something to address the plight of the Honduran workers. Another labor watchdog, United Students Against Sweatshops, staged demonstrations outside Nike shops while chanting "Just Pay It," a play on Nike's commercial slogan, "Just Do It." The University of Wisconsin cancelled its licensing agreement with the company over the matter and other schools, including Cornell University and the University of Washington, indicated they were thinking of following suit. The agreement is the latest involving overseas apparel factories in which an image-conscious brand like Nike responded to campaigns led by college students, who often pressure universities to stand up to producers of college-logo apparel when workers' rights are threatened.

As we have noted above, some public activists and watchdog groups can exert a strong force on organizations and influence decisions that they may make. Strategy Spotlight 9.6 provides two examples of this phenomenon.

Corporate Governance: An International Perspective

The topic of corporate governance has long been dominated by agency theory and based on the explicit assumption of the separation of ownership and control.[115] The central conflicts are principal–agent conflicts between shareholders and management. However, such an underlying assumption seldom applies outside of the United States and the United Kingdom. This is particularly true in emerging economies and continental Europe. Here, there is often concentrated ownership, along with extensive family ownership and control, business group structures, and weak legal protection for minority shareholders. Serious conflicts tend to exist between two classes of principals: controlling shareholders and minority shareholders. Such conflicts can be called **principal–principal (PP) conflicts,** as opposed to *principal–agent* conflicts (see Exhibits 9.9 and 9.10).

Strong family control is one of the leading indicators of concentrated ownership. In East Asia (excluding China), approximately 57 percent of the corporations have board chairmen and CEOs from the controlling families. In continental Europe, this number is 68 percent. A very common practice is the appointment of family members as board chairmen, CEOs, and other top executives. This happens because the families are controlling (not necessarily majority) shareholders. In 2003, 30-year-old James Murdoch was appointed CEO of British Sky Broadcasting (BSkyB), Europe's largest satellite broadcaster. There was very vocal resistance by minority shareholders. Why was he appointed in the first place? James's father just happened to be Rupert Murdoch, who controlled 35 percent of BSkyB and chaired the board. Clearly, this is a case of a PP conflict.

In general, three conditions must be met for PP conflicts to occur:

- A dominant owner or group of owners who have interests that are distinct from minority shareholders.
- Motivation for the controlling shareholders to exercise their dominant positions to their advantage.
- Few formal (such as legislation or regulatory bodies) or informal constraints that would discourage or prevent the controlling shareholders from exploiting their advantageous positions.

principal–principal conflicts conflicts between two classes of principals—controlling shareholders and minority shareholders—within the context of a corporate governance system.

Exhibit 9.9
Traditional Principal–Agent Conflicts versus Principal–Principal Conflicts: How They Differ along Dimensions

	Principal–Agent Conflicts	Principal–Principal Conflicts
Goal Incongruence	Between shareholders and professional managers who own a relatively small portion of the firm's equity.	Between controlling shareholders and minority shareholders.
Ownership Pattern	Dispersed—5%–20% is considered "concentrated ownership."	Concentrated—Often greater than 50% of equity is controlled by controlling shareholders.
Manifestations	Strategies that benefit entrenched managers at the expense of shareholders in general (e.g., shirking, pet projects, excessive compensation, and empire building).	Strategies that benefit controlling shareholders at the expense of minority shareholders (e.g., minority shareholder expropriation, nepotism, and cronyism).
Institutional Protection of Minority Shareholders	Formal constraints (e.g., judicial reviews and courts) set an upper boundary on potential expropriation by majority shareholders. Informal norms generally adhere to shareholder wealth maximization.	Formal institutional protection is often lacking, corrupted, or un-enforced. Informal norms are typically in favor of the interests of controlling shareholders ahead of those of minority investors.

Source: Adapted from Young, M., Peng, M. W., Ahlstrom, D., & Bruton, G. 2002. Governing the Corporation in Emerging Economies: A Principal–Principal Perspective. *Academy of Management Best Papers Proceedings,* Denver.

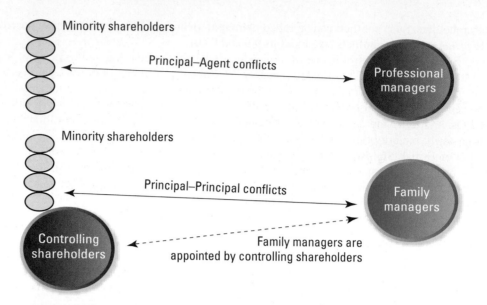

Minority shareholders

Principal–Agent conflicts

Professional managers

Minority shareholders

Principal–Principal conflicts

Family managers

Controlling shareholders

Family managers are appointed by controlling shareholders

Exhibit 9.10 **Principal–Agent Conflicts and Principal–Principal Conflicts: A Diagram**

Source: Young, M. N., Peng, M. W., Ahlstrom, D., Bruton, G. D., & Jiang, 2008. Principal–Principal Conflicts in Corporate Governance. *Journal of Management Studies* 45(1):196–220; and Peng, M. V. 2006. *Global Strategy.* Cincinnati: Thomson South-Western. We are very appreciative of the helpful comments of Mike Young of Hong Kong Baptist University and Mike Peng of the University of Texas at Dallas.

expropriation of minority shareholders activities that enrich the controlling shareholders at the expense of the minority shareholders.

The result is often that family managers, who represent (or actually are) the controlling shareholders, engage in **expropriation of minority shareholders,** which is defined as activities that enrich the controlling shareholders at the expense of minority shareholders. What is their motive? After all, controlling shareholders have incentives to maintain firm value. But controlling shareholders may take actions that decrease aggregate firm performance if their personal gains from expropriation exceed their personal losses from their firm's lowered performance.

Another ubiquitous feature of corporate life outside of the United States and United Kingdom are *business groups* such as the keiretsus of Japan and the chaebols of South Korea. This is particularly dominant in emerging economies. A **business group** is "a set of firms that, though legally independent, are bound together by a constellation of formal and informal ties and are accustomed to taking coordinated action."[116] Business groups are especially common in emerging economies, and they differ from other organizational forms in that they are communities of firms without clear boundaries.

business groups a set of firms that, though legally independent, are bound together by a constellation of formal and informal ties and are accustomed to taking coordinated action.

Business groups have many advantages that can enhance the value of a firm. They often facilitate technology transfer or intergroup capital allocation that otherwise might be impossible because of inadequate institutional infrastructure such as excellent financial services firms. On the other hand, informal ties—such as cross-holdings, board interlocks, and coordinated actions—can often result in intragroup activities and transactions, often at very favorable terms to member firms. Expropriation can be legally done through *related transactions,* which can occur when controlling owners sell firm assets to another firm they own at below market prices or spin off the most profitable part of a public firm and merge it with another of their private firms.

Strategy Spotlight 9.7 provides examples from Latin America of effective corporate governance.

strategy spotlight

Effective and Ineffective Corporate Governance among "Multilatinas"

Latin-owned companies, such as Mexico's Cemex, Argentina's Arcor, and Brazil's Embraer, have been successful in their home markets against U.S. and European competitors. Several of these companies have become "multilatinas," pursuing a strategy of regional and international expansion. Recently, 82 percent of merger and acquisition deals in Latin America were originated by Latin companies. However, while the rise of these Latin firms is promising, it is not enough to ensure they will be competitive globally against large industrialized multinational firms. Access to international capital markets necessary for the "multilatinas" to grow has created a need for a new openness in corporate governance and transparency for these firms.

There are three components emerging-market multinational firms need to implement to succeed:

Sources: Pigorini, P., Ramos, A., & de Souza, I. 2008. Pitting Latin Multinationals against Established Giants. *Strategy + Business,* November 4: *www. strategy business.com/media/file/leading_ideas 20081104.pdf*; Martinez, J., Esperanca, J., & de la Torre, J. 2005. Organizational Change among Emerging Latin American Firms: From "Multilatinas" to Multinationals. *Management Research,* 3(3): 173–188; Krauss, C. 2007. Latin American Companies Make Big U.S. Gains. *New York Times,* May 2: *www.nytimes.com/2007/05/02/-business/worldbusiness/02latin.html.*

- **Shareholder rights.** Minority shareholders must be protected through clear and fair dividend distribution and fair valuation in the event of mergers and acquisitions.
- **Compliance.** The audit committee of the board must be empowered to evaluate the financial statements of the firm and interact with both internal and external auditors.
- **Board and management composition.** Because many multilatinas are still in the process of building effective governance systems, it is important that the board members and top managers have credible professional backgrounds and experience.

These firms need to set up the right board and manager dynamics both to improve access to capital and to implement international management. Many multilatinas were or still are family-owned firms. Boards of these firms tend to be filled with members who have a strong loyalty to the controlling family, but not necessarily exposure to global strategic initiatives and strategies. Many of these firms still use centralized information control systems. In order to grow, some firms may have to consider giving local country managers more authority to make decisions.

Reflecting on Career Implications . . .

- *Behavioral Control:* What sources of behavioral control does your organization employ? In general, too much emphasis on rules and regulations may stifle initiative and be detrimental to your career opportunities.
- *Rewards and Incentives:* Is your organization's reward structure fair and equitable? Does it effectively reward outstanding performance? If not, there may be a long-term erosion of morale which may have long-term adverse career implications for you.
- *Culture:* Consider the type of organization culture that would provide the best work environment for your career goals. How does your organization's culture deviate from this concept? Does your organization have a strong and effective culture? If so, professionals are more likely to develop strong "firm specific" ties, which further enhances collaboration.
- *Corporate Governance:* Does your organization practice effective corporate governance? Such practices will enhance a firm's culture and it will be easier to attract top talent. Operating within governance guidelines is usually a strong indicator of organizational citizenship which, in turn, should be good for your career prospects.

Summary

For firms to be successful, they must practice effective strategic control and corporate governance. Without such controls, the firm will not be able to achieve competitive advantages and outperform rivals in the marketplace.

We began the chapter with the key role of informational control. We contrasted two types of control systems: what we termed "traditional" and "contemporary" information control systems. Whereas traditional control systems may have their place in placid, simple competitive environments, there are fewer of those in today's economy. Instead, we advocated the contemporary approach wherein the internal and external environment are constantly monitored so that when surprises emerge, the firm can modify its strategies, goals, and objectives.

Behavioral controls are also a vital part of effective control systems. We argued that firms must develop the proper balance between culture, rewards and incentives, and boundaries and constraints. Where there are strong and positive cultures and rewards, employees tend to internalize the organization's strategies and objectives. This permits a firm to spend fewer resources on monitoring behavior, and assures the firm that the efforts and initiatives of employees are more consistent with the overall objectives of the organization.

In the final section of this chapter, we addressed corporate governance, which can be defined as the relationship between various participants in determining the direction and performance of the corporation. The primary participants include shareholders, management (led by the chief executive officer), and the board of directors. We reviewed studies that indicated a consistent relationship between effective corporate governance and financial performance. There are also several internal and external control mechanisms that can serve to align managerial interests and shareholder interests. The internal mechanisms include a committed and involved board of directors, shareholder activism, and effective managerial incentives and rewards. The external mechanisms include the market for corporate control, banks and analysts, regulators, the media, and public activists. We also addressed corporate governance from both a United States and an international perspective.

Summary Review Questions

1. Why are effective strategic control systems so important in today's economy?
2. What are the main advantages of "contemporary" control systems over "traditional" control systems? What are the main differences between these two systems?
3. Why is it important to have a balance between the three elements of behavioral control—culture; rewards and incentives; and, boundaries?
4. Discuss the relationship between types of organizations and their primary means of behavioral control.
5. Boundaries become less important as a firm develops a strong culture and reward system. Explain.
6. Why is it important to avoid a "one best way" mentality concerning control systems? What are the consequences of applying the same type of control system to all types of environments?
7. What is the role of effective corporate governance in improving a firm's performance? What are some of the key governance mechanisms that are used to ensure that managerial and shareholder interests are aligned?
8. Define principal–principal (PP) conflicts. What are the implications for corporate governance?

Key Terms

strategic control, 318
traditional approach to strategic control, 319
informational control, 319
behavioral control, 321
organizational culture, 323
reward system, 324
boundaries and constraints, 325
corporate governance, 330
corporation, 332
agency theory, 333
board of directors, 334
shareholder activism, 337
external governance control mechanisms, 340
market for corporate control, 341
takeover constraint, 341
principal–principal conflicts, 345
expropriation of minority shareholders, 346
business groups, 346

Experiential Exercise

McDonald's Corporation, the world's largest fast-food restaurant chain, with 2010 revenues of $24 billion, has recently been on a "roll." Its shareholder value has more than doubled between February 2006 and February 2011. Using the Internet or library sources, evaluate the quality of the corporation in terms of management, the board of directors, and shareholder activism. Are the issues you list favorable or unfavorable for sound corporate governance?

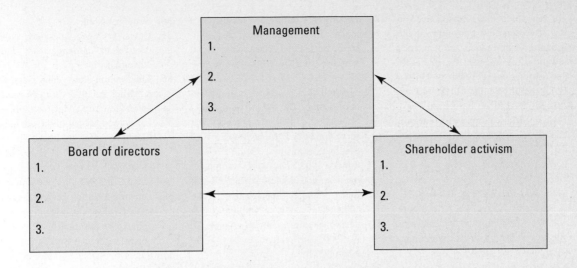

Application Questions & Exercises

1. The problems of many firms may be attributed to a "traditional" control system that failed to continuously monitor the environment and make necessary changes in their strategy and objectives. What companies are you familiar with that responded appropriately (or inappropriately) to environmental change?

2. How can a strong, positive culture enhance a firm's competitive advantage? How can a weak, negative culture erode competitive advantages? Explain and provide examples.

3. Use the Internet to research a firm that has an excellent culture and/or reward and incentive system. What are this firm's main financial and nonfinancial benefits?

4. Using the Internet, go to the website of a large, publicly held corporation in which you are interested. What evidence do you see of effective (or ineffective) corporate governance?

Ethics Questions

1. Strong cultures can have powerful effects on employee behavior. How does this create inadvertent control mechanisms? That is, are strong cultures an ethical way to control behavior?

2. Rules and regulations can help reduce unethical behavior in organizations. To be effective, however, what other systems, mechanisms, and processes are necessary?

References

1. Loomis, C. J. 2010. Directors: Feeding at the trough. *Fortune,* January 18: 20; Schonberger, J. 2009. Why you should care about corporate governance, *www.fool.com.* November 10: np; Hood, H. J. 2009. *Chesapeake Energy Corporation* Schedule 14A; and *www.sec.gov.* November 10: np. We thank Zia Shakir for his valued contributions.

2. This chapter draws upon Picken, J. C. & Dess, G. G. 1997. *Mission critical.* Burr Ridge, IL: Irwin Professional Publishing.

3. For a unique perspective on governance, refer to: Carmeli, A. & Markman, G. D. 2011. Capture, governance, and resilience: Strategy implications from the history of Rome. *Strategic Management Journal,* 32(3):332–341.

4. Argyris, C. 1977. Double-loop learning in organizations. *Harvard Business Review,* 55: 115–125.

5. Simons, R. 1995. Control in an age of empowerment. *Harvard Business Review,* 73: 80–88. This chapter draws on this source in the discussion of informational control.

6. Goold, M. & Quinn, J. B. 1990. The paradox of strategic controls. *Strategic Management Journal,* 11: 43–57.

7. Quinn, J. B. 1980. *Strategies for change.* Homewood, IL: Richard D. Irwin.

8. Mintzberg, H. 1987. Crafting strategy. *Harvard Business Review,* 65: 66–75.

9. Weston, J. S. 1992. Soft stuff matters. *Financial Executive,* July–August: 52–53.

10. This discussion of control systems draws upon Simons, op. cit.

11. Ryan, M. K., Haslam, S. A., & Renneboog, L. D. R. 2011. Who gets the carrot and who gets the stick? Evidence of gender discrimination in executive remuneration. *Strategic Management Journal,* 32(3): 301–321.

12. For an interesting perspective on this issue and how a downturn in the economy can reduce the tendency toward "free agency" by managers and professionals, refer to Morris, B. 2001. White collar blues. *Fortune,* July 23: 98–110.

13. For a colorful example of behavioral control in an organization, see: Beller, P. C. 2009. Activision's unlikely hero. *Forbes.* February 2: 52–58.

14. Ouchi, W. 1981. *Theory Z.* Reading, MA: Addison-Wesley; Deal, T. E. & Kennedy, A. A. 1982. *Corporate cultures.* Reading, MA: Addison-Wesley; Peters, T. J. & Waterman, R. H. 1982. *In search of excellence.* New York: Random House; Collins, J. 2001. *Good to great.* New York: HarperCollins.

15. Collins, J. C. & Porras, J. I. 1994. *Built to last: Successful habits of visionary companies.* New York: Harper Business.

16. Lee, J. & Miller, D. 1999. People matter: Commitment to employees, strategy, and performance in Korean firms. *Strategic Management Journal,* 6: 579–594.

17. For an insightful discussion of IKEA's unique culture, see Kling, K. & Goteman, I. 2003. IKEA CEO Anders Dahlvig on international growth and IKEA's unique corporate culture and brand identity. *Academy of Management Executive,* 17(1): 31–37.

18. For a discussion of how professionals inculcate values, refer to Uhl-Bien, M. & Graen, G. B. 1998. Individual self-management: Analysis of professionals' self-managing activities in functional and cross-functional work teams. *Academy of Management Journal,* 41(3): 340–350.

19. A perspective on how antisocial behavior can erode a firm's culture can be found in Robinson, S. L. & O'Leary-Kelly, A. M. 1998. Monkey see, monkey do: The influence of work groups on the antisocial behavior of employees. *Academy of Management Journal,* 41(6): 658–672.

20. An interesting perspective on organizational culture is in: Mehta, S. N. 2009. UnderArmour reboots. *Fortune,* February 2: 29–33.

21. For insights on social pressure as a means for control, refer to: Goldstein, N. J. 2009. Harnessing social pressure. *Harvard Business Review,* 87(2): 25.

22. Mitchell, R. 1989. Masters of innovation. *BusinessWeek,* April 10: 58–63.

23. Sellers, P. 1993. Companies that serve you best. *Fortune,* May 31: 88.

24. Southwest Airlines Culture Committee. 1993. *Luv Lines* (company publication), March–April: 17–18; for an interesting perspective on the "downside" of strong "cultlike" organizational cultures, refer to Arnott, D. A. 2000. *Corporate cults.* New York: AMACOM.

25. Kerr, J. & Slocum, J. W., Jr. 1987. Managing corporate culture through reward systems. *Academy of Management Executive,* 1(2): 99–107.

26. For a unique perspective on leader challenges in managing wealthy professionals, refer to Wetlaufer, S. 2000. Who wants to manage a millionaire? *Harvard Business Review,* 78(4): 53–60.

27. www.starbucks.com; Wood, Z. 2010. Starbucks' staff set to get free shares in incentive schemes. *www.guardian.co.uk*; December 19: np; and Hammers, M. 2003. Starbucks is pleasing employees and pouring profits. *Workforce Management.* October: 58–59.

28. These next two subsections draw upon Dess, G. G. & Picken, J. C. 1997. *Beyond productivity.* New York: AMACOM.

29. For a discussion of the benefits of stock options as executive compensation, refer to Hall, B. J. 2000. What you need to know about stock options. *Harvard Business Review,* 78(2): 121–129.

30. Tully, S. 1993. Your paycheck gets exciting. *Fortune,* November 13: 89.

31. Carter, N. M. & Silva, C. 2010. Why men still get more promotions than women. *Harvard Business Review,* 88(9): 80–86.

32. Zellner, W., Hof, R. D., Brandt, R., Baker, S., & Greising, D. 1995. Go-go goliaths. *BusinessWeek,* February 13: 64–70.

33. This section draws on Dess & Picken, op. cit.: chap. 5.

34. Simons, op. cit.

35. Davis, E. 1997. Interview: Norman Augustine. *Management Review,* November: 11.

36. This section draws upon Dess, G. G. & Miller, A. 1993. *Strategic management.* New York: McGraw-Hill.

37. For a good review of the goal-setting literature, refer to Locke, E. A. & Latham, G. P. 1990. *A theory of goal setting and task performance.* Englewood Cliffs, NJ: Prentice Hall.

38. For an interesting perspective on the use of rules and regulations that is counter to this industry's (software) norms, refer to Fryer, B. 2001. Tom Siebel of Siebel Systems: High tech the old fashioned way. *Harvard Business Review,* 79(3): 118–130.

39. Thompson, A. A. Jr. & Strickland, A. J., III. 1998. *Strategic management: Concepts and cases* (10th ed.): 313. New York: McGraw-Hill.

40. Ibid.

41. Teitelbaum, R. 1997. Tough guys finish first. *Fortune,* July 21: 82–84.

42. Weaver, G. R., Trevino, L. K., & Cochran, P. L. 1999. Corporate ethics programs as control systems: Influences of executive commitment and environmental factors. *Academy of Management Journal,* 42(1): 41–57.

43. Cadbury, S. A. 1987. Ethical managers make their own rules. *Harvard Business Review,* 65: 3, 69–73.

44. Weber, J. 2003. CFOs on the hot seat. *BusinessWeek,* March 17: 66–70.

45. William Ouchi has written extensively about the use of clan control (which is viewed as an alternate to bureaucratic or market control). Here, a powerful culture results in people aligning their individual interests with those of the firm. Refer to Ouchi, op. cit. This section also draws on Hall, R. H. 2002. *Organizations: Structures, processes, and outcomes* (8th ed.). Upper Saddle River, NJ: Prentice Hall.

46. Poundstone, W. 2003. *How would you move Mount Fuji?* New York: Little, Brown and company, page 59.

47. Interesting insights on corporate governance are in: Kroll, M., Walters, B. A., & Wright, P. 2008. Board vigilance, director experience, and

corporate outcomes. *Strategic Management Journal,* 29(4): 363–382.

48. For a brief review of some central issues in corporate governance research, see: Hambrick, D. C., Werder, A. V., & Zajac, E. J. 2008. New directions in corporate governance research. *Organization Science,* 19(3): 381–385.

49. Monks, R. & Minow, N. 2001. *Corporate governance* (2nd ed.). Malden, MA: Blackwell.

50. Pound, J. 1995. The promise of the governed corporation. *Harvard Business Review,* 73(2): 89–98.

51. Maurer, H. & Linblad, C. 2009. Scandal at Satyam. *BusinessWeek,* January 19: 8; Scheck, J. & Stecklow, S. 2008. Brocade ex-CEO gets 21 months in prison. *The Wall Street Journal,* January 17: A3; Levine, D. & Graybow, M. 2010. Mozilo to pay millions in Countrywide settlement. *finance.yahoo.com.* October 15: np; Ellis, B. 2010. Countrywide's Mozilo to pay $67.5 million settlement. *cnnmoney.com.* October 15: np; Frank, R., Efrati, A., Lucchetti, A. & Bray, C. 2009. Madoff jailed after admitting epic scam. *The Wall Street Journal.* March 13: A1; and Henriques, D. B. 2009. Madoff is sentenced to 150 years for Ponzi scheme. *www.nytimes.com.* June 29: np.

52. Corporate governance and social networks are discussed in: McDonald, M. L., Khanna, P., & Westphal, J. D. 2008. *Academy of Management Journal.* 51(3): 453–475.

53. This discussion draws upon Monks & Minow, op. cit.

54. For an interesting perspective on the politicization of the corporation, read: Palazzo, G. & Scherer, A. G. 2008. Corporate social responsibility, democracy, and the politicization of the corporation. *Academy of Management Review,* 33(3): 773–774.

55. Eisenhardt, K. M. 1989. Agency theory: An assessment and review. *Academy of Management Review,* 14(1): 57–74. Some of the seminal contributions to agency theory include Jensen, M. & Meckling, W. 1976. Theory of the firm: Managerial behavior, agency costs, and ownership

structure. *Journal of Financial Economics,* 3: 305–360; Fama, E. & Jensen, M. 1983. Separation of ownership and control. *Journal of Law and Economics,* 26: 301, 325; and Fama, E. 1980. Agency problems and the theory of the firm. *Journal of Political Economy,* 88: 288–307.

56. Nyberg, A. J., Fulmer, I. S., Gerhart, B. & Carpenter, M. 2010. Agency theory revisited: CEO return and shareholder interest alignment. *Academy of Management Journal,* 53(5): 1029–1049.

57. Managers may also engage in "shirking"—that is, reducing or withholding their efforts. See, for example, Kidwell, R. E., Jr. & Bennett, N. 1993. Employee propensity to withhold effort: A conceptual model to intersect three avenues of research. *Academy of Management Review,* 18(3): 429–456.

58. For an interesting perspective on agency and clarification of many related concepts and terms, visit *www.encycogov.com.*

59. The relationship between corporate ownership structure and export intensity in Chinese firms is discussed in: Filatotchev, I., Stephan, J., & Jindra, B. 2008. Ownership structure, strategic controls and export intensity of foreign-invested firms in transition economies. *Journal of International Business,* 39(7): 1133–1148.

60. Argawal, A. & Mandelker, G. 1987. Managerial incentives and corporate investment and financing decisions. *Journal of Finance,* 42: 823–837.

61. The Carnival and Alliance Semiconductor examples draw upon: MacDonald, E. 2004. Crony capitalism. *Forbes,* June 21: 140–146.

62. For an insightful, recent discussion of the academic research on corporate governance, and in particular the role of boards of directors, refer to Chatterjee, S. & Harrison, J. S. 2001. Corporate governance. In Hitt, M. A., Freeman, R. E., & Harrison, J. S. (Eds.). *Handbook of strategic management:* 543–563. Malden, MA: Blackwell.

63. For an interesting theoretical discussion on corporate governance in

Russia, see: McCarthy, D. J. & Puffer, S. M. 2008. Interpreting the ethicality of corporate governance decisions in Russia: Utilizing integrative social contracts theory to evaluate the relevance of agency theory norms. *Academy of Management Review,* 33(1): 11–31.

64. Haynes, K. T. & Hillman, A. 2010. The effect of board capital and CEO power on strategic change. *Strategic Management Journal,* 31(110): 1145–1163.

65. This opening discussion draws on Monks & Minow, op. cit. 164, 169; see also Pound, op. cit.

66. Business Roundtable. 1990. *Corporate governance and American competitiveness,* March: 7.

67. The director role in acquisition performance is addressed in: Westphal, J. D. & Graebner, M. E. 2008. What do they know? The effects of outside director acquisition experience on firm acquisition performance. *Strategic Management Journal,* 29(11): 1155–1178.

68. Byrne, J. A., Grover, R., & Melcher, R. A. 1997. The best and worst boards. *BusinessWeek,* November 26: 35–47. The three key roles of boards of directors are monitoring the actions of executives, providing advice, and providing links to the external environment to provide resources. See Johnson, J. L., Daily, C. M., & Ellstrand, A. E. 1996. Boards of directors: A review and research agenda. *Academy of Management Review,* 37: 409–438.

69. Pozen, R. C. 2010. The case for professional boards. *Harvard Business Review,* 88(12): 50–58.

70. The role of outside directors is discussed in: Lester, R. H., Hillman, A., Zardkoohi, A., & Cannella, A. A. Jr. 2008. Former government officials as outside directors: The role of human and social capital. *Academy of Management Journal,* 51(5): 999–1013.

71. McGeehan, P. 2003. More chief executives shown the door, study says. *New York Times,* May 12: C2.

72. The examples in this paragraph draw upon Helyar, J. & Hymowitz,

C. 2011. The recession is gone, and the CEO could be next. *Bloomberg Businessweek*. Februrary 7–February 13: 24–26; Stelter, B. 2010. Jonathan Klein to leave CNN. *mediadecoder. blogs.nytimes.com.* September 24: np; Silver, A. 2010. Milestones. *TIME Magazine.* December 20: 28; *www. bp.com* and Mouawad, J. & Krauss, C. 2010. BP is expected to replace Hayward as chief with American. *The New York Times.* July 26: A1.

73. For an analysis of the effects of outside directors' compensation on acquisition decisions, refer to Deutsch, T., Keil, T., & Laamanen, T. 2007. Decision making in acquisitions: The effect of outside directors' compensation ·on acquisition patterns. *Journal of Management,* 33(1): 30–56.

74. Director interlocks are addressed in: Kang, E. 2008. Director interlocks and spillover effects of reputational penalties from financial reporting fraud. *Academy of Management Journal,* 51(3): 537–556.

75. There are benefits, of course, to having some insiders on the board of directors. Inside directors would be more aware of the firm's strategies. Additionally, outsiders may rely too often on financial performance. indicators because of information asymmetries. For an interesting discussion, see Baysinger, B. D. & Hoskisson, R. E. 1990. The composition of boards of directors and strategic control: Effects on corporate strategy. *Academy of Management Review,* 15: 72–87.

76. Hambrick, D. C. & Jackson, E. M. 2000. Outside directors with a stake: The linchpin in improving governance. *California Management Review,* 42(4): 108–127.

77. Ibid.

78. Disney has begun to make many changes to improve its corporate governance, such as assigning only independent directors to important board committees, restricting directors from serving on more than three boards, and appointing a lead director who can convene the board without approval by the CEO. In recent years, the Disney Co. has shown up on some "best" board lists. In addition Eisner has recently relinquished the chairman position.

79. Talk show. 2002. *BusinessWeek,* September 30: 14.

80. Ward, R. D. 2000. *Improving corporate boards.* New York: Wiley.

81. A discussion on the shareholder approval process in executive compensation is presented in: Brandes, P., Goranova, M., & Hall, S. 2008. Navigating shareholder influence: Compensation plans and the shareholder approval process. *Academy of Management Perspectives,* 22(1): 41–57.

82. Monks and Minow, op. cit.: 93.

83. A discussion of the factors that lead to shareholder activism is found in Ryan, L. V. & Schneider, M. 2002. The antecedents of institutional investor activism. *Academy of Management Review,* 27(4): 554–573.

84. For an insightful discussion of investor activism, refer to David, P., Bloom, M., & Hillman, A. 2007. Investor activism, managerial responsiveness, and corporate social performance. *Strategic Management Journal,* 28(1): 91–100.

85. There is strong research support for the idea that the presence of large block shareholders is associated with value-maximizing decisions. For example, refer to Johnson, R. A., Hoskisson, R. E., & Hitt, M. A. 1993. Board of director involvement in restructuring: The effects of board versus managerial controls and characteristics. *Strategic Management Journal,* 14: 33–50.

86. For a discussion of institutional activism and its link to CEO compensation, refer to: Chowdhury, S. D. & Wang, E. Z. 2009. Institutional activism types and CEO compensation. *Journal of Management,* 35(1): 5–36.

87. For an interesting perspective on the impact of institutional ownership on a firm's innovation strategies, see Hoskisson, R. E., Hitt, M. A., Johnson, R. A., & Grossman, W. 2002. *Academy of Management Journal,* 45(4): 697–716.

88. *www.calpers.ca.gov;*

89. Icahn, C. 2007. Icahn: On activist investors and private equity run wild. *BusinessWeek,* March 12: 21–22. For an interesting perspective on Carl Icahn's transition (?) from corporate raider to shareholder activist, read Grover, R. 2007. Just don't call him a raider. *BusinessWeek,* March 5: 68–69. The quote in the text is part of Icahn's response to the article by R. Grover.

90. For a study of the relationship between ownership and diversification, refer to Goranova, M., Alessandri, T. M., Brandes, P., & Dharwadkar, R. 2007. Managerial ownership and corporate diversification: A longitudinal view, *Strategic Management Journal,* 28(3): 211–226.

91. Jensen, M. C. & Murphy, K. J. 1990. CEO incentives—It's not how much you pay, but how. *Harvard Business Review,* 68(3): 138–149.

92. For a perspective on the relative advantages and disadvantages of "duality"—that is, one individual serving as both Chief Executive Office and Chairman of the Board, see Lorsch, J. W. & Zelleke, A. 2005. Should the CEO be the chairman? *MIT Sloan Management Review,* 46(2): 71–74.

93. A discussion of knowledge sharing is addressed in: Fey, C. F. & Furu, P. 2008. Top management incentive compensation and knowledge sharing in multinational corporations. *Strategic Management Journal,* 29(12): 1301–1324.

94. Sasseen, J. 2007. A better look at the boss's pay. *BusinessWeek,* February 26: 44–45; and Weinberg, N., Maiello, M., & Randall, D. 2008. Paying for failure. *Forbes,* May 19: 114, 116.

95. Byrnes, N. & Sasseen, J. 2007. Board of hard knocks. *BusinessWeek,* January 22: 36–39.

96. Research has found that executive compensation is more closely aligned with firm performance in companies with compensation committees and boards dominated by outside directors. See, for example, Conyon, M. J. & Peck, S. I. 1998. Board control, remuneration committees, and top management compensation. *Academy of Management Journal,* 41: 146–157.

97. Lavelle, L., Jespersen, F. F., & Arndt, M. 2002. Executive pay. *Business-Week,* April 15: 66–72.

98. A perspective on whether or not CEOs are overpaid is provided in: Kaplan, S. N. 2008. Are U.S. CEOs overpaid: A response to Bogle and Walsh, J. P. *Academy of Management Perspectives.* 22(3): 28–34.

99. *www.tiaa-cref.org/pubs.*

100. Some insights on CEO compensation—and the importance of ethics—are addressed in: Heineman, B. W. Jr. 2008. The fatal flaw in pay for performance. *Harvard Business Review.* 86(6): 31, 34.

101. Chahine, S. & Tohme, N. S. 2009. Is CEO duality always negative? An exploration of CEO duality and ownership structure in the Arab IPO context. *Corporate Governance: An International Review.* 17(2): 123–141; and McGrath, J. 2009. How CEOs work. *HowStuffWorks.com.* January 28: np.

102. Anonymous. 2009. Someone to watch over them. *The Economist.* October 17: 78; Anonymous. 2004. Splitting up the roles of CEO and Chairman: Reform or red herring? *Knowledge@Wharton.* June 2: np; and Kim, J. 2010. Shareholders reject split of CEO and chairman jobs at JPMorgan. *FierceFinance.com.* May 18: np.

103. Tuggle, C. S., Sirmon, D. G., Reutzel, C. R. & Bierman, L. 2010. Commanding board of director attention: Investigating how organizational performance and CEO duality affect board members' attention to monitoring. *Strategic Management Journal.* 31: 946–968; Weinberg, N. 2010. No more lapdogs. *Forbes.* May 10: 34–36; and Anonymous. 2010. Corporate constitutions. *The Economist.* October 30: 74.

104. Such opportunistic behavior is common in all principal-agent relationships. For a description of agency problems, especially in the context of the relationship between shareholders and managers, see Jensen, M. C. & Meckling, W. H. 1976. Theory of the firm: Managerial behavior, agency costs, and ownership structure. *Journal of Financial Economics,* 3: 305–360.

105. Hoskisson, R. E. & Turk, T. A. 1990. Corporate restructuring: Governance and control limits of the internal market. *Academy of Management Review,* 15: 459–477.

106. For an insightful perspective on the market for corporate control and how it is influenced by knowledge intensity, see Coff, R. 2003. Bidding wars over R&D-intensive firms: Knowledge, opportunism, and the market for corporate control. *Academy of Management Journal,* 46(1): 74–85.

107. Walsh, J. P. & Kosnik, R. D. 1993. Corporate raiders and their disciplinary role in the market for corporate control. *Academy of Management Journal,* 36: 671–700.

108. Gunning for KPMG. 2003. *Economist,* February 1: 63.

109. Timmons, H. 2003. Investment banks: Who will foot their bill? *BusinessWeek,* March 3: 116.

110. The role of regulatory bodies in the banking industry is addressed in: Bhide, A. 2009. Why bankers got so reckless. *BusinessWeek,* February 9: 30–31.

111. Wishy-washy: The SEC pulls its punches on corporate-governance rules. 2003. *Economist,* February 1: 60.

112. McLean, B. 2001. Is Enron overpriced? *Fortune,* March 5: 122–125.

113. Swartz, J. 2010. Timberland's CEO on standing up to 65,000 angry activists. *Harvard Business Review,* 88 (9): 39–43.

114. Bernstein, A. 2000. Too much corporate power. *BusinessWeek,* September 11: 35–37.

115. This section draws upon Young, M. N., Peng, M. W., Ahlstrom, D., Bruton, G. D., & Jiang, Y. 2005. Principal–principal conflicts in corporate governance (un-published manuscript); and, Peng, M. W. 2006. *Globalstrategy.* Cincinnati: Thomson South-Western. We appreciate the helpful comments of Mike Young of Hong Kong Baptist University and Mike Peng of the University of Texas at Dallas.

116. Khanna, T. & Rivkin, J. 2001. Estimating the performance effects of business groups in emerging markets. *Strategic Management Journal,* 22: 45–74.

chapter TEN

Creating Effective Organizational Designs

After reading this chapter, you should have a good understanding of:

LO10.1 The growth patterns of major corporations and the relationship between a firm's strategy and its structure.

LO10.2 Each of the traditional types of organizational structure: simple, functional, divisional, and matrix.

LO10.3 The implications of a firm's international operations for organizational structure.

LO10.4 Why there is no "one best way" to design strategic reward and evaluation systems, and the important contingent roles of business- and corporate-level strategies.

LO10.5 The different types of boundaryless organizations—barrier-free, modular, and virtual—and their relative advantages and disadvantages.

LO10.6 The need for creating ambidextrous organizational designs that enable firms to explore new opportunities and effectively integrate existing operations.

LEARNING OBJECTIVES

To implement strategies successfully, firms must have appropriate organizational designs. These include the processes and integrating mechanisms necessary to ensure that boundaries among internal activities and external parties, such as suppliers, customers, and alliance partners, are flexible and permeable. A firm's performance will suffer if its managers don't carefully consider both of these organizational design attributes.

In the first section, we begin by discussing the growth patterns of large corporations to address the important relationships between the strategy that a firm follows and its corresponding structure. For example, as firms diversify into related product-market areas, they change their structure from functional to divisional. We then address the different types of traditional structures—simple, functional, divisional, and matrix—and their relative advantages and disadvantages. We close with a discussion of the implications of a firm's international operations for the structure of its organization.

The second section takes the perspective that there is no "one best way" to design an organization's strategic reward and evaluation system. Here we address two important contingencies: business- and corporate-level strategy. For example, when strategies require a great deal of collaboration, as well as resource and information sharing, there must be incentives and cultures that encourage and reward such initiatives.

The third section discusses the concept of the "boundaryless" organization. We do *not* argue that organizations should have no internal and external boundaries. Instead, we suggest that in rapidly changing and unpredictable environments, organizations must strive to make their internal and external boundaries both flexible and permeable. We suggest three different types of boundaryless organizations: barrier-free, modular, and virtual.

The fourth section focuses on the need for managers to recognize that they typically face two opposing challenges: (1) being proactive in taking advantage of new opportunities and (2) ensuring the effective coordination and integration of existing operations. This suggests the need for ambidextrous organizations; that is, firms that can both be efficient in how they manage existing assets and competencies and take advantage of opportunities in rapidly changing and unpredictable environments—conditions that are becoming more pronounced in today's global markets. •

Learning from Mistakes

In mid-July 2010, Hong Kong's travel industry was reeling from a wild rant by a commission-based tour guide which was unfortunately captured on video.[1] The video went viral on the Internet and hit television screens across the mainland. More than a dozen television stations picked up the online video and played it constantly over a two-day period. What happened?

The seven-minute clip featured a female guide (nicknamed Ah Zhen) berating a group of mainland visitors and threatening to lock them out of their hotel rooms because they did not spend much at a jewelry store. In effect, this provided a shocking view of what Hong Kong can offer visitors. It followed a series of complaints about visitors being strong-armed by tour guides to go shopping and spend their money.

Ah Zhen is heard scolding the tourists in fluent Mandarin after they boarded their bus. "Don't tell me you don't need to shop," she said. "So later you are going to say you don't need to eat? I will lock you out of your hotel rooms. It's okay for you to stay poor at home, but when you travel outside, don't be like this. In this world there is no such thing as a free lunch."

She went on to talk about how the visitors found money for their airfares and then chides them: "We don't do this for charity. Let me be responsible for charity. I donated 10,500 yuan ($1,500) for Sichuan earthquake victims." She then pointed to shops offering top-quality goods, before adding, "Why did you bother to come to Hong Kong?" She lamented that the group did not look good compared with another group of tourists, who spent HKD137,000 ($17,000). "For a group of 24 people you only just spent HKD13,000 ($2,100). How can you just walk out of the shop like that?"

"It's you who owe me here, not me owing you," the guide continued. "I provided you with food and accommodations, but you people will not give. If you don't repay the debt in this life, you will have to repay it in your next life." She added, "Tonight I will lock all hotel room doors, because you don't need accommodations."

The clip sparked an outcry on the Internet. Some people said that they would no longer dare visit Hong Kong. Travel Industry Council Chairman Michael Wu Siu-ying said he had asked for the names of the travel agency and the tour agent from Guangdong, so that the council could take action.

When contacted, the tour guide became defensive and extremely vocal about mainland tourists condemning tour guides for forcing them to make purchases. "We don't force them to buy. When they sign up for the tour group, they should act responsibly.. . . You can see how much the tour group fees are.. . . You sign up for such a group, then you must do whatever is required. It is that simple. We did not force them to buy anything. We can't force them." She also said, "When they come, they know what they are doing. How much do they pay in fees? How many days are they staying?"

She further said, "Everybody has to earn a living. . . . I did this for the sake of surviving, just like you calling me in order for you to survive. . . . I have to eat. It is very normal for me to tell them about making purchases." Clearly, she was not happy about the media "hyping trivia" so that fewer mainland tour groups are coming. She also threatened the reporter not to write about her. "I will come and hold you accountable. I don't think there is anything wrong with what I did."

The government has given the Travel Industry Council three months to develop concrete measures to address the deteriorating image of Hong Kong as a tourist destination amid anger at the treatment of mainland tourists by commission-hungry guides. The council has set up a special task force to look into the issue.

One person's action has caused a chain reaction and tarnished the image of Hong Kong. One of the pitfalls of outsourcing is that the firm has less control. When companies outsource key activities, an inherent risk is that the quality of the performance of the contractors is not up to the standards of the firm. Further, at times, there are differences in cultural norms and insufficient training in place to ensure that contract employees adhere to standards and expectations.

One of the central concepts in this chapter is the importance of boundaryless organizations. Successful organizations create permeable boundaries among the internal activities as well as between the organization and its external customers, suppliers, and alliance partners. We introduced this idea in Chapter 3 in our discussion of the value-chain concept, which consisted of several primary (e.g., inbound logistics, marketing and sales) and support activities (e.g., procurement, human resource management). There are a number of possible benefits to outsourcing activities as part of becoming an effective boundaryless organization. However, outsourcing can also create challenges. As in the case of the tour operator in Hong Kong, the firm lost a certain amount of control by using independent contractors to provide services. Clearly, the outsourced tour guide was more focused on her personal financial incentives than the welfare of the travel firm or the tourists.

Today's managers are faced with two ongoing and vital activities in structuring and designing their organizations.[2] First, they must decide on the most appropriate type of organizational structure. Second, they need to assess what mechanisms, processes, and techniques are most helpful in enhancing the permeability of both internal and external boundaries.

Traditional Forms of Organizational Structure

Organizational structure refers to the formalized patterns of interactions that link a firm's tasks, technologies, and people.[3] Structures help to ensure that resources are used effectively in accomplishing an organization's mission. Structure provides a means of balancing two conflicting forces: a need for the division of tasks into meaningful groupings and the need to integrate such groupings in order to ensure efficiency and effectiveness.[4] Structure identifies the executive, managerial, and administrative organization of a firm and indicates responsibilities and hierarchical relationships. It also influences the flow of information as well as the context and nature of human interactions.[5]

Most organizations begin very small and either die or remain small. Those that survive and prosper embark on strategies designed to increase the overall scope of operations and enable them to enter new product-market domains. Such growth places additional pressure on executives to control and coordinate the firm's increasing size and diversity. The most appropriate type of structure depends on the nature and magnitude of growth.

Patterns of Growth of Large Corporations: Strategy-Structure Relationships

A firm's strategy and structure change as it increases in size, diversifies into new product markets, and expands its geographic scope.[6] Exhibit 10.1 illustrates common growth patterns of firms.

organizational structure the formalized patterns of interactions that link a firm's tasks, technologies, and people.

>LO10.1
The growth patterns of major corporations and the relationship between a firm's strategy and its structure.

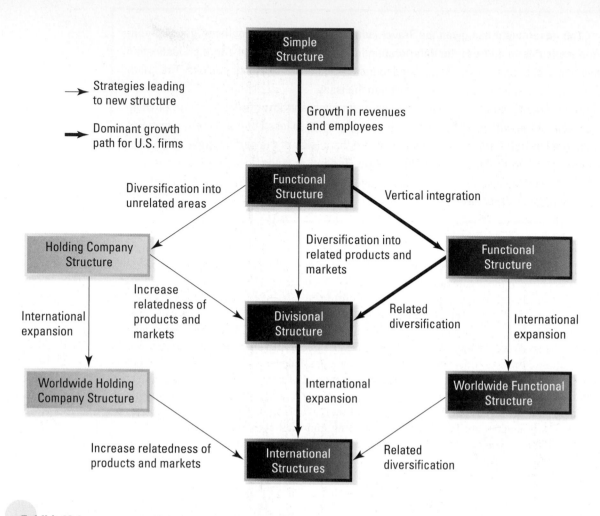

Exhibit 10.1 Dominant Growth Patterns of Large Corporations

Source: Adapted from J. R. Galbraith and R. K. Kazanjian. *Strategy Implementation: Structure, Systems and Process,* 2nd ed. Copyright © 1986.

A new firm with a *simple structure* typically increases its sales revenue and volume of outputs over time. It may also engage in some vertical integration to secure sources of supply (backward integration) as well as channels of distribution (forward integration). The simple-structure firm then implements a *functional structure* to concentrate efforts on both increasing efficiency and enhancing its operations and products. This structure enables the firm to group its operations into either functions, departments, or geographic areas. As its initial markets mature, a firm looks beyond its present products and markets for possible expansion.

A strategy of related diversification requires a need to reorganize around product lines or geographic markets. This leads to a *divisional structure.* As the business expands in terms of sales revenues, and domestic growth opportunities become somewhat limited, a firm may seek opportunities in international markets. A firm has a wide variety of structures to choose from. These include *international division, geographic area, worldwide product division, worldwide functional,* and *worldwide matrix.* Deciding upon the most appropriate structure when a firm has international operations depends on three primary factors: the extent of international expansion, type of strategy (global, multidomestic, or transnational), and the degree of product diversity.[7]

Some firms may find it advantageous to diversify into several product lines rather than focus their efforts on strengthening distributor and supplier relationships through vertical integration. They would organize themselves according to product lines by implementing a divisional structure. Also, some firms may choose to move into unrelated product areas, typically by acquiring existing businesses. Frequently, their rationale is that acquiring assets and competencies is more economical or expedient than developing them internally. Such an unrelated, or conglomerate, strategy requires relatively little integration across businesses and sharing of resources. Thus, a *holding company structure* becomes appropriate. There are many other growth patterns, but these are the most common.[*]

Now we will discuss some of the most common types of organizational structures—simple, functional, divisional (including two variants: *strategic business unit* and *holding company*), and matrix and their advantages and disadvantages. We will close the section with a discussion of the structural implications when a firm expands its operations into international markets.[8]

Simple Structure

The **simple organizational structure** is the oldest, and most common, organizational form. Most organizations are very small and have a single or very narrow product line in which the owner-manager (or top executive) makes most of the decisions. The owner-manager controls all activities, and the staff serves as an extension of the top executive.

Advantages The simple structure is highly informal and the coordination of tasks is accomplished by direct supervision. Decision making is highly centralized, there is little specialization of tasks, few rules and regulations, and an informal evaluation and reward system. Although the owner-manager is intimately involved in almost all phases of the business, a manager is often employed to oversee day-to-day operations.

Disadvantages   A simple structure may foster creativity and individualism since there are generally few rules and regulations. However, such "informality" may lead to problems. Employees may not clearly understand their responsibilities, which can lead to conflict and confusion. Employees may take advantage of the lack of regulations, act in their own self-interest, which can erode motivation and satisfaction and lead to the possible misuse of organizational resources. Small organizations have flat structures that limit opportunities for upward mobility. Without the potential for future advancement, recruiting and retaining talent may become very difficult.

Functional Structure

When an organization is small (15 employees or less), it is not necessary to have a variety of formal arrangements and groupings of activities. However, as firms grow, excessive demands may be placed on the owner-manager in order to obtain and process all of the information necessary to run the business. Chances are the owner will not be skilled in all specialties (e.g., accounting, engineering, production, marketing). Thus, he or she will need to hire specialists in the various functional areas. Such growth in the overall scope and complexity of the business necessitates a **functional organizational structure** wherein the major functions of the firm are grouped internally. The coordination and integration of the functional areas becomes one of the most important responsibilities of the chief executive of the firm (see Exhibit 10.2).

>LO10.2
Each of the traditional types of organizational structure: simple, functional, divisional, and matrix.

simple organizational structure an organizational form in which the owner-manager makes most of the decisions and controls activities, and the staff serves as an extension of the top executive.

functional organizational structure an organizational form in which the major functions of the firm, such as production, marketing, R&D, and accounting, are grouped internally.

---

[*] The lowering of transaction costs and globalization have led to some changes in the common historical patterns that we have discussed. Some firms are, in effect, bypassing the vertical integration stage. Instead, they focus on core competencies and outsource other value-creation activities. Also, even relatively young firms are going global early in their history because of lower communication and transportation costs. For an interesting perspective on global start-ups, see McDougall, P. P. & Oviatt, B. M. 1996. New Venture Internationalization, Strategic Change and Performance: A Follow-Up Study. *Journal of Business Venturing,* 11: 23–40; and McDougall, P. P. & Oviatt, B. M. (Eds.). 2000. The Special Research Forum on International Entrepreneurship. *Academy of Management Journal,* October: 902–1003.

Lower-level managers, specialists, and operating personnel

Exhibit 10.2 Functional Organizational Structure

Functional structures are generally found in organizations in which there is a single or closely related product or service, high production volume, and some vertical integration. Initially, firms tend to expand the overall scope of their operations by penetrating existing markets, introducing similar products in additional markets, or increasing the level of vertical integration. Such expansion activities clearly increase the scope and complexity of the operations. The functional structure provides for a high level of centralization that helps to ensure integration and control over the related product-market activities or multiple primary activities (from inbound logistics to operations to marketing, sales, and service) in the value chain (addressed in Chapters 3 and 4). Strategy Spotlight 10.1 provides an example of an effective functional organization structure—Parkdale Mills.

Advantages By bringing together specialists into functional departments, a firm is able to enhance its coordination and control within each of the functional areas. Decision making in the firm will be centralized at the top of the organization. This enhances the organizational-level (as opposed to functional area) perspective across the various functions in the organization. In addition, the functional structure provides for a more efficient use of managerial and technical talent since functional area expertise is pooled in a single department (e.g., marketing) instead of being spread across a variety of product-market areas. Finally, career paths and professional development in specialized areas are facilitated.

Disadvantages The differences in values and orientations among functional areas may impede communication and coordination. Edgar Schein of MIT has argued that shared assumptions, often based on similar backgrounds and experiences of members, form around functional units in an organization. This leads to what are often called "stove pipes" or "silos," in which departments view themselves as isolated, self-contained units with little need for interaction and coordination with other departments. This erodes communication because functional groups may have not only different goals but also differing meanings of words and concepts. According to Schein:

> The word "marketing" will mean product development to the engineer, studying customers through market research to the product manager, merchandising to the salesperson, and constant change in design to the manufacturing manager. When they try to work together, they will often attribute disagreements to personalities and fail to notice the deeper, shared assumptions that color how each function thinks.[9]

Such narrow functional orientations also may lead to short-term thinking based largely upon what is best for the functional area, not the entire organization. In a manufacturing firm, sales may want to offer a wide range of customized products to appeal to the firm's

strategy spotlight

Parkdale Mills: A Successful Functional Organizational Structure

For more than 80 years, Parkdale Mills, with approximately $1 billion in revenues, has been the industry leader in the production of cotton and cotton blend yarns. Their expertise comes by concentrating on a single product line, perfecting processes, and welcoming innovation. According to CEO Andy Warlick, "I think we've probably

Sources: Stewart, C. 2003. The Perfect Yarn. The Manufacturer.com, July 31; *www.parkdalemills.com*; Berman, P. 1987. The Fast Track Isn't Always the Best Track. *Forbes*, November 2: 60–64; and personal communication with Duke Kimbrell, March 11, 2005.

spent more than any two competitors combined on new equipment and robotics. We do this because we have to compete in a global market where a lot of the competition has a lower wage structure and gets subsidies that we don't receive, so we really have to focus on consistency and cost control." Yarn making is generally considered to be a commodity business, and Parkdale is the industry's low-cost producer.

Tasks are highly standardized and authority is centralized with Duke Kimbrell, founder and chairman, and CEO Andy Warlick. The firm operates a bare-bones staff with a small staff of top executives. Kimbrell and Warlick are considered shrewd about the cotton market, technology, customer loyalty, and incentive pay.

customers; R&D may overdesign products and components to achieve technical elegance; and manufacturing may favor no-frills products that can be produced at low cost by means of long production runs. Functional structures may overburden the top executives in the firm because conflicts have a tendency to be "pushed up" to the top of the organization since there are no managers who are responsible for the specific product lines. Functional structures make it difficult to establish uniform performance standards across the entire organization. It may be relatively easy to evaluate production managers on the basis of production volume and cost control, but establishing performance measures for engineering, R&D, and accounting become more problematic.

Divisional Structure

The **divisional organizational structure** (sometimes called the multidivisional structure or M Form) is organized around products, projects, or markets. Each of the divisions, in turn, includes its own functional specialists who are typically organized into departments.[10] A divisional structure encompasses a set of relatively autonomous units governed by a central corporate office. The operating divisions are relatively independent and consist of products and services that are different from those of the other divisions.[11] Operational decision making in a large business places excessive demands on the firm's top management. In order to attend to broader, longer-term organizational issues, top-level managers must delegate decision making to lower-level managers. Divisional executives play a key role: they help to determine the product-market and financial objectives for the division as well as their division's contribution to overall corporate performance.[12] The rewards are based largely on measures of financial performance such as net income and revenue. Exhibit 10.3 illustrates a divisional structure.

> **divisional organizational structure** an organizational form in which products, projects, or product markets are grouped internally.

General Motors was among the earliest firms to adopt the divisional organizational structure.[13] In the 1920s the company formed five major product divisions (Cadillac, Buick, Oldsmobile, Pontiac, and Chevrolet) as well as several industrial divisions. Since then, many firms have discovered that as they diversified into new product-market activities, functional structures—with their emphasis on single functional departments—were unable to manage the increased complexity of the entire business.

Advantages By creating separate divisions to manage individual product markets, there is a separation of strategic and operating control. Divisional managers can focus

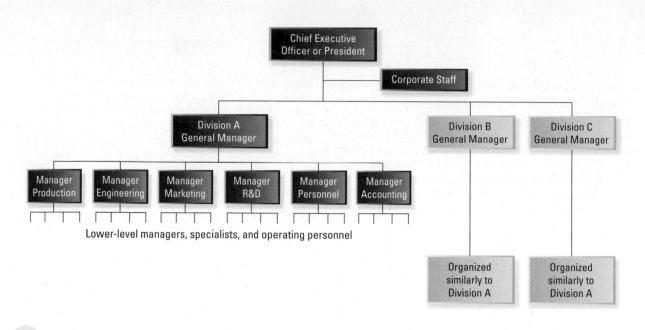

Lower-level managers, specialists, and operating personnel

Exhibit 10.3 Divisional Organizational Structure

their efforts on improving operations in the product markets for which they are responsible, and corporate officers can devote their time to overall strategic issues for the entire corporation. The focus on a division's products and markets—by the divisional executives—provides the corporation with an enhanced ability to respond quickly to important changes. Since there are functional departments within each division of the corporation, the problems associated with sharing resources across functional departments are minimized. Because there are multiple levels of general managers (executives responsible for integrating and coordinating all functional areas), the development of general management talent is enhanced.

Disadvantages   It can be very expensive; there can be increased costs due to the duplication of personnel, operations, and investment since each division must staff multiple functional departments. There also can be dysfunctional competition among divisions since each division tends to become concerned solely about its own operations. Divisional managers are often evaluated on common measures such as return on assets and sales growth. If goals are conflicting, there can be a sense of a "zero-sum" game that would discourage sharing ideas and resources among the divisions for the common good of the corporation. Ghoshal and Bartlett, two leading strategy scholars, note:

> As their label clearly warns, divisions divide. The divisional model fragmented companies' resources; it created vertical communication channels that insulated business units and prevented them from sharing their strengths with one another. Consequently, the whole of the corporation was often less than the sum of its parts.[14]

With many divisions providing different products and services, there is the chance that differences in image and quality may occur across divisions. One division may offer no-frills products of lower quality that may erode the brand reputation of another division that has top quality, highly differentiated offerings. Since each division is evaluated in terms of financial measures such as return on investment and revenue growth, there is often an urge to focus on short-term performance. If corporate management uses quarterly profits as the

Why Sun Microsystems Experienced Major Problems When It Changed Its Organizational Structure

In general, organizational structures don't fail; managers fail at implementing them correctly. For example, in the 1990s, Sun Microsystems (acquired by Oracle in 2010) undertook a major corporate reorganization and changed from a functional structure to a divisional structure. At the time, the rationale seemed quite logical: Management wanted to create miniature Suns to provide autonomy, which would help restore the entrepreneurial spirit of the firm's start-up days.

Separate divisions were created for high-end servers, desktop computers, printers, software, services, and so on. In total, there were nine divisions. Such a configuration led them to call the structure "Sun and the nine planets." However, things certainly didn't work out as planned!

Within a few years, Sun discovered the problems associated with this new structure. Management discovered that they wound up with nine different compensation plans, nine IT systems, nine sales forces calling on the same customers, and so on. In essence, they had nine of everything and, not surprisingly, escalating overhead expenses. As noted by Larry Hambly, Sun's chief quality officer and president of its customer service division, "The planets placed too much visibility on each entity." This resulted in the sales forces competing with each other, while people who were supposed to give customer service passed the buck. Lamented Hambly, "There was too much of, 'I don't know; that is somebody else's problem.'" In addition, it became almost impossible to move talent from one division to the next. As one would expect, Sun soon abandoned this highly autonomous structure and moved back to one similar to what it previously had.

Does this mean that autonomous divisional structures don't work? Of course not. Such a structure works well at diversified firms such as United Technologies and General Electric. Sun simply failed to implement the structure best suited to its particular situation.

Sources: Galbraith, J. 2009. *Designing Matrix Organizations That Actually Work.* San Francisco: Jossey-Bass; Southwick, K. *High Noon: The Inside Story of Scott McNealy and the Rise of Sun Microsystems.* Hoboken, NJ: Wiley; and Shankland, S. 2010. Oracle Buys Sun, Becomes Hardware Company. *www. news.cnet.com.* January 27: np.

key performance indicator, divisional management may tend to put significant emphasis on "making the numbers" and minimizing activities, such as advertising, maintenance, and capital investments, which would detract from short-term performance measures.

When firms change their organization's structure, things don't always work out as planned. In Strategy Spotlight 10.2 we give one example—the problems that Sun Microsystems faced when the firm changed from a functional structure to a divisional structure.

We'll discuss two variations of the divisional form: the strategic business unit (SBU) and holding company structures.

Strategic Business Unit (SBU) Structure Highly diversified corporations such as ConAgra, a $12 billion food producer, may consist of dozens of different divisions.[15] If ConAgra were to use a purely divisional structure, it would be nearly impossible for the corporate office to plan and coordinate activities, because the span of control would be too large. To attain synergies, ConAgra has put its diverse businesses into three primary SBUs: food service (restaurants), retail (grocery stores), and agricultural products.

With an **SBU structure,** divisions with similar products, markets, and/or technologies are grouped into homogeneous units to achieve some synergies. These include those discussed in Chapter 6 for related diversification, such as leveraging core competencies, sharing infrastructures, and market power. Generally the more related businesses are within a corporation, the fewer SBUs will be required. Each of the SBUs in the corporation operates as a profit center.

> **strategic business unit (SBU) structure** an organizational form in which products, projects, or product market divisions are grouped into homogeneous units.

Advantages The SBU structure makes the task of planning and control by the corporate office more manageable. Also, with greater decentralization of authority, individual businesses can react more quickly to important changes in the environment than if all divisions had to report directly to the corporate office.

Disadvantages Since the divisions are grouped into SBUs, it may become difficult to achieve synergies across SBUs. If divisions in different SBUs have potential sources of synergy, it may become difficult for them to be realized. The additional level of management increases the number of personnel and overhead expenses, while the additional hierarchical level removes the corporate office further from the individual divisions. The corporate office may become unaware of key developments that could have a major impact on the corporation.

Holding Company Structure

holding company structure an organizational form that is a variation of the divisional organizational structure in which the divisions have a high degree of autonomy both from other divisions and from corporate headquarters.

The **holding company structure** (sometimes referred to as a *conglomerate*) is also a variation of the divisional structure. Whereas the SBU structure is often used when similarities exist between the individual businesses (or divisions), the holding company structure is appropriate when the businesses in a corporation's portfolio do not have much in common. Thus, the potential for synergies is limited.

Holding company structures are most appropriate for firms with a strategy of unrelated diversification. Companies such as Hanson Trust, ITT, and the CP group of Thailand have used holding company structure to implement their unrelated diversification strategies. Since there are few similarities across the businesses, the corporate offices in these companies provide a great deal of autonomy to operating divisions and rely on financial controls and incentive programs to obtain high levels of performance from the individual businesses. Corporate staffs at these firms tend to be small because of their limited involvement in the overall operation of their various businesses.[16]

Advantages The holding company structure has the cost savings associated with fewer personnel and the lower overhead resulting from a small corporate office and fewer hierarchical levels. The autonomy of the holding company structure increases the motivational level of divisional executives and enables them to respond quickly to market opportunities and threats.

Disadvantages There is an inherent lack of control and dependence that corporate-level executives have on divisional executives. Major problems could arise if key divisional executives leave the firm, because the corporate office has very little "bench strength"— additional managerial talent ready to quickly fill key positions. If problems arise in a division, it may become very difficult to turn around individual businesses because of limited staff support in the corporate office.

Matrix Structure

matrix organizational structure an organizational form in which there are multiple lines of authority and some individuals report to at least two managers.

One approach that tries to overcome the inadequacies inherent in the other structures is the **matrix organizational structure.** It is a combination of the functional and divisional structures. Most commonly, functional departments are combined with product groups on a project basis. For example, a product group may want to develop a new addition to its line; for this project, it obtains personnel from functional departments such as marketing, production, and engineering. These personnel work under the manager of the product group for the duration of the project, which can vary from a few weeks to an open-ended period of time. The individuals who work in a matrix organization become responsible to two managers: the project manager and the manager of their functional area. Exhibit 10.4 illustrates a matrix structure.

Some large multinational corporations rely on a matrix structure to combine product groups and geographical units. Product managers have global responsibility for the development, manufacturing, and distribution of their own line, while managers of geographical regions have responsibility for the profitability of the businesses in their regions. In the mid-1990s, Caterpillar, Inc., implemented this type of structure.

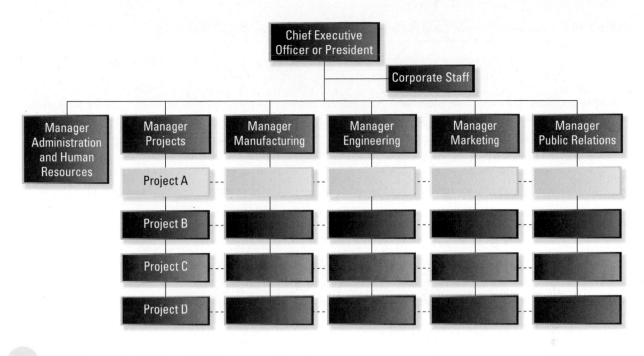

Exhibit 10.4 Matrix Organizational Structure

Advantages   The matrix structure facilitates the use of specialized personnel, equipment, and facilities. Instead of duplicating functions, as would be the case in a divisional structure based on products, the resources are shared. Individuals with high expertise can divide their time among multiple projects. Such resource sharing and collaboration enable a firm to use resources more efficiently and to respond more quickly and effectively to changes in the competitive environment. The flexibility inherent in a matrix structure provides professionals with a broader range of responsibility. Such experience enables them to develop their skills and competencies.

Disadvantages   The dual-reporting structures can result in uncertainty and lead to intense power struggles and conflict over the allocation of personnel and other resources. Working relationships become more complicated. This may result in excessive reliance on group processes and teamwork, along with a diffusion of responsibility, which in turn may erode timely decision making.

Let's look at Procter & Gamble (P&G) to see some of the disadvantages associated with a matrix structure:

> After 50 years with a divisional structure, P&G went to a matrix structure in 1987. In this structure, they had product categories, such as soaps and detergents, on one dimension and functional managers on the other dimension. Within each product category, country managers reported to regional managers who then reported to product managers. The structure became complex to manage, with 13 layers of management and significant power struggles as the functional managers developed their own strategic agendas that often were at odds with the product managers' agendas. After seeing their growth rate decline from 8.5 percent in the 1980s to 2.6 percent in the late 1990s, P&G scrapped the matrix structure to go to a global product structure with three major product categories to offer unity in direction and more responsive decision making.[17]

Exhibit 10.5 Functional, Divisional, and Matrix Organizational Structures: Advantages and Disadvantages

Functional Structure

Advantages	Disadvantages
• Pooling of specialists enhances coordination and control.	• Differences in functional area orientation impede communication and coordination.
• Centralized decision making enhances an organizational perspective across functions.	• Tendency for specialists to develop short-term perspective and narrow functional orientation.
• Efficient use of managerial and technical talent.	• Functional area conflicts may overburden top-level decision makers.
• Facilitates career paths and professional development in specialized areas.	• Difficult to establish uniform performance standards.

Divisional Structure

Advantages	Disadvantages
• Increases strategic and operational control, permitting corporate-level executives to address strategic issues.	• Increased costs incurred through duplication of personnel, operations, and investment.
• Quick response to environmental changes.	• Dysfunctional competition among divisions may detract from overall corporate performance.
• Increases focus on products and markets.	• Difficult to maintain uniform corporate image.
• Minimizes problems associated with sharing resources across functional areas.	• Overemphasis on short-term performance.
• Facilitates development of general managers.	

Matrix Structure

Advantages	Disadvantages
• Increases market responsiveness through collaboration and synergies among professional colleagues.	• Dual-reporting relationships can result in uncertainty regarding accountability.
• Allows more efficient utilization of resources.	• Intense power struggles may lead to increased levels of conflict.
• Improves flexibility, coordination, and communication.	• Working relationships may be more complicated and human resources duplicated
• Increases professional development through a broader range of responsibility.	• Excessive reliance on group processes and teamwork may impede timely decision making.

Exhibit 10.5 briefly summarizes the advantages and disadvantages of the functional, divisional, and matrix organizational structures.

>LO10.3
The implications of a firm's international operations for organizational structure.

International Operations: Implications for Organizational Structure

Today's managers must maintain an international outlook on their firm's businesses and competitive strategies. In the global marketplace, managers must ensure consistency between their strategies (at the business, corporate, and international levels) and the structure of their organization. As firms expand into foreign markets, they generally follow a pattern of change in structure that parallels the changes in their strategies.[18] Three major contingencies that influence the chosen structure are (1) the type of strategy that is driving a firm's foreign operations, (2) product diversity, and (3) the extent to which a firm is dependent on foreign sales.[19]

As international operations become an important part of a firm's overall operations, managers must make changes that are consistent with their firm's structure. The primary types of structures used to manage a firm's international operations are:[20]

- International division
- Geographic-area division
- Worldwide functional
- Worldwide product division
- Worldwide matrix

Multidomestic strategies are driven by political and cultural imperatives requiring managers within each country to respond to local conditions. The structures consistent with such a strategic orientation are the **international division** and **geographic-area division structures.** Here local managers are provided with a high level of autonomy to manage their operations within the constraints and demands of their geographic market. As a firm's foreign sales increase as a percentage of its total sales, it will likely change from an international division to a geographic-area division structure. And, as a firm's product and/or market diversity becomes large, it is likely to benefit from a **worldwide matrix structure.**

Global strategies are driven by economic pressures that require managers to view operations in different geographic areas to be managed for overall efficiency. The structures consistent with the efficiency perspective are the *worldwide functional* and *worldwide product division* structures. Here, division managers view the marketplace as homogeneous and devote relatively little attention to local market, political, and economic factors. The choice between these two types of structures is guided largely by the extent of product diversity. Firms with relatively low levels of product diversity may opt for a worldwide product division structure. However, if significant product–market diversity results from highly unrelated international acquisitions, a worldwide holding company structure should be implemented. Such firms have very little commonality among products, markets, or technologies, and have little need for integration.

Global Start-Ups: A New Phenomenon

International expansion occurs rather late for most corporations, typically after possibilities of domestic growth are exhausted. Increasingly, we are seeing two interrelated phenomena. First, many firms now expand internationally relatively early in their history. Second, some firms are "born global"—that is, from the very beginning, many start-ups are global in their activities. For example, Logitech Inc., a leading producer of personal computer accessories, was global from day one. Founded in 1982 by a Swiss national and two Italians, the company was headquartered both in California and Switzerland. R&D and manufacturing were also conducted in both locations and, subsequently, in Taiwan and Ireland.[21]

The success of companies such as Logitech challenges the conventional wisdom that a company must first build up assets, internal processes, and experience before venturing into faraway lands. It also raises a number of questions: What exactly is a global start-up? Under what conditions should a company start out as a global start-up? What does it take to succeed as a global start-up?

A **global start-up** has been defined as a business organization that, from inception, seeks to derive significant competitive advantage from the use of resources and the sale of outputs in multiple countries. Right from the beginning, it uses in-puts from around the world and sells its products and services to customers around the world. Geographical boundaries of nation-states are irrelevant for a global start-up.

---

international division structure an organizational form in which international operations are in a separate, autonomous division. Most domestic operations are kept in other parts of the organization.

geographic-area division structure a type of divisional organizational structure in which operations in geographical regions are grouped internally.

worldwide matrix structure a type of matrix organizational structure that has one line of authority for geographic-area divisions and another line of authority for worldwide product divisions.

worldwide functional structure a functional structure in which all departments have worldwide reponsibilities.

worldwide product division structure a product division structure in which all divisions have worldwide responsibilities.

global start-up a business organization that, from inception, seeks to derive significant advantage from the use of resources and the sale of outputs in multiple countries.

There is no reason for every start-up to be global. Being global necessarily involves higher communication, coordination, and transportation costs. Therefore, it is important to identify the circumstances under which going global from the beginning is advantageous.[22] First, if the required human resources are globally dispersed, going global may be the best way to access those resources. For example, Italians are masters in fine leather and Europeans in ergonomics. Second, in many cases foreign financing may be easier to obtain and more suitable. Traditionally, U.S. venture capitalists have shown greater willingness to bear risk, but they have shorter time horizons in their expectations for return. If a U.S. start-up is looking for patient capital, it may be better off looking overseas. Third, the target customers in many specialized industries are located in other parts of the world. Fourth, in many industries a gradual move from domestic markets to foreign markets is no longer possible because, if a product is successful, foreign competitors may immediately imitate it. Therefore, preemptive entry into foreign markets may be the only option. Finally, because of high up-front development costs, a global market is often necessary to recover the costs. This is particularly true for start-ups from smaller nations that do not have access to large domestic markets.

Successful management of a global start-up presents many challenges. Communication and coordination across time zones and cultures are always problematic. Since most global start-ups have far less resources than well-established corporations, one key for success is to internalize few activities and outsource the rest. Managers of such firms must have considerable prior international experience so that they can successfully handle the inevitable communication problems and cultural conflicts. Another key for success is to keep the communication and coordination costs low. The only way to achieve this is by creating less costly administrative mechanisms. The boundaryless organizational designs that we discuss in the next section are particularly suitable for global start-ups because of their flexibility and low cost.

Strategy Spotlight 10.3 discusses three global start-ups.

How an Organization's Structure Can Influence Strategy Formulation

Discussions of the relationship between strategy and structure usually strongly imply that structure follows strategy. The strategy that a firm chooses (e.g., related diversification) dictates such structural elements as the division of tasks, the need for integration of activities, and authority relationships within the organization. However, an existing structure can influence strategy formulation. Once a firm's structure is in place, it is very difficult and expensive to change.[23] Executives may not be able to modify their duties and responsibilities greatly, or may not welcome the disruption associated with a transfer to a new location. There are costs associated with hiring, training, and replacing executive, managerial, and operating personnel. Strategy cannot be formulated without considering structural elements.

An organization's structure can also have an important influence on how it competes in the marketplace. It can also strongly influence a firm's strategy, day-to-day operations, and performance.[24] We discussed Brinker International's move to a divisional structure in order to organize its restaurant groups into different units to focus on market niches. This new structure should enable the firm to adapt to change more rapidly and innovate more effectively with the various restaurant brands. Brinker's management did not feel that they were as effective with their previous functional organizational structure.

>LO10.4

Why there is no "one best way" to design strategic reward and evaluation systems, and the important contingent roles of business- and corporate-level strategies.

Linking Strategic Reward and Evaluation Systems to Business-Level and Corporate-Level Strategies

The effective use of reward and evaluation systems can play a critical role in motivating managers to conform to organizational strategies, achieve performance targets, and

Global on Day One

Conventional wisdom would suggest that a firm "get it right" in its home market before venturing abroad. Once established in the home market, a firm could consider the relatively risky move of selling in other countries. However, many new firms are turning conventional wisdom on its head.

More and more start-ups are being born global for two basic reasons. One reason is defensive: to be competitive, many new businesses need to globalize some parts of their business to control costs, access customers, or tap employees from day one. While this might seem an obviously logical choice, until recently many venture capital firms required companies to build locally first, gain a track record, and then branch out. The other reason firms are born global is offensive; many entrepreneurs find that new business opportunities span multiple countries. Going after opportunities in several countries simultaneously from the start can sometimes give firms the operating scope they need to thrive.

Going global is not without significant challenges. Coping with distance in terms of physical, time zone, and cultural dimensions is perhaps a larger hurdle for smaller organizations to tackle. However, start-ups that can articulate a global purpose tend to do better than those with weaker goal orientation toward a global strategy. The following three examples are of start-ups that thought global from day one:

- In 2008, Actavis Pharmaceuticals' revenues were over $2 billion. Robert Wessman took control of this small generic pharmaceutical maker in his native Iceland in 1999. Within weeks of taking over, he realized that to succeed in the generics market, a player had to globalize its core functions, including manufacturing and R&D. Actavis has since entered 60 countries to gain scale and develop a larger portfolio of drugs. By 2009 the company had 650 products on the market and 400 more in development.

- Baradok Pridor, 38, and Yonatan Aumann, 42, Israeli founders of ClearForest, developed an innovative software product—a program that can analyze unstructured electronic data, such as a webpage or a video clip, as if it were already in a spreadsheet or database. Instead of waiting for customers to show up, right from the beginning, they started sending their engineers to make presentations to potential clients around the world. Today, the company's customers include Dow Chemical, Thomson Financial, and the FBI! They have raised $33 million so far in three rounds of venture financing. Interestingly, the headquarters of the 83-person company is in Boston!

- HyperRoll, an Israeli company that makes software for analyzing massive databases, has raised $28 million in venture funding. Referring to the firm's hiring practices, Yossi Matias, founder of Hyper-Roll, says, "We build the strongest team possible, unconstrained by locality, affinity, or culture. It requires every employee to accept and support a multicultural environment." Although the firm is essentially an Israeli start-up, he even banned the use of Hebrew in the office to facilitate greater integration between the American and Israeli employees.

Sources: Isenberg, D. J. 2008. The Global Entrepreneur. *Harvard Business Review*, December: 107–111; Copeland, M. V. 2004. The Start-Up Oasis. *Business 2.0*, August: 46–48.; Brown, E. 2004. Global Start-Up. *Forbes*, November 29: 150–161.

---

reduce the gap between organizational and individual goals. In contrast, reward systems, if improperly designed, can lead to behaviors that either are detrimental to organizational performance or can lower morale and cause employee dissatisfaction.

As we will see in this section, there is no "one best way" to design reward and evaluation systems. Instead, it is contingent on many factors. Two of the most important factors are a firm's business-level strategy (see Chapter 5) and its corporate-level strategy (see Chapter 6).

Business-Level Strategy: Reward and Evaluation Systems

In Chapter 5 we discussed two approaches that firms may take to secure competitive advantages: overall cost leadership and differentiation.[25] As we might expect, implementing these strategies requires fundamentally different organizational arrangements, approaches to control, and reward and incentive systems.

Overall Cost Leadership This strategy requires that product lines remain rather stable and that innovations deal mostly with production processes. Given the emphasis on efficiency, costly changes even in production processes tend to be rare. Since products are quite standardized and change rather infrequently, procedures can be developed to divide work into its basic components—those that are routine, standardized, and ideal for semiskilled and unskilled employees. As such, firms competing on the basis of cost must implement tight cost controls, frequent and comprehensive reports to monitor the costs associated with outputs, and highly structured tasks and responsibilities. Incentives tend to be based on explicit financial targets since innovation and creativity are expensive and might tend to erode competitive advantages.

Nucor a highly successful steel producer with $16 billion in revenues, competes primarily on the basis of cost and has a reward and incentive system that is largely based on financial outputs and financial measures.[26] Nucor uses four incentive compensation systems that correspond to the levels of management.

1. *Production incentive program.* Groups of 20 to 40 people are paid a weekly bonus based on either anticipated product time or tonnage produced. Each shift and production line is in a separate bonus group.
2. *Department managers.* Bonuses are based on divisional performance, primarily measured by return on assets.
3. *Employees not directly involved in production.* These include engineers, accountants, secretaries, receptionists, and others. Bonuses are based on two factors: divisional and corporate return on assets.
4. *Senior incentive programs.* Salaries are lower than comparable companies, but a significant portion of total compensation is based on return on stockholder equity. A portion of pretax earnings is placed in a pool and divided among officers as bonuses that are part cash and part stock.

The culture at Nucor reflects its reward and incentive system. Since incentive compensation can account for more than half of their paychecks, employees become nearly obsessed with productivity and apply a lot of pressure on each other. Ken Iverson, a former CEO, recalled an instance in which one employee arrived at work in sunglasses instead of safety glasses, preventing the team from doing any work. Furious, the other workers chased him around the plant with a piece of angle iron!

Differentiation This strategy involves the development of innovative products and services that require experts who can identify the crucial elements of intricate, creative designs and marketing decisions. Highly trained professionals such as scientists and engineers are essential for devising, assessing, implementing and continually changing complex product designs. This also requires extensive collaboration and cooperation among specialists and functional managers from different areas within a firm. They must evaluate and implement a new design, constantly bearing in mind marketing, financial, production, and engineering considerations.

Given the need for cooperation and coordination in many functional areas, it becomes difficult to evaluate individuals using set quantitative criteria. It also is difficult to measure specific outcomes of such efforts and attribute outcomes to specific individuals. More behavioral measures (how effectively employees collaborate and share information) and intangible incentives and rewards become necessary to support a strong culture and to motivate employees. Consider 3M, a highly innovative company whose core value is innovation.

> Rewards are tied closely to risk-taking and innovation-oriented behavior. Managers are not penalized for product failures. Instead, those same people are encouraged to work on another project that borrows from their shared experience and insight. A culture of creativity and "thinking out of the box" is reinforced by their well-known "15 percent rule," which

permits employees to set aside 15 percent of their work time to pursue personal research interests. And a familiar 3M homily, "Thou shall not kill new ideas for products," is known as the 11th commandment. It is the source of countless stories, including one that tells how L. D. DeSimone (3M's former CEO) tried five times (and failed) to kill the project that yielded the 3M blockbuster product, Thinsulate.[27]

Corporate-Level Strategy: Reward and Evaluation Systems

In Chapter 6 we discussed two broad types of diversification strategies: related and unrelated. The type of diversification strategy that a firm follows has important implications for the type of reward and evaluation systems that it should use.

Sharp Corporation, a $34 billion Japanese consumer electronics giant follows a strategy of *related* diversification.[28] Its most successful technology has been liquid crystal displays (LCDs) that are critical components in nearly all of the firm's products. With their expertise in this area, they are moving into high-end displays for cellular telephones, handheld computers, and digital computers.[29]

Given the need to leverage such technologies across multiple product lines, Sharp needs reward and evaluation systems that foster coordination and sharing. It must focus more on individuals' behavior rather than on short-term financial outcomes. Promotion is a powerful incentive, and it is generally based on seniority and subtle skills exhibited over time, such as teamwork and communication. It helps to ensure that the company's reward system will not reward short-term self-interested orientations.

Like many Japanese companies, Sharp's culture reinforces the view that the firm is a family whose members should cooperate for the greater good. With the policy of lifetime employment, turnover is low. This encourages employees to pursue what is best for the entire company. Such an outlook lessens the inevitable conflict over sharing important resources such as R&D knowledge.

In contrast to Sharp, Hanson PLC (a British conglomerate) followed a strategy of unrelated diversification for most of its history. At one time it owned as many as 150 operating companies in areas such as tobacco, footwear, building products, brewing, and food. There were limited product similarities across businesses and therefore little need for sharing of resources and knowledge across divisional boundaries. James Hanson and Gordon White, founders of the company, actually did not permit any sharing of resources between operating companies even if it was feasible!

Their reward and evaluation system placed such heavy emphasis on individual accountability that they viewed resource sharing, with its potential for mutual blaming, unacceptable. The operating managers had more than 60 percent of their compensation tied to annual financial performance of their subsidiaries. All decision making was decentralized so that subsidiary managers could be held responsible for the return on capital they employed. However, there was one area in which they had to obtain approval from the corporate office. No subsidiary manager was allowed to incur a capital expenditure greater than $3,000 without permission from the corporate office. Hanson managed to be successful with a very small corporate office because of its decentralized structure, tight financial controls, and an incentive system that motivated managers to meet financial goals. Gordon White was proud of claiming that he had never visited any of the operating companies that were part of the Hanson empire.[30]

The key issue becomes the need for *in*dependence versus *inter*dependence. With cost leadership strategies and unrelated diversification, there tends to be less need for interdependence. The reward and evaluation systems focus more on the use of financial indicators because unit costs, profits, and revenues can be rather easily attributed to a given business unit or division.

In contrast, firms that follow related diversification strategies have intense needs for tight interdependencies among the functional areas and business units. Sharing of resources, including raw materials, R&D knowledge, marketing information, and so on, is critical to organizational success. It is more important to achieve synergies with value-creating activities and business units than with cost leadership or unrelated strategies. Reward and evaluation systems tend to incorporate more behavioral indicators.

Although Exhibit 10.6 suggests guidelines on how an organization should match its strategies to its evaluation and reward systems, all organizations must have combinations of both financial and behavioral rewards. Both overall cost leadership and unrelated diversification strategies require a need for collaboration and the sharing of best practices across both value-creating activities and business units. General Electric has developed many integrating mechanisms to enhance sharing "best practices" across what would appear to be rather unrelated businesses such as jet engines, appliances, and network television. For both differentiation and related diversification strategies, financial indicators such as revenue growth and profitability should not be overlooked at both the business-unit and corporate levels.

>LO10.5
The different types of boundaryless organizations— barrier-free, modular, and virtual—and their relative advantages and disadvantages.

boundaryless organizational designs
organizations in which the boundaries, including vertical, horizontal, external, and geographic boundaries, are permeable.

Boundaryless Organizational Designs

The term *boundaryless* may bring to mind a chaotic organizational reality in which "anything goes." This is not the case. As Jack Welch, GE's former CEO, has suggested, boundaryless does not imply that all internal and external boundaries vanish completely, but that they become more open and permeable.[31] Strategy Spotlight 10.4 discusses four types of boundaries.

We are not suggesting that **boundaryless organizational designs** replace the traditional forms of organizational structure, but they should complement them. Sharp Corp. has implemented a functional structure to attain economies of scale with its applied research and manufacturing skills. However, to bring about this key objective, Sharp has relied on several integrating mechanisms and processes:

> To prevent functional groups from becoming vertical chimneys that obstruct product development, Sharp's product managers have responsibility—but not authority—for coordinating the entire set of value-chain activities. And the company convenes enormous numbers of cross-unit and corporate committees to ensure that shared activities, including the corporate R&D unit and sales forces, are optimally configured and allocated among the different product lines. Sharp invests in such time-intensive coordination to minimize the inevitable conflicts that arise when units share important activities.[32]

We will discuss three approaches to making boundaries more permeable, that help to facilitate the widespread sharing of knowledge and information across both the internal and external boundaries of the organization. The *barrier-free* type involves making all organizational boundaries—internal and external—more permeable. Teams are a central building block for implementing the boundaryless organization. The *modular* and *virtual* types of organizations focus on the need to create seamless relationships

Exhibit 10.6
Summary of Relationships between Reward and Evaluation Systems and Business-Level and Corporate-Level Strategies

Level of Strategy	Types of Strategy	Need for Interdependence	Primary Type of Reward and Evaluation System
Business-level	Overall cost leadership	Low	Financial
Business-level	Differentiation	High	Behavioral
Corporate-level	Related diversification	High	Behavioral
Corporate-level	Unrelated diversification	Low	Financial

Boundary Types

There are primarily four types of boundaries that place limits on organizations. In today's dynamic business environment, different types of boundaries are needed to foster high degrees of interaction with outside influences and varying levels of permeability.

1. *Vertical boundaries between levels in the organization's hierarchy.* SmithKline Beecham asks employees at different hierarchical levels to brainstorm ideas for managing clinical trial data. The ideas are incorporated into action plans that significantly cut the new product approval time of its pharmaceuticals. This would not have been possible if the barriers between levels of individuals in the organization had been too high.

2. *Horizontal boundaries between functional areas.* Fidelity Investments makes the functional barriers more porous and flexible among divisions, such as marketing, operations, and customer service, in order to offer customers a more integrated experience when conducting business with the company. Customers can take their questions to one person, reducing the chance that customers will "get the run-around" from employees who feel customer service is not their responsibility. At Fidelity, customer service is everyone's business, regardless of functional area.

3. *External boundaries between the firm and its customers, suppliers, and regulators.* GE Lighting, by working closely with retailers, functions throughout the value chain as a single operation. This allows GE to track point-of-sale purchases, giving it better control over inventory management.

4. *Geographic boundaries between locations, cultures, and markets.* The global nature of today's business environment spurred PricewaterhouseCoopers to use a global groupware system. This allows the company to instantly connect to its 26 worldwide offices.

Source: Ashkenas, R. 1997. The organization's New Clothes. In Hesselbein, F., Goldsmith, M., and Beckhard, R. (Eds.). *The Organization of the Future:* 104–106. San Francisco: Jossey Bass.

with external organizations such as customers or suppliers. While the modular type emphasizes the outsourcing of noncore activities, the virtual (or network) organization focuses on alliances among independent entities formed to exploit specific market opportunities.

The Barrier-Free Organization

The "boundary" mind-set is ingrained deeply into bureaucracies. It is evidenced by such clichés as "That's not my job," "I'm here from corporate to help," or endless battles over transfer pricing. In the traditional company, boundaries are clearly delineated in the design of an organization's structure. Their basic advantage is that the roles of managers and employees are simple, clear, well-defined, and long-lived. A major shortcoming was pointed out to the authors during an interview with a high-tech executive: "Structure tends to be divisive; it leads to territorial fights."

Such structures are being replaced by fluid, ambiguous, and deliberately ill-defined tasks and roles. Just because work roles are no longer clearly defined, however, does not mean that differences in skills, authority, and talent disappear. A **barrier-free organization** enables a firm to bridge real differences in culture, function, and goals to find common ground that facilitates information sharing and other forms of cooperative behavior. Eliminating the multiple boundaries that stifle productivity and innovation can enhance the potential of the entire organization.

Creating Permeable Internal Boundaries For barrier-free organizations to work effectively, the level of trust and shared interests among all parts of the organization must be raised.[33] The organization needs to develop among its employees the skill level needed

barrier-free organization an organizational design in which firms bridge real differences in culture, function, and goals to find common ground that facilitates information sharing and other forms of cooperative behavior.

to work in a more democratic organization. Barrier-free organizations also require a shift in the organization's philosophy from executive to organizational development, and from investments in high-potential individuals to investments in leveraging the talents of all individuals.

Teams can be an important aspect of barrier-free structures.[34] Jeffrey Pfeffer, author of several insightful books, including *The Human Equation,* suggests that teams have three primary advantages.[35] First, teams substitute peer-based control for hierarchical control of work activities. Employees control themselves, reducing the time and energy management needs to devote to control. Second, teams frequently develop more creative solutions to problems because they encourage the sharing of the tacit knowledge held by individuals.[36] Brainstorming, or group problem solving, involves the pooling of ideas and expertise to enhance the chances that at least one group member will think of a way to solve the problems at hand. Third, by substituting peer control for hierarchical control, teams permit the removal of layers of hierarchy and absorption of administrative tasks previously performed by specialists. This avoids the costs of having people whose sole job is to watch the people who watch other people do the work.

● Teams frequently develop more creative solutions to problems because they can share each individual's knowledge.

Effective barrier-free organizations must go beyond achieving close integration and coordination within divisions in a corporation. Research on multidivisional organizations has stressed the importance of interdivisional coordination and resource sharing.[37] This requires interdivisional task forces and committees, reward and incentive systems that emphasize interdivisional cooperation, and common training programs.

Frank Carruba (former head of Hewlett-Packard's labs) found that the difference between mediocre teams and good teams was generally varying levels of motivation and talent.[38] But what explained the difference between good teams and truly superior teams? The key difference—and this explained a 40 percent overall difference in performance—was the way members treated each other: the degree to which they believed in one another and created an atmosphere of encouragement rather than competition. Vision, talent, and motivation could carry a team only so far. What clearly stood out in the "super" teams were higher levels of authenticity and caring, which allowed the full synergy of their individual talents, motivation, and vision.

Developing Effective Relationships with External Constituencies   In barrier-free organizations, managers must also create flexible, porous organizational boundaries and establish communication flows and mutually beneficial relationships with internal (e.g., employees) and external (e.g., customers) constituencies.[39] Michael Dell, founder and CEO of Dell Computer, is a strong believer in fostering close relationships with his customers:

> We're not going to be just your PC vendor anymore. We're going to be your IT department for PCs. Boeing, for example, has 100,000 Dell PCs, and we have 30 people that live at

strategy spotlight

10.5

The Business Roundtable: A Forum for Sharing Best Environmental Sustainability Practices

The Business Roundtable is a group of chief executive officers of major U.S. corporations that was created to promote probusiness public policy. It was formed in 1972 through the merger of three existing organizations: The March Group, the Construction Users Anti-Inflation Roundtable, and the Labor Law Study Committee. The group has been called President Obama's "closest ally in the business community."

The Business Roundtable became the first broad-based business group to agree on the need to address climate change through collective action, and it remains committed to limiting greenhouse gas emissions and setting the United States on a more sustainable path. The organization considers that threats to water quality and quantity, rising greenhouse gas emissions, and the risk of climate change—along with increasing energy prices and growing demand—are of great concern.

Its recent report, "Enhancing Our Commitment to a Sustainable Future 2010" provides best practices and metrics from Business Roundtable member companies that represent nearly all sectors of the economy with $6 trillion in annual revenues. CEOs from Walmart, FedEx, PepsiCo, Whirlpool and Verizon are among the 97 executives from leading U.S. companies that shared some of their best sustainability initiatives in this report. These companies are committed to reducing emissions, increasing energy efficiency, and developing more sustainable business practices.

Let's look, for example, at some of Walmart's initiatives. The firm's CEO, Mike Duke, says it is working with

suppliers, partners, and consumers to drive its sustainability program. It has helped establish the Sustainability Consortium to drive metrics for measuring the environmental effects of consumer products across their life cycle. The retailer also helped lead the creation of a Sustainable Product Index to provide product information to consumers about the environmental impact of the products they purchase.

There are many ways in which Walmart has increased the energy efficiency of its operations:

- It has 30 facilities in California and Hawaii with solar power installations, and it is purchasing 226 million kilowatt hours (kWh) of wind energy annually in Texas.
- It has an agreement in Japan to buy 1 million kWh of clean, renewable energy per year.
- Its trucking fleet in the United Kingdom has cut greenhouse gas emissions (GHG) by 40 percent through the use of new technology, consolidated supplier deliveries, and increased use of rail transportation.

Walmart has also significantly removed GHG emissions from the products that they sell:

- In February 2009, Walmart committed to eliminating 20 million metric tons of GHG emissions from the life cycle of the products they sell worldwide by 2015.
- In 2007, Walmart launched a pilot program to cut supply-chain emissions. Through this program, DVD suppliers reduced packaging and cut more than 28,000 metric tons of GHG.
- Walmart has sold more than 350 million compact fluorescent light bulbs in the United States alone. The firm estimates that during the life of these bulbs, its customers will save more than $13 billion and avoid producing more than 65 million metric tons of GHG emissions.

Sources: Anonymous. 2010. Leading CEOs Share Best Sustainability Practices. www.environmentalleader.com, April 26: np; Hopkins, M. No date. Sustainable Growth. www.businessroundtable, np; Castellani, J. J. 2010. Enhancing our commitment to a sustainable future report. www.businessroundtable.org, March 31: np; and Business Roundtable. www.en.wikipedia.org.

Boeing, and if you look at the things we're doing for them or for other customers, we don't look like a supplier, we look more like Boeing's PC department. We become intimately involved in planning their PC needs and the configuration of their network.

It's not that we make these decisions by ourselves. They're certainly using their own people to get the best answer for the company. But the people working on PCs together, from both Dell and Boeing, understand the needs in a very intimate way. They're right there living it and breathing it, as opposed to the typical vendor who says, "Here are your computers. See you later."[40]

Barrier-free organizations create successful relationships between both internal and external constituencies, but there is one additional constituency—competitors—with whom some organizations have benefited as they developed cooperative relationships. After years of seeing its empty trucks return from warehouses back to production facilities after deliveries, General Mills teamed up with 16 of its competitors. They formed an e-commerce business to help the firms find carriers with empty cargo trailers to piggyback freight loads to distributors near the production facilities.[41] This increases revenue for all network members and reduces fuel costs.

By joining and actively participating in the Business Roundtable—an organization consisting of CEOs of leading U.S. corporations—Walmart has been able to learn about cutting-edge sustainable initiatives of other major firms. This free flow of information has enabled Walmart to undertake a number of steps that increased the energy efficiency of its operations. These are described in Strategy Spotlight 10.5

Risks, Challenges, and Potential Downsides Many firms find that creating and managing a barrier-free organization can be frustrating.[42] Puritan-Bennett Corporation, a manufacturer of respiratory equipment, found that its product development time more than doubled after it adopted team management. Roger J. Dolida, director of R&D, attributed this failure to a lack of top management commitment, high turnover among team members, and infrequent meetings. Often, managers trained in rigid hierarchies find it difficult to make the transition to the more democratic, participative style that teamwork requires.

Christopher Barnes, a consultant with PricewaterhouseCoopers, previously worked as an industrial engineer for Challenger Electrical Distribution (a subsidiary of Westinghouse, now part of CBS) at a plant which produced circuit-breaker boxes. His assignment was to lead a team of workers from the plant's troubled final-assembly operation with the mission: "Make things better." That vague notion set the team up for failure. After a year of futility, the team was disbanded. In retrospect, Barnes identified several reasons for the debacle: (1) limited personal credibility—he was viewed as an "outsider"; (2) a lack of commitment to the team—everyone involved was forced to be on the team; (3) poor communications—nobody was told why the team was important; (4) limited autonomy—line managers refused to give up control over team members; and (5) misaligned incentives—the culture rewarded individual performance over team performance. Barnes's experience has implications for all types of teams, whether they are composed of managerial, professional, clerical, or production personnel.[43] The pros and cons of barrier-free structures are summarized in Exhibit 10.7.

Exhibit 10.7
Pros and Cons of Barrier-Free Structures

Pros	Cons
• Leverages the talents of all employees.	• Difficult to overcome political and authority boundaries inside and outside the organization.
• Enhances cooperation, coordination, and information sharing among functions, divisions, SBUs, and external constituencies.	• Lacks strong leadership and common vision, which can lead to coordination problems.
• Enables a quicker response to market changes through a single-goal focus.	• Time-consuming and difficult-to-manage democratic processes.
• Can lead to coordinated win–win initiatives with key suppliers, customers, and alliance partners.	• Lacks high levels of trust, which can impede performance.

The Modular Organization

As Charles Handy, author of *The Age of Unreason,* has noted:

> While it may be convenient to have everyone around all the time, having all of your work-force's time at your command is an extravagant way of marshaling the necessary resources. It is cheaper to keep them outside the organization . . . and to buy their services when you need them.[44]

The **modular organization** outsources nonvital functions, tapping into the knowledge and expertise of "best in class" suppliers, but retains strategic control. Outsiders may be used to manufacture parts, handle logistics, or perform accounting activities.[45] The value chain can be used to identify the key primary and support activities performed by a firm to create value: Which activities do we keep "in-house" and which activities do we outsource to suppliers?[46] The organization becomes a central hub surrounded by networks of outside suppliers and specialists and parts can be added or taken away. Both manufacturing and service units may be modular.[47]

Apparel is an industry in which the modular type has been widely adopted. Nike and Reebok, for example, concentrate on their strengths: designing and marketing high-tech, fashionable footwear. Nike has few production facilities and Reebok owns no plants. These two companies contract virtually all their footwear production to suppliers in China, Vietnam, and other countries with low-cost labor. Avoiding large investments in fixed assets helps them derive large profits on minor sales increases. Nike and Reebok can keep pace with changing tastes in the marketplace because their suppliers have become expert at rapidly retooling to produce new products.[48]

In a modular company, outsourcing the non-core functions offers three advantages.

1. A firm can decrease overall costs, stimulate new product development by hiring suppliers with superior talent to that of in-house personnel, avoid idle capacity, reduce inventories, and avoid being locked into a particular technology.
2. A company can focus scarce resources on the areas where it holds a competitive advantage. These benefits can translate into more funding for R&D hiring the best engineers, and providing continuous training for sales and service staff.
3. An organization can tap into the knowledge and expertise of its specialized supply-chain partners, adding critical skills and accelerating organizational learning.[49]

The modular type enables a company to leverage relatively small amounts of capital and a small management team to achieve seemingly unattainable strategic objectives.[50] Certain preconditions are necessary before the modular approach can be successful. First, the company must work closely with suppliers to ensure that the interests of each party are being fulfilled. Companies need to find loyal, reliable vendors who can be trusted with trade secrets. They also need assurances that suppliers will dedicate their financial, physical, and human resources to satisfy strategic objectives such as lowering costs or being first to market.

> **modular organization** an organization in which nonvital functions are outsourced, which uses the knowledge and expertise of outside suppliers while retaining strategic control.

● Nike is one of many athletic shoe companies that have outsourced most of its production to low-cost-labor countries such as Indonesia and Vietnam.

Video Games: Microsoft's Outsourcing Strategy

The convergence of Hollywood and Silicon Valley has led to the explosive growth of the worldwide video game industry, with revenues of $66.5 billion. In fact, it has recently overtaken the movie industry's box office receipts. While broadcast TV audiences dwindle and movie attendance stagnates, gaming is emerging as the newest and perhaps the strongest pillar in the media world. So it's no surprise that film studios, media giants, game creators, and Japanese electronics companies are all battling to win the "Game Wars."

Microsoft has dominated the market for computer software with its Windows operating system and its Office and Explorer application software. Seeing the growth in the gaming market, the company diversified into the video game industry with the Xbox and its successor, the Xbox 360. Microsoft faces tough competition from Sony Corp.'s PlayStation 3 and Nintendo Co.'s Wii in the video game industry. However, Microsoft's Xbox 360 beat Wii and PlayStation 3 in sales in the month of February 2010 to become the best-selling video game console in the United States for the first time in more than two years. Microsoft extended their advantage in November 2010 by introducing Kinect, the first motion-sensing system that doesn't require a remote.

Microsoft has a sophisticated approach to outsourcing video game software and hardware. On the software front, since the developmental phase of Xbox 360 in early 2003, Microsoft has reached out to developers by organizing events for the developers to recruit support for the system. Instead of limiting access to video game development software to those with big projects, big budgets, and the backing of the big game labels, Microsoft delivered the necessary tools of game development to hobbyists, students, indie developers, and studios alike. Knowing full well that great game ideas are brewing in the minds of students everywhere, Microsoft has targeted students at colleges, universities, and high schools as game developers. This practice helped bring creative game ideas to life while nurturing game development talent, a collaboration that benefited the entire industry.

For manufacturing the hardware of Xbox 360, Microsoft partnered with companies like Flextronics, Wistron, and Celestica, who produce the game system in their plants in China. According to Jim Sacherman, vice president of business development at Flextronics, "Our goal is to act as a true partner, not just a contractor." The firm showed a willingness to be a team player by collaborating with Microsoft on all aspects of the manufacturing and design process. From the beginning, Microsoft and Flextronics worked together to outline each company's roles and responsibilities and to ensure that all parties knew what was expected of them in all anticipated scenarios. The relationship between Microsoft and Flextronics quickly became a successful hybrid of the two most traditional outsourcing arrangements: Microsoft never turned over complete responsibility to Flextronics or passively waited to hear about progress. Neither did it act as a typical employer, dictating tasks and keeping Flextronics in the dark about its long-term plans for the product. Instead, the two companies worked together collaboratively from the beginning.

Sources: *www.microsoft.com*; Alpeyev, P. & Satariano, A. 2010. Microsoft's Xbox Sales Beat Wii, PS3 in February on "BioShock." *www.businessweek.com*, March 11: np; Grover, R., Edwards, C., Rowley, I., & Moon, I. 2005. Game Wars. *BusinessWeek,* February 28: 35–40; Radd, D. 2005. Xbox 360 Manufacturers Revealed. *www.businessweek.com*, August 16: np; Anonymous. 2002. Outsourcing Xbox Manufacturing: Microsoft Shows the Way for Successful Outsourcing Relationships. *www.goliath.ecnext.com*, np.

Second, the modular company must be sure that it selects the proper competencies to keep in-house. For Nike and Reebok, the core competencies are design and marketing, not shoe manufacturing; for Honda, the core competence is engine technology. An organization must avoid outsourcing components that may compromise its long-term competitive advantages.

Strategic Risks of Outsourcing   The main strategic concerns are (1) loss of critical skills or developing the wrong skills, (2) loss of cross-functional skills, and (3) loss of control over a supplier.[51]

Too much outsourcing can result in a firm "giving away" too much skill and control.[52] Outsourcing relieves companies of the requirement to maintain skill levels needed to manufacture essential components.[53] At one time, semiconductor chips seemed like a simple technology to outsource, but they have now become a critical component of a wide variety of products. Companies that have outsourced the manufacture of these chips run the risk of losing the ability to manufacture them as the technology escalates. They become more dependent upon their suppliers.

Cross-functional skills refer to the skills acquired through the interaction of individuals in various departments within a company.[54] Such interaction assists a department in solving problems as employees interface with others across functional units. However, if a firm outsources key functional responsibilities, such as manufacturing, communication across departments can become more difficult. A firm and its employees must now integrate their activities with a new, outside supplier.

The outsourced products may give suppliers too much power over the manufacturer. Suppliers that are key to a manufacturer's success can, in essence, hold the manufacturer "hostage." Nike manages this potential problem by sending full-time "product expatriates" to work at the plants of its suppliers. Also, Nike often brings top members of supplier management and technical teams to its headquarters. This way, Nike keeps close tabs on the pulse of new developments, builds rapport and trust with suppliers, and develops long-term relationships with suppliers to prevent hostage situations.

Strategy Spotlight 10.6 discusses Microsoft's effective outsourcing strategy for its video games. Exhibit 10.8 summarizes the pros and cons of modular structures.[55]

The Virtual Organization

In contrast to the "self-reliant" thinking that guided traditional organizational designs, the strategic challenge today has become doing more with less and looking outside the firm for opportunities and solutions to problems. The virtual organization provides a new means of leveraging resources and exploiting opportunities.[56]

The **virtual organization** can be viewed as a continually evolving network of independent companies—suppliers, customers, even competitors—linked together to share skills, costs, and access to one another's markets.[57] The members of a virtual organization, by pooling and sharing the knowledge and expertise of each of the component organizations, simultaneously "know" more and can "do" more than any one member of the group

virtual organization a continually evolving network of independent companies that are linked together to share skills, costs, and access to one another's markets.

Pros	Cons
• Directs a firm's managerial and technical talent to the most critical activities.	• Inhibits common vision through reliance on outsiders.
• Maintains full strategic control over most critical activities—core competencies.	• Diminishes future competitive advantages if critical technologies or other competencies are outsourced.
• Achieves "best in class" performance at each link in the value chain.	• Increases the difficulty of bringing back into the firm activities that now add value due to market shifts
• Leverages core competencies by outsourcing with smaller capital commitment.	• Leads to an erosion of cross-functional skills.
• Encourages information sharing and accelerates organizational learning.	• Decreases operational control and potential loss of control over a supplier.

Exhibit 10.8 Pros and Cons of Modular Structures

could do alone. By working closely together, each gains in the long run from individual and organizational learning.[58] The term *virtual,* meaning "being in effect but not actually so," is commonly used in the computer industry. A computer's ability to appear to have more storage capacity than it really possesses is called virtual memory. Similarly, by assembling resources from a variety of entities, a virtual organization may seem to have more capabilities than it really possesses.[59]

The virtual organization is a grouping of units from different organizations that have joined in an alliance to exploit complementary skills in pursuing common strategic objectives. A case in point is Lockheed Martin's use of specialized coalitions between and among three entities—the company, academia, and government—to enhance competitiveness. According to former CEO Norman Augustine:

> The underlying beauty of this approach is that it forces us to reach outward. No matter what your size, you have to look broadly for new ideas, new approaches, new products. Lockheed Martin used this approach in a surprising manner when it set out during the height of the Cold War to make stealth aircraft and missiles. The technical idea came from research done at the Institute of Radio Engineering in Moscow in the 1960s that was published, and publicized, quite openly in the academic media.
>
> Despite the great contrasts among government, academia and private business, we have found ways to work together that have produced very positive results, not the least of which is our ability to compete on a global scale.[60]

Virtual organizations need not be permanent and participating firms may be involved in multiple alliances. Virtual organizations may involve different firms performing complementary value activities, or different firms involved jointly in the same value activities, such as production, R&D, and distribution. The percentage of activities that are jointly performed with partners may vary significantly from alliance to alliance.[61]

How does the virtual type of structure differ from the modular type? Unlike the modular type, in which the focal firm maintains full strategic control, the virtual organization is characterized by participating firms that give up part of their control and accept interdependent destinies. Participating firms pursue a collective strategy that enables them to cope with uncertainty through cooperative efforts. The benefit is that, just as virtual memory increases storage capacity, the virtual organizations enhance the capacity or competitive advantage of participating firms. Strategy Spotlight 10.7 addresses the variety of collaborative relationships in the biotechnology industry.

Each company that links up with others to create a virtual organization contributes only what it considers its core competencies. It will mix and match what it does best with the best of other firms by identifying its critical capabilities and the necessary links to other capabilities.[62]

Challenges and Risks   Such alliances often fail to meet expectations: The alliance between IBM and Microsoft soured in early 1991 when Microsoft began shipping Windows in direct competition to OS/2, which they jointly developed. The runaway success of Windows frustrated IBM's ability to set an industry standard. In retaliation, IBM entered into an alliance with Microsoft's archrival, Novell, to develop network software to compete with Microsoft's LAN Manager.

The virtual organization demands that managers build relationships with other companies, negotiate win–win deals for all parties find the right partners with compatible goals and values, and provide the right balance of freedom and control. Information systems must be designed and integrated to facilitate communication with current and potential partners.

Managers must be clear about the strategic objectives while forming alliances. Some objectives are time bound, and those alliances need to be dissolved once the

How Eli Lilly Used the Collaborative Power of Internet-Based Collaboration to Foster Innovation

The e.Lilly division of pharmaceutical giant Eli Lilly was among the first to harness the collaborative power of the Internet when it launched Innocentive in 2001. Innocentive is the first online, incentive-based scientific network created specifically for the global research and development community. Innocentive's online platform enabled world-class scientists and R&D-based companies to collaborate to attain innovative solutions to complex challenges.

Innocentive offers "seeker companies" the opportunity to increase their R&D potential by posting challenges without violating their confidentiality and intellectual property interests. Seeker companies might be looking for a chemical to be used in art restoration, for example, or the efficient synthesis of butane tetracarboxylic acid. David Bradin, a

patent attorney from Seattle, was recently paid $4,000 for his tetracarboxylic acid formula. And Procter & Gamble claims that Innocentive has increased its share of its new products originating outside the company from 20 to 35 percent.

Often individuals outside of the seeker company find the best solutions to the company's problem. By using Innocentive to post their problems, companies do not have to admit publicly that they need help, yet they get access to a much broader range of ideas than can be generated inside the firm. Within firms, even those firms hiring the best and brightest scientists and engineers, ideas are tossed around by the same few people over and over. This situation can create a narrowing of the possible solutions to a problem (i.e., groupthink can occur) rather than searching over the broadest range of ideas. Anne Goldberg, technical knowledge manager at Solvay Pharmaceuticals, said, "The benefits [of Innocentive] are mainly in the simultaneous access to a lot of different scientific backgrounds that could bring new perspectives on sometimes old problems."

Sources: Libert, B. & Spector, J. 2008. *We Are Smarter Than Me.* Wharton School Publishing, Philadelphia; Lakhani, K. & Jeppesen, L. 2007. Getting Unusual Suspects to Solve R&D Puzzles. *Harvard Business Review*, 85(5). 30–32; Caldwell, T. 2007. R&D Finds Answers in the Crowd. *Information World Review*, 236: 8.

crowdsourcing

---

objective is fulfilled. Some alliances may have relatively long-term objectives and will need to be clearly monitored and nurtured to produce mutual commitment and avoid bitter fights for control. The highly dynamic personal computer industry is characterized by multiple temporary alliances among hardware, operating systems, and software producers.[63] But alliances in the more stable automobile industry, such as those involving Nissan and Volkswagen have long-term objectives and tend to be relatively stable.

The virtual organization is a logical culmination of joint-venture strategies of the past. Shared risks, costs, and rewards are the facts of life in a virtual organization.[64] When virtual organizations are formed, they involve tremendous challenges for strategic planning. As with the modular corporation, it is essential to identify core competencies. However, for virtual structures to be successful, a strategic plan is also needed to determine the effectiveness of combining core competencies.

The strategic plan must address the diminished operational control and overwhelming need for trust and common vision among the partners. This new structure may be appropriate for firms whose strategies require merging technologies (e.g., computing and communication) or for firms exploiting shrinking product life cycles that require simultaneous entry into multiple geographical markets. It may be effective for firms that desire to be quick to the market with a new product or service. The recent profusion of alliances among airlines was primarily motivated by the need to provide seamless travel demanded by the full-fare paying business traveler. Exhibit 10.9 summarizes the advantages and disadvantages.

Exhibit 10.9
Pros and Cons of Virtual Structures

Pros	Cons
• Enables the sharing of costs and skills. • Enhances access to global markets. • Increases market responsiveness. • Creates a "best of everything" organization since each partner brings core competencies to the alliance. • Encourages both individual and organizational knowledge sharing and accelerates organizational learning.	• Harder to determine where one company ends and another begins, due to close interdependencies among players. • Leads to potential loss of operational control among partners. • Results in loss of strategic control over emerging technology. • Requires new and difficult-to-acquire managerial skills.

Source: Miles, R. E., & Snow, C. C. 1986. Organizations: New Concepts for New Forms. *California Management Review,* Spring: 62–73; Miles & Snow. 1999. Causes of Failure in Network Organizations. *California Management Review,* Summer: 53–72; and Bahrami, H. 1991. The Emerging Flexible Organization: Perspectives from Silicon Valley. *California Management Review,* Summer: 33–52.

Boundaryless Organizations: Making Them Work

Designing an organization that simultaneously supports the requirements of an organization's strategy, is consistent with the demands of the environment, and can be effectively implemented by the people around the manager is a tall order for any manager.[65] The most effective solution is usually a combination of organizational types. That is, a firm may outsource many parts of its value chain to reduce costs and increase quality, engage simultaneously in multiple alliances to take advantage of technological developments or penetrate new markets, and break down barriers within the organization to enhance flexibility.

When an organization faces external pressures, resource scarcity, and declining performance, it tends to become more internally focused, rather than directing its efforts toward managing and enhancing relationships with existing and potential external stakeholders. This may be the most opportune time for managers to carefully analyze their value-chain activities and evaluate the potential for adopting elements of modular, virtual, and barrier-free organizational types.

Achieving the coordination and integration necessary to maximize the potential of an organization's human capital involves much more than just creating a new structure. Techniques and processes to ensure the coordination and integration of an organization's key value-chain activities are critical. Teams are key building blocks of the new organizational forms, and teamwork requires new and flexible approaches to coordination and integration.

Managers trained in rigid hierarchies may find it difficult to make the transition to the more democratic, participative style that teamwork requires. As Douglas K. Smith, co-author of *The Wisdom of Teams,* pointed out, "A completely diverse group must agree on a goal, put the notion of individual accountability aside and figure out how to work with each other. Most of all, they must learn that if the team fails, it's everyone's fault."[66] Within the framework of an appropriate organizational design, managers must select a mix and balance of tools and techniques to facilitate the effective coordination and integration of key activities. Some of the factors that must be considered include:

- Common culture and shared values.
- Horizontal organizational structures.
- Horizontal systems and processes.
- Communications and information technologies.
- Human resource practices.

Common Culture and Shared Values   Shared goals, mutual objectives, and a high degree of trust are essential to the success of boundaryless organizations. In the fluid and flexible environments of the new organizational architectures, common cultures, shared values, and carefully aligned incentives are often less expensive to implement and are often a more effective means of strategic control than rules, boundaries, and formal procedures.

Horizontal Organizational Structures   These structures, which group similar or related business units under common management control, facilitate sharing resources and infrastructures to exploit synergies among operating units and help to create a sense of common purpose. Consistency in training and the development of similar structures across business units facilitates job rotation and cross training and enhances understanding of common problems and opportunities. Cross-functional teams and inter-divisional committees and task groups represent important opportunities to improve understanding and foster cooperation among operating units.

horizontal organizational structures organizational forms that group similar or related business units under common management control and facilitate sharing resources and infrastructures to exploit synergies among operating units and help to create a sense of common purpose.

Horizontal Systems and Processes   Organizational systems, policies, and procedures are the traditional mechanisms for achieving integration among functional units. Existing policies and procedures often do little more than institutionalize the barriers that exist from years of managing within the framework of the traditional model. Beginning with an understanding of basic business processes in the context of "a collection of activities that takes one or more kinds of input and creates an output that is of value to the customer," Michael Hammer and James Champy's 1993 best-selling *Reengineering the Corporation* outlined a methodology for redesigning internal systems and procedures that has been embraced by many organizations.[67] Successful reengineering lowers costs, reduces inventories and cycle times, improves quality, speeds response times, and enhances organizational flexibility. Others advocate similar benefits through the reduction of cycle times, total quality management, and the like.

Communications and Information Technologies (IT)   The effective use of IT can play an important role in bridging gaps and breaking down barriers between organizations. Electronic mail and videoconferencing can improve lateral communications across long distances and multiple time zones and circumvent many of the barriers of the traditional model. IT can be a powerful ally in the redesign and streamlining of internal business processes and in improving coordination and integration between suppliers and customers. Internet technologies have eliminated the paperwork in many buyer–supplier relationships, enabling cooperating organizations to reduce inventories, shorten delivery cycles, and reduce operating costs. IT must be viewed more as a prime component of an organization's overall strategy than simply in terms of administrative support.

Human Resource Practices   Change always involves and affects the human dimension of organizations. The attraction, development, and retention of human capital are vital to value creation. As boundaryless structures are implemented, processes are reengineered, and organizations become increasingly dependent on sophisticated ITs, the skills of workers and managers alike must be upgraded to realize the full benefits.

Strategy Spotlight 10.8 discusses Procter & Gamble's successful introduction of Crest Whitestrips. This example shows how P&G's tools and techniques, such as communities of practice, information technology, and human resource practices, help to achieve effective collaboration and integration across the firm's different business units.

>LO10.6
The need for creating ambidextrous organizational designs that enable firms to explore new opportunities and effectively integrate existing operations.

Creating Ambidextrous Organizational Designs

In Chapter 1, we introduced the concept of "ambidexterity," which incorporates two contradictory challenges faced by today's managers.[68] First, managers must explore new opportunities and adjust to volatile markets in order to avoid complacency. They must ensure

Crest's Whitestrips: An Example of How P&G Creates and Derives Benefits from a Boundaryless Organization

Given its breadth of products—soaps, diapers, tooth-paste, potato chips, lotions, detergent—Procter & Gamble (P&G) has an enormous pool of resources it can integrate in various ways to launch exciting new products. For example, the company created a new category, teeth-whitening systems, with Crest Whitestrips. Teeth whitening done at a dentist's office can brighten one's smile in as little as one visit, but it can cost hundreds of dollars. On the other hand, over-the-counter home whitening kits like Crest Whitestrips cost far less and are nearly equally effective.

Whitestrip was created through a combined effort of product developers from three different units in P&G. People at the oral-care division provided teeth-whitening

expertise; experts from the fabric and home-care division supplied bleach expertise; and scientists at corporate research and development provided a novel film technology. Three separate units, by collaborating and combining their technologies, succeeded in developing an affordable product to brighten smiles and, according to the website, bring "greater success in work and love." With $300 million in annual retail sales, the launch of the Whitestrips product has been a big success for P&G, one that would not have been possible without the firm's collaborative ability.

Such collaborations are the outcome of well-established organizational mechanisms. P&G has created more than 20 communities of practice, with 8,000 participants. Each group comprises volunteers from different parts of the company and focuses on an area of expertise (fragrance, packaging, polymer chemistry, skin science, and so on). The groups solve specific problems that are brought to them, and they meet to share best practices. The company also has posted an "ask me" feature on its intranet, where employees can describe a business problem, which is directed to those people with appropriate expertise. At a more fundamental level, P&G promotes from within and rotates people across countries and business units. As a result, its employees build powerful cross-unit networks.

Sources: Hansen, M. T. 2009. *Collaboration: How Leaders Avoid the Traps, Create Unity, and Reap Big Results.* Boston: Harvard Business Press, 24–25; Anonymous. 2004. At P&G, It's 360-Degree Innovation. *www.businessweek. com,* October 11: np; *www.whitestrips.com;* Anonymous. 2009. The Price of a Whiter, Brighter Smile. *www.washingtonpost.com,* July 21: np; Hansen, M. T. & Birkinshaw, J. 2007. The Innovation Value Chain. *Harvard Business Review,* June: 85(6): 121–130.

adaptibility
managers' exploration of new opportunities and adjustment to volatile markets in order to avoid complacency.

alignment
managers' clear sense of how value is being created in the short term and how activities are integrated and properly coordinated.

that they maintain *adaptability* and remain proactive in expanding and/or modifying their product–market scope to anticipate and satisfy market conditions. Such competencies are especially challenging when change is rapid and unpredictable.

Second, managers must also effectively exploit the value of their existing assets and competencies. They need to have *alignment,* which is a clear sense of how value is being created in the short term and how activities are integrated and properly coordinated. Firms that achieve both adaptability and alignment are considered *ambidextrous organizations*— aligned and efficient in how they manage today's business but flexible enough to changes in the environment so that they will prosper tomorrow.

Handling such opposing demands is difficult because there will always be some degree of conflict. Firms often suffer when they place too strong a priority on either adaptability or alignment. If it places too much focus on adaptability, the firm will suffer low profitability in the short term. If managers direct their efforts primarily at alignment, they will likely miss out on promising business opportunities.

Ambidextrous Organizations: Key Design Attributes

A recent study by Charles O'Reilly and Michael Tushman[69] provides some insights into how some firms were able to create successful **ambidextrous organizational designs.** They investigated companies that attempted to simultaneously pursue modest, incremental innovations as well as more dramatic, breakthrough innovations. The team investigated 35 attempts to launch breakthrough innovations undertaken by 15 business units in nine different industries. They studied the organizational designs and the processes, systems, and cultures associated with the breakthrough projects as well as their impact on the operations and performance of the traditional businesses.

Companies structured their breakthrough projects in one of four primary ways:

- Seven were carried out within existing *functional organizational structures*. The projects were completely integrated into the regular organizational and management structure.
- Nine were organized as *cross-functional teams*. The groups operated within the established organization but outside of the existing management structure.
- Four were organized as *unsupported teams*. Here, they became independent units set up outside the established organization and management hierarchy.
- Fifteen were conducted within *ambidextrous organizations*. Here, the breakthrough efforts were organized within structurally independent units, each having its own processes, structures, and cultures. However, they were integrated into the existing senior management structure.

The performance results of the 35 initiatives were tracked along two dimensions:

- Their success in creating desired innovations was measured by either the actual commercial results of the new product or the application of practical market or technical learning.
- The performance of the existing business was evaluated.

The study found that the organizational structure and management practices employed had a direct and significant impact on the performance of both the breakthrough initiative and the traditional business. The ambidextrous organizational designs were more effective than the other three designs on both dimensions: launching breakthrough products or services (i.e., adaptation) and improving the performance of the existing business (i.e., alignment).

Why Was the Ambidextrous Organization the Most Effective Structure?

The study found that there were many factors. A clear and compelling vision, consistently communicated by the company's senior management team was critical in building the ambidextrous designs. The structure enabled cross-fertilization while avoiding cross-contamination. The tight coordination and integration at the managerial levels enabled the newer units to share important resources from the traditional units such as cash, talent, and expertise. Such sharing was encouraged and facilitated by effective reward systems that emphasized overall company goals. The organizational separation ensured that the new units' distinctive processes, structures, and cultures were not overwhelmed by the forces of "business as usual." The established units were shielded from the distractions of launching new businesses, and they continued to focus all of their attention and energy on refining their operations, enhancing their products, and serving their customers.

> **ambidextrous organizational designs** organizational designs that attempt to simultaneously pursue modest, incremental innovations as well as more dramatic, breakthrough innovations.

Reflecting on Career Implications . . .

- *Strategy–Structure:* Is there an effective "fit" between your organization's strategy and its structure? If not, there may be inconsistencies in how you are evaluated which often leads to role ambiguity and confusion. A poor fit could also affect communication among departments as well as across the organization's hierarchy.
- *Matrix Structure:* If your organization employs elements of a matrix structure (e.g., dual reporting relationships), are there effective structural supporting elements (e.g., culture and rewards)? If not, there could be a high level of dysfunctional conflict among managers.
- *The "Fit" between Rewards and Incentives and "Levels of Strategy" (Business- and Corporate-Level):* What metrics are used to evaluate the performance of your work unit? Are there strictly financial measures of success or are you also rewarded for achieving competitive advantages (through effective innovation, organizational learning, or other activities that increase knowledge but may be costly in the short run)?
- *Boundaryless Organizational Designs:* Does your firm have structural mechanisms (e.g., culture, human resource practices) that facilitate sharing of information across boundaries? If so, you should be better able to enhance your human capital by leveraging your talents and competencies.

Summary

Successful organizations must ensure that they have the proper type of organizational structure. Furthermore, they must ensure that their firms incorporate the necessary integration and processes so that the internal and external boundaries of their firms are flexible and permeable. Such a need is increasingly important as the environments of firms become more complex, rapidly changing, and unpredictable.

In the first section of the chapter, we discussed the growth patterns of large corporations. Although most organizations remain small or die, some firms continue to grow in terms of revenues, vertical integration, and diversity of products and services. In addition, their geographical scope may increase to include international operations. We traced the dominant pattern of growth, which evolves from a simple structure to a functional structure as a firm grows in terms of size and increases its level of vertical integration. After a firm expands into related products and services, its structure changes from a functional to a divisional form of organization. Finally, when the firm enters international markets, its structure again changes to accommodate the change in strategy.

We also addressed the different types of organizational structure—simple, functional, divisional (including two variations—strategic business unit and holding company), and matrix—as well as their relative advantages and disadvantages. We closed the section with a discussion of the implications for structure when a firm enters international markets. The three primary factors to take into account when determining the appropriate structure are type of international strategy, product diversity, and the extent to which a firm is dependent on foreign sales.

In the second section, we took a contingency approach to the design of reward and evaluation systems. That is, we argued that there is no one best way to design such systems; rather, it is dependent on a variety of factors. The two that we discussed are business- and corporate-level strategies. With an overall cost leadership strategy and unrelated diversification, it is appropriate to rely primarily on cultures and reward systems that emphasize the production outcomes of the organization, because it is rather easy to quantify such indicators. In contrast, differentiation strategies and related diversification require cultures and incentive systems that encourage and reward creativity initiatives as well as the cooperation among professionals in many different functional areas. Here it becomes more difficult to measure accurately each individual's contribution, and more subjective indicators become essential.

The third section of the chapter introduced the concept of the boundaryless organization. We did not suggest that the concept of the boundaryless organization replaces the traditional forms of organizational structure. Rather, it should complement them. This is necessary to cope with the increasing complexity and change in the competitive environment. We addressed three types of boundaryless organizations. The barrier-free type focuses on the need for the internal and external boundaries of a firm to be more flexible and permeable. The modular type emphasizes the strategic outsourcing of noncore activities. The virtual type centers on the strategic benefits of alliances and the forming of network organizations. We discussed both the advantages and disadvantages of each type of boundaryless organization as well as suggested some techniques and processes that are necessary to successfully implement them. These are common culture and values, horizontal organizational structures, horizontal systems and processes, communications and information technologies, and human resource practices.

The final section addresses the need for managers to develop ambidextrous organizations. In today's rapidly changing global environment, managers must be responsive and proactive in order to take advantage of new opportunities. At the same time, they must effectively integrate and coordinate existing operations. Such requirements call for organizational designs that establish project teams that are structurally independent units, with each having its own processes, structures, and cultures. But, at the same time, each unit needs to be effectively integrated into the existing management hierarchy.

Summary Review Questions

1. Why is it important for managers to carefully consider the type of organizational structure that they use to implement their strategies?
2. Briefly trace the dominant growth pattern of major corporations from simple structure to functional structure to divisional structure. Discuss the relationship between a firm's strategy and its structure.
3. What are the relative advantages and disadvantages of the types of organizational structure—simple, functional, divisional, matrix—discussed in the chapter?
4. When a firm expands its operations into foreign markets, what are the three most important factors to take into account in deciding what type of structure is most appropriate? What are the types of international structures discussed in the text and what are the relationships between strategy and structure?
5. Briefly describe the three different types of boundaryless organizations: barrier-free, modular, and virtual.
6. What are some of the key attributes of effective groups? Ineffective groups?
7. What are the advantages and disadvantages of the three types of boundaryless organizations: barrier-free, modular, and virtual?
8. When are ambidextrous organizational designs necessary? What are some of their key attributes?

Key Terms

organizational structure, 357
simple organizational structure, 359
functional organizational structure, 359
divisional organizational structure, 361
strategic business unit (SBU) structure, 363
holding company structure, 364
matrix organizational structure, 364
international division structure, 367
geographic-area division structure, 367
worldwide matrix structure, 367
worldwide functional structure, 367
worldwide product division structure, 367
global start-up, 367
boundaryless organizational designs, 372,
barrier-free organization, 373
modular organization, 377
virtual organization, 379
horizontal organizational structures, 383
adaptability, 384
alignment, 384
ambidextrous organizational designs, 385

Experiential Exercise

Many firms have recently moved toward a modular structure. For example, they have increasingly outsourced many of their information technology (IT) activities. Identify three such organizations. Using secondary sources, evaluate (1) the firm's rationale for IT outsourcing and (2) the implications for performance.

Firm	Rationale	Implication(s) for Performance
1.		
2.		
3.		

Application Questions & Exercises

1. Select an organization that competes in an industry in which you are particularly interested. Go on the Internet and determine what type of organizational structure this organization has. In your view, is it consistent with the strategy that it has chosen to implement? Why? Why not?

2. Choose an article from *Businessweek, Fortune, Forbes, Fast Company,* or any other well-known publication that deals with a corporation that has undergone a significant change in its strategic direction. What are the implications for the structure of this organization?

3. Go on the Internet and look up some of the public statements or speeches of an executive in a major corporation about a significant initiative such as entering into a joint venture or launching a new product line. What do you feel are the implications for making the internal and external barriers of the firm more flexible and permeable? Does the executive discuss processes, procedures, integrating mechanisms, or cultural issues that should serve this purpose? Or are other issues discussed that enable a firm to become more boundaryless?

4. Look up a recent article in the publications listed in question 2 above that addresses a firm's involvement in outsourcing (modular organization) or in strategic alliance or network organizations (virtual organization). Was the firm successful or unsuccessful in this endeavor? Why? Why not?

Ethics Questions

1. If a firm has a divisional structure and places extreme pressures on its divisional executives to meet short-term profitability goals (e.g., quarterly income), could this raise some ethical considerations? Why? Why not?

2. If a firm enters into a strategic alliance but does not exercise appropriate behavioral control of its employees (in terms of culture, rewards and incentives, and boundaries—as discussed in Chapter 9) that are involved in the alliance, what ethical issues could arise? What could be the potential long-term and short-term downside for the firm?

References

1. Eng, D. 2010. Free tour, new steps to mend HK image. *South China Morning Post,* July 17: A2; Carothers, C. 2010. Hong Kong: Don't shop? Don't come. blogs.wsj.com, November 10: np; and Xinhua, J. 2010. Authority issues travel advisory on trip to Hong Kong. *china.org.cn,* November 10: np. We thank Zia Shakir for his valued contributions.

2. For a unique perspective on organization design, see: Rao, R. 2010. What 17th century pirates can teach us about job design. *Harvard Business Review,* 88(10): 44.

3. This introductory discussion draws upon Hall, R. H. 2002. *Organizations: Structures, processes, and outcomes* (8th ed.). Upper Saddle River, NJ: Prentice Hall; and Duncan,

R. E. 1979. What is the right organization structure? Decision-tree analysis provides the right answer. *Organizational Dynamics,* 7(3): 59–80. For an insightful discussion of strategy-structure relationships in the organization theory and strategic management literatures, refer to Keats, B. & O'Neill, H. M. 2001. Organization structure: Looking through a strategy lens. In Hitt, M. A., Freeman, R. E., & Harrison, J. S. 2001. *The Blackwell handbook of strategic management:* 520–542. Malden, MA: Blackwell.

4. Gratton, L. 2011. The end of the middle manager. *Harvard Business Review,* 89(1/2): 36.

5. An interesting discussion on the role of organizational design in strategy execution is in: Neilson, G. L., Martin, K. L., & Powers, E. 2009. The secrets to successful strategy execution. *Harvard Business Review,* 87(2): 60–70.

6. This discussion draws upon Chandler, A. D. 1962. *Strategy and structure.* Cambridge, MA: MIT Press; Galbraith J. R. & Kazanjian, R. K. 1986. *Strategy implementation: The role of structure and process.* St. Paul, MN: West Publishing; and Scott, B. R. 1971. Stages of corporate development. Intercollegiate Case Clearing House, 9-371-294, BP 998. Harvard Business School.

7. Our discussion of the different types of organizational structures draws on a variety of sources, including Galbraith & Kazanjian, op. cit.; Hrebiniak, L. G. & Joyce, W. F. 1984. *Implementing strategy.* New York: Macmillan; Distelzweig, H. 2000. Organizational structure. In Helms, M. M. (Ed.). *Encyclopedia of management:* 692–699. Farmington Hills, MI: Gale; and Dess, G. G. & Miller, A. 1993. *Strategic management.* New York: McGraw-Hill.

8. A discussion of an innovative organizational design is in: Garvin, D. A. & Levesque, L. C. 2009. The multiunit enterprise. *Harvard Business Review,* 87(2): 106–117.

9. Schein, E. H. 1996. Three cultures of management: The key to organizational learning. *Sloan Management Review,* 38(1): 9–20.

10. Insights on governance implications for multidivisional forms are in: Verbeke, A. & Kenworthy, T. P. 2008. Multidivisional vs. metanational governance. *Journal of International Business,* 39(6): 940–956.

11. Martin, J. A. & Eisenhardt, K. 2010. Rewiring: Cross-business-unit collaborations in multibusiness organizations. *Academy of Management Journal,* 53(2): 265–301.

12. For a discussion of performance implications, refer to Hoskisson, R. E. 1987. Multidivisional structure and performance: The contingency of diversification strategy. *Academy of Management Journal,* 29: 625–644.

13. For a thorough and seminal discussion of the evolution toward the divisional form of organizational structure in the United States, refer to Chandler, op. cit. A rigorous empirical study of the strategy and structure relationship is found in Rumelt, R. P. 1974. *Strategy, structure, and economic performance.* Cambridge, MA: Harvard Business School Press.

14. Ghoshal S. & Bartlett, C. A. 1995. Changing the role of management: Beyond structure to processes. *Harvard Business Review,* 73(1): 88.

15. Koppel, B. 2000. Synergy in ketchup? *Forbes,* February 7: 68–69; and Hitt, M. A., Ireland, R. D., & Hoskisson, R. E. 2001. *Strategic management: Competitiveness and globalization* (4th ed.). Cincinnati, OH. Southwestern Publishing.

16. Pitts, R. A. 1977. Strategies and structures for diversification. *Academy of Management Journal,* 20(2): 197–208.

17. Andersen, M. M., Froholdt, M., Poulfelt, F. 2010. *Return on strategy: How to achieve it.* New York: Routledge.

18. Haas, M. R. 2010. The double edged swords of autonomy and external knowledge: Analyzing team effectiveness in a multinational organization. *Academy of Management Journal,* 53(5): 989–1008.

19. Daniels, J. D., Pitts, R. A., & Tretter, M. J. 1984. Strategy and structure of U.S. multinationals: An exploratory study. *Academy of Management Journal,* 27(2): 292–307.

20. Habib, M. M. & Victor, B. 1991. Strategy, structure, and performance of U.S. manufacturing and service MNCs: A comparative analysis. *Strategic Management Journal,* 12(8): 589–606.

21. Our discussion of global start-ups draws from Oviatt, B. M. & McDougall, P. P. 2005. The internationalization of entrepreneurship. *Journal of International Business Studies,* 36(1): 2–8; Oviatt, B. M. & McDougall, P. P. 1994. Toward a theory of

international new ventures. *Journal of International Business Studies,* 25(1): 45–64; and Oviatt, B. M. & McDougall, P. P. 1995. Global start-ups: Entrepreneurs on a worldwide stage. *Academy of Management Executive,* 9(2): 30–43.

22. Some useful guidelines for global start-ups are provided in Kuemmerle, W. 2005. The entrepreneur's path for global expansion. *MIT Sloan Management Review,* 46(2): 42–50.

23. See, for example, Miller, D. & Friesen, P. H. 1980. Momentum and revolution in organizational structure. *Administrative Science Quarterly,* 13: 65–91.

24. Many authors have argued that a firm's structure can influence its strategy and performance. These include Amburgey, T. L. & Dacin, T. 1995. As the left foot follows the right? The dynamics of strategic and structural change. *Academy of Management Journal,* 37: 1427–1452; Dawn, K. & Amburgey, T. L. 1991. Organizational inertia and momentum: A dynamic model of strategic change. *Academy of Management Journal,* 34: 591–612; Fredrickson, J. W. 1986. The strategic decision process and organization structure. *Academy of Management Review,* 11: 280–297; Hall, D. J. & Saias, M. A. 1980. Strategy follows structure! *Strategic Management Journal,* 1: 149–164; and Burgelman, R. A. 1983. A model of the interaction of strategic behavior, corporate context, and the concept of strategy. *Academy of Management Review,* 8: 61–70.

25. This discussion of generic strategies and their relationship to organizational control draws upon Porter, M. E. 1980. *Competitive strategy.* New York: Free Press; and Miller, D. 1988. Relating Porter's business strategies to environment and structure: Analysis and performance implications. *Academy of Management Journal,* 31(2): 280–308.

26. Rodengen, J. L. 1997. *The legend of Nucor Corporation.* Fort Lauderdale, FL: Write Stuff Enterprises.

27. The 3M example draws upon *Blueprints for service quality.* 1994. New York: American Management Association; personal communication

with Katerine Hagmeier, program manager, external communications, 3M Corporation, March 26, 1998; Lei, D., Slocum, J. W., & Pitts, R. A. 1999. Designing organizations for competitive advantage: The power of unlearning and learning. *Organizational Dynamics,* 27(3): 24–38; and Graham, A. B. & Pizzo, V. G. 1996. A question of balance: Case studies in strategic knowledge management. *European Management Journal,* 14(4): 338–346.

28. The Sharp Corporation and Hanson plc examples are based on Collis, D. J. & Montgomery, C. A. 1998. Creating corporate advantage. *Harvard Business Review,* 76(3): 70–83.

29. Kunii, I. 2002. Japanese companies' survival skills. *BusinessWeek,* November 18: 18.

30. White, G. 1988. How I turned $3,000 into $10 billion. *Fortune,* November 7: 80–89. After the death of the founders, the Hanson plc conglomerate was found to be too unwieldy and was broken up into several separate, publicly traded corporations. For more on its more limited current scope of operations, see www.hansonplc.com.

31. An interesting discussion on how the Internet has affected the boundaries of firms can be found in Afuah, A. 2003. Redefining firm boundaries in the face of the Internet: Are firms really shrinking? *Academy of Management Review,* 28(1): 34–53.

32. Collis & Montgomery, op. cit.

33. Govindarajan, V. G. & Trimble, C. 2010. Stop the innovation wars. *Harvard Business Review,* 88(7/8): 76–83.

34. For a discussion of the role of coaching on developing high performance teams, refer to Kets de Vries, M. F. R. 2005. Leadership group coaching in action: The zen of creating high performance teams. *Academy of Management Executive,* 19(1): 77–89.

35. Pfeffer, J. 1998. *The human equation: Building profits by putting people first.* Cambridge, MA: Harvard Business School Press.

36. For a discussion on how functional area diversity affects performance, see Bunderson, J. S. & Sutcliffe, K.

M. 2002. *Academy of Management Journal,* 45(5): 875–893.

37. See, for example, Hoskisson, R. E., Hill, C. W. L., & Kim, H. 1993. The multidivisional structure: Organizational fossil or source of value? *Journal of Management,* 19(2): 269–298.

38. Pottruck, D. A. 1997. Speech delivered by the co-CEO of Charles Schwab Co., Inc., to the Retail Leadership Meeting, San Francisco, CA, January 30; and Miller, W. 1999. Building the ultimate resource. *Management Review,* January: 42–45.

39. Public-private partnerships are addressed in: Engardio, P. 2009. State capitalism. *BusinessWeek,* February 9: 38–43.

40. Magretta, J. 1998. The power of virtual integration: An interview with Dell Computer's Michael Dell. *Harvard Business Review,* 76(2): 75.

41. Forster, J. 2001. Networking for cash. *BusinessWeek,* January 8: 129.

42. Dess, G. G., Rasheed, A. M. A., McLaughlin, K. J., & Priem, R. 1995. The new corporate architecture. *Academy of Management Executive,* 9(3): 7–20.

43. Barnes, C. 1998. A fatal case. *Fast Company,* February–March: 173.

44. Handy, C. 1989. *The age of unreason.* Boston: Harvard Business School Press; Ramstead, E. 1997. APC maker's low-tech formula: Start with the box. *The Wall Street Journal,* December 29: B1; Mussberg, W. 1997. Thin screen PCs are looking good but still fall flat. *The Wall Street Journal,* January 2: 9; Brown, E. 1997. Monorail: Low cost PCs. *Fortune,* July 7: 106–108; and Young, M. 1996. Ex-Compaq executives start new company. *Computer Reseller News,* November 11: 181.

45. An original discussion on how open-sourcing could help the Big 3 automobile companies is in: Jarvis, J. 2009. How the Google model could help Detroit. *BusinessWeek,* February 9: 32–36.

46. For a discussion of some of the downsides of outsourcing, refer to Rossetti, C. & Choi, T. Y. 2005. On the dark side of strategic sourcing: Experiences from the aerospace industry.

Academy of Management Executive, 19(1): 46–60.

47. Tully, S. 1993. The modular corporation. *Fortune,* February 8: 196.

48. Offshoring in manufacturing firms is addressed in: Coucke, K. & Sleuwaegen, L. 2008. Offshoring as a survival strategy: Evidence from manufacturing firms in Belgium. *Journal of International Business Studies,* 39(8): 1261–1277.

49. Quinn, J. B. 1992. *Intelligent enterprise: A knowledge and service based paradigm for industry.* New York: Free Press.

50. For an insightful perspective on outsourcing and its role in developing capabilities, read Gottfredson, M., Puryear, R., & Phillips, C. 2005. Strategic sourcing: From periphery to the core. *Harvard Business Review,* 83(4): 132–139.

51. This discussion draws upon Quinn, J. B. & Hilmer, F. C. 1994. Strategic outsourcing. *Sloan Management Review,* 35(4): 43–55.

52. Reitzig, M. & Wagner, S. 2010. The hidden costs of outsourcing: Evidence from patent data. *Strategic Management Journal.* 31(11): 1183–1201.

53. Insights on outsourcing and private branding can be found in: Cehn, S-F. S. 2009. A transaction cost rationale for private branding and its implications for the choice of domestic vs. offshore outsourcing. *Journal of International Business Strategy,* 40(1): 156–175.

54. For an insightful perspective on the use of outsourcing for decision analysis, read: Davenport, T. H. & Iyer, B. 2009. Should you outsource your brain? *Harvard Business Review,* 87(2): 38.

55. See also Stuckey, J. & White, D. 1993. When and when not to vertically integrate. *Sloan Management Review,* Spring: 71–81; Harrar, G. 1993. Outsource tales. *Forbes ASAP,* June 7: 37–39, 42; and Davis, E. W. 1992. Global outsourcing: Have U.S. managers thrown the baby out with the bath water? *Business Horizons,* July–August: 58–64.

56. For a discussion of knowledge creation through alliances, refer to

Inkpen, A. C. 1996. Creating knowledge through collaboration. *California Management Review,* 39(1): 123–140; and Mowery, D. C., Oxley, J. E., & Silverman, B. S. 1996. Strategic alliances and interfirm knowledge transfer. *Strategic Management Journal,* 17 (Special Issue, Winter): 77–92.

57. Doz, Y. & Hamel, G. 1998. *Alliance advantage: The art of creating value through partnering.* Boston: Harvard Business School Press.

58. DeSanctis, G., Glass, J. T., & Ensing, I. M. 2002. Organizational designs for R&D. *Academy of Management Executive,* 16(3): 55–66.

59. Barringer, B. R. & Harrison, J. S. 2000. Walking a tightrope: Creating value through interorganizational alliances. *Journal of Management,* 26: 367–403.

60. Davis, E. 1997. Interview: Norman Augustine. *Management Review,* November: 14.

61. One contemporary example of virtual organizations is R&D consortia. For an insightful discussion, refer to Sakaibara, M. 2002. Formation of R&D consortia: Industry and company effects. *Strategic Management Journal,* 23(11): 1033–1050.

62. Bartness, A. & Cerny, K. 1993. Building competitive advantage through a global network of capabilities. *California Management Review,* Winter: 78–103. For an insightful historical discussion of the usefulness of alliances in the computer industry, see Moore, J. F. 1993. Predators and prey: A new ecology of competition. *Harvard Business Review,* 71(3): 75–86.

63. See Lorange, P. & Roos, J. 1991. Why some strategic alliances succeed and others fail. *Journal of Business Strategy,* January–February: 25–30; and Slowinski, G. 1992. The human touch in strategic alliances. *Mergers and Acquisitions,* July–August: 44–47. A compelling argument for strategic alliances is provided by Ohmae, K. 1989. The global logic of strategic alliances. *Harvard Business Review,* 67(2): 143–154.

64. Some of the downsides of alliances are discussed in Das, T. K. & Teng, B. S. 2000. Instabilities of strategic alliances: An internal tensions perspective. *Organization Science,* 11: 77–106.

65. This section draws upon Dess, G. G. & Picken, J. C. 1997. *Mission critical.* Burr Ridge, IL: Irwin Professional Publishing.

66. Katzenbach, J. R. & Smith, D. K. 1994. *The wisdom of teams: Creating the high performance organization.* New York: HarperBusiness.

67. Hammer, M. & Champy, J. 1993. *Reengineering the corporation: A manifesto for business revolution.* New York: HarperCollins.

68. This section draws on Birkinshaw, J. & Gibson, C. 2004. Building ambidexterity into an organization. *MIT Sloan Management Review,* 45(4): 47–55; and Gibson, C. B. & Birkinshaw, J. 2004. The antecedents, consequences, and mediating role of organizational ambidexterity. *Academy of Management Journal,* 47(2): 209–226. Robert Duncan is generally credited with being the first to coin the term "ambidextrous organizations" in his article entitled: Designing dual structures for innovation. In Kilmann, R. II., Pondy, L. R., & Slevin, D. (Eds.). 1976. *The management of organizations,* vol. 1: 167–188. For a seminal academic discussion of the concept of exploration and exploitation, which parallels adaptation and alignment, refer to: March, J. G. 1991. Exploration and exploitation in organizational learning. *Organization Science,* 2: 71–86.

69. This section is based on O'Reilly, C. A. & Tushman, M. L. 2004. The ambidextrous organization. *Harvard Business Review,* 82(4): 74–81.

chapter ELEVEN

Strategic Leadership:

Creating a Learning Organization and an Ethical Organization

After reading this chapter, you should have a good understanding of:

LO11.1   The three key interdependent activities in which all successful leaders must be continually engaged.

LO11.2   Three elements of effective leadership: integrative thinking, overcoming barriers to change, and the effective use of power.

LO11.3   The crucial role of emotional intelligence (EI) in successful leadership as well as its potential drawbacks.

LO11.4   The value of creating and maintaining a learning organization in today's global marketplace.

LO11.5   The leader's role in establishing an ethical organization.

LO11.6   The difference between integrity-based and compliance-based approaches to organizational ethics.

LO11.7   Several key elements that organizations must have to become an ethical organization.

LEARNING OBJECTIVES

To compete in the global marketplace, organizations need to have strong and effective leadership. This involves the active process of both creating and implementing proper strategies. In this chapter we address key activities in which leaders throughout the organization must be involved to be successful in creating and sustaining competitive advantages.

In the first section, we provide a brief overview of the three key leadership activities. These are (1) setting a direction, (2) designing the organization, and (3) nurturing a culture committed to excellence and ethical behavior. Each of these activities is "necessary but not sufficient"; that is, to be effective, leaders must give proper attention to each of them.

Section two addresses practices and capabilities that enable executives to be effective as leaders. To be successful in a complex business environment, leaders must perform a variety of functions and exhibit key strengths. We focus on three capabilities that effective leaders often exhibit—integrative thinking, overcoming barriers to change, and the effective use of power.

The third section discusses the vital role of emotional intelligence (EI) in effective strategic leadership. EI refers to an individual's capacity for recognizing his or her emotions and those of others. It consists of five components: self-awareness, self-regulation, motivation, empathy, and social skills. We also address potential downsides or drawbacks that may result from the ineffective use of EI.

Next we address the important role of a leader in creating a learning organization. Here, leaders must strive to harness the individual and collective talents of individuals throughout the entire organization. Creating a learning organization is particularly important in today's competitive environment, which is increasingly unpredictable, dynamic, and interdependent. The key elements of a learning organization are inspiring and motivating people with a mission or purpose, empowering employees at all levels, accumulating and sharing internal and external information, and challenging the status quo to enable creativity.

The final section discusses a leader's challenge in creating and maintaining an ethical organization. There are many benefits of having an ethical organization. It can provide financial benefits, enhance human capital, and help to ensure positive relationships with suppliers, customers, society at large, and governmental agencies. By contrast failure to operate ethically leading to an ethical crisis can be very costly for many reasons. We address four key elements of an ethical organization: role models, corporate credos and codes of conduct, reward and evaluation systems, and policies and procedures.

⬛ Learning from Mistakes

Duke Energy appeared to be doing the right thing by investing in clean-coal technology. Through a state-of-the-art power plant, Duke Energy would convert coal to flammable gas, a move approved by state regulators, who allowed the firm to pass some of the costs on to consumers. The firm's CEO, Jim Rogers, had even been profiled by the *New York Times* in 2008 as a "green coal baron," who constantly lobbied for a national price on carbon output, seeking to move out of low-tech coal plants to cleaner, more expensive coal plants. Yet in December 2010, the firm was rocked by an ethics scandal caused by e-mail exchanges between some of its executives and state regulators who oversaw its operations, and who decided what rates the utility could charge its customers. What went wrong?[1]

An ethics investigation led to several resignations. These included James Turner (one of Duke Energy's top executives) and two other executives as well as a prominent Indiana state regulator. The press obtained several e-mail exchanges between the four men, relating to alcohol, cars, their wives, and the open mocking of state ethical standards. While the investigation focused on the e-mail exchanges, the main concern was the relationship between Duke and state regulators, raising the question of a possible revolving door between the two entities. The improper relationship between Duke and regulators might have been foreseeable, considering that most big players at Duke had at one point worked for the Indiana government and that the head of Indiana's utility commission had been a lawyer for a local utility acquired by Duke.

While working for Duke, Turner was the second highest paid executive in 2009, totaling $4.3 million in compensation. Even following his resignation, he received a severance and retirement package worth more than $10 million. Turner had frequent e-mail exchanges with the head of Indiana's Utility Regulatory Commission, David Hardy, at times trading up to 10 messages a day. The men frequently ridiculed state ethics rules that were enacted to prevent state-regulated utilities from exerting undue influence on their regulators. In an e-mail, Turner wondered whether the "ethics police would have a cow" if he was visited at his weekend home by a top state regulator. In another published e-mail, Hardy brags about relaxing by the pool in the morning and inquiring about a good breakfast wine, and in reply Turner wrote, "Does anyone know if a desire to 'bitch slap a chairman' violates any state's hate crime laws?" Other e-mails addressed the hiring process of Scott Storm and Mike Reed, as they sought and then obtained jobs with Duke, with Hardy, their former boss, constantly demanding reports on the hiring process and inquiring whether he should try to influence Duke's CEO's decision.

The relationship with state regulators is an important one for Duke, as it invests heavily in the state in an attempt to position itself to prosper in the age of climate politics by investing in a first-of-its-kind clean-coal power plant. Duke received approval from a state commission to raise its rates for Indiana customers by approximately 16 percent, passing on to them costs of almost $2.9 billion when the plant is completed in 2012. Considering that the firm is $1 billion over its previous budget estimates, critics point out that there are cheaper ways to produce energy to meet the state's needs. Some of the matters related to the approval of the clean-coal plant had been overseen by Scott Storm, who was hired by Duke in September 2010.

Storm was a lawyer who had, until then, worked for the Indiana Utility Regulatory Commission as an administrative law judge, as their top legal officer. In that position he had worked on several Duke cases, but there was no indication that he had provided special treatment to the firm. He received an ethics waiver from a state panel to forgo a one-year cooling-off period after leaving state service prior to accepting employment with a company that he had helped regulate. This decision outraged consumer advocates and finally led to the firing of the commission's head, Hardy, by the governor of Indiana and to the reopening of the decision regarding Duke. Both Storm and the Duke executive that hired him, Mike Reed, resigned from the company. Reed had taken the position at Duke as its president for Indiana 16 months after he had himself been the executive director of the Indiana Utility Regulatory Commission. Even after leaving Duke, Storm faced a state ethics panel hearing claiming that he did not recuse himself from cases related to Duke while considering employment with the company.

In response, Duke has drafted new employment guidelines to ensure that they only hire from "regulatory and oversight groups" with no prior affairs related to Duke Energy. However, this seems to be too little, too late.

Clearly, many of the decisions and actions of Duke Energy's top executives were not in the best interests of the firm and its shareholders and were not consistent with norms of ethical behavior. In contrast, effective leaders play an important and often pivotal role in creating and implementing strategies.

This chapter provides insights into the role of strategic leadership in managing, adapting, and coping in the face of increased environmental complexity and uncertainty. First, we define leadership and its components. Then, we identify three elements of leadership that contribute to success—integrative thinking, overcoming barriers to change, and the effective use of power. The third section focuses on emotional intelligence, a trait that is increasingly acknowledged to be critical to successful leadership. Next, we emphasize the importance of developing a learning organization and how leaders can help their firms learn and proactively adapt in the face of accelerating change. Here, we focus on empowerment wherein employees and managers throughout an organization develop a sense of self-determination, competence, meaning, and impact that is centrally important to learning. Finally, we address the leader's role in building an ethical organization and the elements of an ethical culture that contribute to firm effectiveness.

Leadership: Three Interdependent Activities

In today's chaotic world, few would argue against the need for leadership, but how do we go about encouraging it? Is it enough to merely keep an organization afloat, or is it essential to make steady progress toward some well-defined objective? We believe custodial management is not leadership. Leadership is proactive, goal-oriented, and focused on the creation and implementation of a creative vision. **Leadership** is the process of transforming organizations from what they are to what the leader would have them become. This definition implies a lot: *dissatisfaction* with the status quo, a *vision* of what should be, and a *process* for bringing about change. An insurance company executive shared the following insight: "I lead by the Noah Principle: It's all right to know when it's going to rain, but, by God, you had better build the ark."

> **leadership** the process of transforming organizations from what they are to what the leader would have them become.

Doing the right thing is becoming increasingly important. Many industries are declining; the global village is becoming increasingly complex, interconnected, and unpredictable; and product and market life cycles are becoming increasingly compressed. When asked to describe the life cycle of his company's products, the CEO of a supplier of computer components replied, "Seven months from cradle to grave—and that includes three months to design the product and get it into production!" Richard D'Aveni, author of *Hypercompetition,* argued that in a world where all dimensions of competition appear to be compressed in time and heightened in complexity, *sustainable* competitive advantages are no longer possible.

Despite the importance of doing the "right thing," leaders must also be concerned about "doing things right." Charan and Colvin strongly believe that execution, that is, the implementation of strategy, is also essential to success.

> Mastering execution turns out to be the odds-on best way for a CEO to keep his job. So what's the right way to think about that sexier obsession, strategy? It's vitally important—obviously. The problem is that our age's fascination feeds the mistaken belief that developing exactly the right strategy will enable a company to rocket past competitors. In reality, that's less than half the battle.[2]

>LO11.1

The three key interdependent activities in which all successful leaders must be continually engaged.

Thus, leaders are change agents whose success is measured by how effectively they formulate *and* implement a strategic vision and mission.[3]

Many authors contend that successful leaders must recognize three interdependent activities that must be continually reassessed for organizations to succeed. As shown in Exhibit 11.1, these are: (1) setting a direction, (2) designing the organization, and (3) nurturing a culture dedicated to excellence and ethical behavior.[4]

The interdependent nature of these three activities is self-evident. Consider an organization with a great mission and a superb organizational structure, but a culture that implicitly encourages shirking and unethical behavior. Or one with a sound direction and strong culture, but counterproductive teams and a "zero-sum" reward system that leads to the dysfunctional situation in which one party's gain is viewed as another party's loss, and collaboration and sharing are severely hampered. Clearly, such combinations would be ineffective.

A new approach on leadership highlights the importance of being "ambicultural," which emphasizes taking the best elements of the philosophies and practices from multiple cultures while avoiding their negative aspects. Such an approach can be highly effective in performing the three leadership activities in today's increasingly global economy.

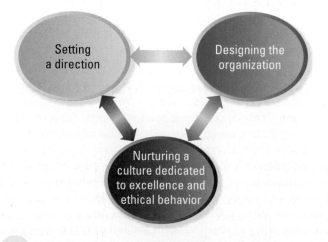

Exhibit 11.1 **Three Interdependent Leadership Activities**

11.1

Julie Gilbert Sets a New Direction for Best Buy

Julie Gilbert is evidence that significant and creative change can be brought about by people who do not happen to be at the very top of an organization. As a senior VP at retailer Best Buy from 2000 to early 2009, she saw a looming crisis in the firm's failure to profit from the greater involvement of women in the male-oriented world of consumer electronics. Women were becoming more influential in purchasing decisions, directly and indirectly. But capitalizing on this trend would require something beyond a smart marketing plan. It would demand a change in the company's orientation.

Getting an organization to adapt to changes in the environment is not easy. You need to confront loyalty to legacy practices and understand that your desire to change them makes you a target of attack. Gilbert believed that instead of simply selling technology products to mostly male customers, Best Buy needed to appeal to women by reflecting the increasing integration of consumer electronics into family life. So Gilbert headed up an initiative to establish in-store boutiques that sold home theater systems along with coordinated furniture and accessories. Stores set up living-room displays to showcase not just electronics but also the entertainment environment. Salespeople were trained to interact with the previously ignored female customers who came in with men to look at systems.

Source: Heifetz, R., Grashow, A. & Linsky, M. 2009. Leadership in a (Permanent) Crisis. *Harvard Business Review,* 87 (7/8): 62–69; and Bustillo, M. & Lloyd, M. 2010. Best Buy Tests New Appeals to Women. *www.wsj.com,* June 16: np.

Gilbert says that championing this approach subjected her to some nasty criticism from managers who viewed Best Buy as a retailer of technology *products,* not experiences. However, focusing on the female purchaser when a man and a woman walked into the store—making eye contact and greeting her, asking about her favorite movies, and demonstrating them on the systems—often resulted in the couple's purchasing a higher-end product than they had originally considered. According to Gilbert, returns and exchanges of purchases made by couples were 60 percent lower than those made by men. With the rethinking of traditional practices, Best Buy's home theater business flourished, growing from two pilot in-store boutiques in mid-2004 to more than 350 five years later.

Such success does not appear to just happen by chance at Best Buy. Consider:

- Best Buy is empowering female workers and consulting teenage girls to suggest new ways to sell to women. The move reflects that women are becoming the most coveted customers in some of the hottest areas of electronic retailing in stores—smart phones and other mobile services.

- Executives say that the best insights on expanding the female customer base come from the company's "Women Leadership Forums," a loose-knit group of female workers and customers that meet around the country. The groups helped increase appliance sales, for example, by suggesting that showrooms be redesigned to resemble kitchens.

Often, failure of today's organizations can be attributed to a lack of equal consideration of these three activities. The imagery of a three-legged stool is instructive: It will collapse if one leg is missing or broken. Let's briefly look at each of these activities as well as the value of an ambicultural approach to leadership.

Setting a Direction

A holistic understanding of an organization's stakeholders requires an ability to scan the environment to develop a knowledge of all of the company's stakeholders and other salient environmental trends and events. Managers must integrate this knowledge into a vision of what the organization could become.[5] It necessitates the capacity to solve increasingly complex problems, become proactive in approach, and develop viable strategic options. A strategic vision provides many benefits: a clear future direction; a framework for the organization's mission and goals; and enhanced employee communication, participation, and commitment.

> **setting a direction**
> a strategic leadership activity of strategy analysis and strategy formulation.

At times the creative process involves what the CEO of Yokogawa, GE's Japanese partner in the Medical Systems business, called "bullet train" thinking.[6] That is, if you want to increase the speed by 10 miles per hour, you look for incremental advances. However, if you want to double the speed, you've got to think "out of the box" (e.g., widen the track, change the overall suspension system). Leaders need more creative solutions than just keeping the same train with a few minor tweaks. Instead, they must come up with more revolutionary visions.

The experience of Julie Gilbert, VP of electronics retailer Best Buy, in changing the orientation of the company to attract more female shoppers is an excellent example of how leaders can overcome resistance and set new directions for their organizations. Strategy Spotlight 11.1 describes her initiatives.

Designing the Organization

designing the organization a strategic leadership activity of building structures, teams, systems, and organizational processes that facilitate the implementation of the leader's vision and strategies.

At times, almost all leaders have difficulty implementing their vision and strategies.[7] Such problems may stem from a variety of sources:

- Lack of understanding of responsibility and accountability among managers.
- Reward systems that do not motivate individuals (or collectives such as groups and divisions) toward desired organizational goals.
- Inadequate or inappropriate budgeting and control systems.
- Insufficient mechanisms to integrate activities across the organization.

Successful leaders are actively involved in building structures, teams, systems, and organizational processes that facilitate the implementation of their vision and strategies. We discussed the necessity for consistency between business-level and corporate-level strategies and organizational control in Chapter 9. Without appropriately structuring organizational activities, a firm would generally be unable to attain an overall low-cost advantage by closely monitoring its costs through detailed and formalized cost and financial control procedures. With regard to corporate-level strategy, a related diversification strategy would necessitate reward systems that emphasize behavioral measures, whereas an unrelated strategy should rely more on financial (or objective) indicators of performance.

These examples illustrate the important role of leadership in creating systems and structures to achieve desired ends. As Jim Collins says about the importance of designing the organization, "Along with figuring out what the company stands for and pushing it to understand what it's really good at, building mechanisms is the CEO's role—the leader as architect."[8]

Nurturing an Excellent and Ethical Culture

excellent and ethical organizational culture an organizational culture focused on core competencies and high ethical standards.

Organizational culture can be an effective means of organizational control.[9] Leaders play a key role in changing, developing, and sustaining an organization's culture. Consider a Chinese firm, Huawei, a highly successful producer of communication network solutions and services.[10] In 2009, it achieved revenues of $21.8 billion and net profits of $2.7 billion. Its strong culture can be attributed to its founder, Ren Zhengfei, and his background in the People's Liberation Army. It is a culture which eliminates individualism and promotes collectivism and the idea of hunting in packs. It is the "wolf culture" of Huawei:

> The culture of Huawei is built on a sense of patriotism, with Mr. Zhengfei frequently citing Mao Zedong's thoughts in his speeches and internal publications such as the employee magazine "Huawei People." Sales teams are referred to as "Market Guerrillas," and battlefield tactics, such as "occupy rural areas first to surround cities," are used internally. In addition to Mao Zedong, Mr. Zhengfei has urged his employees to look to the Japanese and Germans for inspiration on how to conduct themselves. This is exemplified by the words written in a letter to new hires that states, "I hope you abandon the mentality of achieving

IKEA's Founder: "Low Prices—But Not at Any Price"

IKEA's founder, Ingvar Kamprad, although believed to be one of the world's top 10 richest men, is leading his company by example. He flies coach, drives an aging Volvo, and stays in cheap hotels when traveling. Early in his career, Kamprad recognized that promoting a double standard between him and his employees would be detrimental to the health and wealth of the entire company. He contends, "It's a question of good leadership."

His money-pinching habits are thus exemplified and reinforced in the company he founded. As an example of his thriftiness: upon seeing some small pencils in a pile of debris on the floor, Kamprad sent the store manager to recover the pencils, even though their value was less than a penny.

Even though the company is usually tight-fisted, when it comes to environmental issues, IKEA spends millions of dollars in sorting and recycling the various types of plastic, metal, and wood used in packaging its products. Clearly, taking the time to sort the various materials entails significant costs and slows down the replenishment process. However, the processes are considered highly relevant to the firm's spirit of leadership. It is worth mentioning that

● IKEA is well-known for its inexpensive but stylish furniture as well as its concern for the environment.

none of these steps are a regulatory requirement, but are voluntary.

An explanation for IKEA's actions can be found in the company's slogan that is often observed in its offices: "Low prices—but not at any price." For IKEA this is not just another slogan but is reflected in its employees' everyday actions.

Source: Esty, D. C. & Winston, A. S. 2009. *Green to Gold.* Hoboken, NJ: Wiley; and Carmichael, E. undated. Lesson #2: The Best Leadership Is by Example. *www.evancarmichael.com,* np.

---

quick results, learn from the Japanese down-to-earth attitude and the German's spirit of being scrupulous to every detail."

The notion of "wolf culture" stems from the fact that Huawei workers are encouraged to learn from the behavior of wolves, which have a keen sense of smell, are aggressive, and, most important of all, hunt in packs. It is this collective and aggressive spirit that is the center of the Huawei culture. Combining the behavior of wolves with military-style training has been instrumental in building the culture of the company, which, in turn, is widely thought to be instrumental in the company's success.

In sharp contrast, leaders can also have a very detrimental effect on a firm's culture and ethics. Imagine the negative impact that Todd Berman's illegal activities have had on a firm that he cofounded—New York's private equity firm Chartwell Investments.[11] He stole more than $3.6 million from the firm and its investors. Berman pleaded guilty to fraud charges brought by the Justice Department. For 18 months he misled Chartwell's investors concerning the financial condition of one of the firm's portfolio companies by falsely claiming it needed to borrow funds to meet operating expenses. Instead, Berman transferred the money to his personal bank account, along with fees paid by portfolio companies.

Clearly, a leader's behavior and values can make a strong impact on an organization—for good or for bad. Strategy Spotlight 11.2 provides a positive example. It discusses how the values and behavior of Ingvar Kamprad, founder of Swedish furniture retailer IKEA, have resulted in a culture of frugality and environmental consciousness within the company.

Managers and top executives must accept personal responsibility for developing and strengthening ethical behavior throughout the organization. They must consistently demonstrate that such behavior is central to the vision and mission of the organization. Several elements must be present and reinforced for a firm to become highly ethical, including role models, corporate credos and codes of conduct, reward and evaluation systems, and policies and procedures. Given the importance of these elements, we address them in detail in the last section of this chapter.

The Ambicultural Approach: A Key to Successfully Fulfilling the Three Leadership Activities

Highly successful leaders don't rely strictly on one philosophy and its associated set of business practices and apply them to every decision they face. Rather, they endeavor to merge the best from different approaches. For example, leaders can benefit by taking the best of different philosophies and business practices while avoiding the negatives. This is called an "ambicultural" perspective on leadership.[12] For example, a company can try to combine the best of Chinese and Western practices to create a truly ambicultural organization.

Each society has particular strengths and weaknesses as they apply to business practice. The challenge for managers is to utilize the thinking and orientations of both cultures in order to understand, identify with, and benefit from each of them. And we will see that it has important implications for setting an organization's direction, designing structures and processes, as well as instilling a strong culture.

Stan Shih, the legendary founder of the Acer Group, personifies the ambicultural perspective on leadership. Acer is the second-largest computer maker in the world, with revenues for the firm and its sister businesses, BenQ and Winstron, totaling $52 billion. Shih's overall orientation might be best described as a long-term view that values benefits not only for all company stakeholders but the entire global community.[13]

His major influence from the Chinese culture is a patient, holistic, community-driven orientation. From the Western perspective, he has taken a more decentralized and empowering management philosophy. At the same time, he has striven to avoid the mistrust, secrecy, and authoritarian paternalism that have sometimes characterized Eastern practices, and to avoid the short-term, bottom-line-driven focus and grandiosity of some Western companies.

Let's take a closer look at some Western practices that Shih has avoided and some that he has adopted. Most of all, he has avoided short-termism and narrow individualism and its corresponding intolerant, money-driven, up-or-out culture. His concern has never been with short-term profits or kill-or-be-killed competitive reasoning. He has avoided corporate cultures that lavishly reward the very few at the expense of the many. Nor has he focused exclusively on owners at the expense of other stakeholders or society as a whole. In these respects, he has much in common with enduring great Western family businesses.

At the same time, Shih has not universally ignored or dismissed aspects of American or Western management. He has been a strong proponent of decentralization, flat structures, and employee discretion. He has been quick to give up power to the next generations, and he has appreciated the value of brands, branding, and globalization. Unlike most Chinese firms, Acer did not pursue a typical cost-driven strategy or focus on low-end manufacturing. Theirs was more of a Western approach to branding and selling higher-end products. However, Shih did take note of the mistake of so many Western firms of outsourcing too many functions and thereby letting the outsourcers move up the value chain and steal their business. Acer kept total control of the value chain by employing different companies belonging to the same corporate group.

Elements of Effective Leadership

The demands on leaders in today's business environment require them to perform a variety of functions. The success of their organizations often depends on how they as individuals meet challenges and deliver on promises. What practices and skills are needed to get the job done effectively? In this section, we focus on three capabilities that are marks of successful leadership—integrative thinking, overcoming barriers to change, and the effective use of power. Then, in the next section, we will examine an important human trait that helps leaders be more effective—emotional intelligence.

Integrative Thinking

The challenges facing today's leaders require them to confront a host of opposing forces. As the previous section indicated, maintaining consistency across a company's culture, vision, and organizational design can be difficult, especially if the three activities are out of alignment.

> **integrative thinking** a process of reconciling opposing thoughts by generating new alternatives and creative solutions rather than rejecting one thought in favor of another.

How does a leader make good strategic decisions in the face of multiple contingencies and diverse opportunities? A recent study by Roger L. Martin reveals that executives who have a capability known as "integrative thinking" are among the most effective leaders. In his book *The Opposable Mind,* Martin contends that people who can consider two conflicting ideas simultaneously, without dismissing one of the ideas or becoming discouraged about reconciling them, often make the best problem solvers because of their ability to creatively synthesize the opposing thoughts. In explaining the source of his title, Martin quotes F. Scott Fitzgerald, who observed, "The test of a first-rate intelligence is the ability to hold two opposing ideas in mind at the same time and still retain the ability to function. One should, for example, be able to see that things are hopeless yet be determined to make them otherwise."[14]

In contrast to conventional thinking, which tends to focus on making choices between competing ideas from a limited set of alternatives, integrative thinking is the process by which people reconcile opposing thoughts to identify creative solutions that provide them with more options and new alternatives. Exhibit 11.2 outlines the four stages of the integrative thinking and deciding process. Martin uses the admittedly simple example of deciding where to go on vacation to illustrate the stages:

- *Salience*—Take stock of what features of the decision you consider relevant and important. For example: Where will you go? What will you see? Where will you stay? What will it cost? Is it safe? Other features may be less important, but try to think of everything that may matter.
- *Causality*—Make a mental map of the causal relationships between the features, that is, how the various features are related to one another. For example, is it worth it to invite friends to share expenses? Will an exotic destination be less safe?
- *Architecture*—Use the mental map to arrange a sequence of decisions that will lead to a specific outcome. For example, will you make the hotel and flight arrangements first, or focus on which sightseeing tours are available? No particular decision path is right or wrong, but considering multiple options simultaneously may lead to a better decision.
- *Resolution*—Make your selection. For example, choose which destination, which flight, and so forth. You final resolution is linked to how you evaluated the first three stages; if you are dissatisfied with your choices, the dotted arrows in the diagram (Exhibit 11.2) suggest you can go back through the process and revisit your assumptions.

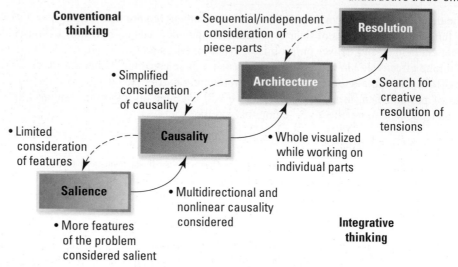

Conventional
thinking

- Ready acceptance of
  unattractive trade-offs

Resolution

- Sequential/independent
  consideration of
  piece-parts

- Simplified
  consideration
  of causality

Architecture

- Search for
  creative
  resolution of
  tensions

- Limited
  consideration
  of features

Causality

- Whole visualized
  while working on
  individual parts

Salience

- Multidirectional and
  nonlinear causality
  considered

**Integrative
thinking**

- More features
  of the problem
  considered salient

Exhibit 11.2 Integrative Thinking: The Process of Thinking and Deciding

Source: Reprinted by permission of Harvard Business School Press from R. L. Martin. *The Opposable Mind*, 2007. Copyright 2007 by the Harvard Business School Publishing Corporation; all rights reserved.

Applied to business, an integrative thinking approach enables decision makers to consider situations not as forced trade-offs—either decrease costs or invest more; either satisfy shareholders or please the community—but as a method for synthesizing opposing ideas into a creative solution. The key is to think in terms of "both-and" rather than "either-or." "Integrative thinking," says Martin, "shows us that there's a way to integrate the advantages of one solution without canceling out the advantages of an alternative solution."

Although Martin found that integrative thinking comes naturally to some people, he also believes it can be taught. But it may be difficult to learn, in part because it requires people to *un*learn old patterns and become aware of how they think. For executives willing to take a deep look at their habits of thought, integrative thinking can be developed into a valuable skill. Strategy Spotlight 11.3 tells how Red Hat Inc. cofounder Bob Young made his company a market leader by using integrative thinking to resolve a major problem in the domain of open-source software.

Overcoming Barriers to Change

What are the **barriers to change** that leaders often encounter, and how can they best bring about organizational change?[15] After all, people generally have some level of choice about how strongly they support or resist a leader's change initiatives. Why is there often so much resistance? Organizations at all levels are prone to inertia and are slow to learn, adapt, and change because:

1. Many people have **vested interests in the status quo.** People tend to be risk averse and resistant to change. There is a broad stream of research on "escalation," wherein certain individuals continue to throw "good money at bad decisions" despite negative performance feedback.[16]

2. There are **systemic barriers.** The design of the organization's structure, information processing, reporting relationships, and so forth impede the proper flow and evaluation of information. A bureaucratic structure with multiple layers, onerous

---

barriers to change
characteristics of
individuals and
organizations that
prevent a leader
from transforming
an organization.

>LO11.2
Three elements
of effective
leadership:
integrative
thinking,
overcoming
barriers to
change, and the
effective use of
power.

**vested intrest in
the status quo** a
barrier to change that
stems from people's
risk aversion.

systemic barriers
barriers to change
that stem from an
organizational
design that impedes
the proper flow
and evaluation of
information.

Integrative Thinking at Red Hat, Inc.

How can a software developer make money giving away free software? That was the dilemma Red Hat founder Bob Young was facing during the early days of the open-source software movement. A Finnish developer named Linus Torvalds, using freely available UNIX software, had developed an operating system dubbed "Linux" that was being widely circulated in the freeware community. The software was intended specifically as an alternative to the pricey proprietary systems sold by Microsoft and Oracle. To use proprietary software, corporations had to pay hefty installation fees and were required to call Microsoft or Oracle engineers to fix it when anything went wrong. In Young's view it was a flawed and unsustainable business model.

But the free model was flawed as well. Although several companies had sprung up to help companies use Linux, there were few opportunities to profit from using it. As Young said, "You couldn't make any money selling [the Linux] operating system because all this stuff was free, and if you started to charge money for it, someone else would come in and price it lower. It was a commodity in the truest sense of the word." To complicate matters, hundreds of developers were part of the software community that was constantly modifying and debugging Linux—at a rate equivalent to three updates per day. As a result, systems administrators at corporations that tried to adopt the software spent so much time keeping track of updates that they didn't enjoy the savings they expected from using free software.

Young saw the appeal of both approaches but also realized a new model was needed. While contemplating the dilemma, he realized a salient feature that others had overlooked—because most major corporations have to live with software decisions for at least ten years, they will nearly always choose to do business with the industry leader. Young realized he had to position Red Hat as the top provider of Linux software. To do that, he proposed a radical solution: provide the authoritative version of Linux and deliver it in a new way—as a download rather than on CD. He hired programmers to create a download-able version—still free—and promised, in essence, to maintain its quality (for a fee, of course) by dealing with all the open-source programmers who were continually suggesting changes. In the process, he created a product companies could trust and then profited by establishing ongoing service relationships with customers. Red Hat's version of Linux became the de facto standard. By 2000, Linux was installed in 25 percent of server operating systems worldwide and Red Hat had captured over 50 percent of the global market for Linux systems.

By recognizing that a synthesis of two flawed business models could provide the best of both worlds, Young exhibited the traits of integrative thinking. He pinpointed the causal relationships between the salient features of the marketplace and Red Hat's path to prosperity. He then crafted an approach that integrated aspects of the two existing approaches into a new alternative. By resolving to provide a free downloadable version, Young also took responsibility for creating his own path to success. The pay-off was substantial: when Red Hat went public in 1999, Young became a billionaire on the first day of trading. And by February 2011 Red Hat had over $850 million in annual revenues and a market capitalization of nearly $9 billion.

Source: Martin, R. L. 2007. *The Opposable Mind*. Boston: Harvard Business School Press; and *www.finance.yahoo.com*.

requirements for documentation, and rigid rules and procedures will often "inoculate" the organization against change.

3. **Behavioral barriers** cause managers to look at issues from a biased or limited perspective due to their education, training, work experiences, and so forth. Consider an incident shared by David Lieberman, marketing director at GVO, an innovation consulting firm:

> A company's creative type had come up with a great idea for a new product. Nearly everybody loved it. However, it was shot down by a high-ranking manufacturing representative who exploded: "A new color? Do you have any idea of the spare-parts problem that it will create?" This was not a dimwit exasperated at having to build a few storage racks at the warehouse. He'd been hearing for years about cost cutting, lean inventories, and "focus." Lieberman's comment: "Good concepts, but not always good for innovation."

behavioral barriers
barriers to change associated with the tendency for managers to look at issues from a biased or limited perspective based on their prior education and experience.

political barriers barriers to change related to conflicts arising from power relationships.

4. **Political barriers** refer to conflicts arising from power relationships. This can be the outcome of a myriad of symptoms such as vested interests, refusal to share information, conflicts over resources, conflicts between departments and divisions, and petty interpersonal differences.

5. **Personal time constraints** bring to mind the old saying about "not having enough time to drain the swamp when you are up to your neck in alligators." Gresham's law of planning states that operational decisions will drive out the time necessary for strategic thinking and reflection. This tendency is accentuated in organizations experiencing severe price competition or retrenchment wherein managers and employees are spread rather thin.

personal time constraints a barrier to change that stems from people's not having sufficient time for strategic thinking and reflection.

Leaders must draw on a range of personal skills as well as organizational mechanisms to move their organizations forward in the face of such barriers. Integrative thinking provides one avenue by equipping leaders with an ability to consider creative alternatives to the kind of resistance and doubt that cause many barriers. Two factors mentioned earlier—building a learning organization and ethical organization—provide the kind of climate within which a leader can advance the organization's aims and make progress toward its goals.

One of the most important tools a leader has for overcoming barriers to change is their personal and organizational power. On the one hand, good leaders must be on guard not to abuse power. On the other hand, successful leadership requires the measured exercise of power. We turn to that topic next.

The Effective Use of Power

Successful leadership requires effective use of power in overcoming barriers to change.[17] As humorously noted by Mark Twain, "I'm all for progress. It's change I object to." **Power** refers to a leader's ability to get things done in a way he or she wants them to be done. It is the ability to influence other people's behavior, to persuade them to do things that they otherwise would not do, and to overcome resistance and opposition to changing direction. Effective exercise of power is essential for successful leadership.[18]

power a leader's ability to get things done in a way he or she wants them to be done.

A leader derives his or her power from several sources or bases. The simplest way to understand the bases of power is by classifying them as organizational and personal, as shown in Exhibit 11.3.

Organizational bases of power refer to the power that a person wields because of holding a formal management position.[19] These include legitimate power, reward power, coercive power, and information power. *Legitimate power* is derived from organizationally conferred decision-making authority and is exercised by virtue of a manager's position in the organization. *Reward power* depends on the ability of the leader or manager to confer rewards for positive behaviors or outcomes. *Coercive power* is the power a manager exercises over employees using fear of punishment for errors of omission or commission. *Information power* arises from a manager's access, control, and distribution of information that is not freely available to everyone in an organization.

organizational bases of power a formal management position that is the basis of a leader's power.

A leader might also be able to influence subordinates because of his or her personality characteristics and behavior. These would be considered the **personal bases of power,** including referent power and expert power. The source of *referent power* is a subordinate's identification with the leader. A leader's personal attributes or charisma might influence subordinates and make them devoted to that leader. The source of *expert power* is the leader's expertise and knowledge in a particular field. The leader is the expert on whom subordinates depend for information that they need to do their jobs successfully.

personal bases of power a leader's personality characteristics and behavior that are the basis of the leader's power.

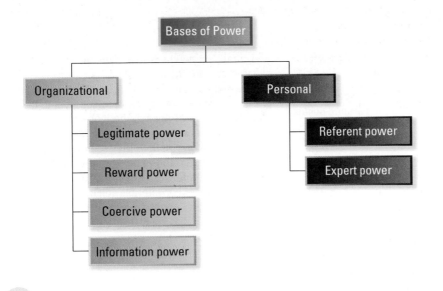

Exhibit 11.3 A Leader's Bases of Power

Successful leaders use the different bases of power, and often a combination of them, as appropriate to meet the demands of a situation, such as the nature of the task, the personality characteristics of the subordinates, the urgency of the issue, and other factors.[20] Leaders must recognize that persuasion and developing consensus are often essential, but so is pressing for action. At some point stragglers must be prodded into line.[21] Peter Georgescu, who recently retired as CEO of Young & Rubicam (an advertising and media subsidiary of the UK-based WPP Group), summarized a leader's dilemma brilliantly (and humorously), "I have knee pads and a .45. I get down and beg a lot, but I shoot people too."[22]

Strategy Spotlight 11.4 addresses some of the subtleties of power. It focuses on William Bratton, Chief of the Los Angeles Police Department, who has enjoyed a very successful career in law enforcement.

Emotional Intelligence: A Key Leadership Trait

>LO11.3
The crucial role of emotional intelligence (EI) in successful leadership as well as its potential drawbacks.

In the previous sections, we discussed skills and activities of strategic leadership. The focus was on "what leaders do and how they do it." Now, the issue becomes "who leaders *are*," that is, what leadership traits are the most important. Clearly, these two issues are related, because successful leaders possess the valuable traits that enable them to perform effectively in order to create value for their organization.[23]

There has been a vast amount of literature on the successful traits of leaders.[24] These traits include integrity, maturity, energy, judgment, motivation, intelligence, expertise, and so on. For simplicity, these traits may be grouped into three broad sets of capabilities:

- Purely technical skills (like accounting or operations research).
- Cognitive abilities (like analytical reasoning or quantitative analysis).
- Emotional intelligence (like self-management and managing relationships).

William Bratton: Using Multiple Bases of Power

William Bratton, Chief of the Los Angeles Police Department has an enviable track record in turning around police departments in crime-ridden cities. First, while running the police division of Massachusetts Bay Transit Authority (MBTA) in Boston, then as police commissioner of New York in the mid-1990s, and with Los Angeles from 2002 to late 2009, Chief Bratton is credited with reducing crime and improving police morale in record time. An analysis of his success at each of these organizations reveals similar patterns both in terms of the problems he faced and the many ways in which he used the different bases of power to engineer a rapid turnaround.

In Boston, New York, and Los Angeles, Chief Bratton faced similar hurdles: organizations wedded to the status quo, limited resources, demotivated staffs, and opposition from powerful vested interests. But he does not give up in the face of these seemingly insurmountable problems. He is persuasive in calls for change, capable of mobilizing the commitment of key players, silencing vocal naysayers, and building rapport with superiors and subordinates while building bridges with external constituencies.

Chief Bratton's persuasion tactics are unconventional, yet effective. When he was running the MBTA police, the Transit Authority decided to buy small squad cars, which are cheaper to buy and to run, but inadequate for the police officer's task. Instead of arguing, Bratton invited the general manager for a tour of the city. He rode with the general manager in exactly the same type of car that was ordered for ordinary officers, and drove over every pothole on the road. He moved the seats forward so that the general manager could feel how little leg room was there. And he put on his belt, cuffs, and gun so that the general manager could understand how limited the space was. After two hours in the cramped car, the general manager was ready to change the order and get more suitable cars for the officers!

Another tactic Bratton used effectively was insisting on community meetings between police officers and citizens. This went against the long-standing practice of detachment between police and community to decrease the chances of corruption. The result was that his department had a better understanding of public concerns and rearranged their priorities, which in turn led to better community relations. For internal communications, he relied mainly on professionally produced videos instead of long, boring memos.

Chief Bratton also shows a remarkable talent for building political bridges and silencing naysayers. As he was introducing his zero-tolerance policing approach that aggressively targets "quality of life" crimes such as panhandling, drunkenness, and prostitution, opposition came from the city's courts, which feared being inundated by a large number of small-crimes cases. Bratton enlisted the support of Rudolph Giuliani, the mayor of New York, who had considerable influence over the district attorneys, the courts, and the city jail. He also took the case to the *New York Times* and managed to get the issue of zero-tolerance on the front pages of the newspaper. The courts were left with no alternative but to cooperate.

To a great extent, Bratton's success can be attributed to his understanding of the subtleties of power, including persuasion, motivation, coalition building, empathy for subordinates, and a focus on goals.

Let's take a quick look at his success during his tenure as Los Angeles's chief of police. Crime dropped significantly: violent crimes were down 53 percent; property crimes were down 33 percent, and gang-related crimes were cut by 34 percent. Connie Rice, a prominent civil-rights lawyer, feels that Bratton's biggest achievement was turning the LAPD's old "warrior culture" into "policing as something not done to people but with people." She says, "Little old ladies who used to shake their head when the cops came around are now calling them about somebody doing crack." This is quite a strong endorsement coming from someone who *The Economist* says "spent much of her career suing the Los Angeles Police Department."

Sources: Exit Bratton. 2009. *The Economist*, October 31:42; Chan Kim, W. & Renee Mauborgne, R. 2003. Tipping Point Leadership. *Harvard Business Review*, 81(4): 60–69; and McCarthy, T. 2004. The Gang Buster. *Time*, January 19: 56–58.

"Emotional intelligence (EI)" has become popular in both the literature and management practice in recent years.[25] *Harvard Business Review* articles published in 1998 and 2000 by psychologist/journalist Daniel Goleman, who is most closely associated with the concept, have become *HBR*'s most highly requested reprint articles. And two of Goleman's recent books, *Emotional Intelligence* and *Working with Emotional Intelligence,* were both on the *New York Times*'s best-seller lists. Goleman defines **emotional intelligence** as the capacity for recognizing one's own emotions and those of others.[26]

Recent studies of successful managers have found that effective leaders consistently have a high level of EI.[27] Findings indicate that EI is a better predictor of life success (economic well-being, satisfaction with life, friendship, family life), including occupational attainments, than IQ. Such evidence has been extrapolated to the catchy phrase: "IQ gets you hired, but EQ (Emotional Quotient) gets you promoted." Human resource managers believe this statement to be true, even for highly technical jobs such as those of scientists and engineers.

This is not to say that IQ and technical skills are irrelevant, but they become "threshold capabilities." They are the necessary requirements for attaining higher-level managerial positions. EI, on the other hand, is essential for leadership success. Without it, Goleman claims, a manager can have excellent training, an incisive analytical mind, and many smart ideas but will still not be a great leader.

Exhibit 11.4 identifies the five components of EI: self-awareness, self-regulation, motivation, empathy, and social skill.

emotional intelligence (EI) an individual's capacity for recognizing his or her own emotions and those of others, including the five components of self-awareness, self-regulation, motivation, empathy, and social skills.

Exhibit 11.4 The Five Components of Emotional Intelligence at Work

	Definition	Hallmarks
Self-management skills:		
Self-awareness	• The ability to recognize and understand your moods, emotions, and drives, as well as their effect on others.	• Self-confidence • Realistic self-assessment • Self-deprecating sense of humor
Self-regulation	• The ability to control or redirect disruptive impulses and moods. • The propensity to suspend judgment—to think before acting.	• Trustworthiness and integrity • Comfort with ambiguity • Openness to change
Motivation	• A passion to work for reasons that go beyond money or status. • A propensity to pursue goals with energy and persistence.	• Strong drive to achieve • Optimism, even in the face of failure • Organizational commitment
Managing relationships:		
Empathy	• The ability to understand the emotional makeup of other people. • Skill in treating people according to their emotional reactions.	• Expertise in building and retaining talent • Cross-cultural sensitivity • Service to clients and customers
Social skill	• Proficiency in managing relationships and building networks. • An ability to find common ground and build rapport.	• Effectiveness in leading change • Persuasiveness • Expertise in building and leading teams

Source: Reprinted by permission of *Harvard Business Review*. Exhibit from "What Makes a Leader," by D. Goleman, January 2004. Copyright © 2004 by the Harvard Business School Publishing Corporation; all rights reserved.

Self-Awareness

Self-awareness is the first component of EI and brings to mind that Delphic oracle who gave the advice "know thyself" thousands of years ago. Self-awareness involves a person having a deep understanding of his or her emotions, strengths, weaknesses, and drives. People with strong self-awareness are neither overly critical nor unrealistically optimistic. Instead, they are honest with themselves and others.

People generally admire and respect candor. Leaders are constantly required to make judgment calls that require a candid assessment of capabilities—their own and those of others. People who assess themselves honestly (i.e., self-aware people) are well suited to do the same for the organizations they run.[28]

Self-Regulation

Biological impulses drive our emotions. Although we cannot do away with them, we can strive to manage them. Self-regulation, which is akin to an ongoing inner conversation, frees us from being prisoners of our feelings.[29] People engaged in such conversation feel bad moods and emotional impulses just as everyone else does. However, they find ways to control them and even channel them in useful ways.

Self-regulated people are able to create an environment of trust and fairness where political behavior and infighting are sharply reduced and productivity tends to be high. People who have mastered their emotions are better able to bring about and implement change in an organization. When a new initiative is announced, they are less likely to panic; they are able to suspend judgment, seek out information, and listen to executives explain the new program.

Motivation

Successful executives are driven to achieve beyond expectations—their own and everyone else's. Although many people are driven by external factors, such as money and prestige, those with leadership potential are driven by a deeply embedded desire to achieve for the sake of achievement.

Motivated people show a passion for the work itself, such as seeking out creative challenges, a love of learning, and taking pride in a job well done. They also have a high level of energy to do things better as well as a restlessness with the status quo. They are eager to explore new approaches to their work.

Empathy

Empathy is probably the most easily recognized component of EI. Empathy means thoughtfully considering an employee's feelings, along with other factors, in the process of making intelligent decisions. Empathy is particularly important in today's business environment for at least three reasons: the increasing use of teams, the rapid pace of globalization, and the growing need to retain talent.[30]

When leading a team, a manager is often charged with arriving at a consensus—often in the face of a high level of emotions. Empathy enables a manager to sense and understand the viewpoints of everyone around the table.

Globalization typically involves cross-cultural dialogue that can easily lead to miscues. Empathetic people are attuned to the subtleties of body language; they can hear the message beneath the words being spoken. They have a deep understanding of the existence and importance of cultural and ethnic differences.

Empathy also plays a key role in retaining talent. Human capital is particularly important to a firm in the knowledge economy when it comes to creating advantages that are sustainable. Leaders need empathy to develop and keep top talent, because when high performers leave, they take their tacit knowledge with them.

Social Skill

While the first three components of EI are all self-management skills, the last two—empathy and social skill—concern a person's ability to manage relationships with others. Social skill may be viewed as friendliness with a purpose: moving people in the direction you desire, whether that's agreement on a new marketing strategy or enthusiasm about a new product.

Socially skilled people tend to have a wide circle of acquaintances as well as a knack for finding common ground and building rapport. They recognize that nothing gets done alone, and they have a network in place when the time for action comes.

Social skill can be viewed as the culmination of the other dimensions of EI. People will be effective at managing relationships when they can understand and control their own emotions and empathize with others' feelings. Motivation also contributes to social skill. People who are driven to achieve tend to be optimistic, even when confronted with setbacks. And when people are upbeat, their "glow" is cast upon conversations and other social encounters. They are popular, and for good reason.

Carol Bartz, CEO of Yahoo!, provides some insights on the importance of emotional intelligence in successfully leading an organization:[31]

> When asked what she had learned over her years leading corporations, Bartz said one mistake was "letting people who didn't fit the culture stay too long because they seemed like such a superstar. . . . You hire for talent but fire for fit."
>
> About hiring, Bartz said, "I have to make it through dinner—without two bottles of wine. And if I can't make it through dinner, then I know I can't work with that person." She added that the dinner test often brought out whether the candidate had the right energy level and personality for her organization.
>
> On changing company culture: "Pick your battles. Changing culture can become like arguing with a teenager, and if you fight over everything—one of you is dead by the end of it."
>
> In a surprising comment, Bartz said she stopped the practice of annual reviews at Yahoo! "Development happens every day. Just like athletes work on their skills every day, managers work on their skills every day."

Emotional Intelligence: Some Potential Drawbacks and Cautionary Notes

Many great leaders have great reserves of empathy, interpersonal astuteness, awareness of their own feelings, and an awareness of their impact on others.[32] More importantly, they know how to apply these capabilities judiciously as best benefits the situation. Having some minimum level of EI will help a person be effective as a leader as long as it is channeled appropriately. However, if a person has a high level of these capabilities it may become "too much of a good thing" if he or she is allowed to drive inappropriate behaviors. Some additional potential drawbacks of EI can be gleaned by considering the flip side of its benefits.

Effective Leaders Have Empathy for Others   However, they also must be able to make the "tough decisions." Leaders must be able to appeal to logic and reason and acknowledge others' feelings so that people feel the decisions are correct. However, it is easy to overidentify with others or confuse empathy with sympathy. This can make it more difficult to make the tough decisions.

Effective Leaders Are Astute Judges of People   A danger is that leaders may become judgmental and overly critical about the shortcomings they perceive in others. They are likely to dismiss other people's insights, making them feel undervalued.

Effective Leaders Are Passionate about What They Do, and They Show It

This doesn't mean that they are always cheerleaders. Rather, they may express their passion as persistence in pursuing an objective or a relentless focus on a valued principle. However, there is a fine line between being excited about something and letting your passion close your mind to other possibilities or cause you to ignore realities that others may see.

Effective Leaders Create Personal Connections with Their People

Most effective leaders take time to engage employees individually and in groups, listening to their ideas, suggestions and concerns, and responding in ways that make people feel that their ideas are respected and appreciated. However, if the leader makes too many unannounced visits, it may create a culture of fear and micromanagement. Clearly, striking a correct balance is essential.

From a moral standpoint, emotional leadership is neither good nor bad. On the one hand, emotional leaders can be altruistic, focused on the general welfare of the company and its employees, and highly principled. On the other hand, they can be manipulative, selfish, and dishonest. For example, if a person is using leadership solely to gain power, that is not leadership at all.[33] Rather, they are using their EI to grasp what people want and pander to those desires in order to gain authority and influence. After all, easy answers sell.

Next, we turn to guidelines for developing a "learning organization." In today's competitive environment, the old saying that "a chain is only as strong as the weakest link" applies more than ever before. To learn and adapt proactively, firms need "eyes, ears, and brains" throughout all parts of the organization. One person, or a small group of individuals, can no longer think and learn for the entire entity.

>LO 11.4
The value of creating and maintaining a learning organization in today's global marketplace.

Developing a Learning Organization

Charles Handy, author of *The Age of Unreason* and *The Age of Paradox* and one of today's most respected business visionaries, shared an amusing story several years ago:

> The other day, a courier could not find my family's remote cottage. He called his base on his radio, and the base called us to ask directions. He was just around the corner, but his base managed to omit a vital part of the directions. So he called them again, and they called us again. Then the courier repeated the cycle a third time to ask whether we had a dangerous dog. When he eventually arrived, we asked whether it would not have been simpler and less aggravating to everyone if he had called us directly from the roadside telephone booth where he had been parked. "I can't do that," he said, "because they won't refund any money I spend." "But it's only pennies!" I exclaimed. "I know," he said, "but that only shows how little they trust us!"[34]

At first glance, it would appear that the story epitomizes the lack of empowerment and trust granted to the hapless courier: Don't ask questions! Do as you're told![35] However, implicit in this scenario is also the message that learning, information sharing, adaptation, decision making, and so on are *not* shared throughout the organization. In contrast, leading-edge organizations recognize the importance of having everyone involved in the process of actively learning and adapting. As noted by today's leading expert on learning organizations, MIT's Peter Senge, the days when Henry Ford, Alfred Sloan, and Tom Watson *"learned for the organization"* are gone.

> In an increasingly dynamic, interdependent, and unpredictable world, it is simply no longer possible for anyone to "figure it all out at the top." The old model, "the top thinks and the local acts," must now give way to integrating thinking and acting at all levels. While the challenge is great, so is the potential payoff. "The person who figures out how to harness the collective genius of the people in his or her organization," according to former Citibank CEO Walter Wriston, "is going to blow the competition away."[36]

Exhibit 11.5 Key Elements of a Learning Organization

These are the five key elements of a learning organization. Each of these items should be viewed as *necessary, but not sufficient.* That is, successful learning organizations need all five elements.

1. Inspiring and motivating people with a mission or purpose.
2. Empowering employees at all levels.
3. Accumulating and sharing internal knowledge.
4. Gathering and integrating external information.
5. Challenging the status quo and enabling creativity.

Learning and change typically involve the ongoing questioning of an organization's status quo or method of procedure. This means that all individuals throughout the organization must be reflective.[37] Many organizations get so caught up in carrying out their day-to-day work that they rarely, if ever, stop to think objectively about themselves and their businesses. They often fail to ask the probing questions that might lead them to call into question their basic assumptions, to refresh their strategies, or to reengineer their work processes. According to Michael Hammer and Steven Stanton, the pioneer consultants who touched off the reengineering movement:

> Reflection entails awareness of self, of competitors, of customers. It means thinking without preconception. It means questioning cherished assumptions and replacing them with new approaches. It is the only way in which a winning company can maintain its leadership position, by which a company with great assets can ensure that they continue to be well deployed.[38]

To adapt to change, foster creativity, and remain competitive, leaders must build learning organizations. Exhibit 11.5 lists the five elements of a learning organization.

Inspiring and Motivating People with a Mission or Purpose

Successful **learning organizations** create a proactive, creative approach to the unknown, actively solicit the involvement of employees at all levels, and enable all employees to use their intelligence and apply their imagination. Higher-level skills are required of everyone, not just those at the top.[39] A learning environment involves organizationwide commitment to change, an action orientation, and applicable tools and methods.[40] It must be viewed by everyone as a guiding philosophy and not simply as another change program.

A critical requirement of all learning organizations is that everyone feels and supports a compelling purpose. In the words of William O'Brien, CEO of Hanover Insurance, "Before there can be meaningful participation, people must share certain values and pictures about where we are trying to go. We discovered that people have a real need to feel that they're part of an enabling mission."[41] Such a perspective is consistent with an intensive study by Kouzes and Posner, authors of *The Leadership Challenge*.[42] They recently analyzed data from nearly one million respondents who were leaders at various levels in many organizations throughout the world. A major finding was that what leaders struggle with most is communicating an image of the future that draws others in, that is, it speaks to what others see and feel. To illustrate:

> Buddy Blanton, a principal program manager at Rockwell Collins, learned this lesson firsthand. He asked his team for feedback on his leadership, and the vast majority of it was positive. However, he got some strong advice from his team about how he could be more effective in inspiring a shared vision. "You would benefit by helping us, as a team, to

learning organizations organizations that create a proactive, creative approach to the unknown, characterized by (1) inspiring and motivating people with a mission and purpose, (2) empowering employees at all levels, (3) accumulating and sharing internal knowledge, (4) gathering and integrating external information, and (5) challenging the status quo and enabling creativity.

understand how you go to your vision. We want to walk with you while you create the goals and vision, so we all get to the end of the vision together."[43]

Inspiring and motivating people with a mission or purpose is a necessary but not sufficient condition for developing an organization that can learn and adapt to a rapidly changing, complex, and interconnected environment.

Empowering Employees at All Levels

"The great leader is a great servant," asserted Ken Melrose, CEO of Toro Company and author of *Making the Grass Greener on Your Side*.[44] A manager's role becomes one of creating an environment where employees can achieve their potential as they help move the organization toward its goals. Instead of viewing themselves as resource controllers and power brokers, leaders must envision themselves as flexible resources willing to assume numerous roles as coaches, information providers, teachers, decision makers, facilitators, supporters, or listeners, depending on the needs of their employees.[45]

The central key to empowerment is effective leadership. Empowerment can't occur in a leadership vacuum. According to Melrose, "You best lead by serving the needs of your people. You don't do their jobs for them; you enable them to learn and progress on the job." Robert Quinn and Gretchen Spreitzer made an interesting point about two diametrically opposite perspectives on empowerment—top-down and bottom-up.[46]

In the top-down perspective, empowerment is about delegation and accountability—senior management has developed a clear vision and has communicated specific plans to the rest of the organization.[47] This strategy for empowerment encompasses the following:

- Start at the top.
- Clarify the organization's mission, vision, and values.
- Clearly specify the tasks, roles, and rewards for employees.
- Delegate responsibility.
- Hold people accountable for results.

By contrast, the bottom-up view looks at empowerment as concerned with risk taking, growth, and change. It involves trusting people to "do the right thing" and having a tolerance for failure. It encourages employees to act with a sense of ownership and typically "ask for forgiveness rather than permission." Here the salient elements of empowerment are:

- Start at the bottom by understanding the needs of employees.
- Teach employees self-management skills and model desired behavior.
- Build teams to encourage cooperative behavior.
- Encourage intelligent risk taking.
- Trust people to perform.

These two perspectives draw a sharp contrast in assumptions that people make about trust and control. Quinn and Spreitzer recently shared these contrasting views of empowerment with a senior management team. After an initial heavy silence, someone from the first group voiced a concern about the second group's perspective, "We can't afford loose cannons around here." A person in the second group retorted, "When was the last time you saw a cannon of any kind around here?"

Many leading-edge organizations are moving in the direction of the second perspective—recognizing the need for trust, cultural control, and expertise at all levels instead of the extensive and cumbersome rules and regulations inherent in hierarchical control.[48] Some have argued that too often organizations fall prey to the "heroes-and-drones syndrome," wherein the value of those in powerful positions is exalted and the value of those who fail to achieve top rank is diminished. Such an attitude is implicit in phrases

A Hospital's Unique Approach to Empowerment

Beth Israel Deaconess is a medical center formed by the merger of two Harvard teaching hospitals. Early in 2009, it was facing a projected $20 million annual loss after several years of profitability. CEO Paul Levy held a meeting to discuss layoffs.

He expressed concern that cutbacks would affect low-wage employees, such as housekeepers, and he floated what he thought would be an unpopular idea: protecting some of those low-paying jobs by reducing the salary and benefits of higher-paid employees—including many sitting in the auditorium. To his surprise, the room erupted in applause!

His candid request for help led to countless suggestions for cost savings. This included an offer by the 13 medical department heads to save 10 jobs through personal donations totaling $350,000. In addition, the plan for reducing layoffs included a combination of delayed raises and a temporary reduction in benefits. Such efforts ultimately reduced the number of planned layoffs by 75 percent.

In the end, the low-wage workers were really taken care of. They were exempt from the salary cuts and even received 3 percent raises.

Sources: Heifetz, R., Grashow, A., & Linsky, M. 2009. Leadership in a (Permanent) Crisis. *Harvard Business Review*, 87(4): 67; and Cooney, E. 2009. Beth Israel Pares Its Plan for Layoffs. *www.bostonglobe.com*, March 25: np.

such as "Lead, follow, or get out of the way" or, even less appealing, "Unless you're the lead horse, the view never changes." Few will ever reach the top hierarchical positions in organizations, but in the information economy, the strongest organizations are those that effectively use the talents of all the players on the team.

Empowering individuals by soliciting their input helps an organization to enjoy better employee morale. It also may help to create a culture of shared sacrifice, which may be critical during difficult economic times, as described in Strategy Spotlight 11.5.

Accumulating and Sharing Internal Knowledge

Effective organizations must also *redistribute information, knowledge* (skills to act on the information), and *rewards.*[49] A company might give frontline employees the power to act as "customer advocates," doing whatever is necessary to satisfy customers. The company needs to disseminate information by sharing customer expectations and feedback as well as financial information. The employees must know about the goals of the business as well as how key value-creating activities in the organization are related to each other. Finally, organizations should allocate rewards on how effectively employees use information, knowledge, and power to improve customer service quality and the company's overall performance.[50]

Let's take a look at Whole Foods Market, Inc., the largest natural foods grocer in the United States.[51] An important benefit of the sharing of internal information at Whole Foods becomes the active process of *internal benchmarking*. Competition is intense at Whole Foods. Teams compete against their own goals for sales, growth, and productivity; they compete against different teams in their stores; and they compete against similar teams at different stores and regions. There is an elaborate system of peer reviews through which teams benchmark each other. The "Store Tour" is the most intense. On a periodic schedule, each Whole Foods store is toured by a group of as many as 40 visitors from another region. Lateral learning—discovering what your colleagues are doing right and carrying those practices into your organization—has become a driving force at Whole Foods.

In addition to enhancing the sharing of company information both up and down as well as across the organization, leaders also have to develop means to tap into some of the more informal sources of internal information. In a recent survey of presidents, CEOs, board members, and top executives in a variety of nonprofit organizations, respondents were asked what differentiated the successful candidates for promotion. The consensus: The executive was seen as a person who listens. According to Peter Meyer, the author of the study, "The value of listening is clear: You cannot succeed in running a company if you do not hear what your people, customers, and suppliers are telling you. . . . Listening and understanding well are key to making good decisions."[52]

Gathering and Integrating External Information

Recognizing opportunities, as well as threats, in the external environment is vital to a firm's success. As organizations *and* environments become more complex and evolve rapidly, it is far more critical for employees and managers to become more aware of environmental trends and events—both general and industry-specific—and more knowledgeable about their firm's competitors and customers. Next, we will discuss some ideas on how to do it.

First, the Internet has dramatically accelerated the speed with which anyone can track down useful information or locate people who might have useful information. Prior to the Net, locating someone who used to work at a company—always a good source of information—was quite a challenge. However, today people post their résumés on the web; they participate in discussion groups and talk openly about where they work.

Marc Friedman, manager of market research at $1 billion Andrew Corporation, a fast-growing manufacturer of wireless communications products provides an example of effective Internet use.[53] One of Friedman's preferred sites to visit is Corptech's website, which provides information on 45,000 high-tech companies and more than 170,000 executives. One of his firm's product lines consisted of antennae for air-traffic control systems. He got a request to provide a country-by-country breakdown of upgrade plans for various airports. He knew nothing about air-traffic control at the time. However, he found a site on the Internet for the International Civil Aviation Organization. Fortunately, it had a great deal of useful data, including several research companies working in his area of interest.

Second, company employees at all levels can use "garden variety" traditional sources to acquire external information. Much can be gleaned by reading trade and professional journals, books, and popular business magazines. Other venues for gathering external information include membership in professional or trade organizations, attendance at meetings and conventions, and networking among colleagues inside and outside of your industry. Intel's Andy Grove gathers information from people like DreamWorks SKG's Steven Spielberg and Tele-Communications Inc.'s John Malone.[54] He believes that such interaction provides insights into how to make personal computers more entertaining and better at communicating. Internally, Grove spends time with the young engineers who run Intel Architecture labs, an Oregon-based facility that Grove hopes will become the de facto R&D lab for the entire PC industry.

Third, benchmarking can be a useful means of employing external information. Here managers seek out the best examples of a particular practice as part of an ongoing effort to improve the corresponding practice in their own organization.[55] There are two primary types of benchmarking. *Competitive benchmarking* restricts the search for best practices to competitors, while *functional benchmarking* endeavors to determine best practices regardless of industry. Industry-specific standards (e.g., response times required to repair power outages in the electric utility industry) are typically best handled through competitive benchmarking, whereas more generic processes (e.g., answering 1-800 calls) lend themselves to functional benchmarking because the function is essentially the same in any industry.

benchmarking
managers seeking out best examples of a particular practice as part of an ongoing effort to improve the corresponding practice in their own organization.

competitive benchmarking
benchmarking where the examples are drawn from competitors in the industry.

functional benchmarking
benchmarking where the examples are drawn from any organization, even those outside the industry.

Ford Motor Company used benchmarking to study Mazda's accounts payable operations.[56] Its initial goal of a 20 percent cut in its 500-employee accounts payable staff was ratcheted up to 75 percent—and met. Ford found that staff spent most of their time trying to match conflicting data in a mass of paper, including purchase orders, invoices, and receipts. Following Mazda's example, Ford created an "invoiceless system" in which invoices no longer trigger payments to suppliers. The receipt does the job.

Fourth, focus directly on customers for information. For example, William McKnight, head of 3M's Chicago sales office, required that salesmen of abrasives products talk directly to the workers in the shop to find out what they needed, instead of calling on only front-office executives.[57] This was very innovative at the time—1909! But it illustrates the need to get to the end user of a product or service. (McKnight went on to become 3M's president from 1929 to 1949 and chairman from 1949 to 1969.) More recently, James Taylor, senior vice president for global marketing at Gateway 2000, discussed the value of customer input in reducing response time, a critical success factor in the PC industry.

> We talk to 100,000 people a day—people calling to order a computer, shopping around, looking for tech support. Our website gets 1.1 million hits per day. The time it takes for an idea to enter this organization, get processed, and then go to customers for feedback is down to minutes. We've designed the company around speed and feedback.[58]

Challenging the Status Quo and Enabling Creativity

Earlier in this chapter we discussed some of the barriers that leaders face when trying to bring about change in an organization: vested interests in the status quo, systemic barriers, behavioral barriers, political barriers, and personal time constraints. For a firm to become a learning organization, it must overcome such barriers in order to foster creativity and enable it to permeate the firm. This becomes quite a challenge if the firm is entrenched in a status quo mentality.

Perhaps the best way to challenge the status quo is for the leader to forcefully create a sense of urgency. For example, when Tom Kasten was vice president of Levi Strauss, he had a direct approach to initiating change.

> You create a compelling picture of the risks of *not* changing. We let our people hear directly from customers. We videotaped interviews with customers and played excerpts. One big customer said, "We trust many of your competitors implicitly. We sample their deliveries. We open *all* Levi's deliveries." Another said, "Your lead times are the worst. If you weren't Levi's, you'd be gone." It was powerful. I wish we had done more of it.[59]

Such initiative, if sincere and credible, establishes a shared mission and the need for major transformations. It can channel energies to bring about both change and creative endeavors.

Establishing a "culture of dissent" can be another effective means of questioning the status quo and serving as a spur toward creativity. Here norms are established whereby dissenters can openly question a superior's perspective without fear of retaliation or retribution. Consider the perspective of Steven Balmer, Microsoft's CEO.

> Bill [Gates] brings to the company the idea that conflict can be a good thing. . . . Bill knows it's important to avoid that gentle civility that keeps you from getting to the heart of an issue quickly. He likes it when anyone, even a junior employee, challenges him, and you know he respects you when he starts shouting back.[60]

Motorola has gone a step further and institutionalized its culture of dissent.[61] By filing a "minority report," an employee can go above his or her immediate supervisor's head and officially lodge a different point of view on a business decision. According to former CEO George Fisher, "I'd call it a healthy spirit of discontent and a freedom by and large to express your discontent around here or to disagree with whoever it is in the company, me or anybody else."

Closely related to the culture of dissent is the fostering of a culture that encourages risk taking. "If you're not making mistakes, you're not taking risks, and that means you're not going anywhere," claimed John Holt, coauthor of *Celebrate Your Mistakes*.[62] "The key is to make errors faster than the competition, so you have more chances to learn and win."

Companies that cultivate cultures of experimentation and curiosity make sure that *failure* is not, in essence, an obscene word. They encourage mistakes as a key part of their competitive advantage. This philosophy was shared by Stan Shih, CEO of Acer, a Taiwan-based computer company. If a manager at Acer took an intelligent risk and made a mistake—even a costly one—Shih wrote off the loss as tuition payment for the manager's education. Such a culture must permeate the entire organization. As a high-tech executive told us during an interview: "Every person has a freedom to fail."

Exhibit 11.6 has insights on how organizations can both embrace risk and learn from failure.

Exhibit 11.6   Best Practices: Learning from Failures

It's innovation's great paradox: Success—that is, true breakthroughs—usually comes through failure. Here are some ideas on how to help your team get comfortable with taking risks and learning from mistakes:

- **Formalize Forums for Failure**
  To keep failures and the valuable lessons they offer from getting swept under the rug, *carve out time for reflection.* GE recently began sharing lessons from failures by bringing together managers whose "Imagination Breakthrough" efforts are put on the shelf.

- **Move the Goalposts**
  Innovation requires flexibility in meeting goals, since early predictions are often little more than educated guesses. Intuit's Scott Cook even suggests that teams developing new products ignore forecasts in the early days. "For every one of our failures, we had spreadsheets that looked awesome," he says.

- **Share Personal Stories**
  If employees hear leaders discussing their own failures, *they'll feel more comfortable talking about their own.* But it's not just the CEO's job. Front-line leaders are even more important, says Harvard Business School professor Amy Edmondson. "That person needs to be inviting, curious, and the first to say: 'I made a mistake.'"

- **Bring in Outsiders**
  Outsiders can *help neutralize the emotions and biases that prop up a flop.* Customers can be the most valuable. After its DNA chip failed, Corning brought pharmaceutical companies in early to test its new drug-discovery technology, Epic.

- **Prove Yourself Wrong, Not Right**
  Development teams tend to look for supporting, rather than countervailing, evidence. "You have to reframe what you're seeking in the early days," says Innosight's Scott Anthony. *"You're not really seeking proof that you have the right answer.* It's more about testing to prove yourself wrong."

- **Celebrate Smart Failures**
  Managers should design performance-management systems that reward risk taking and foster a long-term view. But they should also *celebrate failures that teach something new,* energizing people to try again and offering them closure.

Source: From J. McGregor, "How Failure Breeds Success,". *Bloombarg BusinessWeek*, July 10, 2006, pp. 42–52. used with permission of *Bloombery BusinessWeek*. Copyright © 2006. All rights reserved.

Creating an Ethical Organization

Ethics may be defined as a system of right and wrong.[63] Ethics assists individuals in deciding when an act is moral or immoral, socially desirable or not. The sources for an individual's ethics include religious beliefs, national and ethnic heritage, family practices, community standards, educational experiences, and friends and neighbors. Business ethics is the application of ethical standards to commercial enterprise.

Individual Ethics versus Organizational Ethics

Many leaders think of ethics as a question of personal scruples, a confidential matter between employees and their consciences. Such leaders are quick to describe any wrong-doing as an isolated incident, the work of a rogue employee. They assume the company should not bear any responsibility for individual misdeeds. In their view, ethics has nothing to do with leadership.

Ethics has everything to do with leadership. Seldom does the character flaw of a lone actor completely explain corporate misconduct. Instead, unethical business practices typically involve the tacit, if not explicit, cooperation of others and reflect the values, attitudes, and behavior patterns that define an organization's operating culture. Ethics is as much an organizational as a personal issue. Leaders who fail to provide proper leadership to institute proper systems and controls that facilitate ethical conduct share responsibility with those who conceive, execute, and knowingly benefit from corporate misdeeds.[64]

The **ethical orientation** of a leader is a key factor in promoting ethical behavior. Ethical leaders must take personal, ethical responsibility for their actions and decision making. Leaders who exhibit high ethical standards become role models for others and raise an organization's overall level of ethical behavior. Ethical behavior must start with the leader before the employees can be expected to perform accordingly.

There has been a growing interest in corporate ethical performance. Some reasons for this trend may be the increasing lack of confidence regarding corporate activities, the growing emphasis on quality of life issues, and a spate of recent corporate scandals. Without a strong ethical culture, the chance of ethical crises occurring is enhanced. Ethical crises can be very expensive—both in terms of financial costs and in the erosion of human capital and overall firm reputation. Merely adhering to the minimum regulatory standards may not be enough to remain competitive in a world that is becoming more socially conscious. Strategy Spotlight 11.6 highlights potential ethical problems at utility companies that are trying to capitalize on consumers' desire to participate in efforts to curb global warming.

The past several years have been characterized by numerous examples of unethical and illegal behavior by many top-level corporate executives. These include executives of firms such as Enron, Tyco, WorldCom, Inc., Adelphia, and Healthsouth Corp., who were all forced to resign and are facing (or have been convicted of) criminal charges. Perhaps the most glaring example is Bernie Madoff, whose Ponzi scheme, which unraveled in 2008, defrauded investors of $50 billion in assets they had set aside for retirement and charitable donations.

The ethical organization is characterized by a conception of ethical values and integrity as a driving force of the enterprise.[65] Ethical values shape the search for opportunities, the design of organizational systems, and the decision-making process used by individuals and groups. They provide a common frame of reference that serves as a unifying force across different functions, lines of business, and employee groups. Organizational ethics helps to define what a company is and what it stands for.

There are many potential benefits of an ethical organization, but they are often indirect. Research has found somewhat inconsistent results concerning the overall relationship between ethical performance and measures of financial performance.[66] However, positive

ethics a system of right and wrong that assists individuals in deciding when an act is moral or immoral and/or socially desirable or not.

organizational ethics the values, attitudes, and behavioral patterns that define an organization's operating culture and that determine what an organization holds as acceptable behavior.

ethical orientation the practices that firms use to promote an ethical business culture, including ethical role models, corporate credos and codes of conduct, ethically-based reward and evaluation systems, and consistently enforced ethical policies and procedures.

Green Energy: Real or Just a Marketing Ploy?

Many consumers want to "go green" and are looking for opportunities to do so. Utility companies that provide heat and electricity are one of the most obvious places to turn, because they often use fossil fuels that could be saved through energy conservation or replaced by using alternative energy sources. In fact, some consumers are willing to pay a premium to contribute to environmental sustainability efforts if paying a little more will help curb global warming. Knowing this, many power companies in the United States have developed alternative energy programs and appealed to customers to help pay for them.

Unfortunately, many of the power companies that are offering eco-friendly options are falling short on delivering on them. Some utilities have simply gotten off to a slow start or found it difficult to profitably offer alternative power. Others, however, are suspected of committing a new type of fraud—"greenwashing." This refers to companies that make unsubstantiated claims about how

environmentally friendly their products or services really are. In the case of many power companies, their claims of "green power" are empty promises. Instead of actually generating additional renewable energy, most of the premiums are going for marketing costs. "They are preying on people's goodwill," says Stephen Smith, executive director of the Southern Alliance for Clean Energy, an advocacy group in Knoxville, Tennessee.

Exhibit 11.7 shows what three power companies offered and how the money was actually spent. Unfortunately, utilities that spend only a fraction of voluntary energy premiums on renewable energy are becoming more rather than less common. It will likely be up to consumers or Public Service Commissions to hold the utilities to a higher ethical standard—either by making power companies' advertising more truthful or, better still, by insisting that they deliver on their renewable energy promises. Either way, the idea of defrauding customers who are trying to "do the right thing" makes the utilities' unethical decision even more dishonorable.

 environmental sustainability

Sources: Elgin, B. & Holden, D. 2008. Green Power: Buyers Beware. *Business-Week*, September 29: 68–70; and *www.cleanenergy.org*.

Exhibit 11.7   How "Green" Utilities Actually Used Customer Payments

Company/Program	What Customers Were Told	What Really Happened
Duke Energy of Indiana GoGreen Power	Pay a green energy premium and a specified amount of electricity will be obtained from renewable sources.	Less than 18 percent of voluntary customer contributions in a recent year went to renewable energy development.
Alliant Energy of Iowa Second Nature™	"Support the growth of earth-friendly 'green power' created by wind and biomass."	More than 56 percent of expenditures went to marketing and administrative costs, not green energy development.
Georgia Power Green Energy®	Paying the premium "is equivalent to planting 125 trees or not driving 2,000 miles" and will "help bring more renewable power to Georgia."	Customers pay an annual $54 premium, but green energy is actually cheaper to provide than electricity from conventional sources.

Sources: Elgin, B. & Holden, D. 2008. Green Power: Buyers Beware. *BusinessWeek*, September 29: 68–70; *www.alliantenergy.com; www.duke-energy.com;* and *www.georgiapower.com*.

relationships have generally been found between ethical performance and strong organizational culture, increased employee efforts, lower turnover, higher organizational commitment, and enhanced social responsibility.

The advantages of a strong ethical orientation can have a positive effect on employee commitment and motivation to excel. This is particularly important in today's knowledge-intensive organizations, where human capital is critical in creating value and competitive advantages. Positive, constructive relationships among individuals (i.e., social capital) are vital in leveraging human capital and other resources in an organization. Drawing on the concept of stakeholder management, an ethically sound organization can also strengthen its bonds among its suppliers, customers, and governmental agencies.

Integrity-Based versus Compliance-Based Approaches to Organizational Ethics

Before discussing the key elements of an ethical organization, one must understand the links between organizational integrity and the personal integrity of an organization's members.[67] There cannot be high-integrity organizations without high-integrity individuals. However, individual integrity is rarely self-sustaining. Even good people can lose their bearings when faced with pressures, temptations, and heightened performance expectations in the absence of organizational support systems and ethical boundaries. Organizational integrity rests on a concept of purpose, responsibility, and ideals for an organization as a whole. An important responsibility of leadership is to create this ethical framework and develop the organizational capabilities to make it operational.[68]

Lynn Paine, an ethics scholar at Harvard, identifies two approaches: the compliance-based approach and the integrity-based approach. (See Exhibit 11.8 for a comparison of compliance-based and integrity-based strategies.) Faced with the prospect of litigation, several organizations reactively implement **compliance-based ethics programs.** Such programs are typically designed by a corporate counsel with the goal of preventing, detecting, and punishing legal violations. But being ethical is much more than being legal, and an integrity-based approach addresses the issue of ethics in a more comprehensive manner.

>LO11.6
The difference between integrity-based and compliance-based approaches to organizational ethics.

compliance-based ethics programs programs for building ethical organizations that have the goal of preventing, detecting, and punishing legal violations.

Exhibit 11.8 Approaches to Ethics Management

Characteristics	Compliance-Based Approach	Integrity-Based Approach
Ethos	Conformity with externally imposed standards	Self-governance according to chosen standards
Objective	Prevent criminal misconduct	Enable responsible conduct
Leadership	Lawyer-driven	Management-driven with aid of lawyers, HR, and others
Methods	Education, reduced discretion, auditing and controls, penalties	Education, leadership, accountability, organizational systems and decision processes, auditing and controls, penalties
Behavioral Assumptions	Autonomous beings guided by material self-interest	Social beings guided by material self-interest, values, ideals, peers

Source: Reprinted by permission of *Harvard Business Review*. Exhibit from "Managing Organizational Integrity," by L. S. Paine. Copyright © 1994 by the Harvard Business School Publishing Corporation; all rights reserved.

integrity-based ethics programs

programs for building ethical organizations that combine a concern for law with an emphasis on managerial responsibility for ethical behavior, including (1) enabling ethical conduct; (2) examining the organization's and members' core guiding values, thoughts, and actions; and (3) defining the responsibilities and aspirations that constitute an organization's ethical compass.

Integrity-based ethics programs combine a concern for law with an emphasis on managerial responsibility for ethical behavior. It is broader, deeper, and more demanding than a legal compliance initiative. It is broader in that it seeks to enable responsible conduct. It is deeper in that it cuts to the ethos and operating systems of an organization and its members, their core guiding values, thoughts, and actions. It is more demanding because it requires an active effort to define the responsibilities that constitute an organization's ethical compass. Most importantly, organizational ethics is seen as the responsibility of management.

A corporate counsel may play a role in designing and implementing integrity strategies, but it is managers at all levels and across all functions that are involved in the process. Once integrated into the day-to-day operations, such strategies can prevent damaging ethical lapses, while tapping into powerful human impulses for moral thought and action. Ethics becomes the governing ethos of an organization and not burdensome constraints. Here is an example of an organization that goes beyond mere compliance to laws in building an ethical organization:

> In teaching ethics to its employees, Texas Instruments, the $14 billion chip and electronics manufacturer, asks them to run an issue through the following steps: Is it legal? Is it consistent with the company's stated values? Will the employee feel bad doing it? What will the public think if the action is reported in the press? Does the employee think it is wrong? If the employees are not sure of the ethicality of the issue, they are encouraged to ask someone until they are clear about it. In the process, employees can approach high-level personnel and even the company's lawyers. At TI, the question of ethics goes much beyond merely being legal. It is no surprise, that this company is a benchmark for corporate ethics and has been a recipient of three ethics awards: the David C. Lincoln Award for Ethics and Excellence in Business, American Business Ethics Award, and Bentley College Center for Business Ethics Award.[69]

Compliance-based approaches are externally motivated—that is, based on the fear of punishment for doing something unlawful. On the other hand, integrity-based approaches are driven by a personal and organizational commitment to ethical behavior.

A firm must have several key elements to become a highly ethical organization:

>LO11.7

Several key elements that organizations must have to become an ethical organization.

- Role models.
- Corporate credos and codes of conduct.
- Reward and evaluation systems.
- Policies and procedures.

These elements are highly interrelated. Reward structures and policies will be useless if leaders are not sound role models. That is, leaders who implicitly say, "Do as I say, not as I do," will quickly have their credibility eroded and such actions will sabotage other elements that are essential to building an ethical organization.

Role Models

For good or for bad, leaders are role models in their organizations. Leaders must "walk the talk"; they must be consistent in their words and deeds. The values as well as the character of leaders become transparent to an organization's employees through their behaviors. When leaders do not believe in the ethical standards that they are trying to inspire, they will not be effective as good role models. Being an effective leader often includes taking responsibility for ethical lapses within the organization—even though the executives themselves are not directly involved. Consider the perspective of Dennis Bakke, CEO of AES, the $14 billion global electricity company based in Arlington, Virginia.

> There was a major breach (in 1992) of the AES values. Nine members of the water treatment team in Oklahoma lied to the EPA about water quality at the plant. There was no environmental damage, but they lied about the test results. A new, young chemist at the plant discovered it, told a team leader, and we then were notified. Now, you could argue that the people who lied were responsible and were accountable, but the senior management team also took responsibility by taking pay cuts. My reduction was about 30 percent.[70]

11.7

strategy spotlight

Elements of a Corporate Code

Corporate codes are not simply useful for conveying organizational norms and policies, but they also serve to legitimize an organization in the eyes of others. In the United States, federal guidelines advise judges, when determining how to sentence a company convicted of a crime, to consider whether it had a written code and was out of compliance with its own ethical guidelines. The United Nations and countries around the world have endorsed codes as a way to promote corporate social responsibility. As such, a code provides an increasingly important corporate social contract that signals a company's willingness to act ethically

For employees, codes of conduct serve four key purposes:

1. Help employees from diverse backgrounds work more effectively across cultural backgrounds.

2. Provide a reference point for decision making.

3. Help attract individuals who want to work for a business that embraces high standards.

4. Help a company to manage risk by reducing the likelihood of damaging misconduct.

With recent scandals on Wall Street, many corporations are trying to put more teeth into their codes of conduct. Nasdaq now requires that listed companies distribute a code to all employees. German software giant SAP's code informs employees that violations of the code "can result in consequences that affect employment, and could possibly lead to external investigation, civil law proceedings, or criminal charges." Clearly, codes of conduct are an important part of maintaining an ethical organization.

Sources: Paine, L., Deshpande, R., Margolis, J. D., & Bettcher, K. E. 2005. Up to Code: Does Your Company's Conduct Meet World Class Standards? *Harvard Business Review*, 82(12): 122–126, and Stone, A. 2004. Putting Teeth in Corporate Ethics Codes. *www.businessweek.com*, February 19.

Such action enhances the loyalty and commitment of employees throughout the organization. Many would believe that it would have been much easier (and personally less expensive!) for Bakke and his management team to merely take strong punitive action against the nine individuals who were acting contrary to the behavior expected in AES's ethical culture. However, by taking responsibility for the misdeeds, the top executives—through their highly visible action—made it clear that responsibility and penalties for ethical lapses go well beyond the "guilty" parties. Such courageous behavior by leaders helps to strengthen an organization's ethical environment.

Corporate Credos and Codes of Conduct

Corporate credos and codes of conduct are mechanisms that provide statements of norms and beliefs as well as guidelines for decision making. They provide employees with a clear understanding of the organization's policies and ethical position. Such guidelines also provide the basis for employees to refuse to commit unethical acts and help to make them aware of issues before they are faced with the situation. For such codes to be truly effective, organization members must be aware of them and what behavioral guidelines they contain.[71] Strategy Spotlight 11.7 identifies four key reasons why codes of conduct support organizational efforts to maintain a safe and ethical workplace.

corporate credo a statement of the beliefs typically held by managers in a corporation.

Large corporations are not the only ones to develop and use codes of conduct. Consider the example of Wetherill Associates (WAI), a small, privately held supplier of electrical parts to the automotive market.

Rather than a conventional code of conduct, WAI has a Quality Assurance Manual—a combination of philosophy text, conduct guide, technical manual, and company profile—that describes the company's commitment to honesty, ethical action, and integrity. WAI doesn't have a corporate ethics officer, because the company's corporate ethics officer is

Exhibit 11.9

Johnson & Johnson's
Credo

We believe our first responsibility is to the doctors, nurses and patients, to mothers and fathers and all others who use our products and services. In meeting their needs everything we do must be of high quality. We must constantly strive to reduce our costs in order to maintain reasonable prices. Customers' orders must be serviced promptly and accurately. Our suppliers and distributors must have an opportunity to make a fair profit.

We are responsible to our employees, the men and women who work with us throughout the world. Everyone must be considered as an individual. We must respect their dignity and recognize their merit. They must have a sense of security in their jobs. Compensation must be fair and adequate, and working conditions clean, orderly, and safe. We must be mindful of ways to help our employees fulfill their family responsibilities. Employees must feel free to make suggestions and complaints. There must be equal opportunity for employment, development, and advancement for those qualified. We must provide competent management, and their actions must be just and ethical.

We are responsible to the communities in which we live and work and to the world community as well. We must be good citizens—support good works and charities and bear our fair share of taxes. We must encourage civic improvements and better health and education. We must maintain in good order the property we are privileged to use, protecting the environment and natural resources

Our final responsibility is to our stockholders. Business must make a sound profit. We must experiment with new ideas. Research must be carried on, innovative programs developed, and mistakes paid for. New equipment must be purchased, new facilities provided, and new products launched. Reserves must be created to provide for adverse times. When we operate according to these principles, the stockholders should realize a fair return.

Source: Reprinted with permission of Johnson & Johnson Co.

Marie Bothe, WAI's CEO. She sees her main function as keeping the 350-employee company on the path of ethical behavior and looking for opportunities to help the community. She delegates the "technical" aspects of the business—marketing, finance, personnel, and operations—to other members of the organization.[72]

Perhaps the best-known credo is that of Johnson & Johnson (J&J). It is reprinted in Exhibit 11.9. The credo stresses honesty, integrity, superior products, and putting people before profits. What distinguishes the J&J credo from others is the amount of energy the company's top managers devote to ensuring that employees live by its precepts:

Over a recent three-year period, Johnson & Johnson undertook a massive effort to assure that its original credo, already decades old, was still valid. More than 1,200 managers attended two-day seminars in groups of 25, with explicit instructions to challenge the credo. The president or CEO of the firm presided over each session. The company came out of the process believing that its original document was still valid. However, the questioning process continues. Such "challenge meetings" are still replicated every other year for all new managers. These efforts force J&J to question, internalize, and then implement its credo. Such investments have paid off handsomely many times—most notably in 1982, when eight people died from swallowing capsules of Tylenol, one of its flagship products, that someone had laced with cyanide. Leaders such as James Burke, who without hesitation made an across-the-board recall of the product even though it affected only a limited number of untraceable units, send a strong message throughout the firm.

Reward and Evaluation Systems

It is entirely possible for a highly ethical leader to preside over an organization that commits several unethical acts. How? A flaw in the organization's reward structure may inadvertently cause individuals to act in an inappropriate manner if rewards are seen as being distributed on the basis of outcomes rather than the means by which goals and objectives are achieved.[73]

Consider the example of Sears, Roebuck & Co.'s automotive operations. Here, unethical behavior, rooted in a faulty reward system, took place primarily at the operations level: its automobile repair facilities.[74]

In 1992 Sears was flooded with complaints about its automotive service business. Consumers and attorneys general in more than 40 states accused the firm of misleading customers and selling them unnecessary parts and services, from brake jobs to front-end alignments.

In the face of declining revenues and eroding market share, Sears's management had attempted to spur the performance of its auto centers by introducing new goals and incentives for mechanics. Automotive service advisers were given product-specific quotas for a variety of parts and repairs. Failure to meet the quotas could lead to transfers and reduced hours. Many employees spoke of "pressure, pressure, pressure" to bring in sales.

Not too surprisingly, the judgment of many employees suffered. In essence, employees were left to chart their own course, given the lack of management guidance and customer ignorance. The bottom line: In settling the spate of lawsuits, Sears offered coupons to customers who had purchased certain auto services over the most recent two-year period. The total cost of the settlement, including potential customer refunds, was estimated to be $60 million. The cost in terms of damaged reputation? Difficult to assess, but certainly not trivial.

This example makes two points. First, inappropriate reward systems may cause individuals at all levels throughout an organization to commit unethical acts that they might not otherwise commit. Second, the penalties in terms of damage to reputations, human capital erosion, and financial loss—in the short run and long run—are typically much higher than any gains that could be obtained through such unethical behavior.

Many companies have developed reward and evaluation systems that evaluate whether a manager is acting in an ethical manner. For example, Raytheon, a $20 billion defense contractor, incorporates the following items in its "Leadership Assessment Instrument":[75]

- Maintains unequivocal commitment to honesty, truth, and ethics in every facet of behavior.
- Conforms with the letter and intent of company policies while working to affect any necessary policy changes.
- Actions are consistent with words; follows through on commitments; readily admits mistakes.
- Is trusted and inspires others to be trusted.

Introducing *Johnson's* moisture care baby wash

After bathing about a billion babies, we know there's more to it than just soap and water.

Introducing JOHNSON'S Moisture Care Baby Wash
With a loving touch of baby lotion for soft, irresistible skin, that perfect baby smell, and memories that will last forever. New JOHNSON'S Moisture Care Baby Wash.

this feels right

baby.com

● Johnson & Johnson is well-known for its credo, which stresses honesty, integrity, superior products, and putting people before profits.

As noted by Dan Burnham, Raytheon's former CEO: "What do we look for in a leadership candidate with respect to integrity? What we're really looking for are people who have developed an inner gyroscope of ethical principles. We look for people for whom ethical thinking is part of what they do—no different from 'strategic thinking' or 'tactical thinking.'"

Policies and Procedures

Many situations that a firm faces have regular, identifiable patterns. Leaders tend to handle such routine by establishing a policy or procedure to be followed that can be applied uniformly to each occurrence. Such guidelines can be useful in specifying the proper relationships with a firm's customers and suppliers. For example, Levi Strauss has developed stringent global sourcing guidelines and Chemical Bank (part of J. P. Morgan Chase Bank) has a policy of forbidding any review that would determine if suppliers are Chemical customers when the bank awards contracts.

Carefully developed policies and procedures guide behavior so that all employees will be encouraged to behave in an ethical manner. However, they must be reinforced with effective communication, enforcement, and monitoring, as well as sound corporate governance practices. In addition, the Sarbanes-Oxley Act of 2002 provides considerable legal protection to employees of publicly traded companies who report unethical or illegal practices. Provisions in the Act coauthored by Senator Grassley include:[76]

- Make it unlawful to "discharge, demote, suspend, threaten, harass, or in any manner discriminate against 'a whistleblower.'"
- Establish criminal penalties of up to 10 years in jail for executives who retaliate against whistleblowers.
- Require board audit committees to establish procedures for hearing whistleblower complaints.
- Allow the Secretary of Labor to order a company to rehire a terminated whistleblower with no court hearings whatsoever.
- Give a whistleblower the right to a jury trial, bypassing months or years of cumbersome administrative hearings.

Reflecting on Career Implications . . .

- **Strategic Leadership:** Do managers in your firm effectively set the direction; design the organization; and, instill a culture committed to excellence and ethical behavior? If you are in a position of leadership, do you practice all of these three elements effectively?
- **Power:** What sources of power do managers in your organization use? For example, if there is an overemphasis on organizational sources of power (e.g., position power); there could be negative implications for creativity, morale and turnover among professionals. How much power do you have? What is the basis of it? How might it be used to both advance your career goals and benefit the firm?
- **Emotional Intelligence:** Do leaders of your firm have sufficient levels of EI? Alternatively, are there excessive levels of EI present that have negative implications for your organization? Is your level of EI sufficient to allow you to have effective interpersonal and judgment skills in order to enhance your career success?
- **Learning Organization:** Does your firm effectively practice all five elements of the learning organization? If one or more elements are absent, adaptability and change will be compromised. What can you do to enhance any of the elements that might be lacking?
- **Ethics:** Does your organization practice a compliance-based or integrity-based ethical culture? Integrity-based cultures can enhance your personal growth. In addition, such cultures foster greater loyalty and commitment among all employees.

Summary

Strategic leadership is vital in ensuring that strategies are formulated and implemented in an effective manner. Leaders must play a central role in performing three critical and interdependent activities: setting the direction, designing the organization, and nurturing a culture committed to excellence and ethical behavior. If leaders ignore or are ineffective at performing any one of the three, the organization will not be very successful. We also identified three elements of leadership that contribute to success—integrative thinking, overcoming barriers to change, and the effective use of power.

For leaders to effectively fulfill their activities, emotional intelligence (EI) is very important. Five elements that contribute to EI are self-awareness, self-regulation, motivation, empathy, and social skill. The first three elements pertain to self-management skills, whereas the last two are associated with a person's ability to manage relationships with others. We also addressed some of the potential drawbacks from the ineffective use of EI. These include the dysfunctional use of power as well as a tendency to become overly empathetic, which may result in unreasonably lowered performance expectations.

Leaders must also play a central role in creating a learning organization. Gone are the days when the top-level managers "think" and everyone else in the organization "does." With the rapidly changing, unpredictable, and complex competitive environments that characterize most industries, leaders must engage everyone in the ideas and energies of people throughout the organization. Great ideas can come from anywhere in the organization—from the executive suite to the factory floor. The five elements that we discussed as central to a learning organization are inspiring and motivating people with a mission or purpose, empowering people at all levels throughout the organization, accumulating and sharing internal knowledge, gathering external information, and challenging the status quo to stimulate creativity.

In the final section of the chapter, we addressed a leader's central role in instilling ethical behavior in the organization. We discussed the enormous costs that firms face when ethical crises arise—costs in terms of financial and reputational loss as well as the erosion of human capital and relationships with suppliers, customers, society at large, and governmental agencies. And, as we would expect, the benefits of having a strong ethical organization are also numerous. We contrasted compliance-based and integrity-based approaches to organizational ethics. Compliance-based approaches are largely externally motivated; that is, they are motivated by the fear of punishment for doing something that is unlawful. Integrity-based approaches, on the other hand, are driven by a personal and organizational commitment to ethical behavior. We also addressed the four key elements of an ethical organization: role models, corporate credos and codes of conduct, reward and evaluation systems, and policies and procedures.

Summary Review Questions

1. Three key activities—setting a direction, designing the organization, and nurturing a culture and ethics—are all part of what effective leaders do on a regular basis. Explain how these three activities are interrelated.

2. Define emotional intelligence (EI). What are the key elements of EI? Why is EI so important to successful strategic leadership? Address potential "downsides."

3. The knowledge a firm possesses can be a source of competitive advantage. Describe ways that a firm can continuously learn to maintain its competitive position.

4. How can the five central elements of "learning organizations" be incorporated into global companies?

5. What are the benefits to firms and their shareholders of conducting business in an ethical manner?

6. Firms that fail to behave in an ethical manner can incur high costs. What are these costs and what is their source?

7. What are the most important differences between an "integrity organization" and a "compliance organization" in a firm's approach to organizational ethics?

8. What are some of the important mechanisms for promoting ethics in a firm?

Key Terms

leadership, 395
setting a direction, 397
designing the
    organization, 398
excellent and ethical
    organizational
    culture, 398
integrative thinking, 401
barriers to change, 402
vested intrest in
    the status quo, 402
systemic barriers, 402
behavioral barriers, 403
political barriers, 404
power, 404
organizational bases of
    power, 404
personal bases of
    power, 404
personal time
    constraints, 404

emotional intelligence
    (EI), 407
learning
    organizations, 411
benchmarking, 414
competitive
    benchmarking, 414
functional
    benchmaking, 414
ethics, 417
organizational
    ethics, 417
ethical
    orientation, 417
compliance-based
    ethics programs, 419
integrity-based
    ethics programs, 420
corporate credo, 421

Experiential Exercise

Select two well-known business leaders—one you admire and one you do not. Evaluate each of them on the five characteristics of emotional intelligence.

Emotional Intelligence Characteristics	Admired Leader	Leader Not Admired
Self-awareness		
Self-regulation		
Motivation		
Empathy		
Social skills		

Application Questions & Exercises

1. Identify two CEOs whose leadership you admire. What is it about their skills, attributes, and effective use of power that causes you to admire them?

2. Founders have an important role in developing their organization's culture and values. At times, their influence persists for many years. Identify and describe two organizations in which the cultures and values established by the founder(s) continue to flourish. You may find research on the Internet helpful in answering these questions.

3. Some leaders place a great emphasis on developing superior human capital. In what ways does this help a firm to develop and sustain competitive advantages?

4. In this chapter we discussed the five elements of a "learning organization." Select a firm with which you are familiar and discuss whether or not it epitomizes some (or all) of these elements.

Ethics Questions

1. Sometimes organizations must go outside the firm to hire talent, thus bypassing employees already working for the firm. Are there conditions under which this might raise ethical considerations?

2. Ethical crises can occur in virtually any organization. Describe some of the systems, procedures, and processes that can help to prevent such crises.

References

1. Smith, R. 2010. Another Duke exit amid inquiry. *Wall Street Journal,* December 7: B3; Smith R. 2010. Corporate news: Indiana panel finds Duke wasn't favored. *Wall Street Journal,* December 9: B4; O'Malley, C. 2010. Scandal rocks IURC, Duke. *Indianapolis Business Journal,* December 27: 13A; Jenkins, H. W. 2010. A fine clean coal mess. *Wall Street Journal,* December 15: A19; Anonymous. 2010. Top Duke executive who resigned after ethics flap gets $10 million severance retirement deal. *Associated Press Newswires,* December 10, 11: 11; Henderson, B. 2010. Duke Energy executive resigns over e-mails. *The Herald,* December 7: 11. We thank Ciprian Stan for his valued contribution.

2. Charan, R. & Colvin, G. 1999. Why CEOs fail. *Fortune,* June 21: 68–78.

3. Yukl, G. 2008. How leaders influence organizational effectiveness. *Leadership Quarterly,* 19(6): 708–722.

4. These three activities and our discussion draw from Kotter, J. P. 1990. What leaders really do. *Harvard Business Review,* 68(3): 103–111; Pearson, A. E. 1990. Six basics for general managers. *Harvard Business Review,* 67(4): 94–101; and Covey, S. R. 1996. Three roles of the leader in the new paradigm. In *The leader of the future:* 149–160. Hesselbein, F., Goldsmith, M., & Beckhard, R. (Eds.). San Francisco: Jossey-Bass.

Some of the discussion of each of the three leadership activity concepts draws on Dess, G. G. & Miller, A. 1993. *Strategic management:* 320–325. New York: McGraw-Hill.

5. García-Morales, V. J., Lloréns-Montes, F. J., & Verdú-Jover, A. J. 2008. The effects of transformational leadership on organizational performance through knowledge and innovation. *British Journal of Management,* 19(4): 299–319.

6. Day, C., Jr. & LaBarre, P. 1994. GE: Just your average everyday $60 billion family grocery store. *Industry Week,* May 2: 13–18.

7. Martin, R. 2010. The execution trap. *Harvard Business Review,* 88(7/8): 64–71.

8. Collins, J. 1997. What comes next? *Inc. Magazine.* October: 34–45.

9. Hsieh, T. 2010. Zappos's CEO on going to extremes for customers. *Harvard Business Review,* 88(7/8): 41–44.

10. Andersen, M. M., Froholdt, M. & Poulfelt, F. 2010. *Return on strategy.* New York: Routledge; and 2009 Huawei Annual Report.

11. Anonymous. 2006. Looking out for number one. *BusinessWeek,* October 30: 66.

12. This section draws on: Chen, M.-J. & Miller, D. 2010. West meets East: Toward an ambicultural approach to management. *Academy of Management Perspectives,* 24(4): 17–24.

13. For an interesting, in-depth interview with Stan Shih, read: Lin, H.-C. & Hou, S. T. 2010. Managerial lessons from the East: An interview with Acer's Stan Shih. *Academy of Management Perspectives,* 24(4): 6–16.

14. Evans, R. 2007. The either/or dilemma. *www.ft.com,* December 19; and Martin, R. L. 2007. *The opposable mind.* Boston: Harvard Business School Press.

15. Schaffer, R. H. 2010. Mistakes leaders keep making. *Harvard Business Review,* 88(9): 86–91.

16. For insightful perspectives on escalation, refer to Brockner, J. 1992. The escalation of commitment to a failing course of action. *Academy of Management Review,* 17(1): 39–61; and Staw, B. M. 1976. Knee-deep in the big muddy: A study of commitment to a chosen course of action. *Organizational Behavior and Human Decision Processes,* 16: 27–44. The discussion of systemic, behavioral, and political barriers draws on Lorange, P. & Murphy, D. 1984. Considerations in implementing strategic control. *Journal of Business Strategy,* 5: 27–35. In a similar vein, Noel M. Tichy has addressed three types of resistance to change in the context of General Electric: technical resistance, political resistance, and cultural resistance. See Tichy, N. M. 1993. Revolutionalize your company. *Fortune,* December 13: 114–118. Examples draw from O'Reilly, B. 1997. The secrets of America's most admired corporations: New ideas and new products. *Fortune,* March 3: 60–64.

17. This section draws on Champoux, J. E. 2000. *Organizational behavior: Essential tenets for a new millennium.* London: South-Western; and The mature use of power in organizations. 2003. *RHR International-Executive Insights,* May 29, *12.19.168.197/ execinsights/8-3.htm.*

18. An insightful perspective on the role of power and politics in organizations is provided in Ciampa, K. 2005. Almost ready: How leaders move up. *Harvard Business Review,* 83(1): 46–53.

19. Pfeffer, J. 2010. Power play. *Harvard Business Review,* 88(7/8): 84–92.

20. Westphal, J. D., & Graebner, M. E. 2010. A matter of appearances: How corporate leaders manage the impressions of financial analysts about the conduct of their boards. *Academy of Management Journal,* 53(4): 15–44.

21. A discussion of the importance of persuasion in bringing about change can be found in Garvin, D. A. & Roberto, M. A. 2005. Change through persuasion. *Harvard Business Review,* 83(4): 104–113.

22. Lorsch, J. W. & Tierney, T. J. 2002. *Aligning the stars: How to succeed when professionals drive results.* Boston: Harvard Business School Press.

23. Some consider EI to be a "trait," that is, an attribute that is stable over time. However, many authors, including Daniel Goleman, have argued that it can be developed through motivation, extended practice, and feedback. For example, in D. Goleman, 1998, What makes a leader? *Harvard Business Review,* 76(5): 97, Goleman addresses this issue in a sidebar: "Can emotional intelligence be learned?"

24. For a review of this literature, see Daft, R. 1999. *Leadership: Theory and practice.* Fort Worth, TX: Dryden Press.

25. This section draws on Luthans, F. 2002. Positive organizational behavior: Developing and managing psychological strengths. *Academy of Management Executive,* 16(1): 57–72; and Goleman, D. 1998. What makes a leader? *Harvard Business Review,* 76(6): 92–105.

26. EI has its roots in the concept of "social intelligence" that was first identified by E. L. Thorndike in 1920 (Intelligence and its uses. *Harper's Magazine,* 140: 227–235). Psychologists have been uncovering other intelligences for some time now and have grouped them into such clusters as abstract intelligence (the ability to understand and manipulate verbal and mathematical symbols), concrete intelligence (the ability to understand and manipulate objects), and social intelligence (the ability to understand and relate to people). See Ruisel, I. 1992. Social intelligence: Conception and methodological problems. *Studia Psychologica,* 34(4–5): 281–296. Refer to *trochim.human.cornell.edu/ gallery.*

27. See, for example, Luthans, op. cit.; Mayer, J. D., Salvoney, P., & Caruso, D. 2000. Models of emotional intelligence. In Sternberg, R. J. (Ed.). *Handbook of intelligence.* Cambridge, UK: Cambridge University Press; and Cameron, K. 1999. Developing emotional intelligence at the Weatherhead School of Management. *Strategy: The Magazine of the Weatherhead School of Management,* Winter: 2–3.

28. Tate, B. 2008. A longitudinal study of the relationships among self-monitoring, authentic leadership, and perceptions of leadership. *Journal of Leadership & Organizational Studies,* 15(1): 16–29.

29. Moss, S. A., Dowling, N., & Callanan, J. 2009. Towards an integrated model of leadership and self-regulation. *Leadership Quarterly,* 20(2): 162–176.

30. An insightful perspective on leadership, which involves discovering, developing and celebrating what is unique about each individual, is found in Buckingham, M. 2005. What great managers do. *Harvard Business Review,* 83(3): 70–79.

31. Redefining leadership. 2010. *Foster Business,* Fall: 8.

32. This section draws upon Klemp. G. 2005. *Emotional intelligence and leadership: What really matters.* Cambria Consulting, Inc., *www. cambriaconsulting.com.*

33. Heifetz, R. 2004. Question authority. *Harvard Business Review,* 82(1): 37.

34. Handy, C. 1995. Trust and the virtual organization. *Harvard Business Review,* 73(3): 40–50.

35. This section draws upon Dess, G. G. & Picken, J. C. 1999. *Beyond productivity.* New York: AMACOM. The elements of the learning organization in this section are consistent with the work of Dorothy Leonard-Barton. See, for example, Leonard-Barton, D. 1992. The factory as a learning laboratory. *Sloan Management Review,* 11: 23–38.

36. Senge, P. M. 1990. The leader's new work: Building learning organizations. *Sloan Management Review,* 32(1): 7–23.

37. Bernoff, J. & Schandler, T. 2010. Empowered. *Harvard Business Review,* 88(7/8): 94–101.

38. Hammer, M. & Stanton, S. A. 1997. The power of reflection. *Fortune,* November 24: 291–296.

39. Hannah, S. T. & Lester, P. B. 2009. A multilevel approach to building and leading learning organizations. *Leadership Quarterly,* 20(1): 34–48.

40. For some guidance on how to effectively bring about change in organizations, refer to Wall, S. J. 2005. The protean organization: Learning to love change. *Organizational Dynamics,* 34(1): 37–46.

41. Covey, S. R. 1989. *The seven habits of highly effective people: Powerful lessons in personal change.* New York: Simon & Schuster.

42. Kouzes, J. M. & Posner, B. Z. 2009. To lead, create a shared vision. *Harvard Business Review,* 87(1): 20–21.

43. Kouzes and Posner, op. cit.

44. Melrose, K. 1995. *Making the grass greener on your side: A CEO's journey to leading by servicing.* San Francisco: Barrett-Koehler.

45. Tekleab, A. G., Sims Jr., H. P., Yun, S., Tesluk, P. E., & Cox, J. 2008. Are we on the same page? Effects of self-awareness of empowering and transformational leadership. *Journal of Leadership & Organizational Studies,* 14(3): 185–201.

46. Quinn, R. C. & Spreitzer, G. M. 1997. The road to empowerment: Seven questions every leader should consider. *Organizational Dynamics,* 25: 37–49.

47. For an interesting perspective on top-down approaches to leadership, see Pellegrini, E. K. & Scandura, T. A. 2008. Paternalistic leadership: A review and agenda for future research. *Journal of Management,* 34(3): 566–593.

48. Helgesen, S. 1996. Leading from the grass roots. In *Leader of the future:* 19–24 Hesselbein et al.

49. Bowen, D. E. & Lawler, E. E.,III. 1995. Empowering service employees. *Sloan Management Review,* 37: 73–84.

50. Easterby-Smith, M. & Prieto, I. M. 2008. Dynamic capabilities and knowledge management: An integrative role for learning? *British Journal of Management,* 19(3): 235–249.

51. Schafer, S. 1997. Battling a labor shortage? It's all in your imagination. *Inc.,* August: 24.

52. Meyer, P. 1998. So you want the president's job . . . *Business Horizons,* January–February: 2–8.

53. Imperato, G. 1998. Competitive intelligence: Get smart! *Fast Company,* May: 268–279.

54. Novicki, C. 1998. The best brains in business. *Fast Company,* April: 125.

55. The introductory discussion of benchmarking draws on Miller, A. 1998. *Strategic management:* 142–143. New York: McGraw-Hill.

56. Port, O. & Smith, G. 1992. Beg, borrow—and benchmark. *Business-Week,* November 30: 74–75.

57. Main, J. 1992. How to steal the best ideas around. *Fortune,* October 19: 102–106.

58. Taylor, J. T. 1997. What happens after what comes next? *Fast Company,* December–January: 84–85.

59. Sheff, D. 1996. Levi's changes everything. *Fast Company,* June–July: 65–74.

60. Isaacson, W. 1997. In search of the real Bill Gates. *Time,* January 13: 44–57.

61. Baatz, E. B. 1993. Motorola's secret weapon. *Electronic Business,* April: 51–53.

62. Holt, J. W. 1996. *Celebrate your mistakes.* New York: McGraw-Hill.

63. This opening discussion draws upon Conley, J. H. 2000. Ethics in business. In Helms, M. M. (Ed.). *Encyclopedia of management* (4th ed.): 281–285; Farmington Hills, MI: Gale Group; Paine, L. S. 1994. Managing for organizational integrity. *Harvard Business Review,* 72(2): 106–117; and Carlson, D. S. & Perrewe, P. L. 1995. Institutionalization of organizational ethics through transformational leadership. *Journal of Business Ethics,* 14: 829–838.

64. Pinto, J., Leana, C. R., & Pil, F. K. 2008. Corrupt organizations or organizations of corrupt individuals? Two types of organization-level corruption. *Academy of Management Review,* 33(3): 685–709.

65. Soule, E. 2002. Managerial moral strategies—in search of a few good principles. *Academy of Management Review,* 27(1): 114–124.

66. Carlson & Perrewe, op. cit.

67. This discussion is based upon Paine. Managing for organizational integrity; Paine, L. S. 1997. *Cases in leadership, ethics, and organizational integrity: A Strategic approach.* Burr Ridge, IL: Irwin; and Fontrodona, J. 2002. Business ethics across the Atlantic. Business Ethics Direct, *www.ethicsa.org/ BED_art_fontrodone.html.*

68. For more on operationalizing capabilities to sustain an ethical framework, see Largay III, J. A. & Zhang, R. 2008. Do CEOs worry about being fired when making investment decisions. *Academy of Management Perspectives,* 22(1): 60–61.

69. See *www.ti.com/corp/docs/company/citizen/ethics/benchmark.shtml;* and *www.ti.com/corp/docs/company/citizen/ethics/quicktest.shtml.*

70. Wetlaufer, S. 1999. Organizing for empowerment: An interview with AES's Roger Sant and Dennis Bakke. *Harvard Business Review,* 77(1): 110–126.

71. For an insightful, academic perspective on the impact of ethics codes on executive decision making, refer to Stevens, J. M., Steensma, H. K., Harrison, D. A., & Cochran, P. S. 2005. Symbolic or substantive document? The influence of ethics code on financial executives' decisions. *Strategic Management Journal,* 26(2): 181–195.

72. Paine. Managing for organizational integrity.

73. For a recent study on the effects of goal setting on unethical behavior, read Schweitzer, M. E., Ordonez, L., & Douma, B. 2004. Goal setting as a motivator of unethical behavior. *Academy of Management Journal,* 47(3): 422–432.

74. Paine. Managing for organizational integrity.

75. Fulmer, R. M. 2004. The challenge of ethical leadership. *Organizational Dynamics,* 33 (3): 307–317.

76. *www.sarbanes-oxley.com.*

TWELVE

Managing Innovation and Fostering Corporate Entrepreneurship

After reading this chapter, you should have a good understanding of:

LO12.1   The importance of implementing strategies and practices that foster innovation.

LO12.2   The challenges and pitfalls of managing corporate innovation processes.

LO12.3   How corporations use new venture teams, business incubators, and product champions to create an internal environment and culture that promote entrepreneurial development.

LO12.4   How corporate entrepreneurship achieves both financial goals and strategic goals.

LO12.5   The benefits and potential drawbacks of real options analysis in making resource deployment decisions in corporate entrepreneurship contexts.

LO12.6   How an entrepreneurial orientation can enhance a firm's efforts to develop promising corporate venture initiatives.

LEARNING OBJECTIVES

To remain competitive, established firms must continually seek out opportunities for growth and new methods for strategically renewing their performance. Changes in customer needs, new technologies, and shifts in the competitive landscape require that companies continually innovate and initiate corporate ventures in order to compete effectively. This chapter addresses how entrepreneurial activities can be an avenue for achieving competitive advantages.

In the first section, we address the importance of innovation in identifying venture opportunities and strategic renewal. Innovations can take many forms, including radical breakthroughs, incremental improvements, and disruptive innovations. Innovations often create new markets, update products or services, and help renew organizational processes. We discuss how firms can successfully manage the innovation process. Impediments and challenges to effective innovation are discussed, and examples of good innovation practices are presented.

We discuss the unique role of corporate entrepreneurship in the strategic management process in the second section. Here we highlight two types of activities corporations use to remain competitive—focused and dispersed. New venture groups and business incubators are often used to focus a firm's entrepreneurial activities. In other corporations, the entrepreneurial spirit is dispersed throughout the organization and gives rise to product champions and other autonomous strategic behaviors that organizational members engage in to foster internal corporate venturing. We also discuss the benefits and potential drawbacks of real options analysis in making decisions about which venture activities merit additional investment and which should be abandoned.

In the final section we describe how a firm's entrepreneurial orientation can contribute to its growth and renewal as well as enhance the methods and processes strategic managers use to recognize opportunities and develop initiatives for internal growth and development. The chapter also evaluates the pitfalls that firms may encounter when implementing entrepreneurial strategies. ●

Learning from Mistakes

In April 2006, *Bloomberg Businessweek* described HTC as "the hottest tech outfit you never heard of," but oh how the times have changed.[1]

Founded in 1997 as a contract manufacturer, the company has long been the world's top maker of mobile handsets using Microsoft's Windows Mobile operating system. HTC has several strategic partnerships, including partners such as Intel, Texas Instruments, and Qualcomm. HTC is known for its innovation and is consistently highly ranked by insiders and consumers alike. It is constantly broadening the range of devices it offers—introducing devices to support specific applications that meet the increasingly diverse needs of its customers and partners. Currently *Bloomberg Businessweek* lists HTC as number 47 of the Most Innovative Companies. HTC Chief Executive Peter Chou says, "Innovation is not a one-time job—innovation is a journey. . . . Hardware innovation is less than half the battle," when it comes to the handheld market.

Let's take a look at what happens when corporate entrepreneurship fails to add value through innovation.

HTC paired its proprietary intuitive user interface, Sense, with Windows Mobile version 6.5, Microsoft's mobile operating system, to create the HD2 Smartphone available through T-Mobile. It features a luxurious 4.3-inch touch screen, Qualcomm Snapdragon processor (the same one that powers Google's Nexus One), 5-megapixel camera with flash, and all in sleek design that fits in a shirt pocket! Just one catch, Microsoft's operating system is soon to be obsolete, and its new Windows Mobile 7 is not backward compatible. Bottom line: Consumers are spending $199 on two-year contracts with T-Mobile to have a phone that won't work! What went wrong?

Although Microsoft was one of the first to recognize the power of handhelds, it struggled to look past its ideas of a handheld computer to a more intuitive smartphone. This allowed Microsoft to slip in the market as it attempted to perfect its software. Microsoft—as first mover—was the market leader. However, Blackberry followed and took over the corporate market, while Apple's iPhone ruled the consumer market. In three months, Microsoft smartphone subscribers slipped down to 15.7 percent of the smartphone market by January 2010, according to comScore. HTC has a long history of pairing with Microsoft to innovate in the handheld market. Unfortunately, this partnership of corporate entrepreneurs could not overcome the poor mix of Microsoft's baffling software with HTC's elegant hardware. All of this reinforces the fact that, according to *Bloomberg Businessweek*, "even innovative companies can be hobbled by suppliers peddling out-of-date technology."

>LO12.1
The importance of implementing strategies and practices that foster innovation.

Managing change is one of the most important functions performed by strategic leaders. There are two major avenues through which companies can expand or improve their business—innovation and corporate entrepreneurship. These two activities go hand-in-hand because they both have similar aims. The first is strategic renewal. Innovations help an organization stay fresh and reinvent itself as conditions in the business environment change. This is why managing innovation is such an important strategic implementation issue. The second is the pursuit of venture opportunities. Innovative breakthroughs, as well as new product concepts, evolving technologies, and shifting demand, create opportunities for corporate venturing. In this chapter we will explore these topics—how change and innovation can stimulate strategic renewal and foster corporate entrepreneurship.

Managing Innovation

One of the most important sources of growth opportunities is innovation. **Innovation** involves using new knowledge to transform organizational processes or create commercially viable products and services. The sources of new knowledge may include the latest technology, the results of experiments, creative insights, or competitive information. However it comes about, innovation occurs when new combinations of ideas and information bring about positive change.

The emphasis on newness is a key point. For example, for a patent application to have any chance of success, one of the most important attributes it must possess is novelty. You can't patent an idea that has been copied. This is a central idea. In fact, the root of the word *innovation* is the Latin *novus,* which means new. Innovation involves introducing or changing to something new.[2]

Among the most important sources of new ideas is new technology. Technology creates new possibilities. Technology provides the raw material that firms use to make innovative products and services. But technology is not the only source of innovations. There can be innovations in human resources, firm infrastructure, marketing, service, or in many other value-adding areas that have little to do with anything "high-tech." Strategy Spotlight 12.1 highlights a simple but effective innovation by Dutch Boy paints. As the Dutch Boy example suggests, innovation can take many forms.

Types of Innovation

Although innovations are not always high-tech, changes in technology can be an important source of change and growth. When an innovation is based on a sweeping new technology, it often has a more far-reaching impact. Sometimes even a small innovation can add value and create competitive advantages. Innovation can and should occur throughout an organization—in every department and all aspects of the value chain.

One distinction that is often used when discussing innovation is between process innovation and product innovation.[3] *Product innovation* refers to efforts to create product designs and applications of technology to develop new products for end users. Recall from Chapter 5 how generic strategies were typically different depending on the stage of the industry life cycle. Product innovations tend to be more common during the earlier stages of an industry's life cycle. Product innovations are also commonly associated with a differentiation strategy. Firms that differentiate by providing customers with new products or services that offer unique features or quality enhancements often engage in product innovation.

Process innovation, by contrast, is typically associated with improving the efficiency of an organizational process, especially manufacturing systems and operations. By drawing on new technologies and an organization's accumulated experience (Chapter 5), firms can often improve materials utilization, shorten cycle time, and increase quality. Process innovations are more likely to occur in the later stages of an industry's life cycle as companies seek ways to remain viable in markets where demand has flattened out and competition is more intense. As a result, process innovations are often associated with overall cost leader strategies, because the aim of many process improvements is to lower the costs of operations.

Another way to view the impact of an innovation is in terms of its degree of innovativeness, which falls somewhere on a continuum that extends from incremental to radical.[4]

- *Radical innovations* produce fundamental changes by evoking major departures from existing practices. These breakthrough innovations usually occur because of technological change. They tend to be highly disruptive and can transform a company or even revolutionize a whole industry. They may lead to products or processes that can be patented, giving a firm a strong competitive advantage. Examples include

---

innovation the use of new knowledge to transform organizational processes or create commercially viable products and services.

product innovation efforts to create product designs and applications of technology to develop new products for end users.

process innovation efforts to improve the efficiency of organizational processes, especially manufacturing systems and operations.

radical innovation an innovation that fundamentally changes existing practices.

Dutch Boy's Simple Paint Can Innovation

Sometimes a simple change can make a vast improvement in a product. Any painter knows that getting the paint can open and pouring out paint without drips are two of the challenges of painting. Dutch Boy addressed this issue by developing a twist and pour paint container. The all-plastic container has a large, easy-to-use twist-off top and a handle on the side. The result was a consumer-friendly product that made painting easier and less messy. The handle also reduces the need for a paint stirring stick since you can mix the paint by shaking the container. Even though Dutch Boy's innovation was simple, nontechnological, and had nothing to do with the core product, the launch of the new packaging led to articles in 30 national consumer magazines and 60 major newspapers as well as a story on *Good Morning America.* The Twist and Pour can was also named "Product of the Year" by *USA Today, Bloomberg Businessweek,* and *Better Homes & Gardens.* It was also named a winner of the 2011 Good Housekeeping VIP Awards, which commemorate the most innovative products from the past decade.

Sources: 11 Innovative Products from the Past Decade. 2011 *The Good Housekeeping Research Institute; www.fallscommunications.com.*

electricity, the telephone, the transistor, desktop computers, fiber optics, artificial intelligence, and genetically engineered drugs.

incremental innovation an innovation that enhances existing practices or makes small improvements in products and processes.

- ***Incremental innovations*** enhance existing practices or make small improvements in products and processes. They may represent evolutionary applications within existing paradigms of earlier, more radical innovations. Because they often sustain a company by extending or expanding its product line or manufacturing skills, incremental innovations can be a source of competitive advantage by providing new capabilities that minimize expenses or speed productivity. Examples include frozen food, sports drinks, steel-belted radial tires, electronic bookkeeping, shatterproof glass, and digital telephones.

Some innovations are highly radical; others are only slightly incremental. But most innovations fall somewhere between these two extremes (see Exhibit 12.1).

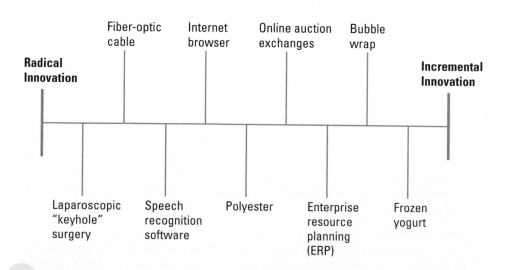

Exhibit 12.1 Continuum of Radical and Incremental Innovations

Harvard Business School Professor Clayton M. Christensen identified another useful approach to characterize types of innovations.[5] Christensen draws a distinction between sustaining and disruptive innovations. *Sustaining innovations* are those that extend sales in an existing market, usually by enabling new products or services to be sold at higher margins. Such innovations may include either incremental or radical innovations. For example, the Internet was a breakthrough technology that transformed retail selling. But rather than disrupting the activities of catalog companies such as Lands' End and L.L. Bean, the Internet energized their existing business by extending their reach and making their operations more efficient.

By contrast, *disruptive innovations* are those that overturn markets by providing an altogether new approach to meeting customer needs. The features of a disruptive innovation make it somewhat counterintuitive. Disruptive innovations:

- Are technologically simpler and less sophisticated than currently available products or services.
- Appeal to less demanding customers who are seeking more convenient, less expensive solutions.
- Take time to take effect and only become disruptive once they have taken root in a new market or low-end part of an existing market.

Christensen cites Walmart and Southwest Airlines as two disruptive examples. Walmart started with a single store, Southwest with a few flights. But because they both represented major departures from existing practices and tapped into unmet needs, they steadily grew into ventures that appealed to a new category of customers and eventually overturned the status quo. "Instead of sustaining the trajectory of improvement that has been established in a market," says Christensen, a disruptive innovation "disrupts it and redefines it by bringing to the market something that is simpler."[6]

The Linux operating system provides a more recent example. When it first became available, few systems administrators used the open-source operating system even though it was free. However, problems with more expensive proprietary operating systems, such as Microsoft Windows, have made Linux increasingly popular. By 2008, the majority of Internet hosting companies and supercomputer operating systems were Linux-based. In addition to being relatively more convenient to use, it is supported by a community of developers.

Seeing the unmet needs of others can also trigger the development of potentially disruptive innovations. One innovator, Dean Kaman, has seen the need for clean water across the globe as a situation crying out for a disruptive innovation. Strategic Spotlight 12.2 describes an innovative product he sees as the solution for the one billion people who don't have access to clean drinking water.

Innovation is a force in both the external environment (technology, competition) and also a factor affecting a firm's internal choices (generic strategy, value-adding activities).[7] Nevertheless, innovation can be quite difficult for some firms to manage, especially those that have become comfortable with the status quo.

Challenges of Innovation

Innovation is essential to sustaining competitive advantages. Recall from Chapter 3 that one of the four elements of the Balanced Scorecard is the innovation and learning perspective. The extent and success of a company's innovation efforts are indicators of its overall performance. As management guru Peter Drucker warned, "An established company which, in an age demanding innovation, is not capable of innovation is doomed to decline and extinction."[8] In today's competitive environment, most firms have only one choice: "Innovate or die."

>LO12.2
The challenges and pitfalls of managing corporate innovation processes.

A Disruptive Innovation: The Slingshot and Affordable Clean Water

Over one billion people have no access to clean water in their homes. Dean Kamen sees this as both a moral dilemma and a business opportunity. Kamen has made innovation his calling. He has had successes, such as developing a pump that improved the delivery of drugs to cancer patients and insulin to diabetics. He also has had notable failures, such as the Segway scooter, which was designed to change how people commute in major cities but, instead, became one of the most overhyped product failures in business history. Now he has focused his attention on clean water.

Providing clean drinking water has been a major point of emphasis for governments and nongovernmental organizations (NGOs) trying to improve living conditions in developing countries. The World Health Organization (WHO) identified universal access to clean water as one of its Millenium Development Goals, goals it aims to reach by 2015. While two-thirds of the earth's surface is covered with water, only 1 percent of this water is safe to drink. To increase the amount of clean, drinkable water, governments and NGOs have invested billions of dollars in major public water projects to take available water from rivers, lakes, and oceans and treat it to provide drinkable water. Still, with all of these efforts, 20 percent of the world's population lives without clean water.

Kamen decided to address this issue by developing a water purification system that is simple, portable, and affordable. Engineers at DEKA Research, Kamen's engineering and design firm, have developed a small water purification system, called the Slingshot. This system has the potential to radically change the method of bringing clean water to developing areas. Rather than relying on major, multimillion dollar water projects, this is a low-cost system (about $2,000 each) that could produce 250 gallons of drinkable water each day, enough water for approximately 100 people or the number of people in a small village. The Slingshot is about the size of a dormitory refrigerator and borrows from a desalination process used to generate drinking water on naval ships. Using a vapor compression distillation process, the system heats water through multiple cycles. This process removes minerals, heavy metals, and other contaminants by evaporating the water away from the contaminants. It also kills bacteria and viruses through pasteurization of the water. It is also a small user of energy, only requiring about the same energy as a coffee maker.

Still, DEKA faces a major challenge bringing this technology to market. To get the cost of the machines down to the $2,000 target, Kamen needs to build scaled facilities to mass manufacture the Slingshot. But how can he build demand for the product? It is hard for Kamen and his backers to tap into governmental investment programs for water to generate sales for his product. Most investment money for clean water is already geared to major projects. Also, it is difficult to generate orders from the potential users. While the target cost for the Slingshot is low by our standards, the cost is still out of reach for many of the potential users, since $2,000 is more than the inhabitants of many small villages can afford, with individual incomes often below $500 a year in the target markets. Kamen has identified a different potential path to build the demand he needs to mass manufacture the product. He is now pitching the benefits of the Slingshot to major corporations, like Coca-Cola, and small business owners, such as the proprietors of bars and restaurants or small manufacturers in areas without clean water. His aim is to build demand from these commercial customers to allow him to build the scale of operations needed to produce the Slingshot at the target cost of $2,000 and to demonstrate the value of the Slingshot to the WHO and others who he hopes would see it as a tool to meet the goal of providing clean water to all.

Sources: Copeland, M. V. 2010. Dean Kamen (Still) Wants to Save the World. *Fortune*, May 3: 61–62; Nasr, S. L. 2009. How the Slingshot Water Purifier Works. *HowStuffWorks.com*, July 27: np;. Segway Creator Unveils His Next Invention, a Magic Water Purifier. 2008. *www.hubpages.com*: np.

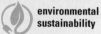

environmental sustainability

As with change, however, firms are often resistant to innovation. Only those companies that actively pursue innovation, even though it is often difficult and uncertain, will get a payoff from their innovation efforts. But managing innovation is challenging.[9] As former Pfizer chairman and CEO William Steere puts it: "In some ways, managing innovation is analogous to breaking in a spirited horse. You are never sure of success until you achieve your goal. In the meantime, everyone takes a few lumps."[10]

What is it that makes innovation so difficult? The uncertainty about outcomes is one factor. Companies are often reluctant to invest time and resources into activities with an unknown future. Another factor is that the innovation process involves so many choices. These choices present five dilemmas that companies must wrestle with when pursuing innovation.[11]

- *Seeds versus Weeds.* Most companies have an abundance of innovative ideas. They must decide which of these is most likely to bear fruit—the "Seeds"—and which should be cast aside—the "Weeds." This is complicated by the fact that some innovation projects require a considerable level of investment before a firm can fully evaluate whether they are worth pursuing. Firms need a mechanism with which they can choose among various innovation projects.

- *Experience versus Initiative.* Companies must decide who will lead an innovation project. Senior managers may have experience and credibility but tend to be more risk averse. Midlevel employees, who may be the innovators themselves, may have more enthusiasm because they can see firsthand how an innovation would address specific problems. Firms need to support and reward organizational members who bring new ideas to light.

- *Internal versus External Staffing.* Innovation projects need competent staffs to succeed. People drawn from inside the company may have greater social capital and know the organization's culture and routines. But this knowledge may actually inhibit them from thinking outside the box. Staffing innovation projects with external personnel requires that project managers justify the hiring and spend time recruiting, training, and relationship building. Firms need to streamline and support the process of staffing innovation efforts.

- *Building Capabilities versus Collaborating.* Innovation projects often require new sets of skills. Firms can seek help from other departments and/or partner with other companies that bring resources and experience as well as share costs of development. However, such arrangements can create dependencies and inhibit internal skills development. Further, struggles over who contributed the most or how the benefits of the project are to be allocated may arise. Firms need a mechanism for forging links with outside parties to the innovation process.

- *Incremental versus Preemptive Launch.* Companies must manage the timing and scale of new innovation projects. An incremental launch is less risky because it requires fewer resources and serves as a market test. But a launch that is too tentative can undermine the project's credibility. It also opens the door for a competitive response. A large-scale launch requires more resources, but it can effectively preempt a competitive response. Firms need to make funding and management arrangements that allow for projects to hit the ground running and be responsive to market feedback.

These dilemmas highlight why the innovation process can be daunting even for highly successful firms. Next, we consider five steps that firms can take to improve the innovation process within the firm.[12]

Cultivating Innovation Skills

Some firms, such as Apple, Google, and Amazon, regularly produce innovative products and services, while other firms struggle to generate new, marketable products. What separates these innovative firms from the rest of the pack? Jeff Dyer, Hal Gregersen, and Clayton Christensen argue it is the Innovative DNA of the leaders of these firms.[13] The leaders of these firms have exhibited "discovery skills" that allow them to see the potential in innovations and to move the organization forward in leveraging the value of those innovations.[14] These leaders spend 50 percent more time on these discovery activities than the leaders of less innovative firms. To improve their innovative processes, firms need to cultivate the innovation skills of their managers.

The key attribute that firms need to develop in their managers in order to improve their innovative potential is creative intelligence. Creative intelligence is driven by a core skill of associating—the ability to see patterns in data and integrating different questions, information, and insights—and four patterns of action: questioning, observing, experimenting, and networking. As managers practice the four patterns of action, they will begin to develop the skill of association. Dyer and his colleagues offer the following illustration to demonstrate that individuals using these skills are going to develop more-creative, higher-potential innovations.

> Imagine that you have an identical twin, endowed with the same brains and natural talents that you have. You're both given one week to come up with a creative new business-venture idea. During that week, you come up with ideas alone in your room. In contrast, your twin (1) talks with 10 people—including an engineer, a musician, a stay-at-home dad, and a designer—about the venture, (2) visits three innovative start-ups to observe what they do, (3) samples five "new to the market" products, (4) shows a prototype he's built to five people, and (5) asks the questions "What if I tried this?" and "Why do you do that?" at least 10 times each day during these networking, observing, and experimenting activities. Who do you bet will come up with the more innovative (and doable) ideas?

The point is that by questioning, observing, experimenting, and networking as part of the innovative process, managers will both make better innovation decisions now but, more importantly, start to build the innovative DNA needed to be more successful innovators in the future. As they get into the practice of these habits, decision makers will see opportunities and be more creative as they associate information from different parts of their life, different people they come in contact with, and different parts of their organizations. The ability to innovate is not hard-wired into our brains at birth. Research suggests that only one-third of our ability to think creatively is genetic. The other two-thirds is developed over time. Neuroscience research indicates that the brain is "plastic," meaning it changes over time due to experiences. As managers build up the ability to ask creative questions, develop a wealth of experiences from diverse settings, and link together insights from different arenas of their lives, their brains will follow suit and will build the ability to easily see situations creatively and draw upon a wide range of experiences and knowledge to identify creative solutions. The five traits of the effective innovator are described and examples of each trait are presented in Exhibit 12.2.

Defining the Scope of Innovation

Firms must have a means to focus their innovation efforts. By defining the "strategic envelope"—the scope of a firm's innovation efforts—firms ensure that their innovation efforts are not wasted on projects that are outside the firm's domain of interest. Strategic enveloping defines the range of acceptable projects. As Alistair Corbett, an innovation expert with the global consulting firm Bain & Company, said, "One man's radical innovation is another man's incremental innovation."[15] A strategic envelope creates a firm-specific view of innovation that defines how a firm can create new knowledge and learn from an innovation initiative even if the project fails. It also gives direction to a firm's innovation efforts, which helps separate seeds from weeds and builds internal capabilities.

One way to determine which projects to work on is to focus on a common technology. Then, innovation efforts across the firm can aim at developing skills and expertise in a given technical area. Another potential focus is on a market theme. Consider how DuPont responded to a growing concern for environmentally sensitive products:

> In the early 1990s, DuPont sought to use its knowledge of plastics to identify products to meet a growing market demand for biodegradable products. It conducted numerous experiments with a biodegradable polyester resin it named Biomax. By trying different applications and formulations demanded by potential customers, the company was finally able to create a product that could be produced economically and had market appeal. DuPont has continued to extend the Biomax brand and now produces a large line of environmentally sensitive plastics.[16]

strategic envelope a firm-specific view of innovation that defines how a firm can create new knowledge and learn from an innovation initiative even if the project fails.

Exhibit 12.2 The Innovator's DNA

Trait	Description	Example
Associating	Innovators have the ability to connect seemingly unrelated questions, problems, and ideas from different fields. This allows them to creatively see opportunities that others miss.	Pierre Omidyar saw the opportunity that led to eBay when he linked three items: (1) a personal fascination with creating more efficient markets, (2) his fiancee's desire to locate hard to find collectible Pez dispensers, and (3) the ineffectiveness of local classified ads in locating such items.
Questioning	Innovators constantly ask questions that challenge common wisdom. Rather than accept the status quo, they ask "Why not?" or "What if?" This gets others around them to challenge the assumptions that limit the possible range of actions the firm can take.	After witnessing the emergence of eBay and Amazon, Marc Benioff questioned why computer software was still sold in boxes rather than leased with a subscription and downloaded through the Internet. This was the genesis of Salesforce.com, a firm with over $1.3 billion in sales in 2010.
Observing	Discovery-driven executives produce innovative business ideas by observing regular behavior of individuals, especially customers and potential customers. Such observations often identify challenges customers face and previously unidentified opportunities.	From watching his wife struggle to keep track of the family's finances, Intuit founder Scott Cook identified the need for easy-to-use financial software that provided a single place for managing bills, bank accounts, and investments.
Experimenting	Thomas Edison once said, "I haven't failed. I've simply found 10,000 ways that do not work." Innovators regularly experiment with new possibilities, accepting that many of their ideas will fail. Experimentation can include new jobs, living in different countries, and new ideas for their businesses.	Founders Larry Page and Sergey Brin provide time and resources for Google employees to experiment. Some, such as the Android cell phone platform, have been big winners. Others, such as the Orkut and Buzz social networking systems, have failed. But Google will continue to experiment with new products and services.
Networking	Innovators develop broad personal networks. They use this diverse set of individuals to find and test radical ideas. This can be done by developing a diverse set of friends. It can also be done by attending idea conferences where individuals from a broad set of backgrounds come together to share their perspectives and ideas, such as the Technology, Entertainment, and Design (TED) Conference or the Aspen Ideas Festival.	Michael Lazaridis got the idea for a wireless e-mail device that led him to found Research in Motion from a conference he attended. At the conference, a speaker was discussing a wireless system Coca-Cola was using that allowed vending machines to send a signal when they needed refilling. Lazaridis saw the opportunity to use the same concept with e-mail communications, and the idea for the Blackberry was hatched.

Source: Reprinted by permission of Harvard Business Review. Exhibit from "The Innovator's DNA," by J. H. Dyer, H. G. Gregerson and C. M. Christensen. Copyright 2009 by The Harvard Business School Publishing Corporation; all rights reserved.

Companies must be clear not only about the kinds of innovation they are looking for but also the expected results. Each company needs to develop a set of questions to ask itself about its innovation efforts:

- How much will the innovation initiative cost?
- How likely is it to actually become commercially viable?
- How much value will it add; that is, what will it be worth if it works?
- What will be learned if it does not pan out?

However a firm envisions its innovation goals, it needs to develop a systematic approach to evaluating its results and learning from its innovation initiatives. Viewing innovation from this perspective helps firms manage the process.[17]

Managing the Pace of Innovation

Along with clarifying the scope of an innovation by defining a strategic envelope, firms also need to regulate the pace of innovation. How long will it take for an innovation initiative to realistically come to fruition? The project time line of an incremental innovation may be 6 months to 2 years, whereas a more radical innovation is typically long term—10 years or more.[18] Radical innovations often begin with a long period of exploration in which experimentation makes strict timelines unrealistic. In contrast, firms that are innovating incrementally in order to exploit a window of opportunity may use a milestone approach that is more stringently driven by goals and deadlines. This kind of sensitivity to realistic time frames helps companies separate dilemmas temporally so they are easier to manage.

Time pacing can also be a source of competitive advantage because it helps a company manage transitions and develop an internal rhythm.[19] Time pacing does not mean the company ignores the demands of market timing; instead, companies have a sense of their own internal clock in a way that allows them to thwart competitors by controlling the innovation process.

Not all innovation lends itself to speedy development, however. Radical innovation often involves open-ended experimentation and time-consuming mistakes. The creative aspects of innovation are often difficult to time. When software maker Intuit's new CEO, Steve Bennett, began to turn around that troubled business, he required every department to implement Six Sigma, a quality control management technique that focuses on being responsive to customer needs. Everybody, that is, but the techies.

> "We're not GE, we're not a company where Jack says 'Do it,' and everyone salutes," says Bill Hensler, Intuit's vice president for process excellence. That's because software development, according to many, is more of an art than a science. At the Six Sigma Academy, president of operations Phil Samuel says even companies that have embraced Six Sigma across every other aspect of their organization usually maintain a hands-off policy when it comes to software developers. Techies, it turns out, like to go at their own pace.[20]

Some projects can't be rushed. Companies that hurry up their research efforts or go to market before they are ready can damage their ability to innovate—and their reputation. Thus, managing the pace of innovation can be an important factor in long-term success.

Staffing to Capture Value from Innovation

People are central to the processes of identifying, developing, and commercializing innovations effectively. They need broad sets of skills as well as experience—experience working with teams and experience working on successful innovation projects. To capture value from innovation activities, companies must provide strategic decision makers with staff members who make it possible.

This insight led strategy experts Rita Gunther McGrath and Thomas Keil to research the types of human resource management practices that effective firms use to capture value from their innovation efforts.[21] Four practices are especially important:

- Create innovation teams with experienced players who know what it is like to deal with uncertainty and can help new staff members learn venture management skills.
- Require that employees seeking to advance their career with the organization serve in the new venture group as part of their career climb.
- Once people have experience with the new venture group, transfer them to main-stream management positions where they can use their skills and knowledge to revitalize the company's core business.
- Separate the performance of individuals from the performance of the innovation. Otherwise, strong players may feel stigmatized if the innovation effort they worked on fails.

There are other staffing practices that may sound as if they would benefit a firm's innovation activities but may, in fact, be counterproductive:

- Creating a staff that consists only of strong players whose primary experience is related to the company's core business. This provides too few people to deal with the uncertainty of innovation projects and may cause good ideas to be dismissed because they do not appear to fit with the core business.
- Creating a staff that consists only of volunteers who want to work on projects they find interesting. Such players are often overzealous about new technologies or overly attached to product concepts, which can lead to poor decisions about which projects to pursue or drop.
- Creating a climate where innovation team members are considered second-class citizens. In companies where achievements are rewarded, the brightest and most ambitious players may avoid innovation projects with uncertain outcomes.

Unless an organization can align its key players into effective new venture teams, it is unlikely to create any differentiating advantages from its innovation efforts.[22] An enlightened approach to staffing a company's innovation efforts provides one of the best ways to ensure that the challenges of innovation will be effectively met. Strategy Spotlight 12.3 describes the approach Air Products and Chemicals Inc. is using to enhance its innovation efforts.

Collaborating with Innovation Partners

It is rare for any one organization to have all the information it needs to carry an innovation from concept to commercialization. Even a company that is highly competent with its current operations usually needs new capabilities to achieve new results. Innovation partners provide the skills and insights that are needed to make innovation projects succeed.[23]

Innovation partners may come from many sources, including research universities and the federal government. Each year the federal government issues requests for proposals (RFPs) asking private companies for assistance in improving services or finding solutions to public problems. Universities are another type of innovation partner. Chip-maker Intel, for example, has benefited from underwriting substantial amounts of university research. Rather than hand universities a blank check, Intel bargains for rights to patents that emerge from Intel-sponsored research. The university retains ownership of the patent, but Intel gets royalty-free use of it.[24]

Strategic partnering requires firms to identify their strengths and weaknesses and make choices about which capabilities to leverage, which need further development, and which are outside the firm's current or projected scope of operations.

Staffing for Innovation Success at Air Products

When it comes to implementing its innovation efforts, Air Products and Chemicals, Inc. (APCI) recognizes the importance of staffing for achieving success. Air Products is a global manufacturer of industrial gases, chemicals, and related equipment. Headquartered in Allentown, Pennsylvania, Air Products has annual sales of $10 billion, manufacturing facilities in over 30 countries, and 22,000 employees worldwide. The company has a strong reputation for effectively embedding innovation into its culture through its unique employee engagement processes.

Ron Pierantozzi, a 30-year veteran of the company and its director of innovation and new product development, says, "Innovation is about discipline. . . . It

requires a different type of training, different tools and new approaches to experimentation." To enact this philosophy, Pierantozzi begins with his people. He recruits people with diverse backgrounds and a wide range of expertise including engineers, entrepreneurs, and government officials. It is made clear to those on his innovation teams that they will return to mainstream operations after four years—a fact that most consider a plus since working in the innovation unit usually provides a career boost. He also assures players that there is no stigma associated with a failed venture because experimentation is highly valued.

Innovation teams are created to manage the company's intellectual assets and determine which technologies have the most potential value. A key benefit of this approach has been to more effectively leverage its human resources to achieve innovative outcomes without increasing its R&D expenses. These efforts resulted in an innovation award from APQC (formerly known as the American Productivity and Quality Center) which recognizes companies for exemplary practices that increase productivity.

Sources: Chesbrough, H. 2007. Why Bad Things Happen to Good Technology. *The Wall Street Journal:* April 28–29, R11; Leavitt, P. 2005. Delivering the Difference: Business Process Management at APCI. *APQC, www.apqc.com*; McGrath, R. G. & Keil, T. 2007. The Value Captor's Process: Getting the Most Out of Your New Business Ventures. *Harvard Business Review,* May: 128–136; and *www.apci.com.*

To choose partners, firms need to ask what competencies they are looking for and what the innovation partner will contribute.[25] These might include knowledge of markets, technology expertise, or contacts with key players in an industry. Innovation partnerships also typically need to specify how the rewards of the innovation will be shared and who will own the intellectual property that is developed.[26]

Innovation efforts that involve multiple partners and the speed and ease with which partners can network and collaborate are changing the way innovation is conducted.[27] Strategy Spotlight 12.4 outlines how IBM is using crowdsourcing technologies to foster collaboration between employees, customers, suppliers, and other stakeholders to enhance its innovation efforts.

Successful innovation involves a companywide commitment because the results of innovation affect every part of the organization. Innovation also requires an entrepreneurial spirit and skill set to be effective. Few companies have a more exemplary reputation than W. L. Gore. Exhibit 12.3 highlights the policies that help make Gore an innovation leader. One of the most important ways that companies improve and grow is when innovation is put to the task of creating new corporate ventures.

corporate entrepreneurship
the creation of new value for a corporation, through investments that create either new sources of competitive advantage or renewal of the value proposition.

Corporate Entrepreneurship

Corporate entrepreneurship (CE) has two primary aims: the pursuit of new venture opportunities and strategic renewal.[28] The innovation process keeps firms alert by exposing them to new technologies, making them aware of marketplace trends, and helping them

Crowdsourcing: IBM's Innovation Jam

IBM is one of the best known corporations in the world, but their CEO, Samuel Palmisano, saw a major challenge for the firm. Though IBM had great ability to do basic scientific research and owned the rights to over 40,000 patents, they had struggled to translate their patented knowledge into marketable products. Also, they had built a reputation with investors as a firm with incremental product development, not the reputation needed in dynamic technological markets. Palmisano saw crowdsourcing as a means to move IBM forward in a bold way.

In 2006, IBM hosted an Innovation Jam, an open event that involved 150,000 IBM employees, family members, business partners, clients, and university researchers. The jam took place over two 72-hour sessions. Participants from over 100 countries jammed for 24 hours a day over three days. The discussions were organized around 25 technologies in six broad categories. While the jam discussions were rich in content, it was a challenge for IBM to pull meaningful data from them. The 24-hour format meant that no single moderator could follow any discussion, and the volume of posts to the discussion threads left IBM with a huge amount of data to wade through. The discussions yielded 46,000 potential business ideas. To make sense of the data, IBM organized the discussion threads using sophisticated text analysis software and had a team of 50 managers read through the organized data. Using data from the first session, the managers identified 31 "big ideas." They further explored these 31 ideas in the second jam session. IBM then used another set of 50 global managers to review the discussions from the jam. Teams of managers focused on related groups of ideas, such as health care and the environment.

IBM's managers saw the jam as serving three purposes. First, it gave individuals both inside and outside IBM who already had big ideas a forum in which to share their vision with top managers. Second, it gave individuals with smaller ideas a venue to link up with others with related ideas, resulting in larger major initiatives. For example, individuals who had ideas about better local weather forecasting, sensing devices for water utilities, and long-term climate forecasting came together to create "Predictive Water Management," a comprehensive solution for water authorities to manage their resources, a business solution no one at IBM had thought of before the jam. Third, the global structure of the jam allowed IBM, early on, to see how employees, partners, and customers from different regions had different goals and concerns about possible new businesses. For example, what customers wanted from systems to manage health care records varied greatly across regions.

Based on the jam sessions, IBM launched 10 new businesses using $100 million in funding. One, the Intelligent Transportation System, a system that gathers, manages, and disseminates real-time information about metropolitan transportation systems to optimize traffic flow, has been sold to transportation authorities in Sweden, the UK, Singapore, Dubai, and Australia. Another, Intelligent Utility Networks, became a core product in IBM's public utility business. A third, Big Green, became part of the largest initiative in IBM's history, a billion-dollar project on better managing energy and other resources.

Sources: Bjelland, O. M. & Wood, R. C. 2008. An Inside View of IBM's Innovation Jam. *Sloan Management Review.* Fall: 32–40; Hempel, J. 2006. Big Blue Brainstorm. *BusinessWeek,* August 7: 70; Takahashi, D. 2008 IBM's Innovation Jam 2008 Shows How Far Crowdsourcing Has Come. *Businessweek.com,* October 9: np.

crowdsourcing

evaluate new possibilities. CE uses the fruits of the innovation process to help firms build new sources of competitive advantage and renew their value propositions. Just as the innovation process helps firms to make positive improvements, corporate entrepreneurship helps firms identify opportunities and launch new ventures. Strategy Spotlight 12.5 outlines how Cisco is being entrepreneurial by expanding into new, growing product segments.

Corporate new venture creation was labeled "intrapreneuring" by Gifford Pinchot because it refers to building entrepreneurial businesses within existing corporations.[29] However, to engage in corporate entrepreneurship that yields above-average returns and

Exhibit 12.3
W. L. Gore's New Rules
for Fostering Innovation

Rule	Implications
The power of small teams	Gore believes that small teams promote familiarity and autonomy. Even its manufacturing plants are capped at just 200 people. That way everyone can get to know one another on a first-name basis and work together with minimal rules. This also helps to cultivate "an environment where creativity can flourish," according to CEO Chuck Carroll.
No ranks, no titles, no bosses	Because Gore believes in maximizing individual potential, employees, dubbed "associates," decide for themselves what new commitments to take on. Associates have "sponsors," rather than bosses, and there are no standardized job descriptions or categories. Everyone is supposed to take on a unique role. Committees of co-workers evaluate each team member's contribution and decide on compensation.
Take the long view	Although impatient about the status quo, Gore exhibits great patience with the time—often years, sometimes decades—it takes to nurture and develop breakthrough products and bring them to market.
Make time for face time	Gore avoids the traditional hierarchical chain of command, opting instead for a team-based environment that fosters personal initiative. Gore also discourages memos and e-mail and promotes direct, person-to-person communication among all associates—anyone in the company can talk to anyone else.
Lead by leading	Associates are encouraged to spend about 10 percent of their time pursuing speculative new ideas. Anyone is free to champion products, as long as they have the passion and ideas to attract followers. Many of Gore's breakthroughs started with one person acting on his or her own initiative and developed as colleagues helped in their spare time.
Celebrate failure	When a project doesn't work out and the team decides to kill it, they celebrate just as they would if it had been a success— with some beer and maybe a glass of champagne. Rather than condemning failure, Gore figures that celebrating it encourages experimentation and risk taking.

Source: Deutschman, A. 2004. The Fabric of Creativity. *Fast Company,* 89: 54–62; Levering, R. & Moskowitz, M. 2006. The 100 Best Companies to Work For. *Fortune, www.fortune.com*, January; and *www.gore.com*.

contributes to sustainable advantages, it must be done effectively. In this section we will examine the sources of entrepreneurial activity within established firms and the methods large corporations use to stimulate entrepreneurial behavior.

In a typical corporation, what determines how entrepreneurial projects will be pursued? That depends on many factors, including:

- Corporate culture.
- Leadership.

Cisco Looks to Video to Spur Demand

Cisco produces both hardware and software used to manage network and communication systems. Cisco, which was founded in San Francisco in 1984, began by manufacturing routers to manage Internet communications. It has expanded from its original market position in computer routers by acquiring firms that make network switches, Voice over Internet Protocol (VOIP) systems, home networking equipment, and other information technology products and services. Today, Cisco dominates the market for Internet protocol-based networking equipment and provides routers and switches used to direct data, voice, and video traffic. Cisco has had a nice run over the last 10 years, with sales growing from $19 billion in 2001 to $40 billion in 2010 and net income growing from $2.7 billion to $7.8 billion over the same period.

Even with this success, Cisco is not one to rest on its laurels. Managers at Cisco retain an entrepreneurial orientation and look to expand their product portfolio to meet where the market is going. A few years ago, Cisco introduced Teleprescence, an Internet-based videoconference technology. This has been a winning product during the recent recessionary years, since many corporations have turned to videoconferencing as a means to host meetings without the travel expense of bringing employees together. From this experience, John Chambers, the firm's CEO, began to believe that the Internet's primary payload going forward will be video and has placed a big bet on Internet video.

As the Internet moves toward being primarily a video-based medium, communications hardware and software to manage video traffic will be valued resources, because HD video takes about 50 times as much Internet bandwidth as audio data. To meet the challenge of this new Internet era, Cisco has developed a technology, called Medianet, that facilitates the flow of video media across all devices transferring, delivering, or receiving Internet-based videos. For example, a smartphone could tell a Medianet-enabled network the phone's screen size and connection speed. The network would then tailor how it delivered the media to the phone to optimize the transfer and to use the network hardware as efficiently as possible.

Sources: Fortt, J. 2010. Cisco's Online Video Gamble. *Fortune*, November 1: 43; Lawson, S. 2008. Cisco Plays Up Video for Business, Carriers. *IDG News Service*, September 16: np; www.hoovers.com; www.cisco.com.

● Cisco Systems is developing its Internet-based video media products.

Cisco's ultimate objective with this new product is to extend its dominance in the network business. As Cisco develops systems that increase the use of Internet-based video, it stokes up demand for its core products. Telecommunication service providers and corporations will need to ramp up their investment in network gear to meet the growing demand for Internet video. These firms will likely to turn to Cisco to purchase Medianet-enabled network gear as they expand their network systems. As Robert Hagerty, the former CEO of Polycom, a competitor of Cisco, commented, Cisco's "real motivation is to sell more routers and switches on the enterprise side." In line with this, Procter & Gamble has expanded its purchasing of Cisco's network equipment as it has worked to double its network capacity in 2010 in anticipation of greater video traffic. Thus, Cisco's entrepreneurial entry into the Internet-video business has fostered growth in the value of its core markets.

- Structural features that guide and constrain action.
- Organizational systems that foster learning and manage rewards.

All of the factors that influence the strategy implementation process will also shape how corporations engage in internal venturing.

Other factors will also affect how entrepreneurial ventures will be pursued.

- The use of teams in strategic decision making.
- Whether the company is product or service oriented.
- Whether its innovation efforts are aimed at product or process improvements.
- The extent to which it is high-tech or low-tech.

Because these factors are different in every organization, some companies may be more involved than others in identifying and developing new venture opportunities.[30] These factors will also influence the nature of the CE process.

Successful CE typically requires firms to reach beyond their current operations and markets in the pursuit of new opportunities. It is often the breakthrough opportunities that provide the greatest returns. Such strategies are not without risks, however. In the sections that follow, we will address some of the strategic choice and implementation issues that influence the success or failure of CE activities.

Two distinct approaches to corporate venturing are found among firms that pursue entrepreneurial aims. The first is *focused* corporate venturing, in which CE activities are isolated from a firm's existing operations and worked on by independent work units. The second approach is *dispersed,* in which all parts of the organization and every organization member are engaged in intrapreneurial activities.

Focused Approaches to Corporate Entrepreneurship

Firms using a focused approach typically separate the corporate venturing activity from the other ongoing operations of the firm. CE is usually the domain of autonomous work groups that pursue entrepreneurial aims independent of the rest of the firm. The advantage of this approach is that it frees entrepreneurial team members to think and act without the constraints imposed by existing organizational norms and routines. This independence is often necessary for the kind of open-minded creativity that leads to strategic breakthroughs. The disadvantage is that, because of their isolation from the corporate mainstream, the work groups that concentrate on internal ventures may fail to obtain the resources or support needed to carry an entrepreneurial project through to completion. Two forms—new venture groups (NVGs) and business incubators—are among the most common types of focused approaches.

New Venture Groups (NVGs)   Corporations often form NVGs whose goal is to identify, evaluate, and cultivate venture opportunities. These groups typically function as semi-autonomous units with little formal structure. The **new venture group** may simply be a committee that reports to the president on potential new ventures. Or it may be organized as a corporate division with its own staff and budget. The aims of the NVG may be open-ended in terms of what ventures it may consider. Alternatively, some corporations use them to promote concentrated effort on a specific problem. In both cases, they usually have a substantial amount of freedom to take risks and a supply of resources to do it with.[31]

NVGs usually have a larger mandate than a typical R&D department. Their involvement extends beyond innovation and experimentation to coordinating with other corporate divisions, identifying potential venture partners, gathering resources, and actually launching the venture. Strategy Spotlight 12.6 shows how WD-40 has used an NVG to improve its CE efforts.

>LO12.3

How corporations use new venture teams, business incubators, and product champions to create an internal environment and culture that promote entrepreneurial development.

focused approches to corporate entrepreneurship corporate entrepreneurship in which the venturing entity is seperated from the other ongoing operations of the firm.

new venture group a group of individuals, or a division within a corporation, that identifies, evaluates, and cultivates venture opportunities.

Using Team Tomorrow to Grow WD-40

When a hinge squeaks, most people reach for a can of WD-40. The iconic lubricant in the blue cans has been around for over 50 years and commands a 70 percent market share in the spray lubricant business. Garry Ridge, the CEO of WD-40, quips that "more people use WD-40 every day than use dental floss." Still, Ridge wanted the firm to look forward, searching for growth opportunities. Historically, WD-40's marketing team was responsible for new product development, but this typically involved minor product changes or new packaging for existing products.

Knowing the incremental focus of the current structure and wanting to get WD-40 focused on bolder new product opportunities, Ridge created a multifunctional team, dubbed Team Tomorrow, to manage its global CE efforts. This team includes members from marketing, research, supply chain, purchasing, and distribution. To head the team, Ridge tapped an experienced executive, Graham Milner, who thought globally and had a marketing

background. There was some resistance from the marketing staff, because they lost power in the new product-development process. Ridge overcame this in a number of ways. He was active in forming the team, got involved during times of conflict between Team Tomorrow and other groups in the organization, and carried around an early prototype of the team's first product, the No Mess Pen, to show how interested he was in the new product. His involvement signaled the importance of the team to WD-40. By placing a marketing executive in charge of Team Tomorrow, he signaled the importance of marketing to the organization. Milner and the other team leader, Stephanie Barry, worked collaboratively with the head of marketing, instituted an open-door policy, and shared information with marketing. Collectively, these actions broke down resistance to Team Tomorrow.

Ridge also gave the team a bold goal. He charged the team to create new products that would generate $100 million in sales per year from products developed and launched within the previous three years. As of 2010, the team had created products that generate $165 million in sales. Ridge also sees a large change in the rest of the firm as a result of this effort. He sees the firm's employees as being members of a "tribe" and the organization as a "living learning laboratory."

Sources: Ferrarini, E. 2010. WD-40 Company CEO Talks about Rebuilding an Innovative Brand and Taking It Global. *Enterprise Leadership*, February 27: np; Bounds, G. 2006. WD-40 CEO Repackages a Core Product. *Pittsburgh Post Gazette*, May 23: np; Govindarajan, V. & Trimble, D. 2010. Stop the Innovation Wars. *Harvard Business Review*, July–August: 76–83; www.intheboardroom.com.

Business Incubators The term *incubator* was originally used to describe a device in which eggs are hatched. **Business incubators** are designed to "hatch" new businesses. They are a type of corporate NVG with a somewhat more specialized purpose—to support and nurture fledgling entrepreneurial ventures until they can thrive on their own as stand-alone businesses. Corporations use incubators as a way to grow businesses identified by the NVG. Although they often receive support from many parts of the corporation, they still operate independently until they are strong enough to go it alone. Depending on the type of business, they are either integrated into an existing corporate division or continue to operate as a subsidiary of the parent firm.

Incubators typically provide some or all of the following five functions.[32]

business incubator
a corporate new venture group that supports and nurtures fledgling entrepreneurial ventures until they can thrive on their own as stand-alone businesses.

- *Funding.* Includes capital investments as well as in-kind investments and loans.
- *Physical space.* Incubators in which several start-ups share space often provide fertile ground for new ideas and collaboration.
- *Business services.* Along with office space, young ventures need basic services and infrastructure; may include anything from phone systems and computer networks to public relations and personnel management.
- *Mentoring.* Senior executives and skilled technical personnel often provide coaching and experience-based advice.

- *Networking.* Contact with other parts of the firm and external resources such as suppliers, industry experts, and potential customers facilitates problem solving and knowledge sharing.

The risks associated with incubating ventures should not be overlooked. Companies have at times spent millions on new ideas with very little to show for it. Major corporations such as Lucent, British Airways, and Hewlett-Packard deactivated their incubators and scaled back new venture portfolios after experiencing major declines in value during recent financial downturns.[33]

To encourage entrepreneurship, corporations sometimes need to do more than create independent work groups or venture incubators to generate new enterprises. In some firms, the entrepreneurial spirit is spread throughout the organization.

Dispersed Approaches to Corporate Entrepreneurship

The second type of CE is dispersed. For some companies, a dedication to the principles and practices of entrepreneurship is spread throughout the organization. One advantage of this approach is that organizational members don't have to be reminded to think entrepreneurially or be willing to change. The ability to change is considered to be a core capability. This leads to a second advantage: Because of the firm's entrepreneurial reputation, stakeholders such as vendors, customers, or alliance partners can bring new ideas or venture opportunities to anyone in the organization and expect them to be well-received. Such opportunities make it possible for the firm to stay ahead of the competition. However, there are disadvantages as well. Firms that are overzealous about CE sometimes feel they must change for the sake of change, causing them to lose vital competencies or spend heavily on R&D and innovation to the detriment of the bottom line. Two related aspects of dispersed entrepreneurship include entrepreneurial cultures that have an overarching commitment to CE activities and the use of product champions in promoting entrepreneurial behaviors.

Entrepreneurial Culture   In some large corporations, the corporate culture embodies the spirit of entrepreneurship. A culture of entrepreneurship is one in which the search for venture opportunities permeates every part of the organization. The key to creating value successfully is viewing every value-chain activity as a source of competitive advantage. The effect of CE on a firm's strategic success is strongest when it animates all parts of an organization. It is found in companies where the strategic leaders and the culture together generate a strong impetus to innovate, take risks, and seek out new venture opportunities.[34]

In companies with an entrepreneurial culture, everyone in the organization is attuned to opportunities to help create new businesses. Many such firms use a top-down approach to stimulate entrepreneurial activity. The top leaders of the organization support programs and incentives that foster a climate of entrepreneurship. Many of the best ideas for new corporate ventures, however, come from the bottom up. Here's what Martin Sorrell, CEO of the WPP Group, a London-based global communication services group, says about drawing on the talents of lower-level employees:

> The people at the so-called bottom of an organization know more about what's going on than the people at the top. The people in the trenches are the ones in the best position to make critical decisions. It's up to the leaders to give those people the freedom and the resources they need.[35]

An entrepreneurial culture is one in which change and renewal are on everybody's mind. Sony, 3M, Intel, and Cisco are among the corporations best known for their corporate venturing activities. Many fast-growing young corporations also attribute much of their success to an entrepreneurial culture. But other successful firms struggle in their efforts to remain entrepreneurial. Strategy Spotlight 12.7 describes Microsoft's struggles with its CE efforts.

dispersed approaches to corporate entrepreneurship corporate entrepreunership in which a dedication to the principles and policies of entrepreunership is spread throughout the organization.

entrepreneurial culture corpotate culture in which change and renewal are a constant focus of attention.

Microsoft's Struggles with Corporate Entrepreneurship

Microsoft generated $62 billion in sales and nearly $19 billion in profits in 2010 and dominates the market for PC operating system and office suite application software, yet its stock languishes at a price lower than it was 10 years ago. Why is this the case? Investors have little confidence that Microsoft will produce blockbuster products that will replace its core PC software products as the information technology market moves into the post-PC phase.

It isn't that Microsoft has failed to generate innovative ideas. The firm spends $9 billion a year on R&D. Over 10 years ago, engineers at Microsoft developed a tablet PC and an e-book system, two of the hottest technology products today. They also pioneered Web-TV. But they failed to turn these pioneering efforts into marketable products. In other markets, they have not pioneered, but have seen limited success with products they've designed to meet emerging challengers. The Zune music player was supposed to challenge the iPod but was a flop in the market. Recently, they introduced the Kin One and Kin Two, smartphones with flashy designs and social networking capabilities, but they pulled the phones from the market within two months. The Xbox 360 has arguably been Microsoft's most successful product launch designed to take on a pioneering rival, but even there, the firm is competitive but not dominating the market.

With all of its resources, why has Microsoft struggled to translate its innovations into market successes? Let's look at three reasons that have been talked about in the business press.

First, the dominance of the Windows and Office software has made it difficult to launch new products. Developers of new products have, at times, had to justify how their new product fit into the core Microsoft product line. Dick Brass, a former VP at Microsoft, states, "The company routinely manages to frustrate the efforts of its visionary leaders." For example, when Brass and his team developed an innovative technology to display text on a screen, called ClearType, engineers in the Windows group hampered the product by falsely arguing it had bugs and wouldn't display some colors properly. Others in the firm stated they would support the technology only if they could control it. In the end, it took 10 years to get ClearType integrated into Windows.

Second, Microsoft has a difficult time attracting the top software designers. The firm is not seen as a hip place to work. It is seen by developers as too bureaucratic. And their flat stock price makes it hard to entice top designers with promises of wealth from rising stock options—a common compensation element for technology talent.

Third, great innovations are increasingly the output of collaborative, open-source design, but Microsoft is reluctant to fully embrace the open-source development model. They developed a system where start-up firms can sign onto a program to gain access to free Microsoft software and provide development ideas to Microsoft and have signed up 35,000 firms, but its system is still more bureaucratic than those of its competitors. As one entrepreneur commented about working with Microsoft, "We got introduced to Microsoft through our investors. They don't do this for just anybody." As a result, Microsoft has lost those "anybodies" as development partners and future customers.

Sources: Vance, A. 2010. At Top of Business but Just Not Cool. *International Herald Tribune*, July 6: 2; Clarke, G. 2010. Inside Microsoft's Innovation Crisis. *Theregister.co.uk*, February 5: np; Brass, D. 2010. Microsoft's Creative Destruction. *NYTimes.com*, February 4: np.

Product Champions   CE does not always involve making large investments in start-ups or establishing incubators to spawn new divisions. Often, innovative ideas emerge in the normal course of business and are brought forth and become part of the way of doing business. Entrepreneurial champions are often needed to take charge of internally generated ventures. **Product** (or project) **champions** are those individuals working within a corporation who bring entrepreneurial ideas forward, identify what kind of market exists for the product or service, find resources to support the venture, and promote the venture concept to upper management.[36]

When lower-level employees identify a product idea or novel solution, they will take it to their supervisor or someone in authority. A new idea that is generated in a technology lab may be introduced to others by its inventor. If the idea has merit, it gains support

> **product champion**
> an individual working within a corporation who brings entrepreneurial ideas forward, identifies what kind of market exists for the product or service, finds resources to support the venture, and promotes the venture concept to upper management.

and builds momentum across the organization.[37] Even though the corporation may not be looking for new ideas or have a program for cultivating internal ventures, the independent behaviors of a few organizational members can have important strategic consequences.

No matter how an entrepreneurial idea comes to light, however, a new venture concept must pass through two critical stages or it may never get off the ground:

1. *Project definition.* An opportunity has to be justified in terms of its attractiveness in the marketplace and how well it fits with the corporation's other strategic objectives.
2. *Project impetus.* For a project to gain impetus, its strategic and economic impact must be supported by senior managers who have experience with similar projects. It then becomes an embryonic business with its own organization and budget.

For a project to advance through these stages of definition and impetus, a product champion is often needed to generate support and encouragement. Champions are especially important during the time after a new project has been defined but before it gains momentum. They form a link between the definition and impetus stages of internal development, which they do by procuring resources and stimulating interest for the product among potential customers.[38] Often, they must work quietly and alone. Consider the example of Ken Kutaragi, the Sony engineer who championed the PlayStation.

> Even though Sony had made the processor that powered the first Nintendo video games, no one at Sony in the mid-1980s saw any future in such products. "It was a kind of snobbery," Kutaragi recalled. "For Sony people, the Nintendo product would have been very embarrassing to make because it was only a toy." But Kutaragi was convinced he could make a better product. He began working secretly on a video game. Kutaragi said, "I realized that if it was visible, it would be killed." He quietly began enlisting the support of senior executives, such as the head of R&D. He made a case that Sony could use his project to develop capabilities in digital technologies that would be important in the future. It was not until 1994, after years of "underground" development and quiet building of support, that Sony introduced the PlayStation. By the year 2000, Sony had sold 55 million of them, and Kutaragi became CEO of Sony Computer Entertainment. By 2005, Kutagari was Sony's Chief Operating Officer, and was supervising efforts to launch PS3, the next generation version of the market-leading PlayStation video game console.[39]

Product champions play an important entrepreneurial role in a corporate setting by encouraging others to take a chance on promising new ideas.[40]

Measuring the Success of Corporate Entrepreneurship Activities

At this point in the discussion, it is reasonable to ask whether CE is successful. Corporate venturing, like the innovation process, usually requires a tremendous effort. Is it worth it? We consider factors that corporations need to take into consideration when evaluating the success of CE programs. We also examine techniques that companies can use to limit the expense of venturing or to cut their losses when CE initiatives appear doomed.

>LO12.4

How corporate entrepreneurship achieves both financial goals and strategic goals.

Comparing Strategic and Financial CE Goals   Not all corporate venturing efforts are financially rewarding. In terms of financial performance, slightly more than 50 percent of corporate venturing efforts reach profitability (measured by ROI) within six years of their launch.[41] If this were the only criterion for success, it would seem to be a rather poor return. On the one hand, these results should be expected, because CE is riskier than other investments such as expanding ongoing operations. On the other hand, corporations expect a higher return from corporate venturing projects than from normal operations. Thus, in terms of the risk–return trade-off, it seems that CE often falls short of expectations.[42]

There are several other important criteria, however, for judging the success of a corporate venture initiative. Most CE programs have strategic goals.[43] The strategic reasons for undertaking a corporate venture include strengthening competitive position, entering into new markets, expanding capabilities by learning and acquiring new knowledge, and building the corporation's base of resources and experience. Three questions should be used to assess the effectiveness of a corporation's venturing initiatives:[44]

1. *Are the products or services offered by the venture accepted in the marketplace?* Is the venture considered to be a market success? If so, the financial returns are likely to be satisfactory. The venture may also open doors into other markets and suggest avenues for other venture projects.

2. *Are the contributions of the venture to the corporation's internal competencies and experience valuable?* Does the venture add to the worth of the firm internally? If so, strategic goals such as leveraging existing assets, building new knowledge, and enhancing firm capabilities are likely to be met.[45]

3. *Is the venture able to sustain its basis of competitive advantage?* Does the value proposition offered by the venture insulate it from competitive attack? If so, it is likely to place the corporation in a stronger position relative to competitors and provide a base from which to build other advantages.

These criteria include both strategic and financial goals of CE. Another way to evaluate a corporate venture is in terms of the four criteria from the Balanced Scorecard (Chapter 3). In a successful venture, not only are financial and market acceptance (customer) goals met but so are the internal business and innovation and learning goals. Thus, when assessing the success of corporate venturing, it is important to look beyond simple financial returns and consider a well-rounded set of criteria.[46]

Exit Champions   Although a culture of championing venture projects is advantageous for stimulating an ongoing stream of entrepreneurial initiatives, many—in fact, most—of the ideas will not work out. At some point in the process, a majority of initiatives will be abandoned. Sometimes, however, companies wait too long to terminate a new venture and do so only after large sums of resources are used up or, worse, result in a marketplace failure. Motorola's costly global satellite telecom project known as Iridium provides a useful illustration. Even though problems with the project existed during the lengthy development process, Motorola refused to pull the plug. Only after investing $5 billion and years of effort was the project abandoned.[47]

One way to avoid these costly and discouraging defeats is to support a key role in the CE process: **exit champions.** In contrast to product champions and other entrepreneurial enthusiasts within the corporation, exit champions are willing to question the viability of a venture project.[48] By demanding hard evidence and challenging the belief system that is carrying an idea forward, exit champions hold the line on ventures that appear shaky.

Both product champions and exit champions must be willing to energetically stand up for what they believe. Both put their reputations on the line. But they also differ in important ways.[49] Product champions deal in uncertainty and ambiguity. Exit champions reduce ambiguity by gathering hard data and developing a strong case for why a project should be killed. Product champions are often thought to be willing to violate procedures and operate outside normal channels. Exit champions often have to reinstate procedures and re-assert the decision-making criteria that are supposed to guide venture decisions. Whereas product champions often emerge as heroes, exit champions run the risk of losing status by opposing popular projects.

The role of exit champion may seem unappealing. But it is one that could save a corporation both financially and in terms of its reputation in the marketplace. It is especially important because one measure of the success of a firm's CE efforts is the extent to which it knows when to cut its losses and move on.

> **exit champion** an individual working within a corporation who is willing to question the viability of a venture project by demanding hard evidence of venture success and challenging the belief system that carries a venture forward.

real options analysis an investment analysis tool that looks at an investment or activity as a series of sequential steps, and for each step the investor has the option of (a) investing additional funds to grow or accelerate, (b) delaying, (c) shrinking the scale of, or (d) abandoning the activity.

Real Options Analysis: A Useful Tool

One way firms can minimize failure and avoid losses from pursuing faulty ideas is to apply the logic of real options. **Real options analysis** (ROA) is an investment analysis tool from the field of finance. It has been slowly, but increasingly, adopted by consultants and executives to support strategic decision making in firms. What does ROA consist of and how can it be appropriately applied to the investments required to initiate strategic decisions? To understand *real* options it is first necessary to have a basic understanding of what *options* are.

Options exist when the owner of the option has the right but not the obligation to engage in certain types of transactions. The most common are stock options. A stock option grants the holder the right to buy (call option) or sell (put option) shares of the stock at a fixed price (strike price) at some time in the future.[50] The investment to be made immediately is small, whereas the investment to be made in the future is generally larger. An option to buy a rapidly rising stock currently priced at $50 might cost as little as $.50.[51] Owners of such a stock option have limited their losses to $.50 per share, while the upside potential is unlimited. This aspect of options is attractive, because options offer the prospect of high gains with relatively small up-front investments that represent limited losses.

The phrase "real options" applies to situations where options theory and valuation techniques are applied to real assets or physical things as opposed to financial assets. Applied to entrepreneurship, real options suggest a path that companies can use to manage the uncertainty associated with launching new ventures. Some of the most common applications of real options are with property and insurance. A real estate option grants the holder the right to buy or sell a piece of property at an established price some time in the future. The actual market price of the property may rise above the established (or strike) price—or the market value may sink below the strike price. If the price of the property goes up, the owner of the option is likely to buy it. If the market value of the property drops below the strike price, the option holder is unlikely to execute the purchase. In the latter circumstance, the option holder has limited his or her loss to the cost of the option, but during the life of the option retains the right to participate in whatever the upside potential might be.

Applications of Real Options Analysis to Strategic Decisions

The concept of options can also be applied to strategic decisions where management has flexibility. Situations arise where management must decide whether to invest additional funds to grow or accelerate the activity, perhaps delay in order to learn more, shrink the scale of the activity, or even abandon it. Decisions to invest in new ventures or other business activities such as R&D, motion pictures, exploration and production of oil wells, and the opening and closing of copper mines often have this flexibility.[52] Important issues to note are:

- ROA is appropriate to use when investments can be staged; a smaller investment up front can be followed by subsequent investments. Real options can be applied to an investment decision that gives the company the right, but not the obligation, to make follow-on investments.
- Strategic decision makers have "tollgates," or key points at which they can decide whether to continue, delay, or abandon the project. Executives have flexibility. There are opportunities to make other go or no-go decisions associated with each phase.
- It is expected that there will be increased knowledge about outcomes at the time of the next investment and that additional knowledge will help inform the decision makers about whether to make additional investments (i.e., whether the option is in the money or out of the money).

Many strategic decisions have the characteristic of containing a series of options. The phenomenon is called "embedded options," a series of investments in which at each stage of the investment there is a go/no–go decision. Consider the real options logic that Johnson Controls, a maker of car seats, instrument panels, and interior control systems uses to advance or eliminate entrepreneurial ideas.[53] Johnson options each new innovative idea by making a small investment in it. To decide whether to exercise an option, the idea must continue to prove itself at each stage of development. Here's how Jim Geschke, vice president and general manager of electronics integration at Johnson, describes the process:

> Think of Johnson as an innovation machine. The front end has a robust series of gates that each idea must pass through. Early on, we'll have many ideas and spend a little money on each of them. As they get more fleshed out, the ideas go through a gate where a go or no-go decision is made. A lot of ideas get filtered out, so there are far fewer items, and the spending on each goes up. . . . Several months later each idea will face another gate. If it passes, that means it's a serious idea that we are going to develop. Then the spending goes way up, and the number of ideas goes way down. By the time you reach the final gate, you need to have a credible business case in order to be accepted. At a certain point in the development process, we take our idea to customers and ask them what they think. Sometimes they say, "That's a terrible idea. Forget it." Other times they say, "That's fabulous. I want a million of them."

This process of evaluating ideas by separating winning ideas from losing ones in a way that keeps investments low has helped Johnson Controls grow its revenues to over $34 billion a year. Using real options logic to advance the development process is a key way that firms reduce uncertainty and minimize innovation-related failures.[54]

Potential Pitfalls of Real Options Analysis

Despite the many benefits that can be gained from using ROA, managers must be aware of its potential limitations or pitfalls. Below we will address three major issues.[55]

Agency Theory and the Back-Solver Dilemma   Let's assume that companies adopting a real-options perspective invest heavily in training and that their people understand how to effectively estimate variance—the amount of dispersion or range that is estimated for potential outcomes. Such training can help them use ROA. However, it does not solve another inherent problem: managers may have an incentive and the know-how to "game the system." Most electronic spreadsheets permit users to simply back-solve any formula; that is, you can type in the answer you want and ask what values are needed in a formula to get that answer. If managers know that a certain option value must be met in order for the proposal to get approved, they can back-solve the model to find a variance estimate needed to arrive at the answer that upper management desires.

Agency problems are typically inherent in investment decisions. They may occur when the managers of a firm are separated from its owners—when managers act as "agents" rather than "principals" (owners). A manager may have something to gain by not acting in the owner's best interests, or the interests of managers and owners are not co-aligned. Agency theory suggests that as managerial and owner interests diverge, managers will follow the path of their own self-interests. Sometimes this is to secure better compensation: Managers who propose projects may believe that if their projects are approved, they stand a much better chance of getting promoted. So while managers have an incentive to propose projects that *should* be successful, they also have an incentive to propose projects that *might* be successful. And because of the subjectivity involved in formally modeling a real option, managers may have an incentive to choose variance values that increase the likelihood of approval.

Managerial Conceit: Overconfidence and the Illusion of Control   Often, poor decisions are the result of such traps as biases, blind spots, and other human frailties. Much of this literature falls under the concept of **managerial conceit**.[56]

First, managerial conceit occurs when decision makers who have made successful choices in the past come to believe that they possess superior expertise for managing uncertainty. They believe that their abilities can reduce the risks inherent in decision making to a much greater extent than they actually can. Such managers are more likely to shift

back-solver dilemma
problem with investment decisions in which managers scheme to have a project meet investment approval criteria, even though the investment may not enhance firm value.

managerial conceit biases, blind spots, and other human frailties that lead to poor managerial decisions.

away from analysis to trusting their own judgment. In the case of real options, they can simply declare that any given decision is a real option and proceed as before. If asked to formally model their decision, they are more likely to employ variance estimates that support their viewpoint.

Second, employing the real-options perspective can encourage decision makers toward a bias for action. Such a bias may lead to carelessness. Managerial conceit is as much a problem (if not more so) for small decisions as for big ones. Why? The cost to write the first stage of an option is much smaller than the cost of full commitment, and managers pay less attention to small decisions than to large ones. Because real options are designed to minimize potential losses while preserving potential gains, any problems that arise are likely to be smaller at first, causing less concern for the manager. Managerial conceit could suggest that managers will assume that those problems are the easiest to solve and control—a concern referred to as the illusion of control. Managers may fail to respond appropriately because they overlook the problem or believe that since it is small, they can easily resolve it. Thus, managers may approach each real-option decision with less care and diligence than if they had made a full commitment to a larger investment.

Managerial Conceit: Irrational Escalation of Commitment   A strength of a real options perspective is also one of its Achilles heels. Both real options and decisions involving escalation of commitment require specific environments with sequential decisions.[57] As the escalation-of-commitment literature indicates, simply separating a decision into multiple parts does not guarantee that decisions made will turn out well. This condition is potentially present whenever the exercise decision retains some uncertainty, which most still do. The decision to abandon also has strong psychological factors associated with it that affect the ability of managers to make correct exercise decisions.[58]

An option to exit requires reversing an initial decision made by someone in the organization. Organizations typically encourage managers to "own their decisions" in order to motivate them. As managers invest themselves in their decision, it proves harder for them to lose face by reversing course. For managers making the decision, it feels as if they made the wrong decision in the first place, even if it was initially a good decision. The more specific the manager's human capital becomes, the harder it is to transfer it to other organizations. Hence, there is a greater likelihood that managers will stick around and try to make an existing decision work. They are more likely to continue an existing project even if it should perhaps be ended.[59]

Despite the potential pitfalls of a real options approach, many of the strategic decisions that product champions and top managers must make are enhanced when decision makers have an entrepreneurial mind-set.

Entrepreneurial Orientation

Firms that want to engage in successful CE need to have an entrepreneurial orientation (EO).[60] EO refers to the strategy-making practices that businesses use in identifying and launching corporate ventures. It represents a frame of mind and a perspective toward entrepreneurship that is reflected in a firm's ongoing processes and corporate culture.[61]

An EO has five dimensions that permeate the decision-making styles and practices of the firm's members: autonomy, innovativeness, proactiveness, competitive aggressiveness, and risk taking. These factors work together to enhance a firm's entrepreneurial performance. But even those firms that are strong in only a few aspects of EO can be very successful.[62] Exhibit 12.4 summarizes the dimensions of **entrepreneurial orientation.** Below, we discuss the five dimensions of EO and how they have been used to enhance internal venture development.

escalation of commitment the tendency for managers to irrationally stick with an investment, even one that is broken down into a sequential series of decisions, when investment criteria are not be met.

>LO12.6

How an entrepreneurial orientation can enhance a firm's efforts to develop promising corporate venture initiatives.

entrepreneurial orientation the strategy-making practices that businesses use in identifying and launching new ventures, consisting of autonomy, innovativeness, proactiveness, competitive aggressiveness, and risk taking.

Dimension	Definition
Autonomy	Independent action by an individual or team aimed at bringing forth a business concept or vision and carrying it through to completion.
Innovativeness	A willingness to introduce novelty through experimentation and creative processes aimed at developing new products and services as well as new processes.
Proactiveness	A forward-looking perspective characteristic of a market-place leader that has the foresight to seize opportunities in anticipation of future demand.
Competitive aggressiveness	An intense effort to outperform industry rivals characterized by a combative posture or an aggressive response aimed at improving position or overcoming a threat in a competitive marketplace.
Risk taking	Making decisions and taking action without certain knowledge of probable outcomes; some undertakings may also involve making substantial resource commitments in the process of venturing forward.

Sources: Dess, G. G. & Lumpkin, G. T. 2005. The Role of Entrepreneurial Orientation in Stimulating Effective Corporate Entrepreneurship. *Academy of Management Executive,* 19(1): 147–156; Covin, J. G. & Slevin, D. P. 1991. A Conceptual Model of Entrepreneurship as Firm Behavior. *Entrepreneurship Theory & Practice,* Fall: 7–25; Lumpkin, G. T. and Dess, G. G. 1996. Clarifying the Entrepreneurial Orientation Construct and Linking It to Performance. *Academy of Management Review,* 21: 135–172; Miller, D. 1983. The Correlates of Entrepreneurship in Three Types of Firms. *Management Science,* 29: 770–791.

Exhibit 12.4
Dimensions of Entrepreneurial Orientation

Autonomy

Autonomy refers to a willingness to act independently in order to carry forward an entrepreneurial vision or opportunity. It applies to both individuals and teams that operate outside an organization's existing norms and strategies. In the context of corporate entrepreneurship, autonomous work units are often used to leverage existing strengths in new arenas, identify opportunities that are beyond the organization's current capabilities, and encourage development of new ventures or improved business practices.[63]

The need for autonomy may apply to either dispersed or focused entrepreneurial efforts. Because of the emphasis on venture projects that are being developed outside of the normal flow of business, a focused approach suggests a working environment that is relatively autonomous. But autonomy may also be important in an organization where entrepreneurship is part of the corporate culture. Everything from the methods of group interaction to the firm's reward system must make organizational members feel as if they can think freely about venture opportunities, take time to investigate them, and act without fear of condemnation. This implies a respect for the autonomy of each individual and an openness to the independent thinking that goes into championing a corporate venture idea. Thus, autonomy represents a type of empowerment (see Chapter 11) that is directed at identifying and leveraging entrepreneurial opportunities. Exhibit 12.5 identifies two techniques that organizations often use to promote autonomy.

autonomy
independent action by an individual or team aimed at bringing forth a business concept or vision and carrying it through to completion.

Exhibit 12.5 Autonomy Techniques

	Autonomy	
Technique	**Description/Purpose**	**Example**
Use skunkworks to foster entrepreneurial thinking	Skunkworks are independent work units, often physically separate from corporate headquarters. They allow employees to get out from under the pressures of their daily routines to engage in creative problem solving.	Overstock.com created a skunkworks to address the problem of returned merchandise. The solution was a business within-a-business: Overstock auctions. The unit has grown by selling products returned to Overstock and offers fees 30 percent lower than eBay's auction service.
Design organizational structures that support independent action	Established companies with traditional structures often need to break out of such old forms to compete more effectively.	Deloitte Consulting, a division of Deloitte Touche Tohmatsu, found it difficult to compete against young agile firms. So it broke the firm into small autonomous units called "chip-aways" that operate with the flexibility of a start-up. In its first year, revenues were $40 million—10 percent higher than its projections.

Sources: Conlin, M. 2006. Square Feet. Oh How Square! *BusinessWeek, www.businessweek.com*, July 3; Cross, K. 2001. Bang the Drum Quickly. *Business 2.0*, May: 28–30; Sweeney, J. 2004. A Firm for All Reasons. *Consulting Magazine, www.consultingmag.com*; and Wagner, M. 2005. Out of the Skunkworks. *Internet Retailer*, January, *www.internetretailer.com*.

Creating autonomous work units and encouraging independent action may have pitfalls that can jeopardize their effectiveness. Autonomous teams often lack coordination. Excessive decentralization has a strong potential to create inefficiencies, such as duplication of effort and wasting resources on projects with questionable feasibility. For example, Chris Galvin, former CEO of Motorola, scrapped the skunkworks approach the company had been using to develop new wireless phones. Fifteen teams had created 128 different phones, which led to spiraling costs and overly complex operations.[64]

For autonomous work units and independent projects to be effective, such efforts have to be measured and monitored. This requires a delicate balance: companies must have the patience and budget to tolerate the explorations of autonomous groups and the strength to cut back efforts that are not bearing fruit. It must be undertaken with a clear sense of purpose—namely, to generate new sources of competitive advantage.

Innovativeness

innovativeness a willingness to introduce novelty through experimentation and creative processes aimed at developing new products and services as well as new processes.

Innovativeness refers to a firm's efforts to find new opportunities and novel solutions. In the beginning of this chapter we discussed innovation; here the focus is on innovativeness—a firm's attitude toward innovation and willingness to innovate. It involves creativity and experimentation that result in new products, new services, or improved technological processes.[65] Innovativeness is one of the major components of an entrepreneurial strategy. As indicated at the beginning of the chapter, however, the job of managing innovativeness can be very challenging.

Innovativeness requires that firms depart from existing technologies and practices and venture beyond the current state of the art. Inventions and new ideas need to be nurtured

Best Buy Finds Social Responsibility Drives Business

In the storage areas of a Best Buy store, you might find old-style analog TVs, desktop computers, and outmoded cell phones, and possibly an eight-track tape player or ham radio. Best Buy believes that social responsibility and good business sense meet at the recycling bin. With this perspective, Best Buy is at the forefront of a growing business trend—firms that see social responsibility as a means toward competitive success. Firms increasingly see entrepreneurial opportunities in taking a leading role on issues such as the environment, product safety, and fair trade. In focusing on Corporate Social Responsibility (CSR), they are leveraging new technologies, environmentally friendly ventures, and entrepreneurial practices to motivate workers in their firm, meet the interests and demands of their customers, and differentiate themselves from their rivals—while also meeting their societal responsibilities.

With Best Buy, we see this trend in multiple ways. The most obvious example is with their recycling program. Starting in early 2009, Best Buy began offering free recycling of a wide range of electronic products. In the first nine months of the program, Best Buy took in 25 million pounds of used electronics. To insure responsible manufacturing of new products, Best Buy instituted an auditing program of their suppliers' manufacturing facilities to insure they don't exploit their workers or damage the environment. This is an audit with teeth. They canceled relationships with 26 of their approximately 200 supplier factories in 2008 as a result of the audits. They also work to create a positive environment for their employees and to promote diversity by creating social networks for groups of their employees. Best Buy has groups for women, Hispanic, African American, Asian American, and gay and lesbian employees. The firm has also targeted their charitable giving toward teens, a key customer group, and offers scholarships and grants to teenagers working for social change.

Best Buy doesn't take these actions simply to be a "good" company. They also see these actions as a means toward success. "We don't budget for corporate responsibility," said Paul Prahl, vice president of Best Buy public affairs. "We're really trying to drive it through the business model of the company. We only feel we'll be successful in the marketplace if we are socially responsible."

● Best Buy, well-known as an innovative electronics retailer, is also pioneering the recycling of electronics products.

With the recycling program, they are driving traffic to the store. An individual dropping off an old stereo that just broke is likely shopping for a new surround sound system. For some product trade-ins, Best Buy will even give a gift card to the person bringing in the old product for recycling. This also offers a way to differentiate from more bottom-line competitors, such as Walmart. Some customers will prefer to buy from Best Buy because of their recycling program. Their auditing program is also designed to insure they maintain a positive reputation with their customers. The worker social groups are designed to motivate workers, lower turnover, and connect with customer communities. For example, one of the groups, the women's leadership forum (WoLF), reaches out to female customers.

Best Buy's CEO, Brian Dunn, believes that Best Buy can benefit by listening to employees and customers for socially responsible ventures. Best Buy initiated the recycling program after employees asked what the firm was doing to become more socially responsible. Dunn now posts questions to an employee website called the Water Cooler, monitors customer comments on Facebook and Twitter, and invites customers to leadership meetings to get stakeholder input on socially responsible actions Best Buy should take. With their success, Best Buy's experience supports the view that being a good corporate citizen does make business sense.

Sources: Gunther, M. 2009. Best Buy Wants Your Junk. *Fortune*, December 7: 96–100; Kirdahy, M. 2007. Responsibility Pays. *Forbes.com*, November 13: np.

 environmental sustainability ethics

even when their benefits are unclear. However, in today's climate of rapid change, effectively producing, assimilating, and exploiting innovations can be an important avenue for achieving competitive advantages. Interest in global warming and other ecological concerns has led many corporations to focus their innovativeness efforts on solving environmental problems. Strategy Spotlight 12.8 describes how Best Buy is using entrepreneurial thinking and innovative practices to deliver socially responsible solutions.

As our earlier discussion of CE indicated, many corporations owe their success to an active program of innovation-based corporate venturing.[66] Exhibit 12.6 highlights two of the methods companies can use to enhance their competitive position through innovativeness.

Innovativeness can be a source of great progress and strong corporate growth, but there are also major pitfalls for firms that invest in innovation. Expenditures on R&D aimed at identifying new products or processes can be a waste of resources if the effort does not yield results. Another danger is related to the competitive climate. Even if a company innovates a new capability or successfully applies a technological breakthrough, another company may develop a similar innovation or find a use for it that is more profitable. Finally R&D and other innovation efforts are among the first to be cut back during an economic downturn.

Even though innovativeness is an important means of internal corporate venturing, it also involves major risks, because investments in innovations may not pay off. For strategic managers of entrepreneurial firms, successfully developing and adopting innovations can generate competitive advantages and provide a major source of growth for the firm.

Proactiveness

Proactiveness refers to a firm's efforts to seize new opportunities. Proactive organizations monitor trends, identify the future needs of existing customers, and anticipate changes

> **proactiveness** a forward-looking perspective characteristic of a marketplace leader that has the foresight to seize opportunities in anticipation of future demand.

Exhibit 12.6 Innovativeness Techniques

Innovativeness		
Technique	**Description/Purpose**	**Example**
Foster creativity and experimentation	Companies that support idea exploration and allow employees to express themselves creatively enhance innovation outcomes.	To tap into its reserves of innovative talent, Royal Dutch/Shell created "GameChanger" to help employees develop promising ideas. The process provides funding up to $600,000 for would-be entrepreneurs to pursue innovative projects and conduct experiments.
Invest in new technology, R&D, and continuous improvement	The latest technologies often provide sources of new competitive advantages. To extract value from a new technology, companies must invest in it.	Dell Computer Corporation's new OptiPlex manufacturing system revolutionized the traditional assembly line. Hundreds of custom-built computers can be made in an eight-hour shift using state of the art automation techniques that have increased productivity per person by 160 percent.

Sources: Breen, B. 2004. Living in Dell Time. *Fast Company,* November: 88–92: Hammonds, K. H. 2002. Size Is Not a Strategy. *Fast Company,* August: 78–83; Perman, S. 2001. Automate or Die. *eCompanyNow.com,* July; Dell, M. 1999. *Direct from Dell.* New York: HarperBusiness; and Watson, R. 2006. Expand Your Innovation Horizons. *Fast Company, www.fastcompany.com,* May.

in demand or emerging problems that can lead to new venture opportunities. Proactiveness involves not only recognizing changes but also being willing to act on those insights ahead of the competition.[67] Strategic managers who practice proactiveness have their eye on the future in a search for new possibilities for growth and development. Such a forward-looking perspective is important for companies that seek to be industry leaders. Many proactive firms seek out ways not only to be future oriented but also to change the very nature of competition in their industry.

Proactiveness puts competitors in the position of having to respond to successful initiatives. The benefit gained by firms that are the first to enter new markets, establish brand identity, implement administrative techniques, or adopt new operating technologies in an industry is called first mover advantage.[68]

First movers usually have several advantages. First, industry pioneers, especially in new industries, often capture unusually high profits because there are no competitors to drive prices down. Second, first movers that establish brand recognition are usually able to retain their image and hold on to the market share gains they earned by being first. Sometimes these benefits also accrue to other early movers in an industry, but, generally speaking, first movers have an advantage that can be sustained until firms enter the maturity phase of an industry's life cycle.[69]

First movers are not always successful. The customers of companies that introduce novel products or embrace breakthrough technologies may be reluctant to commit to a new way of doing things. In his book *Crossing the Chasm,* Geoffrey A. Moore noted that most firms seek evolution, not revolution, in their operations. This makes it difficult for a first mover to sell promising new technologies.[70]

Even with these caveats, however, companies that are first movers can enhance their competitive position. Exhibit 12.7 illustrates two methods firms can use to act proactively.

Exhibit 12.7   **Proactiveness Techniques**

Proactiveness		
Technique	**Description/Purpose**	**Example**
Introduce new products or technological capabilities ahead of the competition.	Being a first mover provides companies with an ability to shape the playing field and shift competitive advantages in their favor.	Sony's mission states, "We should always be the pioneers with our products—out front leading the market." This philosophy has made Sony technologically strong with industry-leading products such as the PlayStation and Vaio laptop computers.
Continuously seek out new product or service offerings.	Firms that provide new resources or sources of supply can benefit from a proactive stance.	Costco seized a chance to leverage its success as a warehouse club that sells premium brands when it introduced Costco Home Stores. The home stores are usually located near its warehouse stores and its rapid inventory turnover gives it a cost advantage of 15 to 25 percent over close competitors such as Bassett Furniture and the Bombay Company.

Sources: Bryce, D. J. & Dyer, J. H. 2007. Strategies to Crack Well-Guarded Markets. *Harvard Business Review,* May: 84–92; Collins, J. C. & Porras, J. I. 1997. *Built to Last.* New York: HarperBusiness; Robinson, D. 2005. Sony Pushes Reliability in Vaio Laptops. *IT Week, www.itweek.co.uk,* October 12; and *www.sony.com.*

Being an industry leader does not always lead to competitive advantages. Some firms that have launched pioneering new products or staked their reputation on new brands have failed to get the hoped-for payoff. Coca-Cola and PepsiCo invested $75 million to launch sodas that would capitalize on the low-carb diet trend. But with half the carbohydrates taken out, neither *C2,* Coke's entry, nor *Pepsi Edge* tasted very good. The two new brands combined never achieved more than one percent market share. PepsiCo halted production in 2005 and Coca-Cola followed suit in 2007.[71] Such missteps are indicative of the dangers of trying to proactively anticipate demand. Another danger for opportunity-seeking companies is that they will take their proactiveness efforts too far. For example, Porsche has tried to extend its brand images outside of the automotive arena. While some efforts have worked, such as Porsche-designed T-shirts and sunglasses, other efforts have failed, such as the Porsche-branded golf clubs.

Careful monitoring and scanning of the environment, as well as extensive feasibility research, are needed for a proactive strategy to lead to competitive advantages. Firms that do it well usually have substantial growth and internal development to show for it. Many of them have been able to sustain the advantages of proactiveness for years.

Competitive Aggressiveness

competitive aggressiveness an intense effort to outperform industry rivals characterized by a combative posture or an aggressive response aimed at improving position or overcoming a threat in a competitive marketplace.

Competitive aggressiveness refers to a firm's efforts to outperform its industry rivals. Companies with an aggressive orientation are willing to "do battle" with competitors. They might slash prices and sacrifice profitability to gain market share or spend aggressively to obtain manufacturing capacity. As an avenue of firm development and growth, competitive aggressiveness may involve being very assertive in leveraging the results of other entrepreneurial activities such as innovativeness or proactiveness.

Competitive aggressiveness is directed toward competitors. The SWOT analysis discussed in Chapters 2 and 3 provides a useful way to distinguish between these different approaches to CE. Proactiveness, as we saw in the last section, is a response to opportunities—the O in SWOT. Competitive aggressiveness, by contrast, is a response to threats—the T in SWOT. A competitively aggressive posture is important for firms that seek to enter new markets in the face of intense rivalry.

Strategic managers can use competitive aggressiveness to combat industry trends that threaten their survival or market position. Sometimes firms need to be forceful in defending the competitive position that has made them an industry leader. Firms often need to be aggressive to ensure their advantage by capitalizing on new technologies or serving new market needs. Exhibit 12.8 suggests two of the ways competitively aggressive firms enhance their entrepreneurial position.

Another practice companies use to overcome the competition is to make preannouncements of new products or technologies. This type of signaling is aimed not only at potential customers but also at competitors to see how they will react or to discourage them from launching similar initiatives. Sometimes the preannouncements are made just to scare off competitors, an action that has potential ethical implications.

Competitive aggressiveness may not always lead to competitive advantages. Some companies (or their CEOs) have severely damaged their reputations by being overly aggressive. Although it continues to be a dominant player, Microsoft's highly aggressive profile makes it the subject of scorn by some businesses and individuals. Efforts to find viable replacements for the Microsoft products have helped fuel interest in alternative options provided by Google, Apple, and the open-source software movement.[72]

Competitive aggressiveness is a strategy that is best used in moderation. Companies that aggressively establish their competitive position and vigorously exploit opportunities to achieve profitability may, over the long run, be better able to sustain their competitive advantages if their goal is to defeat, rather than decimate, their competitors.

Exhibit 12.8 Competitive Aggressiveness Techniques

Competitive Aggressiveness		
Technique	**Description/Purpose**	**Example**
Enter markets with drastically lower prices.	Narrow operating margins make companies vulnerable to extended price competition.	Using open-source software, California-based Zimbra, Inc. has become a leader in messaging and collaboration software. Its product costs about one-third less than its direct competitor Microsoft Exchange. Zimbra now has over 60 million users.
Find successful business models and copy them.	As long as a practice is not protected by intellectual property laws, it's probably okay to imitate it. Finding solutions to existing problems is generally quicker and cheaper than inventing them.	Best Practices LLC is a North Carolina consulting group that seeks out best practices and then repackages and resells them. With annual revenues in excess of $8 million, Best Practices has become a leader in continuous improvement and benchmarking strategies.

Sources: Guth, R. A. 2006. Trolling the Web for Free Labor, Software Upstarts Are New Force. *The Wall Street Journal*, November 12: 1; Mochari, I. 2001. Steal This Strategy, *Inc.*, July: 62–67; www.bestpractices.com, and www.zimbra.com.

Risk Taking

Risk taking refers to a firm's willingness to seize a venture opportunity even though it does not know whether the venture will be successful—to act boldly without knowing the consequences. To be successful through corporate entrepreneurship, firms usually have to take on riskier alternatives, even if it means forgoing the methods or products that have worked in the past. To obtain high financial returns, firms take such risks as assuming high levels of debt, committing large amounts of firm resources, introducing new products into new markets, and investing in unexplored technologies.

All of the approaches to internal development that we have discussed are potentially risky. Whether they are being aggressive, proactive, or innovative, firms on the path of CE must act without knowing how their actions will turn out. Before launching their strategies, corporate entrepreneurs must know their firm's appetite for risk.[73]

Three types of risk that organizations and their executives face are business risk, financial risk, and personal risk:

- *Business risk taking* involves venturing into the unknown without knowing the probability of success. This is the risk associated with entering untested markets or committing to unproven technologies.
- *Financial risk taking* requires that a company borrow heavily or commit a large portion of its resources in order to grow. In this context, risk is used to refer to the risk/return trade-off that is familiar in financial analysis.
- *Personal risk taking* refers to the risks that an executive assumes in taking a stand in favor of a strategic course of action. Executives who take such risks stand to influence the course of their whole company, and their decisions also can have significant implications for their careers.

risk taking making decisions and taking action without certain knowledge of probable outcomes. Some undertakings may also involve making substantial resource commitments in the process of venturing forward.

Exhibit 12.9 Risk-Taking Techniques

Risk Taking		
Technique	**Description/Purpose**	**Example**
Research and assess risk factors to minimize uncertainty	Companies that "do their homework"—that is, carefully evaluate the implications of bold actions—reduce the likelihood of failure.	Graybar Electric Co. took a risk when it invested $144 million to revamp its distribution system. It consolidated 231 small centers into 16 supply warehouses and installed the latest communications network. Graybar is now considered a leader in facility redesign and its sales have increased steadily since the consolidation, topping $5 billion in sales in a recent year.
Use techniques that have worked in other domains	Risky methods that other companies have tried may provide an avenue for advancing company goals.	Autobytel.com, one of the first companies to sell cars online, decided on an approach that worked well for others—advertising during the Super Bowl. It was the first dot-com ever to do so and its $1.2 million 30-second ad paid off well by generating weeks of free publicity and favorable business press.

Sources: Anonymous. 2006. Graybar Offers Data Center Redesign Seminars. *Cabling Installation and Maintenance, www.cim.pennnet.com*, September 1; Keenan, F. & Mullaney, T. J. 2001. Clicking at Graybar. *BusinessWeek,* June 18: 132–34; Weintraub, A. 2001. Make or break for Autobytel. *BusinessWeek e.biz,* July 9: EB30-EB32; *www.autobytel.com*; and *www.graybar.com*.

Even though risk taking involves taking chances, it is not gambling. The best-run companies investigate the consequences of various opportunities and create scenarios of likely outcomes. A key to managing entrepreneurial risks is to evaluate new venture opportunities thoroughly enough to reduce the uncertainty surrounding them. Exhibit 12.9 indicates two methods companies can use to strengthen their competitive position through risk taking.

Risk taking, by its nature, involves potential dangers and pitfalls. Only carefully managed risk is likely to lead to competitive advantages. Actions that are taken without sufficient forethought, research, and planning may prove to be very costly. Therefore, strategic managers must always remain mindful of potential risks. In his book *Innovation and Entrepreneurship,* Peter Drucker argued that successful entrepreneurs are typically not risk takers. Instead, they take steps to minimize risks by carefully understanding them. That is how they avoid focusing on risk and remain focused on opportunity.[74] Risk taking is a good place to close this chapter on corporate entrepreneurship. Companies that choose to grow through internal corporate venturing must remember that entrepreneurship always involves embracing what is new and uncertain.

Reflecting on Career Implications . . .

- *Innovation:* Look around at the types of innovations being pursued by your company. Do they tend to be incremental or radical? Product-related or process-related? What new types of innovations might benefit your organization? How can you add value to such innovations?
- *Managing Innovation:* How might your organization's chances of a successful innovation increase through collaboration with innovation partners? Your ability to collaborate with individuals from other departments and firms will make you more receptive to and capable of innovation initiatives and enhance your career opportunities.
- *Corporate Entrepreneurship:* Do you consider the company you work for to be entrepreneurial? If not, what actions might you take to enhance its entrepreneurial spirit? If so, what have been the keys to its entrepreneurial success? Can these practices be repeated to achieve future successes?
- *Entrepreneurial Orientation:* Consider the five dimensions of entrepreneurial orientation. Is your organization especially strong at any of these? Especially weak? What are the career implications of your company's entrepreneurial strengths or weaknesses?

Summary

To remain competitive in today's economy, established firms must find new avenues for development and growth. This chapter has addressed how innovation and corporate entrepreneurship can be a means of internal venture creation and strategic renewal, and how an entrepreneurial orientation can help corporations enhance their competitive position.

Innovation is one of the primary means by which corporations grow and strengthen their strategic position. Innovations can take several forms, ranging from radical breakthrough innovations to incremental improvement innovations. Innovations are often used to update products and services or for improving organizational processes. Managing the innovation process is often challenging, because it involves a great deal of uncertainty and there are many choices to be made about the extent and type of innovations to pursue. By cultivating innovation skills, defining the scope of innovation, managing the pace of innovation, staffing to capture value from innovation, and collaborating with innovation partners, firms can more effectively manage the innovation process.

We also discussed the role of corporate entrepreneurship in venture development and strategic renewal. Corporations usually take either a focused or dispersed approach to corporate venturing. Firms with a focused approach usually separate the corporate venturing activity

from the ongoing operations of the firm in order to foster independent thinking and encourage entrepreneurial team members to think and act without the constraints imposed by the corporation. In corporations where venturing activities are dispersed, a culture of entrepreneurship permeates all parts of the company in order to induce strategic behaviors by all organizational members. In measuring the success of corporate venturing activities, both financial and strategic objectives should be considered. Real options analysis is often used to make better quality decisions in uncertain entrepreneurial situations. However, a real options approach has potential drawbacks.

Most entrepreneurial firms need to have an entrepreneurial orientation: the methods, practices, and decision-making styles that strategic managers use to act entrepreneurially. Five dimensions of entrepreneurial orientation are found in firms that pursue corporate venture strategies. Autonomy, innovativeness, proactiveness, competitive aggressiveness, and risk taking each make a unique contribution to the pursuit of new opportunities. When deployed effectively, the methods and practices of an entrepreneurial orientation can be used to engage successfully in corporate entrepreneurship and new venture creation. However, strategic managers must remain mindful of the pitfalls associated with each of these approaches.

Summary Review Questions

1. What is meant by the concept of a continuum of radical and incremental innovations?

2. What are the dilemmas that organizations face when deciding what innovation projects to pursue? What steps can organizations take to effectively manage the innovation process?

3. What is the difference between focused and dispersed approaches to corporate entrepreneurship?

4. How are business incubators used to foster internal corporate venturing?

5. What is the role of the product champion in bringing a new product or service into existence in a corporation? How can companies use product champions to enhance their venture development efforts?

6. Explain the difference between proactiveness and competitive aggressiveness in terms of achieving and sustaining competitive advantage.

7. Describe how the entrepreneurial orientation (EO) dimensions of innovativeness, proactiveness, and risk taking can be combined to create competitive advantages for entrepreneurial firms.

Key Terms

innovation, 433
radical innovation, 433
product innovation, 433
process innovation, 433
incremental
    innovation, 434
strategic envelope, 438
corporate
    entrepreneurship, 442
new venture group, 446
focused approaches
    to corporate
    entrepreneurship, 446
business incubator, 447
dispersed approaches
    to corporate
    entrepreneurship, 448
entrepreneurial
    culture, 448

product champion, 449
exit champion, 451
real options
    analysis, 452
back-solver
    dilemma, 453
managerial
    conceit, 453
entrepreneurial
    orientation, 454
escalation of
    commitment, 454
autonomy, 455
innovativeness, 456
proactiveness, 458
competitive
    aggressiveness, 460
risk taking, 461

Entrepreneurial Orientation	Company A	Company B
Autonomy		
Innovativeness		
Proactiveness		
Competitive Aggressiveness		
Risk Taking		

Experiential Exercise

Select two different major corporations from two different industries (you might use Fortune 500 companies to make your selection). Compare and contrast these organizations in terms of their entrepreneurial orientation.

Based on Your Comparison:

1. How is the corporation's entrepreneurial orientation reflected in its strategy?

2. Which corporation would you say has the stronger entrepreneurial orientation?

3. Is the corporation with the stronger entrepreneurial orientation also stronger in terms of financial performance?

Application Questions & Exercises

1. Select a firm known for its corporate entrepreneurship activities. Research the company and discuss how it has positioned itself relative to its close competitors.

Does it have a unique strategic advantage? Disadvantage? Explain.

2. Explain the difference between product innovations and process innovations. Provide examples of firms that have recently introduced each type of innovation. What are the types of innovations related to the strategies of each firm?

3. Using the Internet, select a company that is listed on the NASDAQ or New York Stock Exchange. Research the extent to which the company has an entrepreneurial culture. Does the company use product champions? Does it have a corporate venture capital fund? Do you believe its entrepreneurial efforts are sufficient to generate sustainable advantages?

4. How can an established firm use an entrepreneurial orientation to enhance its overall strategic position? Provide examples.

Ethics Questions

1. Innovation activities are often aimed at making a discovery or commercializing a technology ahead of the competition. What are some of the unethical practices that companies could engage in during the innovation process? What are the potential long-term consequences of such actions?

2. Discuss the ethical implications of using entrepreneurial policies and practices to pursue corporate social responsibility goals. Are these efforts authentic and genuine or just an attempt to attract more customers?

References

1. HTC. 2010. About HTC. *HTC.com*, np; Einhorn, M. and Arndt, B. 2010. The 50 most innovative companies. *Bloomberg Businessweek*, April 25: 34–40; and Jaroslovsky, R. 2010. HTC's elegant dead-end phone. *Bloomberg Businessweek*, April 25: 42. We thank Kimberly Kentfield for her valued contributions.

2. For an interesting discussion, see Johannessen, J. A., Olsen, B., & Lumpkin, G. T. 2001. Innovation as newness: What is new, how new, and new to whom? *European Journal of Innovation Management*, 4(1): 20–31.

3. The discussion of product and process innovation is based on Roberts, E. B. (Ed.). 2002. *Innovation: Driving product, process, and market change*. San Francisco: Jossey-Bass; Hayes, R. & Wheelwright, S. 1985. Competing through manufacturing. *Harvard Business Review*, 63(1): 99–109; and Hayes, R. & Wheelwright, S. 1979. Dynamics of product–process life cycles. *Harvard Business Review*, 57(2): 127–136.

4. The discussion of radical and incremental innovations draws from Leifer, R., McDermott, C. M., Colarelli, G., O'Connor, G. C., Peters, L. S., Rice, M. P., & Veryzer, R. W. 2000. *Radical innovation: How mature companies can outsmart upstarts*. Boston: Harvard Business School Press; Damanpour, F. 1996. Organizational complexity and innovation: Developing and testing multiple contingency models. *Management Science*, 42(5): 693–716; and Hage, J. 1980. *Theories of organizations*. New York: Wiley.

5. Christensen, C. M. & Raynor, M. E. 2003. *The innovator's solution*. Boston: Harvard Business School Press.

6. Dressner, H. 2004. The Gartner Fellows interview: Clayton M. Christensen. *www.gartner.com*, April 26.

7. For another perspective on how different types of innovation affect organizational choices, see Wolter, C. & Veloso, F. M. 2008. The effects of innovation on vertical structure: Perspectives on transactions costs and competences. *Academy of Management Review*, 33(3): 586–605.

8. Drucker, P. F. 1985. *Innovation and entrepreneurship: 2000* New York: Harper & Row.

9. Birkinshaw, J., Hamel, G., & Mol, M. J. 2008. Management innovation. *Academy of Management Review*, 33(4): 825–845.

10. Steere, W. C., Jr. & Niblack, J. 1997. Pfizer, Inc. In Kanter, R. M., Kao, J., & Wiersema, F. (Eds.), *Innovation: Breakthrough thinking at 3M, DuPont, GE, Pfizer, and Rubbermaid*: 123–145. New York: HarperCollins.

11. Morrissey, C. A. 2000. Managing innovation through corporate venturing. *Graziadio Business Report*, Spring, gbr.pepperdine.edu; and Sharma, A. 1999. Central dilemmas of managing innovation in large firms. *California Management Review*, 41(3): 147–164.

12. Sharma, op. cit.

13. Dyer, J. H., Gregerson, H. B., & Christensen, C. M. 2009. The innovator's DNA. *Harvard Business Review*, December: 61-67.

14. Eggers, J. P., & Kaplan, S. 2009. Cognition and renewal: Comparing CEO and organizational effects on incumbent adaptation to technical change. *Organization Science*, 20: 461–477.

15. Canabou, C. 2003. Fast ideas for slow times. *Fast Company*, May: 52.

16. Biodegradable Products Institute. 2003. "Compostable Logo" of the Biodegradable Products Institute gains momentum with approval of DuPont Biomax resin, *www.bpiworld.org*, June 12; Leifer et al., op. cit.

17. For more on defining the scope of innovation, see Valikangas, L. & Gibbert, M. 2005. Boundary-setting strategies for escaping innovation traps. *MIT Sloan Management Review*, 46(3): 58–65.

18. Leifer et al., op. cit.

19. Bhide, A. V. 2000. *The origin and evolution of new businesses*. New York: Oxford University Press; Brown, S. L. & Eisenhardt, K. M. 1998. *Competing on the edge: Strategy as structured chaos*. Cambridge, MA: Harvard Business School Press.

20. Caulfield, B. 2003. Why techies don't get Six Sigma. *Business 2.0*, June: 90.

21. McGrath, R. G. & Keil, T. 2007. The value captor's process: Getting

the most out of your new business ventures. *Harvard Business Review,* May: 128–136.

22. For an interesting discussion of how sharing technology knowledge with different divisions in an organization can contribute to innovation processes, see Miller, D. J., Fern, M. J., & Cardinal, L. B. 2007. The use of knowledge for technological innovation within diversified firms. *Academy of Management Journal,* 50(2): 308–326.

23. Ketchen Jr., D. J., Ireland, R. D., & Snow, C. C. 2007 Strategic entrepreneurship, collaborative innovation, and wealth creation. *Strategic Entrepreneurship Journal,* 1(3–4): 371–385.

24. Chesbrough, H. 2003. *Open innovation: The new imperative for creating and profiting from technology.* Boston: Harvard Business School Press.

25. For a recent study of what makes alliance partnerships successful, see Sampson, R. C. 2007. R&D alliances and firm performance: The impact of technological diversity and alliance organization on innovation. *Academy of Management Journal,* 50(2): 364–386.

26. For an interesting perspective on the role of collaboration among multinational corporations see Hansen, M. T. & Nohria, N. 2004. How to build collaborative advantage. *MIT Sloan Management Review,* 46(1): 22–30.

27. Wells, R. M. J. 2008. The product innovation process: Are managing information flows and cross-functional collaboration key? *Academy of Management Perspectives,* 22(1): 58–60. Dougherty, D., & Dunne, D. D. 2011. Organizing ecologies of complex innovation. *Organization Science,* forthcoming. Kim, H. E., Pennings, J. M. 2009. Innovation and strategic renewal in mature markets: A study of the tennis racket industry. *Organization Science,* 20: 368–383.

28. Guth, W. D. & Ginsberg, A. 1990. Guest editor's introduction: Corporate entrepreneurship. *Strategic Management Journal,* 11: 5–15.

29. Pinchot, G. 1985. *Intrapreneuring.* New York: Harper & Row.

30. For an interesting perspective on the role of context on the discovery and creation of opportunities, see Zahra, S. A. 2008. The virtuous cycle of discovery and creation of entrepreneurial opportunities. *Strategic Entrepreneurship Journal,* 2(3): 243–257.

31. Birkinshaw, J. 1997. Entrepreneurship in multinational corporations: The characteristics of subsidiary initiatives. *Strategic Management Journal,* 18(3): 207–229; and Kanter, R. M. 1985. *The change masters.* New York: Simon & Schuster.

32. Hansen, M. T., Chesbrough, H. W., Nohria, N., & Sull, D. 2000. Networked incubators: Hothouses of the new economy. *Harvard Business Review,* 78(5): 74–84.

33. Stein, T. 2002. Corporate venture investors are bailing out. *Red Herring,* December: 74–75.

34. For more on the importance of leadership in fostering a climate of entrepreneurship, see Ling, Y., Simsek, Z., Lubatkin, M. H., & Veiga, J. F. 2008. Transformational leadership's role in promoting corporate entrepreneurship: Examining the CEO-TMT interface. *Academy of Management Journal,* 51(3): 557–576.

35. Is your company up to speed? 2003. *Fast Company,* June: 86.

36. For an interesting discussion, see Davenport, T. H., Prusak, L., & Wilson, H. J. 2003. Who's bringing you hot ideas and how are you responding? *Harvard Business Review,* 80(1): 58–64.

37. Howell, J. M. 2005. The right stuff. Identifying and developing effective champions of innovation. *Academy of Management Executive,* 19(2): 108–119. See also Greene, P., Brush, C., & Hart, M. 1999. The corporate venture champion: A resource-based approach to role and process. *Entrepreneurship Theory & Practice,* 23(3): 103–122; and Markham, S. K. & Aiman-Smith, L. 2001. Product champions: Truths, myths and management. *Research Technology Management,* May–June: 44–50.

38. Burgelman, R. A. 1983. A process model of internal corporate venturing in the diversified major firm. *Administrative Science Quarterly,* 28: 223–244.

39. Hamel, G. 2000. *Leading the revolution.* Boston: Harvard Business School Press.

40. Greene, Brush, & Hart, op. cit.; and Shane, S. 1994. Are champions different from non-champions? *Journal of Business Venturing,* 9(5): 397–421.

41. Block, Z. & MacMillan, I. C. 1993. *Corporate venturing—Creating new businesses with the firm.* Cambridge, MA: Harvard Business School Press.

42. For an interesting discussion of these trade-offs, see Stringer, R. 2000. How to manage radical innovation. *California Management Review,* 42(4): 70–88; and Gompers, P. A. & Lerner, J. 1999. *The venture capital cycle.* Cambridge, MA: MIT Press.

43. Cardinal, L. B., Turner, S. F., Fern, M. J., & Burton, R. M. 2011. Organizing for product development across technological environments: Performance trade-offs and priorities. *Organization Science,* Forthcoming.

44. Albrinck, J., Hornery, J., Kletter, D., & Neilson, G. 2001. Adventures in corporate venturing. *Strategy + Business,* 22: 119–129; and McGrath, R. G. & MacMillan, I. C. 2000. *The entrepreneurial mind-set.* Cambridge, MA: Harvard Business School Press.

45. Kiel, T., McGrath, R. G., Tukiainen, T., 2009. Gems from the ashes: Capability creation and transforming in internal corporate venturing. *Organization Science,* 20: 601–620.

46. For an interesting discussion of how different outcome goals affect organizational learning and employee motivation, see Seijts, G. H. & Latham, G. P. 2005. Learning versus performance goals: When should each be used? *Academy of Management Executive,* 19(1): 124–131.

47. Crockett, R. O. 2001. Motorola. *BusinessWeek,* July 15: 72–78.

48. The ideas in this section are drawn from Royer, I. 2003. Why bad projects are so hard to kill. *Harvard Business Review,* 80(1): 48–56.

49. For an interesting perspective on the different roles that individuals play in the entrepreneurial process, see Baron, R. A. 2008. The role of affect in the entrepreneurial process. *Academy of Management Review,* 33(2): 328–340.

50. Hoskin, R. E. 1994. *Financial accounting.* New York: Wiley.

51. We know stock options as derivative assets—that is, "an asset whose value depends on or is derived from the value of another, the underlying asset": Amram, M. & Kulatilaka, N. 1999. *Real options: Managing strategic investment in an uncertain world: 34.* Boston: Harvard Business School Press.

52. For an interesting discussion on why it is difficult to "kill options," refer to Royer, I. 2003. Why bad projects are so hard to kill. *Harvard Business Review,* 81(2): 48–57.

53. Slywotzky, A. & Wise, R. 2003. Double-digit growth in no-growth times. *Fast Company,* April: 66–72; *www.hoovers.com;* and *www.johnsoncontrols.com.*

54. For more on the role of real options in entrepreneurial decision making, see Folta, T. B. & O'Brien, J. P. 2004. Entry in the presence of dueling options. *Strategic Management Journal,* 25: 121–138.

55. This section draws on Janney, J. J. & Dess, G. G. 2004. Can real options analysis improve decision-making? Promises and pitfalls. *Academy of Management Executive,* 18(4): 60–75. For additional insights on pitfalls of real options, consider McGrath, R. G. 1997. A real options logic for initiating technology positioning investment. *Academy of Management Review,* 22(4): 974–994; Coff, R. W. & Laverty, K. J. 2001. Real options on knowledge assets: Panacea or Pandora's box. *Business Horizons,* 73: 79, McGrath, R. G. 1999. Falling forward: Real options reasoning and entrepreneurial failure. *Academy of Management Review,* 24(1): 13–30; and, Zardkoohi, A. 2004.

56. For an understanding of the differences between how managers say they approach decisions and how they actually do, March and Shapira's discussion is perhaps the best. March, J. G. & Shapira, Z. 1987. Managerial perspectives on risk and risk-taking. *Management Science,* 33(11): 1404–1418.

57. A discussion of some factors that may lead to escalation in decision making is included in Choo, C. W. 2005. Information failures and organizational disasters. *MIT Sloan Management Review,* 46(3): 8–10.

58. For an interesting discussion of the use of real options analysis in the application of wireless communications, which helped to lower the potential for escalation, refer to McGrath, R. G., Ferrier, W. J., & Mendelow, A. L. 2004. Real options as engines of choice and heterogeneity. *Academy of Management Review,* 29(1): 86–101.

59. One very useful solution for reducing the effects of managerial conceit is to incorporate an "exit champion" into the decision process. Exit champions provide arguments for killing off the firm's commitment to a decision. For a very insightful discussion on exit champions, refer to Royer, I. 2003. Why bad projects are so hard to kill. *Harvard Business Review,* 81(2): 49–56.

60. For more on how entrepreneurial orientation influences organizational performance, see Wang, L. 2008. Entrepreneurial orientation, learning orientation, and firm performance. *Entrepreneurship Theory & Practice,* 32(4): 635–657; and Runyan, R., Droge, C., & Swinney, J. 2008. Entrepreneurial orientation versus small business orientation: What are their relationships to firm performance? *Journal of Small Business Management,* 46(4): 567–588.

61. Covin, J. G. & Slevin, D. P. 1991. A conceptual model of entrepreneurship as firm behavior. *Entrepreneurship Theory and Practice,* 16(1): 7–24; Lumpkin, G. T. & Dess, G. G. 1996. Clarifying the entrepreneurial orientation construct and linking it to performance. *Academy of Management Review,* 21(1): 135–172; and McGrath, R. G. & MacMillan, I. C. 2000. *The entrepreneurial mind-set.* Cambridge, MA: Harvard Business School Press.

62. Lumpkin, G. T. & Dess, G. G. 2001. Linking two dimensions of entrepreneurial orientation to firm performance: The moderating role of

environment and life cycle. *Journal of Business Venturing,* 16: 429–451.

63. For an interesting discussion, see Day, J. D., Mang, P. Y., Richter, A., & Roberts, J. 2001. The innovative organization: Why new ventures need more than a room of their own, *McKinsey Quarterly,* 2: 21–31.

64. Crockett, R. O. 2001. Chris Galvin shakes things up—again. *BusinessWeek,* May 28: 38–39.

65. For insights into the role of information technology in innovativeness, see Dibrell, C., Davis, P. S., & Craig, J. 2008. Fueling innovation through information technology in SMEs. *Journal of Small Business Management,* 46(2): 203–218.

66. For an interesting discussion of the impact of innovativeness on organizational outcomes see Cho, H. J. & Pucik, V. 2005. Relationship between innovativeness, quality, growth, profitability, and market value. *Strategic Management Journal,* 26(6): 555–575.

67. Danneels, E., & Sethi, R. 2011. New product exploration under environmental turbulence. *Organization Science,* forthcoming.

68. Lieberman, M. B. & Montgomery, D. B. 1988. First mover advantages. *Strategic Management Journal,* 9 (Special Issue): 41–58.

69. The discussion of first mover advantages is based on several articles, including Lambkin, M. 1988. Order of entry and performance in new markets. *Strategic Management Journal,* 9: 127–140; Lieberman & Montgomery, op. cit.: 41–58; and Miller, A. & Camp, B. 1985. Exploring determinants of success in corporate ventures. *Journal of Business Venturing,* 1(2): 87–105.

70. Moore, G. A. 1999. *Crossing the chasm* (2nd ed.). New York: HarperBusiness.

71. Mallas, S. 2005. PepsiCo loses its Edge. *Motley Fool,* June 1, *www.fool.com.*

72. Lyons, D. 2006. The cheap revolution. *Forbes,* September 18: 102–111.

73. Miller, K. D. 2007. Risk and rationality in entrepreneurial processes. *Strategic Entrepreneurship Journal,* 1(1–2): 57–74.

74. Drucker, op. cit., pp. 109–110.

chapter THIRTEEN

Analyzing Strategic Management Cases

After reading this chapter, you should have a good understanding of:

LO13.1 How strategic case analysis is used to simulate real-world experiences.

LO13.2 How analyzing strategic management cases can help develop the ability to differentiate, speculate, and integrate when evaluating complex business problems.

LO13.3 The steps involved in conducting a strategic management case analysis.

LO13.4 How to get the most out of case analysis.

LO13.5 How conflict-inducing discussion techniques can lead to better decisions.

LO13.6 How to use the strategic insights and material from each of the 12 previous chapters in the text to analyze issues posed by strategic management cases.

LEARNING OBJECTIVES

Case analysis is one of the most effective ways to learn strategic management. It provides a complement to other methods of instruction by asking you to use the tools and techniques of strategic management to deal with an actual business situation. Strategy cases include detailed descriptions of management challenges faced by executives and business owners. By studying the background and analyzing the strategic predicaments posed by a case, you first see that the circumstances businesses confront are often difficult and complex. Then you are asked what decisions you would make to address the situation in the case and how the actions you recommend will affect the company. Thus, the processes of analysis, formulation, and implementation that have been addressed in this textbook can be applied in a real-life situation.

In this chapter we will discuss the role of case analysis as a learning tool in both the classroom and the real world. One of the benefits of strategic case analysis is to develop the ability to differentiate, speculate, and integrate. We will also describe how to conduct a case analysis and address techniques for deriving the greatest benefit from the process, including the effective use of conflict-inducing decision techniques. Finally, we will discuss how case analysis in a classroom setting can enhance the process of analyzing, making decisions, and taking action in real-world strategic situations.

Why Analyze Strategic Management Cases?

>LO13.1

How strategic case analysis is used to simulate real-world experiences.

It is often said that the key to finding good answers is to ask good questions. Strategic managers and business leaders are required to evaluate options, make choices, and find solutions to the challenges they face every day. To do so, they must learn to ask the right questions. The study of strategic management poses the same challenge. The process of analyzing, decision making, and implementing strategic actions raises many good questions.

- Why do some firms succeed and others fail?
- Why are some companies higher performers than others?
- What information is needed in the strategic planning process?
- How do competing values and beliefs affect strategic decision making?
- What skills and capabilities are needed to implement a strategy effectively?

case analysis a method of learning complex strategic management concepts—such as environmental analysis, the process of decision making, and implementing strategic actions—through placing students in the middle of an actual situation and challenging them to figure out what to do.

How does a student of strategic management answer these questions? By strategic case analysis. **Case analysis** simulates the real-world experience that strategic managers and company leaders face as they try to determine how best to run their companies. It places students in the middle of an actual situation and challenges them to figure out what to do.[1]

Asking the right questions is just the beginning of case analysis. In the previous chapters we have discussed issues and challenges that managers face and provided analytical frameworks for understanding the situation. But once the analysis is complete, decisions have to be made. Case analysis forces you to choose among different options and set forth a plan of action based on your choices. But even then the job is not done. Strategic case analysis also requires that you address how you will implement the plan and the implications of choosing one course of action over another.

A strategic management case is a detailed description of a challenging situation faced by an organization.[2] It usually includes a chronology of events and extensive support materials, such as financial statements, product lists, and transcripts of interviews with employees. Although names or locations are sometimes changed to provide anonymity, cases usually report the facts of a situation as authentically as possible.

One of the main reasons to analyze strategic management cases is to develop an ability to evaluate business situations critically. In case analysis, memorizing key terms and conceptual frameworks is not enough. To analyze a case, it is important that you go beyond textbook prescriptions and quick answers. It requires you to look deeply into the information that is provided and root out the essential issues and causes of a company's problems.

>LO13.2

How analyzing strategic management cases can help develop the ability to differentiate, speculate, and integrate when evaluating complex business problems.

The types of skills that are required to prepare an effective strategic case analysis can benefit you in actual business situations. Case analysis adds to the overall learning experience by helping you acquire or improve skills that may not be taught in a typical lecture course. Three capabilities that can be learned by conducting case analysis are especially useful to strategic managers—the ability to differentiate, speculate, and integrate.[3] Here's how case analysis can enhance those skills.

1. *Differentiate.* Effective strategic management requires that many different elements of a situation be evaluated at once. This is also true in case analysis. When analyzing cases, it is important to isolate critical facts, evaluate whether assumptions are useful or faulty, and distinguish between good and bad information. Differentiating between the factors that are influencing the situation presented by a case is necessary for making a good analysis. Strategic management also involves understanding that problems are often complex and multilayered. This applies to case analysis as well. Ask whether the case deals with operational, business-level, or corporate issues. Do the problems stem from weaknesses in the internal value chain or threats in

the external environment? Dig deep. Being too quick to accept the easiest or least controversial answer will usually fail to get to the heart of the problem.

2. ***Speculate.*** Strategic managers need to be able to use their imagination to envision an explanation or solution that might not readily be apparent. The same is true with case analysis. Being able to imagine different scenarios or contemplate the outcome of a decision can aid the analysis. Managers also have to deal with uncertainty since most decisions are made without complete knowledge of the circumstances. This is also true in case analysis. Case materials often seem to be missing data or the information provided is contradictory. The ability to speculate about details that are unknown or the consequences of an action can be helpful.

3. ***Integrate.*** Strategy involves looking at the big picture and having an organization-wide perspective. Strategic case analysis is no different. Even though the chapters in this textbook divide the material into various topics that may apply to different parts of an organization, all of this information must be integrated into one set of recommendations that will affect the whole company. A strategic manager needs to comprehend how all the factors that influence the organization will interact. This also applies to case analysis. Changes made in one part of the organization affect other parts. Thus, a holistic perspective that integrates the impact of various decisions and environmental influences on all parts of the organization is needed.

In business, these three activities sometimes "compete" with each other for your attention. For example, some decision makers may have a natural ability to differentiate among elements of a problem but are not able to integrate them very well. Others have enough innate creativity to imagine solutions or fill in the blanks when information is missing. But they may have a difficult time when faced with hard numbers or cold facts. Even so, each of these skills is important. The mark of a good strategic manager is the ability to simultaneously make distinctions and envision the whole, and to imagine a future scenario while staying focused on the present. Thus, another reason to conduct case analysis is

to help you develop and exercise your ability to differentiate, speculate, and integrate.

Case analysis takes the student through the whole cycle of activity that a manager would face. Beyond the textbook descriptions of concepts and examples, case analysis asks you to "walk a mile in the shoes" of the strategic decision maker and learn to evaluate situations critically. Executives and owners must make decisions every day with limited information and a swirl of business activity going on around them. Consider the example of Sapient Health Network, an Internet start-up that had to undergo some analysis and problem solving just to survive. Strategy Spotlight 13.1 describes how this company transformed itself after a serious self-examination during a time of crisis.

As you can see from the experience of Sapient Health Network, businesses are often faced with immediate challenges that threaten their lives. The Sapient case illustrates how the strategic management process helped it survive. First, the company realistically assessed the environment, evaluated the marketplace, and analyzed its resources. Then it made tough decisions, which included shifting its market focus, hiring and firing, and redeploying its assets. Finally, it took action. The result was not only firm survival, but also a quick turnaround leading to rapid success.

How to Conduct a Case Analysis

>LO13.3
The steps involved in conducting a strategic management case analysis.

The process of analyzing strategic management cases involves several steps. In this section we will review the mechanics of preparing a case analysis. Before beginning, there are two things to keep in mind that will clarify your understanding of the process and make the results of the process more meaningful.

Analysis, Decision Making, and Change at Sapient Health Network

Sapient Health Network (SHN) had gotten off to a good start. CEO Jim Kean and his two cofounders had raised $5 million in investor capital to launch their vision: an Internet-based health care information subscription service. The idea was to create an Internet community for people suffering from chronic diseases. It would provide members with expert information, resources, a message board, and chat rooms so that people suffering from the same ailments could provide each other with information and support. "Who would be more voracious consumers of information than people who are faced with life-changing, life-threatening illnesses?" thought Bill Kelly, one of SHN's cofounders. Initial market research and beta tests had supported that view.

During the beta tests, however, the service had been offered for free. The troubles began when SHN tried to convert its trial subscribers into paying ones. Fewer than 5 percent signed on, far less than the 15 percent the company had projected. Sapient hired a vice president of marketing who launched an aggressive promotion, but after three months of campaigning SHN still had only 500 members. SHN was now burning through $400,000 per month, with little revenue to show for it.

At that point, according to SHN board member Susan Clymer, "there was a lot of scrambling around trying to figure out how we could wring value out of what we'd already accomplished." One thing SHN had created was

an expert software system which had two components: an "intelligent profile engine" (IPE) and an "intelligent query engine" (IQE). SHN used this system to collect detailed information from its subscribers.

SHN was sure that the expert system was its biggest selling point. But how could they use it? Then the founders remembered that the original business plan had suggested there might be a market for aggregate data about patient populations gathered from the website. Could they turn the business around by selling patient data? To analyze the possibility, Kean tried out the idea on the market research arm of a huge East Coast health care conglomerate. The officials were intrigued. SHN realized that its expert system could become a market research tool.

Once the analysis was completed, the founders made the decision: They would still create Internet communities for chronically ill patients, but the service would be free. And they would transform SHN from a company that processed subscriptions to one that sold market research.

Finally, they enacted the changes. Some of it was painful, including laying off 18 employees. Instead, SHN needed more health care industry expertise. It even hired an interim CEO, Craig Davenport, a 25-year veteran of the industry, to steer the company in its new direction. Finally, SHN had to communicate a new message to its members. It began by reimbursing the $10,000 of subscription fees they had paid.

All of this paid off dramatically in a matter of just two years. Revenues jumped to $1.9 million and early in the third year, SHN was purchased by WebMD. Less than a year after that, WebMD merged with Healtheon. The combined company still operates a thriving office out of SHN's original location in Portland, Oregon.

Sources: Ferguson, S. 2007. Health Care Gets a Better IT Prescription. *Baseline*, www.baselinemag.com, May 24. Brenneman, K. 2000. Healtheon/WebMD's Local Office Is Thriving. *Business Journal of Portland*, June 2; Raths, D. 1998. Reversal of Fortune. *Inc. Technology*, 2: 52–62.

First, unless you prepare for a case discussion, there is little you can gain from the discussion and even less that you can offer. Effective strategic managers don't enter into problem-solving situations without doing some homework—investigating the situation, analyzing and researching possible solutions, and sometimes gathering the advice of others. Good problem solving often requires that decision makers be immersed in the facts, options, and implications surrounding the problem. In case analysis, this means reading and thoroughly comprehending the case materials before trying to make an analysis.

The second point is related to the first. To get the most out of a case analysis you must place yourself "inside" the case—that is, think like an actual participant in the case situation. However, there are several positions you can take. These are discussed in the following paragraphs:

- **Strategic decision maker.** This is the position of the senior executive responsible for resolving the situation described in the case. It may be the CEO, the business owner, or a strategic manager in a key executive position.

- **Board of directors.** Since the board of directors represents the owners of a corporation, it has a responsibility to step in when a management crisis threatens the company. As a board member, you may be in a unique position to solve problems.
- **Outside consultant.** Either the board or top management may decide to bring in outsiders. Consultants often have an advantage because they can look at a situation objectively. But they also may be at a disadvantage since they have no power to enforce changes.

Before beginning the analysis, it may be helpful to envision yourself assuming one of these roles. Then, as you study and analyze the case materials, you can make a diagnosis and recommend solutions in a way that is consistent with your position. Try different perspectives. You may find that your view of the situation changes depending on the role you play. As an outside consultant, for example, it may be easy for you to conclude that certain individuals should be replaced in order to solve a problem presented in the case. However, if you take the role of the CEO who knows the individuals and the challenges they have been facing, you may be reluctant to fire them and will seek another solution instead.

The idea of assuming a particular role is similar to the real world in various ways. In your career, you may work in an organization where outside accountants, bankers, lawyers, or other professionals are advising you about how to resolve business situations or improve your practices. Their perspective will be different from yours but it is useful to understand things from their point of view. Conversely, you may work as a member of the audit team of an accounting firm or the loan committee of a bank. In those situations, it would be helpful if you understood the situation from the perspective of the business leader who must weigh your views against all the other advice that he or she receives. Case analysis can help develop an ability to appreciate such multiple perspectives.

One of the most challenging roles to play in business is as a business founder or owner. For small businesses or entrepreneurial start-ups, the founder may wear all hats at once—key decision maker, primary stockholder, and CEO. Hiring an outside consultant may not be an option. However, the issues faced by young firms and established firms are often not that different, especially when it comes to formulating a plan of action. Business plans that entrepreneurial firms use to raise money or propose a business expansion typically revolve around a few key issues that must be addressed no matter what the size or age of the business. Strategy Spotlight 13.2 reviews business planning issues that are most important to consider when evaluating any case, especially from the perspective of the business founder or owner.

Next we will review five steps to follow when conducting a strategic management case analysis: becoming familiar with the material, identifying the problems, analyzing the strategic issues using the tools and insights of strategic management, proposing alternative solutions, and making recommendations.[4]

Become Familiar with the Material

Written cases often include a lot of material. They may be complex and include detailed financials or long passages. Even so, to understand a case and its implications, you must become familiar with its content. Sometimes key information is not immediately apparent. It may be contained in the footnotes to an exhibit or an interview with a lower-level employee. In other cases the important points may be difficult to grasp because the subject matter is so unfamiliar. When you approach a strategic case try the following technique to enhance comprehension:

- Read quickly through the case one time to get an overall sense of the material.
- Use the initial read-through to assess possible links to strategic concepts.
- Read through the case again, in depth. Make written notes as you read.

strategy spotlight

Using a Business Plan Framework to Analyze Strategic Cases

Established businesses often have to change what they are doing in order to improve their competitive position or sometimes simply to survive. To make the changes effectively, businesses usually need a plan. Business plans are no longer just for entrepreneurs. The kind of market analysis, decision making, and action planning that is considered standard practice among new ventures can also benefit going concerns that want to make changes, seize an opportunity, or head in a new direction.

The best business plans, however, are not those loaded with decades of month-by-month financial projections or that depend on rigid adherence to a schedule of events that is impossible to predict. The good ones are focused on four factors that are critical to new-venture success. These same factors are important in case analysis as well because they get to the heart of many of the problems found in strategic cases.

1. *The People.* "When I receive a business plan, I always read the résumé section first," says Harvard Professor William Sahlman. The people questions that are critically important to investors include: What are their skills? How much experience do they have? What is their reputation? Have they worked together as a team? These same questions also may be used in case analysis to evaluate the role of individuals in the strategic case.

2. *The Opportunity.* Business opportunities come in many forms. They are not limited to new ventures.

Sources: Wasserman, E. 2003. A Simple Plan. *MBA Jungle*, February: 50–55; DeKluyver, C. A. 2000. *Strategic Thinking: An Executive Perspective.* Upper Saddle River, NJ: Prentice Hall; and Sahlman, W. A. 1997. How to Write a Great Business Plan. *Harvard Business Review*, 75(4): 98–108.

The chance to enter new markets, introduce new products, or merge with a competitor provides many of the challenges that are found in strategic management cases. What are the consequences of such actions? Will the proposed changes affect the firm's business concept? What factors might stand in the way of success? The same issues are also present in most strategic cases.

3. *The Context.* Things happen in contexts that cannot be controlled by a firm's managers. This is particularly true of the general environment where social trends, economic changes, or events such as the September 11, 2001, terrorist attacks can change business overnight. When evaluating strategic cases, ask: Is the company aware of the impact of context on the business? What will it do if the context changes? Can it influence the context in a way that favors the company?

4. *Risk and Reward.* With a new venture, the entrepreneurs and investors take the risks and get the rewards. In strategic cases, the risks and rewards often extend to many other stakeholders, such as employees, customers, and suppliers. When analyzing a case, ask: Are the managers making choices that will pay off in the future? Are the rewards evenly distributed? Will some stakeholders be put at risk if the situation in the case changes? What if the situation remains the same? Could that be even riskier?

Whether a business is growing or shrinking, large or small, industrial or service oriented, the issues of people, opportunities, context, and risks and rewards will have a large impact on its performance. Therefore, you should always consider these four factors when evaluating strategic management cases.

- Evaluate how strategic concepts might inform key decisions or suggest alternative solutions.
- After formulating an initial recommendation, thumb through the case again quickly to help assess the consequences of the actions you propose.

Identify Problems

When conducting case analysis, one of your most important tasks is to identify the problem. Earlier we noted that one of the main reasons to conduct case analysis was to find solutions. But you cannot find a solution unless you know the problem. Another saying you may have heard is, "A good diagnosis is half the cure." In other words, once you have determined what the problem is, you are well on your way to identifying a reasonable solution.

Some cases have more than one problem. But the problems are usually related. For a hypothetical example, consider the following: Company A was losing customers to a new competitor. Upon analysis, it was determined that the competitor had a 50 percent faster delivery time even though its product was of lower quality. The managers of company A could not understand why customers would settle for an inferior product. It turns out that no one was marketing to company A's customers that its product was superior. A second problem was that falling sales resulted in cuts in company A's sales force. Thus, there were two related problems: inferior delivery technology and insufficient sales effort.

When trying to determine the problem, avoid getting hung up on symptoms. Zero in on the problem. For example, in the company A example above, the symptom was losing customers. But the problems were an underfunded, understaffed sales force combined with an outdated delivery technology. Try to see beyond the immediate symptoms to the more fundamental problems.

Another tip when preparing a case analysis is to articulate the problem.[5] Writing down a problem statement gives you a reference point to turn to as you proceed through the case analysis. This is important because the process of formulating strategies or evaluating implementation methods may lead you away from the initial problem. Make sure your recommendation actually addresses the problems you have identified.

One more thing about identifying problems: Sometimes problems are not apparent until *after* you do the analysis. In some cases the problem will be presented plainly, perhaps in the opening paragraph or on the last page of the case. But in other cases the problem does not emerge until after the issues in the case have been analyzed. We turn next to the subject of strategic case analysis.

case symptoms observable and concrete information in a case analysis that indicates an undesirable state of affairs.

case problems inferred causes of case symptoms.

Conduct Strategic Analyses

This textbook has presented numerous analytical tools (e.g., five-forces analysis and value-chain analysis), contingency frameworks (e.g., when to use related rather than unrelated diversification strategies), and other techniques that can be used to evaluate strategic situations. The previous 12 chapters have addressed practices that are common in strategic management, but only so much can be learned by studying the practices and concepts. The best way to understand these methods is to apply them by conducting analyses of specific cases.

The first step is to determine which strategic issues are involved. Is there a problem in the company's competitive environment? Or is it an internal problem? If it is internal, does it have to do with organizational structure? Strategic controls? Uses of technology? Or perhaps the company has overworked its employees or underutilized its intellectual capital. Has the company mishandled a merger? Chosen the wrong diversification strategy? Botched a new product introduction? Each of these issues is linked to one or more of the concepts discussed earlier in the text. Determine what strategic issues are associated with the problems you have identified. Remember also that most real-life case situations involve issues that are highly interrelated. Even in cases where there is only one major problem, the strategic processes required to solve it may involve several parts of the organization.

Once you have identified the issues that apply to the case, conduct the analysis. For example, you may need to conduct a five-forces analysis or dissect the company's competitive strategy. Perhaps you need to evaluate whether its resources are rare, valuable, difficult to imitate, or difficult to substitute. Financial analysis may be needed to assess the company's economic prospects. Perhaps the international entry mode needs to be reevaluated because of changing conditions in the host country. Employee empowerment techniques may need to be improved to enhance organizational learning. Whatever the case, all the strategic concepts introduced in the text include insights for assessing their effectiveness. Determining how well a company is doing these things is central to the case analysis process.

financial ratio analysis a method of evaluating a company's performance and financial well-being through ratios of accounting values, including short-term solvency, long-term solvency, asset utilization, profitability, and market value ratios.

Financial ratio analysis is one of the primary tools used to conduct case analysis. Appendix 1 to Chapter 13 includes a discussion and examples of the financial ratios that are often used to evaluate a company's performance and financial well-being. Exhibit 13.1 provides a summary of the financial ratios presented in Appendix 1 to this chapter.

In this part of the overall strategic analysis process, it is also important to test your own assumptions about the case.[6] First, what assumptions are you making about the case materials? It may be that you have interpreted the case content differently than your team members or classmates. Being clear about these assumptions will be important in determining how to analyze the case. Second, what assumptions have you made about the best way to resolve the problems? Ask yourself why you have chosen one type of analysis over another. This process of assumption checking can also help determine if you have gotten to the heart of the problem or are still just dealing with symptoms.

Exhibit 13.1   Summary of Financial Ratio Analysis Techniques

Ratio	What It Measures
Short-term solvency, or liquidity, ratios:	
Current ratio	Ability to use assets to pay off liabilities.
Quick ratio	Ability to use liquid assets to pay off liabilities quickly.
Cash ratio	Ability to pay off liabilities with cash on hand.
Long-term solvency, or financial leverage, ratios:	
Total debt ratio	How much of a company's total assets are financed by debt.
Debt-equity ratio	Compares how much a company is financed by debt with how much it is financed by equity.
Equity multiplier	How much debt is being used to finance assets.
Times interest earned ratio	How well a company has its interest obligations covered.
Cash coverage ratio	A company's ability to generate cash from operations.
Asset utilization, or turnover, ratios:	
Inventory turnover	How many times each year a company sells its entire inventory.
Days' sales in inventory	How many days on average inventory is on hand before it is sold.
Receivables turnover	How frequently each year a company collects on its credit sales.
Days' sales in receivables	How many days on average it takes to collect on credit sales (average collection period).
Total asset turnover	How much of sales is generated for every dollar in assets.
Capital intensity	The dollar investment in assets needed to generate $1 in sales.
Profitability ratios:	
Profit margin	How much profit is generated by every dollar of sales.
Return on assets (ROA)	How effectively assets are being used to generate a return.
Return on equity (ROE)	How effectively amounts invested in the business by its owners are being used to generate a return.
Market value ratios:	
Price-earnings ratio	How much investors are willing to pay per dollar of current earnings.
Market-to-book ratio	Compares market value of the company's investments to the cost of those investments.

As mentioned earlier, sometimes the critical diagnosis in a case can only be made after the analysis is conducted. However, by the end of this stage in the process, you should know the problems and have completed a thorough analysis of them. You can now move to the next step: finding solutions.

Propose Alternative Solutions

It is important to remember that in strategic management case analysis, there is rarely one right answer or one best way. Even when members of a class or a team agree on what the problem is, they may not agree upon how to solve the problem. Therefore, it is helpful to consider several different solutions.

After conducting strategic analysis and identifying the problem, develop a list of options. What are the possible solutions? What are the alternatives? First, generate a list of all the options you can think of without prejudging any one of them. Remember that not all cases call for dramatic decisions or sweeping changes. Some companies just need to make small adjustments. In fact, "Do nothing" may be a reasonable alternative in some cases. Although that is rare, it might be useful to consider what will happen if the company does nothing. This point illustrates the purpose of developing alternatives: to evaluate what will happen if a company chooses one solution over another.

Thus, during this step of a case analysis, you will evaluate choices and the implications of those choices. One aspect of any business that is likely to be highlighted in this part of the analysis is strategy implementation. Ask how the choices made will be implemented. It may be that what seems like an obvious choice for solving a problem creates an even bigger problem when implemented. But remember also that no strategy or strategic "fix" is going to work if it cannot be implemented. Once a list of alternatives is generated, ask:

- Can the company afford it? How will it affect the bottom line?
- Is the solution likely to evoke a competitive response?
- Will employees throughout the company accept the changes? What impact will the solution have on morale?
- How will the decision affect other stakeholders? Will customers, suppliers, and others buy into it?
- How does this solution fit with the company's vision, mission, and objectives?
- Will the culture or values of the company be changed by the solution? Is it a positive change?

The point of this step in the case analysis process is to find a solution that both solves the problem and is realistic. A consideration of the implications of various alternative solutions will generally lead you to a final recommendation that is more thoughtful and complete.

Make Recommendations

The basic aim of case analysis is to find solutions. Your analysis is not complete until you have recommended a course of action. In this step the task is to make a set of recommendations that your analysis supports. Describe exactly what needs to be done. Explain why this course of action will solve the problem. The recommendation should also include suggestions for how best to implement the proposed solution because the recommended actions and their implications for the performance and future of the firm are interrelated.

Recall that the solution you propose must solve the problem you identified. This point cannot be overemphasized; too often students make recommendations that treat only symptoms or fail to tackle the central problems in the case. Make a logical argument that shows how the problem led to the analysis and the analysis led to the recommendations you are proposing. Remember, an analysis is not an end in itself; it is useful only if it leads to a solution.

The actions you propose should describe the very next steps that the company needs to take. Don't say, for example, "If the company does more market research, then I would recommend the following course of action. . . ." Instead, make conducting the research part of your recommendation. Taking the example a step further, if you also want to suggest subsequent actions that may be different *depending* on the outcome of the market research, that's OK. But don't make your initial recommendation conditional on actions the company may or may not take.

In summary, case analysis can be a very rewarding process but, as you might imagine, it can also be frustrating and challenging. If you will follow the steps described above, you will address the different elements of a thorough analysis. This approach can give your analysis a solid footing. Then, even if there are differences of opinion about how to interpret the facts, analyze the situation, or solve the problems, you can feel confident that you have not missed any important steps in finding the best course of action.

Students are often asked to prepare oral presentations of the information in a case and their analysis of the best remedies. This is frequently assigned as a group project. Or you may be called upon in class to present your ideas about the circumstances or solutions for a case the class is discussing. Exhibit 13.2 provides some tips for preparing an oral case presentation.

How to Get the Most from Case Analysis

>LO13.4
How to get the most out of case analysis.

One of the reasons case analysis is so enriching as a learning tool is that it draws on many resources and skills besides just what is in the textbook. This is especially true in the study of strategy. Why? Because strategic management itself is a highly integrative task that draws on many areas of specialization at several levels, from the individual to the whole of society. Therefore, to get the most out of case analysis, expand your horizons beyond the concepts in this text and seek insights from your own reservoir of knowledge. Here are some tips for how to do that.[7]

- *Keep an open mind.* Like any good discussion, a case analysis discussion often evokes strong opinions and high emotions. But it's the variety of perspectives that makes case analysis so valuable: Many viewpoints usually lead to a more complete analysis. Therefore, avoid letting an emotional response to another person's style or opinion keep you from hearing what he or she has to say. Once you evaluate what is said, you may disagree with it or dismiss it as faulty. But unless you keep an open mind in the first place, you may miss the importance of the other person's contribution. Also, people often place a higher value on the opinions of those they consider to be good listeners.

- *Take a stand for what you believe.* Although it is vital to keep an open mind, it is also important to state your views proactively. Don't try to figure out what your friends or the instructor wants to hear. Analyze the case from the perspective of your own background and belief system. For example, perhaps you feel that a decision is unethical or that the managers in a case have misinterpreted the facts. Don't be afraid to assert that in the discussion. For one thing, when a person takes a strong stand, it often encourages others to evaluate the issues more closely. This can lead to a more thorough investigation and a more meaningful class discussion.

- *Draw on your personal experience.* You may have experiences from work or as a customer that shed light on some of the issues in a case. Even though one of the purposes of case analysis is to apply the analytical tools from this text, you may be able to add to the discussion by drawing on your outside experiences and background. Of course, you need to guard against carrying that to extremes. In other words, don't think that your perspective is the only viewpoint that matters! Simply recognize that

Exhibit 13.2 Preparing an Oral Case Presentation

Rule	Description
Organize your thoughts.	Begin by becoming familiar with the material. If you are working with a team, compare notes about the key points of the case and share insights that other team members may have gleaned from tables and exhibits. Then make an outline. This is one of the best ways to organize the flow and content of the presentation.
Emphasize strategic analysis.	The purpose of case analysis is to diagnose problems and find solutions. In the process, you may need to unravel the case material as presented and reconfigure it in a fashion that can be more effectively analyzed. Present the material in a way that lends itself to analysis—don't simply restate what is in the case. This involves three major categories with the following emphasis: Background/Problem Statement 10–20% Strategic Analysis/Options 60–75% Recommendations/Action Plan 10–20% As you can see, the emphasis of your presentation should be on analysis. This will probably require you to reorganize the material so that the tools of strategic analysis can be applied.
Be logical and consistent.	A presentation that is rambling and hard to follow may confuse the listener and fail to evoke a good discussion. Present your arguments and explanations in a logical sequence. Support your claims with facts. Include financial analysis where appropriate. Be sure that the solutions you recommend address the problems you have identified.
Defend your position.	Usually an oral presentation is followed by a class discussion. Anticipate what others might disagree with and be prepared to defend your views. This means being aware of the choices you made and the implications of your recommendations. Be clear about your assumptions. Be able to expand on your analysis.
Share presentation responsibilities.	Strategic management case analyses are often conducted by teams. Each member of the team should have a clear role in the oral presentation, preferably a speaking role. It's also important to coordinate the different parts of the presentation into a logical, smooth-flowing whole. How well a team works together is usually very apparent during an oral presentation.

firsthand experience usually represents a welcome contribution to the overall quality of case discussions.

- ***Participate and persuade.*** Have you heard the phrase, "Vote early . . . and often"? Among loyal members of certain political parties, it has become rather a joke. Why? Because a democratic system is built on the concept of one person, one vote. Even though some voters may want to vote often enough to get their candidate elected, it is against the law. Not so in a case discussion. People who are persuasive and speak their mind can often influence the views of others. But to do so, you have to be prepared and convincing. Being persuasive is more than being loud or long-winded. It involves understanding all sides of an argument and being able to overcome objections to your own point of view. These efforts can make a case discussion more lively. And they parallel what happens in the real world; in business, people frequently share their opinions and attempt to persuade others to see things their way.

- *Be concise and to the point.* In the previous point, we encouraged you to speak up and "sell" your ideas to others in a case discussion. But you must be clear about what you are selling. Make your arguments in a way that is explicit and direct. Zero in on the most important points. Be brief. Don't try to make a lot of points at once by jumping around between topics. Avoid trying to explain the whole case situation at once. Remember, other students usually resent classmates who go on and on, take up a lot of "airtime," or repeat themselves unnecessarily. The best way to avoid this is to stay focused and be specific.

- *Think out of the box.* It's OK to be a little provocative; sometimes that is the consequence of taking a stand on issues. But it may be equally important to be imaginative and creative when making a recommendation or determining how to implement a solution. Albert Einstein once stated, "Imagination is more important than knowledge." The reason is that managing strategically requires more than memorizing concepts. Strategic management insights must be applied to each case differently—just knowing the principles is not enough. Imagination and out-of-the-box thinking help to apply strategic knowledge in novel and unique ways.

- *Learn from the insights of others.* Before you make up your mind about a case, hear what other students have to say. Get a second opinion, and a third, and so forth. Of course, in a situation where you have to put your analysis in writing, you may not be able to learn from others ahead of time. But in a case discussion, observe how various students attack the issues and engage in problem solving. Such observation skills also may be a key to finding answers within the case. For example, people tend to believe authority figures, so they would place a higher value on what a company president says. In some cases, however, the statements of middle managers may represent a point of view that is even more helpful for finding a solution to the problems presented by the case.

- *Apply insights from other case analyses.* Throughout the text, we have used examples of actual businesses to illustrate strategy concepts. The aim has been to show you how firms think about and deal with business problems. During the course, you may be asked to conduct several case analyses as part of the learning experience. Once you have performed a few case analyses, you will see how the concepts from the text apply in real-life business situations. Incorporate the insights learned from the text examples and your own previous case discussions into each new case that you analyze.

- *Critically analyze your own performance.* Performance appraisals are a standard part of many workplace situations. They are used to determine promotions, raises, and work assignments. In some organizations, everyone from the top executive down is subject to such reviews. Even in situations where the owner or CEO is not evaluated by others, they often find it useful to ask themselves regularly, Am I being effective? The same can be applied to your performance in a case analysis situation. Ask yourself, Were my comments insightful? Did I make a good contribution? How might I improve next time? Use the same criteria on yourself that you use to evaluate others. What grade would you give yourself? This technique will not only make you more fair in your assessment of others but also will indicate how your own performance can improve.

- *Conduct outside research.* Many times, you can enhance your understanding of a case situation by investigating sources outside the case materials. For example, you may want to study an industry more closely or research a company's close competitors. Recent moves such as mergers and acquisitions or product introductions may be reported in the business press. The company itself may provide useful information on its website or in its annual reports. Such information can usually spur additional discussion and enrich the case analysis. (*Caution:* It is best to check with your instructor in advance to be sure this kind of additional research is encouraged. Bringing in outside research may conflict with the instructor's learning objectives.)

Several of the points suggested above for how to get the most out of case analysis apply only to an open discussion of a case, like that in a classroom setting. Exhibit 13.3 provides some additional guidelines for preparing a written case analysis.

Using Conflict-Inducing Decision-Making Techniques in Case Analysis

>LO13.5
How conflict-inducing discussion techniques can lead to better decisions.

Next we address some techniques often used to improve case analyses that involve the constructive use of conflict. In the classroom—as well as in the business world—you will

Exhibit 13.3   **Preparing a Written Case Analysis**

Rule	Description
Be thorough.	Many of the ideas presented in Exhibit 13.2 about oral presentations also apply to written case analysis. However, a written analysis typically has to be more complete. This means writing out the problem statement and articulating assumptions. It is also important to provide support for your arguments and reference case materials or other facts more specifically.
Coordinate team efforts.	Written cases are often prepared by small groups. Within a group, just as in a class discussion, you may disagree about the diagnosis or the recommended plan of action. This can be healthy if it leads to a richer understanding of the case material. But before committing your ideas to writing, make sure you have coordinated your responses. Don't prepare a written analysis that appears contradictory or looks like a patchwork of disconnected thoughts.
Avoid restating the obvious.	There is no reason to restate material that everyone is familiar with already, namely, the case content. It is too easy for students to use up space in a written analysis with a recapitulation of the details of the case—this accomplishes very little. Stay focused on the key points. Only restate the information that is most central to your analysis.
Present information graphically.	Tables, graphs, and other exhibits are usually one of the best ways to present factual material that supports your arguments. For example, financial calculations such as break-even analysis, sensitivity analysis, or return on investment are best presented graphically. Even qualitative information such as product lists or rosters of employees can be summarized effectively and viewed quickly by using a table or graph.
Exercise quality control.	When presenting a case analysis in writing, it is especially important to use good grammar, avoid misspelling words, and eliminate typos and other visual distractions. Mistakes that can be glossed over in an oral presentation or class discussion are often highlighted when they appear in writing. Make your written presentation appear as professional as possible. Don't let the appearance of your written case keep the reader from recognizing the importance and quality of your analysis.

frequently be analyzing cases or solving problems in groups. While the word *conflict* often has a negative connotation (e.g., rude behavior, personal affronts), it can be very helpful in arriving at better solutions to cases. It can provide an effective means for new insights as well as for rigorously questioning and analyzing assumptions and strategic alternatives. In fact, if you don't have constructive conflict, you may only get consensus. When this happens, decisions tend to be based on compromise rather than collaboration.

In your organizational behavior classes, you probably learned the concept of "groupthink."[8] Groupthink, a term coined by Irving Janis after he conducted numerous studies on executive decision making, is a condition in which group members strive to reach agreement or consensus without realistically considering other viable alternatives. In effect, group norms bolster morale at the expense of critical thinking and decision making is impaired.[9]

Many of us have probably been "victims" of groupthink at one time or another in our life. We may be confronted with situations when social pressure, politics, or "not wanting to stand out" may prevent us from voicing our concerns about a chosen course of action. Nevertheless, decision making in groups is a common practice in the management of many businesses. Most companies, especially large ones, rely on input from various top managers to provide valuable information and experience from their specialty area as well as their unique perspectives. Chapter 11 emphasized the importance of empowering individuals at all levels to participate in decision-making processes. In terms of this course, case analysis involves a type of decision making that is often conducted in groups. Strategy Spotlight 13.3 provides guidelines for making team-based approaches to case analysis more effective.

Clearly, understanding how to work in groups and the potential problems associated with group decision processes can benefit the case analysis process. Therefore, let's first look at some of the symptoms of groupthink and suggest ways of preventing it. Then, we will suggest some conflict-inducing decision-making techniques—devil's advocacy and dialectical inquiry—that can help to prevent groupthink and lead to better decisions.

● Effectively working in teams is a critical skill— both in the classroom and in business organizations.

Symptoms of Groupthink and How to Prevent It

Irving Janis identified several symptoms of groupthink, including:

- *An illusion of invulnerability.* This reassures people about possible dangers and leads to overoptimism and failure to heed warnings of danger.
- *A belief in the inherent morality of the group.* Because individuals think that what they are doing is right, they tend to ignore ethical or moral consequences of their decisions.
- *Stereotyped views of members of opposing groups.* Members of other groups are viewed as weak or not intelligent.
- *The application of pressure to members who express doubts about the group's shared illusions or question the validity of arguments proposed.*
- *The practice of self-censorship.* Members keep silent about their opposing views and downplay to themselves the value of their perspectives.

Making Case Analysis Teams More Effective

Working in teams can be very challenging. Not all team members have the same skills, interests, or motivations. Some team members just want to get the work done. Others see teams as an opportunity to socialize. Occasionally, there are team members who think they should be in charge and make all the decisions; other teams have freeloaders—team members who don't want to do anything except get credit for the team's work.

One consequence of these various styles is that team meetings can become time wasters. Disagreements about how to proceed, how to share the work, or what to do at the next meeting tend to slow down teams and impede progress toward the goal. While the dynamics of case analysis teams are likely to always be challenging depending on the personalities involved, one thing nearly all members realize is that, ultimately, the team's work must be completed. Most team members also aim to do the highest quality work possible. The following guidelines provide some useful insights about how to get the work of a team done more effectively.

Spend More Time Together

One of the factors that prevents teams from doing a good job with case analysis is their failure to put in the necessary time. Unless teams really tackle the issues surrounding case analysis—both the issues in the case itself and organizing how the work is to be conducted—the end result will probably be lacking because decisions that are made too quickly are unlikely to get to the heart of the problem(s) in the case. "Meetings should be a precious resource, but they're treated like a necessary evil," says Kenneth Sole, a consultant who specializes in organizational behavior. As a result, teams that care more about finishing the analysis than getting the analysis right often make poor decisions.

Therefore, expect to have a few meetings that run long, especially at the beginning of the project when the work is being organized and the issues in the case are being sorted out, and again at the end when the team must coordinate the components of the case analysis that will be presented. Without spending this kind of time together, it is doubtful that the analysis will be comprehensive and the presentation is likely to be choppy and incomplete.

Make a Focused and Disciplined Agenda

To complete tasks and avoid wasting time, meetings need to have a clear purpose. To accomplish this at Roche, the Swiss drug and diagnostic product maker, CEO Franz Humer implemented a "decision agenda." The agenda focuses only on Roche's highest value issues and discussions are limited to these major topics. In terms of case analysis, the major topics include sorting out the issues of the case, linking elements of the case to the strategic issues presented in class or the text, and assigning roles to various team members. Such objectives help keep team members on track.

Agendas also can be used to address issues such as the time line for accomplishing work. Otherwise the purpose of meetings may only be to manage the "crisis" of getting the case analysis finished on time. One solution is to assign a team member to manage the agenda. That person could make sure the team stays focused on the tasks at hand and remains mindful of time constraints. Another role could be to link the team's efforts to the steps presented in Exhibits 13.2 and Exhibit 13.3 on how to prepare a case analysis.

Pay More Attention to Strategy

Teams often waste time by focusing on unimportant aspects of a case. These may include details that are interesting but irrelevant or operational issues rather than strategic issues. It is true that useful clues to the issues in the case are sometimes embedded in the conversations of key managers or the trends evident in a financial statement. But once such insights are discovered, teams need to focus on the underlying strategic problems in the case. To solve such problems, major corporations such as Cadbury Schweppes and Boeing hold meetings just to generate strategic alternatives for solving their problems. This gives managers time to consider the implications of various courses of action. Separate meetings are held to evaluate alternatives, make strategic decisions, and approve an action plan.

Once the strategic solutions or "course corrections" are identified—as is common in most cases assigned—the operational implications and details of implementation will flow from the strategic decisions that companies make. Therefore, focusing primarily on strategic issues will provide teams with insights for making recommendations that are based on a deeper understanding of the issues in the case.

Produce Real Decisions

Too often, meetings are about discussing rather than deciding. Teams often spend a lot of time talking without reaching any conclusions. As Raymond Sanchez, CEO of Florida-based Security Mortgage Group, says, meetings are often used to "rehash the hash that's already been hashed." To be efficient and productive, team meetings

(continued)

(continued)

need to be about more than just information sharing and group input. For example, an initial meeting may result in the team realizing that it needs to study the case in greater depth and examine links to strategic issues more carefully. Once more analysis is conducted, the team needs to reach a consensus so that the decisions that are made will last once the meeting is over. Lasting decisions are more actionable because it frees team members to take the next steps.

One technique for making progress in this way is recapping each meeting with a five-minute synthesis report. According to Pamela Schindler, director of the

Sources: Mankins, M. C. 2004. Stop Wasting Valuable Time. *Harvard Business Review*, September: 58–65; and Sauer, P. J. 2004. Escape from Meeting Hell. *Inc. Magazine*, May, www.inc.com.

Center for Applied Management at Wittenberg University, it's important to think through the implications of the meeting before ending it. "The real joy of synthesis," says Schindler, "is realizing how many meetings you won't need."

Not only are these guidelines useful for helping teams finish their work, but they can also help resolve some of the difficulties that teams often face. By involving every team member, using a meeting agenda, and focusing on the strategic issues that are critical to nearly every case, the discussion is limited and the criteria for making decisions become clearer. This allows the task to dominate rather than any one personality. And if the team finishes its work faster, this frees up time to focus on other projects or put the finishing touches on a case analysis presentation.

- *An illusion of unanimity.* People assume that judgments expressed by members are shared by all.
- *The appointment of mindguards.* People sometimes appoint themselves as mindguards to protect the group from adverse information that might break the climate of consensus (or agreement).

Clearly, groupthink is an undesirable and negative phenomenon that can lead to poor decisions. Irving Janis considers it to be a key contributor to such faulty decisions as the failure to prepare for the attack on Pearl Harbor, the escalation of the Vietnam conflict, and the failure to prepare for the consequences of the Iraqi invasion. Many of the same sorts of flawed decision making occur in business organizations—as we discussed above with the EDS example. Janis has provided several suggestions for preventing groupthink that can be used as valuable guides in decision making and problem solving:

- Leaders must encourage group members to address their concerns and objectives.
- When higher-level managers assign a problem for a group to solve, they should adopt an impartial stance and not mention their preferences.
- Before a group reaches its final decision, the leader should encourage members to discuss their deliberations with trusted associates and then report the perspectives back to the group.
- The group should invite outside experts and encourage them to challenge the group's viewpoints and positions.
- The group should divide into subgroups, meet at various times under different chairpersons, and then get together to resolve differences.
- After reaching a preliminary agreement, the group should hold a "second chance" meeting which provides members a forum to express any remaining concerns and rethink the issue prior to making a final decision.

Using Conflict to Improve Decision Making

In addition to the above suggestions, the effective use of conflict can be a means of improving decision making. Although conflict can have negative outcomes, such as ill will, anger, tension, and lowered motivation, both leaders and group members must strive to assure that it is managed properly and used in a constructive manner.

Two conflict-inducing decision-making approaches that have become quite popular are *devil's advocacy* and *dialectical inquiry.* Both approaches incorporate conflict into the decision-making process through formalized debate. A group charged with making a decision or solving a problem is divided into two subgroups and each will be involved in the analysis and solution.

Devil's Advocacy   With the devil's advocate approach, one of the groups (or individuals) acts as a critic to the plan. The devil's advocate tries to come up with problems with the proposed alternative and suggest reasons why it should not be adopted. The role of the devil's advocate is to create dissonance. This ensures that the group will take a hard look at its original proposal or alternative. By having a group (or individual) assigned the role of devil's advocate, it becomes clear that such an adversarial stance is legitimized. It brings out criticisms that might otherwise not be made.

Some authors have suggested that the use of a devil's advocate can be very helpful in helping boards of directors to ensure that decisions are addressed comprehensively and to avoid groupthink.[10] And Charles Elson, a director of Sunbeam Corporation, has argued that:

> Devil's advocates are terrific in any situation because they help you to figure a decision's numerous implications. . . . The better you think out the implications prior to making the decision, the better the decision ultimately turns out to be. That's why a devil's advocate is always a great person, irritating sometimes, but a great person.

As one might expect, there can be some potential problems with using the devil's advocate approach. If one's views are constantly criticized, one may become demoralized. Thus, that person may come up with "safe solutions" in order to minimize embarrassment or personal risk and become less subject to criticism. Additionally, even if the devil's advocate is successful with finding problems with the proposed course of action, there may be no new ideas or counterproposals to take its place. Thus, the approach sometimes may simply focus on what is wrong without suggesting other ideas.

Dialectical Inquiry   Dialectical inquiry attempts to accomplish the goals of the devil's advocate in a more constructive manner. It is a technique whereby a problem is approached from two alternative points of view. The idea is that out of a critique of the opposing perspectives—a thesis and an antithesis—a creative synthesis will occur. Dialectical inquiry involves the following steps:

1. Identify a proposal and the information that was used to derive it.
2. State the underlying assumptions of the proposal.
3. Identify a counterplan (antithesis) that is believed to be feasible, politically viable, and generally credible. However, it rests on assumptions that are opposite to the original proposal.
4. Engage in a debate in which individuals favoring each plan provide their arguments and support.
5. Identify a synthesis which, hopefully, includes the best components of each alternative.

There are some potential downsides associated with dialectical inquiry. It can be quite time consuming and involve a good deal of training. Further, it may result in a series of compromises between the initial proposal and the counterplan. In cases where the original proposal was the best approach, this would be unfortunate.

● Conflict-inducing decision-making techniques, such as devil's advocacy, can be very effective.

devil's advocacy a method of introducing conflict into a decision-making process by having specific individuals or groups act as a critic to an analysis or planned solution.

dialectical inquiry a method of introducing conflict into a decision-making process by devising different proposals that are feasible, politically viable, and credible, but rely on different assumptions; and debating the merits of each.

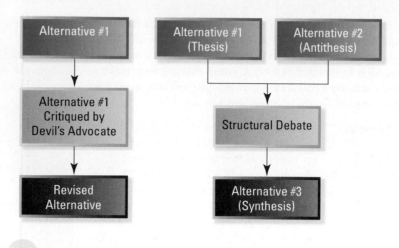

Exhibit 13.4 Two Conflict-Inducing Decision-Making Processes

Despite some possible limitations associated with these conflict-inducing decision-making techniques, they have many benefits. Both techniques force debate about underlying assumptions, data, and recommendations between subgroups. Such debate tends to prevent the uncritical acceptance of a plan that may seem to be satisfactory after a cursory analysis. The approach serves to tap the knowledge and perspectives of group members and continues until group members agree on both assumptions and recommended actions. Given that both approaches serve to use, rather than minimize or suppress, conflict, higher quality decisions should result. Exhibit 13.4 briefly summarizes these techniques.

Following the Analysis-Decision-Action Cycle in Case Analysis

In Chapter 1 we defined strategic management as the analysis, decisions, and actions that organizations undertake to create and sustain competitive advantages. It is no accident that we chose that sequence of words because it corresponds to the sequence of events that typically occurs in the strategic management process. In case analysis, as in the real world, this cycle of events can provide a useful framework. First, an analysis of the case in terms of the business environment and current events is needed. To make such an analysis, the case background must be considered. Next, based on that analysis, decisions must be made. This may involve formulating a strategy, choosing between difficult options, moving forward aggressively, or retreating from a bad situation. There are many possible decisions, depending on the case situation. Finally, action is required. Once decisions are made and plans are set, the action begins. The recommended action steps and the consequences of implementing these actions are the final stage.

Each of the previous 12 chapters of this book includes techniques and information that may be useful in a case analysis. However, not all of the issues presented will be important in every case. As noted earlier, one of the challenges of case analysis is to identify the most critical points and sort through material that may be ambiguous or unimportant.

In this section we draw on the material presented in each of the 12 chapters to show how it informs the case analysis process. The ideas are linked sequentially and in terms of an overarching strategic perspective. One of your jobs when conducting case analysis is to see how the parts of a case fit together and how the insights from the study of strategy can help you understand the case situation.

>LO13.6

How to use the strategic insights and material from each of the 12 previous chapters in the text to analyze issues posed by strategic management cases.

1. *Analyzing organizational goals and objectives.* A company's vision, mission, and objectives keep organization members focused on a common purpose. They also influence how an organization deploys its resources, relates to its stakeholders, and matches its short-term objectives with its long-term goals. The goals may even impact how a company formulates and implements strategies. When exploring issues of goals and objectives, you might ask:

   - Has the company developed short-term objectives that are inconsistent with its long-term mission? If so, how can management realign its vision, mission, and objectives?
   - Has the company considered all of its stakeholders equally in making critical decisions? If not, should the views of all stakeholders be treated the same or are some stakeholders more important than others?
   - Is the company being faced with an issue that conflicts with one of its long-standing policies? If so, how should it compare its existing policies to the potential new situation?

2. *Analyzing the external environment.* The business environment has two components. The general environment consists of demographic, sociocultural, political/legal, technological, economic, and global conditions. The competitive environment includes rivals, suppliers, customers, and other factors that may directly affect a company's success. Strategic managers must monitor the environment to identify opportunities and threats that may have an impact on performance. When investigating a firm's external environment, you might ask:

   - Does the company follow trends and events in the general environment? If not, how can these influences be made part of the company's strategic analysis process?
   - Is the company effectively scanning and monitoring the competitive environment? If so, how is it using the competitive intelligence it is gathering to enhance its competitive advantage?
   - Has the company correctly analyzed the impact of the competitive forces in its industry on profitability? If so, how can it improve its competitive position relative to these forces?

3. *Analyzing the internal environment.* A firm's internal environment consists of its resources and other value-adding capabilities. Value-chain analysis and a resource-based approach to analysis can be used to identify a company's strengths and weaknesses and determine how they are contributing to its competitive advantages. Evaluating firm performance can also help make meaningful comparisons with competitors. When researching a company's internal analysis, you might ask:

   - Does the company know how the various components of its value chain are adding value to the firm? If not, what internal analysis is needed to determine its strengths and weakness?
   - Has the company accurately analyzed the source and vitality of its resources? If so, is it deploying its resources in a way that contributes to competitive advantages?
   - Is the company's financial performance as good as or better than that of its close competitors? If so, has it balanced its financial success with the performance criteria of other stakeholders such as customers and employees?

4. *Assessing a firm's intellectual assets.* Human capital is a major resource in today's knowledge economy. As a result, attracting, developing, and retaining talented workers is a key strategic challenge. Other assets such as patents and trademarks are also critical. How companies leverage their intellectual assets through social networks and strategic alliances, and how technology is used to manage knowledge may be a major

influence on a firm's competitive advantage. When analyzing a firm's intellectual assets, you might ask:

- Does the company have underutilized human capital? If so, what steps are needed to develop and leverage its intellectual assets?
- Is the company missing opportunities to forge strategic alliances? If so, how can it use its social capital to network more effectively?
- Has the company developed knowledge-management systems that capture what it learns? If not, what technologies can it employ to retain new knowledge?

5. ***Formulating business-level strategies.*** Firms use the competitive strategies of differentiation, focus, and overall cost leadership as a basis for overcoming the five competitive forces and developing sustainable competitive advantages. Combinations of these strategies may work best in some competitive environments. Additionally, an industry's life cycle is an important contingency that may affect a company's choice of business-level strategies. When assessing business-level strategies, you might ask:

- Has the company chosen the correct competitive strategy given its industry environment and competitive situation? If not, how should it use its strengths and resources to improve its performance?
- Does the company use combination strategies effectively? If so, what capabilities can it cultivate to further enhance profitability?
- Is the company using a strategy that is appropriate for the industry life cycle in which it is competing? If not, how can it realign itself to match its efforts to the current stage of industry growth?

6. ***Formulating corporate-level strategies.*** Large firms often own and manage portfolios of businesses. Corporate strategies address methods for achieving synergies among these businesses. Related and unrelated diversification techniques are alternative approaches to deciding which business should be added to or removed from a portfolio. Companies can diversify by means of mergers, acquisitions, joint ventures, strategic alliances, and internal development. When analyzing corporate-level strategies, you might ask:

- Is the company competing in the right businesses given the opportunities and threats that are present in the environment? If not, how can it realign its diversification strategy to achieve competitive advantages?
- Is the corporation managing its portfolio of businesses in a way that creates synergies among the businesses? If so, what additional business should it consider adding to its portfolio?
- Are the motives of the top corporate executives who are pushing diversification strategies appropriate? If not, what action can be taken to curb their activities or align them with the best interests of all stakeholders?

7. ***Formulating international-level strategies.*** Foreign markets provide both opportunities and potential dangers for companies that want to expand globally. To decide which entry strategy is most appropriate, companies have to evaluate the trade-offs between two factors that firms face when entering foreign markets: cost reduction and local adaptation. To achieve competitive advantages, firms will typically choose one of three strategies: global, multidomestic, or transnational. When evaluating international-level strategies, you might ask:

- Is the company's entry into an international marketplace threatened by the actions of local competitors? If so, how can cultural differences be minimized to give the firm a better chance of succeeding?
- Has the company made the appropriate choices between cost reduction and local adaptation to foreign markets? If not, how can it adjust its strategy to achieve competitive advantages?

- Can the company improve its effectiveness by embracing one international strategy over another? If so, how should it choose between a global, multidomestic, or transnational strategy?

8. **Formulating entrepreneurial strategies.** New ventures add jobs and create new wealth. To do so, they must identify opportunities that will be viable in the marketplace as well as gather resources and assemble an entrepreneurial team to enact the opportunity. New entrants often evoke a strong competitive response from incumbent firms in a given marketplace. When examining the role of strategic thinking on the success of entrepreneurial ventures and the role of competitive dynamics, you might ask:
   - Is the company engaged in an ongoing process of opportunity recognition? If not, how can it enhance its ability to recognize opportunities?
   - Do the entrepreneurs who are launching new ventures have vision, dedication and drive, and a commitment to excellence? If so, how have these affected the performance and dedication of other employees involved in the venture?
   - Have strategic principles been used in the process of developing strategies to pursue the entrepreneurial opportunity? If not, how can the venture apply tools such as five-forces analysis and value-chain analysis to improve its competitive position and performance?

9. **Achieving effective strategic control.** Strategic controls enable a firm to implement strategies effectively. Informational controls involve comparing performance to stated goals and scanning, monitoring, and being responsive to the environment. Behavioral controls emerge from a company's culture, reward systems, and organizational boundaries. When assessing the impact of strategic controls on implementation, you might ask:
   - Is the company employing the appropriate informational control systems? If not, how can it implement a more interactive approach to enhance learning and minimize response times?
   - Does the company have a strong and effective culture? If not, what steps can it take to align its values and rewards system with its goals and objectives?
   - Has the company implemented control systems that match its strategies? If so, what additional steps can be taken to improve performance?

10. **Creating effective organizational designs.** Organizational designs that align with competitive strategies can enhance performance. As companies grow and change, their structures must also evolve to meet new demands. In today's economy, firm boundaries must be flexible and permeable to facilitate smoother interactions with external parties such as customers, suppliers, and alliance partners. New forms of organizing are becoming more common. When evaluating the role of organizational structure on strategy implementation, you might ask:
   - Has the company implemented organizational structures that are suited to the type of business it is in? If not, how can it alter the design in ways that enhance its competitiveness?
   - Is the company employing boundaryless organizational designs where appropriate? If so, how are senior managers maintaining control of lower-level employees?
   - Does the company use outsourcing to achieve the best possible results? If not, what criteria should it use to decide which functions can be outsourced?

11. **Creating a learning organization and an ethical organization.** Strong leadership is essential for achieving competitive advantages. Two leadership roles are especially important. The first is creating a learning organization by harnessing talent and encouraging the development of new knowledge. Second, leaders play a vital role in

motivating employees to excellence and inspiring ethical behavior. When exploring the impact of effective strategic leadership, you might ask:

- Do company leaders promote excellence as part of the overall culture? If so, how has this influenced the performance of the firm and the individuals in it?
- Is the company committed to being a learning organization? If not, what can it do to capitalize on the individual and collective talents of organizational members?
- Have company leaders exhibited an ethical attitude in their own behavior? If not, how has their behavior influenced the actions of other employees?

12. *Fostering corporate entrepreneurship.* Many firms continually seek new growth opportunities and avenues for strategic renewal. In some corporations, autonomous work units such as business incubators and new-venture groups are used to focus corporate venturing activities. In other corporate settings, product champions and other firm members provide companies with the impetus to expand into new areas. When investigating the impact of entrepreneurship on strategic effectiveness, you might ask:

- Has the company resolved the dilemmas associated with managing innovation? If so, is it effectively defining and pacing its innovation efforts?
- Has the company developed autonomous work units that have the freedom to bring forth new product ideas? If so, has it used product champions to implement new venture initiatives?
- Does the company have an entrepreneurial orientation? If not, what can it do to encourage entrepreneurial attitudes in the strategic behavior of its organizational members?

Summary

Strategic management case analysis provides an effective method of learning how companies analyze problems, make decisions, and resolve challenges. Strategic cases include detailed accounts of actual business situations. The purpose of analyzing such cases is to gain exposure to a wide variety of organizational and managerial situations. By putting yourself in the place of a strategic decision maker, you can gain an appreciation of the difficulty and complexity of many strategic situations. In the process you can learn how to ask good strategic questions and enhance your analytical skills. Presenting case analyses can also help develop oral and written communication skills.

In this chapter we have discussed the importance of strategic case analysis and described the five steps involved in conducting a case analysis: becoming familiar with the material, identifying problems, analyzing strategic issues, proposing alternative solutions, and making recommendations. We have also discussed how to get the most from case analysis. Finally, we have described how the case analysis process follows the analysis-decision-action cycle of strategic management and outlined issues and questions that are associated with each of the previous 12 chapters of the text.

Key Terms

case analysis, 470	devil's
case symptoms, 475	advocacy, 485
case problems, 475	dialectical
financial ratio	inquiry, 485
analysis, 476	

References

1. The material in this chapter is based on several sources, including Barnes, L. A., Nelson, A. J., & Christensen, C. R. 1994. *Teaching and the case method: Text, cases and readings.* Boston: Harvard Business School Press: Guth, W. D. 1985. Central concepts of business unit and corporate strategy. In W. D. Guth (Ed.). *Handbook of business strategy:* 1–9. Boston: Warren, Gorham & Lamont; Lundberg, C. C., & Enz, C. 1993. A framework for student case preparation. *Case Research Journal,* 13 (Summer): 129–140; and Ronstadt, R. 1980. *The art of case analysis: A guide to the diagnosis of business situations.* Dover, MA: Lord Publishing.

2. Edge, A. G. & Coleman, D. R. 1986. *The guide to case analysis and reporting* (3rd ed.). Honolulu, HI: System Logistics.

3. Morris, E. 1987. Vision and strategy: A focus for the future. *Journal of Business Strategy* 8: 51–58.

4. This section is based on Lundberg & Enz, op. cit., and Ronstadt, op. cit.

5. The importance of problem definition was emphasized in Mintzberg, H., Raisinghani, D. & Theoret, A. 1976. The structure of "unstructured" decision processes. *Administrative Science Quarterly,* 21(2): 246–275.

6. Drucker, P. F. 1994. The theory of the business. *Harvard Business Review,* 72(5): 95–104.

7. This section draws on Edge & Coleman, op. cit.

8. Irving Janis is credited with coining the term *groupthink,* and he applied it primarily to fiascos in government (such as the Bay of Pigs incident in 1961). Refer to Janis, I. L. 1982. *Victims of groupthink* (2nd ed.). Boston: Houghton Mifflin.

9. Much of our discussion is based upon Finkelstein, S. & Mooney, A. C. 2003. Not the usual suspects: How to use board process to make boards better. *Academy of Management Executive,* 17(2): 101–113; Schweiger, D. M., Sandberg, W. R., & Rechner, P. L. 1989. Experiential effects of dialectical inquiry, devil's advocacy, and consensus approaches to strategic decision making. *Academy of Management Journal,* 32(4): 745–772; and Aldag, R. J. & Stearns, T. M. 1987. *Management.* Cincinnati: South-Western Publishing.

10. Finkelstein and Mooney, op. cit.

APPENDIX 1 TO CHAPTER 13

Financial Ratio Analysis*

Standard Financial Statements

One obvious thing we might want to do with a company's financial statements is to compare them to those of other, similar companies. We would immediately have a problem, however. It's almost impossible to directly compare the financial statements for two companies because of differences in size.

For example, Oracle and IBM are obviously serious rivals in the computer software market, but IBM is much larger (in terms of assets), so it is difficult to compare them directly. For that matter, it's difficult to even compare financial statements from different points in time for the same company if the company's size has changed. The size problem is compounded if we try to compare IBM and, say, SAP (of Germany). If SAP's financial statements are denominated in German marks, then we have a size *and* a currency difference.

To start making comparisons, one obvious thing we might try to do is to somehow standardize the financial statements. One very common and useful way of doing this is to work with percentages instead of total dollars. The resulting financial statements are called *common-size statements.* We consider these next.

Common-Size Balance Sheets

For easy reference, Prufrock Corporation's 2010 and 2011 balance sheets are provided in Exhibit 13A.1. Using these, we construct common-size balance sheets by expressing each item as a percentage of total assets. Prufrock's 2010 and 2011 common-size balance sheets are shown in Exhibit 13A.2.

*This entire Appendix is adapted from Rows, S. A., Westerfield, R. W., & Jordan, B. D. 1999. *Essentials of Corporate Finance* (2nd ed.). chap. 3. New York: McGraw-Hill.

Exhibit 13A.1

Prufrock Corporation
Balance Sheets as of December 31, 2010 and 2011 ($ in millions)

	2010	2011
Assets		
Current assets		
Cash	$ 84	$ 98
Accounts receivable	165	188
Inventory	393	422
Total	$ 642	$ 708
Fixed assets		
Net plant and equipment	$2,731	$2,880
Total assets	$3,373	$3,588
Liabilities and Owners' Equity		
Current liabilities		
Accounts payable	$ 312	$ 344
Notes payable	231	196
Total	$ 543	$ 540
Long-term debt	$ 531	$ 457
Owners' equity		
Common stock and paid-in surplus	$ 500	$ 550
Retained earnings	1,799	2,041
Total	$2,299	$2,591
Total liabilities and owners' equity	$3,373	$3,588

Notice that some of the totals don't check exactly because of rounding errors. Also notice that the total change has to be zero since the beginning and ending numbers must add up to 100 percent.

In this form, financial statements are relatively easy to read and compare. For example, just looking at the two balance sheets for Prufrock, we see that current assets were 19.7 percent of total assets in 2011, up from 19.1 percent in 2010. Current liabilities declined from 16.0 percent to 15.1 percent of total liabilities and equity over that same time. Similarly, total equity rose from 68.1 percent of total liabilities and equity to 72.2 percent.

Overall, Prufrock's liquidity, as measured by current assets compared to current liabilities, increased over the year. Simultaneously, Prufrock's indebtedness diminished as a percentage of total assets. We might be tempted to conclude that the balance sheet has grown "stronger."

Common-Size Income Statements

A useful way of standardizing the income statement, shown in Exhibit 13A.3, is to express each item as a percentage of total sales, as illustrated for Prufrock in Exhibit 13A.4.

This income statement tells us what happens to each dollar in sales. For Prufrock, interest expense eats up $.061 out of every sales dollar and taxes take another $.081. When all is said and done, $.157 of each dollar flows through to the bottom line (net income), and that amount is split into $.105 retained in the business and $.052 paid out in dividends.

Exhibit 13A.2
Prufrock Corporation
Common-Size
Balance Sheets as of
December 31, 2010
and 2011 (%)

	2010	2011	Change
Assets			
Current assets			
Cash	2.5%	2.7%	+ .2%
Accounts receivable	4.9	5.2	+ .3
Inventory	11.7	11.8	+ .1
Total	19.1	19.7	+ .6
Fixed assets			
Net plant and equipment	80.9	80.3	− .6
Total assets	100.0%	100.0%	.0%
Liabilities and Owners' Equity			
Current liabilities			
Accounts payable	9.2%	9.6%	+ .4%
Notes payable	6.8	5.5	−1.3
Total	16.0	15.1	− .9
Long-term debt	15.7	12.7	−3.0
Owners' equity			
Common stock and paid-in surplus	14.8	15.3	+ .5
Retained earnings	53.3	56.9	+3.6
Total	68.1	72.2	+4.1
Total liabilities and owners' equities	100.0%	100.0%	.0%

Note: Numbers may not add up to 100.0% due to rounding.

These percentages are very useful in comparisons. For example, a relevant figure is the cost percentage. For Prufrock, $.582 of each $1.00 in sales goes to pay for goods sold. It would be interesting to compute the same percentage for Prufrock's main competitors to see how Prufrock stacks up in terms of cost control.

Ratio Analysis

Another way of avoiding the problems involved in comparing companies of different sizes is to calculate and compare *financial ratios*. Such ratios are ways of comparing and investigating the relationships between different pieces of financial information. We cover some of the more common ratios next, but there are many others that we don't touch on.

One problem with ratios is that different people and different sources frequently don't compute them in exactly the same way, and this leads to much confusion. The specific definitions we use here may or may not be the same as others you have seen or will see elsewhere. If you ever use ratios as a tool for analysis, you should be careful to document how you calculate each one, and, if you are comparing your numbers to those of another source, be sure you know how its numbers are computed.

For each of the ratios we discuss, several questions come to mind:

1. How is it computed?
2. What is it intended to measure, and why might we be interested?
3. What is the unit of measurement?

Exhibit 13A.3

Prufrock Corporation

2011 Income Statement
($ in millions)

Sales	$2,311
Cost of goods sold	1,344
Depreciation	276
Earnings before interest and taxes	$ 691
Interest paid	141
Taxable income	$ 550
Taxes (34%)	187
Net income	$ 363

Dividends	$121	
Addition to retained earnings	242	

Exhibit 13A.4

Prufrock Corporation

2011 Common-Size
Income Statement (%)

Sales	100.0%
Cost of goods sold	58.2
Depreciation	11.9
Earnings before interest and taxes	29.9
Interest paid	6.1
Taxable income	23.8
Taxes (34%)	8.1
Net income	15.7%

Dividends	5.2%	
Addition to retained earnings	10.5	

4. What might a high or low value be telling us? How might such values be misleading?
5. How could this measure be improved?

Financial ratios are traditionally grouped into the following categories:

1. Short-term solvency, or liquidity, ratios.
2. Long-term solvency, or financial leverage, ratios.
3. Asset management, or turnover, ratios.
4. Profitability ratios.
5. Market value ratios.

We will consider each of these in turn. In calculating these numbers for Prufrock, we will use the ending balance sheet (2011) figures unless we explicitly say otherwise. The numbers for the various ratios come from the income statement and the balance sheet.

Short-Term Solvency, or Liquidity, Measures

As the name suggests, short-term solvency ratios as a group are intended to provide information about a firm's liquidity, and these ratios are sometimes called *liquidity measures*. The primary concern is the firm's ability to pay its bills over the short run without undue stress. Consequently, these ratios focus on current assets and current liabilities.

For obvious reasons, liquidity ratios are particularly interesting to short-term creditors. Since financial managers are constantly working with banks and other short-term lenders, an understanding of these ratios is essential.

One advantage of looking at current assets and liabilities is that their book values and market values are likely to be similar. Often (though not always), these assets and liabilities just don't live long enough for the two to get seriously out of step. On the other hand, like any type of near cash, current assets and liabilities can and do change fairly rapidly, so today's amounts may not be a reliable guide to the future.

Current Ratio One of the best-known and most widely used ratios is the *current ratio.* As you might guess, the current ratio is defined as:

$$\text{Current ratio} = \frac{\text{Current assets}}{\text{Current liabilities}}$$

For Prufrock, the 2011 current ratio is:

$$\text{Current ratio} = \frac{\$708}{\$540} = 1.31 \text{ times}$$

Because current assets and liabilities are, in principle, converted to cash over the following 12 months, the current ratio is a measure of short-term liquidity. The unit of measurement is either dollars or times. So, we could say Prufrock has $1.31 in current assets for every $1 in current liabilities, or we could say Prufrock has its current liabilities covered 1.31 times over.

To a creditor, particularly a short-term creditor such as a supplier, the higher the current ratio, the better. To the firm, a high current ratio indicates liquidity, but it also may indicate an inefficient use of cash and other short-term assets. Absent some extraordinary circumstances, we would expect to see a current ratio of at least 1, because a current ratio of less than 1 would mean that net working capital (current assets less current liabilities) is negative. This would be unusual in a healthy firm, at least for most types of businesses.

The current ratio, like any ratio, is affected by various types of transactions. For example, suppose the firm borrows over the long term to raise money. The short-run effect would be an increase in cash from the issue proceeds and an increase in long-term debt. Current liabilities would not be affected, so the current ratio would rise.

Finally, note that an apparently low current ratio may not be a bad sign for a company with a large reserve of untapped borrowing power.

Quick (or Acid-Test) Ratio Inventory is often the least liquid current asset. It's also the one for which the book values are least reliable as measures of market value, since the quality of the inventory isn't considered. Some of the inventory may later turn out to be damaged, obsolete, or lost.

More to the point, relatively large inventories are often a sign of short-term trouble. The firm may have overestimated sales and overbought or overproduced as a result. In this case, the firm may have a substantial portion of its liquidity tied up in slow-moving inventory.

To further evaluate liquidity, the *quick,* or *acid-test, ratio* is computed just like the current ratio, except inventory is omitted:

$$\text{Quick ratio} = \frac{\text{Current assets} - \text{Inventory}}{\text{Current liabilities}}$$

Notice that using cash to buy inventory does not affect the current ratio, but it reduces the quick ratio. Again, the idea is that inventory is relatively illiquid compared to cash.

For Prufrock, this ratio in 2011 was:

$$\text{Quick ratio} = \frac{\$708 - 422}{\$540} = .53 \text{ times}$$

The quick ratio here tells a somewhat different story than the current ratio, because inventory accounts for more than half of Prufrock's current assets. To exaggerate the point, if this inventory consisted of, say, unsold nuclear power plants, then this would be a cause for concern.

Cash Ratio A very short-term creditor might be interested in the *cash ratio:*

$$\text{Cash ratio} = \frac{\text{Cash}}{\text{Current liabilities}}$$

You can verify that this works out to be .18 times for Prufrock.

Long-Term Solvency Measures

Long-term solvency ratios are intended to address the firm's long-run ability to meet its obligations, or, more generally, its financial leverage. These ratios are sometimes called *financial leverage ratios* or just *leverage ratios.* We consider three commonly used measures and some variations.

Total Debt Ratio The *total debt ratio* takes into account all debts of all maturities to all creditors. It can be defined in several ways, the easiest of which is:

$$\text{Total debt ratio} = \frac{\text{Total assets} - \text{Total equity}}{\text{Total assets}}$$

$$= \frac{\$3,588 - 2,591}{\$3,588} = .28 \text{ times}$$

In this case, an analyst might say that Prufrock uses 28 percent debt.[1] Whether this is high or low or whether it even makes any difference depends on whether or not capital structure matters.

Prufrock has $.28 in debt for every $1 in assets. Therefore, there is $.72 in equity ($1 − .28) for every $.28 in debt. With this in mind, we can define two useful variations on the total debt ratio, the *debt-equity ratio* and the *equity multiplier:*

$$\text{Debt-equity ratio} = \text{Total debt/Total equity}$$
$$= \$.28/\$.72 = .39 \text{ times}$$
$$\text{Equity multiplier} = \text{Total assets/Total equity}$$
$$= \$1/\$.72 = 1.39 \text{ times}$$

The fact that the equity multiplier is 1 plus the debt-equity ratio is not a coincidence:

$$\text{Equity multiplier} = \text{Total assets/Total equity} = \$1/\$.72 = 1.39$$
$$= (\text{Total equity} + \text{Total debt})/\text{Total equity}$$
$$= 1 + \text{Debt-equity ratio} = 1.39 \text{ times}$$

The thing to notice here is that given any one of these three ratios, you can immediately calculate the other two, so they all say exactly the same thing.

Times Interest Earned Another common measure of long-term solvency is the *times interest earned* (TIE) *ratio.* Once again, there are several possible (and common) definitions, but we'll stick with the most traditional:

$$\text{Times interest earned ratio} = \frac{\text{EBIT}}{\text{Interest}}$$

$$= \frac{\$691}{\$141} = 4.9 \text{ times}$$

As the name suggests, this ratio measures how well a company has its interest obligations covered, and it is often called the interest coverage ratio. For Prufrock, the interest bill is covered 4.9 times over.

Cash Coverage A problem with the TIE ratio is that it is based on earnings before interest and taxes (EBIT), which is not really a measure of cash available to pay interest. The reason is that

---

[1] Total equity here includes preferred stock, if there is any. An equivalent numerator in this ratio would be (Current liabilities + Long-term debt).

depreciation, a noncash expense, has been deducted. Since interest is most definitely a cash outflow (to creditors), one way to define the *cash coverage ratio* is:

$$\text{Cash coverage ratio} = \frac{\text{EBIT} + \text{Depreciation}}{\text{Interest}}$$

$$= \frac{\$691 + 276}{\$141} = \frac{\$967}{\$141} = 6.9 \text{ times}$$

The numerator here, EBIT plus depreciation, is often abbreviated EBDIT (earnings before depreciation, interest, and taxes). It is a basic measure of the firm's ability to generate cash from operations, and it is frequently used as a measure of cash flow available to meet financial obligations.

Asset Management, or Turnover, Measures

We next turn our attention to the efficiency with which Prufrock uses its assets. The measures in this section are sometimes called *asset utilization ratios.* The specific ratios we discuss can all be interpreted as measures of turnover. What they are intended to describe is how efficiently, or intensively, a firm uses its assets to generate sales. We first look at two important current assets: inventory and receivables.

Inventory Turnover and Days' Sales in Inventory   During the year, Prufrock had a cost of goods sold of $1,344. Inventory at the end of the year was $422. With these numbers, *inventory turnover* can be calculated as:

$$\text{Inventory turnover} = \frac{\text{Cost of goods sold}}{\text{Inventory}}$$

$$= \frac{\$1,344}{\$422} = 3.2 \text{ times}$$

In a sense, we sold off, or turned over, the entire inventory 3.2 times. As long as we are not running out of stock and thereby forgoing sales, the higher this ratio is, the more efficiently we are managing inventory.

If we know that we turned our inventory over 3.2 times during the year, then we can immediately figure out how long it took us to turn it over on average. The result is the average *days' sales in inventory.*

$$\text{Days' sales in inventory} = \frac{365 \text{ days}}{\text{Inventory turnover}}$$

$$= \frac{365}{3.2} = 114 \text{ days}$$

This tells us that, on average, inventory sits 114 days before it is sold. Alternatively, assuming we used the most recent inventory and cost figures, it will take about 114 days to work off our current inventory.

For example, we frequently hear things like "Majestic Motors has a 60 days' supply of cars." This means that, at current daily sales, it would take 60 days to deplete the available inventory. We could also say that Majestic has 60 days of sales in inventory.

Receivables Turnover and Days' Sales in Receivables   Our inventory measures give some indication of how fast we can sell products. We now look at how fast we collect on those sales. The *receivables turnover* is defined in the same way as inventory turnover:

$$\text{Receivables turnover} = \frac{\text{Sales}}{\text{Accounts receivable}}$$

$$= \frac{\$2,311}{\$188} = 12.3 \text{ times}$$

Loosely speaking, we collected our outstanding credit accounts and reloaned the money 12.3 times during the year.[2]

This ratio makes more sense if we convert it to days, so the *days' sales in receivables* is:

$$\text{Days' sales in receivables} = \frac{365 \text{ days}}{\text{Receivables turnover}}$$

$$= \frac{365}{12.3} = 30 \text{ days}$$

Therefore, on average, we collect on our credit sales in 30 days. For obvious reasons, this ratio is very frequently called the *average collection period* (ACP).

Also note that if we are using the most recent figures, we can also say that we have 30 days' worth of sales currently uncollected.

Total Asset Turnover   Moving away from specific accounts like inventory or receivables, we can consider an important "big picture" ratio, the *total asset turnover ratio.* As the name suggests, total asset turnover is:

$$\text{Total asset turnover} = \frac{\text{Sales}}{\text{Total assets}}$$

$$= \frac{\$2,311}{\$3,588} = .64 \text{ times}$$

In other words, for every dollar in assets, we generated $.64 in sales.

A closely related ratio, the *capital intensity ratio,* is simply the reciprocal of (i.e., 1 divided by) total asset turnover. It can be interpreted as the dollar investment in assets needed to generate $1 in sales. High values correspond to capital intensive industries (e.g., public utilities). For Prufrock, total asset turnover is .64, so, if we flip this over, we get that capital intensity is $1/.64 = $1.56. That is, it takes Prufrock $1.56 in assets to create $1 in sales.

Profitability Measures

The three measures we discuss in this section are probably the best known and most widely used of all financial ratios. In one form or another, they are intended to measure how efficiently the firm uses its assets and how efficiently the firm manages its operations. The focus in this group is on the bottom line, net income.

Profit Margin   Companies pay a great deal of attention to their *profit margin:*

$$\text{Profit margin} = \frac{\text{Net income}}{\text{Sales}}$$

$$= \frac{\$363}{\$2,311} = 15.7\%$$

This tells us that Prufrock, in an accounting sense, generates a little less than 16 cents in profit for every dollar in sales.

All other things being equal, a relatively high profit margin is obviously desirable. This situation corresponds to low expense ratios relative to sales. However, we hasten to add that other things are often not equal.

For example, lowering our sales price will usually increase unit volume, but will normally cause profit margins to shrink. Total profit (or, more importantly, operating cash flow) may go up or down; so the fact that margins are smaller isn't necessarily bad. After all, isn't it possible that, as the saying goes, "Our prices are so low that we lose money on everything we sell, but we make it up in volume!"[3]

---

[2] Here we have implicitly assumed that all sales are credit sales. If they were not, then we would simply use total credit sales in these calculations, not total sales.

[3] No, it's not; margins can be small, but they do need to be positive!

Return on Assets *Return on assets* (ROA) is a measure of profit per dollar of assets. It can be defined several ways, but the most common is:

$$\text{Return on assets} = \frac{\text{Net income}}{\text{Total assets}}$$

$$= \frac{\$363}{\$3,588} = 10.12\%$$

Return on Equity *Return on equity* (ROE) is a measure of how the stockholders fared during the year. Since benefiting shareholders is our goal, ROE is, in an accounting sense, the true bottom-line measure of performance. ROE is usually measured as:

$$\text{Return on equity} = \frac{\text{Net income}}{\text{Total equity}}$$

$$= \frac{\$363}{\$2,591} = 14\%$$

For every dollar in equity, therefore, Prufrock generated 14 cents in profit, but, again, this is only correct in accounting terms.

Because ROA and ROE are such commonly cited numbers, we stress that it is important to remember they are accounting rates of return. For this reason, these measures should properly be called *return on book assets* and *return on book equity*. In addition, ROE is sometimes called *return on net worth*. Whatever it's called, it would be inappropriate to compare the results to, for example, an interest rate observed in the financial markets.

The fact that ROE exceeds ROA reflects Prufrock's use of financial leverage. We will examine the relationship between these two measures in more detail below.

Market Value Measures

Our final group of measures is based, in part, on information not necessarily contained in financial statements—the market price per share of the stock. Obviously, these measures can only be calculated directly for publicly traded companies.

We assume that Prufrock has 33 million shares outstanding and the stock sold for $88 per share at the end of the year. If we recall that Prufrock's net income was $363 million, then we can calculate that its earnings per share were:

$$\text{EPS} = \frac{\text{Net income}}{\text{Shares outstanding}} = \frac{\$363}{33} = \$11$$

Price-Earnings Ratio The first of our market value measures, the *price-earnings,* or PE, *ratio* (or multiple), is defined as:

$$\text{PE ratio} = \frac{\text{Price per share}}{\text{Earnings per share}}$$

$$= \frac{\$88}{\$11} = 8 \text{ times}$$

In the vernacular, we would say that Prufrock shares sell for eight times earnings, or we might say that Prufrock shares have, or "carry," a PE multiple of 8.

Since the PE ratio measures how much investors are willing to pay per dollar of current earnings, higher PEs are often taken to mean that the firm has significant prospects for future growth. Of course, if a firm had no or almost no earnings, its PE would probably be quite large; so, as always, be careful when interpreting this ratio.

Market-to-Book Ratio A second commonly quoted measure is the *market-to-book ratio*:

$$\text{Market-to-book ratio} = \frac{\text{Market value per share}}{\text{Book value per share}}$$

$$= \frac{\$88}{(\$2{,}591/33)} = \frac{\$88}{\$78.5} = 1.12 \text{ times}$$

Notice that book value per share is total equity (not just common stock) divided by the number of shares outstanding.

Since book value per share is an accounting number, it reflects historical costs. In a loose sense, the market-to-book ratio therefore compares the market value of the firm's investments to their cost. A value less than 1 could mean that the firm has not been successful overall in creating value for its stockholders.

Conclusion

This completes our definition of some common ratios. Exhibit 13A.5 summarizes the ratios we've discussed.

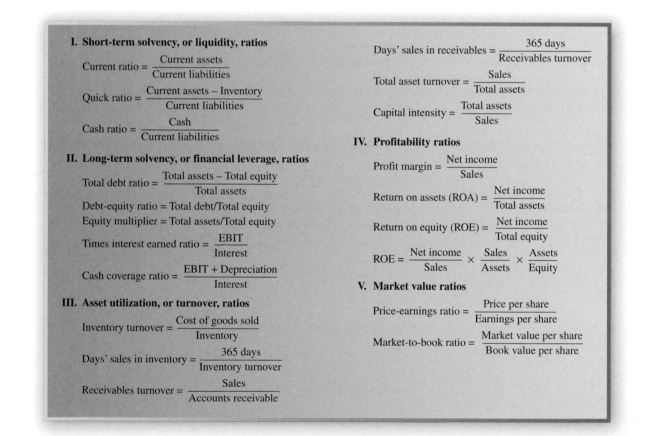

I. Short-term solvency, or liquidity, ratios

$$\text{Current ratio} = \frac{\text{Current assets}}{\text{Current liabilities}}$$

$$\text{Quick ratio} = \frac{\text{Current assets} - \text{Inventory}}{\text{Current liabilities}}$$

$$\text{Cash ratio} = \frac{\text{Cash}}{\text{Current liabilities}}$$

II. Long-term solvency, or financial leverage, ratios

$$\text{Total debt ratio} = \frac{\text{Total assets} - \text{Total equity}}{\text{Total assets}}$$

Debt-equity ratio = Total debt/Total equity

Equity multiplier = Total assets/Total equity

$$\text{Times interest earned ratio} = \frac{\text{EBIT}}{\text{Interest}}$$

$$\text{Cash coverage ratio} = \frac{\text{EBIT} + \text{Depreciation}}{\text{Interest}}$$

III. Asset utilization, or turnover, ratios

$$\text{Inventory turnover} = \frac{\text{Cost of goods sold}}{\text{Inventory}}$$

$$\text{Days' sales in inventory} = \frac{365 \text{ days}}{\text{Inventory turnover}}$$

$$\text{Receivables turnover} = \frac{\text{Sales}}{\text{Accounts receivable}}$$

$$\text{Days' sales in receivables} = \frac{365 \text{ days}}{\text{Receivables turnover}}$$

$$\text{Total asset turnover} = \frac{\text{Sales}}{\text{Total assets}}$$

$$\text{Capital intensity} = \frac{\text{Total assets}}{\text{Sales}}$$

IV. Profitability ratios

$$\text{Profit margin} = \frac{\text{Net income}}{\text{Sales}}$$

$$\text{Return on assets (ROA)} = \frac{\text{Net income}}{\text{Total assets}}$$

$$\text{Return on equity (ROE)} = \frac{\text{Net income}}{\text{Total equity}}$$

$$\text{ROE} = \frac{\text{Net income}}{\text{Sales}} \times \frac{\text{Sales}}{\text{Assets}} \times \frac{\text{Assets}}{\text{Equity}}$$

V. Market value ratios

$$\text{Price-earnings ratio} = \frac{\text{Price per share}}{\text{Earnings per share}}$$

$$\text{Market-to-book ratio} = \frac{\text{Market value per share}}{\text{Book value per share}}$$

Exhibit 13A.5 A Summary of Five Types of Financial Ratios

APPENDIX 2 TO CHAPTER 13

Sources of Company and Industry Information*

In order for business executives to make the best decisions when developing corporate strategy, it is critical for them to be knowledgeable about their competitors and about the industries in which they compete. The process used by corporations to learn as much as possible about competitors is often called "competitive intelligence." This appendix provides an overview of important and widely available sources of information that may be useful in conducting basic competitive intelligence. Much information of this nature is available in libraries in article databases, business reference books, and on websites. This list will recommend a variety of them. Ask a librarian for assistance, because library collections and resources vary.

The information sources are organized into 10 categories:

Competitive Intelligence

Public or Private—Subsidiary or Division—U.S. or Foreign?

Annual Report Collections—Public Companies

Guides and Tutorials

SEC Filings/EDGAR—Company Disclosure Reports

Company Rankings

Business Websites

Strategic and Competitive Analysis—Information Sources

Sources for Industry Research and Analysis

Search Engines

Competitive Intelligence

Students and other researchers who want to learn more about the value and process of competitive intelligence should see four recent books on this subject.

Mike Biere. *The New Era of Enterprise Business Intelligence: Using Analytics to Achieve a Global Competitive Advantage.* Upper Saddle River, NJ: IBM Press/Pearson, 2011.

Seena Sharp. *Competitive Intelligence Advantage: How to Minimize Risk, Avoid Surprises, and Grow Your Business in a Changing World.* Hoboken, NJ: Wiley, 2009.

T. J. Waters. *Hyperformance: Using Competitive Intelligence for Better Strategy and Execution.* San Francisco: Jossey-Bass, 2010.

Benjamin Gilad. *Early Warning: Using Competitive Intelligence to Anticipate Market Shifts, Control Risk, and Create Powerful Strategies.* New York: American Management Association, 2004.

Public or Private—Subsidiary or Division—U.S. or Foreign?

Companies traded on stock exchanges in the United States are required to file a variety of reports that disclose information about the company. This begins the process that produces a wealth of data on public companies and at the same time distinguishes them from private companies, which often lack available data. Similarly, financial data of subsidiaries and divisions are typically filed in a

---

* This information was compiled by Ruthie Brock and Carol Byrne, Business Librarians at The University of Texas at Arlington. We greatly appreciate their valuable contribution.

consolidated financial statement by the parent company, rather than treated independently, thus limiting the kind of data available on them. On the other hand, foreign companies that trade on U.S. stock exchanges are required to file 20F reports, similar to the 10-K for U.S. companies, the most comprehensive of the required reports. The following directories provide brief facts about companies, including whether they are public or private, subsidiary or division, U.S. or foreign.

> *Corporate Directory of U.S. Public Companies.* San Mateo, CA: Walker's Research, LLC, 2010.
> The *Corporate Directory* provides company profiles of more than 9,000 publicly traded companies in the United States, including foreign companies trading on the U.S. exchanges (ADRs). Some libraries may subscribe to an alternative online version at *www. walkersresearch.com*.

> *Corporate Affiliations.* New Providence, NJ: LexisNexis, 2010.
> This 8-volume directory features brief profiles of major U.S. and foreign corporations, both public and private, as well as their subsidiaries, divisions, and affiliates. The directory also indicates hierarchies of corporate relationships. An online version of the directory allows retrieval of a list of companies that meet specific criteria. Results can be downloaded to a spreadsheet. The online version requires a subscription, available in some libraries.

> *ReferenceUSA.* Omaha, NE: Infogroup.Inc.
> *ReferenceUSA* is an online directory of more than 14 million businesses located in the United States. One of the unique features is that it includes public and private companies, both large and small. Custom and Guided search tabs are available. Also, results can be analyzed using Quick, the data summary feature, which allows for a snapshot of how the industry breaks down by size, geographic location, etc. Other subscription options are available using the ReferenceUSA interface and may be available in some libraries.

> *Ward's Business Directory of U.S. Private and Public Companies.* Farmington Hills, MI: Gale CENGAGE Learning, 2010. 8 vols.
> *Ward's Business Directory* lists brief profiles on more than 112,000 public and private companies and indicates whether they are public or private, a subsidiary or division. Two volumes of the set are arranged using the Standard Industrial Classifications (SIC) and the North American Industry Classification System (NAICS) and feature company rankings within industries. Some libraries may offer this business directory as part of a database called *Gale Directory Library.*

Finding Public Company Information

Most companies have their annual report to shareholders and other financial reports available on their corporate website. Note that some companies use a variation of their company name in their Web address, such as Procter & Gamble: *www.pg.com.* A few "aggregators" have also conveniently provided an accumulation of links to many reports of U.S. and international corporations or include a PDF document as part of their database, although these generally do not attempt to be comprehensive.

> *The Public Register Online.* Woodstock Valley, CT: Bay Tact Corp.
> *Public Register Online* includes over 5,000 public company shareholder annual reports and 10-K filings for online viewing. Links are provided to reports on individual companies' websites, official filings from the Securities and Exchange Commission website, stock information from the NYSE Euronext exchange, or some combination of these sources. A link is also provided on this website for ordering personal copies of hard copy annual reports.
> *http://www.annualreportservice.com/*

> *Mergent Online.* New York: Mergent, Inc.
> *Mergent Online* is a database that provides company reports and financial statements for both U.S. and foreign public companies. Mergent's database has up to 25 years of quarterly and annual financial data that can be downloaded into a spreadsheet for analysis across time or across companies. Students should check with a librarian to determine the availability of this database at their college or university library.
> *http://mergentonline.com*

Guides & Tutorials for Researching Companies and Industries

Researching Companies Online. Debbie Flanagan. Fort Lauderdale, FL
This site provides a step-by-step process for finding free company and industry information on the web.
www.learnwebskills.com/company/

Guide to Financial Statements and *How to Read Annual Reports.* Armonk, NY: IBM
These two educational guides, located on IBM's website, provide basic information on how to read and make sense of financial statements and other information in 10-K and shareholder annual reports for companies in general, not IBM specifically.
www.ibm.com/investor/help/guide/introduction.wss
www.ibm.com/investor/help/reports/introduction.wss

EDGAR Full-Text Search Frequently Asked Questions (FAQ). Washington DC: U.S. Securities and Exchange Commission
The capability to search full-text SEC filings (popularly known as EDGAR filings), was vastly improved when the SEC launched its new search form in late 2006. Features are explained at the FAQ page.
www.sec.gov/edgar/searchedgar/edgarfulltextfaq.htm

Locating Company Information. Tutorial. William and Joan Schreyer Business Library, Penn State University, University Park, PA
Created by librarians at Penn State, this outstanding tutorial provides suggestions for online and print resources for company information. Click on "how to" links for each item to view a brief instruction vignette.
www.libraries.psu.edu/psul/researchguides/business.html

Ten Steps to Industry Intelligence. Industry Tutorial. George A. Smathers Libraries, University of Florida, Gainesville, FL
Provides a step-by-step approach for finding information about industries, with embedded links to recommended sources.
http://businesslibrary.uflib.ufl.edu/industryresearch

SEC Filings/EDGAR—Company Disclosure Reports

SEC Filings are the various reports that publicly traded companies must file with the Securities and Exchange Commission to disclose information about their corporation. These are often referred to as "EDGAR" filings, an acronym for the Electronic Data Gathering, Analysis and Retrieval System. Some websites and commercial databases improve access to these reports by offering additional retrieval features not available on the official (*www.sec.gov*) website.

EDGAR Database Full-Text Search. U.S. Securities and Exchange Commission (SEC), Washington, DC
10-K reports and other required corporate documents are made available in the SEC's EDGAR database within 24 hours after being filed. Annual reports, on the other hand, are typically sent directly to shareholders and are not required as part of EDGAR by the SEC, although some companies voluntarily include them. Both 10-Ks and shareholder's annual reports are considered basic sources of company research. The SEC offers a search interface for full-text searching of the content and exhibits of EDGAR SEC filings. The advanced search is recommended to locate "hard-to-find" information within documents filed by corporations and their competitors. Searches for specific types of reports or certain industries can also be performed.
http://searchwww.sec.gov/EDGARFSClient/jsp/EDGAR_MainAccess.jsp

LexisNexis Academic—SEC Filings & Reports. Bethesda, MD: LexisNexis.
Company Securities Exchange Commission filings and reports are available through a database called LexisNexis Academic. These reports and filings can be retrieved by company name, industry code, or ticker symbol for a particular time period or by a specific report. Proxy, 10-Ks, prospectus, and registration filings are also available.

Mergent Online—EDGAR Search. New York: Mergent, Inc.
As an alternative to *sec.gov,* the Securities and Exchange Commission website, it is possible to use the *Mergent Online* database to search for official company filings. Check to be sure if your library subscribes to the *Mergent Online* database. Select the "Filings" tab and then click on the "EDGAR Search" link. Next, Mergent's Government Filings search allows searching by company name, ticker, CIK (Central Index Key) number, or industry SIC number. The search can be limited by date and by type of SEC filing. The URL below should also work if your library subscribes to the Mergent Online database.
http://www.mergentonline.com/filingsearch.php?type=edgar&criteriatype=findall& submitvalues

Company Rankings

Fortune 500. New York: Time Inc.
The *Fortune 500* list and other company rankings are published in the printed edition of *Fortune* magazine and are also available online.
http://money.cnn.com/magazines/fortune/fortune500/2008/full_list/index.html

Forbes Global 2000. Forbes, Inc.
The companies listed on The Forbes Global 2000 are the biggest and most powerful in the world.
http://www.forbes.com/lists

Ward's Business Directory of U.S. Private and Public Companies. Farmington Hills, MI: Gale CENGAGE Learning, 2008, 8 vols.
Ward's Business Directory is one of the few directories to rank both public and private companies together by sales within an industry, using both the Standard Industrial Classification system (in vol. 5 only) and the North American Industry Classification System (in vol. 8 only). With this information, it is easy to spot who the big "players" are in a particular product or industry category. Market share within an industry group can be calculated by determining what percentage a company's sales figure is of the total given by Ward's for that industry group. Some libraries may offer this business directory as part of a database called *Gale Directory Library.*

Business Websites

Big Charts. San Francisco: MarketWatch, Inc.
BigCharts is a comprehensive and easy-to-use investment research website, providing access to professional-level research tools such as interactive charts, current and historical quotes, industry analysis, and intraday stock screeners, as well as market news and commentary. MarketWatch operates this website, a service of Dow Jones & Company. Supported by site sponsors, it is free to self-directed investors.
http://bigcharts.marketwatch.com/

GlobalEdge. East Lansing, MI: Michigan State University
GlobalEdge is a web portal providing a significant amount of information about international business, countries around the globe, the U.S. states, industries, and news.
http://globaledge.msu.edu/

Hoover's Online. Hoover's, Inc., Short Hills, NJ: Dun & Bradstreet Corp.
Hoover's includes a limited amount of free information on companies and industries. The subscribers' edition provides more in-depth information, especially for competitors and industries.
www.hoovers.com/free

Yahoo Finance. Sunnyvale, CA: Yahoo! Inc.
This website links to information on U.S. markets, world markets, data sources, finance references, investment editorials, financial news, and other helpful websites.
http://finance.yahoo.com

Strategic and Competitive Analysis—Information Sources

Analyzing a company can take the form of examining its internal and external environment. In the process, it is useful to identify the company's strengths, weaknesses, opportunities and threats (SWOT). Sources for this kind of analysis are varied, but perhaps the best would be to locate articles from *The Wall Street Journal,* business magazines and industry trade publications. Publications such as these can be found in the following databases available at many public and academic libraries. When using a database that is structured to allow it, try searching the company name combined with one or more keywords, such as "IBM and competition" or "Microsoft and lawsuits" or "AMR and fuel costs" to retrieve articles relating to the external environment.

ABI/Inform Complete. Ann Arbor, MI: ProQuest LLC
ABI/Inform Complete provides abstracts and full-text articles covering management, law, taxation, human resources, and company and industry information from more than 5,400 business and management journals. *ABI/Inform* includes market condition reports, corporate strategies, case studies, executive profiles, and global industry conditions.

Business & Company Resource Center. Farmington Hills, MI: Gale CENGAGE Learning
Business & Company Resource Center provides company and industry intelligence for a selection of public and private companies. Company profiles include parent-subsidiary relationships, industry rankings, products and brands, investment reports, industry statistics, and financial ratios. A selection of full-text investment reports and SWOT analysis reports are also available.

Business Source Complete. Ipswich, MA: EBSCO Publishing
Business Source Complete is a full-text database with over 3,800 scholarly business journals covering management, economics, finance, accounting, international business, and more. The database also includes detailed company profiles for the world's 10,000 largest companies, as well as selected country economic reports provided by the Economist Intelligence Unit (EIU). The database includes case studies, investment and market research reports, SWOT analyses, and more. *Business Source Complete* contains over 1,850 peer-reviewed business journals.

Investext Research Reports. Detroit, MI: Thomson Reuters Corp.
Investext Research Reports offer full-text analytical reports on more than 65,000 companies worldwide. The research reports are excellent sources for strategic and financial profiles of a company and its competitors and of industry trends. Developed by a global roster of brokerage, investment banking, and research firms, these full-text investment reports include a wealth of current and historical information useful for evaluating a company or industry over time.

International Directory of Company Histories. Detroit, MI: St. James Press, 1988–present. 120 volumes to date.
This directory covers more than 11,000 multinational companies, and the series is still adding volumes. Each company history is approximately three to five pages in length and provides a summary of the company's mission, goals, and ideals, followed by company milestones, principal subsidiaries, and competitors. Strategic decisions made during the company's period of existence are usually noted. This series covers public and private companies and nonprofit entities. Entry information includes a company's legal name, headquarters information, URL, incorporation date, ticker symbol, stock exchange, sales figures, and the primary North American Industry Classification System (NAICS) code. Further reading selections complete the entry information. Volume 59 to current date, is available electronically in the Gale Virtual Reference Library database from Gale CENCAGE Learning.

LexisNexis Academic. Bethesda, MD: LexisNexis
The "business" category in *LexisNexis Academic* provides access to timely business articles from newspapers, magazines, journals, wires, and broadcast transcripts. Other information available in this section includes detailed company financials, company comparisons, and database industry and market information for over 25 industries. The Company Dossier research tool allows a researcher to compare up to five companies' financial statements at one time with download capabilities.

The Wall Street Journal. New York: Dow Jones & Co.

This respected business newspaper is available in searchable full-text from 1984 to the present in the *Factiva* database. The "News Pages" link provides access to current articles and issues of *The Wall Street Journal.* Dow Jones, publisher of the print version of the *Wall Street Journal,* also has an online subscription available at wsj.com. Some libraries provide access to *The Wall Street Journal* through the ProQuest Newspapers database.

Sources for Industry Research and Analysis

Factiva. New York: Dow Jones & Co.

The *Factiva* database has several options for researching an industry. One would be to search the database for articles in the business magazines and industry trade publications. A second option in *Factiva* would be to search in the Companies/Markets category for company/industry comparison reports.

Mergent Online. New York: Mergent Inc.

Mergent Online is a searchable database of over 60,000 global public companies. The database offers worldwide industry reports, U.S. and global competitors, and executive biographical information. *Mergent*'s Basic Search option permits searching by primary industry codes (either SIC or NAICS). Once the search is executed, companies in that industry should be listed. A comparison or standard peer group analysis can be created to analyze companies in the same industry on various criteria. The Advanced Search allows the user to search a wider range of financial and textual information. Results, including ratios for a company and its competitors, can be downloaded to a spreadsheet.

North American Industry Classification System (NAICS)

The North American Industry Classification System has officially replaced the Standard Industrial Classification (SIC) as the numerical structure used to define and analyze industries, although some publications and databases offer both classification systems. The NAICS codes are used in Canada, the United States, and Mexico. In the United States, the NAICS codes are used to conduct an Economic Census every five years providing a snapshot of the U.S. economy at a given moment in time.

NAICS: *www.census.gov/eos/www/naics/*

Economic Census: *www.census.gov/econ/census07/*

NetAdvantage. New York: Standard & Poor's

The database includes company, financial, and investment information as well as the well-known publication called *Industry Surveys.* Each industry report includes information on the current environment, industry trends, key industry ratios and statistics, and comparative company financial analysis. Available in HTML, PDF, or Excel formats.

Search Engines

Google. Mountain View, CA: Google, Inc.

Recognized for its advanced technology, quality of results, and simplicity, the search engine Google is highly recommended by librarians and other expert Web surfers.

www.google.com

Dogpile. Bellevue, WA: InfoSpace, Inc.

Dogpile is a metasearch engine that searches and compiles the most relevant results from more than 12 individual search engines.

http://www.dogpile.com/

photo credits

company index

Page numbers followed by n refer to footnotes.

General Motors, 7, 25, 67, 70–71, 285, 309, 319, 343, 361
  mistakes made by, 320
Genzyme, 257
Georgia Power, 418
Gerber Products Company, 98
Gibson's guitars, 172–173
Gillette Company, 173, 206, 220, 222, 224
GlaxoSmithKline, 132, 266
Glaxo Wellcome, 222
Glidden, 216
Global Crossing, 229, 342
Global Logistic Properties Ltd., 49
GoGreenSolar.com, 60
Goldcorp, crowdsourcing at, 20
Goodyear Aerospace, 192
Google Inc., 4, 25, 28, 43, 117, 126, 130, 131, 302, 432, 437, 439, 460
  interactive control system, 322
Graybar Electric Company, 462
Green Careers, 129
Greenpeace, 19
Green Tree Financial, 203, 223
Gucci, 90, 173–174
Guidant, 220
Gulfstream, 327
GVO, 403

h

H. H. Cutler, 209
Hafts, 232
Hamilton, 190
H&M, 43
Hangzhou Wahaha Company Ltd., 100
Hanover Insurance, 411
Hanson Trust PLC, 214, 216, 364, 371
Hantz Farms, 285
Hantz Financial Services, 285
Harley-Davidson, 95, 170–171, 257
Harley-Davidson Café, 95
Hauwei, 398–399
HCI Direct, 86
Headhunter.com, 97
HealthSouth Corporation, 417
Heidrick & Struggles, 335
Hewlett-Packard, 6, 26, 102, 135, 143, 146, 176, 179–180, 227, 244, 248, 271, 323, 374, 448
Hill & Knowlton/Harris Interactive, 21
Hill-Rom Holdings, 337
Hindustan Unilever, 22, 132, 242
Hitachi-GE joint venture, 124
Hitachi Ltd., problems at, 124
Home Depot, 50, 176, 220, 324, 328, 330
Honda motorcycles, 169, 260
Honda Motors, 7, 70–71, 83, 213, 266
Honeywell Corporation, 46, 88
  merger prevented in European Union, 209
Honeywell ElectroOptics, 192

Hong Kong Travel Industry Council, problems at, 356–357
Hospitality Properties Trust, 337
Hotjobs.com, 97
Household International, 223
HTC, innovation failure, 432
H2bid.com, 285
Hudson Square Research, 99
Human Genome Sciences, 256
HyperRoll, 369
Hyundai, 68, 70–71

i

IBM, 25, 46, 59, 103, 137, 193, 204n, 244, 246, 259, 266, 271, 343, 380, 442, 491
IBM Global, 90
ICI, 207
Icos Corporation, 61
Ignition Corporation, 138
IKEA, 8
  pricing policy, 399
ImClone Systems, 16
IMS Health, 337
InBev, 220
Indymac, 16
iNest.com, 119
Infosys, 246
ING Group, 266
ING SRI, 25
Innosight, 416
Intel Capital, 204n
Intel Corporation, 5, 15, 54, 89, 126, 132, 204n, 254, 262, 271, 301, 308, 309, 330, 336, 414, 441, 448
  competition from AMD, 306
Interland, 54
International Franchise Association, 283
International Paper, 126
Intuit, 135, 193–195, 439, 440
Iowa Beef Processors, 97
iSold, problems at, 280
ITT, 364
ITT China, 89
iTunes Music Store, 69

j

J. D. Power & Associates, 71, 171, 179
Jaguar, 209
James Irvine Foundation, 30
  mission redefined, 31
Jantzen, 209
JCPenney, 69
JetBlue Airways, 88, 301
Jobsearch.com, 97
Johnson & Johnson, 22, 42, 154, 423
  credo, 422
Johnson Controls, 453

JPMorgan Chase, 139, 204, 339, 424
Juno Online Services, 86
Jupitermedia Corporation, 184

k

Kaufmann Foundation, 285, 289
Kazaa, 69
Kellogg, 258
Kentucky Fried Chicken, 210
  management-franchisers disagreement, 162
KFC-National Council and Advertising Cooperative, 162
Kia, 70
Kidder Peabody, 230
Kiva Systems, 300
Kmart, 68, 188–189, 211
Kmart Holding Group, 220
KMPG, 131
K'Netix, 145
Kodak, 266
Kohlberg, Kravis, Roberts & Company, 214
Korn/Ferry International, 335
KPMG, 341
Kraft Foods, 220

l

Labor Law Study Committee, 375
Lacoste, 90
Lafarge, 266
Lamborghini, 69, 70, 175
  strategic alliance, 270
Land Rover, 194
Lands' End, 177, 435
LaPage's Inc., 211
Lee jeans, 209
Lego, 45 46
Lehman Brothers, 16, 131
Lending Tree, 311, 312
Lenovo, 306
Levi Strauss, 415, 424
Lexus, 169, 171, 323
Liberty Mutual Group, 187
  combination strategies, 186
LinkedIn, 139
Litton Industries, 46
L.L.Bean, 435
Lockheed Martin, 10, 131, 192, 213, 326, 380
Loews Corporation, 215
Logitech Inc., 367
Longines, 190
Loral Corporation, 213
L'Oréal, 266, 297
Lotus Corporation, 103, 271
Lowe's, 50, 176
Lucent Technologies, 448
LVMH, 266

name index

Page numbers followed by n refer to footnotes.

Lerner, J., 466
Lester, P. B., 428
Lester, R. H., 351
Leung, W., 49
Levering, R., 444
Levesque, L. C., 36, 389
Levine, D., 351
Levitt, Theodore, 255, 276
Levy, A., 294
Levy, Paul, 413
Lewin, A. Y., 276
Lewis, Ken, 230
Li, C., 96
Li, J. J., 115, 158, 237
Li, J. T., 277
Lian, R., 49
Libert, B., 20, 36, 172, 288, 381
Lichtenthal, John, 254
Lieber, N., 256
Lieberman, David, 403
Lieberman, M. B., 467
Lieberthal, K., 275, 276
Light, D. A., 74, 158
Light, L., 198
Lim, Y., 198
Lin, H.-C., 314, 427
Lin, John, 158
Linblad, C., 351
Ling, C. S., 49
Ling, Y., 466
Linn, A., 194
Linsky, M., 397, 413
Lipin, S., 235, 237
Lipparini, A., 115
Lipton, M., 37
Litz, R. A., 36
Liu, S. X. Y., 115
Lloréns Montes, F. J., 427
Lloyd, M., 397
Locke, Edwin A., 350
Loeb, M., 35
Logan, Natalie, 221–222
Lohr, S., 199
London, T., 35
Long, W., 313
Loomis, C. J., 349
Lopez, José Ignacio, 157
Lorange, P., 73, 391, 427
Lore, Marc, 300
Lorenzoni, G., 115
Lorsch, J. W., 352, 427
Low, C. K., 331
Lowery, T., 197, 235, 237
Lu, J., 275, 313
Lubatkin, M. H., 466
Lucchetti, A., 351
Luchs, K., 236
Luehrman, T. A., 116
Luhby, Y., 129
Lumpkin, G. T., 157, 313, 455, 465, 467
Lundberg, C. C., 491
Lunnan, R., 237

Luthans, Fred, 427
Lutz, Robert, 16
Lynn, M., 35
Lyons, D., 467

m

Ma, H., 197
Mabey, C., 156
MacCormack, A., 36, 277
MacDonald, E., 351
MacDonald, I., 51
MacMillan, I. C., 198, 199, 275, 466, 467
Madhok, A., 277
Madoff, Bernard L., 45, 332, 417
Magretta, J., 390
Mahmood, I., 276
Maiello, M., 314, 352
Main, J., 428
Majluf, N. S., 235, 236
Makino, S., 275, 277
Makri, M., 235
Malhotra, D., 235
Malkin, E., 275
Mallas, S., 467
Malone, John, 414
Malone, Michael S., 155, 156
Malone, Tom, 138
Maloney, Sean, 306
Mandel, M., 74, 275
Mandelker, G., 351
Mandl, Alex, 221–222
Mang, P. Y., 467
Mankins, M. M., 37, 237
Manning, S., 276
Mao Zedong, 398
March, J. G., 391, 467
Marcial, G., 75
Marcus, Bernard, 324
Margolis, J. D., 36
Margolis, J. R., 421
Markham, S. K., 466
Markides, C. C., 73, 198
Markman, G. D., 349
Marks, M. S., 115, 199
Marriott, J. W., Jr., 166, 197
Martin, A., 207
Martin, J., 156, 277
Martin, J. A., 389
Martin, J. E., 159
Martin, K. D., 276
Martin, K. L., 36, 389
Martin, Roger L., 401, 402, 403, 427
Martin, X., 277
Martinez, Arthur, 4
Martinez, J., 347
Mass, N. J., 116
Massini, S., 276
Mathur, S., 74
Mathur, S. K., 245
Matias, Yossi, 369

Matlack, C., 76
Matthews, C. H., 313
Mauborgne, Renee, 296, 314, 406
Mauborgne, W., 406
Maurer, H., 351
May, R. C., 74
Mayer, J. D., 427
Maynard, M., 114, 320
McAfee, A., 115
McCarthy, D. J., 351
McCarthy, T., 406
McCartney, S., 303
McClellan, S., 227
McClendon, Aubrey, 318
McCune, J. C., 277
McDermott, C. M., 465
McDonald, M. L., 235, 351
McDonald, Mackey, 209
McDonald, Robert, 242
McDougall, P. P., 359n, 389
McEwen, Robert, 20
McGahan, Anita, 75
McGalian, A. M., 115
McGann, R., 54, 75
McGeehan, P., 351
McGrath, C., 158
McGrath, J., 353
McGrath, Rita Gunther, 198, 199, 275, 441,
    442, 465, 466, 467
McGregor, J., 89, 135, 242
McKnight, William, 415
McLaughlin, K. J., 390
McLean, Bethany, 343, 353
McMullan, W. E., 313
McNamara, G., 199
McNamee, M., 116
McNerney, James, 6
McNicol, J. P., 276
McVae, J., 36
McVey, Henry, 168
Means, Gardiner C., 333
Meckling, W. H., 351, 353
Meehan, Sean, 157
Mehra, Sanjiv, 207
Mehta, S. N., 198, 350
Meier, D., 235
Meindl, J. R., 35
Melcher, R. A., 351
Melrose, Ken, 412, 428
Mendelow, A. L., 467
Merchant, H., 277
Meredith, R., 275
Mero, J., 250
Meyer, A. D., 313
Meyer, K. E., 277
Meyer, Peter, 414, 428
Michael, D. C., 276
Michel, J. G., 314
Miles, R. E., 382
Millan, Julio, 85
Miller, A., 35, 197, 236, 350, 389, 427, 428,
    467

subject index

Page numbers followed by n refer to footnotes.

Commoditized products, 65
Common-size balance sheet, 490–491
Common-size income statement, 492–493
Communications, organizational, 383
Companies; *see also* Organizations
  alumni networks, 139
  array of technologies used by, 88
  book vs. market value, 125–126
  environmental values, 24
  fallen stars, 4–5
  global dispersion of value chains, 254–255
  global vs. regional, 266
  information sources, 501–506
  intellectual capital, 123
  motives for international expansion, 244–249
  perspective of balanced scorecard, 108
  risks of international expansion
    currency risks, 252–253
    economic risk, 251–252
    management risks, 253–254
    political risk, 249–251
Company rankings, 504
Comparison shopping, online, 117, 186
Compensation plans, incentive, 370
Competencies
  in-house at modular organizations, 378
  in innovation partners, 442
  for new ventures, 451
  ought for innovation partners, 442
Competing for the Future (Hamel & Prahalad), 40
Competition
  based on price, 61
  and blue ocean strategy, 296
  deceiving, 303
  dysfunctional, 362
  globalization of, 255
  innovation for, 431
  in maturity stage, 189
  soft drink industry, 100
Competitive actions
  defensive actions, 308
  forms of, 309
  frontal assault, 306
  guerrilla offensive, 307–308
  selective attacks, 307–308
  strategic, 307
  tactical, 306, 307
Competitive advantage
  from bundle of resources, 79
  and business performance, 163
  creating, 8–9, 180–181
  by creating factors of production, 243
  criteria for firm's resources, 95–101
  in diamond of national advantage, 241–244
  and diversion of firm's profits, 103–104
  from dynamic capabilities, 151–152
  eroded at Dell Inc., 101–102
  exploiting profit pool for, 177, 178
  focus of business-level strategy, 161

forces eroding, 180
from general administration, 89
generic strategies for
  combination strategies, 176–179
  differentiation, 162, 169–174
  focus, 162, 174–176
  overall cost leadership, 162, 164–169
in global markets
  cost reductions, 255–257
  global strategy, 259–260
  international strategy, 257–259
  local adaptation, 255–257
  multidomestic strategy, 260–263
  transnational strategy, 263–265
goal in global start-ups, 367
from Internet, 116–120
  business model types, 119–120
  customer feedback, 118
  entertainment programming, 118
  evaluation activities, 117
  expertise, 118
  problem-solving activities, 117–118
  search activities, 117
  transaction activities, 118
and nature of globalization, 265–267
of new ventures, 451
often short-lived, 179–180
and proactiveness, 460
by protecting intellectual assets, 149–151
in resource-based view of the firm, 93
sustainable, 181–182, 396
value-chain analysis, 81
in workforce diversity, 136
Competitive Advantage (Porter), 81
Competitive aggressiveness, 455
  combat industry trends, 460
  and competitive advantage, 460
  definition, 460
  preannouncement, 460
  SWOT analysis for, 460
  techniques
    copy successful business models, 461
    low prices, 461
  used in moderation, 460
Competitive analysis
  checklist, 62
  information sources, 505
Competitive attack
  choosing not to react, 309
  hardball strategies, 303
  likelihood of reaction, 308–309
  motivation and capability to respond, 304–305
  newspaper business, 304, 305
  protection from, 68–69
  sources of, 301–302
  threat analysis, 302–304
  types of, 305–308
Competitive benchmarking, 414
Competitive dynamics, 14, 279, 299–309
  choosing not to react
    co-opetition, 309, 310

    forbearance, 309, 310
  definition, 300
  hardball strategies, 303
  likelihood of competitive reaction
    actor's reputation, 308–309
    competitor's resources, 308
    market dependence, 308
  model, 301
  motivation and capability to respond, 304–305
  new competitive actions, 301–302
  threat analysis, 302–304
  types of competitive actions, 305–308
Competitive environment
  in case analysis, 487
  components, 39, 55
  definition, 55
  effect of Internet, 61–65
  five-forces model of industry competition, 55–61
  industry analysis, 65–68
  rewards and culture, 323
  strategic industry groups, 68–71
Competitive intelligence
  definition and function, 42
  examples, 42–43
  ignoring new competitors, 44
  information sources, 501
  via Internet, 43
  unethical or illegal behaviors, 43–44
  at United Technologies, 44
Competitiveness, 368
Competitive parity, 166–167
  with combination strategies, 178
Competitive position
  enhanced by divestment, 225
  eroded at Dell Inc., 84
  improved by differentiation strategy, 171
  improved by focus strategy, 175
  improved with overall cost leadership, 168
  low-cost, 168
  in strategic groups, 69
Competitive reaction
  alternatives to
    co-opetition, 309, 310
    forbearance, 309, 310
  likelihood factors
    actor's reputation, 308–309
    competitor's resources, 308
    market dependence, 308
Competitive strategies, 161
  applying strategic management concepts
    creating competitive advantage, 180–181
    easily imitated or substituted strategies, 181–182
    short-lived competitive advantage, 179–180
    sustainable advantage, 181
  in decline stage, 191–193
  effect of Internet, 182–187
  generic
    combination strategies, 176–179

varying perceptions of differentiation, 174
requirements, 162
reward and evaluation systems, 370–371
value chain activities, 170
varying means of achieving, 170–171
Digital Reverse Mentoring, 133
Digital technologies; *see also* Internet
effects on five-forces model, 61–65
impact on businesses, 54
Discovery skills, 347
Disintermediation, 64
effect of Internet, 183
Disparities of wealth, 241
Dispersal approach to corporate entrepreneurship; *see* Corporate entrepreneurship
Disruptive innovation
definition, 435
examples, 435–436
Dissatisfaction, 395
Dissolution, 225n
Distribution channels
as barrier to entry, 56
effect of Internet, 61, 63
in sharing activities, 209
in vertical integration, 213
Distribution networks, 100
Distributors, partnerships with, 100
Diversification; *see also* Related diversification; Unrelated diversification
by corporate entrepreneurship, 228
failed efforts, 202–204
by internal development, 228
risk reduction goal, 218–219
successful initiatives, 204–205
synergies from, 201
types of initiatives, 204
by vertical integration, 358–359
Diversity management
benefits of, 136
cost argument, 136
creativity argument, 136
marketing argument, 136
organizational flexibility argument, 136
problem-solving argument, 136
resource acquisition argument, 136
Divestments
acquisitions resulting in, 204
criteria for, 226
definition, 224
to enhance competitive position, 225
examples, 224–225
objectives achieved by, 225
Tyco International, 225
types of, 225n
Divisional organizational structure
advantages, 361–362
decision making in, 361
definition, 361
disadvantages, 362–363
focus on products and markets, 362

functions in, 358
at General Motors, 361
holding company structure, 364
for international operations
geographic-area division, 367
international division, 367
worldwide product division, 367
organizational chart, 362
problem at Sun Microsystems, 363
strategic business unit structure, 363–364
Dogs, 217
Doing Both (Sidhu), 102
Dollar, weakness of, 221
Domestic rivalry, 244
Double-loop learning, 321
Dow Jones Industrial Average, 52
Downstream activities, 213, 243
Drive, of entrepreneurs, 290–292
Drug cartels, Mexican, 85
Durable opportunity, 286
Dynamic capabilities
definition, 151
examples, 151
Dysfunctional competition, 362

e

East Asia
corporate governance in, 345
industrial power, 241
E-business
combination strategies, 185–187
differentiation strategy, 183–184
erosion of profits, 95
focus strategy, 184–185
overall cost leadership, 182–183
Echo boom generation, 131
Ecological problems, 23
Economic indicators
alcoholic beverage sales, 52
kinds of, 51–52
Economic integration, 267
Economic risks, 251–252
Economic segment of the general environment
definition, 51
economic indicators, 51–52
impact on industries, 53
key trends and events, 48
Economies of scale
as barrier to entry, 56
and capacity additions, 60
in China, 246
in global strategy, 259
in International expansions, 247
lacking in start-ups, 297
and local adaptation, 257
Economies of scope
definition, 206
in related diversification, 205
Economist, 4, 119

Economy
broader economic factors, 241
human capital, 126
intellectual capital, 126
knowledge-based Gross domestic product, 125
leveraging human capital, 145–149
role of human capital, 127–136
role of knowledge, 124–127
role of social capital, 137–144
social capital, 126
value of the firm, 125–126
EDGAR database, 503–504
Effectiveness, 10
Effectiveness–efficiency trade-off, 10
Efficiency, 10
Egotism, examples of, 229–230, 231
Electronic invoice system, 186
Electronic networks, 84
Electronic storage, 64–65
Electronic teams
advantages, 146
challenges, 147
definition, 146
generating social capital, 146
less restrained by geography, 146
versus traditional teams, 146
E-mail, excessive use, 145
Embedded options, 452–453
Emerging markets, multinational corporations in, 347
Emotional intelligence, 393
components
relationship management skills, 407, 408–409
self-management skills, 407–409
definition, 407
and IQ, 407
for leading organizations, 409
potential drawbacks, 408–410
sets of capabilities, 405
studies on, 406–407
Empathy, 407, 408
Employee bargaining power, 103
Employee empowerment, 26
at all levels, 412–413
at Beth Israel Deaconess, 413
from effective leadership, 412
versus heroes and drones syndrome, 412–413
salient elements of, 412
strategy for, 412
Employee exit costs, 103
Employee loyalty, 323
Employee replacement costs, 103
Employee retention, 127–128
Employees
access to boards, 336
as customer advocates, 413
development of, 150
diversion of profits to, 103–104
empowerment, 26

g

Gallup poll on corporations, 16
General administration
  assessment factor, 87
  definition, 89
  information systems, 89
  leadership by top executives, 89
  source of competitive advantage, 89
General Agreement on Tariffs and Trade, 52
General environment
  in case analysis, 487
  components, 12, 39, 47
  definition, 47
  demographic segment, 47–49
  economic segment, 51–52
  global segment, 52
  impact on industries, 53
  Internet/digital technologies, 54
  key trends and events, 48
  political/legal segment, 50
  relationships among segments, 52–55
  sociocultural segment, 49–50
  technological segment, 50–51
Generation Y, 131
Generic strategies, 161
  differentiation, 162, 169–174
  effect of Internet, 182–187
  focus, 162, 174–176
  in industry life cycle, 187–195
  in new ventures
    combination strategies, 299–300
    differentiation, 297–298
    focus, 298–299
    overall cost leadership, 297
  overall cost leadership, 162, 164–169
Geographic-area division structure, 358, 367
Geographic boundaries, 373
Germany, population, 246
Getting from College to Career (Pollack), 129
Glass-Steagall Act repeal, 48, 50
Global economy; *see also* International expansion
  achieving competitive advantage, 255–257
  business-friendly policies, 241
  Carrefour's problems, 240
  effect on poverty levels, 241
  factors affecting competitiveness, 241–244
  global dispersion of value chains, 254–255
  India's place in, 245–246
  market capitalism, 241
  marketing to bottom of the pyramid, 241, 242
  and meaning of globalization, 265–267
  motivation for expansion, 244–249
  opportunities in, 239
  recent trade increases, 240
  risks in expansion, 249–254
  strategies for
    global, 259–260

    international, 257–259
    multidomestic, 250–263
    transnational, 263–265
  sustainable, 23–24
  worldwide talent pool, 240–241
Globalization
  of competition, 255
  cross-cultural dialogue, 408
  definition, 241
  meaning of, 265
  opportunities from, 52
  versus regionalization, 265–267
Global marketplace, leadership challenges, 5–7
Global segment of the general environment
  costs of terrorism, 52
  definition, 52
  elements of, 52
  growth of middle class, 52
  impact on industries, 53
  key trends and events, 48
  regional trade blocs, 52
Global start-ups
  boundaryless design, 368
  challenges of, 369
  defensive motive, 369
  definition, 367
  examples, 369
  Logitech success, 367
  management challenges, 368
  offensive motive, 369
  organizational requirements, 368
  outsourcing by, 368
Global strategy
  cost control emphasis, 259
  definition, 259
  economies of scale, 259
  and organizational structure, 367
  risks and challenges, 260
  standard quality, 259–260
  strengths and limitations, 261
Global value of mergers and acquisitions, 221
Goals
  dysfunctional, 319
  organizational, 26
Going green, 129, 418
Golden parachute, 232, 341
Good Housekeeping VIP Awards, 434
Good Morning America, 434
Good to Great (Collins), 292, 323
Gorillas in the Mist, 27
Government
  business-friendly policies, 241
  as innovation partner, 441
Government resources for start-ups, 290
Great Pacific Garbage Patch, 287
Green Berets, 330
Green employment, 129
Greenmail, 230–232, 341
Green plastic, 287
Green to Gold (Esty & Winston), 24

Greenwashing, 418
Gross domestic product
  generated by family businesses, 283
  information technology percentage in India, 245
  knowledge-based, 125
Group problem solving, 374
Groups, belief in inherent morality of, 482
Groupthink, 143
  symptoms and prevention of, 482–484
  victims of, 482
Growth for growth's sake, 228–229
Growth/share matrix, 216–217
  limitations, 218–219
Growth stage
  definition, 189
  strategies for, 189
Guatemala, poverty in, 241
Guerrilla offensive, 307–308
Guidelines, 328
Gulf oil spill of 2010, 335

h

Hardball strategies, 303
Harvard Business Review, 11, 23, 127, 165, 180
Harvesting, 192
Hierarchical relationships, 205, 214
Hierarchy of goals, 3, 12
  definition, 26
  mission statement, 29–30
  strategic objectives, 30–32
  vision, 26–29
High-technology industry, H-1B visa program, 50, 51
Hiring
  advice for candidates, 131
  for attitude, 129–130
  bozo filter, 129–130, 329–330
  matching approach, 128–129
  via personal networks, 137–138
  and retention, 127–128
  star performers, 144
Hispanic Americans, 136
Historical comparison of financial ratios, 105–106
Hoarding barrier, 141
Holding company structure, 359
  advantages and disadvantages, 364
  definition, 364
Home-based businesses, 283
H-1B visa program
  for high-tech industries, 50
  and Microsoft, 51
Hong Kong
  doing business in, 253–254
  Travel Industry Council, 356–357
Horizontal boundaries, 373
Horizontal organizational structure, 383
Horizontal relationships, 204, 214

benefits of, 206
Horizontal systems and processes, 383
Hostile takeovers, 230
Human capital
  attracting
    best practices, 131
    by going green, 129
    hiring for attitude, training for skill,
      129–130
    matching approach, 128–129
    recruiting approaches, 130
  definition, 126
  developing
    as company obligation, 130
    knowledge transfer, 132
    leadership involvement, 132
    mentoring programs, 132
  enhancing, 136
  evaluating, 132–133
  foundation of intellectual capital,
    127–136
  in Generation Y, 131
  mentoring programs, 133
  for new ventures, 289
  organizational protection of, 127
  prominence of knowledge workers, 127
  retaining, 123, 127–128
    challenging work environment,
      134–135
    creating incentives, 133
    identification with mission and values,
      134
    retention rules, 135
    rewards and incentives, 135
  technology for leveraging, 145–149
  value creation through, 150
  workforce diversity, 136
Human capital mobility, 138
Human Equation (Pfeffer), 374
Human resource management
  assessment factor, 87
  components, 88
  in differentiation strategy, 170
  at JetBlue Airways, 88
  in multidomestic strategy, 261–262
  in overall cost leadership, 164
  and performance evaluations, 89
Human resource practices, 383
  to capture value from innovation, 441
  dysfunctional, 143–144
Human resource professionals, lock and key
  mentality, 128
Human resources, 94
Hurricane Katrina, 7
Hypercompetition (D'Aveni), 396

I

Iceland, volcanic eruption, 7
Iconoclast (Berns), 142

Identification and combination activities,
  147
Illegal actions/behavior, 417
  in competitive intelligence, 43, 44
  in marketing and sales, 86
Illusion of control, 453–454
Imitation
  of differentiation, 173
  of focus strategy, 176
  intensified by Internet, 183
Imitative new entry, 293–294
Improper conduct, 328
Inbound logistics
  assessment factors, 83
  definition, 83
  in differentiation strategy, 170
  just-in-time systems, 83–84
  in overall cost leadership, 164
  in service organizations, 92–93
Incentive compensation systems, 370
Incentives
  financial and nonfinancial, 135
  in recruitment, 130
Incentive systems
  characteristics, 325
  in corporate governance, 338–339
  effective, 325
  as motivator, 324–325
  with multiple divisions, 325
  potential downside, 324–325
  at Starbucks, 324
  and subcultures, 325
Income disparities, 241
  and reverse innovation, 249
Incremental innovation, 434
  time line for, 440
Incremental launch, 437
Incremental management, 7–8
India
  diamond of national advantage, 245–246
  PepsiCo joint venture, 272
  population, 246
  software services industry, 245–246
Indiana, Utility Regulatory Commission,
  394–395
Industries
  co-opetition, 309
  impact of trends in general environment,
    53
  information sources, 501–506
  low-profit, 65–66
  mature, 299
  related and supporting, 243–244
  strategic groups, 39, 68–71
Industry analysis
  basic assumptions, 68
  caveats on
    no avoidance of low-profit industries,
      65–66
    static analysis, 67–68
    zero-sum game assumption, 66–67
  quantification of five-forces model, 68

strategic groups, 68–71
  time horizon, 68
  value net concept, 67–68
Industry consolidation, 222
Industry environment, 12
Industry growth, 60
Industry life cycle, 161, 165
  decline stage, 191–193
  definition, 187
  generic strategies, 187, 188
  growth stage, 189
  introduction stage, 187–189
  limitations, 187
  maturity stage, 189–191
  and process innovation, 433
  reasons for importance, 187
  turnaround strategies, 193–195
Industry norms, for financial ratios,
  106–107
Industry research analysis, 506
Industry trends
  combating, 460
  implications, 69–70
Infomediary services, 65
Information
  private, 142–143
  redistribution of, 413–414
Informational control
  approaches to, 317
  and attribution bias, 320
  characteristics, 321
  compared to behavioral control,
    319–321
  and confirmation bias, 320
  contemporary approach, 319–322
  definition, 319–321
  feedback loop, 319
  interactive system, 321–322
  key issues, 321
  operation of, 321
  organizational learning, 321
  and strategic change, 319
  traditional approach, 319
Information power, 405
Information systems, 89
Information technology
  alternative to offshoring, 256
  to break down barriers, 383
  effect on productivity, 53
  to extend value chain, 177–178
  in India, 245–246
  at Zara, 43
Inimitability
  of blue ocean strategies, 296–297
  of core competencies, 207–208
  of resources
    at Amazon Prime, 99
    causal ambiguity, 98
    key to value creation, 97
    path dependency, 98
    physical uniqueness, 97
    social complexity, 98

Innovation, 94; *see also* Corporate
    entrepreneurship
  aims of, 432
  breakthrough, 385
  challenges of, 435–437
    capabilities vs. collaboration, 437
    experience vs. expertise, 437
    incremental vs. preemptive launch, 437
    internal vs. external staffing, 437
    meeting resistance, 436
    seeds vs. weeds problem, 437
  at Cisco Systems, 445
  by collaboration, 441–442
  in control systems, 88
  from creative abrasion, 143
  by crowdsourcing, 442
  cultivating skills for
    creative intelligence, 438
    discovery skills, 437
  defining scope of
    focus on common technology, 438
    focus on market theme, 438
    questions to consider, 440
    strategic envelope, 438
  definition, 433
  at Dutch Boy, 434
  entrepreneurial orientation, 454–462
  failure for Shell Oil, 261
  forms of, 431
  from Internet-based collaboration, 382
  managing, 433–442
  new industries from, 50–51
  in performance materials, 88
  perspective of balanced scorecard, 108
  real options analysis, 452–454
  reverse, 248–249, 250
  rules for fostering, 444
  staffing to capture value from, 440–441
  for successful competition, 431
  at 3M Corporation, 5–6
  types of
    continuum of, 434
    disruptive, 435–436
    incremental, 434
    process innovation, 433
    product innovation, 433
    radical, 433–434
    sustaining, 435
Innovation partners, 441–442
Innovation teams, 442
Innovativeness, 455
  and corporate social responsibility, 457
  definition, 456
  pitfalls and risks, 458
  requirements, 456–458
  techniques
    foster creativity, 458
    invest in technology, 458
Innovator's DNA
  creative intelligence, 438
  discovery skills, 437
  traits, 439

Inputs in common with rivals, 168
In Search of Excellence (Peters &
    Waterman), 323
Institutional investors, 337–338, 339
Intangible assets, 108
Intangible resources, 79
  definition, 95
  kinds of, 94, 95
Integrating, 471
Integrative thinking
  ability to learn, 402
  versus conventional thinking, 401
  for decision making, 402
  definition, 401
  to overcome barriers to change, 404
  at Red Hat, Inc., 403
  stages, 401–402
Integrity-based ethics programs, 419, 420
Intellectual assets
  analysis of, 14
  in case analysis, 487
  protecting, 149–152
Intellectual capital, 123
  definition, 126
Intellectual property, 123
  litigation over, 152
  patent litigation, 124
  stealing or counterfeiting, 151
  and value creation, 124
Intellectual property rights
  lack of enforcement, 251–252
  versus physical property rights, 151
  protection of, 149–151
  Research in Motion, 152
Intelligence quotient (IQ), 407
Intended strategy, 11–12
Intensity of rivalry among competitors
  based on price, 61
  causes
    capacity additions, 60
    high exit barriers, 60
    high fixed/storage costs, 60
    lack of differentiation, 60
    lack of switching costs, 60
    numerous/evenly balanced competition,
      59
    slow industry growth, 60
  definition, 59
  effects of Internet, 65
Interactive control system, 321–322
Interlocking directorships, 335
Internal benchmarking, 413
Internal development, 228
Internal environment
  analysis of, 14
  in case analysis, 487
  performance evaluation tools
    balanced scorecard, 107–110
    financial ratio analysis, 104–107
  perspective of balanced scorecard, 108
  problems at Toyota, 80
  resource-based view of the firm, 93–104

  and strategic control, 319–321
  value-chain analysis, 81–93
Internal knowledge
  accumulating and sharing, 413–414
  informal sources of, 414
Internal networkers, 25
Internal staffing, 437
International Air Transport Association, 49
International Anti-Counterfeiting Coalition,
  252
International Civil Aviation Organization,
  414
International country risk ratings, 251
International division structure, 367
  functions, 358
International expansion
  achieving competitive advantage,
    255–267
  entry modes, 267–272
  global value chain dispersion, 254–255
  modes of entry
    exporting, 258
    franchising, 268–269
    joint ventures, 269–271
    licensing, 268–269
    strategic alliances, 269–271
    wholly owned subsidiaries, 271–272
  motivation for
    arbitrage, 247
    explore reverse innovation, 248–249,
      250
    extend product life cycle, 247–248
    increased market size, 244–247
    optimization of value chain activities,
      248
  potential risks
    currency risks, 252–253
    economic risk, 251–252
    management risk, 253–254
    political risk, 249–251
  by Walmart, 247
International-level strategy
  basis and suitability, 258
  in case analysis, 488–489
  definition, 257
  formulation of, 14
  risks and challenges, 258–259
  strengths and limitations, 259
International operations, organizational
    structures
  contingencies influencing, 367
  geographic-area structure, 367
  global start-ups, 367–368, 369
  international division structure, 367
  management outlook, 366–367
  worldwide functional structure, 367
  worldwide matrix structure, 367
  worldwide product division, 367
International trade
  exporting, 268
  recent increases in., 240
International Trade Commission, 124

Internet
 business model types, 119–120
 challenges faced by, 54
 competitive advantage from
  customer feedback, 118
  entertainment programming, 118
  evaluation activities, 117
  expertise, 118
  problem-solving activities, 117–118
  search activities, 117
  transaction activities, 118
 effects on five-forces model
  bargaining power of buyers, 61–63
  bargaining power of suppliers, 63–64
  intensity of competitive rivalry, 65
  threat of new entrants, 61
  threat of substitutes, 64–65
 impact on businesses, 54
 influences on industry, 66
 infomediary services, 65
 as information source, 414
 number of users worldwide, 54
 use by small and medium-sized businesses, 54
 as video-based medium, 445
Internet-based collaboration, 382
Interrelationships among value chain
  activities, 89–90
Intrapreneuring, 443
Introduction stage
 definition, 187
 strategies for, 187–189
Inventory management, 83–84, 243
Inventory turnover, 105, 476, 497
Investing, socially responsible, 25
Investment analysis, 452
Investment banks, as corporate governance
  mechanism, 341–342
Investment decisions
 agency problems, 453
 and corporate governance, 330
Investments, transaction-specific, 214
Investors Business Daily, 343
Invulnerability illusion, 482
Irrational escalation of commitment, 454
Israel, strong currency, 253

J

Jam event at IBM, 443
Japan
 business groups, 346
 earthquake and tsunami, 7
 just-in-time systems, 243
 population, 246
Job creation
 by multinational corporations, 52
 by small businesses, 282–283
Joint ventures, 220
 benefits, 269
 definition, 226

to develop and diffuse technologies, 227
to enter new markets, 226
Lamborghini and Callaway, 270
PepsiCo in India, 272
potential downsides, 227–228
to reduce value chain costs, 226–227
risks and limitations, 270–271
Telles, 287
and virtual organizations, 381
Just-in-time systems, 66, 83–84, 243

K

Keiretsu, 346
Kickbacks, 328
Knowledge
 explicit, 127, 147
 redistribution of, 413–414
 role in economy, 124–127
 of socially complex processes, 127
 sources for new, 433
 tacit, 127, 147
Knowledge-based gross domestic product,
  125
Knowledge economy
 characteristics, 124–127
 definition, 125
Knowledge management, 138–143
Knowledge sharing
 codification for competitive advantage,
  147–149
 electronic teams, 146–147
 using networks, 145–146
Knowledge transfer
 to develop human capital, 132
 not automatic, 265
Knowledge workers, 123
 personal goals, 127

L

Labor force, changes in U.S., 49
Last-gasp technologies, 192–193
Late-mover advantage, 188–189
Latin America
 corporate governance in, 347
 number of Internet users, 54
 personal income, 241
Lawyers (corporate), Sarbanes-Oxley Act
  on, 342
Leaders
 challenge of global marketplace, 5–7
 dealing with unanticipated events, 7
 types needed, 25
 vision development, 27–28
Leadership
 ambicultural approach, 400
 at Best Buy, 397
 capabilities, 393

for competing in global economy, 393
creating ethical organizations, 417–424
definition, 395
designing the organization, 398
to develop learning organizations,
  410–416
 challenging status quo, 415–416
 empowering employees, 412–413
 enabling creativity, 415–416
 integrating external information,
  414–415
 sharing internal knowledge, 413–414
doing the right thing, 395–396
elements of effectiveness
 integrative thinking, 401–402
 overcoming barriers to change, 402–404
 uses of power, 404–405
emotional intelligence, 393, 405–410
entrepreneurial, 290–292
ethical orientation, 417
by example, 399
external control view of, 6–7
at IKEA, 399
involved in training, 132
key activities, 393
key interdependent activities, 396–397
learning from failure, 415
mistakes at Duke Energy, 394–395
nurturing ethical culture, 398–400
romantic view of, 5–6
setting a direction, 397–398
Leadership Challenge (Kouzes & Posner),
  411
Learning organizations, 15, 393, 410–416
 accumulating and sharing internal knowledge, 413–414
 in case analysis, 489–490
 challenging status quo, 415–416
 definition, 411
 empowering employees, 412–413
 enabling creativity, 415–416
 gathering and integrating external information, 414–415
 key elements, 411
 learning from failure, 416
 motivating people, 411–412
Learning perspective of balanced scorecard,
  108
Legacy costs, 179
Legislation
 antitakeover, 232
 effects on business, 50
Legitimate power, 405
Libya, 249–251
Licensing
 benefits and risks, 269
 definition, 268
Licensing agreements, 291
Limit costs, 257
Linux, 403
Liquidity ratios, 105
Litigation, antitrust, 211

Organizational design, 15
    ambidextrous, 383–385
    in case analysis, 489
    composition of, 355
    leadership task, 398
Organizational ethics
    definition, 417
    fraud potential, 418
    versus individual ethics, 417–419
Organizational flexibility argument, 136
Organizational goals, 9
    aligned with reward systems, 330
    analysis of, 12
    in case analysis, 487
    flexibility in meeting, 416
    strategic–financial comparison, 450–451
    3M Corporation, 6
Organizational integrity, 419
Organizational learning, 321
Organizational resources, 94
Organizational structure, 15
    ambidextrous designs, 383–385
    boundaryless designs, 372–383
        barrier-free organizations, 373–376
        factors to consider, 382–383
        modular, 377–379
        virtual organization, 379–382
    created by leadership, 398
    definition and function, 357
    divisional structure, 361–366
    functional structure, 359–361
    horizontal, 383
    independent action in, 456
    influence on strategy formulation, 368
    in international operations, 366–368
    matrix structure, 364–365
    patterns of corporate growth
        conglomerate strategy, 359
        functional structure, 358
        holding company structure, 359
        for international markets, 358
        simple structure, 358
        strategic business units, 359
        vertical integration, 358–359
    problems at Sun Microsystems, 363
    reward and evaluation systems, 368–372
        business-level strategy, 369–371
        corporate-level strategy, 371–372
    simple structure, 359
    and strategy, 355
    strategy–structure relationships, 357–359
    types of, 355
Organizational vision; *see* Vision
Organizations; *see also* Companies
    barriers to change, 402–404
    boundaryless, 355
    code of conduct, 421–422
    conflicting demands on, 18
    conflicts within, 326
    diversity management, 136
    dynamic capabilities, 151–152
    entrepreneurial orientation, 431

environmentally aware
    competitive intelligence, 42–44
    environmental forecasting, 44–45
    environmental monitoring, 42
    environmental scanning, 41–42
    scenario analysis, 45–46
    SWOT analysis, 46–47
external boundaries, 373
geographic boundaries, 373
hierarchy of goals, 26–32
horizontal boundaries, 373
integrative view of, 24
key stakeholders, 17
long- vs. short-term perspective, 9–10
mission statements, 29–30
performance evaluation
    balanced scorecard, 107–110
    financial ratio analysis, 104–107
permeable boundaries, 357
protecting intellectual assets, 149–151
protection of human capital, 127
resource-based view of, 93–104
strategic management perspective, 24–26
strategic objectives, 30–32
structural holes, 141
subcultures in, 325
tribal loyalty, 134
understanding stakeholders, 397–398
value-chain analysis, 81–93
vertical boundaries, 373
vision, 26–29
Outbound logistics, 84–85
    assessment factors, 83
    definition, 84
    in differentiation strategy, 170
    electronic networks, 84
    in overall cost leadership, 164
    in service organizations, 92–93
Outside consultants, 473
Outside directors, 335, 336, 343
Outsiders, to neutralize biases, 416
Outsourcing, 213, 291
    in boundaryless organizations, 357
    definition, 254
    manufacturing volume of industries, 255
    Microsoft strategy, 378
    by modular organizations
        advantages, 377
        strategic risks, 378–379
    recent explosion in, 254–255
Overall cost leadership, 163
    absolute cost advantage, 168
    basis of, 162
    in combination strategies, 176–179
    competitive parity, 166–167
    effect of Internet, 182–183
    from electronic invoice system, 186
    experience curve, 165
    and five-forces model, 168
    in new ventures, 297
    often unattainable for start-ups, 297
    pitfalls

common inputs with rivals, 168
    easily imitated, 168–169
    erosion of cost advantage, 169
    lack of parity on differentiation, 169
    too much focus on few value chain
        activities, 168
reward and evaluation systems, 370
    at Ryanair, 167
    summary of, 174
    tactics, 164–165
    value chain activities, 164
    at Vizio, Inc., 298

P

Parenting advantage, 214–215
    in unrelated diversification, 206
Partnerships with distributors, 100
Patent litigation, 124
Path dependency, 98
Pay for performance, 338
Peer-to-peer lending, 287, 288
Pension Rights Center, 343
People for the Ethical Treatment of Animals,
    344
People lever, 141
People's Liberation Army, 398
Pep talks, 324
Performance, and competitive advantage,
    163
Performance enhancement by value chain
    location, 248
Performance evaluation
    for breakthrough innovations, 385
    in case analysis, 487
    of companies
        balanced scorecard, 107–110
        financial ratio analysis, 104–107
    and employee turnover, 89
    for human capital
        360-degree feedback system, 133, 134
        traditional system, 132
Performance materials, 88
Personal integrity, 419
Personal time constraints, 404
Pharmaceutical industry, 257–258
Physical property rights, 151
Physical resources, 94
Physical technology, 98
Physical uniqueness, 97
Pied Piper effect, 137–138
Pioneering new entry
    definition, 293
    differentiation in, 297–298
    example, 294
Piracy, 251
Plagiarize, 303
Plastics, 287
Poison pill, 232, 341
Policies for ethical organizations, 424

prosumer concept, 90–91
  in service organizations, 92–93
Value-chain concept, 80
Value/cost trade-off, blue ocean strategy, 296
Value-creating opportunity, 286
Value creation, 81
  at Apple Inc., 208
  criteria for core competencies
    difficult to imitate, 207–208
    lack of substitutes, 207–208
    similarity of businesses, 207
    superior customer value, 206–207
  by entrepreneurship
    leadership, 290–292
    recognizing opportunities, 281–286
    resources, 286–290
  eroded by managerial motives
    antitakeover tactics, 230–232
    egotism, 229–230
    growth for growth's sake, 228–229
  with human capital, 150
  by inimitability, 97
  by internal development, 228
  by related diversification, 201, 205
  with social capital, 150
  with technology, 150
  underestimating challenge of, 179
  by unrelated diversification, 201, 205
Value net concept, 67–68
Value of the firm, 125–126
  book vs. market value, 125–126
  from business groups, 346
  examples, 126
  policies to maximize, 338
Values
  employee identification with, 134
  ethical, 417
  in organizational cultures, 323
Venture capital, 289
Vertical boundaries, 373
Vertical integration

administrative costs, 214
benefits, 210–212
definition and types, 210
for diversification, 358–359
risks, 212–213
at Shaw Industries, 211, 212
transaction cost perspective, 213–214
Vertical relationships, 214
Videoconferencing, 148
Video game industry, 67–68
  competitors in, 378
Virtual organizations
  challenges and risks, 380–381
  compared to modular organizations, 380
  composition of, 380
  definition, 379–380
  demands on managers, 380–381
  and joint ventures, 381
  pros and cons, 382
  strategic plan, 381
Vision, 3, 12, 395
  benefits of, 397–398
  contrasted with mission, 29
  definition, 26
  developed by leaders, 27–28
  of entrepreneurs, 290
  examples, 28
  obstacles to implementing, 398
  reasons for failure, 28–29
Vision statements, 28, 30
Voice over Internet Protocol, 61, 445
Volcanic eruption, Iceland, 7

W

Wall Street Journal, 42, 85, 137, 224, 304, 343
Wealth
  creation in knowledge economy, 125
  disparities of, 241

Web of Inclusion (Helgesen), 25–26
Western culture, 400
Wholesalers, as stakeholders, 18
Wholly owned subsidiaries
  definition, 271
  risks and limitations, 271
Wind energy industry, 12
Wired magazine, 18
Wisdom of Teams (Smith), 382
Wolf culture, 398–399
Women
  assessing employers, 144
  educational attainment, 50
  in work force, 49–50
Work
  challenging, 134–135
  decentralized model, 138
  undefined roles, 373
Workers Rights Consortium, 344
Workforce diversity, 136
Workplace environment, 134–135
World Bank, 241, 249
World Health Organization, 252, 436
World population, 244, 246
World Trade Organization, 48
  report on value chain dispersion, 254
Worldwide functional structure, 358, 367
Worldwide matrix structure, 358, 367
Worldwide product division structure, 358, 367
Written case presentation, 481

Z

Zero-sum game assumption, 66–67
Zero-sum game sense, 362
Zero-sum view of stakeholder management, 17–18